CITY SENSE AND CITY DESIGN

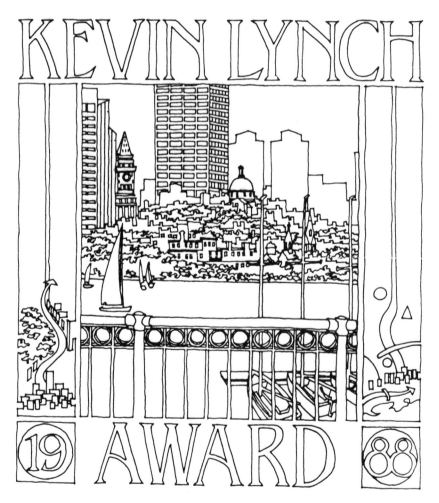

The Kevin Lynch Book Award (facsimile).
Designed by Randall Imai.

CITY SENSE
AND
CITY DESIGN

Writings and Projects of Kevin Lynch

edited by

Tridib Banerjee and

Michael Southworth

The MIT Press

Cambridge, Massachusetts

London, England

This book was set in Univers and Palatino by Asco Trade Typesetting Ltd. in Hong Kong and was printed and bound by Halliday Lithograph in the United States of America.

Library of Congress Cataloging-in-Publication Data

Lynch, Kevin, 1918–
   City sense and city design: writings and projects of Kevin Lynch/edited by Tridib Banerjee and Michael Southworth.
      p.   cm.
   Includes bibliographical references.
   ISBN 0-262-12143-3
   1. Lynch, Kevin, 1918– —Philosophy.   2. City planning—United
States—History—20th century.   3. City Planning—History—20th
century.   I. Banerjee, Tridib.   II. Southworth, Michael.
III. Title.
NA9085.,L96A4   1990
711'.4'092—dc20   89-38350
                                                              CIP

Passage from *In My Father's Court*, on page 23, © 1962, 1964, 1965, 1966 Isaac Bashevis Singer; reprinted by permission of Farrar, Straus, and Giroux, Inc.

Contents

Acknowledgments

The idea of putting together a collection of Kevin Lynch's work was first considered in the summer of 1986 in a conversation with Gary Hack of MIT's Department of Urban Studies and Planning. It was Gary's encouragement that led us to pursue the idea and to approach the Lynch family for approval. The book was discussed with Mrs. Anne Lynch and her daughter Catherine (a professor of history at Case Western Reserve University) over lunch during the 1986 Christmas season. With the endorsement and support of the family, we proceeded to develop a formal prospectus for the book, which ultimately became the basis for this publication.

We owe thanks to many individuals and several institutions for their help. But first and foremost we must acknowledge the very special role that Mrs. Anne Lynch played in the creation of this book, as she helped us in finding unpublished materials and sketches by Kevin that we did not know about. Her warmth and enthusiasm made the effort a very rewarding experience for us. Furthermore, it was Anne who influenced us to focus more on the early life of Kevin Lynch, and who made us see his intellectual contributions and his design philosophy in a proper biographical context. Indeed, much of our material for the biographical sketch came from a taped interview with Anne Lynch, conducted in the summer of 1987.

We also thank the Lynch children—Catherine, David, Laura, and Peter—for their interest in the project and their support. Their comments have been constructive, providing information we did not have and occasionally cautioning us against misinterpreting their father's ideas and restraining our penchant for academic jargon.

We would like to thank James Lynch, Kevin's elder brother, for his financial contribution toward this project. We also thank Hamilton and Peggy Marston of San Diego for their financial contribution and for making available materials on the San Diego study.

Several colleagues provided encouragement and support in the project and read our early prospectus for this book: Randolph Hester of the University of California at Berkeley, John DeMoncheaux, Gary Hack, and Tunney Lee of the Massachusetts Institute of Technology, and Ralph Knowles and Martin Krieger of the University of Southern California.

Institutional support and service were also crucial to the completion of various phases of this project. The College of Environmental Design at the University of California at Berkeley, the Institute Archives and the Rotch Library at MIT, and the School of Urban and Regional Planning at the University of Southern California provided various materials and services. Helen Samuels of the Institute Archives and Special Collections and Margaret De Popolo of the Rotch Library (both at MIT) deserve thanks for their cooperation in obtaining various items included in this publication.

We owe special thanks to Stephen Carr, a colleague and associate of Kevin Lynch and the principal partner of Carr/Lynch Associates. Not only did he make available to us the reports on various projects in which Kevin was involved; he also gave us important background information and insights related to these projects.

We are grateful to Ann Simunovic, a former staff member of MIT's Department of Urban Studies and Planning, for graciously agreeing to type from the handwritten pages of the Florence Journals. Several students in our respective departments helped us at various stages of the research and the preparation of the manuscript: Rajeev Bhatia and Amita Sinha of the University of California at Berkeley and Kanishka Goonawerdena, Wei Jer Hsu, and Thomas Lew of the University of Southern California.

Finally, we thank Roger Conover, Paul Bethge, and the staff of The MIT Press.

Tridib Banerjee and Michael Southworth

Publisher's note

Although they have been reset, the articles are presented essentially in their original form. They have been set from copies provided by the volume editors. Trivial errors, such as misspellings and the mixing of plural nouns and singular verb forms, have been corrected. The spellings of certain words (e.g. *traveling*, *buses*, and *center*) have been standardized, and the serial comma has been employed consistently. In a few places, clarity seemed to require the insertion of *and* or some slightly greater correction; such corrections have been made economically and have been bracketed to indicate their origin. Most of the handwritten alterations that were evident in the archival copies of manuscripts have been implemented. All true idiosyncrasies and other aspects of Kevin Lynch's style have been preserved.

CITY SENSE
AND
CITY DESIGN

Kevin Lynch: His Life and Work

Tridib Banerjee
and
Michael Southworth

Kevin Lynch (1918–1984) was the leading environmental design theorist of our time. His productive career was devoted to research, writing, and teaching, as well as to consulting in city design and planning. He has left behind a rich legacy of ideas and insights about human purposes and values in built form, and possibilities for designing humane environments. His published work includes seven books (eight, including a posthumous volume) and some twenty-five journal articles and essays written for various anthologies edited by others. Although Lynch's books will continue to represent his major contributions, they are by no means exhaustive of his ideas. To fully appreciate his distinctively humanistic design philosophy, which evolved over a period of more than thirty years, one must know of his other work. Much of his design philosophy was developed and elaborated in many different essays written on different occasions. Until now, these other previously published works were buried in the shadowy depths of journal stacks or in sundry anthologies and symposium proceedings. Many of these materials are not readily accessible to the public, to the professional community, or to the younger generation of design and planning students. Then there are various studies and reports from his professional practice, very few of which have ever been published. Much of this material remains in the archives of the Massachusetts Institute of Technology, available only to the hardy and inquisitive scholar. Some of these examples not only represent a less well known side of Lynch's many-faceted talents, but also show how he was able to translate his ideas and theories into practice. Moreover, these are important case studies of design and planning projects; they will be valuable in teaching and in practice.

In this volume we have assembled almost all of Lynch's previously published journal and anthology articles, as well as a broad selection of his unpublished work, including drawings and sketches, essays, and excerpts from professional reports and travel journals.[1] We include the published articles in this volume so that they will be easily accessible to students, teachers, and practitioners of city design and planning. Moreover, many of the journal articles are not readily available abroad—especially in the Third World, where library collections are often limited. By including both published and unpublished materials, this collection becomes an important supplement to the books of Kevin Lynch and essentially completes the published record of his written contributions.

The Contributions of Kevin Lynch

To understand the contributions of Kevin Lynch we must look at his work in the context of the planning practices of earlier decades. It takes some effort to remember today, in the waning years of the twentieth century, that city planning in America at the turn of the century was rooted in the grand traditions of civic, landscape, and garden city design set forth by such stalwarts as Daniel Burnham, Ebenezer Howard, and Frederick Law Olmsted. Not only could cities be designed; the belief was that they should be designed, because aesthetic and orderly environments were essential for the health and well-being of the people. A good and beautiful city was believed to mirror—in fact, to shape—a good society; it instilled civic pride and responsibility in its citizens, and promoted their moral and social development.

This turn-of-the-century design philosophy was influenced by the thinking of anti-urbanist social reformers who were worried that the individual and the family were likely to be lost in the incipient urban transition, and that the wholesomeness of rural community life and values would be replaced by an anomic urban social order. The proliferation of smokestack industries and the attendant urban sprawl along the Eastern Seaboard further reinforced the anxieties and anti-city biases of the reformists.[2] Restoring family, neighborhood, and community values was seen as crucial to countering the impersonal tendencies of urban life. Such important social thinkers of the time as the psychologist William James, the philosopher and educator John Dewey, the sociologist Robert Park, and the social worker Jane Addams all spoke of establishing local communities, neighborhoods, and a sense of place so that the individual and the family would not get lost in the great emerging urban agglomerations. Clarence Perry's "neighborhood unit" formula, although a physical planning principle, grew out of this movement. Across the Atlantic came Ebenezer Howard's "garden city" idea, formulated to create healthy communities in industrial Britain. Clarence Stein's "superblock" concept, which was meant to create large, safe pedestrian domains free from auto traffic, was another design idea that came out of similar reactions to the expanding metropolis. Together these ideas gave legitimacy to the notion that physical planning could indeed create safe, decent, and wholesome community environments, even within seemingly faceless urban regions.[3]

In the 1950s and the 1960s, this view faced a serious challenge from social scientists who openly questioned what they called the "physical determinism" of design. They argued, sometimes convincingly, that the physical form had very little to do with the social form of our environments, and they exhorted designers to understand how social forces actually influence the physical city. They further argued that designers' sense of physical order had nothing to do with the social or the moral order of society, pointing to debacles such as Boston's West End and St. Louis's Pruitt-Igoe and to the social "blues" of the British (and, later, the American) new towns. The role of urban design was seen essentially as a matter of aesthetics. In the long list of social and economic priorities, design values were relegated to the status of window dressing—something frivolous and worth attending to only after the "real" problems were solved.

Cities were seen essentially as an outcome of the locational organization of market demand for urban space, mediated by local politics.

Beyond that, the city was recognized to be a highly complex phenomenon. And since this complex entity was yet to be fully fathomed by the social sciences, any proposition that cities could be shaped by deliberate design appeared too perverse an idea. To the strong systems orientation of the social sciences, which was shaping the direction of city planning, the idea of city design was seen as anachronistic, impudent, and megalomaniac. Yet by the early 1960s the impact of the federal urban renewal program was beginning to be felt across the country. Entire urban districts were being leveled with little concern for the social life and roots of places, to be replaced with anonymous forms on a new scale. These changes in the urban physical environment continued to have major impacts on people's life experiences.

It was against this background that Kevin Lynch began his early research on city form and city design as a young instructor at MIT. He was fascinated and intrigued by the physical city and the urban experience generally, and by the interaction between physical space and its human use. He quickly became engrossed in describing and understanding the form of the modern metropolis. Between the mid-1950s and the mid-1960s he wrote a set of articles on this subject in rather quick succession: "The Form of Cities" (1954), "The Pattern of the Metropolis" (1961), "A Theory of Urban Form" (with Lloyd Rodwin, 1958), and "The City As Environment" (1965). In these articles Lynch was beginning to chart a whole new way of looking at the large-scale built environment and was searching for a taxonomy to describe the physical city.

He was also curious to know how the public, not the trained designer, saw and understood the everyday environment, what they valued in it, how it shaped their lives and activities, and how they in turn shaped the urban form. After a year of travel and research in Europe, a major grant from the Rockefeller Foundation allowed him to continue his research on how people perceive and organize their environment.

Gyorgy Kepes, a well-known painter and professor of design at MIT whom Kevin considered a great man and a great teacher, had in part inspired the research and worked with Lynch on the project. The study, conducted in three cities—Boston, Jersey City, and Los Angeles— culminated in the all-time classic of the planning literature, *The Image of the City* (1960). This book earned Lynch national and international renown. No other book in this field has touched so many, or sparked so much interest both inside and outside the field.

In other writings, Lynch had begun to present different aspects of his research findings on the perception of environments and related discussions of users' needs: "Some Childhood Memories of the City" (with Alvin Lukashok, 1956), "Environmental Adaptability" (1958), and "A Walk Around the Block" (with Malcolm Rivkin, 1959). His interest in how people perceive and evaluate their environments remained strong. When asked by UNESCO to write a paper on perception of environmental quality, he quickly produced a cross-cultural comparison of childhood environments, utilizing interviews with children and naturalistic field studies. Eventually the study was published as an edited book, *Growing Up In Cities* (1977), but before that it was reported in abbreviated form in two journal articles: "Growing Up in Cities" (1976) and "On People and Places: A Comparative Study of the Spatial Environment of Adolescence" (1976), both with Tridib Banerjee.[4]

In the years that followed the publication of *The Image of the City*, the contributions of Kevin Lynch as a design theorist continued to become known and appreciated through his other books. *Site Planning* (1962), written as a textbook, proved to be quite popular. *The View from the Road* (1964), which Lynch wrote with Donald Appleyard and John Myer, was a study of the visual environment of the city as experienced while in motion, inspired by the massive freeway development in American cities. Another sabbatical in the late 1960s led to a revised and expanded edition of *Site Planning* that included new materials on design methods and behavioral research. Lynch also began the work on what was to became his favorite book, *What Time Is This Place?* (1972). In 1976 he published *Managing the Sense of a Region*, an exploration of how the form of a large metropolitan area might be designed and controlled.

By the mid-1960s Lynch had already begun his work on theories of city form and city design. In a way this work was the most significant of his contributions, because it attempted to integrate many previously unconnected branches of planning theory. In articles such as "Environmental Adaptability" and "A Theory of Urban Form" he had already begun to address specific requirements of "good city form" and how these requirements interacted with various elements of the physical city. In the 1960s and the 1970s Lynch devoted a major part of his writing to proposing what the goals of city design and ideal city form might be. The essays "Quality in City Design" (1966), "City Design and City Appearance" (1968), "The Openness of Open Space" (1965), and "Open Space: Freedom and Control" (with Stephen Carr, 1979) are examples of his efforts to define the qualities of a good urban environment.

Some of these papers were written in a speculative vein; others bordered on romanticism and utopian thinking. Yet these pieces were often engaging and inspiring, suggesting a completely different way of defining the scope of city design. Although the physical environment itself was very much the focus of Lynch's writing, his ideas had nothing to do with the "grand" and deterministic turn-of-the-century design traditions, which the social scientists openly scorned. What was distinctive about Lynch's philosophy was that he dealt with the immediate experiential qualities of place—which he was fond of referring to as the "sensuous qualities," or simply "sense"—and their importance in people's lives. He made his case simply and forcefully, yet in a rich and elegant way that was characteristic of his writing. Drawing liberally from the tradition of the social sciences, he convinced even the most skeptical of the contemporary social scientists and policy makers that the physical city mattered, and that it mattered in a very fundamental and important way. City design is not window dressing!

Lynch took care to differentiate what he preferred to call "city design" from "urban design." In contrast to urban design, which was more architectural and more project-oriented at that time, he felt that city design should address the quality and character of the entire public city, or at least large sectors of it. However, his term "city design" never really took hold; the profession continues to use the term "urban design," regardless of scale or focus. While reestablishing the importance of the physical environment in the context of policy, Lynch also revived the normative aspects of city design—the standards or ideals that urban form should achieve and the reasons for doing so. Here he parted company with the social sciences and drew inspiration from the humanities. He emphasized that city design is not just about the physical arrangement or rearrangement of things to satisfy today's needs, but that it also has to do with fundamental human values and rights: justice, freedom, control, learning, access, dignity, and creativity. He emphasized that city design is not the reproduction of environments in the images of the present order, but is really about what should be and what could be. During this period he wrote such memorable essays as "Where Learning Happens" (with Stephen Carr, 1968), "The Possible City" (1968), and "Grounds for Utopia" (1975). Eventually many of these ideas were abridged and incorporated in his last major book, *Good City Form* (1981), which is in many ways the most complete treatise on his philosophy of good city form and city design. It is a culmination of many decades of research, thinking, and writing on the performance characteristics of city form that serve human purposes and values best.

By the late 1960s Lynch was considered the leading expert on city design. He was asked to write essays on design practice and education for several publications and symposia. "Urban Design," written for the *Encyclopaedia Britannica* (1974), and "City and Regional Planning," written for the *Enciclopedia Italiana* (1973), are cases in point; "City Design: What It Is and How It Might Be Taught" (1980) is another. Two interesting essays on growth management that proved to have considerable practical significance were also published in the 1970s: "Performance Zoning: The Small Town of Gay Head Tries It" (with Philip Herr, 1973) and "Controlling the Location and Timing of Development by the Distribution of Marketable Development Rights" (1975). However, only a few of Kevin Lynch's practice-oriented writings have been published before now. A large number of his design and planning studies—some of them national award winners—remained unpublished and therefore generally inaccessible. Lynch was particularly proud of his contribution to the development of Boston's Government Center and waterfront. Although the results deviated from Lynch's plans in some ways and were not always to his liking, the basic concepts of creating a system of public open spaces, opening up public access to the waterfront, and preserving historic places have made the Government Center and Haymarket area of Boston one of the more successful urban places in the contemporary American city. Also special to Lynch was a study of the San Diego region he did with Donald Appleyard in the early 1970s under a grant from the Marston family. This study, based largely on public perceptions and community concerns about declining environmental quality, was written as a white paper for public discussion. It brought out ideas and presented scenarios for the future of the San Diego community, and it continues to serve as a rallying point for local groups. Other examples of Lynch's professional work include "Analysis of the Visual Form of Brookline, Massachusetts" (1965), "Sensuous Criteria for Highway Design" (with Donald Appleyard, 1966), "The Urban Landscape of San Salvador: Environmental Quality in an Urbanizing Region" (1968), "Looking at the Vineyard" (with Sasaki, Dawson & Demay, 1973), and "Designing and Managing the Strip" (with Michael Southworth, 1974). These works illustrate how Lynch tried to translate his ideas and his philosophy into proposals for specific settings and contexts.

Toward the end of Lynch's career it was clear to those who were close to him that he wanted to focus on applying some of his ideas to practice. Yet he continued to write, producing some moving essays in the final years of his life. "Reconsidering *The Image of the City*" (1985) is a brief but poignant essay on what Lynch himself thought of the work that had won him international recognition. He was deeply disturbed by world events, and in particular by the escalating nuclear arms race and the attendant prospects of a nuclear war. He chose to address this chilling prospect in "What Will Happen To Us?" (1983), written with Tunney Lee and Peter Droege. Asked to comment on what role planners and designers could play in the event of such a catastrophe, Lynch wrote a hauntingly sad scenario of a "cacotopia"—the word he used to describe the opposite of a utopia[5]—in which he tries to find his way home to Watertown after a nuclear explosion has leveled the entire Boston urban region ("Coming Home," 1984). These are powerful articles which most designers and planners probably have not yet read. Lynch also prepared the third edition of *Site Planning* (1984, co-authored with Gary Hack) shortly before his death.

Lynch's last book, *Wasting Away* (edited by Michael Southworth), was nearing completion at the time of his death and was published posthumously. In it he reflects on the processes of decline, decay, and renewal in our lives and environments. While it does deal with waste and the environment, the book goes beyond these boundaries to explore the subject from many points of view.

These works stand out as one of most significant contributions to the field to date, linking theory and research with a strong philosophy of the human purposes of environmental form and of design as social action.

A Biographical Sketch

Kevin Lynch was born in Chicago in 1918. His parents were second-generation Irish-Americans, his grandparents having emigrated from Ireland after the famine. They struggled at first, but by the time Kevin was born his parents were well-to-do. By his own account his father's side of the family had "boom" and "bust" years. At one time the family lived on South Parkway, then an upper-class neighborhood.

Kevin was the youngest of three brothers. He grew up in the Hazel Avenue neighborhood on the North Side of Chicago, near Lake Michigan. This was a mixed but stable city neighborhood of apartments and single-family homes, with tree-lined streets. Swimming, playing, and walking along the lake shore always remained among his most treasured childhood memories. In 1953 he returned to this neighborhood of his youth and noted the following impressions of what he described as a "sentimental journey":

> . . . [the] Hazel Avenue neighborhood [is] surprisingly unchanged despite a few store alterations, a new house in Cummings' yard. . . . Still a little island of green and solid one family houses; the trees [are] thicker and higher, the buildings much as remembered, though the open spaces seem smaller. Here [is] an example of a stable mixed neighborhood; the apartments jostle the houses, but the latter [are] still well kept and well-to-do. . . . Remarkable that though remembered buildings were sharply remembered, yet memory (and presumably attention) operate only on a few points: our apartment, that next door that we saw in construction, the Holmeiers, the Cummings, the Walshes, the big house that once had rabbis, the drug store, the apartment hotel, the church and school, the el and the cemetery, Robbins Terrace and its big wild lot. The rest [is] just vaguely familiar, and probably [was] never experienced as much more than a collection to pass through. . . . The area is quiet and relaxed, and sometimes successful in its juxtaposition of different houses, but basically dull and often cramped and ugly. Strange to feel at home in it and to realize its ugliness or dullness. The church tower that I used to look on so long in the late sunlight is only a colorless copy. The circle by the parochial school is a dusty playground, heavily equipped and used but dirty and unsupervised. . . . many of the kids play in the street by preference. . . .[6]

Young Kevin's early education began at home, with private tutors. He then attended a Catholic parish school for several years with his brothers. But his mother, who was quite free-thinking and knowledgeable about education, later sent her children to the Francis W. Parker School, one of the first progressive schools in the country. This was quite a courageous thing for an Irish Catholic mother to do at that time, since Catholic children were expected to attend parochial schools. Lynch recalled later: "Everytime I went to confession I was asked why I wasn't attending Catholic school." This school, attended by Lynch all the way through his high school years, had been founded by Francis Parker, a former school superintendant from Quincy, Massachusetts, and a disciple of John Dewey. The curriculum and the instructional methods were innovative, inspired by Dewey's philosophy of learning by doing. The learning environment was enormously engaging and stimulating, and the teachers were excellent. Throughout his life Lynch treasured his education at the Parker School. There he met Anne Borders, his future wife, and they shared many of the same learning experiences. She recalls that "children loved going to that school and never forgot what they learned there."

The Parker School experience had a major effect on Kevin Lynch's early intellectual development—more than college—and shaped his future interests in human environments and social justice. His interest in architecture grew out of a course in Egyptian history taught by Hazel Cornell, his seventh-grade teacher. Another teacher, James Mitchell, interested Lynch in reading Bacon, Hobbes, Descartes, Hegel, Spinoza, Schopenhauer, Locke, and Mill. Also influential was his eighth-grade teacher, Sarah Greenbaum, who continued to be an advisor and a friend long after he left the Parker School. (She introduced Anne and Kevin to the island of Martha's Vineyard, off Cape Cod, where she had a summer cottage and where the Lynches later built a summer house of their own.)

Lynch's high school days coincided with the Great Depression, picket lines and bread lines, a general climate of political upheaval, and talk of social and political change. The Parker School, with its progressive educational philosophy, engaged its students in those larger social and political questions. But the Spanish Civil War was the "first real political influence" on Lynch's life. It stimulated his interest in questions of socialism and communism and other contemporary political matters. "It was one of the great times of my life," he commented to one interviewer.[7]

After graduation from high school in 1935, Kevin Lynch decided to study architecture. Not certain where to apply, he went to see John A. Holabird, Jr., of Chicago—the only architect he knew at the time—for advice. Holabird, who believed in the old-fashioned, conservative, Beaux-Arts tradition, as Lynch later discovered, suggested that he should go to Yale, the last bastion of that tradition in the United States. Thus, Lynch began his study of architecture at Yale, but he was disappointed and discouraged by the Beaux-Arts approach—he once described the Yale architecture program as "the most conservative and backward" of its time.

It was at this point that Lynch read about Frank Lloyd Wright and wrote to inquire about studying architecture with him[8]:

Mr. F.L. Wright,
Taliesin,
Spring Green, Wis.

Dear Mr. Wright,

I had heard of your school before, and considered it an interesting possibility for the study of architecture, but a few days ago I got hold of one of your bulletins, and was filled with enthusiasm to go to a place with such an atmosphere of freedom and creation. So I am writing you for some advice and a little information.

At present I am a student at Yale, entering my Sophomore year. Yale's school of architecture has a large reputation, but after one course in the history of architecture and a look at the work being done there, I think it is academic and stifling. Of course there are many things to be learned there such as technique in the drawing and the science of construction, but it seems a waste of time. One of my major deficiencies is lack of ability in drawing, but I am taking a course in freehand drawing, and I imagine that if it is only a technique that I can master it with hard work. But does your school give sufficient instruction in engineering and materials, which are so vital in architecture? Or would you advise me to take some engineering courses before applying for admission at Taliesin?

I have another question. I have hopes of qualifying myself not only for architecture, but for city-planning, although that is somewhat of a big order. Does Taliesin give adequate training for work in that field, not

Kevin Lynch (seated, second from left)
with Frank Lloyd Wright at Taliesin.
Photo: Hedrich-Blessing.

only in its theoretical but its practical aspects? Or again would you
advise me to get further training in some school of city planning (as at
Harvard) before applying to work with you?

Perhaps I could finish my Sophomore year at Yale, and then enter
Taliesin. Do you think that that would be advisable? I am now eighteen
years old, never have had any practical architectural experience, despite attempts this summer to get such a job. I hope that I may join the
fellowship soon or within a few years. I will appreciate it very much if
you would advise me and send me any further information about
Taliesin that you can. As your answer will not probably arrive before the
end of this week, please send it to my college address below.

Sincerely yours,
Kevin Lynch
1440 Yale Station
New Haven, Conn.

Monday, Sept. 21

Wright replied as follows:

September 25, 1936
Kevin Lynch
New Haven, Conn.

My dear Kevin Lynch:

Answering your questions about Fellowship at Taliesin—
1. Your stay at Yale could be no possible help to your work at Taliesin.
2. Your lack of ability to draw is soon rectified.
3. We have no course nor any curriculum at Taliesin. Only performance under my direction and alongside other apprentices.
4. No engineering course will help you here except as they are not anterior but posterior to experience in learning the nature of the thing to which they apply. The sense of the whole and its philosophy first. Technique first is the cart before the horse.
5. Theory and practice are one at Taliesin.
6. City planning is natural feature of our work at Taliesin (Broadacre City).
7. The best time for an architect in embryo to join the Fellowship is before any time is wasted along conventional educational lines in architecture or engineering.
We should want to see you and talk with you personally and have you see us before we agree to take you into Fellowship. And you would be welcome at any time for that interview.[9]

Even after receiving this letter from Wright which answered most of his questions and after he had visited Taliesin, Lynch had further inquiries prompted largely by questions raised by various advisors. The following letter captures some of his predicaments, yet confirms his determination to leave Yale.

Kevin Lynch – Yale University – New Haven, Conn.
1440 Yale Station

Sunday, Jan. 10

Dear Mr. Wright,

Since I have been to see you different people have been giving me advice about my architectural education as if I had a cold and they had an infinite number of home remedies. I went up to see Cranbrook Academy near Detroit on my way back East, since I had heard so much favorable comment about it. I found out that it was an ultra-graduate school, seemingly good in certain specialized fields but definitely depending on a good deal of technical knowledge.

Kevin Lynch, in U.S. Army uniform,
with his bride Anne in the summer
of 1943.

I also talked with several men here, and they stressed the need for a general cultural background and a college degree before going to work with you. There is something of value to be gotten out of college (I remember you asked me about that) from the group life, from the stimulation of certain people, from the mere quantity of activities and loose ideas that lie scattered about. And could not the knowledge of drafting and of construction well come after a general development in the field?

But they did bring up one rather solid objection, that it is necessary to have a degree from a school of architecture to become a registered architect, unless one goes through something like ten or twelve years of apprenticeship. Does that then make it at least legally necessary to go thru an architectural school? You said something about that; I don't remember what it was.

I am still pretty definite that I want to leave Yale at the end of this year; perhaps I can come to Taliesin sometime in the summer, if that is agreeable to you.

I hope you can answer my question about the state requirements.

Sincerely,
Kevin Lynch

Correspondence continued between Lynch and Taliesin. In one of the subsequent letters (dated April 12, 1937) Lynch asked Wright about fees and the appropriate time for joining the Fellowship. In this letter he also commented on an article that Wright had sent him. The following excerpt captures young Lynch's sentiments about the city and the country, an attitude that endured throughout his later work:

. . . If I have not written since I received your article about Taliesin and its cultural background, I like it very much. The realization that the country is a very vital part of our cultural tradition is a stimulating idea, although I do think that the city contributes another vital part to our culture. The real problem is to strip all that is unhealthy out of the city and the country too, and try to integrate those two traditions and give them a common basis and a common expression. . . .

The Taliesin experience came at a critical point in Lynch's professional schooling. The experience of Yale—not just the Beaux-Arts approach to architecture, but the university education as a whole—had set him against the conventional college education. Although going to Taliesin required some initial adjustment, he liked its "hands-on" approach to architectural education, which was very much like the Parker School's approach. Shortly after he started his apprenticeship with

Wright in the fall of 1937, Lynch wrote a short essay for the *Capital Times*, a local newspaper published in Madison. The following ex-cerpts, written when Lynch was 19, capture rather well his joy of being

at Taliesin and his views of conventional university education.

Life for a new apprentice at Taliesin is a welter of new impressions, new stimulations, new jobs to handle, new friends who have much to teach you, new tensions to measure up to what is being done around you. The new apprentice must learn how to handle a tall bundle of corn-stalks, or how to cut a green oak plank, or how to translate a drawing for a building, or how to lay plaster, or even the most efficient method of scraping oatmeal out of the pot. There are new horizons of work, of creation, of meaning, lifting all around you. . . .

. . . while I was making up my mind to leave my course at Yale half-finished and come to Taliesin, my nebulous convictions as to the value of university training were hammered out into pretty definite shape. An initial vague dissatisfaction with college grew slowly into the disillusioning idea that something was radically wrong with the whole method of doling out education in standardized bucketfuls, five buckets per year per man. . . .

College as a preparation for creative activity later in life is only a period of "watchful waiting," and not very watchful at that. . . . It is an attempt by society to cast men into a mould leavened with inertia and lack of enthusiasm, so that they may not question the glaring flaws in the social structure. College is most logically considered from the stu-dent's point of view as four years of fun before the hard and unpleasant job of living begins. . . .

That is my conviction regarding university education. Taliesin, at first glance, was something entirely different and had a different ideal. It is the attempt to grasp the new ideal of hard work, of creative activity, of "learning by doing," of enthusiastic cooperation in solving common problems, that makes the life of the new apprentice so full and so fascinating here. I am afraid that a candid comparison of the large and famous university with five thousand students housed in expensive new Gothic buildings, with the small group studying and working with a great architect in a building nowhere adequate for their needs, but surrounded by beauty, might make wish he had given his money and his books to the Iroquois Indians.[10]

Kevin Lynch studied with Wright for a year and a half during an important time in Taliesin's history: 1937–38, when Wright was moving Taliesin from Wisconsin to Arizona, largely for personal health reasons. Lynch, a wonderful storyteller, recalled the amusing experiences of traveling for days in a caravan of cars and trucks laden with everything from drawings to frozen sides of beef. (As the caravan moved southwest to warmer temperatures, the beef began to thaw, forcing the entourage to eat steak three meals a day[11]) Construction of the new school began immediately upon arrival at the Arizona site, and according to Lynch's own account he and the other "apprentices" were all required to participate in the construction work.

Lynch considered Frank Lloyd Wright another great influence on his life. He did not agree with Wright's social philosophy, which he considered "backward looking" and of the "arts and crafts tradition" with a view of "individualistic society"; however, he respected Wright's genius for form and design, and he once said that Wright had made him "see the world for the first time."

Lynch left Taliesin after a year and a half because he felt that "one can get swallowed up" by the establishment, and he wanted to be on his own. According to Lynch, Wright did not always treat his apprentices gently. He could be quite harsh and rude in his criticisms, often devastating for young designers. This treatment must have troubled Kevin, who always believed in human potentialities and who himself became a gentle, fair, and kind teacher. Lynch felt that many of Wright's apprentices had missed the opportunity to blossom on their own. "You became only a small Mr. Wright if you stayed," he once commented. He never regretted leaving Taliesin, but Wright did not take his departure kindly. ". . . he cursed me up and down. That was the most wonderful bit of cursing I have ever received: it was really poetic."[12]

After he left Taliesin, Lynch felt that he needed some engineering background. He went to Rensselaer Polytechnic Institute to study civil and structural engineering. It turned out that engineering was not quite suited to his taste. He got bored and decided to discontinue his engineering studies. He stayed at RPI to study biology under Professor Bray (a self-taught man), who became another of Lynch's mentors. He then worked for a while as an assistant to Paul Schweicker, an architect in Chicago.

On June 7, 1941, Lynch married Anne Borders at the Chicago Commons, a settlement house where Anne's parents had been social workers. Three weeks later he was drafted into the Army. In the spring of 1944 he was sent to the South Pacific. He served in the Army Corps of Engineers in the Palau Islands, in the Philippines, and in Japan during the occupation.

After returning to the United States, Lynch went back to college under the G.I. Bill, pursuing a bachelor's degree in city planning at MIT. His interest in the field had been aroused in part by his reading of The Culture of Cities, by Lewis Mumford. His Bachelor of City Planning thesis (1947), "Controlling the Flow of Rebuilding and Replanning in Residential Areas," made a strong impression on MIT faculty members Lloyd Rodwin, Burnham Kelly, and John Burchard and was an important factor in his later being asked to teach at MIT. Interestingly, the thesis touched on the themes of change, decay, and renewal that Lynch developed many years later in What Time is This Place? and Wasting Away.

After graduation Lynch went to North Carolina to work for the Greensboro Planning Commission—his first planning job. He was quite happy there, and apparently he intended to go on working as a planner. To his surprise, he got a call from MIT offering him a faculty position, even though he did not have a higher degree. At first Lynch was ambivalent about a teaching career and was quite content to stay at Greensboro. Anne Lynch, unhappy with this possibility, persuaded him to accept the MIT job. He joined the faculty in 1948 and continued teaching into the early 1980s, although he had formally retired in 1978. Soon after he joined the planning program at MIT, Lynch became interested in the form and the visual environment of the city. Lloyd Rodwin recalled that Lynch was remarkably capable in every area of planning—not just one or two—and that he could have taught any course in the program. However, there was no particular focus, no passion. This changed when a Ford Foundation grant allowed him to spend a year in Europe with his family, based mainly in Florence. For Lynch this was a period of observing, questioning, discussing with friends and colleagues the essential nature of city experience, probing others about their reactions to Italian urban settings, and interpreting his own intuitions and feelings about what he saw and experienced. He kept a daily journal in which he recorded his travels, encounters, reflections, and occasional sketches. We have included in this collection some segments from the travel journals that capture the essence of Lynch's inquiry. These pages are interesting reading in their own right, but they should also give the reader a sense of how Lynch's early ideas were formed. According to Rodwin, "Lynch came back to MIT transformed; the fire was burning and from that point on his course was set."

The MIT years were truly remarkable. With his colleagues Fred Adams, Jack Howard, and Lloyd Rodwin, Lynch helped build the planning program into one of the most distinguished in the world. The emphasis on city and metropolitan design within the field of planning was a creation of Lynch, shaped by his own evolving philosophy of city design. Bright and creative students from all over the world came to study with Lynch, who nurtured their creativity and stimulated them to branch out into new areas of inquiry. His teaching method was Socratic; he always asked the strategic question that would go to the heart of the problem. Those who came to him for design solutions or "answers" might have been disappointed, for he was more interested in teaching ways of asking the right questions. He enjoyed the company of his students and was always interested in them and their work. He respected their views, and was willing to listen to their ideas and to learn from them. He often said that his students were his best teachers and the part of his MIT experience that he valued most. Long after they left MIT, Lynch kept in touch with many of his students. He was interested in their work and their career developments, which in many cases he himself supported and advanced. Former students also kept in touch with him for their own intellectual stimulation and sustenance. Throughout his life he received an enormous amount of correspondence and many examples of professional and scholarly work to review or comment on, from former students as well as from practitioners and scholars all over the world. He answered every letter and reviewed almost every manuscript, no matter how busy he was. His students remember him as a great teacher, a friend, a sounding board, a source of inspiration, and a great influence on their lives.

Throughout his academic career at MIT, Lynch maintained an active involvement in planning practice. In the early years he was associated with the Cambridge-based consulting firm of Adams, Howard and Greeley. In the middle years he worked largely as an independent consultant. After he retired from MIT, besides continuing his research and writing he became more actively involved in practice as a principal partner of Carr/Lynch Associates, with a former student and colleague at MIT, Stephen Carr. Notable examples of their work are the redesign of Columbia Point (one of the worst public housing projects in the Boston area) and a plan for a linear regional park and urban development along forty miles of the Rio Salado corridor in Phoenix. He was also involved in several international projects, many in the Third World (one such project is included in this collection). His interest in the planning and development of Third World cities took him to Africa, Cuba, China, El Salvador, and Morocco. His interest in the future of human settlements was indeed global in scope.

Lynch particularly enjoyed projects in which the present or future users of the environment were directly involved. He always recommended what he felt would be best for the "substantive" clients—the actual users—even though at times they might be at odds with the desires of the "nominal" or institutional clients.[13] He felt quite strongly

Kevin Lynch receiving the Rexford Tugwell Award at the Bonaventure Hotel in Los Angeles in April 1984. With him is Alan Kreditor, dean of the University of Southern California School of Urban and Regional Planning. Photo: David Dubuque.

Kevin Lynch with Mrs. Tugwell at the Tugwell Award ceremony. Photo: David Dubuque.

that ultimately it is the people who make a place successful, not the designer.

Kevin Lynch was honored by a number of professional societies. He received the American Institute of Planners' Fiftieth Anniversary Award in 1967 and the American Institute of Architects' Allied Professions Medal in 1974. He was conferred honorary doctorate degrees by Stuttgart University and Ball State University. In 1984, shortly before his death, he became the first recipient of the most prestigious recognition in the field of planning: the Rexford G. Tugwell Award.[14]

On the evening of April 23, 1984, at his Watertown house, Lynch was happily talking with Professor Zhu Zixuan, making plans for Lynch to teach a course at Tsinghua University, in Beijing, that November. He left the next morning for his summer home on Martha's Vineyard, where he died suddenly, alone, on April 25, 1984. He had spent the time immediately before his death reading, writing, and planting a garden according to his carefully drawn plan. At his side was *In My Father's Court*, by Isaac Bashevis Singer, opened to the passage where Singer describes his first visit to the country as a boy:

I had not seen any wild cows, but what I had already seen was wonderful and strange. The sky here was not a narrow strip as on Krochmalna Street, but broad, spread out like the ocean, and it descended to the earth like a supernatural curtain. Birds flew overhead in swarms, with a twittering, a cawing, a whistling—large birds and small birds. Two storks were circling above one of the hills of the Citadel. Butterflies of all colors fluttered above the grass: white, yellow, brown, with all kinds of dots and patterns. The air smelled of earth, of grass, of the smoke of locomotives, and of something more that intoxicated me and made my head reel. There was a strange stillness here, and yet everything murmured, rustled, chirped. Blossoms fell from somewhere and settled on the lapels of my jacket. I looked up at the sky, saw the sun, the clouds, and suddenly I understood more clearly the meaning of the words of Genesis. This, then, was the world God had created: the earth, the heaven, the waters above that are separated by the firmaments from the waters below.

The Organization of the Book

We have organized this book into seven major parts, each of which focuses on a major facet of Lynch's work. Part I, "The Form of Cities," includes papers in which he speculates on urban form—what it is, its scale, its patterns, and its characteristics. Part II, "Experiencing Cities," focuses on how the city is perceived and interpreted; it includes Lynch's

The last design: a carefully laid-out plan for a kitchen garden on Martha's Vineyard.

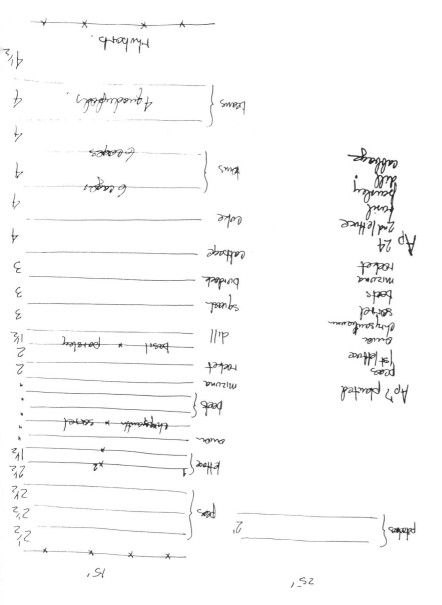

personal impressions of several cities, reports on his research with children, and his assessments of environmental perception research. Part III, "Analysis of Visual Form," contains Lynch's work on ways of describing and analyzing urban form. Part IV, "City Design: Theory," includes his more theoretical papers on the performance criteria for good form, such as openness and adaptability. Part V, "City Design: Education and Practice," contains papers on the teaching and practice of city design, particularly the operational principles and guidelines. Part VI, "City Design: Projects," presents several examples of Lynch's professional work, especially those projects in which he took particular pride. Part VII, "Utopias and Cacotopias," includes several of his fantasy pieces exploring what the city might aspire to and what might occur if things go wrong.

We believe that the works of Kevin Lynch, which have appealed to different audiences for their research, analytical, theoretical, and application values, can be seen as constituting the only extant philosophy of large-scale design. Our hope is that this collection will make it easier to interpret this unique design philosophy, which seeks to define the functions and the purposes of urban form and city design in terms of fundamental human values.

For practicing professionals, this collection offers models for the analysis and the solution of problems as well as techniques of large-scale design. Also, we hope these projects will inspire innovative approaches to seemingly stereotypical problems.

For students of architecture, landscape architecture, and urban and regional planning, this book may serve as a textbook. The field of city design, at least as it is commonly practiced and understood today, does not yet have a complete and definitive textbook. Some books have covered the historical perspectives, the practical side of design, or the implementation aspects of the field, but we do not know of a book that has included the theories and philosophies as well as the research and

practice of city design. If such a book were to be compiled, many of the materials would have to come from the writings of Kevin Lynch.

There is a need for a special group of talented designers who can conceptualize design issues at a scale larger than that of buildings or projects. "Urban design" continues to be defined as large-scale architecture, because many design practitioners—mainly architects— choose to define it that way. The architecture profession does not deal with policy; it deals with forms that can be built. Thus, any concept of large-scale design that extends beyond project-scale site plans and collections of buildings becomes too unwieldy for the vast majority of practitioners. Yet, as the quality of the urban experience continues to decline all around the world, there is a growing and urgent need for thinking about design at the city scale. Lynch has not only written exten- sively in this vein but also has shown, as in the San Diego study, how design guidelines can be developed for landscapes and built environ- ments at the regional scale. This collection may help to inspire and teach those designers who will dedicate their professional careers to large-scale environments.

But even more fundamentally this collection can be seen as a tribute to Kevin Lynch. His genius was many-faceted, yet our sense is that the common conception of his thoughts and works may be very limited and superficial. Many people know Lynch only as the author of *The Image of the City*. Even within the design profession, few are fully aware of his talents as a designer. And yet, in the words of his col- leagues at MIT, he was "a brilliant and subtle designer, always looking for those few simple strokes which would give both form to a place and open it to the creativity of its users."[15]

Asked to talk about the failures and successes of planning on the occasion of the Tugwell Award presentation in Los Angeles in April 1984, Kevin Lynch gave a speech entitled "Localities." In this speech— his last, as it turned out—he spoke of the need to understand the bond between place and community. He spoke of how the most successful

Kevin Lynch, Charlotte, North Carolina,
1981. Photo: Mark B. Sluder.

places are those that are owned, cared for, and intensely loved by people. He felt that planning and planners had not been very effective in creating localities, and that where localities exist they have happened without much formal planning. The point, which Lynch had made in many of his writings, is that planning and design must begin with community participation, local control, and individual engagements with the immediate environment. The success of planning and design will ultimately depend on our ability to create such opportunities and environments.

It is our hope that through the presentation of the materials assembled in this book, in the particular organization we have chosen, the genius of Kevin Lynch and the different facets of his intellectual contributions will become widely known and understood.

Notes

1. Two published articles and several unpublished materials have not been included. The subject matter of "On People and Places: A Comparative Study of the Spatial Environment of Adolescence" (*Town Planning Review* 47 [1975]: 105–115, co-authored with Tridib Banerjee) is generally covered by the article "Growing Up in Cities." "Some Comments on the Work of Donald Appleyard" (from *Places*) is not central to Lynch's own work. The decisions not to include other materials were also based on considerations of redundancy and relevance.

2. See, for example, Morton and Lucia White, *The Intellectual Versus the City* (New York: Mentor, 1962).

3. For a more detailed discussion of these points see Tridib Banerjee and William C. Baer, *Beyond the Neighborhood Unit* (New York: Plenum, 1984), chapter 2.

4. See note 1 above.

5. See *Good City Form*, p. 69.

6. "Florence Journals" (unpublished), MIT Archives.

7. In a video interview by Ann Buttimer, then of Clark University, conducted at MIT.

8. The letters from Kevin Lynch to Frank Lloyd Wright are reprinted by courtesy of the Frank Lloyd Wright Foundation and the Archives of the History of Art at the Getty Center for the History of Art and the Humanities.

9. Frank Lloyd Wright, *Letters to Apprentices/Frank Lloyd Wright; selected and with commentary by Bruce Brook Pfeiffer* (Fresno: The Press at California State University, 1982). Reprinted by permission of the publisher.

10. This essay was brought to our attention by Anne Lynch, and was made available by Randolph Henning, an architect from Winston-Salem, North Carolina. Reprinted by permission of the *Capital Times*, Madison, Wisconsin.

11. From personal conversations with Tridib Banerjee.

12. Interview by Ann Buttimer.

13. This distinction between substantive and nominal clients is taken from Koichi Mera, "Consumer Sovereignty in Urban Design", *Town Planning Review 37*, no. 4 (1967): 305–312.

14. Established by the colleagues and students of Rexford G. Tugwell (a member of FDR's "brain trust" and the founder of the prestigious planning program at the University of Chicago), the award is administered by the School of Urban and Regional Planning of the University of Southern California.

15. From a tribute written by MIT alumnus Stephen Carr and faculty members Lloyd Rodwin and Gary Hack for the memorial service held at Trinity Church, Copley Square, Boston, on May 14, 1984.

I The Form of Cities

In these articles Lynch sets forth the premises that underlie much of his work: that designers and planners should deal with the form of the entire city and region, not just the small spaces and individual structures of civic significance; that the urban landscape can and should be just as meaningful and delightful as the natural landscape and should be designed to be so; and that there should be an intimate connection between the forms of places and the values and needs of their users.

"The Form of Cities," one of Lynch's earliest published articles, lays the groundwork for many of his later interests. In it he examines the city, historically and morphologically, in terms of various attributes of urban form, such as size, density, grain, and pattern. Already he is interested in analyzing the visual experience while moving along a path, an idea later developed in depth in the book *The View From the Road*. He presents the notion that the city might be "a work of art, fitted to human purpose"—an ideal that he never abandoned.

Lynch's strong normative stance comes into focus in "The Pattern of the Metropolis." As a society, he writes, we must go beyond tracking and projecting urban trends and say what kind of city we really desire. He states that "realistic action without purpose can be as useless as idealism without power." His interest in analyzing urban form continues in this article, and he begins to examine large-scale metropolitan form. He discusses several regional patterns, from the dispersed sheet and galaxy to the urban star and ring. The goals and values of urban form are examined as well, hinting at what is to come much later in *Good City Form*. Lynch's favored metropolitan form is what he calls "the polycentered net."

"The Visual Shape of the Shapeless Metropolis," which has not been published before, further explores in a very systematic way Lynch's interest in the forms of regions, with an emphasis on the importance of "imageability" at the regional scale. What elements of re- gional form contribute to imageability? What metropolitan patterns are more conducive to imageability? An extension of *The Image of the City*, this work leads to the book *Managing the Sense of A Region*, in which Lynch discusses the importance of form at the regional scale and the ways that regional form might be analyzed and managed.

The final article in this part, "The City as Environment," presents an application of the "polycentered net" developed by Lynch's students at MIT. This article addresses "quality of life" issues—the problems of stress, the lack of identity and legibility, and the lack of openness in the contemporary metropolis. How might regional form be improved? Here Lynch's concern with the intimate connection between human values and the form of the environment is clear, and his interests in waste space and open space surface.

The world's first cities arose between 4500 and 3500 B.C. in the valleys of the Tigris-Euphrates, the Nile, and the Indus. The coming of the city marked a sudden alteration in the character of human existence: with it came the invention of writing, the specialization of labor, the acceleration of technology, and the beginnings of science. Today in every advanced country the city is man's principal way of organizing his living space. In the U.S., for instance, two-thirds of the population lives in cities, and by the year 2000 some 80 or 90 percent may do so.

We are increasingly aware of the effects of the city's physical form on the human activities that go on inside it. In making decisions as to how to build, enlarge, or renew this complicated piece of equipment, we are faced with many controversial issues and questions to which neither history nor planning theory [has] yet given us final answers.

Take, for example, the question of city size, a key issue in planning theory today. It was an important question for the Greek philosophers, who were concerned with the conditions under which a city-state becomes a healthy political and social unit. "Ten people would not make a city and with 100,000 it is a city no longer," wrote Aristotle. In the 20th century attempts have been made to control or reverse the growth of the metropolis, notably in the cases of London and Moscow.

In a city of what size can we produce most efficiently, best facilitate cultural development, live the most satisfying lives? Let us consider some examples, taken on an ascending scale of size of population.

Size

The little town of Ortonovo in the foothills of the Italian Apennines has a population of some 500 people. Beautifully set on the point of a mountain spur, it depends for its living on olive groves that stretch down the steep mountain slopes. It is closely related to its countryside, intimate, and protective. Everyone knows everyone else; gossip is strong. More a village than a town, it means social security for the inhabitants and charm for the visitor. It also means isolation and poverty of life. The village settlements of Neolithic man may almost have reached this size.

Ancient Priene, a planned Greek city of Asia Minor, had in the fourth century B.C. a population of about 5,000. Its temples, agora, and stadium give evidence of an organized cultural life, though still on a provincial scale. Presumably nearly all its inhabitants were at least acquainted with one another by sight and its leaders knew each other well. Man's first cities were of this order of size. In modern terms the size of Priene corresponds closely to the "neighborhood unit," a separate residential district equipped with all the basic daily services except employment. Those who favor this type of unit assert that it would assure services within reasonable distances and would reestablish a sound social structure in our great anonymous metropolitan areas. Its opponents argue that 5,000 is already too large a number for any real intimacy, and too small for cultural life in modern terms.

When we come to a town the size of Greensboro, N.C., with 70,000 people, we begin to approach a city as we think of one today. Greensboro deals with the entire Piedmont region and sells some of its products throughout the U.S. The citizens of such a city no longer are generally acquainted with one another but often meet friends on the downtown streets. A specialized cultural life appears, and so do contending social divisions. There is a reasonable variety of jobs and shopping facilities. Public services—police protection, health, education—approach an efficient size. Such towns, once the backbone of American life, still figure deeply in our literature and our popular attitudes, expressed either as nostalgia or revolt. Planning theorists of classical Greece apparently thought this was about the right size for a city—large enough to be self-sufficient for the purpose of living the good life but small enough to allow the citizens to know one another's personal characters. Some modern city planners refer to this size as "ideal."

The next jump is represented by Italy's world-famous Florence, whose population is 350,000. Its size brings to its inhabitants a new freedom and a marked economic and cultural variety. It exerts a strong influence on its region and has a characteristic flavor all its own. Its contributions to man's culture have been tremendous. Although the city is big and anonymous, its whole central area is familiar to all its citizens. The open countryside is 10 minutes away by motorbike, within walking distance in some directions. This size may be near or just over the optimum for efficient urban services. It provides a good variety of economic opportunity. Some problems of urban congestion begin to appear. Many theorists believe, however, that this is the optimum city size for modern society.

Finally we come to the world metropolis: New York, say, with its 13 millions. Here is a tremendous concentration of specialties and specialists, a vast economic and physical network. Products of any kind can be produced or purchased; activities of all types can be found. The city environment completely encompasses the citizen; rural land is far away. There is high stimulus in such a city, and cultural innovation proceeds at a rapid rate, setting the pace for the world. Only 10 cities on earth approximate this size: New York, Chicago, London, Berlin, Paris, Moscow, Leningrad, Tokyo, Shanghai, and Buenos Aires. The problems of congestion here appear in acute form, and the city is attacked for its anonymity, loneliness, and social disorganization. But it is also defended with equal fire as an efficient structure in a market economy. What is required, say its advocates, is not its abolition but restructing into more manageable units.

The optimum size for a city is difficult to reduce to a formula. Any principle must be tempered by the purpose and character of the city, its location, and the society for which it is built. The definition of a "big" city has changed with history. Lagash in ancient Sumer had 20,000 people; Babylon under Nebuchadnezzar had 80,000; Periclean Athens, perhaps 200,000. Carthage during the Punic Wars was a city of 500,000; imperial Rome, a metropolis of a million.

A factor importantly related to a city's size is its population density: the number of persons occupying a given unit of city ground. Florence, because of its relatively high density, can have green hills close to its center and work places within walking distance of its homes. The endless spread of Los Angeles is a product of low density and a large population.

Density directly affects the life of the city-dweller, since it controls the bulk and height of buildings, the living space inside and out, even the light and air. If the city's size is often beyond our rational control at present, its density is determined daily by every act of construction or regulation.

Density

We can weight our experience with various densities just as we have compared size. At the lower end of the scale is a town with a density of about 1,000 persons per square mile. This verges on rural land; it would be the density of a community of single-family houses on lots of an acre or more. Few cities have densities this low; one of the few examples is Canberra, the capital of Australia. It is a planned town, set out in 1913 by Walter Griffin, a U.S. architect chosen by international competition. His aim was a plan in the grand manner, with plenty of open space and room for expansion. Its ultimate density was to be 3,000 to 4,000 persons per square mile, but it is still only 500, and the town of 20,000 occupies an area 7 by 5 miles. In Canberra the minor roads have a 100-foot right of way; the major roads, 200 feet. Shops are a mile or more from most homes, and many people must travel 5 miles to work. The open areas are distances to overcome rather than countryside to enjoy. Densities of this order mean waste of land and inevitable problems of transportation and social cohesion. Only wealth and two cars per family can begin to overcome the difficulties.

At 3,500 persons per square mile we approach the density of a typical U.S. suburb, with single houses on generous lots. This is the American dream becoming reality: a home of one's own, a measure of privacy and freedom, room for the children to grow in. Surveys indicate that more than

60 percent of our population would prefer to live in areas like this. (There are some large cities with densities of this order, Los Angeles for an example.) The present impulse toward the suburbs is too strong to be denied. Yet it raises important problems: the giant mushrooming of cities, long travel times to work, the impracticability of frequent bus service because of the population dispersal, some isolation of group from group, insufficiency of social stimuli. Many of those who move out from the city remark on the loneliness of outer suburbia.

At 10,000 persons per square mile we reach an urban structure in which the dominant residential type is group housing: row houses, two-family houses, and the like. Baltimore and Washington are cities of this order; Chicago is just above it (average overall density: 16,000). A city that has been planned for a 10,000 density is the new English town of Harlow. There are still private gardens, but the layout is tighter and more economical than in single-family suburbs, with greater visual and social cohesion. Efficient public transport, even rail transit, can be supplied. Theoretically each of the jumps in density we have reviewed reduces travel time to work by 75 percent. But in a great metropolitan center an average density of 10,000 still means a substantial journey from the periphery to the center. And in a land-starved nation such as England it may be wasteful of land. Few cities of the past were so dispersed, for defense was paramount and transportation primitive.

At 35,000 persons per square mile we come to crowded walk-up apartments three and four stories high. Florence (among the older cities) and the central areas of most of our own major cities are in this range. Congestion begins here: it spells a more difficult environment for growing children, a surrender of light and air. Yet there are also positive values: better social intercourse, a strong feeling of "urbanity," short journeys to work or to the open country, efficient mass transportation. If we waive direct access to the ground, modern design can meet this density and satisfy basic standards by the open use of six story and nine-story elevator apartments.

At 100,000 per square mile, the upper end of our scale, we find the most congested parts of Manhattan, the modern city of Damascus, the slums of Naples or of ancient Rome. Such concentrations are formed by densely set elevator apartments or hopelessly dark and overcrowded tenements. There is loss of privacy, light, air, circulation, recreational space. Minimum standards cannot be met at this scale today without the use of 40- to 60-story buildings, suspended open spaces such as balconies and terraces, tiered circulation and parking areas. Such a metropolis may be tolerable at the center only for certain special individuals.

We cannot pick any one density as "best." Below a certain point acute difficulties of physical and social communication appear; above another point come inescapable problems of congestion. Within the toler-

times the city had a rigidly enforced ghetto, separate precincts for clergy or ironmongers; locations were controlled by guilds or the city. Some-pational and class lines. There was a street of butchers, another of men often lived over their shops, but there were sharp cleavages on occu-The medieval city had a well-developed sorting-out of uses. Crafts-though often called chaotic, represent a much higher level of organization. Such a town astonishes and confuses a visitor from our own cities, which, large-scale functions, to locate any particular activity or to service it easily. mixed together; there are few distinct focal points. It is difficult to perform may spread out indiscriminately along the streets. Houses of all kinds are some agricultural occupations. Buying and selling may go on there, too, or East are cases in point. Production is carried on in the home, mixed with pattern. The "city villages" of West Africa and some towns of the Middle Some of the primitive city types have relatively little differentiation or

Grain

uses. ner normally begins his design with a plan for the distribution of special efficiency, reduce or aggravate conflicts. It is so important that a city plan-of racial groups. The pattern of differentiation may promote or thwart housing, of large and small dwellings, of segregation or non-segregation tions in a city give it a "grain" or texture—a pattern of work places and power and effectiveness. The extent and distribution of such specializa-carried far in modern cities, and this is one of the chief sources of their residence, trade, ceremony, production, recreation. Specialization is tion in the way it uses structures and space. There are separate places for density. Every city, however small or primitive, shows a certain specializa-The arrangement of the city's parts is just as important as its size and communication.

low-density suburb is raising its own problems of obsolescence and left them disorganized and decaying. Our contemporary flight to the Conversely, the depopulation of cities at the beginning of the Dark Ages sanitary and safety problems took on new and alarming proportions. immigrants poured into the tenements of Boston and New York; the floors were added, leaning out over the streets. This happened again when walls. Gardens disappeared, houses were packed together and upper changes came as the population gradually increased within static city acter and functioning of a city. In most medieval cities fundamental The act of setting or changing densities directly influences the char-town, may impose a cracking strain on the circulation of a big one. appropriate density and total size. A low density, excellent in a small different social groups. Above all, there is a close relation between able range are various types of development which may be better for

or lawyers. It had one or more precise focal points: the market square, a cathedral, or a castle. Rich and poor might live close together but grouped by guilds or dominant families. On the other hand, Florence had a section of workers' houses across the Arno River; imperial Rome had a similar "poor" district on the far side of the Tiber which persists to the present day.

The "grain" of a medieval city was relatively fine and sharp. The Florentine ghetto occupied a small city block, and abutted directly on the market center. Street names changed from block to block, or even in mid-block, according to the trade or family occupying the frontage. Producers were in close contact with their fellows of the same trade, and comparative shopping was easy. Areas adapted to special uses had strong emotional associations with their activity, be it weaving or worship. The fine grain, the small areas, provided easy accessibility, good social contact, and great visual richness.

This medieval organization, however, has features against which we rebel: the fixed definition of a man's position in society, the restrictive control over the productive process, the segregation of the ghetto—though we have our own examples of these today. The fine grain, too, can develop frictions. Medieval Paris made repeated efforts to move the butchers out of the center of town. A convent in 14th-century Béziers protested against nearby tanneries producing "infected air." In addition, small areas may prevent growth and efficient development of a specific activity Florence's celebrated textile-finishing industry was carried on in dark, cramped shops, with the goods stored on floors above, difficult to handle and exposed to ruinous fires.

Modern cities exhibit differentiation on a much broader scale. The grain is coarse rather than fine. For instance, Chicago has a large Negro section on the South Side, an extensive upper middle class housing area in its North Shore suburbs. Manhattan has a section for the garment industry, a long avenue of department stores, and so on. Such large-scale differentiation may have marked advantages. Residential areas can have quiet local streets, with open areas for children and family life. Factory districts can be supplied with rail and road connections; interdependent industries can be kept in close proximity. Both types of area may have room to grow and to develop without interference from other uses.

In U.S. cities the boundaries between areas are generally blurred and indistinct. This indecisive physical transition can be painful: blighted housing mixed with outworn factories or stores; the notorious belt of decay which borders the major commercial center; tense areas on the edge of a racial ghetto where a struggle between expansion and containment goes on constantly. To avoid such conflicts contemporary designers try to make boundaries as sharp and frictionless as possible. Thus in a new town such as Harlow, industry is concentrated in two areas, separated from the residential sections by topography and wide open spaces. Shops are placed in marked-off centers. Even the residential areas are broken up by wide greenbelts. The patterns resemble those of ancient towns which conquerors divided to forestall conflicts. An example is Peking, with its Chinese and Manchu cities and separate quarters for the emperor, noble-men, and commoners. Kahun, the ancient construction camp for the Egyptian pyramids, had a wall separating the workmen from officials. Shanghai is divided into "foreign" and "native" settlements.

Indeed, broad segregation may make population groups hostile strangers to one another, place necessary facilities beyond easy reach and overload transportation systems. In the suburbs the lack of nearby neigh-borhood stores is a common complaint, and the public library may have little patronage because it is beautifully isolated in a "civic center." Thus segregation is a matter of controversy in planning theory. The need for specialization is accepted, but there is sharp disagreement over how far it should go. For example, heavy industry must be kept in its own area, but is it wrong to put certain light industries in the midst of housing? Each use must be examined to see why its functioning calls for a special area, since segregation is not a good in itself. No reasoned stand can be made for residential division by race, for example, yet this is still a common practice even in new developments.

Some of the argument over specialization can be resolved if each use is studied to find the minimum cluster that will give functional efficiency for that use. For example, houses for families with small children may best be grouped in clusters, so that the young may have playmates (and the adults, fellow-sufferers), but it may be wrong to extend to such an area beyond a square mile, forming a one-class section from which it is not easy to escape.

Shape

Besides size, density and grain, there is the matter of the shape of cities. Even the silhouette of a city tells us a great deal about its living quality. The old cities usually were roughly circular or rectangular in outline, with a sharp boundary commonly marked by a wall. Such is the medieval town of Lucca or a great city like Peking. The compelling motive was protection—the carving out of a special environment in an alien world. In the Etruscan ritual of city-founding, the first act after consulting the omens was to cut a furrow marking the new city boundary. For centuries towns were built first by throwing up a wall, then filling in with development.

Beyond its defensive value, the compact mass is a logical form when it is not too large. The center is close to all sectors of the periphery; the town has a solid, visible unity. It is particularly delightful when the countryside can readily be seen, giving the sense that it can be entered easily. The English city of Bath, ringed with green hills, is a fine example of this.

As the population grows, the compact shape begins to exhibit diffi-culties. Growth must occur by crowding within or by annular accretion, like the growth rings of a tree. Unlike a tree, however, the center cannot be left to die. It must continue to function, and its obsolescence is increasingly difficult to remedy. It becomes a critical problem to serve the spreading mass with transportation. The open country recedes farther and farther away.

A second city form is the long, narrow ribbon, usually lying along a road or river. The typical "street village" is a good example. The road or river is the primary fact, and the town has developed along it. Topography also may dictate this shape, as in coastal towns or in a settlement like Colle di Val d'Elsa, on a narrow ridge in Italian Umbria. The linear city rarely grows very large. An exception is Stalingrad, which developed this way partly because of the importance of river transport to it and partly for theoretical considerations. On a regional scale the ribbon form may take in a string of towns, such as the urban "corridor" running from Springfield, Mass., through New York and Philadelphia to Washington.

The advantage of the linear shape is that all structures are close to the main line, and readily accessible in terms of time or effort, given efficient transportation. Expansion can go on indefinitely, without losing touch with the open country. Louisiana parishes and many New England settle-ments were laid out in this way, requiring a minimum of road to service farms which ran back in deep strips. In Colle di Val d'Elsa most houses front directly on the main street and have green landscape at their backs. Easy communication and closeness to rural land are the motivations be-hind theoretical proposals of this type. An example is the *Ciudad Lineal* of the 19th-century Spanish engineer Raphael Soria, based on a trolley line. Similar proposals were made by Arthur Comey of the U.S. in 1923 and more recently by the noted French architect Le Corbusier.

Overextension of the linear form risks throttling the main artery, particularly if too much local movement and access to the road is allowed. On a giant scale it cuts the countryside into the kind of isolated patches which may now be seen in the environs of big cities. There is an inherent lack of focus in this form, a lack of centers around which identification and activities can group themselves. Yet on a smaller scale or for particular uses this ancient form has value today.

The shape of a metropolis is something else again. From a central mass extend long arms of development. It is often likened to a star or an octopus, depending on one's emotions. This stellar shape is a natural one for peaceful communication cities, growing from within outwards along fast rail lines or high-speed roads. It is markedly the outline of Chicago. The star shape combines a strong center with the advantages of linear extensibility and close contact with open country between the fingers. If open land is brought in close to the center, then the entire mass can be "aerated" without destruction of convenience or urbanity. Copenhagen's new regional plan has taken this shape. It is advocated by the U.S. planner Hans Blumenfeld in his *Theory of City Form*. Its inherent problems are the difficulty of moving around the circumference, of avoiding the overtaxing of the single center and of seeing the city as a whole. If this form today is associated with overloaded radial highways, blurred boundaries, the gradual melting of houses into scattered dwellings, unoccupied subdivisions and roadside stands, these defects can be prevented by good design and regulation. The blundering fringe which is our first sight on approaching a modern metropolis is the visual evidence of a careless, indecisive relation of the city to rural land.

Each of these city shapes has its problems, particularly as the urban complex grows to great size. For such a complex a new form, called the "constellation," has been proposed. Many separate units, distributed over a large region, would be held together by a web of fast transportation lines. If one unit is clearly dominant and the others are connected with it radially, we have the "satellite" form proposed by the English reformer Ebenezer Howard. Or there might be several more or less equal but specialized centers, each supporting the others, as in the "regional city" of the planner Clarence Stein.

There are no large, thoroughgoing examples yet of the constellation form. A few satellite units have been built, principally near London; the new town of Harlow is one of these. Elsewhere we may see suggestive forms, as in the Boston [and] Copenhagen regions, where peripheral small towns, anciently independent, have been drawn into the expanding influence of a big city. In some heavily urbanized regions we find close groupings of independent cities, as in the Dutch ring Amsterdam-Haarlem-Hague-Rotterdam-Utrecht or the German cluster Wiesbaden-Frankfurt-Mainz-Darmstadt. Or we may see the form struggling to be born in some of our metropolises, where shopping and employment centers are moving out into the suburbs. The form presupposes fast, flexible transport systems. It would presumably retain the advantages of the great metropolis and yet avoid congestion. Growth and special areas can be provided for, and close contact with open land can be regained. Most city planners today probably hold some variant of this form as their objective. There are still other possible forms which await imaginative study. Cities might be conceived in a ring shape, with open centers. Or one might turn the old pattern inside out, putting residence on the inside and normally central functions on the periphery, as suggested by the planner Alexander Klein, now working in Israel.

A big city of course resists rapid and sweeping changes. The physical and social investment in its existing structures is too high. Yet growth and change occur perpetually. There is constant opportunity for decisions which in time could completely reorganize the shape of the city.

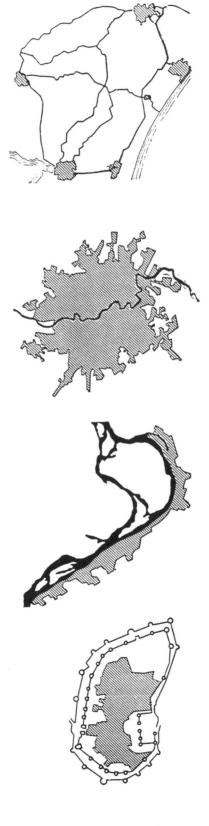

Outline types are compact (Carcassonne in France), linear (Stalingrad), star (London), constellation (Haarlem, Amsterdam, Utrecht, Rotterdam, The Hague, Leiden).

The Internal Pattern

Every city has its intimate inner pattern: the streets, squares, and other openings that make buildings accessible and livable. In ancient cities and those of North Africa today the pattern is highly irregular. Buildings or high-walled private gardens are dominant; the public way is simply the land left over. This intricate capillary mass may be perforated occasionally by larger open spaces for gatherings, exchange or ceremonials. Where such a system is not too extensive, it may have its values. There is visual fascination in its intricacy. Its very complication protects the citizen from violent weather, from heavy traffic, or from the sudden foray of an enemy. But over any large area it poses tremendous difficulties of movement, unity, and living standards. The agonies of circulation in ancient Rome and the desperate efforts to alleviate them are a matter of historical record.

Equally ancient is the pattern of enclosure in which buildings are wrapped around the community heart; there are ring streets with few breaks into the center. The ring village is a form natural to small settlements in warlike periods. The modern residential or shopping court repeats it. Its modern values are not military defense but social intimacy, segregation of traffic, and visual satisfaction. It is difficult to apply on a large scale, although organization of a city as a system of courts of various sizes has been suggested.

More important for city planning today is the axial pattern of streets leading to and from important centers. It is a pattern made for movement. Indeed, the earliest instances, in Egypt and Babylonia, seem to have been designed for religious processions. The axial pattern may appear as a very simple linear arrangement, or be expanded into a spindle consisting of a bundle of parallel roads. Berne is such a city. In Rome the axial lines are scattered irregularly through the city. In many cities the main lines converge from several directions on a center or crossing, or are organized in a perfect form. Karlsruhe is a classic example of this axial geometry, which pervaded the ideal city plans of the Renaissance and Baroque periods.

The advantages are obvious. It is easy to locate one's self in such a city if the lines are not too numerous. The long vistas may be imposing, as from the Arc de Triomphe in Paris, or infinitely dreary, as in Chicago. Converging lines have the disadvantage of producing triangular plots, difficult to develop efficiently, and of making intersections hazardous. Yet the axial form is so natural to great cities with dominant city centers that city plans repeat it again and again.

A common alternate method of street arrangement is the grid. Although it could take other forms, such as triangular or hexagonal, in practice the grid has always been rectangular. It has very ancient roots. The Bronze Age villages of northern Italy were laid out in a clear rectangular grid and so was the ancient Indus city of Mohenjo-Daro; Greek colonial cities, Roman camps, and medieval towns such as Villeneuve-sur-Lot were all planned on it. It has been the preferred form for new communities. It is systematic, easy to lay out, and provides equal, rectangular building sites. It allows a numbering system for easy location. The motives for choosing a grid may be philosophic, as in Peking, where it was adopted to promote regularity and harmony in a city conceived to be the center of the universe, or they may be strictly utilitarian, as when the Commissioners laying out Manhattan in 1811 rejected circles, ovals, and stars and decided that "strait-sided and right-angled houses are the most cheap to build and the most convenient to live in."

Among designers there is now a reaction against the grid, mainly because of its lack of adaptability and its "monotony." It causes difficulties on irregular ground, as in San Francisco and Priene. When diagonal motion must be applied over it, as in Washington, it produces confusing intersections and awkward pieces of land. If used unthinkingly, it may allot the same kind of ground for factories as for homes, the same width for main arteries as for local streets. Sensitive design can avoid this, but not without departing from a uniform grid. The impression of monotony arises in part from the lack of necessary specialization; it is not inherent in the pattern.

Another pattern of interior space developing in modern towns makes open spaces instead of buildings dominant, with the building masses as isolated points. Examples may be found both in new low-density suburbs and in relatively high-density "open" developments. Modern transportation allows dispersal of the city and also demands more ground area for its facilities. At the same time modern building technology permits tall, concentrated structures which free the land around them.

This pattern provides a new freedom of movement and of use of the ground. Yet towering buildings set on open ground may have only an illusory advantage if overall densities remain high and the open spaces are overloaded. In certain sections, particularly shopping and office areas, there is both a technical and a psychological need for concentration which the open pattern cannot supply. The sense of urbanity and the function of the city as a meeting place for large numbers would be destroyed if an entire city were given over to this new pattern. The new town of Harlow, for all its open-space advantages, has a "flat" taste. The modern city requires a rhythmical balance between enclosure and openness, [between] concentration and freedom.

Size, density, grain, outline, pattern—all are basic aspects of the city's physical form. All have a powerful effect on the quality of life that goes on in it. Decisions about them must be faced with increasing frequency as we rebuild and enlarge man's peculiar environment.

The pattern of urban development critically affects a surprising number of problems, by reason of the spacing of buildings, the location of activities, the disposition of the lines of circulation. Some of these problems might be eliminated if only we would begin to coordinate metropolitan develop- ment so as to balance services and growth, prevent premature abandon- ment or inefficient use, and see that decisions do not negate one another. In such cases, the form of the urban area, whether concentrated or dis- persed, becomes of relatively minor importance.

There are other problems, however, that are subtler and go deeper. Their degree of seriousness seems to be related to the particular pattern of development which has arisen. To cope with such difficulties, one must begin by evaluating the range of possible alternatives of form, on the arbitrary assumption that the metropolis can be molded as desired. For it is as necessary to learn what is desirable as to study what is possible; realistic action without purpose can be as useless as idealism without power. Even the range of what is possible may sometimes be extended by fresh knowl- edge of what is desirable.

Let us, therefore, consider the form of the metropolis as if it existed in a world free of pressures or special interests and on the assumption that massive forces can be harnessed for reshaping the metropolis for the com- mon good—provided this good can be discovered. The question then is, how should such power be applied? We must begin by deciding which aspects of the metropolitan pattern are crucial. We can then review the commonly recognized alternative patterns, as well as the criteria that might persuade us to choose one over another. Finally, we may hope to see the question as a whole. Then we will be ready to suggest new alternatives and will have the means of choosing the best one for any particular purpose.

The Critical Aspects of Metropolitan Form

There are at least three vital factors in our judging the adequacy of the form of the metropolis, once its total size is known. The first of all is the magni- tude and pattern of both the structural density (the ratio of floor space in buildings to the area of the site) and the structural condition (the state of obsolescence or repair). These aspects can be illustrated on a map by plotting the locations of the various classes of density ranging from high concentration to wide dispersion, and the various classes of structural condition ranging from poor to excellent. Density and condition provide a fundamental index of the physical resources an urban region possesses.

Reprinted, with permission, from *Daedalus* 90, no. 1, pp. 79–98.

A second factor is the capacity, type, and pattern of the facilities for the circulation of persons, road, railways, airlines, transit systems, and pathways of all sorts. Circulation and intercommunication perhaps consti- tute the most essential function of a city, and the free movement of persons happens to be the most difficult kind of circulation to achieve, the service most susceptible to malfunction in large urban areas.

The third factor that makes up the spatial pattern of a city is the location of fixed activities that draw on or serve large portions of the population, such as large department stores, factories, office and govern- ment buildings, warehouses, colleges, hospitals, theaters, parks, and museums. The spatial pattern of a city is made up of the location of fixed activities as well as the patterns of circulation and physical structure. However, the distribution of locally based activities, such as residence, local shopping, neighborhood services, [and] elementary and high schools is for our purpose sufficiently indicated by mapping the density of people or of buildings. Hence, if we have already specified structural density and the circulation system, the remaining critical fact at the metropolitan scale

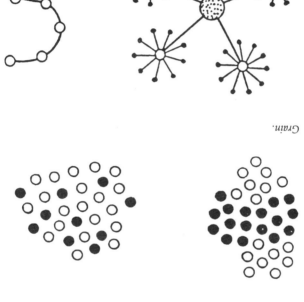

Grain.

Focal organization.

is the location of the city-wide activities which interact with large portions of the whole.

When we come to analyze any one of these three elements of spatial pattern, we find that the most significant features of such patterns are the grain (the degree of intimacy with which the various elements such as stores and residences are related), the focal organization (the interrelation of the nodes of concentration and interchange as contrasted with the general background), and the accessibility (the general proximity in terms of time of all points in the region to a given kind of activity or facility). In this sense, one might judge that from every point the accessibility to drug-stores was low, uneven, or uniformly high, or that it varied in some regular way, for example, high at the center and low at the periphery of the region. All three aspects of pattern (focal organization, grain, and accessibility) can be mapped, and the latter two can be treated quantitatively if desired.

It is often said that the metropolis today is deficient as a living environment. It has suffered from uncontrolled development, from too rapid growth and change, from obsolescence and instability. Circulation is congested, requiring substantial time and a major effort. Accessibility is uneven, particularly to open rural land. The use of facilities is unbalanced, and they become increasingly obsolete. Residential segregation according to social groups seems to be growing, while the choice of residence for the individual remains restricted and unsatisfactory. The pattern of activities is unstable, and running costs are high. Visually, the city is characterless and confused, as well as noisy and uncomfortable.

Yet the metropolis has tremendous economic and social advantages that override its problems and induce millions to bear with the discomforts. Rather than dwindle or collapse, it is more likely to become the normal human habitat. If so, the question then is, what particular patterns can best realize the potential of metropolitan life?

The Dispersed Sheet

One alternative is to allow the present growth at the periphery to proceed to its logical conclusion but at a more rapid pace. Let new growth occur at the lowest densities practicable, with substantial interstices of open land

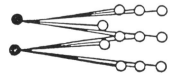 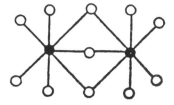

Accessibility.

kept in reserve. Let older sections be rebuilt at much lower densities, so that the metropolitan region would rapidly spread over a vast continuous tract, perhaps coextensive with adjacent metropolitan regions. At the low densities of the outer suburbs, a metropolis of twenty million might require a circle of land one hundred miles in diameter.

The old center and most subcenters could be dissolved, allowing city-wide activities to disperse throughout the region, with a fine grain. Factories, offices, museums, universities, hospitals would appear everywhere in the suburban landscape. The low density and the dispersion of activities would depend on and allow circulation in individual vehicles, as well as a substantial use of distant symbolic communication such as telephone, television, mail, [and] coded messages. Accessibility to rural land would become unnecessary, since outdoor recreational facilities would be plentiful and close at hand. The permanent low-density residence would displace the summer cottage.

The system of flow, concerned solely with individual land (and perhaps air) vehicles, should be highly dispersed in a continuous grid designed for an even movement in all directions. There would be no

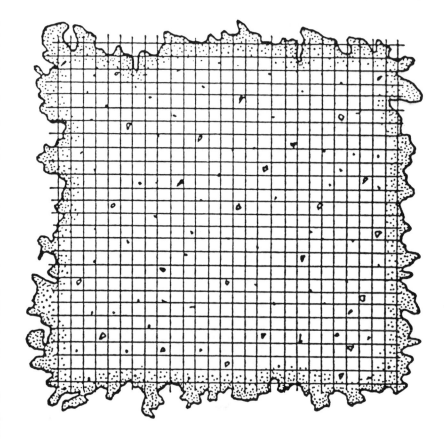

The dispersed sheet.

outstanding nodal points, no major terminals. Since different densities or activities would therefore be associated in a very fine grain, the physical pattern similarly might encourage a balanced cross-section of the population. Work place and residence might be adjacent or miles apart. Automatic factories and intensive food production might be dispersed throughout the region.

Frank Lloyd Wright dreamed of such a world in his Broadacre City.[1] It is this pattern toward which cities like Los Angeles appear to be moving, although they are hampered and corrupted by the vestiges of older city forms. Such a pattern might not only raise flexibility, local participation, personal comfort, and independence to a maximum, but also go far toward solving traffic congestion through the total dispersion and balancing of loads. Its cost would be high, however, and distances remain long. Accessibility would be good, given high speeds of travel and low terminal times (convenient parking, rapid starting); at the very least it would be evenly distributed. Thus communication in the sense of purposeful trips ("I am going out to buy a fur coat") might not be hindered, but spontaneous or accidental communication ("Oh, look at that fur coat in the window!"), which is one of the advantages of present city life, might be impaired by the lack of concentration.

Although such a pattern would require massive movements of the population and the extensive abandonment of equipment at the beginning, in the end it might promote population stability and the conservation of resources, since all areas would be favored alike. It gives no promise, however, of heightening of sense of political identity in the metropolitan community nor of producing a visually vivid and well-knit image of environment. Moreover, the choice of the type of residence would be restricted, although the choice of facility to be patronized (churches, stores, etc.) might be sufficiently wide.

The Galaxy of Settlements

We might follow a slightly different tack while at the same time encouraging dispersion. Instead of guiding growth into an even distribution, let development be bunched into relatively small units, each with an internal peak of density and each separated from the next by a zone of low or zero structural density. Depending on the transport system, this separation might be as great as several miles. The ground occupied by the whole metropolis would increase proportionately; even if the interspaces were of minimum size, the linear dimensions of the metropolis would increase from 30 to 50 percent.

City-wide activities could also be concentrated at the density peak within each urban cluster, thus forming an overall system of centers, each of which would be relatively equal in importance to any of the others. Such a metropolitan pattern may be called an "urban galaxy." The centers might be balanced in composition or they might vary by specializing in a type of activity, so that one might be a cultural center, another a financial center.

The system of flow would also be dispersed but would converge locally at the center of each cluster. It might be organized in a triangular grid, which provides such a series of foci while maintaining an easy flow in all directions over the total area. Since median densities remain low, while the centers of activity are divided into relatively small units, the individual vehicle must be the major mode of transportation, but some supplementary public transportation such as buses or aircraft running from center to center would now be feasible.

While it retains many of the advantages of the dispersed sheet, such as comfort, independence, and stability, this scheme probably enhances general communication, and certainly spontaneous communication, through creating centers of activity. It would presumably encourage participation in local affairs by favoring the organization of small communities, though this might work equally against participation and coordination on the metropolitan scale. In the same sense, the visual image at the local level would be sharpened, though the metropolitan image might be only slightly improved. Flexibility might be lost, since local clusters would of necessi-

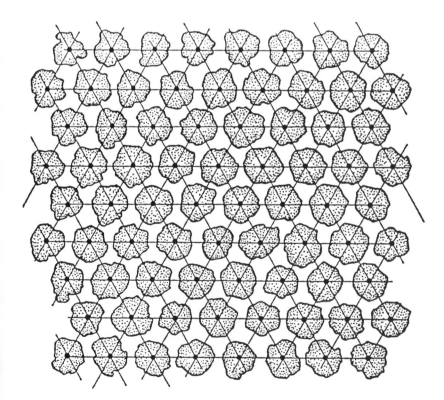

The galaxy.

ty have relatively fixed boundaries, if interstitial spaces were preserved, and the city-wide activities would be confined to one kind of location.

The factor of time-distance might remain rather high, unless people could be persuaded to work and shop within their own cluster, which would then become relatively independent with regard to commutation. Such independent communities, of course, would largely negate many metropolitan advantages: choice of work for the employee, choice of social contacts, of services, and so on. If the transportation system were very good, then "independence" would be difficult to enforce.

This pattern, however, can be considered without assuming such local independence. It is essentially the proposal advocated by the proponents of satellite towns, pushed to a more radical conclusion, as in Clarence Stein's diagram.[2] Some of its features would appear to have been incorporated into the contemporary development of Stockholm.

The pattern of an urban galaxy provides a wider range of choice than does pure dispersion, and a greater accessibility to open country, of the kind that can be maintained between clusters. This pattern has a somewhat parochial complexion and lacks the opportunities for intensive, spontaneous communication and for the very specialized activities that might exist in larger centers. Local centers, too, might develop a monotonous similarity, unless they were given some specific individuality. That might not be easy, however, since central activities tend to support and depend on one another (wholesaling and entertainment, government and business services, headquarters offices and shopping). A compromise would be the satellite proposal proper: a swarm of such unit clusters around an older metropolitan mass.

The Core City

There are those who, enamored with the advantages of concentration, favor a completely opposite policy that would set median structural densities fairly high, perhaps at 1.0 instead of 0.1; in other words, let there be as much interior floor space in buildings as there is total ground area in the city, instead of only one-tenth as much. If we consider the open land that must be set aside for streets, parks, and other such uses, this means in practice the construction of elevator apartments instead of one-family houses. The metropolis would then be packed into one continuous body, with a very intensive peak of density and activity at its center. A metropolis of 20 million could be put within a circle 10 miles in radius, under the building practice normal today.

Parts of the city might even become "solid," with a continuous occupation of space in three dimensions and a cubical grid of transportation lines. (The full application of this plan could cram a metropolis within a surprisingly small compass: 20 million people, with generous spacing, could be accommodated within a cube less than 3 miles on a side.) Most probably there would be a fine grain of specialized activities, all at high intensity, so that apartments would occur over factories, or there might also be stores on upper levels. The system of flow would necessarily be highly specialized, sorting each kind of traffic into its own channel. Such a city would depend almost entirely on public transport, rather than individual vehicles, or on devices that facilitated pedestrian movement, such as moving sidewalks or flying belts. Accessibility would be very high, both to special activities and to the open country at the edges of the city. Each family might have a second house for weekends; these would be widely dispersed throughout the countryside and used regularly three or four days during the week, or even longer, by mothers and their young children. The city itself, then, would evolve into a place for periodic gathering. Some of the great European cities, such as Paris or Moscow, which are currently building large numbers of high-density housing as compact extensions to their peripheries, are approximating this pattern without its more radical features.

Such a pattern would have an effect on living quite different from that of the previous solutions. Spontaneous communication would be high, so high that it might become necessary to impede it so as to preserve privacy. Accessibility would be excellent and time-distance low, although the channels might be crowded. The high density might increase discomfort because of noise or poor climate, although these problems could perhaps be met by the invention of new technical devices. As with the previous patterns, the choice of habitat would be restricted to a single general type within the city proper, although the population could enjoy a strong contrast on weekends or holidays. The nearness of open country and the many kinds of special services should on the whole extend individual choice. Once established, the pattern should be stable, since each point would be a highly favored location. However, a very great dislocation of people and equipment, in this country at least, would be required to achieve this pattern.

Such a metropolis would indeed produce a vivid image and would contribute to a strong sense of the community as a whole. Individual

The core.

participation, on the other hand, might be very difficult. It is not clear how running costs would be affected; perhaps they would be lower because of the more efficient use of services and transportation, but initial costs would undoubtedly be very high. The segregation of social groups, as far as physical disposition can influence it, might be discouraged, although there is a level of density above which intercommunication among people begins to decline again. Certainly this solution is a highly rigid and unadaptable one in which change of function could be brought about only by a costly rearrangement.

The Urban Star

A fourth proposal would retain the dominant core without so drastic a reversion to the compact city. Present densities would be kept, or perhaps revised upward a little, while low-density development at the outer fringe would no longer be allowed. Tongues of open land would be incorporated into the metropolitan area to produce a density pattern that is star-shaped in the central region and linear at the fringes. These lines of dense development along the radials might in time extend to other metropolitan centers, thus becoming linear cities between the main centers. The dominant core, however, would remain, surrounded by a series of secondary centers distributed along the main radials. At moderate densities (less than the core pattern, and more than the sheet), the radial arms of a metropolis of comparable size might extend for 50 miles from its own center.

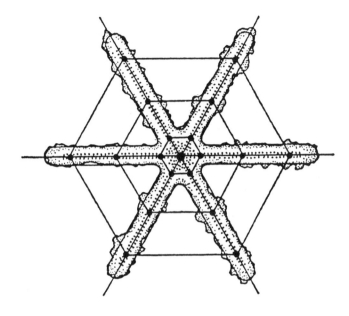

The star.

The metropolitan center of the star pattern would again contain the most intensive types of city-wide activity. Elsewhere, either in the subcenters or in linear formations along the main radials—whichever proved the more suitable—these activities would be carried on at a less intense level. The system of flow would logically be organized on the same radial pattern, with supplementary concentric rings. An efficient public transportation system of high capacity could operate along the main radials, whereas the ring roads could accommodate public transit of lower intensity. To some degree, travel by individual vehicles, although discouraged for centrally bound flows, would be practicable in other directions.

This pattern is a rationalization of the manner in which metropolitan areas were developing till the individual vehicle became the usual means of travel. It is the form the city of Copenhagen has adopted as its pattern for future growth[3]; Blumenfeld has discussed it at length.[4] This form retains the central core, with its advantages of other kinds of major activities. Lower residential densities are also possible. Individual choice should be fairly wide, in regard to living habitat, access to services, and access to open land—this land lies directly behind each tongue of development, even at the core, and leads continuously outward to rural land.

Movement along a sector would be fairly fast and efficient, although terminals at the core might continue to be congested and, with continued growth, the main radials might become overloaded. Movement between sectors, however, would be less favored, especially in the outer regions; there distances are great, transit hard to maintain, and channels costly, since they would span long distances over land they do not directly serve. Accessibility to services would be unequal as between inner and outer locations.

The visual image is potentially a strong one and should be conducive to a sense of the metropolis as a whole, or at least to the sense of one unified sector leading up to a common center. Growth could occur radially outward, and future change could be accomplished with less difficulty than in the compact pattern, since densities would be lower and open land would back up each strip of development. The principal problems with this form are probably those of circumferential movement, of potential congestion at the core and along the main radials, and of the wide dispersion of the pattern as it recedes from the original center.

The Ring

In the foregoing, the most discussed alternatives for metropolitan growth have been given in a highly simplified form. Other possibilities certainly exist—e.g., the compact high-density core pattern might be turned inside out, producing a doughnut-like form. In this case the center would be kept open, or at very low density, while high densities and special activities

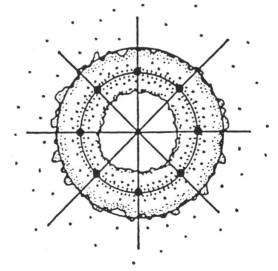

The ring.

surround it, like the rim of a wheel. The principal channels of the flow system would then be a series of annular rings serving the high-intensity rim, supplemented by a set of feeder radials that would converge at the empty center. In fact, this is essentially a linear system, but one that circles back on itself and is bypassed by the "spokes" crossing the "hub." This system is well-adapted to public transportation, both on the ring roads and the cross radials, while individual vehicles might be used for circulation outside the rim.

Densities within the rim would have to be rather high, while those beyond the rim could be low. A system of weekend houses might also be effectively employed here. The central area could either be kept quite open or devoted to special uses at low densities. City-wide activities could be spotted round the rim in a series of intense centers, supplemented by linear patterns along the annular roadways. There would be no single dominant center but rather a limited number of strong centers (an aristocracy rather than a monarchy). These centers might also be specialized in regard to activity—finance, government, culture, etc.

This pseudo-linear form, like the radial tongues of the star plan, has the linear advantages: a high accessibility, both to services and to open land; a wide choice of habitat and location of activities; and a good foundation for efficient public transit. Congestion at any single center is avoided, yet there is a high concentration. In contrast to the galaxy or satellite form, the variety and strong character inherent in the specialized centers would have some hope of survival because of the relatively close proximity of those centers.

The visual image would be strong (though perhaps a little confusing because of its circularity), producing a particularly clear impression of the centers around the rim, in contrast to the central openness, and of their successive interconnections. The whole metropolis would seem more nearly like one community. One of the most difficult problems would be that of growth, since much development beyond the rim would soon blur the contour and require a new transportation system. A second concentric ring might be developed beyond the first, but it would negate some of the advantages of the first ring and would demand massive initiative by the central government to undertake its development. Another difficulty would be that of control. How can the belts of open land or the accessible center be kept free of building? Even if this problem [is] solved satisfactorily, a dilemma is also likely to arise in regard to the size of the ring: should it be small enough for the major centers to be in close proximity to one another, or big enough to allow all the residences and other local activities to be related to it?

One classic example of this form exists, although on a very large scale—the ring of specialized Dutch cities that surround a central area of agricultural land: Haarlem, Amsterdam, Utrecht, Rotterdam, The Hague, and Leiden. This general pattern is now being rationalized and preserved as a matter of national policy in the Netherlands. In our own country, the San Francisco Bay region appears to be developing in this same direction. The ring tends to be rather rigid and unadaptable as a form. It would require an extreme reshaping of the present metropolis, particularly with regard to transportation and the central business district; but it might dovetail with an observable trend toward emptying and abandoning the central areas. The plan could be modified by retaining a single major center, separated by a wide belt of open space from all other city-wide activities to be disposed along the rim. It may be noted that this use of open land in concentric belts ("green belts") is exactly opposite to its use as radial tongues in the star form.

The Objectives of Metropolitan Arrangement

Many other metropolitan forms are hypothetically possible, but the five patterns described (the sheet, the galaxy, the core, the star, and the ring) indicate the variation possible. One of the interesting results of the discussion is to see the appearance of a particular set of values as criteria for evaluating these forms. It begins to be clear that some human objectives are intimately connected with the physical pattern of a city, while others are very little affected by it. For example, there has been little discussion of the healthfulness of the environment or of its safety. Although these are influenced by the detailed design of the environment, such as the spacing of buildings or the provision for utilities, it is not obvious that the specific metropolitan pattern has any significant effect on them so long as we keep well ahead of the problems of pollution and supply. Psychological well-being, on the other hand, may be affected by the shape of the urban environment. But again, we are too ignorant of this aspect at present to discuss it further.

We have not referred to the efficiency of the environment in regard to production and distribution. This represents another basic criterion that probably is substantially affected by metropolitan pattern, but unfortunately no one seems to know what the effect is. "Pleasure" and "beauty" have not been mentioned, but these terms are nebulous and hard to apply accurately. A number of criteria have appeared, however, and it may well be worthwhile to summarize them. They might be considered the goals of metropolitan form, its fundamental objectives, either facilitated or frustrated in some significant way by the physical pattern of the metropolis.

The criterion of choice heads the list. As far as possible, the individual should have the greatest variety of goods, services, and facilities readily accessible to him. He should be able to choose the kind of habitat he prefers; he should be able to enter many kinds of environment at will, including the open country; he should have the maximum of personal control over his world. These advantages appear in an environment of great variety and of fine grain, one in which transportation and communication are as quick and effortless as possible. There may very likely be some eventual limit to the desirable increase of choice, since people can be overloaded by too many alternatives, but we do not as yet operate near that limit for most people. In practice, of course, to maximize one choice may entail minimizing another, and compromises will have to be made.

The ideal of personal interaction ranks as high as choice, although it is not quite so clear how the optimum should be defined. We often say that we want the greatest number of social contacts, so as to promote neighborliness and community organization, minimize segregation and social isolation, increase the velocity and decrease the effort of social exchange. And yet, while the evils of isolation are known, we are nevertheless beginning to see problems at the other end of the scale as well. Too much personal communication may cause breakdown, just as surely as too little. Even in moderate quantities, constant "neighborliness" can interfere with other valuable activities such as reflection, independent thought, or creative work. A high level of local community organization may mean civic indifference or intergovernmental rivalry when the large community is involved.

In this dilemma, a compromise could be found in saying that potential interaction between people should be as high as possible, as long as the individual can control it and shield himself whenever desired. His front door, figuratively speaking, should open on a bustling square, and his back door on a secluded park. Thus this ideal is seen as related to the ideal of choice.

Put differently, individuals require a rhythmical alternation of stimulus and rest—periods when personal interchange is high and to some degree is forced upon them, to be followed by other periods when stimulus is low and individually controlled. A potentially high level of interaction, individually controlled, is not the whole story; we also need some degree of spontaneous or unpremeditated exchange, of the kind that is so often useful in making new associations.

The goal of interaction, therefore, is forwarded by many of the same physical features as the goal of choice: variety, fine grain, efficient communication; but it puts special emphasis on the oscillation between stimulus and repose (centers of high activity versus quiet parks), and requires that communication be controllable. In addition, it calls for situations conducive to spontaneous exchange. Storehouses of communication, such as libraries or museums, should be highly accessible and inviting, their exterior forms clearly articulated and expressive of their function.

These two objectives of choice and interaction may be the most important goals of metropolitan form, but there are others of major importance, such as minimum first cost and minimum operating cost. These seem to depend particularly on continuous occupation along the major transportation channels, on a balanced use of the flow system, both in regard to time and [in regard to] direction of flow, a moderately high structural density, and a maximum reliance on collective transport.

Objectives of comfort, on the other hand, related principally to a good climate, the absence of distracting noise, and adequate indoor and outdoor space, may point either toward generally lower densities or toward expensive ameliorative works, such as sound barriers, air conditioning, and roof-top play areas. The important goal of individual participation may also indicate lower densities and an environment that promotes active relation between an individual and his social and physical milieu, thus giving him a world that to some extent he can manage and modify by his own initiative.

We must also consider that the urban pattern will necessarily shift and expand, and therefore it is important to ask whether the adjustment to new functions will be relatively easy, and whether growth, as well as the initial state, is achievable with a minimum of control and central initiative and intervention. Adaptability to change seems to be greater at lower densities, since scattered small structures are readily demolished or converted. Both an efficient transport system and some form of separation of one kind of activity from another are also conducive to flexibility. Discontinuous forms like the galaxy or the ring require special efforts to control growth, for these patterns raise problems such as the appearance of squatters and the preservation and use of intervening open land.

Stability is a somewhat contradictory goal; it takes into account the critical social and economic costs of obsolescence, movement of population, and change of function. It is very possible that stability in the modern world will be impossible to maintain, and it runs counter to many of the values cited above. Yet stability may be qualified in this light: if change is inevitable, then it should be moderated and controlled so as to prevent violent dislocations and preserve a maximum of continuity with the past. This criterion would have important implications as to how the metropolis should grow and change.

Finally, there are many esthetic goals the metropolis can satisfy. The most clear-cut is that the metropolis should be "imageable"—that is, it should be visually vivid and well structured; its component parts should be easily recognized and easily interrelated. This objective would encourage the use of intensive centers, variety, sharp grain (clear outlines between parts), and a differentiated but well-patterned flow system.

The Relation of Forms to Goals

We have now treated a number of objectives that are crucial, that are on the whole rather generally accepted, and that seem to be significantly affected by the pattern of the metropolis: the goals of choice, interaction, cost, comfort, participation, growth and adaptability, continuity, and imageability. Other goals may develop as we increase our knowledge of city form. What even these few imply for city form is not yet obvious; moreover, they often conflict, as when interaction and cost appear to call for higher densities, while comfort, participation, and adaptability achieve optimal realization at lower levels. Nevertheless, we have immediate decisions to make regarding the growth of urban areas; and if we marshall our goals and our alternatives as best we can, we can the better make these decisions.

The clarifying of alternatives and objectives has an obvious value, for this will permit public debate and the speculative analysis of the probable results of policy as related to any given form. Yet this kind of approach will soon reach a limit of usefulness unless it is supported by experimental data. Such experimentation is peculiarly difficult in regard to so large and complex an organism as a metropolis. To some degree we can form judgments drawn from such different urban regions as Los Angeles, Stockholm, and Paris, but these judgments are necessarily distorted by various cultural and environmental disparities. Possibly we can study certain partial aspects of city form, such as the effects of varying density or the varying composition of centers, but the key questions pertain to the metropolitan pattern as an operating whole. Since we cannot build a metropolis purely for experimental purpose, we can only build and test models, with some simplified code to designate pattern. By simulating basic urban functions in these models, tests might be run for such criteria as cost, accessibility, imageability, [and] adaptability. Such tests will be hard to relate to the real situation, and it is difficult to see how certain objectives (such as interaction or participation) can be tested, yet this technique is our best current hope for experimental data on the implications of the total metropolitan pattern.

Dynamic and Complex Forms

Until we have such experimental data, what can we conclude from our imaginary juxtaposition of metropolitan form and human goals? Each of the alternatives proposed has its drawbacks, its failures in meeting some basic objectives. A radical, consistent dispersion of the metropolis appears to restrict choice, impair spontaneous interaction, entail high cost, and inhibit a vivid metropolitan image. A galaxy of small communities promises better, but would still be substandard as regards choice, interaction, and cost, besides being harder to realize. A recentralization of the metropolis in an intensive core appears to entail almost fatal disadvantages in cost, comfort, individual participation, and adaptability. The rationalization of the old metropolis in a star would work better if central congestion could be avoided and free accessibility maintained, but this form is less and less usable as size increases. The ring has many special advantages but raises great difficulties in cost, adaptability, and continuity with present form.

Of course, these are all "pure" types that make no concessions to the complications of reality, and they have been described as though they were states of perfection to be maintained forever. In actuality, a plan for a metropolis is more likely to be a complex and mixed one, to be realized as an episode in some continuous process, whose form involves rate and direction of changes as well as a momentary pattern.

For example, let us consider, on the basis of the little we know, a form that might better satisfy our aspirations, if we accept the fact of metropolitan agglomeration: this form is in essence a variant of the dispersed urban sheet. Imagine a metropolis in which the flow system becomes more specialized and complex, assuming a triangular grid pattern that grows at the edges and becomes more specialized in the interior. Many types of flow would be provided for. Densities would have a wide range and a fine grain, with intensive peaks at junctions in the circulation system and with linear concentrations along major channels, but with extensive regions of low density inside the grid. Through the interstices of this network belts and tongues of open land would form another kind of grid. Thus the general pattern would resemble a fisherman's net, with a system of dispersed centers and intervening spaces.

City-wide activities would concentrate in these knots of density, which would be graded in size. In the smaller centers the activities would not be specialized, but the larger centers would be increasingly dominated

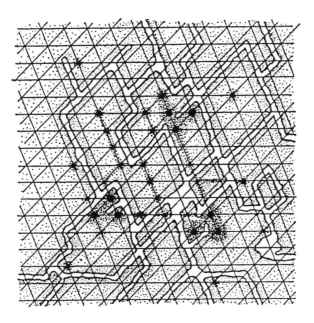

The polycentered net.

by some special activity. Therefore the major centers would be highly specialized—although never completely "pure"—and would be arranged in a loose central cluster, each highly accessible to another.

A metropolis of 20 million might have, not one such cluster, but two or three whose spheres of influence would overlap. These clusters might be so dense as to be served by transportation grids organized in three dimensions, like a skeletal framework in space. Elsewhere, the network would thin out and adapt itself to local configurations of topography. This general pattern would continue to specialize and to grow, perhaps in a rhythmically pulsating fashion. With growth and decay, parts of the whole would undergo periodic renewal. Such a form might satisfy many of the general criteria, but each particular metropolis is likely to encounter special problems. Even so, the description illustrates the complexity, the indeterminacy, and the dynamic nature of city form that are inherent in any such generalization.

Perhaps we can make such a proposal more concrete by stating it as a set of actions rather than as a static pattern. If this were the form desired, then the agencies of control would adopt certain definite policies. First, they would encourage continued metropolitan agglomeration. Second, they would begin to construct a generalized triangular grid of channels for transportation, adapting its interspacing and alignment to circumstances but aiming at raising accessibility throughout the area as a whole. This grid would provide for many different kinds of flow and would have a hierarchy of its own—that is, the lines of circulation would be differentiated with respect to the intensity and speed of their traffic. Third, peaks of activity and density would be encouraged, but in sharply defined areas, not in rings whose density gradually declines from the center. The present metropolitan center would be encouraged to specialize and thus loosen into a cluster, while one or two major rival centers might develop elsewhere in the network, rather than allowing a general dispersal of city-wide activities. Such major specialized centers might be given even greater local intensity, with multi-level circulation, perhaps as a three-dimensional system of public rights-of-way.

Fourth, every effort would be made to retain, acquire, or clear a system of linked open spaces of generous size that pervaded the network, Fifth, a wide variety of activities, of accommodation and structural character, dispersed in a fine-grained pattern, would be encouraged. Once the concentration of special activities and the arrangement of higher densities in centers and along major channels had been provided for, then zoning and other controls would be employed only to maintain the minimum grain needed to preserve the character and efficency of the various types of use and density, and large single-purpose areas would be avoided. Sixth, the form of centers, transportation channels, and major open spaces would be controlled so as to give as vivid a visual image as possible. Seventh, the agency would be committed to continuous rebuilding and reorganization of successive parts of the pattern.

Such a set of policies would mean a radical redirection of metropolitan growth. Whether this plan is feasible or worth the cost would require serious consideration. Even if this pattern were chosen, there would still be many crucial questions of relative emphasis and timing to be weighed. If life in the future metropolis is to be worthy of the massive effort necessary to build it, the physical pattern must satisfy human values. The coordination of metropolitan development, however obligatory, will not of itself ensure this happy result. Coordination must be directed toward some desired general pattern, and, to define this, we must clarify our alternatives and the goals they are meant to serve.

References

1. Frank Lloyd Wright, "Broadacre City," *Taliesin*, October 1940, vol. 1, no. 1.

2. Clarence Stein, "City Patterns, Past and Future," *Pencil Points*, June 1942.

3. *Skitseforslag til egnsplan for Stockobenhaven* (Copenhagen regional plan). Summary of the preliminary proposal, 1948–1949, with list of contents and notes explaining all illustrations of the preliminary proposal, translated into English.

4. Hans Blumenfeld, "A Theory of City Form," *Society of Architectural Historians Journal*, July 1949.

The Visual Shape of the Shapeless Metropolis

A number of recent attempts have been made to describe, influence, or propose solutions for the physical form of metropolitan regions. Without entering into their specific merits, the proposals have certain general form defects:

1. Their apparent form depends on a very simple and arbitrary classification and separation of use and intensity and a simple geometry of outline and street pattern, which rarely exist, and are undesirable when they do. They have none of the complexity and subtlety of a true city, and many designers secretly consider the existing land use map of a real place to be a more interesting object than a proposed future layout.

2. These proposed forms seem to be static ones which do not easily grow or change, except by additions in restricted directions, or by major jumps. There is little reflection of the cyclic, process nature of a city.

3. The suggested large-scale regional pattern is a self-contained one, relatively independent of local patterns, which are organized at a totally different level of scale. It would be difficult to conceive of these different patterns as being part of any continuous whole (as indeed it normally is in a metropolis today).

In addition to these formal problems, which will be our main concern in what is to follow, there are of course many serious questions about the relevance of these forms to substantive goals of city-building: economy, comfort, adequacy of facilities, choice, or whatever. The connection between city form and objectives has been discussed elsewhere[1] in a very speculative way. I am more interested here in the issue of patterned, conceivable form itself, and its direct relevance, if any, at the metropolitan scale.

Therefore we begin with two questions: is it possible to find or provide perceptible metropolitan form, and, if so, does it have any significance? To take the latter question first, a perceivable large-scale form is not a necessary condition for optimizing or improving city performance. Intuition whispers that some sort of organization is required for efficient function, or even for any function at all, simply because all things which function adaptively, in our experience, are somehow organized. But it does not follow that this organization would be evident in map form, or even on the ground. An economically efficient city might seem utterly chaotic when seen or recorded in the ordinary way. The organization may be a hidden one, only apparent when the environment is analyzed by some indirect means, such as mathematically or historically.

No date. Courtesy of Institute Archives and Special Collections, MIT Libraries.

However, we can feel more confident that an efficient environment must have a perceptible form for another reason: as long as its function depends on human actions, [the] inhabitants must be able to perceive it and to conceive it in their minds in some economical way if they are to act efficiently in it. And since individuals do in fact move and act frequently over metropolitan distances, we can argue that perceivable metropolitan form (in the actual city experience, and not on paper) is a significant issue.

We can also argue that a perceivable form on paper is also of some, although of much lesser, importance. Those who are setting or influencing metropolitan policy, of whom the designers are only a small group, must also be able to represent to themselves the area they are working with. Thus it is common to use the map of a large region as "background" for a group discussion which may never refer to the features of the map as such. This need for the professional or policy maker to conceive his area of discourse is undoubtedly a principal motive behind many attempts to systematize metropolitan form. Although not an important motive at the community level, it is nevertheless important simply because of the strategic position of this small group. It is probable that some of the aversion to the large metropolis, so often expressed, is in fact an esthetic and conceptual aversion, a discomfort due to the inability to represent it in any orderly way in relation to oneself. It seems chaotic and incomprehensible, therefore it must be a bad place. On the other hand, even larger regions— river valleys or islands or mountain ranges—can seem orderly and related to self despite their size and complexity, and thus appear to be good places.

I prefer, however, to argue from the need to make the environment conceivable to the "man in the street," as a prerequisite for intelligent and enjoyable behavior in the street. This requirement may not entirely coincide with the features that make that environment orderly when drawn as a map. Or, more correctly, we will probably have to revise our technique of recording city pattern, so that a perceptible diagrammatic form coincides with a perceptible form in actual experience.

But if this kind of large-scale form is significant, is it also possible? That is, does it sometimes exist, and, more important, can it be created, controlled, or improved? As to its existence, we can baldly say Yes, based not only on our everyday experience but also on a more careful study of the Boston region and its conception by some of its inhabitants. These people *do* have an organized conception of the region, however imperfect; physical conformations have a strong influence on that conception, and the quality of the conception is of importance to them.

The Criteria of Legibility

Whether this type of mental organization at the metropolitan scale can realistically be imporved is a more difficult question, and this is what I would like to explore. More specifically, would it be possible to create a metropolitan pattern which satisfied the following criteria in regard to its perceptual form?

1. It is an imageable region, composed of vivid differentiated elements, legibly organized. A crude test for this might be that the majority of normal, familiar adult inhabitants are able to conceive of and fit together the major metropolitan elements.

2. This structured image is an extensible one, not only legible at a very general level, but one that can be explored and known at deeper and more detailed levels. Let us say that this condition is satisfied if it is possible for a normal inhabitant, if he chooses to attend to it, to recognize and structure the environment at the community level (say perhaps 10 or 20,000 people), and to be able to fit this structure into the metropolitan picture.

3. The metropolitan region is capable of being imaged in various ways, according to the desires or capabilities of the particular observer (as a system of paths, as well as a constellation of linked focal points, for example). We will arbitrarily say here that there must be at least different general ways to organize the region. Ideally, one of these should enable an observer to image the area as a static map, and another as a system of sequences.

4. The image must be adaptable to the growth and change of physical features, activities, and their interconnections and be able to survive a degree of functional disorganization and waste. The test would be to see if the perceptual image could survive certain arbitrary changes, for example:

a. doubling the current rate of change, or the reversal of its direction,

b. a radical transformation of the dominant mode of the circulation system (from ground to air, or from movement of people to symbolic communication),

c. a radical shift in the preferred life style, or of the production system (suburb to central residence, complete industrial automation).

5. Finally, this metropolitan image should be congruent, having a form which can easily be associated with the form of the existing social and functional organizations, there being a recognizable formal correspondence, without any gross mismatch. Assume for our purpose that the following are the principal characteristics of the metropolitan social and functional structure which must be corresponded to formally:

a. the essential components of the region are interacting people distributed in a system of adapted spaces;

b. these people and these spaces are grouped in relatively normal, recognizable units (firms, families, structures, etc.), and these units are very small and numerous relative to the scale of the region;

c. there is a great diversity of function, styles of life, and values;

d. communication and interchange is the dominant process, which is relatively complex, dense and diffuse, occurring in an overlapping pattern of channels, with nodes where interaction rises to peaks of intensity;

e. this system is mobile and changing;

f. decision is diffused, but with some key points of partial control;

g. technical capabilities are large, but there are many problems of deprivation, frustration and disorganization.

All these characteristics have formal dimensions (density, diffusion, diversity, dynamism, scale, peaking, web-like form, contrast) to which perceptual form can correlate without requiring the more elusive "expression" of these characteristics. In a specific city, of course, social and functional patterns can be stated more specifically.

Other Performance Characteristics

These are our principal criteria, which we will attempt to satisfy in developing metropolitan form possibilities. But since any form has many non-perceptual effects, it is necessary to indicate at least vaguely the non-perceptual performance characteristics which will hover in the background, as restraints to our fantasy. Briefly, we want to be sure, while concentrating on the visual quality of the region, that we are suggesting models which also have the following features:

1. Accessibility: low cost of movement or communication between activity locations.

2. Adequacy: sufficient quantity and quality of such basic facilities as houses, roads, schools, recreation areas, shopping, offices, and factories.

3. Diversity: a wide range of variation of facilities and activities, these varieties being rather finely mixed in space.

4. Adaptability: low cost of adaptation to new functions, and the ability to absorb sudden shock.

5. Comfort: an environment which does not place undue stress on the individual, particularly in regard to communication, climate, noise, and pollution.

The Crucial Elements of Metropolitan Form

If we intend to manipulate (at least in imagination) the form of the metropolitan region to improve perceptual performance, what elements of that form will we operate upon? We abstract from the vast array of characteristics just those dimensions which seem to be most crucial in perception at that scale, and which also have some likelihood for manipulation by planned action. In other words, what would be the content of a proposal for the perceptual form of a metropolitan region? I suggest the following as the crucial elements:

1. *The major path system, the streets, rail lines, canals, promenades, airways.* These are perhaps the most crucial elements of all. Here I include the choice of the general types of channels and vehicles for movement of people; the relative roles they are assigned; the differentiation of major pathways, using both visual and symbolic means; the spatial organization of these paths and their pattern of interconnection; the expected flows along these channels; the relation of these paths to the major centers, open areas, natural features, and special use districts. A plan would specify the general sequence form of the various paths (progressive, recurrent, climactic, etc.), as well as the principal entry and climax points. It would set general policy for more specific plans, such as intersection and terminal design, the detailing of pathways and their borders, connections to local paths, visibility to and from the paths, and the character of the spatial, movement, and activity rhythms.

2. *The major centers, focal points or nodes*: the peaks of density, special activity, or access, such as shopping centers and major terminals. The plan would be concerned with the location of these nodal points; their general perceptual character; their relation to each other, to the path system, and to the natural features; their sense of local connection or of contrast with their surroundings. It would set policy on such elements of visual character as lighting, the mix of visible activity, spatial texture, the use of associated landmarks, skylines, distant visibility, entrance points, microclimate, and noise.

3. *Special districts*: areas of appreciable size associated with memorable activities, character, or associations. In particular these include the large special institutions (universities, hospitals, etc.), ports and the regions of heavy industry, the CBD or other principal office districts, the major open spaces or recreation zones, and the special historical areas. The plan would be concerned with the location of these districts, their visibility and accessibility from the path system, and their general visual character (in terms of such dimensions as the spatial and activity texture, silhouette, landscaping, light, climate, and noise).

These three elements—the paths, nodes, and special districts—seem to be the keys to metropolitan form. The designer also pays attention to the background on which these elements are set forth—the visible character, diversity, and mix of the districts which make up the bulk of the metropolis. Occasionally, where there is a sharp discontinuity in this background character (built-up to open, land to water, industrial to residential), another visual element at the metropolitan scale will result: an edge. Or there may be a consistent gradient of character which is perceptible at the metropolitan scale—a continuous increase of age and density toward the center, for example.

Metropolitan form will also be concerned with the large natural features of the site: hills, mountains, rivers, lakes, and seas. In fact, the paths, nodes, and special districts will achieve much of their character from the way they use and relate to these big topographic features. It is even possible to create such landscape features at the metropolitan scale (reservoirs, canal systems, large fills, pits, or spoil heaps), but this will be rare.

Any designer who is attempting to manipulate metropolitan visual form is working in two ways: the direct design of large features, such as the path system, the constellation of foci, or the location of special districts; and on the other hand, the setting of visual policy for more specific, local designs: the character of sequence rhythms along the paths, the visual character of nodes and districts, and so on.

The visual form has a temporal dimension as well as an "instantaneous" one, rhythms which are both cyclic (the variation of visible activity through 24 hours) and also secular (the change of the metropolitan visual form over the decades, and how these past associations and future anticipations affect the experience of the region at any one time). Therefore our models of metropolitan form must also include a time dimension—something notably lacking in many previous visual proposals.

A Canvass of Models for Metropolitan Form

Having stated our criteria for metropolitan form, and the principal elements which will be manipulated to those ends, the next step is to canvass some of the possibilities. Let us begin by listing some of the form alternatives in a sketch manner, and then we can develop and discuss some of the more likely ones. This initial list is drawn from many previous suggestions by others,[2] with a few speculative additions of my own. Most of them do not deal with all of the form elements together, and are limited to static, two-dimensional patterns. These deficiencies must be dealt with later in developing the chosen possibilities.

1. First come the linear forms, extended in one dimension and relatively narrow in the other, which may be organized either by a single dominant path, [by] a set of parallel paths, or [by] a dominant edge, such as a seacoast. Places are located by reference to their serial position along the major line, and are linked to it by short perpendicular paths or open

spaces. There may be a series of distinctive nodes along the line. This is a rather unusual form at the metropolitan scale, although it is found in smaller settlements, and again at the super metropolitan scale, such as the line of cities between Hartford and Washington. But in the latter the width of the band is at such a different scale that it is doubtful if it is psychologically the same thing at all. At the metropolitan or city level it is a rarity but not unknown, particularly under topographic constraints (e.g. Caracas, Stalingrad).

2. Secondly, we may use a set of focal points to organize the region. In this case, these foci must be rooted, connected somehow to their immediate environs, so that these environs can be organized around them.

> a. The simplest form is simply a collection of distinctive foci, each of which confers a sense of place to its hinterland, without there being any large-scale system of connection. If the foci are sufficiently dense, and sufficiently differentiated, one can memorize the set, and every location in the region is now "placed."[3] But, at the metropolitan scale, a sufficiently dense set would be too numerous to be remembered as distinctive, or organized in spatial relation to each other.

> b. These foci may be organized into a hierarchy: a main center, subcenters, sub-subcenters, and so on. Now the nodes are systematically related to each other, the main features of the region can be simply remembered, while the observer can go more deeply into parts of the system as he chooses. Subcenters need not be completely distinguished from all other centers, but only from those in their subset. In some degree, our city areas are now organized by hierarchical sets of centers, although imperfectly so, while subcenters are barely distinguishable from each other. While partly realistic, such a rank ordering may not long endure, in any complete form, in our complex, fluid cities.

> c. The foci, while not systematically ranked, may be systematically linked together by a triangular web of paths going from center to center. Ideally, these centers are not only distinct but also intervisible, whether by axial views along connecting avenues or by tall dominant landmarks. The former technique is the baroque city model, used so successfully, and for so long a period, in the small to moderate-sized city. It is still useful today.[4] City areas can be referenced not only to the nodes, but also the the linking avenues between them. It is more difficult to apply this system to very large regions, due to the strain of remembering all the centers and all the linked pairs and their links. It is also doubtful if such a triangular network, going through each center, could efficiently carry modern traffic, or allow for all the necessary variety of personal movement.

d. A system which seems strangely disorderly on paper, but which may be closer to existing methods of imaging environments, would be a series of overlapping but independent linkages, each with its proper foci and terminals. If each linkage is imageable within itself and spans the entire region, and if each node is recognizably placed within its proper linkage, as well as being recognizably part of the family of centers belonging to that linkage, then all places can be referenced by the nearest node, or by the nearest node in any given linkage. Inhabitants can either use the linkage of their choice, or, if they can remember more than one linkage system, they can cover the region more finely with recognizable places. Something like this happens today when people remember expressway and subway systems which have little in common geometrically. To go from one system to another, one simply strikes out "blind" to find the nearest node of the other family. If there is some rule for the grouping of unlike nodes (such as that they always occur in close clusters, or nodes A are usually to be found at the other end of an open space from nodes B, then transitions can be made throughout the system, even if it cannot be imagined as a single whole.

3. A third general system of organization is the radial star, having a single dominant center, from which a series of radials goes out, along which there are subsidiary centers.

a. As usually proposed in the ideal form, the built-up areas run out along the radials like thick fingers, and between each finger is an ever-widening wedge of open space or, in some cases, industrial use. The radial paths may be supplemented by circumferential ones, and the inter-sectorial open wedges may in a less rigid model be filled in by low-density uses, at least near the center. This is a pattern approximated by many 19th-century cities, expanding outward along a set of rail or canal lines. It is less and less suited to the multi-centered, multi-directional interactions of contemporary cities, and will entail difficult control problems if the open wedges are to be maintained. Nevertheless it is perceptually clear, as long as there is some way of distinguishing the various sectors and of maintaining a sense of outward progression on each. Conceptual linkages between sectors, however, are more difficult to achieve.[5]

b. A possible variant is a branching star, in which outgoing radials branch successively in order to "fill" the expanding radial space. This form raises such difficulties in circulation, and such problems of remembering successive branchings, that it does not seem to be worth serious attention.

4. The inverse of the radial star is the ring form, in which the built-up strips, the dominant paths, and the open space circle around the center.

There may be only a single ring with an open center, or an entire series of concentric rings. While this form has interesting perceptual qualities (of recurrent, endless sequences in one direction, and a continuous outward gradient in the other), it seems to be so incongruent with metropolitan function that we will shelve it, too.

5. A metropolis might be organized as a group of districts—indeed many of them are so organized today. We can distinguish at least two types (which correspond to the first two types of the focal organization):

a. The total region may be remembered as a mosaic or patchwork of relatively equal smaller districts, each one distinctive. The Boston region is partly conceived of in this way; territories of nesting birds show a similar pattern (although it is unlikely that birds bother themselves with conceiving the whole pattern). These small districts may correspond to historical communities, social gatherings, civil divisions, areas of homogeneous physical character, sharply bounded areas, and so on. It is a very congenial way for many people to imagine their world. In part, it can reflect real social or political organizations, but must in some degree be incongruent to overlapping communication and function, and to some degree inadaptable to change. It has the perceptual defect that it may be difficult to apply over very large areas, due to the numerous unranked elements to be remembered and the ambiguous way they relate to each other in space. A variant of this system is to "explode" the mosaic, allowing each distinctive district to be set in a neutral background, separate from its peers. The district is more sharply bounded for being bordered by "empty" space. If that background space is actually empty or open, we have the constellation of small communities proposed by Stein[6]; if the background is a neutral, unrecognized urban area, we have a common contemporary city image: a few distinctive places floating in a gray sea.

b. These districts may be grouped in some more systematic fashion. They could be organized geometrically, as in a checkerboard, to improve the conception of their spatial interrelations. But this is very unlikely to fit the variety and complexity of functional districts. They can be ranked and nested or clustered so that the region contains subregions which contain sub-subregions, or so that sub-subregions cluster about a more important subregion, and so on. The former solution, the nesting of hierarchically ranked areas, is a favorite model for many planners. Some ranking of functional districts does in fact occur in real cities, but it is even less systematic than the ranking of centers. It is very unlikely that any overall systematic organization of districts can be made congruent with the function of the modern city, and it is sure to be highly inadaptable.

6. The last major category depends on the organization of the paths throughout a region. In general, some variant of this is perhaps the way most people orient themselves within large regions today. It can be flexible yet generalized, and is congruent with the dominance of communication and its diffuse, web-like pattern. The perceptual difficulties arise in differentiating a large number of paths visually, in tying them to other urban features, and in a certain "impersonality" which focuses attention on features only temporarily occupied, which are not vital to an individual, as a local center or a home district might be.

a. To begin again with the most primitive variant, the organization can simply consist of an irregular web of intersecting major paths, each of which has a name and some recognizable character. The recognition signs and the spatial inter-relations are memorized by main force. The intersections may play a special role. Here is a system which is common to many of our less regularly laid out cities. It is workable, but difficult to grasp if extended far.

b. The next step is to organize these paths into some geometric system: a radial network, or a grid. The grid may in theory be triangular, but is more likely to be rectangular, the staple basis of organization in American cities. The geometry is often quite regular, with standardized directions and interspacings, but this is not necessary for field recognition. Paths may in fact curve irregularly, as long as they intersect one another in some regular, predictable way. This allows for adaptation to topography, historical forms, variations in block sizes, etc. But if there are major directional changes, or sharp variations in interspacings, the user will be unable to use any other clues for orientation, such as cardinal directions or approximate distances. While many of our cities have this grid system, the members of the grid are not differentiated, except perhaps by some arbitrary naming or numbering. Thus it may be hard to distinguish one street from another, or the N/S streets from the E/W ones, or to discover which way one is going. The organization is regular but faceless, confusing in its own sweet way. Other features which may be added, therefore, are visual distinctions between one set of parallels and their cross-streets (Manhattan's "streets and avenues"); or the visual differentiation of individual paths (which may, however, become very numerous); or a ranking and distinction of dominant paths; or a progressive sequence of names or visual conditions which facilitates remembering the serial order of successive streets, or facilitates recognizing which way one is traveling on any one street.

c. Paths may be (and in fact, often are) remembered, not as a geometric system, an abstracted map, but as a sequence of visual events. Many observers seem to prefer to organize their world in this way, which is, after all, the way it is experienced.[7] Paths may be given their individual character, and a sense of their direction and the distance traversed, by a sequential pattern rather than by an unvarying characteristic. When using either a grid, a radio-concentric net, or an irregular web, such organized individual sequences may be introduced as integral features of the pattern. A more speculative idea is a total coordinated network of sequences in which any movement through the system seems to be an organized one, and perhaps in which any such movement seems to be part of some larger "sequence form." A simple-minded way of achieving the latter is to endow all the sequences running in parallel in a rectangular grid with some progressive gradient directed in the same way. Thus N/S streets might all run north uphill, and E/W streets all run east into more densely wooded land. Then various diagonal sequences going southwesterly in the grid might all have the common gradient "downhill and away from the woods." Presumably there are more sophisticated devices for generalized sequential form, but they remain to be developed.[8]

d. Finally, as a further complication, it is not necessary that all paths belong to a common set. There may be two or more internally organized systems covering the region, which only intersect here and there, or not at all. Subways and surface streets are an example. The discussion of this type would be similar to that on the system of non-coordinate foci (our second).

7. All the above systems assume that it will be necessary to organize the metropolis as a conceivable unit, if it is to be lived in. This is logically unnecessary, however desirable. For many purposes, it is enough if the environment is simply *continuous*, one part linking to the next so that eventually any part can be reached or conceived, and that the "known world" can be enlarged as far as is desired. In this case, the designer is concerned with local differentiation and local continuity, rather than with general form. Distinctive paths should lead into other paths through clear joints, foci be linked legibly to neighboring foci, districts be clearly bounded by other districts, that there be legible sequences in every direction in which it is locally possible to go.

Undoubtedly such local continuity is a necessity in any case, and it is logically sufficient for metropolitan orientation. It fails to provide for emergencies or unusual movements, for occasions when it is politically, technically, or even esthetically desirable to think of the region as a whole, and it would allow only the gifted person to range conceptually or physically beyond his habitual ground. It is an adequate but limiting technique, although it may be perceptually quite satisfying in direct experience. It is analogous to that parlor game in which one imagines how he would reach the Queen of England through a chain of mutual acquaintances.

8. To go farther, it is not even necessary that there be any visible organization in the environment at all, as long as there is some unseen organization which can be called up at will, as in the telephone system. Imagine, for example, that the city appeared chaotic and its parts indistinguishable (or need we imagine it?). If sought-for locations would on request light up or emit a broadcast recognition signal, one could still get about. There could be orientation experts (there are), systematic means of random search, etc. However fantastic, they serve to remind us that other devices are possible, and are to some extent used in visually unfavorable circumstances. They make the observer dependent on the well functioning of an outside system, and deprive him of the pleasure and security of constructing his own mental image. We will pursue them no further.

Looking back over this compilation, we find that only a handful have escaped such common difficulties as gross incongruence with metropolitan function, lack of adaptability, inability to organize very large areas, or psychological inadequacy to our basic purpose. These few seem to be the linear form based on the dominant edge or path, the interlinked and partly hierarchical set of nodes, the radial star, and the general grid. Many features of the other systems, of course, may be incorporated into these four systems, or may be useful for smaller-scale organization.

Four General Models for Metropolitan Form

The next step, then, is to develop these four models as more comprehensive systems. All of them are restricted in form—different observers cannot organize them in different ways. They are primarily two-dimensional. Their coordination with sequential form has only been touched upon. What follows is an attempt to enrich the models in these several dimensions, while still keeping them abstract and general, and to then evaluate them speculatively.

1. The Linear System

Organized by a set of parallel, relatively close, dominant paths, which are reinforced by the presence of a dominant edge or edges. The interplay between path and edge is an important aspect of the visual form. The paths are organized into rhythmically recurrent visual sequences, although there is also some continuous characteristic (such as the presence of the edge) which distinguishes one direction from the other. Along the paths are a chain of distinct focal points, perhaps changing progressively in any one direction, and perhaps with some ranking of importance. Between the centers on the parallel lines run short cross-paths. Foci, cross-paths, and sequential rhythms are coordinated so that progress along one main path can mentally be correlated with that along the other main paths. There may be one main center, or several, distributed along the lines—one main path, or two or three. Some of the paths may be of different modes, or at different levels. In areas of high intensity, a single path may diverge horizontally or vertically, like a spindle, to make several paths. Here the path may be enclosed by a complete "sheath" of activity, above and below, as well as right and left. As intense regions are passed by, this spindle of paths will reconverge to one. Cross-paths will lead in from low-intensity zones at the sides, each one having a directed linear sequence (i.e., going from a beginning to a climax in one direction). There will also be local gradients within the general built-up areas which connect them to the dominant lines. Major open spaces are also linear, and probably part of the edge system. They have sequential patterns along their lengths, which are also correlated with the path sequences.

This form can grow indefinitely in either longitudinal direction without losing its integrity, but can grow laterally very little. Thus it may be best fitted to sites (as on a narrow sea-coast) where lateral expansion is permanently restricted, unless it is proposed to shift over to another model at a later date. Major changes in the direction or mode of flow may be troublesome. The form is not conducive to progressive change by means of infilling, since development is from the beginning likely to be compact along the line. On the other hand, it may be possible to rebuild and modify continuously by moving down the line in small increments. In this way, intact centers may "roll" along the line. Large-scale clearances, however, will cause serious gaps in the system. The city may also be changed more radically by building new parallel paths along the old linear open spaces, or be shifted bodily sidewise to occupy new parallel ground, if not restricted by the site.

Here we have a model powerful enough to organize a large complex region, without hampering or being incongruent with its communications-dominated function (as long as the region is otherwise constrained at the sides or attracted to the central line). Vivid visual contrasts between open spaces and intense linear development (as well as the physical access to diversity that would go with this contrast) are built in to the form. It is extensible, since many small and complexly varying parts can be brought into contact with the simple main form. It gives the observer the choice of several means of organization: map shape, major correlated sequences, succession of centers, relation to an edge, etc. It is reasonably adaptable to certain kinds of change, but not to others. It does not seem to preclude achievement of the background criteria, except for difficulties with accessibility due to overload of the main corridors or susceptibility to disaster, if those same main corridors should be blocked. It may therefore be a useful perceptual model in particular cases.

2. The Linkage System

The outstanding feature of this model (which derives from the old baroque idea, as already mentioned) is a distributed set of focal points, interlinked by paths to form an irregular, usually triangular, network. The foci are each of distinctive character, and are contrasted to their immediate hinterlands but rooted in them. There is some ranking of centers, although incomplete, so that more important centers can occasionally be found throughout the region, and they tend to cluster toward the geographical center of the region. The succession of links leading from one major center to another, through a series of minor centers, can be read as a major link, so that the region can be imagined more simply as a few major centers and their connections. The linking paths have symmetrical linear sequences (which lead up to the centers at both ends), and they have some pervasive character which reflects those of both termini, so that the node connected to can be read anywhere along the path. Associated with the nodes are dominant landmarks, visible from a distance and particularly from neighboring nodes and approaching paths. Local gradients lead up to the foci. Special districts and open spaces of small to medium size are also associated with these centers. The foci have well-marked entrances. Where uses in these centers become quite intense, they are disposed in vertical layers, with linkages in three dimensions and special local systems of movement, such as beltways. Densities tend to fall off away from the nodes, and particularly away from the links, toward the interior of the triangular blocks, where there may be major open spaces. A special subsidiary movement system may also move through these open interiors: a pleasureway, or a series of bypasses. Centers on the periphery may be satellite communities, connected by their links into the whole region, but surrounded by substantial open space.

Since this form is a generalized linkage throughout the field, a certain amount of clearance, and a degree of disorganization and waste, can occur without disrupting the system. These flows can simply be bypassed. The form is well suited to in-filling and gradual change, as long as the loci of the centers are preserved. The region may easily grow outward at the edges. It may even be possible to invert the entire structure by locating new centers with their links in the old open spaces, then "plowing under" the old linkage system. There is some adaptability to shifts in circulation, but this must continue to be destined primarily for the center.

This second model is one of proven value at a smaller scale, and might work at a larger one if developed as outlined above. The principal perceptual difficulty will be to create a sufficient number of recognizable nodes to cover the region, without straining the observer's capacity to retain the whole, and while making it possible to remember the interconnections of these points. The model provides choices for preferred ways of organizing (by centers, by special districts, by landmarks, by sequences); it is easily extensible to small localities; it is very flexible. It is congruent to the multi-centered nature of our urban environment, the peaking and the diffuse interactions. Since local centers are often a locus of social, political, and activity attachments, this match can produce a "warm" image. It may be somewhat lacking in contrast, due to the interior locations of the major open spaces. It is also difficult to convey any sense of general direction: in versus out, or north versus south. Its only difficulty in regard to the general criteria that is immediately apparent is the concentration of flows on the links that run from center to center—an invitation to congestion and discouraging for long-range traffic.

3. The Radial System

There is a single dominant metropolitan focus, centrally placed. Into it run a series of major radial paths, including various modes of circulation. Between these ribbons of development there are wedges of open space, within which may run special pleasure ways. There are a series of secondary centers along the radial paths, and these are interconnected by circumferential ways. The radial paths are directed linear sequences, climaxing at the main center but with rhythmic punctuations at each secondary center. There should be a clear differentiation of the *in* and *out* directions. The successive centers will act as scaling devices—can they also be given a character which changes progressively with distance from the center? The visual characters of centers around the same circumferential, and the sequential rhythms of the radials, are coordinated, to aid the conception of how the different radials interrelate. The circumferentials have a recurrent sequence arising from their periodic passage of the sectorial open space, followed by approach to a new center. This will probably be sufficient to mark them off from the radials. They should also be given some progressively changing characteristic which will indicate how far out they are from the center. The relative length of the open space traversed might do this, but would it be perceptually apparent in the outer areas? On the periphery of the region, on extensions of the radial paths, there may be separate satellite communities. Pedestrian routes or pleasure ways along the open wedges may also have interesting sequences with close access to the development and subcenters at the sides, connection to the "outside" country at one end, and a climactic approach to the metro center at the other. The metro center itself will have special treatment: dominant landmarks, massive termini and interchanges for the incoming radials, which act as gateways; intensive development accompanied by the distribution of activity and circulation in three-dimensional space; and a very particular visual character, or more likely a complex of characters caused by the close packing of a wide range of activities. Small open spaces, connected to the radial wedges, can provide a high visual contrast.

The star form may easily grow outward along its rays, although as it gets very large the sense of radial form changes to a linear one, isolated from other rays and running toward a distant center. It is also possible to renew progressively along the rays, allowing the centers to "roll" along the line, but any large clearances will disrupt the continuity. It is difficult to restructure this form, or to shift to a new location, particularly in regard to the main center. It might be possible to renew the model by building new rays in the open wedges and abandoning the old rays—obviously a radical move and one which will cause upheavals in the center itself. Major changes in the characteristics of flow will be troublesome, as will anything which reduces the dominance of the center.

In sum, the radial model is a perceptually powerful form which marked many nineteenth-century cities and still marks some today. For all its simplicity, it can organize large areas. It provides high visual contrast and close access both to open land and to concentrated centers. It conveys a strong sense of in and out, and a single point to which the whole metropolitan area may be associated. Its difficulties lie in distinguishing one radial from another, in clarifying their directions (since many will be at angles to the cardinal points), and in making a satisfactory visual connection to the center under conditions of massive traffic. Near the periphery the radial form loses some of its force, and the circumferentials pass through wide regions of open space. It is difficult to maintain any sense of direction when traveling on these endlessly circling circumferentials. It will not be easy to correlate visually the various positions along one radial with positions along another, and thus mental connections except those passing through the center will be difficult to make. But relations to and from the center are very powerful.

There are alternate ways to image the city: it is easy to extend this organization to smaller parts. Adaptability is not so high if the central dominance fades, or if an individual's interests connect across the radial lines. Although highly congruent to the city of the recent past, the form is less so to the more diffuse interactions of today. The problems in terms of the general criteria center principally on the lack of adaptability, and on the defects in accessibility arising from the massive central convergence, and the relative isolation of the radial aims at their outer ends. The access to open space, however, is uniformly high, and the use of high-density transit systems is made possible.

Since centers have very similar locational characteristics along the radials, there may be some lack of diverstiy. On the other hand, rather wide social and physical divergences between radials may occur, which may be undesirable when coupled with the relative isolation of the sectors. Existing Washington is an example of this effect. As in the linear system, average densities will tend to be higher than they can be in more diffuse organizations such as the linkage or the grid. There are likely to be serious problems of control involved in keeping open the intervening wedges, since accessibility is good along the circumferentials.

4. The Grid System

Our last example depends for its form on a general rectangular grid of major ways. The grid lines may be distorted to adapt to particular conditions, but the topographic relation of one parallel set of ways to the intersecting set are maintained as well as the general sense of direction. The grid interspacing may vary, but only in some systematic way. The two perpendicular sets of paths are clearly distinguished from each other. There can be some ranking of importance among the ways, and the dominant ways in particular have an individual character. The paths are ordered progressively from each side of the region to the other, and there is some visible gradient that clarifies the sense of direction in both dimensions. Paths have recurrent rhythmic sequences which reinforce each other at their intersections. Intersections are legible, clearly indicating the cross-path and its two directions.

Foci occur at or near the intersections but do not straddle them. Local connections and visual gradients root them to their surroundings. They will have differentiated visual characters, and also be ranked in importance, relating to the intersections of the dominant grid lines. Major grid lines and major foci may cluster together toward the center of the region, where the grid interspacing may become smaller. In this relatively intense central area the grid may become three dimensional, and the centers will have a vertical layering of uses. Major open spaces occur in the block interiors of the grid, and near the periphery the grid may open sufficiently to allow large tracts of rural land. These interior open spaces may be interconnected with pleasureways, also sequentially organized, or may have fingers giving access to the nodes at grid corners. Densities fall off away from the foci, but especially toward the interior of the grid.

The basic form is simple, and a very old one. It has clarity and indefinite coverage. It can organize a very complex environment, as well as a very large one, and is extremely adaptable to shifts in function and circulation. It can be imaged either as a map or as a set of sequences, although it may be troublesome for those accustomed to think in terms of bounded districts. The metropolitan form can be extended down into local visual organization, although these local forms may have a very different character. Access to, and contrast with, open space can be provided. A sense of general location, direction, and scaling is easily provided anywhere. The form seems congruent to the multiform, shifting, overlapping functions of the contemporary city, and to the dominance of communication. Centers may be varied in their relation to the grid, have diverse characters and functions, and yet not be isolated from one another.

The principal conceptual difficulties are twofold. First, it is difficult to differentiate the individual lines sufficiently, since they have been distinguished into two intersecting sets and given some general visual gradient across the field. The designer must rely on association with distinctive places visible from the grid, or on making just a few super-paths distinctive, or on some arbitrary naming and numbering system. Second, the relations between grid lines and the foci are difficult. The centers must lie alongside the lines, and not straddle or interrupt them. Major circulation works more easily if access to the centers occurs between the major intersections rather than at them. Thus there is a sense of isolation between the grid and the rest of the fabric, and an ambiguous relation between the centers and the grid corners which requires special techniques of visibility to overcome. Local movements are likely to follow quite a different pattern than the grid (perhaps a center-to-center linkage as in the linkage system), increasing the sense of dichotomy. The visual sequences along the main paths may be delightful, but if the path is only temporarily occupied, and not a focus of personal associations, the basic image may be "cold." It is an endless, repetitive form, rather than a centrally oriented, limited one, which may be congenial to some temperaments and not to others, however congruent to reality.

The grid model relates very well to growth and change, both as an image and as a reality. Development may in-fill or rebuild gradually, centers may shift location or change their dominance. Even a shift backwards to a single dominant center can be accommodated. Growth may occur at the edges; there can be cyclical renewal. Large clearances, abandoned sections, or areas of disorganization [may] be bypassed. Flow changes can be accommodated. It is possible to create a new structure by shifting to a new grid intermediate between the old. This generalized flexibility, and the congruence with present function, is indeed the model's major asset. There seem to be no particular problems in terms of the other general criteria.

Certainly there are other potential models for metropolitan form, and features of these that have been given may be recombined or modified to meet particular circumstances. But the previous four have been developed as examples of the many interlocking features that such models must have, abstract as they are. Even in such abstract form, these models can be evaluated for their legibility and are useful conceptual devices for attacking real problems, just as the baroque model facilitated many plans. Each model, of course, has its own advantages and disadvantages, and situations to which it is most applicable.

The Application of a Composite Model

It may be interesting to go one step further while still at this level of abstraction: how would such a model be applied to a real city, with all its existing chaos, rich historical overlappings, and sunk investments? Even without considering costs, or political problems, or social dislocations, is it possible to see how one of these forms might be adapted to, and evolve out of, an existing, accidental form? Or are these models useful only for planning cities on virgin ground?

While we are at it, we can not only illustrate evolution and adaptation, but also show how particular features from separate models may be recombined. I will put together the main features from the linkage and the grid systems, to gain diversity, and also to ameliorate certain inherent deficiencies in both. Rather than producing a crystal-clear map form, the result will illustrate complex continuity and consistent character developing from systematic visual policy.

Assume we begin with a semi-radial system: a partly random collection of nodes which nevertheless cluster and become more dominant closer to the center of the region. They are associated with a partly radial, partly triangular, partly random system of arterials. Densities are diffuse but increase near the major nodes. Many activities are mixed but there is a broad gradient of residential type and age, outward from the center. There are a few random major open spaces, special uses, historic areas, and large natural features. However abstract, this is not too unlike many existing situations, although it is more random than most communities will be, shaped as they are by historical forces.

Due to a desire for a large legible form which is nevertheless rich, diverse, and flexible, and in accord with a sense of the increasing complexity, diffusion, and dynamism in the city, a future form is projected which is a combination of the grid and linkage systems. It might be described as an open-ended, interconnected triple movement system: a grid of freeways, a triangular network of arterials linking differentiated centers, and an independent, looping mesh of pleasureways connecting the open spaces, the large institutions, and natural features. One form may evolve into the other, as a process of evolution guided by the following consistent visual policies.

1. A rectangular grid of limited-access freeways will be inserted into the existing fabric, usually passing near but not through existing centers, and maintaining visual contact with these centers and with open spaces and special-use districts. There are two types of intersections, the one with sister freeways, the other with local arterials. Usually these two intersections will succeed one another in an a-b-a-b-a rhythm, but sometimes it will become a-b-b-a-b-a-a-b, etc. Wherever the freeway is in visual contact with a center, it will have an arterial intersection clearly associated with

that center. Along the grid lines run transit systems as well as individual but automated vehicles. The transit lines loop off the grid lines to pass through the nearby centers. A few of the grid lines will be visually dominant and carry heavier traffic. They will be associated with the dominant centers and will converge toward the center of the region. The transit lines associated with them will be higher [in] capacity. While the detailed structures, and even the modes of circulation, will change within the grid, the right-of-way pattern is expected to be a stable feature.

2. The two perpendicular sets of grid lines will have two distinct visual characters. In addition, each of the few dominant grid lines will be given some individual distinction. Each grid line will have a single name throughout, and those names will be systematized to indicate the serial order of successive parallel lines. There will be a gradient of character along each line, to distinguish one direction from its opposite. Each line will have a strong recurrent "endless" visual sequence so arranged as to reinforce the intersecting sequences, and its rhythm will increase in tempo near the center of the region. Grid intersections will connect legibly to the crossing lines, with the two different directions clearly expressed.

3. The arterial streets will gradually be relocated and improved to form an irregular triangular network, running from center to center. Each portion of the network between a pair of centers will be given an individual name and have an individual visual character. The street will have a symmetrical visual sequence, coming to a climax at the nodes at either end. On this channel run transit and individual vehicles, the former being routed back and forth between the pair of centers. Typically, there will be an intersection with a freeway on each arterial between each pair of centers, allowing a transit transfer and an entrance for individual vehicles onto the automated system. Along the arterials will be concentrated the special, non-central uses (institutional, auto-oriented retail, footloose offices and industries, etc). Into the street will run many local collectors. The arterials may be remodeled or occasionally replaced by a new link between the same pair of centers.

4. Dispersion of central functions will be encouraged or tolerated, but usually only into other centers, however widely distributed over the region. Where needed, the growth of new multi-purpose centers will be stimulated or supported, and coordinated with the arterial street network. Old centers will not be frozen in size or function, since continued adjustment and specialization of central function is desirable, but they will be maintained as active places, if well-established and strategically located. All centers designated as part of the regional system will be kept concentrated, and of sufficient size for diversity and visual weight. Mixture of use will be encouraged, a special local movement system may be provided, and a sense of connection to the local surroundings will be developed. Each center will be furnished with distant landmarks, with entrance points

and one or more focus points. In each center a special mixture of visible activity, a unique spatial texture, and other particular visual characters will be encouraged, so that each node can have its own individual recognizable personality.

5. The system of major open spaces will be expanded, using the natural features available and aiming to achieve a balanced distribution throughout the region. Typically, there will be a large open space within each triangular block of arterials, and these open spaces will often be visible from the freeway lines. Interconnecting the open spaces, there will, in time, be created a system of pleasureways, patterned like a series of coinciding loops. These ways, wandering throughout the region from open space to open space, will pass close by the nodes and can be entered from them. They will also be accessible from many local points, but not from the arterials or the freeways. Typically, they will pass through the centers of the open spaces, and three-way junctions will often occur there. Although they touch each node, they never go directly between them, nor do they parallel an arterial for any great distance. These channels are restricted to pedestrians or to certain special transit or individual vehicles designed for pleasure in movement rather than efficient communication— vehicles which are slow, quiet, and open—boats, horses, bicycles, moving benches, open trolleys, carriages. Each complete loop will have a name and an identifiable character, and as a consequence each part of the path has two names and a mixed character. The lines tend to follow natural features, or interesting landscapes are created for them. The sequences are intricate, somewhat mysterious. An attempt will be made to preserve the pleasureways and large open spaces over long periods of time, as links with the past in contrast to the changing urban areas. But where it becomes necessary to occupy an open space by a new center, in a major shift of structure, then equivalent open space and pleasureways will be opened within the new triangular blocks resulting therefrom.

6. In general, densities are rather low, but not uniform, tending to increase along the arterials and particularly near the centers. While central functions are encouraged to remain in clusters, and other access-oriented or large special activities are guided to locations along the arterials, remaining uses are allowed to locate rather freely, under general density rules, as long as service levels are maintained and nuisance effects controlled. Diversity and individual action is encouraged, and rebuilding is kept dispersed and locally small in scale, however large in total quantity.

Here we have a set of general policies which, when applied consistently over a period of time, would result in a legible but complex metropolitan form, a form which satisfies most of our criteria. It could develop gradually, need not be applied rigidly, and furnishes guidance for plans and designs developed at smaller scales. It is not meant to be the optimum solution—there is no such thing—but to be an illustration of a workable one, and how it could grow out of a present situation. However much it may sound like the outline for a superficial comprehensive plan, it is actually designed solely for visual ends, with only background consideration being given to other purposes. It indicates the complexity of required policy, the range of considerations involved in metropolitan visual form, and at the same time how much "play" and looseness there can be.

It seems clear that a model like this would help to illuminate many decisions, and to make metropolitan perceptual form a manageable topic. Such models would have to be tested in at least two ways:

a. Can they be applied in a concrete case; would they bear on decisions?

b. If applied, will they improve the metropolitan image, and, if so, which model would be best for that purpose in a given situation?

The latter question is too difficult to answer directly. Since we are unable to build experimental metropolises and lack the time to test them, we are constrained to make inferences from the images and behavior arising in parts of existing cities. Comparative studies between cities of different form, and analyses of image changes which follow after physical change, would be of great value to us in making these inferences.

As to the first question, it may soon be possible to apply one of these models, or to compare several of them, in preparing metropolitan highway policy or even a comprehensive metropolitan plan. How or if these ideas are able to sway metropolitan decisions in a way that previous ideas about city esthetics have been unable to do will be revealing in itself.

Notes

1. See "The Form of the Metropolis" and "The Quality of City Design."

2. Some of these are evaluated by more general criteria in "The Pattern of the Metropolis."

3. Jane Jacobs recommends this as the most realistic model for city organization; see *Death and Life of Great American Cities* (New York: Random House, 1961).

4. See Christopher Tunnard, *American Skyline* (Boston: Houghton Mifflin, 1955).

5. See National Capitol Planning Commission, "Washington Year 2000."

6. Clarence Stein, *Toward New Towns for America* (New York: Reinhold, 1957).

7. See Kevin Lynch, Donald Appleyard, and John Myer, *The View From the Road* (Cambridge: MIT Press, 1964).

8. See chapter 4 of *The View From the Road*.

The City as Environment (1965)

Imagine that the growth of population and the evolution of technology have urbanized the entire globe—that a single world city covers the usable surface of the earth. The prospect is a nightmare. One instantly has a vision of being trapped in endless rows of tenements or little suburban houses, of no escape from the continual presence and pressure of other people. The city would be monotonous, faceless, bewildering. It would be abstract, out of contact with nature; even the man-made things could not be handled or changed. The air would be foul, the water murky, the streets crowded and dangerous. Billboards and loudspeakers would force their attentions on everyone. One could be at home in a sealed room, but how could one farm or hunt or explore? Where could one find a wilderness or start a revolution? Would there be anything to challenge or excite the human spirit? Would not this world, entirely man-made, be utterly alien to every man? Surely it would be a vulnerable place: any shift of conditions would sweep it all away.

As a prediction of the quality of life in a world city these fears may be wildy irrational. We magnify the city we know, and this is what horrifies us. Our fright is too quick to be based on reasoning—even indirect reasoning. Cities have many human implications, and the articles in this issue of *Scientific American* consider a number of them: history, economics, physical and social organization, problems of communication, transportation, land use, and so on. Our fears, however, rise from another quarter: the way in which the environment affects our lives through our immediate perception and daily use of it. The physical form of a city has a sensuous impact that profoundly conditions the lives of its people, and this is often ignored in the task of city-building. By attempting, in our imagination, to make a world city habitable, we may discover policies that could humanize the real metropolis.

The cities we live in have many admirable features, at least in the affluent, highly developed countries. The incidence of disease is low and the material standard of living higher than it has ever been in mankind's history. The modern metropolis provides unprecedented opportunities for education and entertainment. For millions of people it offers new ways of life that seem far more attractive to them than the old ones from which they are breaking away. Nonetheless, the metropolis has begotten problems that are monumental and notorious. Many of these are social and economic problems, but not the least of them is the harsh and confusing physical environment that has been created, which in itself aggravates social and personal problems.

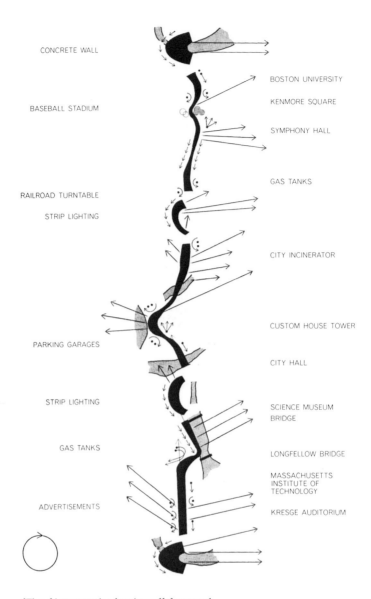

CONCRETE WALL

BOSTON UNIVERSITY

KENMORE SQUARE

BASEBALL STADIUM

SYMPHONY HALL

GAS TANKS

RAILROAD TURNTABLE

STRIP LIGHTING

CITY INCINERATOR

CUSTOM HOUSE TOWER

PARKING GARAGES

CITY HALL

STRIP LIGHTING

SCIENCE MUSEUM
BRIDGE

GAS TANKS

LONGFELLOW BRIDGE

MASSACHUSETTS
INSTITUTE OF
TECHNOLOGY

ADVERTISEMENTS

KRESGE AUDITORIUM

[These] interpretative drawings of [a] proposed
expressway route are intended to represent the
complete, sequential experience of motion,
space, light, texture and orientation in an abstract, shorthand way. The roughly triangular
route has been straightened out by breaking it at
the corner intersections, so that it can be read as
a continuous linear sequence. The drawings at
left represent the sensations of space, motion
and view for a clockwise trip around the route.
Widening of roadway signifies ascent; narrowing, descent. The small black arrows beside the
route indicate the apparent motion of the visual
field at various points; where a single important object is being referred to a dot is appended

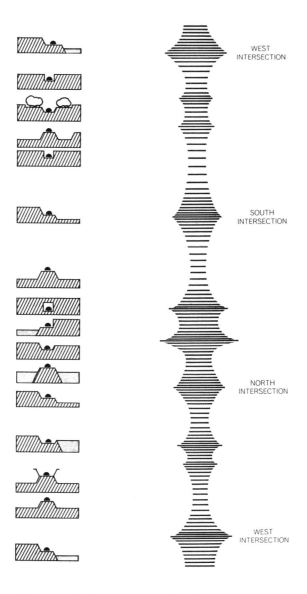

WEST
INTERSECTION

SOUTH
INTERSECTION

NORTH
INTERSECTION

WEST
INTERSECTION

to the arrow. The [long] arrows point toward particularly interesting land-marks several of which are named. The drawings at center are cross sections that show some of the characteristics of the space being traversed (enclosing surfaces and so on): here a half-dot indicates the elevation of the traveler. At right is an even more abstract notation, which merely shows the location and timing of major visual events, or the level of general visual density, without further specification. Basic visual rhythm of this particular route is set by recurrent intersections, each followed by a double climax of visual intensity.

Imagine, then, that we have been required to develop a sector of the hypothetical world city and to ameliorate as best we can the conditions it sets for the quality of life. What could we do to make it a more human place? What physical deficiencies make the great metropolises we know less than satisfying as places in which to live? There are perhaps four faults that stand out most sharply.

First and most obvious is the burden of perceptual stress imposed by the city. In particular we suffer from omnipresent noise (symbolic as well as acoustic) and an uncomfortable climate, including polluted air. The city is too hot, too noisy, too confusing; the air is unpleasant to breathe. Too often the sensations we experience go beyond our limits of comfort or even of tolerance.

The second fault is a lack of visible identity. A good environment is richly diverse: its parts have distinct, identifiable character; they are marked by visible differences that allow choice and sensuous exploration, and they give a sense of place and home. A city is inherently a much richer and more diverse habitat than most rural areas, but it rarely appears to be so. Objective differences of activity, history and culture are glossed over and submerged. Large areas are zoned for similar land occupancy, which tends to separate different populations in a coarse grain. The physical setting could be managed to express and allow human diversity, and to bring those differences within sight of each other. We sense that the world city would be a trap because we are now trapped in a monotone city.

A third source of distress in our cities is their illegibility. In order to feel at home and to function easily we must be able to read the environment as a system of signs. It should be possible to relate one part to another and to ourselves, to locate these parts in time and space, and to understand their function, the activities they contain, and the social position of their users. When the parts of the city lack visible relation to one another, their incoherence can contribute to a sense of alienation—of being lost in an environment with which one cannot carry on any sort of dialogue. Our cities display many ambiguities, confusions, and discontinuities; significant activities are hidden from sight; history and natural setting are obscured. The language of the cityscape is as baffling as a news release.

The fourth disability of the city is its rigidity, its lack of openness. For his satisfaction and growth an individual needs opportunities to engage in active interchange with his environment: to use it, change it, organize it, even destroy it. His physical surroundings should be accessible and open-ended, challenging, wayward, responsive to effort. Individual action is a road to personal growth; cooperative action leads to satisfying interpersonal relations. These require a plastic physical setting, with opportunities for seclusion and for risk, and with a degree of ambiguity and waste. Woods, water and lonely places work this way, but so do empty buildings, back alleys, waste heaps, vegetable gardens, pits, caves, and construction sites. They are not usually regarded as being beautiful, but this is a narrow view. They are the physical basis of an open society.

What might be done to correct these ills: discomfort, lack of diversity, illegibility, rigidity?

Discomfort must be attacked by taking the measure of the noxious sources and applying technology to control them. These questions have been scandalously neglected by the technological establishment of the advanced countries, hyperactive as it is in many other fields. We still lack detailed, quantitative knowledge about noise and pollution levels and human tolerances to them. In no large city has there been a systematic mapping of even the clearly definable qualities, such as the variations in microclimate, lighting, or noise level. We will want to go further than suppression, to consider the possibilities for diversity and a stimulating rhythm of change. A universal hush or eternally mild sunny weather would be equally deadening.

In dealing with the other physical problems of the city (diversity, legibility, openness) I would concentrate to begin with on the character of the urban centers. These peaks of activity and interest, which dominate the urban scene because of their symbolic importance and the frequency with which they are occupied and seen, are the meeting ground of the diverse population of the metropolis, and they give character to large areas around themselves. They stand for the quality of the whole, and they act as foci for organization and memory. It would be my policy to sharpen whatever is unique in the physical character of each center and to increase the diversity between centers. Studies would be made of their existing differences and of their hidden potentialities—studies of each center's history, landform, building type, population, and mix of activities. A program for visible character could be set for each focus, dealing with such qualities as the nature of exterior spaces, lighting, planting, and even the texture of the pavements. Each center could have an identifying focal point: a plaza, a crossroads, a terrace, or a public room. The entrances to each center would be clarified, and its presence would be made visible from a distance. For the symbolic effect of contrast and for relief from the intensity of the central activities, I would take care to locate each center next to some natural feature: a rocky hill, a broad lake, a hidden stream, a tranquil garden.

High-intensity uses are currently moving outward from the central area to follow the movement of population. Often these uses seize on random suburban locations where land happens to be available and cars can be parked. In the process we are losing social and visual meeting points and the functional advantages of supporting interactivity. Some retail uses are relocating in compact regional shopping centers, but these are visually isolated from their surroundings and very limited in their range of activities. At other locations more comprehensive centers are gradually developing, but in a piecemeal fashion. Elsewhere old foci are expiring. Old or new, centers everywhere are incoherent and repetitious. (How many American shopping centers can be distinguished from one another from their photographs?)

What is happening suggests a twofold program: conserving and building up the old centers (or helping them to die gracefully if that is inevitable) and encouraging in the outer areas the coalescence of new centers with a wide range of activity. My goal would be a city-wide system of differentiated, compact centers, each reinforced by high-density housing and new educational or recreational institutions. The centers would be stable in location, giving the city continuity in time, but they would be changeable in form, reflecting the city's flux of activities and aspirations. It would be policy to preserve historic symbols and to limit locational drift, but not to freeze the patterns of use, whether within or between centers. We need not be bound by the structure of the past. Shifts in use should be encouraged, surfaces should be scarred by past traces and premonitory signs. The daily rhythm of activity could be made visible, the landscape charged with communications. These centers are the stable focal points of stimulus and change; I would make them visibly so.

Although the land in built-up centers in the U.S. typically is privately owned, this does not preclude planned change. Much can be achieved by zoning and other regulations, by the design of streets, open spaces, and other public facilities, by the public renewal of strategic sections, by the provision of land or access, and by other positive or negative inducements to private developers. Moreover, there is room for the development of new centers in the outlying areas of our metropolitan regions by public or semipublic agencies. These new centers might also serve as reception areas for low-income or segregated families escaping from inner-city ghettos. The inner centers may be preferred places in which to introduce new types of housing or recreational activity.

Open space is more easily accepted as being of public concern than is the planning of city centers, but our range of ideas in dealing with this feature is extremely narrow. Public open space usually means an athletic field, a beach, a lawn with trees and shrubs, a woodland with trails and picnic areas, perhaps a central plaza. Many other kinds can easily be imagined: mazes, heaths, thickets, canyons, rooftops, caves, marshes, canals, undersea gardens, yards for certain hobbies. We should design for diversity, experiment with new types, open recreational choices, fit opportunities to the real diversity of city people and their values.

Thinking of an endless world city reminds us how important it is that much of this be truly open space, permitting freely chosen activity, allowing us to manipulate things and make our own mark. Hobby yards could be provided, or sites for temporary gardens or self-help buildings. In this sense a dirt pile, a junkyard, or a waste lot may be preferable to a rose garden, unless the roses are your own. We might present opportunities for adventure, [for] challenge, even for real risk, if adjusted to individual ability. There could be difficult rock climbs, or dense brush for games of war or hunting. For much of this we can look to the present wastelands of our cities: the vacant lots, abandoned buildings, tidal flats, swamps, dumps, fields of weed and scrub, odd bits of land. We see in them the unhappy sign of neglect and decay; they are in fact a magnificent resource for recreation.

Open lands should be distributed throughout the metropolis in a fine-grained pattern, in contrast with the active urban areas, producing a varied texture of dense and free. A secluded park or a quiet walk, immediately adjacent to a center or to compact housing, can be more valuable to the city dweller than a remote preserve. Five-acre lots and many areas colored green on the map—estates, institutions, reservations—are of little use for public recreation. I would even try to create urban analogues of wilderness, open to the public but secluded, difficult of access, lean in human symbols. Spaces might be opened up to display characteristic views of city elements, to lay bare geologic formations, to dramatize the weather and the sky. There could be opportunities for observing and interacting with other species, or for studying the ecology of the city, including its human ecology. Camps could provide for experiments in social roles or for the innovation of new life styles. We may find that a prime use for obsolete inner-city land is for such diverse activities of recreation and education. Going to the inner city, with its full complement of intense urban use and diverse open space, could become an even more widespread way of enjoying vacation time than it is today.

The character of the centers and of the open spaces are two aspects of the city that influence the quality of living. There is a third, no less important: the system of paths along which people move and from which they perceive their environment. This is their observation platform for seeing the city, their principal means of comprehending it. It is from the path network that the city dweller sees the relations among the city's parts, recognizes its organization, becomes familiar with its landmarks, and develops a sense of being at home instead of lost in the city's immensity. Since communication and meeting are the fundamental functions of the modern city, it is appropriate that their physical facilities provide the best means of understanding it.

I would give each path an identifiable character and make the network memorable as a system of clear and coherent sequences. The views from the system would expose the city's major physical parts, its dominant functions, and its principal social areas. They would reveal its most interesting activities, its historical points, its geology (as in a cut for a roadway), its local fauna (the road traverses a huge aviary). Signs of impending change would be displayed, or symbols of community cooperation, celebration, or even conflict. The movement system would be used not only as the visual organizer of the city but also as a prime source of information.

Many new highways and transit lines will be built by public agencies in our metropolitan areas in the next 20 years. The alignments and details of these routes could easily be planned to make traveling a delight as well as a necessity. The sequence of activities, open spaces, motions, and details experienced along the route could be managed for the aesthetic pleasure of the moving observer. Each road could be given a coherent form, and the intersections with other paths made clear. Names and visible character might be used to differentiate various roads and to explain their directions and destinations. This is a new art form that could add immeasurable richness to city life.

I would press hard for a diversity of routes, vehicles, and styles of movement. The network would offer a variety of sequences that might be played in many combinations. Some routes would be designed as pleasureways, planned more for the motion along them to be enjoyed than for the simple function of circulation. There would be direct lines for people in a hurry and slow, leisurely journeys for people on tour; challenging roads that tested a driver's skill and safe, easy means of transport for the infirm. Independent networks would be built not only for rail and automobile traffic but also for walking, bicycling, riding, and movement by water. New modes of travel could be developed, for example an economical transit system for the low-density suburbs (where a person without a car is now immobilized), or a safe, easily controlled vehicle (locatable on call by radio) in which children might roam with the freedom they once had in rural areas or small towns. Innovations in the means of travel might well be a public planning function.

The kind of action I am urging is not confined to developing new methods for new roads. It applies also to our present streets and highways, which—unpleasant, illegible, and dangerous as they are—will be with us for at least another generation. Much could be done to improve these roads, by opening attractive views and closing ugly ones, by changing lighting and pavement textures, by adding interesting roadside detail, by planting, and by designing more informative and meaningful signs.

We need not look forward with gloom to the future of the city. None of these proposals depend on freezing the city as it is or turning it back to some imaginary golden past. Metropolitan growth and "scatteration" at low densities, which is an expression of overriding preference on the part of a great majority of our people, could be welcomed, not bemoaned.

There is no inherent reason why life in a metropolis, however large the city, should be unpleasant or restrictive, why it cannot be a satisfactory ground for human survival and development, why its people should be unable to look on it as a beloved landscape.

We cling to the notion of a world with an urban inside and a rural outside, divided between the exciting but dirty and disagreeable city and the placid countryside where people live in dull good health. The contrast is ceasing to have any validity. There have been artificial environments in the past that were cherished by their inhabitants with passionate attachment; most farm landscapes were of this kind. The sense of being at home does not depend on tidiness or tininess but on an active relation between men and their landscape, a pervasive meaningfulness in what they see. This meaningfulness is as possible in the city as in any other place, and probably more so.

For perhaps the first time in history we have the means of producing an enjoyable environment for everyone. It need not be saved for vacations but can be achieved in the world into which we wake every day. At the same moment we are becoming highly aware of the ugliness and discomfort the urban colossus now imposes on most of its inhabitants. Means and conscience should go together. Vast, drab, and chaotic, the colossus looks permanent but is in fact changing rapidly. Its enormity, its complexity and changefulness, the diversity of function and life style, our scale of control in relation to the whole—all cause us to doubt our ability to manage the quality of our surroundings. Strategic action at the metropolitan scale is desperately needed. It is easy to criticize the city. What is not so obvious are its potentialities for satisfaction and delight, potentialities arising not just from the quality of the intimate setting—but from the form of the city on the large scale. Although the quality of the local environment is also important, I have emphasized the large-scale possibilities since they are new and not so well known.

Our speculations on the problems of a world city have picked out at least three points of leverage for improving large-scale environmental quality: the movement system, the array of centers, and the pattern of open spaces. We can imagine new possibilities for each of these, attractive directions for innovation in public policy. To this must be added the more traditional concerns for the adequacy and equity of housing and local services, the quality of site design, [and] the control of noise, climate, and the pollution of water and air. We could now begin to convert the real, existing metropolis into an environment in which men would take pride and pleasure. It could be made into something artificial in the old-fashioned sense of the word: a work of art, fitted to human purpose.

II Experiencing Cities

This part of the volume opens with excerpts from Lynch's travel journals of 1952–53, an important documentation of his early observations and ideas on urban form. The journals are a rich account of Lynch's perceptions of places, his thoughts of what makes a good city, and his delight in the life of the city. "Notes on City Satisfactions," written shortly after his return to the United States and never published, distills these travel experiences and represents the first formulation of the ideas that led to *The Image of the City*.

The next three articles address perception and use of the environment. Many people hold the misconception that Lynch was primarily concerned with the superficial visual image of the environment, since he dealt primarily with visual structure and legibility in *The Image of the City*. However, his writings and his professional work, particularly the later work, make clear that he was concerned with the total environment—its use and meaning, as well as its sensuous form. He had a special interest in the role that the physical environment plays in human development, and in what design could do to support such development. "Some Childhood Memories of the City" looks at the environments of childhood and at what attributes of places are particularly important to children from the point of view of adults looking back. "Growing Up in Cities," on the other hand, examines the actual experience of children in Argentina, Australia, Mexico, and Poland. The research was part of a UNESCO project (designed with Tridib Banerjee) that resulted in Lynch's book by the same title. The research for "A Walk Around the Block" was done at the same time as the research for *The Image of the City*. It attempts to record the actual perceptions of people as they walk through a section of Boston's Back Bay and then compares their immediate perceptions with later memories of that experience. What do people notice, and how do they structure their observations? Lynch notes that his research methods may not only be useful in research and design but also have educational value in heightening awareness of one's surroundings.

In "The Urban Landscape of San Salvador" and "Nanjing" we read Lynch's own impressions of two Third World cities. The San Salvador work is particularly interesting because in it Lynch proposes policies for managing the form of the regional city similar to those proposed in his later work on San Diego. It is frequently assumed that urban design is not (and should not be) a concern in Third World countries. However, Lynch stresses the importance of environmental planning and design in the cities of developing countries, emphasizing that environmental quality is not secondary to economic development and should not be a luxury reserved for wealthy countries. Reacting to the bland new buildings he saw shooting up, he goes on to explain that "esthetics" must be related to how people actually use and perceive their environment and should not be imposed upon a place from the outside. He admonishes San Salvador not to copy the "developed" countries but to create environments well suited to its own needs and culture.

In the final three articles, Lynch reflects on his pioneering work in environmental perception and on how it might have affected research and practice. In the foreword to *Environmental Knowing* he criticizes environmental psychologists for being too detached from the places they are studying and for emphasizing verbal rather than visual languages in their research methods. In fact, his original manuscript for the foreword contained the subtitle "In Defense of Pictures." Clearly Lynch was also disappointed that the design professions seem not to have been affected in more than a superficial way. (For further discussion of the influence of Lynch's work on planning practice, see Michael Southworth, "Shaping the City Image," *Journal of Planning Education and Research* 5, no.1 (1985), pp. 52–59, and Michael Southworth, "Theory and Practice of Contemporary Urban Design: A Look At American Urban Design Plans," *Town Planning Review* 60, no. 4 (1990).)

Although a wave of research was generated by *The Image of the City*, the effects on design and planning are less pronounced and more subtle. While the notion that designers and planners should take into account the environmental conceptions and needs of those who would be affected by those designs and plans is usually—but certainly not universally—acknowledged as important, few professionals actually do this, or even know how to do it, in a meaningful way. It can be time consuming, as well as expensive, and it requires special training. Perhaps more important, it can be unsettling, undermining the preconceptions and training of the design professions. That it can be educational is perhaps one of its great values, both for the citizen/user and for the professional.

The Travel Journals (1952–53)

In 1952–53 Kevin Lynch received a one-year fellowship from the Ford Foundation for travel and research abroad. He chose to spend most of this time studying urban form in Florence, Venice, and Rome, and to a lesser extent in Pisa, Siena, Bologna, and Lucca. He also made a week-long visit to Tripoli and West Africa, and he spent three weeks in England before returning to the United States. He recorded his thoughts and observations almost daily, producing four handwritten travel journals. These are interesting for their colorful and astute observations of cities, landscapes, architecture, art, people, and politics, and for their occasional trashing of some of the sacred notions of design.

Lynch's concern for the plight of the common man is evident throughout, and he often seeks out the impressions of seasoned residents. In these journals one can find the seeds of his developing ideas on city design. Already he has strong notions about the role of design and about what good design is. His interest in approaching urban design in an analytical way is evident as he considers the various ways of recording urban activity and form. At one point in Florence he spends a day observing and describing the flow of human activity from dawn to dusk; at another he takes cross-section walks through the city to describe how the street-level experience changed with different periods of growth.

Limitations of space do not allow us to include Lynch's notes on all of these places. We include his notes on three cities where he spent much time and which are known for their urban form and their architecture: Florence, Venice, and Rome. These notes are reproduced verbatim, except for the most idiosyncratic abbreviations. They are reprinted courtesy of the Institute Archives and Special Collections of the MIT Libraries.

Florence

a. Impressions

October 4—Cloudless sun—Giardino dei Semplice, Santa Maria Novella, Oltrarno (Pza. del Carmine).

Semplice a very pleasant spot visible through iron fence in street, actually a series of planting plots defined by grid of gravel walks with pool in center. Plots partly grass, partly experimental plantings, partly graves (why? war dead?). On edges specimen plants in pots and large trees. Whole has a simple air of open shade, yet complex with various leaves. Cool, quiet, the sound of falling water.

Novella a striking bold facade, true stage set. No connection [with] interior, or building, but dominates trapezoidal square. Square also heavily used as San Marco.

Oltrarno poorer section, streets not kept clean here. In Piazza del Carmine two groups children, one of 15 boys, bunched, some play leap frog or with ball. Also group little children in another corner, sitting or dancing in ring. Elsewhere saw boys playing game like duck on rock, without duck.

October 6—Cloudy sun. Pza. San Marco and S. Spirito. Both of these are "used" squares, but greatly different. San Marco small, neat, busy, comfortable green benches and clean gravel, full of quiet bench sitters. S. Spirito, in the poor Oltrarno, larger, dirt surfaced, the scene of a great range of functions: selling, games, lounging, work.

Spirito dominated by the blank baroque scroll facade of church (where plain, the bold heavy silhouette rather striking), opening at that corner to raised terrace by church. In center an eroded fountain, edged by streets but little traffic, border of cottonwoods and trees of heaven, surface plain dirt. Urinal in corner, several shops along the building fronts, which 4 stories, yellowed and stained. Plain stone benches under trees. Building heights just right to confine square. At 1–2 P.M., last stalls which take one border street just moving out. School children returning (the girls usually with father). Mostly boys playing: running with dog, peering through gratings, pissing on fountain. A few girls less active. Aimless bicycling. Adults poorly dressed, but children well, and even boys concerned about dirt on clothes. Tending babies in streamlined carriages. Like a worn but familiar and friendly great common room.

Spend a day in each?

Pza. Vittoria a feeble effort with pine trees—no users. Under the railroad (no more beautiful than ours). Via Stibbert a typical ending of city at the hills edge. All large estates. Pleasure of transition marred by the continuous walling of street (broken glass-topped), which shuts you in narrow passage with no turning. This type of walled street would be pleasant if not so long.

Pza. Leopoldo breaks out in all directions. This star scheme must only be successful if the lines of sight are impressive. Square itself merely gravelled ovals, infant trees, in midst traffic. But occupied with young middle-class mothers and children. Whole area here more American than have yet seen.

By S. Donato, a strange contrast with factories (an old monastery now occupied with low income housing?). Down pleasant treed street and across a fine canal (open sewer), fast-flowing, bordered by rich growth, The dirtier the water the better it is handled scenically. By the Hippodrome and the Agricultural school to the Pza. delle Cassine and Sul. Arno. A pleasant geometric garden, and then the trees along the river bank.

The Cassine no great shakes in itself, but a fine ending to the line of the Arno through the city. To the W. (on the S. bank) a rural setting. Huge poplars line the grassy flood-bank, a fine walk into the city, seen with the S. hills as a romantic backdrop.

Near S. Donato at noon: first the factory whistles, then the gun and bells of central Florence. Even in this industrial area, the dome and tower are visible to the N., marking the city center.

Note Porta S. Frediano coming down Via Pisana; the excitement of the huge gate: within is the city.

Signoria at 1:45. Pleasure of a large paved square occupied by freely moving pedestrians. Like the huge sculpture which also peoples it. Good or bad, it is strong enough to give life. Perhaps as Greeks used statues at Olympia, not axially, but to people the area. Continuous roar and sputter of the motorcycles and Vespas.

Public transportation seems very difficult and irregularly plotted— hard to move in a given direction though number of circumferentials.

October 9—Clear bright sun (like Arizona)—retraced yesterday's steps for pictures. Also a very pleasant formal park by fort at Viale Strozzi. Women marketing at open stalls. Pza. Muratori. What is relation of these to regular stores and what determines their position?

Bank of the Arno along the Cassine one of the finest places in Florence. The old poplars on one side, the muddy river on the other. Grass you can walk on, weeds, wild flowers and their scent in the air. Fishing, bicycling, lying in the sun, children playing, others just wandering. One of the most relaxed places I have seen, and evidently a great favorite with the Florentines. But not overcrowded, room to move, and the view connects to rural land on one side, the city's heart on the other. Work also going on to watch: hand excavation of the bank—clay digging, netting for fish.

October 10—The central market is wonderful—the smell and sight of such variety of food, piled up in the market building and the outer stands.

Crowds and activity. [Thought] how much of the pleasure and value of a city is in shopping, the choosing and acquisition and review of all the possibilities. How much of the "knowledge" of a city consists in knowing where to buy what, where to eat, etc. This S. Lorenzo is certainly one of the great active centers.

Saw the show of Leonardo at the Biblioteca Medicea Laurenziana. The drawings (tiny sketches, fragmentary) are beautiful: delicate, accurate, a wonderful fusion of art and science, "thinking" in forms as well as words. Many of the faces are violent, strained, cartooned.

The entrance to stairs by Michelangelo are in the white and gray-brown, somewhat over-blown, strange vertical proportions. . . .

Down to SS Apostoli, one of oldest churches, on a little place off narrow street paralleling Arno. Church closed, but interesting to see how houses crowd around it, one even building over the roof on the right. Narrow crooked streets here, but must have had some feeling of protection when open country close.

Saw Sargrestia Vecchia, S. Lorenzo, of Brunelleschi. Square high room, dim and gray, of curious mixed and imperfect feeling. Donatello medallions dull. But hemispherical ribbed dome with little windows in cusps and a lantern, soars elegantly over the round wall arches.

Stopped in to enjoy Baptistery mosaics. Thought again how more dramatic it would be if gallery arcade omitted and the golden dome brought down over the dark main walls, with their primitive geometric marble patterns. Then the dome would enclose you, and fill the world.

October 26—Reading Schevill's Florence (not top-notch,) impressed not only by the waste and violence (as well as the real growth that he hardly reflects), but by the constant changes of the city. At its prime young strength (c. 1300–50) it was still largely wood, overcrowded, filled with a confusion of private towers, expanding rapidly beyond its 2nd walls in strings, and beginning many important works in a burst of energy. Also many ruins, where houses destroyed by fire or political quarrels.

Planning was in the walls, the bridges, and the individual buildings. Locations not integrated, as Palazzo Vecchio, put there because land could be opened before it over ruined Uberti houses. Piazzas were holes cut in the crowded city. Traffic problems and the widening of streets and bridges. Haphazard relation to food supply. But the city was alive then, if not beautiful, and the desire was generally to make its outward appearance fit its economic power. Note delight of Villani in the improvements he was involved in.

3rd walls included much open land, a bold sweep. Note the continuous rebuilding of the city, due to fires, war and growth. 5/6 of the city revenue went into war: poverty of the general mass, famines every decade, pestilence and bad sanitation.

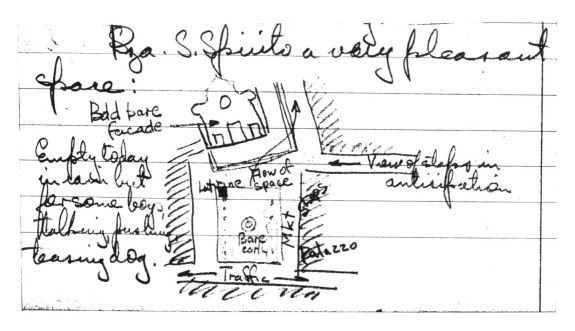

Piazza San Spirito (October 13).

Still no good indication of reasons for city's growth. Seems more like an act of will and prior technique, like some of the early New England shipbuilding locations. . . .

Need to think of basic questions to ask Florentines to evoke their reaction to their physical city, as: sketch a map, or panorama; what do you think of first; where would you prefer to live; where do you go in free time or to meet people, or to spend a little time outdoors; where is the center of the city; what is your favorite part of Florence, what changes would you make; what is your local section and how do you recognize it, etc.

Perhaps one thing I can do here besides evaluating the Italian cities is to clearly formulate the problem, and develop a technique of analysis which, tested here, can then be employed at home.

Also to formulate my ideas of City Planning education.

Make a map of Florence showing the different localities of active outdoor congregation, and its type (N. Pza. Signoria, arcade Pza. Republ. San Marco, S.M. Novella, San Spirito, Mercato Centrale, etc.).

Early afternoon photos in Boboli. The many different effects of space there: the terraced amphitheater, the long plunging valley, the gravelled area completely under tree cover, the tree-ringed meadow, the green tunnel, the curving hedge-bordered walk, large tree-trunks right against house walls, the islanded lake, the tree-lined allee, the tortuous path through thicket growth, the open garden peopled with potted flowers, etc. Not unified, but full of surprises and play of light and form. . . .

November 3—brisk, sunny, then cloudy. Errands most of A.M., then S. Croce, S. Spirito, Carmine.

The weather pleasant, and with some feeling that I know my way about the city. I find myself more at home in the city and more inclined to look at it pleasantly. A *good* history of the social and physical development of the city would make it much more meaningful.

Note the projecting eaves at different heights down the long narrow streets, giving a protected look as though comfortable hats are on. Saw the curve of streets that preserve the lines of the old amphitheater (Bentaccordi, etc.). The streets leading out the W. end of Pza. Santa Croce do not break the continuity of its enclosure, since they are narrow and bend quickly out of sight. Rather they give interest and air of activity, focussing on square (which by itself is very poor).

S. Croce itself is plain, well lighted spacious and warm enough, but to me it has no form. Only a great interior walled and covered by whatever means handy. Old frescoes in rear chapels (must have missed Giotto) are dull and stiff, without stylized power of medieval work; but are interesting in their views of cities: always small in relation to figures, but vertical in emphasis, showing walls and projecting tops of a collection of public buildings. Like a jewel box rather than an organism. Backgrounds at closer range always emphasize loggias, arcades, steps and other open architectural features as stages for the action.

S. Spirito by Brunelleschi is disappointing after all the eulogies. The side aisles are fine with their pietra serena columns arches and vaults, in perfect order. But the main aisle has a flat painted ceiling high up, no relation to arches and columns. The arcades bend back at the crossing, leaving peculiar corners. The crossing itself is fine (forgetting the baldachino), with the dome on pendentives, a soaring thing of opposed curves. By the crossing the feeling is better, the vaults and arches take over, the cusped walls repeat the curves and emphasize the screen of the walls. How fine this would have been as a square or Greek cross, high and small, all arches, vaults and domes, with the light all from above! Seems typical to me of Renaissance work: promises, but the execution is confused, half-done, unable to face itself, uncertain of direction.

Note the many small chapels devoted to various saints, at the most popular the walls are covered with votive medals. One small girl brings in her tiny sister to show her the life of a saint in realistic photos. Something is here which is needed in cities: an over-all order which mutes the complexity, but with many nooks which people can choose as their own and embellish themselves.

Carmine is a horrible baroque church with false perspectives and cut outs on the ceilings. Back in side chapel, no relation to rest, the Masaccio frescoes (also Masolino and Lippi). Frescoes are dulled, not specially noteworthy for color or relation to walls or each other, and hard to see, but they are quite wonderful in their portrayal of powerful *individuals* with psychological realism. The bodies act naturally and powerfully, the faces are compelling. Many portraits. This must have been a humanistic revolution in painting. Here the city scenes are real ones of Florence, perhaps less exciting than the earlier frescoes, but with a flavor of life: the familiar and accepted background.

Sunset was magnificent over Florence that night: the sky a dusty pink, the hills lavender, the Arno reflecting both colors; a sprinkling of lights already showing, but the forms of the Duomo, etc. still apparent, the sides bathed in light coming up from the streets below. Followed by a clear cold moon.

Down into the valley leading to Poggibonsi. The hills are crowned with little towns, castles, monasteries, all like illustrations in a fairy book. Wonderful feeling of relation, where one town looks over to the next, some miles off. . . .

November 19—Went by the other market area just N.W. of Santa Croce Piazza, a second but smaller Mercato Centrale. Florence is almost in a way cut into two parts, with these 2 sub-centers on either side of the old center, now tourists and more expensive shops. Thought again how much of the character of the city is in the narrow streets with dark but fascinating stores and workshops opening off the rain, the uneven and puddled stone pavement, the eaves finishing off the street walls like arrows pointing down the street directions. The cold and the wet and the dark, and the life that beats here in spite of it. Umbrellas, narrow sidewalks, and the rosticcerias. . . .

Went to S. Spirito and started a sketch, but driven off by rain. Stopped in S. Stefano, with its fine facade. Inside a peculiar barn space, rising in clerestory rear, with baroque applications on wall. The sense of space and light above and beyond in altar end good, despite the detail. Liked the peculiar tormented altar steps.

April 2—The trip to Florence very crowded and tiring. Home at 8 P.M. Pleasant to be in Florence again, the narrow streets full of quiet but not sad movement. Anne says the town no longer cold and depressing to her. She likes the presence of dominants, the ability to grasp it which she did not feel of Rome.

Wondering why our feeling towards Florence is changing. Is it simply habituation? Not entirely, though partly, since I have no feeling for Camp Rucker [army camp, Ozark, Alabama], and not as much for Greensboro. Familiarity with these complex entities certainly gives pleasure, but why in the case of Rucker did it give so little? Perhaps because there was so little to know and discover? Florence certainly offers the pleasure of familiarity with a new world, and one complex and varied. But other elements too? The contrast of life in the narrow hard environment? Sense of history

Approach to Piazza Signore along Via di Ninna, Florence (November 19).

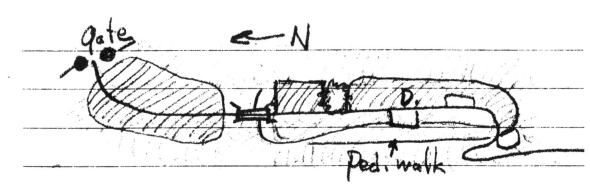

Town of Colle Val d'Elsa near Florence (December 8).

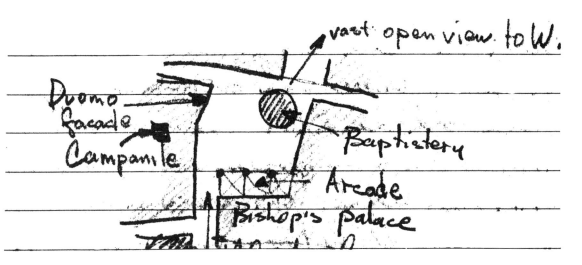

Piazza, Volterra (December 8).

(which is most of Pza. Signoria's pleasure for me)? Ability to see and grasp easily as a whole symbol?

Anne remarked on the pleasure of watching traffic here, due to its mixture of cars, trucks, carts, horses, cycles, scooters, etc.

April 24—I wonder why, as I go about, that I have gotten fond of the dirty weary stones of the old city? Not the very center, nor the great monuments, but the medieval body of the city: such places as S. Piero Maggiore. Perhaps for their richness of texture and life, and sense of what has gone on, and how life still carries on in them?

April 25—in P.M. noticed Palazzo Vecchio alight (today is anniversary of surrender of German armies in Italy), and rushed down. The whole upper structure set with flickering flames, a wonderful sight against night sky. Small oil pots. The building looks tremendous, and the soft glow reveals new detail. Christmasy and cruel and medieval at once. Especially effective from close under, with the smoke and glare above the battlements; also from the Uffizi or from Corso du v. d'Cerchi. Flags out all over town, even on the busses, a big rally in A.M., left wing. Conservative papers do not play this day up very much.

b. A Walk

December 15—Christmas shopping A.M. in wonderful crowded toy store. Via Cavoni. Then up for walk down old Cardo, from Via Bolognese to Via Senesa, then heart of town. Notes as follows:

2 P.M. —V. Bolognese and V. Trieste. 3 city buildings broken by garden walls. Feeling of down to Florence, with view of hills ahead, and

also through to right. Ugly tan modern apartment like jaws to catch. Heavy traffic but trees give openness and movement. Windy and cloudy.

Road snakes sharply down, with walls and barred gates either side. At last turn on slope: view of Renaissance facade on left, dark overhanging trees right. The light dirty tan of walls. Roar of down-going cycles, hum of filobus. As slope eases, garden walls give way to city facades. A narrow slot for a major approach. V. Trieste right. gives piece of sky.

Ugly fake Roman gate revealed, and Bellosguardo above and beyond. Railroad heard under but not seen.

People collect bicycles and street discussions. At Mugnone the sky and a traffic wilderness. Fiesole seen backward left. A block of stores: Bar-Tabacchi, Macelleria, Calzative, Cuoieria, "A. Beni"(?), restaurant equipment, Cicli, Cartoleria, Parrucehiere, Orologiario, vacant, scales,? (only a waiting room visible), Merceria, shoe repair, garage, Bar Tab., Vini, Macelleria.

A big opening at the Viale Circumvallazione, the instinctive direction runs off to right. Oblique view of medieval gate obscured by "Roman." A formless space.

The Viale views seem to embrace the town. Walk under gigantic gates, but Cardo no longer main entrance now. V. S. Gallo abruptly narrows and quiet. This is now city.

Calm meandering house fronts, under a slanting back light. Shutters and wavy plaster. Arcade ahead. Dusty pavement. Spotted yellow walls. Calm space under the arcade (questura!).

Solid 4–5 story fronts now, tired and old and shutter-cluttered, but with air of decency. Glimpse inner garden left. Street does see-through meanders, but no feeling of urgent direction.

Side views left to S. Marco, right. to Indipendenza. Walls ahead like bluffs with dark rock projections and growths giving shadows. Street visibly narrows ahead.

At V. Guelfa street narrows, darkens, roofs reach over. Moving pedestrians thicken, cycles again. The narrow worn sidewalk stones. The clutter that is on our pavements is on their side walls.

S. Lorenzo and the markets, open right, cheerless in this windy cold. Iron shutters, food and clothing, shops and sidewalk stands. Many people moving leisurely.

Duomo space opens up ahead, also light from Repubblica as street straightens out and heads to projecting corner Mercato Nouvo.

The Baptistery (which should not have the Duomo behind it) is here, and the streetcars. 2:50. Hills beyond Mercato N. and raw new construction. Large glass shop fronts, 5 story monumental facades on a broader even line, crowds.

The Repubblica parking lot where a vital center should be. Mercato N. abruptly narrows the street, which becomes confused and seems to end ahead. Michele di Lando bars the way.

Street bends and heads into ruins over Arno, and the sagging awnings of Ponte Vecchio. Sounds of construction, slick shops, confusion. Side view to Signoria left, seems flat.

3:00 Pza. Vecc. Tawdry jewelry. At mid-bridge the momentary great river view. Then ruins, mud and gravel. Road winds off again.

A tall elegant crane and the rich brick-and-stone rough walking. Now horse, donkey, and man-carts appear.

The clumsy Pitti space murders the street.

Street quietens: buildings lower, shabbier, workshops as well as stores on groundspace. A funeral turns into the church: 5 white robed and hooded pall bearers, and the priest in front, the black-and-gold hearse and unconcerned driver and seven mourners (6 women). Rain begins.

Smell of refuse and cold wet earth and stone. Streets of the poor lead off, wash on the canyon walls. Then a garden on right, Boboli backward left, and a hilltop ahead.

Umbrella-dodging. A narrow turn and the great Porta Romana ahead.

Under the great gates 3:25. Another traffic wilderness, and sky again. Viale Colli invites to left, but my road straight ahead, lower, car-tracked, dull.

Up a gentle incline. Little old house encroaches on street right, and then newer houses break back over retaining walls. Seedy stores and workshops. Small plant left (millstones?). Washing clothes right at public basin, long trough dirty soapy water and cold spigot at one end.

Garden walls and trees again, though dustier than on N. side. Road goes up up, gently straight, seeming a tiring climb.

Looking back, the mountains visible behind, and the Cestello dome. Shell-pocked walls. New gravel streets and little walled villas, leading off. Bend at top with Esso sign.

Here at top 3:40 (Asilio San Gaggio). Strong wind over crest. Partial view red roofs Florence with Torrigiani trees and Porta Romana on looking back. The street seems more inviting downwards to N. Ahead is ribbon development, and silhouetted on hill tops the peculiar pines like smoke puffs that begin on way to Siena.

Coming back, noted fine view down V. Serragli from Porta Romana: a narrow, strongly directed street with car tracks, but the buildings are relatively low in proportion, and in mid-distance trees burst out and lean over street. Invitation.

c. Uses of Space

May 7—clearing mackerel sky.

SPM 7:45 A—half the shops open or opening—fish, eggs, vegetables, cosmetics, etc. A few in bars. Largest group of dozen on bikes around headline sheets of newsstands. Bikes and pedestrians moving in on Borgo Albizzi, otherwise fairly quiet, no cars, no parking, no open stands as yet. No or very few shoppers.

SS 8:15—here the stands already out, though a few at lower end, of clothes, etc. still opening up. The vegetable market very fresh and green (asparagus, artichokes, salad, peas, new onions). Some 30 stands here, another 20 on the E. street. Quiet and not too many buyers on arrival, rapidly thickening. Horses, mules and donkeys hitched to carts and facing in on island, a country air especially at first when not so many people.

Children with schoolbags cutting diagonally to N.E., women with shopping bags converging. 3–4 clothes stands, 1 flowers, 2 household goods, 1 candy and baked goods, rest fruit and vegetables. By 8:30 noise has raised to [murmur] of voices and passing feet. Flow is along S street and diagonally N.E.–S.W. Sun, pale and hazy, striking W. side and half of island. Street sweepers at work with their bicycle carts. One or two hand market carts still moving in. W. side almost empty, except for passers-by and knot at newsstand. I [am the] only loiterer.

Girls in white school uniforms going S.W. One small boy carried playfully by thin mother—only small child in square. Horses are restless being fed and watered. Women walk straight to stands, men pass more casually, some now loitering.

As people come into S.W. corner, none look up—most glance to newsstand. A cart in motion with pots flying, strange sight. An umbrella repair man with his box strapped to shoulder passes by chanting. Old man with shopping bag and child with running nose sits down next to me. One or two dogs taken for walk. By now several groups of 2 or 3 gossiping. One group all in black smocks, another in sweaters and skirts. More business on E. street now (9A).

Typical stands on E. street—fancy (!) pottery, cloth and table covers, underwear and trimmings, wool yarn, household goods (small, especially soap, etc.), wine and cheese, rabbits, dresses, shoes. Group of men talking at the N.W. corner by gate where truck just unloaded. How few take notice of anything but details of surroundings, except for some going out N.E. corner who glance up at church facade.

SPM 9:40, stores all open, shoppers in and out. Only two stands, fruit and vegetable (not so good as SS?) and coats and dresses 2nd. Constant flow pedestrians and cycles down Borga Albizzi, movement through square to S. But despite size seems somewhat quiet compared to SS. One group women gossip, but in general moving through. Baby carriage by

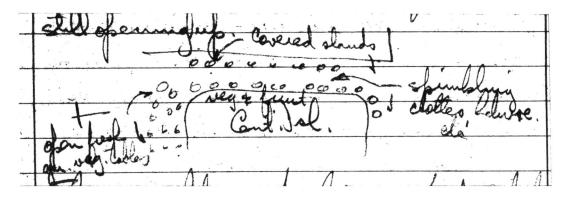

Market, Florence (May 7).

me, baby crying. Store owner woman, woman with small boy and own market basket, contadino with donkey cart, all stop to coo. [Tripe cart moves in.?]

Here reg. [?] stores more important, and people shopping over a wider area. In general better dressed. Man pushing handcart wool underwear, shirt sleeves, vest. Another in plastered work smock pushing streamlined baby carriage empty. Motorized tricycle truck with water hoses, cans, in to clean street. A truck of milk cans.

Most windows shuttered, but a few open, with laundry. One woman on balcony over old church, beating rug. People rarely look up on entering square (only saw one). But most sweep it from side as they enter. They move freely through space—not much concern for vehicles.

Standing at N.E. just beyond entrance tunnel, can see through old porch (now egg store) and get pleasant glimpse square beyond, framing tower base. This sort of interrupted view of a continuity good. Turned and N.E. corner seen active part of square.

SS 11:05—sun now behind clouds. Loudspeaker at N.E. corner going full blast, election propaganda and music. Ironic dialogues (anticommunist?). Certainly all on Togliatti, N.[euni?] doves of peace, etc.

Traffic on S street, but less diagonal flow. Green market at N. somewhat worn down, street market still full. Mothers and children on two benches, old man dozing another (sack by side, feather in hat). Radio noise dominates, reechoing from walls. Several middle-aged men loitering in center, or gossip. Radio shuts off, and you hear again vendor's cues, voices, cycles and now a street organ at S.W. corner. Sentimental, with a painting of volcano at Napoli. The organ moves up the market street, collecting from the stands. Children delighted.

Green market beginning to pack up 11:30. Many people buy flowers along with their bag vegetables. The organ donkey has a hat and pants on the front legs, which amuses everyone and causes friendly jokes. Newly varnished chairs carried through the street. Bottegles have piles unfinished small tables, not too well done in underparts. Election posters everywhere. The whole atmosphere seems relaxed, with much stopping for a joke or talk. Boys and men group about stand owners, watching selling, talking. Contadini, in packing up green market, carefully scrape up morning's manure and pack home. Carts and stand parts put in the porteggio.

May 8—Summer clouds, sunny but cool.

SPM 1:50—most stores just closing up, some desultory shopping. Vegetables, tripe, and 2nd clothes carts as yesterday, also another closed. Tradesmen eating by their stalls, trattoria full, couple eating at table foot of tower. Some parking, but square taken over by pedestrians and cycles. Pedestrians move easily through it, as through an outdoor hall. Two groups young men loitering, one front bar N. side, another near vegetable stand E. side. All with bicycles, narrow shoes, but poorly dressed. Children home from school and odd passers-by. Election posters here all PCI and PSI. No one at the windows, which are closed. The bright light, reflected, eases grimness of narrow streets—in places the city has a toy-like air.

SS 2:20—sun full on square and the shade of trees, in full but not heavy leaf, over benches is grateful. Last cart tying up to go, and sweepers shovelling and brushing off street. A few handcarts stand about, and 1–2 cars. A few children back from school, mostly younger, with their mothers. A small group in front of bar, E. side, men and a woman. Three men on seats of palazzo. On the benches, from urinal S. around: 8 older boys, chattering and reading some torn comic; myself and an older man, very still; a man resting, tool box by his side; a mother and her idiot son in a special seat, two empty: 4 young men sitting with bottle wine and some glasses; 2 men talking, feet on bench. A group of small boys near newsstand, in constant motion, with comics. The sun goes in and out, it is cool and warm.

The half torn election posters give a ragged look to the lower stories, the island floor and the facades are varying shades of earth brown. Girls go by, arm in arm. A vendors cart, with cheap small popsicles. A girl sits at one bench, sketching (probably the man next to me). An older man with cane and pipe. A leisurely flow. Others with briefcases, probably returning to work. Two women, one with baby, sit at front to church. The center of the square a little empty, especially without the children running—the life goes on around the edges.

Both bars full; there is a billiard parlor in between. The [hat-block?] shop already working.

SPM 4:00—stores open again, and extra cart turns out to be small candies, like taffy. Man with tie loose sits there hopelessly, watching people pass his dusty glass jars. Slowly splinters some wood, kindles charcoal fire, rinses pot and puts sugar in. Long discussion going on at 2nd clothes cart, 2 men and vendor. They examine own clothes, look at stuff on stall, argue with a sly look, adjourn to bar, come out, begin to go away several times. Finally no sale. Have never seen sale from this cart, only one from candy cart.

Same group young men outside N. bar, strutting a little and swinging at each other. Another in front bar W. side. Two pairs of men talk quietly, standing in square, traffic around. One discussing bad painting, with much animation. Others stop to look at news, but in general a passing through—more like a crossroads now. Flow on Borg. Albizzi in continuous conflict with people on narrow sidewalk, but still this one of favorite spots to stand. Several near bumps between cycles, people, cars, Bike carts come through, one of [hemp?] by old man, brown face, white hair, handsome and spare. No children, except passing through.

Young platinum blonde comes by with black sweater and slacks, causing much amusement and amazement and by-play between loiterers. Almost two worlds here: the people of SPM and the passers-by on Borg. Albizzi, but these last not quite so heavy as to utterly disrupt square.

SS 5:15—half in shade and the rest speckled. Now it is the children's: 4 girls chase each other around the statue, a troop of boys with "guns" hunt along the street, 2 small boys get water from the fountain to play in the mud. Mothers and children sit on the sunny benches. A line of women, children and old men sit along facade S. Spirito in sun. Two boys hit pegs in air with sticks. A group of adults at one of sunny benches talking and watching baby in arms.

Principal noise is children's voices. They are better dressed than parents. A little traffic on S street, otherwise only a few slow cycles. The water a constant fascination—splashing, carrying, throwing things in.

Another truck unloads N.W. corner; military. There is a vegetable stand down by newsstand, closed up earlier. People look very small against church facade, this seems more like big free space. Many windows unshuttered and a few with curtains, which kills the black hole. A few heads out, and some calling, "Viene qua!"

The light falling strong on N.E. corner, leaving foreground in shade, emphasizes depth and distance. One or two young girls trot their baby sisters about. Men and women hail each other across square, and walk over easily to talk. A light wind blows the dust, and torn paper.

At end of day brought pictures to the little girl, Milvia Pecchioli, whom I photographed in SS two months ago. She not in, and the pictures taken by a young man much puzzled and slightly defensive. Glimpse of their apartment (up some dark narrow stairs), seemed fairly big, a dark wide strong hall with rooms opening off.

d. Sensuous Form: An Analysis

January 27—In to Florence to survey "characteristic elements." Windy, clear and cold.

Area 1 : (within 1st circle W. of Calzainoli, the central redevelopment):

a. *Spaces* (including light and atmosphere)—deep but not narrow corridors; even walls and eave lines; ending abruptly in short lengths at tees or winding corridors. Area 2 eminently rectangular, characteristic open space the oblong Pza. Repubblica of non-directional static space; light on one side, dark on the other, hazy air.

b. *Orientation*—by gridiron pattern and by feeling that here is center, though relation to rest of city and Arno not clear; rarely by landmarks.

c. *Middle distance picture* (the characteristic views seen in one fixing of eye, ahead and slightly above horizon, most often obliquely across the space, characteristically of street facades at 2nd and 3rd story one or two blocks down street)—stone, heavily moulded with cornices, architraves, balconies, rustication, coats of arms, etc., but all generally within one plane—a shadow pattern principally, heavy but not grim, proper.

d. *Eye level detail* (just ahead or abreast of walker, seen in interrupted snatches)—store windows set back in pilasters, so that disappear in enfilade, and appear abreast staccato; fascinating variety of goods in windows which are crowded but orderly, shown with little imagination or concentration, all pieces exhibited equally: cloth, optical goods, rich foods, etc; posters to some extent, rough wall textures; names of firms and products, difficult to read. (The familiar strain of locating a shop until you are right on it.)

e. *Floor* (visual texture and form and color, extension and levels as a place, feel to feet)—smooth, large stories; medium wide sidewalks, clean but dusty; smooth but hard to feet, metal buttons in street, walkways, warning posts and sewer tops; level and spreading equally at intersections.

f. *Human activity*—medium heavy passage of pedestrians, mostly elegantly dressed but a few quite poorly, moving through but without great haste; a minor proportion standing and talking, expressive gestures.

g. *Traffic*—constant and rather haphazard movement cars and motorbikes, streets not overloaded but requiring constant attention; parked cars and bikes; the overriding tension at crossings, the policeman's hands and the glance up to awkwardly high street lights, bunching and weaving at curb corners.

h. *Noise and smells*—(should noises go with traffic etc., with which allied?)—constant hum of traffic, though rarely at high pitch, and sputter of motorbikes; some loudspeaker music and announcing; less often the footfall or a voice. Smell of car fumes and some coal smoke.

Area 2 : (remainder within 2nd circle, the medieval):

a. *Spaces*—narrow, deep corridors, overhung and "perspectivized" by eaves, turning and closed in middle distance where not hopelesly intricate; undulating walls and uneven roof line; sudden bursts out into Arno or closed spaces ranging from tiny openings like Croce al Trebbio to large piazzas like S. Croce; angular intersections and the sense of convergence or divergence; irregular more dynamic spaces such as SM Novella, S Spirito, Signoria, Duomo apse. Dark, with sudden lights heralding an opening.

b. *Orientation*—by linear direction or often by landmarks seen above, more rarely by approach to a space.

c. *Middle distance*—tan plaster and stone sometimes rusticated with great barred windows, more often decaying plaster cluttered with shutters, drain pipes, eaves, sometimes old stone work. Generally in one plane, but this changes direction.

d. *Eye level*—blank walls punctured by cavernous doors or windows; occasional store windows set flush in walls; workshop-eaves; merchandise spills out into streets; cheaper goods and rosticcerias; near wall uncomfortably close; open air stands.

e. *Floor*—stone, worn, sloping and undulating; very narrow sidewalks; dirt-film and some refuse; puddles and pools on wet days; general plane often rising or falling gently; frequent attention required.

f. *Human activity*—moving through but also discussion, selling, work or play; fewer in numbers but seemingly more intense; poorer dress, many land loads.

g. *Traffic*—generally lower, but in some narrow streets. Streets of even greater intensity than 1; wagon and carts mix in; fewer parked vehicles; more haphazard; less attention by pedestrians and much walking and street and mixture.

h. *Noises* of traffic at times very intense, especially chatter of bikes, but generally lower, more oscillating; footfalls and voices; some work noises. Smell of wood smoke, food, and some of decay.

Area 3 (remainder within 3rd circle—basically late Renaissance and some later growth). Area has many similarities with 1 and 2, in many ways a sort of compromise between the two, in a lower key.

a. *Spaces*—generally long corridors, but lower and broader than 1, straight or gently curving, even facades, but varied eave heights. Entering typically into traffic seas and broad formless spaces such as Stazione Indipendenza, Carmine, Tasso, but also into ordered refined spaces such as S. Spirito, S. Marco, Annunziata. Light falling in most streets, but as usual hazy.

b. *Orientation*—linear, to spaces, and to some extent by landmarks. First glimpses of topo relation. Contains typically many points of confusion. Little or no disorientation, but frequent areas of indifference.

c. *Middle distance*—the dusty light tan or grey, stone and plaster. Much more in one flat plane, but the shutter and cornice-eave lines still a part. Trees and plants occasionally visible for first time, over high walls or in courts.

d. *Eye-level*—the blank walls with little relief—few store windows and these with scanty goods, the profusion being in the darkness within. Many shops and work places of negative interest: coal and wood, garages, etc. Posters are dominant. But this also the area of the most intense detail: the open-air markets (Centrale, S. Ambrogio, Borgo Pinti, S. Spirito, etc.). Spotted plaster and dirty stone. A few flashes into interior gardens.

e. *Floor*—stone walls and stone (some asphalt) roads, stones uneven to feet, but as broad as 1. Generally level.

f. *Human activity*—plentiful movement, but little discussion or free use, except in piazzas. Intense activity in markets. Medium to poor dressing.

g. *Traffic*—a substantial amount, but moving faster and more freely in broader streets. Parked vehicles occasionally.

h. *Noises and smells*—traffic noise predominant, but is undulating. Footfalls and voices join the background. Smell mostly coal smoke again, and some food.

Area 4 (urban beyond 3rd circle, principally 19th century, and a little modern growth)

a. *Spaces*—long straight corridors, basically gridiron, with some stars. House fronts begin to break up into cubes, or fall back from street line (though this always preserved with at least a low wall). Thus space becomes diffused and uncertain. Full light and a clearer air. The typical piazza rectangle, characterless and with spindly planting.

b. *Orientation*—almost entirely indifferent, except for wealth of topo relation. Local orientation in one neighborhood may be fair, due to grid pattern, but turning and twisting and lack of differentiation of these makes for complete lack to larger whole.

c. *Middle distance*—gardens over walls occasionally, and street planting. Low walls, high walls, cubical houses and pieces of street facade. Conscious of end walls and some backs with balconies and laundry. Facades have newer, cleaner, duller look: paperboard arch, and sham style varieties in an overall similarity of form. Strangely empty streets. In places, intensely cold and monotonous.

d. *Eye level*—Almost completely closed with few doors and little but residential use. The unending walls: stone base molding and plaster above; self-effacing doors. Scribblings and slogans.

e. *Floor*—broad, level, tile and asphalt as well as stone: little but chisel marks to divert eye. Almost no furniture—street is swept clean of any projections.

f. *Human activity*—sparse movement, little stopping except delivery-men and occasional children. People seem lost in this open strong waste.

g. *Traffic*—also sparse and passing at high speed, to get it over with. Rare parkings.

h. *Noise and smell*—Background is the occasional car and especially the noise of bus and train one street away. Some voices and footfalls, but now also birds! Air is fresher, emptier of smell.

Some interesting comments: That originally there were only 3 "wide" streets in the city: Calzzurole connecting Duomo and Signoria, Fornabuoni from Arno to V. Strozzi, and Verbarga (near Palazzo Medici). Pza. S. Giovanni was much more confined, due to Bishop's Palace, and Merc. Vecchio was almost completely encumbered with market buildings, so that Pza. Signoria was actually almost only open space in center. (other spaces: Pza. Strozzi, and the Fondamenti around Duomo). Garden S. side V. dei Bieni was only planted area in center (the result of a private redevelopment). . . . Block just N. Merc. Vecchio was the Ghetto, with internal streets and spaces entered by 3 gates locked at night. Jews enclosed here by the Medici.

February 2—Through Fiesole in A.M., taking some photos until the haze rose. Then into Florence in P.M., walking to S. Domenico, very pleasant. This area typical of Area 5 (rural-suburban outskirts). Elements:

a. *Spaces*—generally the very narrow rather oppressive, but not too deep hallway of the walled street; turning rising and falling plastically. Infinite sky overhead. Breaking occasionally into the wide space of the countryside, with long views; yet even here the space molded and contained in hills and open valleys. Air clear.

b. *Orientation*—by topography, and by the views, since the natural topography converges on the city.

c. *Middle distance*—mossy tile roofs, irregular blocks of houses, gardens, countryside and wall. Accidental and sculptural.

d. *Eye level*—Either long stretches of overgrown wall, rich in texture, or the plants: feathery olive, dark cypress, and the tilled soil. Occasionally the fantastic and yet rather arid villa gates: steps, balustrades, ironwork, carving. Many stone street and landmark signs.

e. *Floor*—steeply sloping and twisting. Generally gravel or earth, some irregular paving, guttering, ramped steps. Freshly broken stone road fill. Constant attention to placing of feet, and of touch sensations.

f. *Human activity*—very quiet, often empty. Passers generally single, peasants and city people, many carrying loads. Encounters are small events. Domestic activity seen through gates and windows.

g. *Traffic*—little. Often wagons and carts or busses and trucks on few major roads. Almost zero parking. Traffic when it comes almost fills the road, and causes momentary cessation of other activity.

h. *Noise and smell*—smell of fresh country air above all, with some scents of wood smoke and manure. Noises are of birds, leaves in wind, small animals, distant hum of city (traffic and children at play), and the startlingly loud noise of the occasional car or of people's voices.

Took photo of Fiesole from S. Domenico, and then into Florence, catching D's bus. Picked up more material from Aranguren, checked on Alinari and boat ticket, and other chores. Returned to find children coming back from Summer's birthday party, complete with hats, masks, and horns. Tonight they staged a parade with floats!

Venice

OCTOBER 18—to Venice—hazy sun. A $4\frac{1}{2}$ hour train trip over the mountains. Amazing rapid change of countryside: just over the ridge the little terraces of olives and grapes disappear for larger fields interspersed in more powerful mountains of tawny chalky outcrop. The small strip fields reassert themselves down on the plain at Bologna, to give way to large square fields, plowed and open, at Ferrara and the Po. Later small fields come back and then near Padova and Ven. the crops become very varied: a beautiful sight, a square of deep green cover against dark plowed ground, bright orange fruit (persimmon) in purple brown leaves, occasional patches of mature trees. Last a great relief to me, after the miles of growth kept down to 10–15'.

Approach to Venice not beautiful, but yet exciting as you catch glimpse of distant silhouette, and go out over water. Then from railroad station you are suddenly on the canal. Take a gondola, long black narrow, beautifully shaped to balance oarsman and his thrust. Plunge into small canals: decaying house fronts, color and individual design, watery light, strange like a flooded city.

Walked out into San Marco. Tremendous! A great crowd wandering freely, a band concert in the center. Colonnades all around, the church a jewel box at back, flanked by tower, clean and fine though somewhat squatter than had thought. Glimpse of Doge's Palace then.

Went slowly around the crowd at concert, there were hundreds of pigeons. One little girl in the middle, squealing with joy, picking them up. The river of pigeons swept through the square. Many children active and joyous.

Through into the church, its lacy outside delightful, the interior dim and mysterious: lights behind silk, screens, dull light glinting on the domes and curves swinging overhead. Rolling floor. Nooks everywhere, and women and children coming in to pray. Little girl kissing foot of crucifix. Sat down and the bells sounded. Felt very moved: sad and tender.

From church out to the sea steps, with the gondolas rocking and dancing by their poles, S. Giorgio framed across the water. Doge's Pza. is perfect, contrast of lacy and wall. Color: white and tawny. Doge Pza., warm brick tower (subtly tapered), white and gold and blue church, dirty gray colonnades, crimson flag poles. Colonnades do not match at sides in height or style, but this invisible, all you see is the innumerable repetition of columns.

Then into a narrow street (pedestrians only) 15 ft. from lighted store to lighted store, with a river of humanity. The ways wind and turn, going up and down the stepped bridges, and through little squares. The acme of the accidental.

OCTOBER 19—cloudy—left the hotel to walk through San Marco and back to the Rialto through the crowded streets. The Rialto is relatively small, and full of people (more Venetians) standing and watching. No seats. A feeling that everyone sees everyone else here sooner or later.

There seem to be more children here and running more freely on the streets, with more laughter. The only play place is the streets, and the little irregular paved squares. The occasional tree is very striking, but the houses have many vines and potted plants. Living conditions must be very bad: overcrowding, decay and poor sanitation (canals are the sewers).

The walkways are fascinating in that they continually twist, rise and fall over bridges, break out into little squares. In detail a maze, but general orientation not difficult since water or bell-towers soon visible. It takes a great time to traverse a small space.

Freight carried by canals. Saw a family moving by gondola, a difficult business. The gondola themselves are beautiful, an exactly shaped tool, warped to right to balance weight of oarsman, etc. Also barges, large sailboats (gaily painted), motor boats, etc. The movement of the sea is very gentle, and is almost on a level with the city pavements. A magnificent setting for architecture like San Giorgio.

Took some pictures around S. Marco, though light poor. Sat in the small park (first I saw), on the Bacino just behind S. Marco. Here is Venice's traffic problem: all the children use their bikes here, a tremendous tangle.

Up to the railroad station by motoscapo, then dinner for L500, watching the passersby. Many stopped to peer in the restaurant windows and discuss the food—much time is spent in choosing preparing and disposing of it. Down the dark streets, with points of light flowing with people, 2 or 3 small children's fairs, a booth where raffling liquor, dolls, etc. Venice spends much more of its life on the streets than Florence.

Reached Florence after a tiring ride, almost with a feeling of homecoming. . . .

January 17: The clean sweep of floor, with the buildings set in or along it, the theatrical facades, the up and down, out and under, twisting and turning, the lively crowds are delightful.

The kids are out late. Why do they skip and look so happy in this slum. The young men sing (they began this on the train, about at Ferrara). The older people are more stern or sad, but still forceful in movement and speech. . . .

April 14: Returned to San Marco in P.M. for more pigeon feeding, then up top Campanile. From above Venice a dense network of roofs, have no idea of presence canals and squares. A city not made for the air view, but the close ground view.

Then Anne and I out for long walk to S. Marco via Accademia, and return by boat. Venice best by night, a city where electric lights really fit, where the light and darkness adds to the drama, and the shadow hides the decay.

Best of Venice really in its pedestrian ways, the big open squares, the irregular footways, the people, the buildings and storefronts scaled to the pedestrian. Anne surprised at size of squares (seemed to her biggest and most frequent she had seen), and feels this a city really made for people.

A boatload of young men passing through canals, with a candle, accordion and tambourines, singing. The fine early sculptures worked into the walls of S. Marco. High tide, water lapping at the edge of the piazza and over many of the sills of the water doors, the half submerged look.

April 17—to railroad station again, the canal full of activity, especially at the wholesale food market by the Rialto. The variety of loads carried in the barges (food, lumber, furniture, sand, metal, pianos, flowers, etc. etc.) make a fascinating sight.

For an hour's gondola ride (1500 L!), the last part through the crowded narrow [rii?], working through the barges, gondolas, motor-boats, between the peeling walls. These boats ride beautifully, breasting the waves.

Pigeons again at S. Marco's, rides on the red stone lions, ice cream cones and souvenirs. In P.M. a visit to J. Fraci, a great brick Italian Gothic interior, encumbered with enormous monuments on the sides. Most common games are ball, hopscotch, a race of bottle tops (or what have you), through a twisting course chalked on paving. Or just drawing on walls and pavement.

Now the evening bells are ringing, and time for supper.

Anne and I out for a last night stroll together. Interesting that we can already follow these twisting routes without even thinking of them. Also that I could follow the Accademia-S. Marco run from memory of last fall, without hesitation. Complex as they are, these sequences of sharply individual detail seem easy for mind to absorb and retain.

April 18—Started toward Accademia, turned off at S. Trovaso to follow Rio to Giudecca side. Here a small patch of 2-story decayed houses, now a gondola repair station, probably real medieval stuff. The "zattere" here are wide and open, sunny and pleasant, though the Giudecca view quite ordinary. Note the freighters coming in loaded and going out empty.

Back to Accademia and then the wonderful S. Marco trail, twisting, turning, over bridges and under "sotto. portici," along with the throng. Note the difficulty of getting baby carriages or any loads up the stepped bridges. They have same "level" problems as we with divided traffic: pedestrians must mount 4–5 feet, boat loads descent 3–4.

Lounged in piazza, and into the Basilica. Above it is a wonderful, creation, with its main dome and four surrounding domes, separated and flanked by barrel vaults, and with intersecting galleries: diverse and mysterious, and yet spatially unified. Light and shadow, gold and brown. Below it is more cluttered, and the sinking floor gives an uneasy feeling. Some of the 12th century mosaics nice, in a comic strip fashion.

By the Merceria to the Rialto and over to the markets, which fun as usual but not quite as exciting as S. Lorenzo.

Thence to the Stazione, passing through Campo S. Giacomo dall'Orio, a very fine open space around the church, ample, with a few good trees, and full of children and older boys at soccer.

By boat down through whole length Can. Grande to Giardini stop. US battleship "Roanoke" in, a tremendous bulk against the city. The gardens look good after all the paving, but not actually fine, since a thin and sprawling string.

Around by the naval school, and an area back of the Exposition which quite strange: plaster houses, home made. A street icon surrounded by an amateur mural.

Back to the Riva, to see a new Italian passenger ship ("Asia") brought alongside and then by back streets to S. Marco. Some of these narrow streets, where they lack the color and life of the shopping and crowds, very dreary and depressing. Saw one 3 feet wide.

Find I can orient and find my way fairly well with the sun to give direction, but where completely cut out, can very easily lose it. Once made 180 degree change without realizing it. But very soon you come to a recognizable place, due to small size of town, especially in breadth. Orientation here is basically linear (a very crooked "linear"), i.e., by a sequence of remembered objects; secondarily by references to water, which soon corrects you if you go astray. Also by sun direction and rarely, by tower landmarks. Nothing else. It could be difficult to find a specific point, but you are never long lost in general orientation.

Boat back to S. Toma and Camp. Mosca. Brief rest, and off to S. Marco again, to watch evening come on and bells to strike seven. "D" boat through new canal to station (past Pzle. Roma, a shock to see busses, cars and neon signs again), and dinner. Walk home to Rialto and across through the evening crowds and the shop lights. You can follow almost automatically even in new areas.

Leonardo's proposal for a city with water running through it for power, transportation, and sanitation (April 19).

April 19—The room of city views (principally Bellini and Carpaccio) fascinating to me in their illustrative detail. Seem to be quite accurate, except for old trick of widening spaces and heightening main buildings. Bellini's S. Marco pushes away N. well and lowers it. Shows S wall as in line with campanile. Standpoint must be half way back in present square. Obviously these painters enjoy the color and quality of their city as a background.

Also took in a good Leonardo show, explaining critically his achievements in various fields with notes and drawings. In fields related to planning, he developed the accurate bird's eye view, and worked on whole compact spaces in architecture. In cities, he developed an idea for a 2-level circulation, the upper for gentry, the lower for commoners and goods and waste. The lower might be canals, a system he thought much of. Impulse: the pestilence in Milan, and the need for sanitation (for the upper classes). Also stated that streets should be as broad as the height of bounding buildings.

Worked much on canal systems (did not invent lock, but developed it), and irrigation, drainage and hydraulics. Suggested cities of basic type [illustrated in sketch] with water running through (power, transportation, sanitation). Developed accurate bird's eye maps (as well as his work in geology) and could express and thus design complex projects (including a diversion of water from Tiber to Arno via L. Trasimene and Val di Chiana).

To me he seems at his best with practical, factual things backed by scientific generalization, whether machines for war, engineering, industry, etc. or descriptive botany or anatomy. Here his precise drafting is a powerful tool. In his sketching, painting, knot designs, caricature, etc., there is a mystic, inturned quality, somewhat sly and evil. They say his mirror writing not for secrecy, but because he was "mancino" (look up). A very interesting show, by Min. Publ. Instruction.

Then walked route: Accademia-S. Marco, photographing it in series at every new space compartment. This should be interesting, since it to me one of most significant qualities of Venice, but a hurried job, lacking careful notation of the sequence of detail, or side views (thus little water), etc. More mechanically descriptive. Route Campo S. Vidal-Campo S. Stefano-

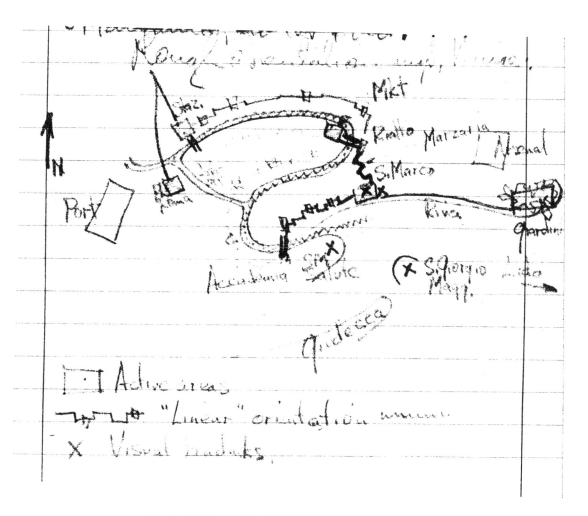

Rough orientation map, Venice (April 19).

Calle de Spezieri-Campo S. Maurizio-Calle Zugari-Campo S. M. del Giglio-Calle delle Ostreglia-Calle Lurga-Campo S. Moise-Saluta S. Moise-Arcade, Fabbrica, Nuova, Pza. S. Marco.

The square almost full, several thousand people, quiet and orderly with many children. Not a policeman in sight. A clear but not brilliant speech, attacking government for electoral law, danger fascist revival, war policy, and lack or slowness economic reform. Proposed internal reforms on speeded land distribution: nationalization electricity utilities and Montecatini and import of coffee and sugar; houses for lowest income class (most reaction from crowd); tax reform to make half revenue from direct taxes (now 15%), abolish indirect on food and many of other minor taxes. A moderate speech, except for hints that there might be fighting if center gets its 2/3 and uses it to further modify constitution or declare war. Crowd favorable but quiet.

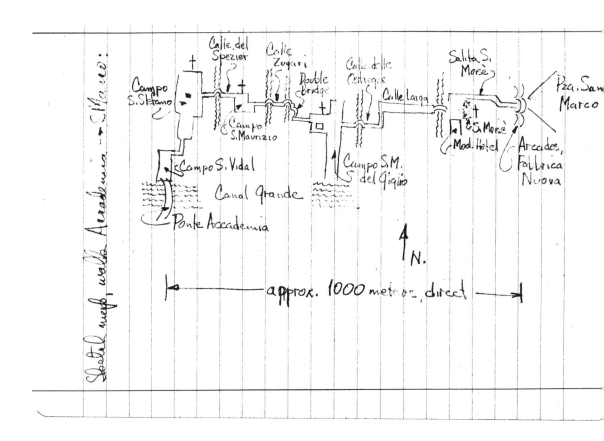

Sketch map, walk from Accademia to San Marco (April 19).

April 20—Through Doge's Palace, an imposing horror. The facade masks an architectural sewer. To S. Giorgio Maggiore, one of those vast cold churches, and up Campanile for a fine view of Venice and lagoon. Best spot to see it in relation to its environment.

Down through streets back S. Marco for some element photos. Venice begins to wear on me (as must almost any city that you simply walk in and look at without action), but also because of the damp despair in its interior.

Characteristic elements, central Venice:

Space—constantly changing narrow slits to broad openings, dark to light, suddenly terminating and suddenly renewed. Constant turns. A chain of beads.

Middle distance—rarely evident; occasionally the decayed shutters, peeling plaster, wash, rusted bars, faded color.

Eye-level—greatly heightened, due to suppression of above and closeness of spaces. Shop fronts varied but subdued signs, crumbling brick, doors, water and weed at edge steps and walls.

Floor—constantly varied, though basically all square stone block. Rising, turning falling over dirty water, spreading and contracting irregularly. The string on which the space beads strung. Often wet or sinking.

Human activity—lively and free: the rivers in narrow streets sweeping you along, the sudden encounters at sharp corners. Children, much singing, poor (or tourist) clothes, hoarse anxious voices, lively faces. Free movement.

Traffic—none, except the varied canal loads and the very occasional small barrow or baby carriages, and the heavy loads hand-carried. These have difficulties, but the freedom for pedestrian is immense. Long walks are possible without conscious attention. Jams in the narrow canals: goods capacity probably limited.

Noise and smell—wonderful absence motor noises. Voices and feet, singing, seeming especially loud. Smells sewage and dirty water. Damp. Occasionally the clean sea air.

April 21—Thinking that the walk from one spot to another in Venice is always a "something," not a negative quality. It may be a pleasure, or the weary effort to push through a dense medium but never an empty gap of time between arrival and departure. It exists as well as the termini.

Rome

February 23—Out to seek a home. Day bright and warm, the sunlight very clear and sharp. Now Rome seemed very fine, totally different than Florence.

I kept to main streets, and here all the activity of a big city, plus the Italian use of the street. The spaces are very broad, irregular and in constant motion. The overwhelming impresion is of great dynamic masses in the light, seen at odd angles and perspectives, strikingly juxtaposed. The mix of Roman ruins and baroque splendor is exciting, and the movement of people equally so.

Although the plan is quite irregular, orientation seems easy on the main streets, since long axes cut through and you go from easily recognizable point to point. The interruption and misjoining of axes causes much roundabout movement, however, both for pedestrian and traffic (which must have a hell of a time).

The hills are not prominent as I had thought, but half-buried in the buildings. Their effect is not as orientation points, but rather the sudden throwing up of a building or a garden in a street vista, adding to the crag-like play of contrasting masses. Also results the concave sweep of axial streets, usually with some columns, monument or fountain at the end.

Commented on the many centeredness of Rome: that each product has its shopping center, that each piazza has its own character and life, that

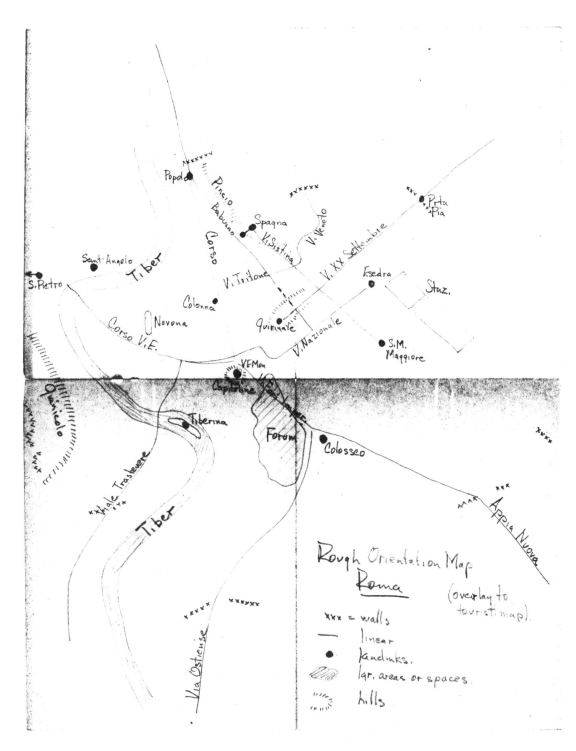

Rough orientation map, Rome (April 2).

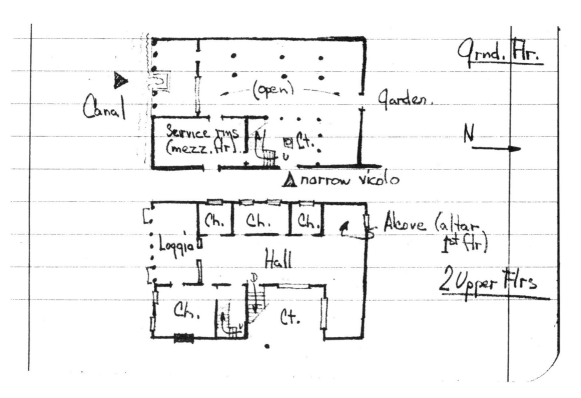

Ca d'Oro, Venice (April 20).

it is hard to find any one center in the city. The city seems to be structured on the piazzas as cohesive nuclei and the irregular set of avenues: only secondarily on the ring of hills (volcanic), which now being submerged in expansion and grading operations.

Blake says Rome located here because at head of primitive navigation on Tiber, yet away from sea raiders; that at important crossing of land routes; and that protected from land attack by ring of hills, which then much more prominent.

Then walked back to American sector on Via Veneto, but found consulate, USIS, and Fulbright all closed for some unknown festa. Over to Pza. Spagna from above, coming on it by Via Sistina, which ends in burst of light at obelisk. The stairs cascade down from here in curving, interrupted jumps; broadening and narrowing within its banks of houses. The platforms, steps, and balustrades dotted with people resting, playing, strolling: a manmade pleasure hill. Must photo this use. Ends abruptly in the narrow piazza traffic passing at right, with the strange little short foundation at the foot, half-sunk in the street paving. A sense as if tottering, as if must catch balance at bottom. Not sure this is not right—adding to dynamism—the stairs are the event, not a monument base.

Back down Corso, jammed with pedestrians. After several futile calls up to Campidoglio, behind the disgusting V. E. Monument. The two great step-slides at the entrance are very exciting in their juxtaposition and the strange bare curving facade of S. Mn. [illegible]. But disappear in Campi-doglio itself. The splayed sides make me uneasy, and shorten perspective to that central facade seems to be at your nose. Nor are the facades im-pressive as architecture. The Roman and medieval structures covered up by the central facade are much more powerful. The convex, patterned oval floor is nice, however. Best are the strange views out through corners: AMArac. [?] hunching its shoulders, Roman fragments, stairs, a deeply-etched little dome. Back through Foro, interesting as ruins and a puzzle to reconstruct mentally, and over to see Pantheon. Too late and dark to be worth going inside; outside just big.

Pza. Navona, old stadium, hence its fine regular shape: A very pleasant space in the evening, full of loiterers and children. Two streets on either long side, which do not bother, interior protected by bollards, chains and paved. A fantastic baroque church on middle W.-E. side—seems right to have a dominant here, though do not like it individually. Would be fine if all remaining facades were like E. side; rosy, [cozy?] human in scale, even in roofline and restrained. Two things spoil: the street at the N. end that shatters the hemicycle, and the gigantic Bernini fountain in the middle, which almost destroys everything. Here would be a low fountain perhaps just a pool, or something like the Spagna boat. At the ends should be higher features, though slender. But still a good space, and much used.

February 24—Over to Pantheon in warm bright sun. The concrete dome is impressive, especially the hole in ceiling, the sense of sky and shaft of light. Interior spoiled by later [?] marble panelling, niches, etc. lower walls.

To fountains Pza. Trevi. This baroque rockwork is magnificent. A wild jumble of stone and plunging statues, water and great pool, set down below street level and closely contained. Many people enjoying water and sun. The piazza walls warm colored and at one corner a baroque church facade peers in. Fine set of stairs, platforms and bollards leading down to it, rich effect from simple means and in close space.

Along V. del Babuino to Pza. Popolo with its obelisk, a good terminal feature. Past Pza. Spagna, smell flowers, people in sun, water gurgling over stone boat. Pza. Popolo big and difficult to cross but looking at it towards center, very impressive gate to city, though right hand street (Ripetta) sems to have no particular destination. A great stage set; though diverging, not too confusing, probably because angles of divergence are wide, regular, and the long straight streets give you a sense of what they lead to.

Down Ripetto past Marco Augustus, a gloomy pile, and over Tevere to Pza. Cavoni, a be-palmed nonentity. To Castello Sant'Angelo, from outside, just a big picturesque medieval fortress. Has much used park and playground alongside.

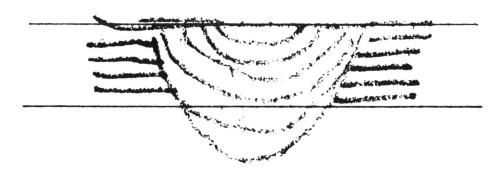

St. Peter's steps, Rome (February 24).

Down V. Conciliazione (horrible) to S. Peter's. The great colonnades not so impressive after all, and the pitching of the floor very disturbing. But the feathery fountains are fine, and along the colonnade is a good place to sit in the sun, or move back in checkered shade of columns. I did for a good space, half dreaming in light. Every column base taken.

Up to S. Peter's, no emotion. One detail, the delta-like flow of ramped steps over old steep ones on central axis is good. They flow out.

Inside the basilica is impressive by its size (not fully realized) and the clean newness of completely finished gold and white interior. On baldechin, the spiral columns even taper, very queer and plant-like. But it in general leaves me cold.

Then down papal walls to Pita S. Pancrazio. One side high brick masses topped with umbrella pines and gardens on other, a steep rubbish filled slope to shacks and backs apartments. Must have been fine when open country. But waste space and sun here, so occasional people.

March 27—Out with Barringer in A.M. to see some current Italian work. My God! A sick fantasy of forms and materials, "expressing" to top of ability. A street of these apartments (like California) the shapes seem to lean out over street, and choke your way, screaming for attention. Streamlines, abstractions, exaggerated structure, "plasticity," a restless movement. A few by Monaco the best, at least the front elevations decent, but the old faults of lack of tie with the other parts and neglect of everything but the show pieces: front facade, lobby, living rooms, and with everything going on up in the air, often little is done at the pavement and eye level, a real desolation. These the luxury residences, but they are pretty poor. Some of the materials are fine: hammered concrete, mosaic tile, etc.

Of all these, the Trevi is outstanding to me. Partly for the rockwork but mostly for the unique space: let down below the street level, it almost fills the space from side to side. The sides irregular but make a dynamic closure, with some narrow slit-like views out at dramatic angles, and down below your eyes are filled with the great pool and the rushing water, around which the people gather. A protective, enveloping enclave.

Navona is calm and pleasant, and a good urban opening. Would be much better if the enclosing sides more regular, simple and refined, since this kind of space seems to call for order.

The Quattro Fontane crossroads not as exciting as I had imagined, since none of the terminal features very strong, and the topography drops sharply away to Esquiline and Trinità dei Monti while N.E.–S.W. road runs on ridge top. But see where this could be a fine feature if the termini were actually key features of town.

The VE Monument is of course ugly, and the view disappointing. Possibly Rome cannot be seen as satisfying a panorama as Florence, due to its size, and the up and down of hills without any dominance. But Rome still seems a city of sparkle to me, with its variety of features, its activity, its light, its surprising spaces and rich surfaces.

In p.m. back to town to Roman Forum, a fairly dull affair, since mostly massive ruins, in a great jumble. S.M. Antiqua interesting for its 7–10th century frescoes. Those, especially in left chapel, already have a medieval spirit, but others have more "realistic" faces, to me more early Christian.

To Pza. da Spagna for many pictures—this is a wonderful spot to me, equal to Fontana di Trevi, and much enjoyed by people. Note most of walkers going up. People of all sorts and conditions sit and stroll here.

March 31. To Vatican to see Sistine. Up a double spiral staircase, which widens and becomes less steep as it rises, very peculiar from below, since it seems to spin off to one side. Then galleries and galleries, painted and crammed with antiquities and art. Some of the Limoges ware and glass quite fascinating. Several maps and views of Rome. Best (should get), one of Leonardo Bufalini, 1551, sketchy but probably fairly accurate and a true plan; another, by Gianbattista Nolli, 1748, a beautiful precise job.

The Sistine hell to look at, all wrong in its general scheme: its relation to observer, false architecture, disorder of figures and scenes. But when can concentrate on individual parts, some are magnificent, especially the giving of life to Adam, and the expulsion, floating electric mysterious. Also the figures of Jeremiah, Isaiah, Ezekiel, and the Delphic oracle.

Notes on City Satisfactions (1953)

We are concerned here with the psychological and sensual effects of the physical form of the city—drawing the line (though an uncertain one) to exclude the direct functional effects (job security, social groups, good housing, etc.), and the provision of adequate quantities of the environmental elements (houses, stores, playfields, etc.). Note, of course, the overbearing importance of these "functional" effects: that people choose residential areas for cost, safety for children, "good neighbors," distance to work, etc.; that a Trieste engineer called a city good because it had fine bars and night clubs, beautiful girls, and plenty of work.

In this more limited sector, then, the city can provide several satisfactions, which are summarized here as orientation, warmth, stimulus, sensual delight, and interest; and, in addition, several more directly "functional" satisfactions, which however have such a direct emotional impact as to be worth including: movement, shopping and climate.

1. *Orientation*—the sense of clear relation of the observer with the city and its parts, and with the larger world around it. In the simplest sense it may be taken as knowing where one is at any time, and how to reach any other part. This self-location is largely achieved by:

a. Directed lines: strongly organized lines, with a visible or felt direction, concentrating transport and intensive uses, from which other points can be related as from a spine or axis (Corso, Roma; Borgo Albizzi; Halsted St.). Mass transport lines may in themselves create such lines or systems of lines (London underground), and if confused, muddy the orientation of the entire city (Firenze). These lines are particularly strong if they lead to an important terminal area (Via Mazzini). Orientation must be to something worth noting: great streets which lead to nothing are a disappointing fraud. Close angles of divergence between such streets may be confusing (Porta Romana; diagonals on a grid system), as may be constant and gradual shift of direction (Riverside).

b. Sequences—also linear but not necessarily directed: the memory of a sequence of detail, of which the mind can absorb a vast amount if the sequence is maintained (Venezia; any habitual path).

c. Landmarks—isolated objects of peculiar form associated with key locations, and to which observers can be radially oriented by sight. They are especially useful when they can be seen from great distances, at high objects over lower ones (Duomo, Firenze). They can also operate on a smaller scale, as the color of a house, or the pleasure of central Firenze arising from the several distinctive buildings which are imporant for their contents or history. The power is increased where the structures are expressive, monumentally or functionally.

1:8000

0   100   2ᵒ0   300   400   500 m.

The Urban Pattern, Florence.

d. Spaces or areas—several locations which have key importance and are of significant form (spatial, topographical, character of structure, etc.). Once in them, the observer is oriented, knowing "where he is". It is especially useful if the spaces themselves are oriented (have direction), and are related to the exterior. Then the observer senses how to proceed outwards, and can note their presence from some distance away (Signoria; SS. Annunziata). Even more useful if distributed rather thickly, so that brief searching brings one into one of them (London). Area orientation may expand, to include, for example, the entire central section. Here the boundary becomes important, with the sense of "now I am entering the city".

e. Grid systems—coordinate street systems, which give compass directions and a basis for measure of distance and location by coordinates. This is intellectual rather than intuitive, but is useful in the location of vast numbers of minor points (Manhattan, Chicago). It is very confusing when the grid breaks off or shifts direction (E. London). Two directions is the limit that can be grasped (Palmanova).

f. Diffuse—compass orientation only, from various effects: streets which run in one or two general directions, though not on a grid (Bologna); large topographic features visible outside the city (Udine, Chicago); sunlight, etc.

g. Topographic—orientation from the slope and configuration of ground in the city (Oltrarno; Perugia).

h. Symbolic—use of maps, street signs, numbers, shop signs, directional symbols, etc. These are inevitable in a large city, but are fatal if too much reliance is put on them, since they require minute conscious attention. Where used, they must be as clear, simple, and bold as possible, and not in conflict with others and thus self-defeating. When used alone, they provide no emotional satisfaction, and are accompanied by uneasiness.

Beyond this simple sense of orientation, it can also mean the satisfactions arising out of an intuition of the city as a unified whole, with a major structure and a relation to its larger structure. There is a delight in grasping a complex thing as a unity, of assigning it a character, of "knowing" it, of seeing its setting, of identifying oneself with it. In a city, it may be achieved in many ways, including most of those above, plus:

a. Panoramic views of the whole or a large part of it (Pzle. Michealangiolo; Ortonovo; S. Gimignano). The effect is heightened by a sharp boundary (city walls). It may be panoramic in time rather than instantaneous, as in the ability to walk around a city (Lucca).

b. Repetition of features or forms, "harmony," "character" (Florentine facades; Bologna; central Roma; Boston; San Francisco).

c. Sense of the outer setting, which can be achieved by elevation, or gaps thru which the exterior can be seen (Perugia; Colle Val d'Elsa). Also by bringing open country very close to a high density center, which also has the value of contrast (Boboli; Lake Michigan). Or by the penetration of wide linear spaces (Arno). Sharpness of boundary generally increases the sense of relation. All this, of course, has functional values, in allowing citizens to reach open country quickly. Relation can also be made to large natural phenomena, such as weather and sky (of which one is more aware in certain cities), the flow of a river coming from great distances, or astronomical devices such as the huge sun altimeter in the Duomo, Bologna.

d. City size, in the sense that the smaller the city the easier to grasp it. In part it is self-defeating, since, in the lower ranges, the smaller the community the less exciting or worthwhile it is to know (Assisi).

e. Sound—the sense of "city" from bells, the urban hum, etc.
and, of course,

f. Time and familiarity.

Within this general subject, the approach is an exciting moment, full of anticipation but also anxiety (Siena; Firenze; Venezia). Orientation is particularly important in large cities, where the approaching stranger must look forward to a period of confusion and strain. Loss either of excitement or of direction in the approach can be unpleasant (Chicago; Verona; Palmanova; Venezia from Chioggia). Perhaps there are two effective methods:

a. Approach on a clear line, during which orientation gradually unfolds, and the observer is never in doubt about his destination (Fiesole).

b. Making the approach (completely or after a distant hint), until one suddenly bursts in on the destination (Grand Central Station). This pares down the period of doubt from confusing signs, and then takes the values of surprise and contrast.

Orientation is distinct from order or unity, since one can be well oriented in an area lacking in unity. Order usually aids orientation, but variety is also necessary, to allow the distinguishing of parts.

2. *Warmth and Attachment*—a feeling of response projected onto the physical surroundings, of its intimate adjustment to humanity, a sense of protection, ease, and affection. In part it springs automatically from familiarity and the sense of history, but it is reinforced by physical forms:

a. Evidence of human care and adaptation, as in the Tuscan landscape, with the proviso that "too perfect" an adaptation implies rigidity and lack of free maneuver room: it is difficult to wander in Tuscany. Lack of such care is unpleasant in inhabited country; in a city it may appear as careless use of land, neglect and decay, litter and worse. Forms which are carefully tended or which are patently adapted to their use, i.e. "functional," have the opposite effect.

b. If there are plentiful distinctive forms, even though they have no symbolic content at first, associations can more readily adhere than if all is undifferentiated. If my street has a big house, with gingerbread, it is easier both to distinguish that street and to sense its local history, and also to recall it with its associations (Firenze's Duomo; the hill of Fiesole; 345's yellow door; Venezia's campi).

c. "Human scale," in which the individual has some significance, and can impress outward marks of his personality on the environment. This is in general a term too vaguely used, but it is pleasant to be where people in top floors can be seen easily (say 3–4 stories), where there are small openings and gardens, where spaces are not too vast for the individual figure. However, occasional areas of "superhuman" scale, with a feeling of power and awe, serve to set off the more intimate areas and to magnify

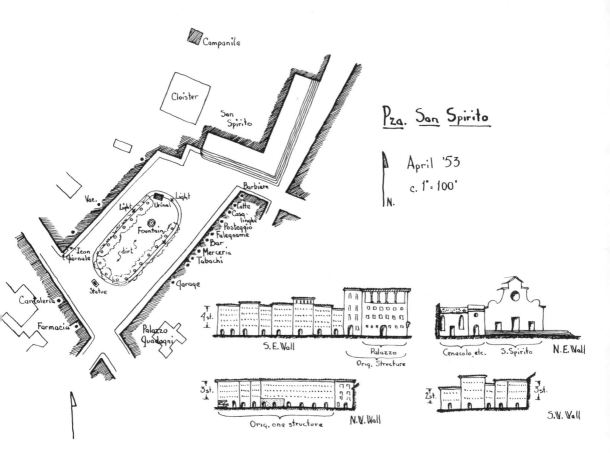

Piazza San Spirito (April 1957).

men. Note the value of seeing marks of individual effort (doors, gardens), but especially the opportunity of making the individual mark, and thus achieving concrete self-expression. There is a tie here with orientation, since it is a very great pleasure to have a spot that is markedly "one's own," and which is yet visibly set in a larger organization which is the "city." Certain features, such as arcades, which have a general unified form yet are capable of limitless detailed variation, can be employed in this way (Bologna).

d. Enclosure gives a sense of warmth and protection, especially if related to a wide open space thru a quick transition, while complete and continuous enclosure is stifling (cloister S. Marco; Monteggiori; various narrow curving medieval streets).

e. There is a warmth in intricacy of detail, if well set off so as to focus attention, and if within easy visual reach. It is enjoyable and interesting to look at detail, to see fantasy forms in complicated shapes and to read double meanings. There may be unconscious analogies to the complexity of life, and in itself complicated detail reflects human care (door, Ca'd'Oro; Victorian gingerbread; Neapolitan stairs).

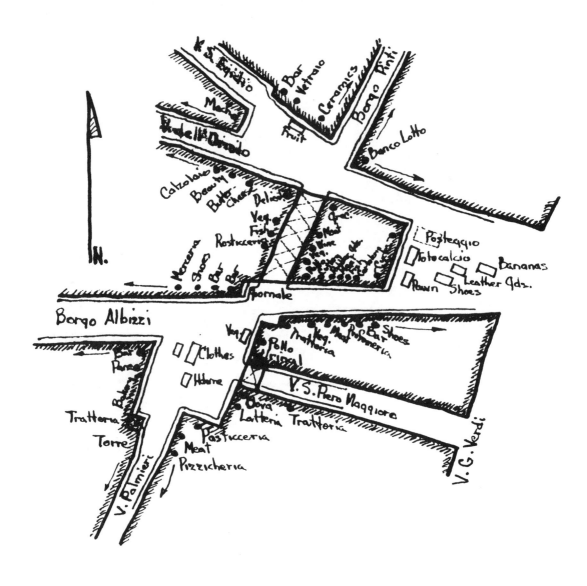

Pza. S. Piero Maggiore   Apr. 1953

plan c. 1"= 100'
elevs. larger scale

Piazza San Piero Maggiore (April 1953).

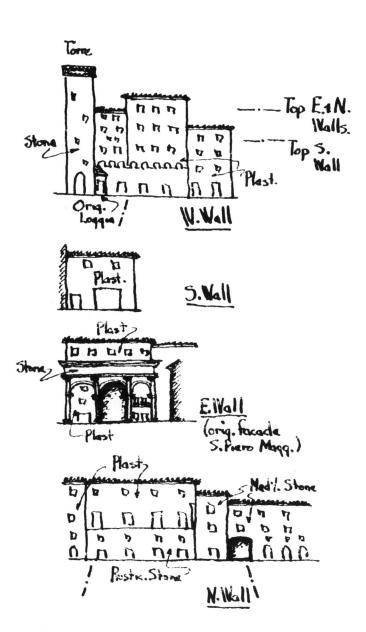

f. Warmth is also heightened by "signs of life": open furnished windows; interior glimpses; benches; laundry; etc. The sight of people and their activity is a fundamental impression.

Note the deep feeling of attachment of Italians to their cities, especially to Firenze, Bologna, Roma, Venezia. Why not to Milano or London? Personal happiness and situation will, of course, profoundly modify these attitudes toward a city (early days in Firenze; 2nd trip to Roma). There is also a contrary stimulus in strong life going on in a "cold" or resistant environment, if the life has held on over time, and left some mark of its existence (medieval Firenze).

3. *Stimulus and Relaxation*—the proper balance between the stimulus of activity and participation, and on the other hand the release of pressure, the freedom for casual "private" activity.

One of the great delights is the stimulus of a city; the sight of and participation in groups; the range of personal friendships and contacts available; the variety of activities, services and goods offered; the sight of many different ways of life; the excitement of being in intense and powerful urban centers (Corso, Firenze; Piazza di Spagna; Burlington Arcade; the "bright light").

Children delight in new experiences and in the contact with trade and activity, if the stimulus is not too strong. Thus the need for urban centers, not only for orientation, but for the excitement, activity, services, intercommunication, that only dense concentrations can give. Cities that are too small may not be able to build up a pleasurable level of stimulation or communication.

There are theoretical advantages of neatness in monocentered cities, with a hierarchy of well-defined sub-centers. They imply questionable assumptions as to standardized relative values of the different central functions, as well as undesirable congestion (Milano; CIAM conference). Poly-centeredness has more probable advantages, especially in larger cities: specialization and "character" of centers; greater availability to population; flexibility (London; Paris; Roma). Different people may have very different ideas as to "the" center (Pernabuoni; Signoria, and the Borgo Pinti). Indecisiveness of center or centers may raise problems, however (Firenze). Formlessness and monotony result from the lack of nuclei (Rifredi; parts of Chicago). There are various advantages both to the linear centers and to the nuclear ones. Linear centers which terminate in nuclei are particularly valuable (Corso, Perugia; Via Mazzini).

The pleasure of observing high activity is the greater when it is made more visible or apparent (Piazza di Spagna; Sala dei Notari); or when animation is contrasted with old, restrictive, or "cold" forms (Scioppio del Carro, Battistero). Structures and spaces must also be proportionate to their use and designed to insure the necessary concentration (outlying

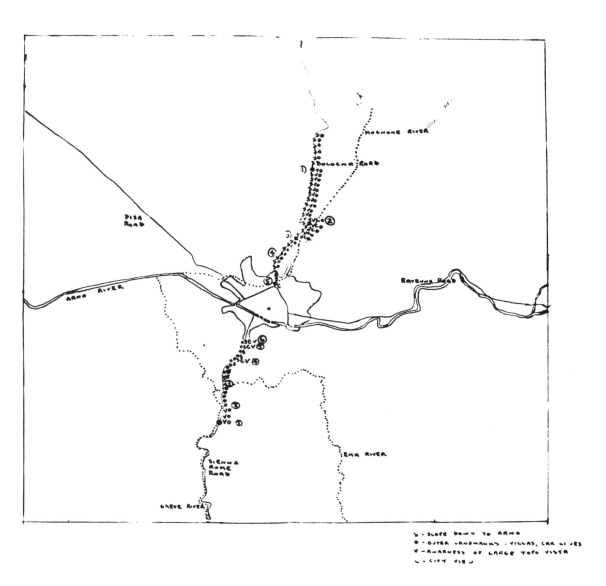

Approaches to Florence. [See accompanying
sketches on pp. 147 and 150.]

arcades, Bologna; Signoria, Verona; S. S. Annunziata; Venetian calle;
Chicago's lakefront). Overdesigned low-use areas are "dead," and the
opposite oppressive. The city can be looked upon as a setting for action
(medieval painting). City size influences the "life," in that those too
small may be "dead," "dull," or "provincial" (Perugia, Welwyn).

At the same time, continuous stimulus or concentration is madden-
ing (Venezia); there is strong need for times and areas of low pressure and
low concentration. Here activity can be unmindful of its reaction on others,
and movement relatively free, and open to whim (pressure of Firenze).
Thus the value not only of private spaces, but also rural, open, or "waste"

Notes on City Satisfactions

lands, over which no one has strong concern (vacant lots; Firenze roofs). Density has much to do with this, also a little carelessness in use or design.

The pleasure comes in the rhythmical alternation of these two states, in time and space. Spasmodic changes are also delightful, as the great festas which transform and stir up the whole city. There is enjoyment in "low pressure" areas which are very close to "highs" (Temple; Arno banks). This rhythm is closely tied to movement and communication: its relative ease or difficulty. Complete isolation and complete permeability are both murderous (Monteggori; Venezia). Good rhythm will only be possible when it is easy to move from one area to another. The optimum is thus both stimulus and freedom, implying variety of environment, fluctuation of intensity, strong centers and waste spaces, and easy communication.

4. *Sensual delight*—All the satisfactions of order, variety, rhythm, contrast, relation: thru all the senses. The major impressions may be summarized as spaces, floor, detail, texture and silhouette, plastic form, smell, sound, and the use of natural elements (of which the first three are perhaps the strongest):

a. Spaces—To the observer, a city is basically a pattern of spaces, defined by enclosure or otherwise, and he is probably conscious of these volumes even when most preoccupied. The greatest physical impressions in a city spring from these space sensations, and, when strong, they can have very powerful emotional effects. "Spaces," of course, refer not just to formal squares, but to all volumes in the city: streets, parks, courts, tunnels, etc. In existing communities we already possess a rich vocabulary of forms.

Their basic quality is determined by the shape and proportions of the volume: both intrinsic proportions and proportion to their use and to the human being (S. Spirito). Many details of color, texture, floor, silhouette, etc., can be used to underline or modify this fundamental shape (Florentine eaves: Campidoglio). Certain forms can be used to "articulate" the space, to explain its volume intuitively: either by putting up measuring rods; showing what can be put into it; or dividing it up for better comprehension (Torcello; S. Marco). Significant objects may be used as space foci, or "condensation nuclei" for human activity. As in all exterior work, vertical dimensions have exaggerated importance, and small level changes, fluctuations of height, and lapses from the perpendicular, can all exert strong effects (Pisa; S. M. Trastevere; Trevi). Thus a *plan* may have small bearing on the final quality of a space, and an interesting plan pattern may have dreary results (Bath; Mantova; Palmanova; greenbelts, Harlow).

Space can be looked at as volume of potential movement, thus the dynamic feelings, and the frustration or giddiness, protection or exhilaration of closed or open spaces. Blocks to movement exercise an influence:

barriers, ditches, etc. can by themselves define a space. Spaces can have a sense of motion, and be static (S. M. Trastevere) or dynamic (Piazza di Spagna); and have direction, and thus be oriented or unoriented to other directed things (Arno).

Spatial forms are only partly sensed from one viewpoint, and require movement and a succession of views to be fully enjoyed. The fluctuations in the space as you move about, the sight of the same objects in different relations, the sensations of near and far, closed and open, turning and straight, over and under, are one of the delights. Thus a greater degree of irregularity and variety is tolerable and pleasant (S. Spirito). Transitions from one kind of space to another make strong impressions (Venezia). Very rigid control and harmony can be desolate (Circus, Bath).

While this is so, the form must have general unity or clarity. A lack can cause irritation and fatigue (Lucca), or the space may not be sensed at all, the city being merely a collection of buildings and people attached to a pavement (Chicago; Accra).

As one space or linked chain is sensed by movement, so is the spatial pattern of the city as whole, which should have some rhythmical quality geared to the speed of motion. Such a pattern may have much to do with the city's "character". Spaces are much more delightful if related to one another, sometimes directly and openly (Bergamo; S. Marco), sometimes with hinted openings, light, or connecting links (Signoria; SS. Annunziata), sometimes with no visible link, but with the memory of a brief, oriented connection (market, Pisa; cloister, S. Marco). All the techniques which promise more on approach, or give a partial, interrupted view of a known continuity, give pleasure. Thus light, or characteristic detail, coming around a corner; truncated forms; or a space seen spottily thru an arcade, can be enjoyable (Venezia; Trevi; Firenze's Duomo from Certosa; S. Pietra Maggiore). A sense of infinite extent can be gained from the gradually dissolving view of one space beyond another (ceiling, Duomo, Pisa; fields, Po Valley), or a feeling of undefined connection with a larger whole by the focussing of corridors whose depth is obscure (S. Croce; S. Pietra Maggiore at night). Spaces have perhaps two basic characters, depending on whether they are relatively closed and self-sufficient, or open and expanding.

The relations of the exterior public spaces to the smaller interior or private spaces is also important: the connection or contrast between a room and a square, the entrance of outdoor light and sound, the sudden transition from street to inner garden, from market to quiet church (Bologna; Palazzo Vecchio; S. Lorenzo; Orsanmichele; Loggia del Saturno). A consistency in the relations of exterior to interior may again have much to do with city character.

If space can be considered as potential movement it can also be thought of as volume of light. Thus the quality, intensity, location and diffusion of the light has a sweeping effect on the spatial sensation, and there are marked changes in the form of a space with darkness or a shift of daylight (S. M. Novella; Piazza di Spagna). By itself, light can define a space, especially at night (S. Marco).

Apparent proportions can also be shifted by temporary changes of use or furnishing (Uffizi; S. Marco; city posters). That human attitudes on preferred types of space have also shifted markedly in history can be seen from paintings, literature, "space styles," etc. We seem to be confronted with a hesitancy of taste between pleasure in the enclosed or clearly defined space, or, on the other hand in the free-flowing space, moving fluidly around objects without final stop.

b. The floor—While moving thru the city streets, the frequent posture is with eyes on the ground, which thus gets constant if distracted attention. And, as the surface of physical contact, each change in texture or level of the floor must be examined with care, if only to stay upright. Thus the great visual importance of the "floor": street paving, walk, yard or square.

Color and texture in this surface can give a great deal of pleasure, or changing touch sensations to the feet. (Torcello; medieval Firenze). Textures can be used to guide movement (Verona), or to give direction or spatial unity in irregular surroundings (Orvieto). Litter, waste, or breaks in the floor immediately reflect their character over the entire scene (Accra; Chicago), and this is particularly unpleasant in areas that are normally associated with cleanliness (parks and grass, water).

As a surface of stability, changes in level are greatly exaggerated in importance. Irregular swells or sinking can give a feeling of great uneasiness (S. Pietro, Roma; S. Marco, Venezia). The play and detailed form of level changes can be exciting (S. Gimignano; Perugia; Aracoeli; Royal Festival Hall), and also fatiguing in daily use. Too strong a level change in a static space may be destructive (SS. Annunziata; Duomo Siena; lower Arno). and very slight changes can modify or enhance the sensation of a space (S. M. Trastevere; Campidoglio; S. Gimigmano; Bologna). Steep slopes can be put to exciting use (park, Volterra; Piazza di Spagna; Posetano). Bringing two very unlike surfaces together at, or very near, the same level, is surprising and delightful (Venezia). This is a widely neglected aspect in our present cities.

c. Detail—The small expressive objects nearby (doors, shop window contents, signs, ornaments, etc.) typically close to eye level from the floor: Often a fortuitous collection in a city, they get relatively great attention and are more noticeable than any grand effects higher up or at a distance. Whether beautiful or not, they must at any rate be interesting: the eye demands material to work on. Here arises the pleasure of walking thru market or work areas, and the monotony of long smooth walls close at hand. The "density" of detail may of course become too high, as in a

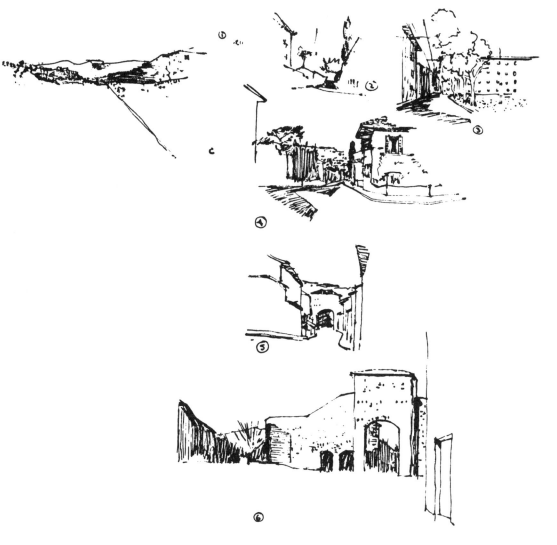

Florence, Sequential Views from the South.

cluttered street or signboard, or an extensive busy area without breaks of lower intensity. But even in low intensity areas, there is need for occasional rich detail.

The city is continually "talking" to the observer; it is full of written or pictorial symbols, directing, informing, exhorting. The chatter must be controlled so that the voices can be heard.

d. Texture and Silhouette—To some extent, the observer is aware of the city as a series of planes, with textured surface and definite edges. This is particularly true of the "middle distance view": the look of the street in the upper stories perhaps a block ahead, to which the observer is occasionally glancing. This may have a distinctive color and texture, from such features as windows, shutters, mouldings, signs, wires, etc., all usually seen in sharp foreshortening. It often fades into a general tone that characterizes the city or one part (Perugia; Bologna; Roma). These textures can have rhythm (Procuratie), strong contrast (Palazzo Ducale), urbane delicacy and harmony (Cheltenham). Here enter in the qualities of material (Firenze) and of plane composition (Burano).

In this same view, the skyline is usually the dominant edge, very pleasant if organized—if senselessly broken, the reverse (Milwaukee Ave.). Other elements may also be seen as a texture, roofs for example (Firenze; Pisa). The occasional view of a city as a silhouette can be very dramatic (Ravenna; New York; Back Bay, Boston).

e. Plastic Form—Less often, a solid form is sensed as a whole: an important structure skillfully set off, turning the space "inside out" (Salisbury; Pisa); a bold sensational facade (S. Peter's, Chicago); rarely but very dramatically an entire community (Ortonovo); more often again some important object set in the city space and acting as a focus (market cross, wellhead, monument, tree, small building, etc).

f. Smells—limitlessly and subtly varying, unclassified and indescribable. They seem, nevertheless, to have the most direct emotional effect of all the sense perceptions, and are the most closely tied to memory. Much of the impression of buildings comes from their smell (chapels, Oxford), and passage down a street is punctuated by smells of bread, beer, flowers, antiseptic, smoke, garbage, car fumes, etc. Cities or their parts seem to have characteristic odors (Oltrarno; lake fringe, Chicago; Venezia), certainly much of the pleasure or displeasure in certain sections is their smell (Mercato Centrale; autumn suburbs; Fiesole; lower Clark St.). The "fresh air" that lightens everyone is as much a smell as a reaction to temperature and humidity. Clearly, massive offending odors may be eliminated; may it not also be possible to "plant" and arrange pleasant ones?

g. Sound—Except for painful levels of intensity, pitch, or monotonous repetition, sounds seem generally to be associated with the activities producing them, and to borrow their emotional effects from these activities. There seems to be a strong ability to become inattentive to unpleasant sound not associated with threatening activity. Principal problems are the preferred maximum and minimum levels, and sounds which are an intrusion on privacy or communication. Other sounds, of course, have pleasant connotation: especially the "natural" rhythmical ones (waves, leaves in wind); those indicative of not too intense human activity (voices, feet); and those musical in nature (bells, singing).

h. "Natural" Elements—Beyond their functional values for shade, ground cover, privacy, recreation, and climate control,—water, plants, earth and rocks are important materials in the esthetic design. Vegetation in particular, with its variety and intricacy of form and color, its seasonal growth and change, is a necessary adjunct in low intensity areas (old vs.

new subdivisions; Florentine suburbs). In high intensity areas, it can be ruled out, or, better, used sparingly for the effect of contrast (S. Giacoro dall'Orio; Promenade, Cheltenham; Cestello). Water, a basically simple material, has the connotations of coolness, refreshment, and free liquid motion, and can be enjoyed in an endless variety of delightful forms: fountains, pools, jets, sheets, streams, cascades, seas—each with its own character of form, motion, and reflected light. It possesses, with fire, the fascination of intricate, repetitive, flickering motion.

Beyond the purely esthetic effects, these materials have emotional connotations of growth, life, and contact with a larger, or more ancient, world. The polemics on the subject of "natural" and "artificial" are slippery ones, however.

5. *Interest*—the intellectual pleasures of curiosity, new experiences and new impressions, the savoring of distinct character springing from concrete differences of background and function. A real pleasure in a big city, it is in part an automatic result of its size and complexity, but also depends on good intercommunication. Isolation and picturesqueness vs. communication and standardization is an antithesis only half valid, since differences must be experienced to be of any value, and isolation means rigidity and lack of the new rather than the reverse. This topic connects with the concept of stimulus, and with the use of detail.

There is this delight in watching a market place or a specialized center (Mercato Centrale; Charing Cross Rd.); in visiting a new section of the city; in spasmodic changes or the introduction of "movable" scenery (festa, Lucca; Uffizi flower show; battleship, Venezia). Equally interesting can be the changes in the known environment due to night and day and the seasons, and the new detail then apparent. It should be emphasized that human activity is, in itself, the fundamental source of interest.

There is perhaps a certain "density" of detail or interesting objects, which makes a street worth looking at. This density can, of course, be too high and thus confusing, or too little related to a general frame on which it can be compared (Accra). Designers with a "variety complex" can be quite dangerous, when they are led to force variation at any cost (Harlow). But distinct and interrelated sets of variations, having a real basis, are very delightful (regional variety of Italian cities and landscapes).

In addition, some "functional" satisfactions with direct emotional impact:

6. *Movement*—communication is perhaps the fundamental city function, but beyond this crucial aspect it has two kinds of immediate psychological effect:

a. On the mover: the ease and "naturalness" of motion is important, and obvious unnecessary blocks are irritating (Roma); the partial blocks, in which the way thru or around is clear, may add interest. It is not necessary

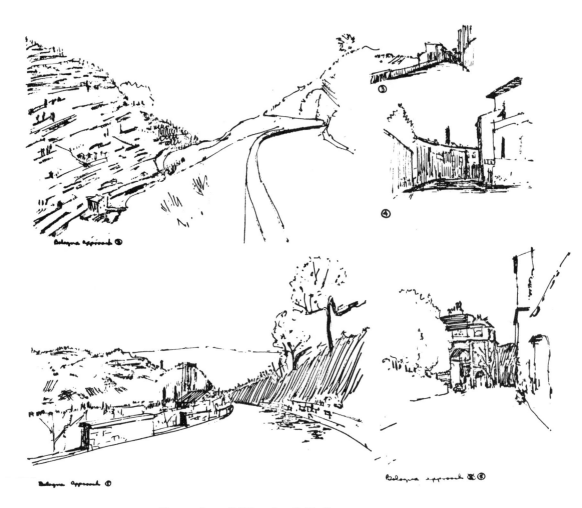

Florence, Sequential Views from the North.

to provide bee-straight motion; smooth irregularities can be rhythmical and give variety. The pedestrian path may be even more tortuous, as long as not confusing or frustrating (Venezia). Motion is a basic way of seeing the city, and the time sequences of pictures is a vital impression, varying with the speed of motion. There is pleasure in motion over and under, in and out; in contact and breakaway from spaces and centers.

Such vehicles as horse carriages or gondola are particularly pleasant: effortless for the rider yet having the change in dynamic scale; related to the surroundings by proximity and the open view; rhythmic in motion and sound. There are losses involved in individually operated vehicles, where attention is absorbed in maneuver. For contrary reasons, it is enjoyable to ride in mass transit vehicles, when they are in contact with pedestrians and activity (State Street cars; double-decker buses). Disorganized patterns of mass transport routes may induce disorientation and frustration.

In general, motion should be directed (except for the opposite case of free aimless wandering)—thus the displeasure of low-density unclear circulation (Whipshade), and of the "traffic wilderness" (Porta Seccaria). There are difficulties in complete traffic segregation: functional problems of separation and contact, lack of orientation and stimulus, problems of isolation and fatigue. There are similar problems in terminal locations at the transfer or stoppage of vehicles: disorientation, frustration, and break of continuity.

There is fun in the play of levels, but always the possibility of strain; lack of space, vision, or clarity may be other blocks to movement. Movement is often a gap, a vacant (or slightly irritating) time between arrival and departure. It is a great pleasure when the motion is an experience in itself (Venezia). Methods must be found of contact with protection, of free movement compatible with intensive use.

b. On the bystander: Not only does group activity receive vital support from circulation; there is stimulation in observing it, particularly if it is a mixed or varied form (canal loads, Venezia; Florentine traffic; "street corner" gangs). Complete exclusion of traffic, long maintained, has isolating and deadening effects.

Nevertheless, traffic is one of the principal preoccupations of the man on foot, due to its danger and its dominant noise and motion. Beyond the functional dangers and discomforts, the anxiety and sharp attention evoked by traffic can destroy urban delight and prevent other observation. Heavy cross-cutting traffic can shatter an otherwise pleasant space (Erbe; SS. Annunziata; S. Giovanni). Relatively thin lines of moving traffic, however, passing at right angles to vision, and not too difficult to cross, seem to have little effect (Via Massini; Union Pass; even Lake Shore Drive). The stored "dead" vehicle is more depressing than the live one.

A rhythm of segregation and mixture, with partial pedestrian networks and cores is one solution (Mazzini; Bath; London). Various devices of protection yet contact can be used: arcades (Bologna); grade separations, which have their problems (Venezia; Milano; Lake Shore Drive); tangential feeding and by-passing (S. M. Forisportam; S. Spirito; Communale, Siena).

There can be no question of the delight of completely pedestrian streets: freedom, safety, the new level of noise, the ability to pay attention to new things (Venezia; Bath). But universal application brings monotony as well as physical problems. Juxtaposition of the big, long-range mass vehicle with pedestrians and the heart of the city can be quite exciting (trains, ships, airplanes).

7. *Shopping and Entertainment*—A big city may be looked at as a great center for recreation, acquisition, and consumption. If we must assign a hierarchy, shopping is "the" central function, and provides the "live",

most broadly used foci. "Window shopping" (the ability to choose or daydream among a variety of goods) and "the bright lights" are two fundamental urban pleasures. Lack of range in these activities are the common complaints in small or new towns (Welwyn; Perugia). Specialization is essential, requiring concentration and a large supporting population. To be able to find a peculiar good or service quickly is a matter of pride. The quality of shops is also a very sensitive index of the character of a city.

Concentration on a relatively narrow corridor, with a mutual reinforcement of stimulus, is one of the most exciting methods (Burlington Arcade; Merceria), or the exposure of goods for smell and touch as well as sight (Mercato Centrale). In large cities, division and specialization of shopping areas is advisable both for the functional problems of traffic, and for good orientation and "character" (London; Roma).

Store fronts in general should not be hidden and retired (Verona), but bold, urbane, or colorful, inviting to enter, their display windows full of interesting and concrete objects (Venezia; Cheltenham). Projecting and legible signs are both a necessity and a pleasure (Firenze; Chicago).

8. *Climate*—the immediate environment in contact with the individual, and whose temperature, humidity, pressure, light, pollution, noise, smell, etc. are his constant concern. Its importance is evidenced by frequent reference, by the effects on activity, by the use of areas.

There are marked microclimatic effects (lake shore vs. interior; Fiesole vs. Firenze). They can be manipulated by siting and structures, both inviting weather and protecting from it: shelters, orientation, size and direction of spaces, use of plants, use of levels, etc. It is especially desirable to have alternate locations or detail for different weathers (two sides of Fiesole; Arno and Loggia dei Lanzi).

If protection and the avoidance of weather extremes is desirable a completely sheltered and equable climate is not. There is also a delight in weather changes; in the observation of its movements thru vistas and open views of sky; and of the detailed effects of rain, snow, fog and sun.

It will be noted that certain general, abstract themes have been running thru all the above:

A. The problem of order and variety, the pleasure of differentiations on an underlying ground. There must be an organized whole holding within it a rich complexity: neither disorder nor an imposed "too perfect" order is pleasing. There are connections with the broader problem of freedom and authority. It recurs here in the esthetic impression; in the ability to sense the whole city with a common character and an organized structure; in environmental release for individual expression coupled with organization for group action; in the interest of varied detail but necessity of a general frame of reference; in the necessity for clear form or statement.

B. Contrast and Relation: the delight and tension of two unlike things brought closely and sharply together; the not incompatible delight of seeing the connection hinted between them. Thus arises the tension and importance of the boundary, where two unlike phases come together, which should be sharp yet with an echo of one in the other. Here enters the key nature of intercommunication, and the problem of regulating its flow. Also involved is the question of the "grain" of the mixture of unlikes, which may be so fine as to dissolve any contrast in a general melting, or so coarse as to eliminate it except at one remote and over-intense division line.

C. Intensity: or the concept of optimum, maximum, and minimum; or proportion. There can be too much detail (a notice board) or too little (a blank wall); too much activity (a subway crush), or too little; too strong an enclosure; too many trees; too few latrines; etc. There is a certain optimum range of densities for each type of use, proportioned to the men, their city, their culture, etc.

D. Rhythm: periodic fluctuation of intensities or qualities within an optimum range—a fundamental satisfaction and a basic means of tackling many apparent dilemmas (open *and* closed spaces; order *and* variety; stimulus *and* relaxation; etc). Rhythm as inherent in life. It is a principal mode of observing the city while moving through it, and important in another way: the pleasure of watching the city through the rhythm of night and day, winter and summer, or the spasmodic ones of special events.

Additional note: We might consider the objectives of the esthetic ordering of the city as threefold, i.e., increasing, for the individual, his:

1. perception of himself, the things outside him, and their relations;
2. range and ease of choice;
3. pleasure.

Some Childhood Memories of the City (1956)

with Alvin K. Lukashok

What does a child notice in his city? What elements of the physical environment leave the deepest impression? A class of architects and planners at MIT wrote short papers on their memories of the environment in which they lived as children. Their homes were dispersed from Bangkok to Brooklyn, their play spaces from country lawns to slum pavements, and yet there were striking similarities in the reports. They spoke of trees, or the lack thereof; the ground under their feet, or what had been substituted for it. They made mention of hills and water and streetcars, of space and of the physical marks of social status. Many other elements, such as buildings and traffic, schools and playgrounds, took a distinctly secondary place if they appeared at all. Some interesting light was also thrown on a child's idea of the neighborhood and of the city as a whole.

All of this was tempting enough to suggest a somewhat more methodical study of childhood memories, with the objective of answering two questions: first and primarily, to what does the child pay attention in his outdoor physical world; and, secondly, how does he respond emotionally to these features?

In the summer of 1955, forty subjects were interviewed for their memories, and their responses tape recorded. Twenty-two were MIT students, eighteen were nonstudents, with occupations ranging from sociologist to cab driver. Seven were women. None were professionally involved in urbanism or design. The ages ranged from eighteen to thirty-two, and all but four or five were middle class. The majority were born and raised in Boston, but there was a sprinkling of outlanders from New York or even more distant cities such as Lisbon, Riga, Warsaw, Berlin, and Vienna.

The basic assumption was that present adult memories reflect actual childhood preoccupations, i.e., that items which persist over such a long time span are records of the real, salient, emotionally important experiences of youth. There are, of course, at least four other possibilities:

a. The memory is of an actual but not important experience; it is an accidental retention. This seemed unlikely, particularly where the memory is supported by vivid detail.

b. It is a false memory, a product of what others have said, or otherwise the result of experience after childhood. This probably occurs, and is difficult to detect.

c. Consciously or not, the memories are employed to cover something else, or are selected and marshaled to impress the interviewer. Some

Reprinted, with permission, from *Journal of the American Institute of Planners* 22, no. 3 (1956), pp. 144–152. Illustrations for this article were prepared by Mr. Gardner Ertmann. The original work was aided by funds from a grant of the Rockefeller Foundation.

attempts to impress the interviewer did, in fact, occur and in the analysis this distortion of emphasis has been taken into account as much as possible.

d. Finally, while retained memories may indicate important experiences, nevertheless many other truly important events may have been forgotten.

Features in the landscape may be important for many reasons, of course: because the experience occurs frequently; because of strong emotional ties; because of the relation to the child's needs. In any case, these items are worth the attention of the city builder.

Method

Each interview began with a question concerning the person's home and street, encouraging him to continue from this, telling his memories as he pleased, so long as he did not wander too far afield from perceptual material. Then direct questions were asked on such subjects as traffic, the neighborhood, and attitude to the city as a whole, or on other questions growing out of preceding answers. These questions might deal with strong likes and dislikes that the person expressed concerning any part of the city scene. Preferences in downtown areas were discussed, or the kind of street on which the subject would live if he could. Elementary and naive as these direct questions may seem, yet by experience it was found that they produced the most satisfactory, honest and exhaustive answers. Very little has been done previously to apply this simple method to urban design.

As a first step in the analysis, these interviews were broken down into arbitrary topics, ranked in their frequency of spontaneous or especially vivid mention, depending upon the judgment of the experimenter:

Frequency of mention of various topics
(out of a total of 40 interviews)

Lawns	27	Ground surface
Other ground surfaces	25	in general, 36
Topography	24	
Wall materials	23	
Trees	21	
Mass transport	21	
Color	20	
Families per house	19	
Sense of space	17	
Water	15	
Cleanliness	15	
Crowdedness	13	

City floor.

Awareness of a neighborhood	12
Play in "waste" areas	12
Order and maintenance	11
Traffic	9
Shopping	8
Historical association	7
Orientation to the city:	
through	
High school	14
Wandering	8
Parent's occupation	7
Transportation lines	7
After-school occupation	5
Play	4

The City "Floor"

Among the items mentioned most often are the lawns. A lawn is associated with spaciousness and a sense of freedom. The positive effect associated with this was expressed, for example, in the following:

"I was very happy. I remember the first day we got there I was running over the lawns, up the slopes because it was so much of a change.

The size of the lawn and its upkeep indicates the status of an area. For instance:

"After you ride along Cleary Square the houses become nicer, they have lawns, some are set up on a hill, a little off the street."

In one interview on Scarsdale, two neighborhoods are compared in terms of house set-back and what the subject calls the "estate" quality of some properties. Even small front lawns are mentioned and when the subject has lived in a house with no yard or lawn around it, he is still aware of the lawn as being a status indicator in other, presumably better, neighborhoods. The lawn provides play space, and for many subjects the front or back yard is their earliest play area, and, as will become more and more evident, a child remembers what he can play on or with.

Not only just the lawns, but the entire "floor" of his environment is of great importance to the child. Very few things are so close to him for play. Of all the various types of floor coverings mentioned, grass is the best liked, then dirt that can be dug or molded, and after that any smooth surface that allows roller skating or bicycling. Driveways are occasionally mentioned in this regard.

The floor surfaces that a child seems to dislike are asphalt on open spaces that otherwise would remain grassy, and brick, gravel and cobblestones placed where he can suffer a fall. Of the few people who mention brick-paved surfaces, none talk about the visual qualities of such surfaces, all dislike the uneven texture it provides. A typical attitude is expressed by a girl who said when describing a street:

"It had a hill and brick sidewalk, which is not good for roller skating."

Another subject refers to Beacon Hill:

"I remember distinctly the brick sidewalks. I didn't like that at all. I was strictly for cement sidewalks, didn't like brick; they jibbled and jabbled all ways."

The child is sensitive to the floor and its various coverings because it is the prime condition of his main activity—play. This surface, rarely the conscious concern of the designer, so often left to surveyor, contractor or sheer custom, thus turns out to be the most important sensuous element of all.

Texture and Color

The city floor is the textured surface which has the most powerful impact on the child. While another type of surface, the material of the building walls, was also often mentioned, it is nevertheless clear that it had a totally different significance. Comments on wall materials almost always convey the impression that they are one of the standard and expected ingredients of the description of a region and rarely seem to carry much emotional significance. In a few cases they are used to convey a sense of shabbiness, or of darkness and thus of gloominess. "The usual red brick" is also an epithet of dislike applied to schoolhouses.

Trees.

Color, which was brought up in some twenty of the interviews, is almost invariably an inseparable part of the descriptive term for the wall material, and seems to have little life of its own in memory. Occasionally "green" is used as a synonym for foliage or grass, in a purely conceptual way. Only in a few cases did color seem to have much impact, usually by characterizing the tone of a dreary area, as "gray." Another remembers being disgusted by "yellow" grass in Franklin Park.

Foliage

Trees are mentioned with great frequency. With few minor exceptions trees and foliage are remembered with great warmth. When describing an ideal street these are usually included, and they are mentioned in the preferred downtown sections. Children like trees and foliage for many reasons. They provide the ideal environment for play. Offering shade in the summer, they can be climbed, they can be carved, they are hiding places. They are places where children can create their own fantasies. Here is a memory that expresses this:

"We had a big oak tree in front of our house which was sort of a favorite. Then they were planting these small ones which were supposed to grow into these big ones someday but never got a chance because we'd hang on them or try to climb them and break them off. During the latter part of the spring, when they used to get real bushy, they almost covered the street in sort of a tunnel. It gave a nice feeling of security. You could walk on the outside of the trees and be blocked off from the road. Yet it wasn't the same thing as barriers you encountered in Brookline, it was sort of

a friendly thing. We carved our initials in them. You could do a lot of things with them, climb them, hit them, hide behind them . . . you could see out between the trees but none could see in, and we used to hide in there and watch people. . . I always liked to watch people.''

There are those who remember the pleasure of being shaded by trees.

"I can remember in the summertime it was beautiful along Saratoga and Bennington Streets because it was shaded. We used to play on the front stoop of somebody's house, and it was so nice to get under the trees for shade.''

Of course, not everybody feels this way, especially if their experience living among trees is limited. Here is a comment of a New Yorker:

"There were very few trees, occasionally thin trees . . . I remember wondering when I was young why they bothered, because it seemed obvious that the trees had absolutely nothing to do. I really didn't miss them. What little foliage there was in the city would seem to interfere.''

But the majority are so at ease in their love of trees and green that there is hardly an interview that in some way does not take them into account. Trees are alive, they move but are always there. They regularly change their form in step with the great seasons. For some subjects the trees are the dominant impression of their childhood:

"There were maple trees along our street . . . It's about the only tree I've ever been conscious of; it's the first tree I remember the name of, I've thought of it all my life. White birch trees, too, have a special meaning . . . But when I think of Scarsdale, I think of maple trees.''

Play Areas

One of the interesting things coming out of the interviews is that children seem to prefer to play anywhere but the playground. Some of the following comments will illustrate the feelings of many children. A boy from Jersey City played in the park

"near the bushes to get away from the playgrounds.''

A girl remembers:

"We would rather play in the foliage. I think it represented a certain amount of mystery and imagination. You could invent things. Bushes sort of formed a clump surrounding an open space, and this can begin to mean something to you, such as a house.''

Another person:

"Our idea, when I was 9 or 10 years old, was not to play on the playground but to find some place where there were rocks and broken bottles . . . a lot of trees and holes to fall into.''

Play areas.

In commenting on the extensive program of playground construction that took place in Manhattan under the direction of Robert Moses, one person said:

"I remember Riverside Park before it turned into . . . developed areas . . . I remember there being a lot more space to play in. The big change, the big spurt of playground building had gone up. I was sort of pleased with having all these nice places to play in, the nice things that moved and worked, etc., but there simply wasn't enough space just to go and play in and do idiotic things in. You couldn't dig, for example; I like to dig. There weren't many places to dig because of the hard asphalt on the playground."

Another, in referring to where he used to play, said:

"Out in back was a big field where the grass was over your head. They have cut that down now and made a playground out of it so it isn't as romantic.

Referring to some empty land, one person said:

"The land surrounding the school was sort of jungle—trees and brush growing up, very unkempt . . . It wasn't much outside but I remember we used to play there a lot and have a great time there."

One girl remembers:

"I really liked to play most of all in the back alleys. It was interesting. There were all kinds of doorways to go under. Very colorful place. I'd feel like an adventurer. That seemed to be the main place of activity for children . . . It was a wonderful place to hide, you see, because of all kinds of doors and passageways."

The garage and garage area, so often the insoluble part of many architectural design problems, is usually remembered by the child with great affection. Children remember garage roofs as places to climb to and jump off from. Garages seem to have the importance of enclosed spaces without the accompanying authority of adult organization.

These are positive statements and nowhere do we find them contradicted. A child's play is most satisfactory when it allows him the greatest opportunity to manipulate his environment according to his needs: to imagine, create, and hide. A well-differentiated world, and one that is plastic to his hands and mind, is his desire. That is perhaps why so many people remember with pleasure the overgrown lot, thick brush and woods. It is sufficient to give us pause in our treatment of "waste" or "untidy" areas, or in the design of play spaces. Naturally, as the child grows older, the type of organized activity he wants demands a different type of open space. In some of the interviews we find the conventional open playground, mentioned without any negative effect, but again not with any positive effect either. Most often it is in reference to the organized games of adolescence.

Hills

The majority of the interviews mention the local topography in one way or another. The hilliness or flatness of an area is noted in the basic descriptions, and, on the whole, people remember keenly and with pleasure the hills that were in the vicinity. A typical example is the person from Scarsdale who makes comparisons of her hills in Westchester to the disliked flatness of Long Island. There are some who include hilliness as part of their requirement for an ideal location of their home. More usually, the memory of a hill is part of the play area, lending itself to many types of activity such as coasting. Because so often a hill is not the best site for building, it is the last part of the area developed, allowing it to remain wild and therefore attractive to children. If there is any negative effect toward hills it is in terms of their inconvenience—the difficulties of getting up them in winter and the number of accidents which take place because of them. But on the whole this variation in topography is strongly desired. And yet, although the child is sensitive to hills, it is surprising how little the *general* hilliness of such a place as Chelsea affected the memories. The subjects mentioned that certain places were on hills or that they played on certain hills but nowhere were we given any indication that the central characteristic of Chelsea is its hills.

Transport and Traffic

Frequently mentioned were the mass transport vehicles. This includes trolleys, buses, trains, or even ships. It is here distinguished from traffic. The flow of vehicles as a total pattern. In the interviews there is a strong but ambivalent feeling toward mass transport vehicles. The delight of watching trains, buses or trolleys is usually paired with impressions of dirt and noise. One person, decribing with pleasure his memories of watching trains in the Jersey City station, still remarks that:

" . . . it seemed very dirty and black."

The excitement that this type of experience affords is illustrated by the following memories:

"One thing I can remember very clearly is going to the subway and being very impressed by subway trains. I remember that it was rather dingy and rather filthy, and the big cold tracks were very interesting, always the signs . . . 'Danger—Third Rail'."

And:

" . . . the elevated, that was miserable. When you stand at the corner of the street, even with your father, with all these cars honking, darkness from the buildings and the elevated cutting it off, and then one of these things would come roaring down the tracks, clattering and clashing."

The last impression is undeniably negative in effect, yet there is that tension and excitement in the description that reflects the child's closely held interest.

Impressions and memories of trolleys and trains are often associated with the noise they make. These are the noises children often hear, especially at night.

"Talbot St., I can remember, had these streetcars on it. It was cobblestone, a pretty noisy street; if a car went down you heard the car. I used to live on the top floor and could hear the streetcars ten blocks away, and after a while you can tell exactly where they were, what stop, just by the sound."

It may be that we sometimes make mistakes in isolating our railroads or burying our transit vehicles. For a child at least, these seem to be a very adventurous part of city life.

As far as traffic in general is concerned, it is mentioned much less often. Most of the people remember being warned by their parents about its dangers, but there is no evidence that they had or retained strong feelings about it. Traffic seems to be taken for granted in childhood. It may be, of course, that in the last ten or fifteen years traffic has increased from the stage of mild discomfort to one of near crisis for some of our major cities. But in these memories, traffic is remembered as a mild interference with play rather than a more serious threat. It is also, like mass transport, a source of pleasure to the child. It was for the one who said:

"I got over the hill and went down the square, and maybe I liked the increased activity that I came upon—the streetcars, all the people and everything.

Or the girl from Berlin:

"Part of our apartment was facing the street, and the balcony, and my room was facing the street. I remember looking out before bedtime at night and watching the traffic. I liked that very much. Our street was leading into a main street where they had a trolley car and I even could see that."

It is of some interest that the two interviews that deal with Manhattan never mention traffic. In answer to a direct question about traffic, one person said:

"I don't remember noticing traffic; there wasn't that much."

This, about uptown Manhattan! Is the great volume of traffic on Manhattan streets such an ordinary part of the environment that it goes unnoticed?

Space and the Sense of Crowdedness

The sense of space is put in strong terms, and with positive effect, in at least seventeen of the forty interviews. This consideration, often felt to be restricted to technical conversations among professional architects and planners, is keenly felt, and often articulated as such, by people who rarely think of these problems technically. At times the word might not be used, but the sense is expressed, as in the following comment:

"Take Franklin Field especially. It was quite a big field, being wide open there, Now when I look at it, it's closing in on you."

Often it is one of the earliest impressions mentioned. Here are a number of examples, the first referring to a park:

" . . . It was a very nice place to walk around; it was larger; it gave you the impression of having more space and more green."

Another from Vienna:

"The first thing I remember about Vienna physically? There are are two things— one is the wide spaces, wide airy squares . . ."

A girl from Scarsdale:

"I remember having the great big playground with space to move and play. I remember no feeling of closeness, which I have noticed later on in my life as I have moved into cities."

Referring to Lisbon:

"But you don't get the confined feeling that you do in New York, for example, because none of the buildings were that high. Most of the streets in residential areas were wide, or they seemed wide anyway."

Space.

Or to Baltimore:

"The downtown area was not very pretty to me at all and I didn't like it very well, except for one street which is the longest street . . . in Baltimore. It runs from the suburbs all the way downtown, very broad . . . I tend to like broad streets, the one where I first lived and this one."

This is indeed a common theme:

"The upper Concourse had no shops on it, was very much wider, and could be seen to stretch for greater distance, and I liked this very much."

Occasionally spaces of a different quality are remarked upon:

"Boston was almost like a maze. You felt you were at the bottom of a maze with high walls, noisy with echoes from cars beeping their horns."

"One street was interlocked with another so that you would climb stairs or step down and move around in a labyrinth of little streets, and one house almost embracing or sitting on the other house so that you never get the feeling of separate units, but one continuum of little streets which was moving like a path. All of these were descending toward the Vistula." (of old Warsaw)

Crowdedness has an overwhelming effect on the impression formed of the physical environment. The fact that it occurs only thirteen times out of forty does not give a strong enough indication of how widely this feeling pervades the memory. It is the obverse of space, but its more pressing and immediate aspect. As in the case of space, it is one of the earliest things mentioned and there is little mistaking the effect. In the first paragraph of one interview:

"The district I lived in was notably apartment and tenement houses, usually crowded."

Another interview, after the question, "What's the first thing you remember?", begins:

"Very crowded. Everybody knows everybody."

It is interesting to note that in no interview does the subject complain about too much space. Rarely is there even a reference to the emptiness or the loneliness of great spaces, and although it is generally felt by designers that public squares can be too large to be comfortable and by their excessive dimensions destroy just those qualities for which they are designed, yet in none of these interviews do we see any reaction remotely echoing this objection—with perhaps the exception of the Warsaw interview where one might infer that some of the courtyards in the wealthier parts of Warsaw had a deserted and empty feeling or again in the following:

"Both Berkeley and Arlington used to run down to the Charles. This was a bit larger sensation than the Public Gardens because the river is very broad. You feel a bit more lonely there."

If one might hazard a generalization, it is that there is so little open space left in our cities that, in their hunger for it, most people cannot afford to be concerned with the quality of the space, they are grateful that it is there. This feeling of gratitude, and complementary feelings of resentment toward any elimination of open space, was expressed by a cab driver whose last sentiment during the interview was:

"Boston Common is one of the best parks in all New England. They'll never get that."

Marks of Social Status

An aspect of the city environment that is constantly mentioned is the number of families per dwelling. When describing a street or a neighborhood this is one of the first things to which a person will refer. Whether there is one family, two families or three families per house is of great importance and is closely related to feelings of crowdedness. The number of families per house is the usual indicator of social boundaries. It is fundamental in describing the differences between one neighborhood and another, or between one street and another. Closely allied to this is the feeling of cleanliness, as well as the order and maintenance apparent in the neighborhood.

The emotions lying behind the adjectives of "clean" and "dirty" were universal among the subjects and perhaps only surprising in their frequency of mention and in the strength of the feelings that go with them.

"I remember the section of our city was rather nice. It was clean. I never saw any accumulated dirt. They had a man clean the streets every morning and empty garbage. Everything was done, there was nothing left, and it was always clean looking."

"The buildings were sort of old, not in the sense that they were built a long while ago but that they were actually beginning to fall down; they were dirty; some of the structure was breaking down and falling away. The streets were bad, as I recall. They had pavement on them but were broken down and needed repairs, and the sidewalks in the same fashion. It gave me the appearance of being all cluttered up, dirty."

"Around this neighborhood were the best residential areas in the city. They were centrally located. Streets were extremely clean, with trees, and houses were well kept." (of Riga) "The most clear memory I have of it was that it was confusing— everything seemed to be big and dirty and ugly. I was afraid, I think, of this house."

We'd go into Franklin Park which was right across the street, which I didn't like very much because it was a grubby park, not well kept. Sometimes you like dirt when you're out in the woods—it's good and clean. But in Franklin Park it looked as if the earth was layed there by some contractor, and the grass was yellow, spotted, and the ground was hard, and it was really dirty."
"Just a straight street . . . but clean. It was a nice clean street."

"What part of Boston?"

"The dirty part! Big four-decker house. There was an ash heap in the back and I used to climb on it. It was a dirty street, long street . . . In Somerville we lived in a three-decker, nice house—nice because it was so different from the other one. It was clean . . ."

It is only to be expected that judgments as to crowdedness, cleanliness, upkeep of areas be expressed in social terms. There is nothing subtle about this; the people who express themselves so are quite aware of what they mean and are at pains to let you know it. For instance:

"All around that area, up the hill to the Chelsea border going into Everett, the homes are far better, the people are much richer or more well-to-do. I don't think you'll find any three-family houses, more one-family houses, and the two-family houses are very nice . . . The exteriors might possibly be newly shingled or freshly painted. The grass is well kept. All the homes in this area have at least small plots in front of the house with grass and bushes. The cleanliness of the houses makes them look decent, and the fact that you know the people do have a certain amount of money probably will produce a psychological effect . . . When I say 'nice' I think it may have to do with the psychological aspect of it, because you know the people there are

very nice, their kids go to college, and to varying degrees their houses are well kept on the insides as well as painted on the outside every now and then."

Another person, in reference to Huntington, Long Island:

"I thought and think that the Village is a lot prettier than the Station because the type of person that lives in the Village is more of the business capacity, whereas the person that lives in the Station is more of the working type of person, and consequently there is a great deal of difference in the homes."

Here is a comment that brings together a number of the above considerations:

"Orient Heights seemed nicer in the sense that the houses were nicer, newer houses. There were more brick houses—very attractive looking. In our neighborhood, for example, the street would go down, right off the street you would have two or three-story tenement houses. There would be no grass in the front yard, and in the back yard there used to be just dozens of clotheslines. When I was a kid, I often wondered how the people in Orient Heights ever got their clothes washed because we used to have these clotheslines, and you go through Orient Heights where the people own their own homes, they didn't have any clotheslines, and it was always in my mind how they got their clothes washed and dried. They never seemed to hang them out. This was quite a contrast, the absence of dozens and dozens of clotheslines. In front of the house they would have a plot of grass. Instead of just walking along the street and falling into the house, you would go up five or six stairs, you'd have grass in the front and flowers around. Many people would have flagpoles in front of the houses. We didn't have those things. The clothesline question stuck in my mind. The houses were smaller, that is, single-family homes; two-family homes were kept up much nicer."

He also says:

"The people in Orient Heights, a much nicer section, with nicer homes, more grass—there was a feeling of resentment for those people."

It is of interest to contrast the above account of this section of Boston with that of another person who was interviewed:

"Then there was the Orient Heights section. That's still East Boston. That's definitely way out of our class. That's where the rich people would be living. That's where you would have your home with trees, yards and gardens. I used to go up there as a kid and steal apples off the trees. I never felt any envy about that section a bit. I used to enjoy going up there and stealing apples and peaches, but as far as wanting to live there it never occurred to me. I used to remark about the fact as how they could just live and sit and do nothing. Too quiet, that's what I always said. I thought I'd never want to live in a place like that, too quiet for me."

All three of the comments show how strongly the sense of space is reflected in lawns and yards. They also reflect the sense of upkeep and neatness. Two out of the three comments stress the number of families per house as an index of crowdedness or its lack. But all three cannot describe the differences in neighborhood without bringing in the term of social comparison. It would be interesting to know how much of what is perceived about a neighborhood is based on preconceived notions of the habits of the class that lives there. This is a whole area which is largely outside the control of city planners, which cannot help but make its effect on their designs.

The interaction of social status and perception is a part of the interview material that deserves further study. One suspects that for many people no area, no matter how delightfully planned, can ever compete aesthetically with other areas of higher status. For architects and planners who are increasingly called upon to design housing projects, which by their very nature have class labels, this type of information is critical. So far, the results in income-limited housing are far from reassuring architecturally. The relative segregation and scale of housing projects—whether they should be scattered in such a way as to minimize their presence—is immediately brought into focus by these considerations, even though superficially such reasoning seems to surrender to what some people might call an unattractive snobbery.

Associations

This leads us to consideration of the role of historical and cultural associations in the city scene. An obvious example where these are strong is Beacon Hill in Boston, an area that is enjoyed by many who consider it beautiful mainly because of its associations. Although there were not many who talked of the physical environment in those terms, this type of perception played a large part in the most imaginative interviews, especially those about European cities. Many people, because of such linkages, will enjoy or remark upon elements that they otherwise think unpleasant or insignificant. Here are two examples:

"There were individual things in the city which started to acquire a great deal of emotional values for me. I can't say it was really the things in themselves that did it. It was also the literary associations which would make me want to think they were good—such things as Brooklyn Bridge . . . But Brooklyn Bridge was always very, very strange and somewhat foreboding . . . I started to walk across it myself more than once or twice, and I really did get interested in it, knowing a little bit about the history of it. I came to think of it as beautiful, whereas I hadn't before."

"Louisburg Square—I like the square itself, the history of it. I was up there a couple of times . . ."

Of course, for many, such as the person who commented on the brick sidewalk on Beacon Hill, such knowledge is merely another reason why the building or neighborhood should be torn down. To them it is proof of its age and therefore of its obsolescence.

The theme of *wandering*, though not mentioned often and then always linked to adolescence, is yet of great interest because it reflects a certain fascination in the city for its own sake. It is often stimulated by an interest in historical monuments, or in the appearance of different class areas, or in the literary associations of certain neighborhoods like Beacon Hill in Boston or Greenwich Village in New York. Sometimes there are those who will wander for pleasures of curiosity alone. The comments which follow will illustrate some of these delights:

"A lot of my sense of the city came from looking at it at night, especially later on in high school. My friends and I used to walk through the city when it was still . . . even so far as to go down, on weekends, to the Battery and walk all the way uptown to 86th Street. . . . "It was actually from this part of the city (Lafayette Street) I would explore, walking westward and wind up in the Village . . . My first sense of the Village (was) . . . simply looking at it itself and noticing how marvelous it was to find a place like this . . . The crookedness and apparent randomness of the path of the street, an escape from the gridiron pattern, fascinated me very much."

"At about the age of 12 or 11 I started the custom of spending Saturday mornings walking from the West End through Scollay Square along Tremont and the Common and down to the Boston Public Library which I began to know. I liked the city and it was a walk that had so many different experiences in it—to go from the slums of the West End, very picturesque ones they were. Then to walk through the business district and go around the Common and down to the quieter and a little bit more Bostonian business district of Boylston Street to the Library where I'd spend the afternoon."

The American subjects who indulged in this type of activity were in the minority and often, as children, in some way unhappy with their home environment, using this as a form of play. In the interviews with the subjects from Riga, and Warsaw and Vienna, however, this activity was more frequently mentioned and seemed more directly stimulated by interest in the excitement of the urban areas themselves.

Most of the people interviewed do not express such feelings about the city, except for the early reactions to the downtown area. If the children go downtown it usually is for some specific purpose such as a job or entertainment, taking in a movie or a ball game. They do not express a feeling of enjoying the city for its own sake.

The desire to wander and take pleasure in the city presumes that there is a city worth wandering about. The absence of pleasure in the city for itself, the pleasure we have seen in the above comments and which comes through the interviews pertaining to Riga, Warsaw and Vienna, suggests that there may be a diffuseness in the American city that makes this difficult. It suggests that greater satisfactions in this direction might be possible with a more concentrated or differentiated urban environment. Incidentally, the majority of persons interviewed were engineering students, and their reaction to such satisfactions might be somewhat more negative than what would be shown by a wider sampling of the population.

Orientation

We were interested in finding out how people think of their city as a whole, how they gain a conception of its over-all pattern. The majority of the people interviewed oriented themselves to the city, not by wandering, but through the more ordinary processes of going to high school or having after-school jobs that sent them to various sections. Here are comments that illustrate these two ways in which children get to know the larger city:

"I had a job in Boston. My father was a tailor . . . and he got me a job with another tailor . . . who wanted someone to carry coats to different places in town. That's how I learned how to get from one spot to another. Then, of course, you're always looking for something new or adventure and you try going around a different block to get there and in that way you know different parts of town."

"I went to Boston Trade High School and I would leave East Boston to go to Roxbury to school. That would more or less make me aware of other sections of the city. For example, I never had any occasion to go to Dorchester; I still don't know anything about Dorchester; I'm not aware of it and I feel nothing towards it or against it . . . Trade School made me aware of certain sections of Roxbury. I would meet people there, fellows from high school, and I would go to their homes. If we had common interests we would get to know each others' districts that way."

As can be seen from the table [above], going to high school is the most common way by which people start to grasp the city in its completeness.

In general, the people interviewed who came from the Boston area showed a lack of appreciation of the city as a whole. If any one attitude comes out, it is a hatred for and desire to avoid the downtown areas. Under questioning they will admit that certain areas are not too bad, usually the Common and the Commonwealth Avenue or the Beacon Street area, but their desires run to the suburbs.

Occasionally there are hints of how the parts of a city seem to "fit together," or on the contrary to take on a confusing pattern:

"I remember it had a sort of square with two or three streets running into it, except the square was not in the center of things but off to one side. That was really confusing. You got to one spot and you were afraid to move because you were afraid you'd get lost."

"You could locate yourself by landmarks. There was a series of hotels so you knew you were here, and on the other side you would be near a certain park. The land-

marks in the city . . . were historical buildings or historical sites, natural kinds of locations like parks or hills, and in the downtown area there were, of course, movies, theater, opera. . . . If you remember the locality you can locate yourself quickly . . . Sections that I knew I knew well, and the rest sort of fit in."

"It was pretty massive and confusing when I was a youngster, very difficult to find my way around."

Neighborhoods

It is also interesting to see that the sense of neighborhood, although fairly well developed, does not seem to follow lines that many planners refer to as "the neighborhood." To begin with, the conception of the neighborhood in any given physical area seems to differ according to the age and personality of the child perceiving it. The twelve-year-old's neighborhood does not coincide with that of the high school student nor with the adult's. The employment of unique and fixed physical boundaries to define the neighborhood for all groups may be of doubtful validity. Secondly, it becomes clear how small and sharply limited is the "neighborhood" of a child; how it is sometimes determined by minor physical irregularities:

"There wasn't any other kid my age on the street; they were all older, two or three years older, or younger. A couple of streets away there were a lot of kids my age. Occasionally I'd go over there, but I sort of had the feeling that they were different; they lived on that street. I don't know why. There might have been a reason because my street was the only street in the area with all single-family houses, and everyone knows each other. On these other streets they were longer in the first place and are all three to six-family houses."

"We more or less considered the neighborhood constituted a block. Your gang constituted a block and then there was a group down in the other block . . . Within our block we were the ones. Everybody in their own block within that area, five or six blocks, felt that way. Another sort of feeling of a neighborhood was that in our block there was a drug store, a First National, two or three candy stores, and that constituted a sort of cohesiveness; we were a unit. Each block, come to think of it, had a store—a grocery store, maybe not a drug store, a gasoline station, which added a little bit of unity to the group. These trading areas seemed to more or less unify people."

"I had a friend way down the other end of the street. That was sort of no-man's land. By the time you got there you were in a different neighborhood altogether. The whole—all the surroundings seemed to be chopped up into little bits, so that as soon as you went any distance at all you were somewhere else altogether. Maybe it was because I was so young that it seemed such a long distance. But you rounded sort of a bend and your house was out. Although the houses looked somewhat the same, they just weren't."

Other Topics

Water is brought up in a quarter of the interviews and always with an expression of pleasure. The pleasure seems to be associated with the potentialities for play and physical activity:

"Around lunch time I'd go out to the Public Gardens which also became very important to me. I loved going there. I liked to watch the swan boats. I'd follow a whole string of ducks along the bank, go fishing for guppies or pick up snails along the retaining wall . . ."

"I loved the ocean. I used to do a lot of swimming. When I started swimming, Wood Island Park was really the big place."

Commercial activity is mentioned in a few of the interviews, usually either in a purely descriptive way or with conflicting emotions of excitement or exhaustion. It is clear, however, that "going downtown" is an event of some importance in a child's life:

"There was another big area, a big thing, a very big area. There's a movie there—Coolidge Corner. I went there before I went downtown."

"In other parts, which served as market places, they were colorful with all the things sold, and the noise and variety of people—I liked them because I liked to move around in the large crowds and get lost."

"It seemed like there was a million people there, pushcarts and what-have-you . . . It was pretty run-down, very dirty . . . I hated to go there. I hated it because it was crowded and I was usually tired at the end of the day."

"I remember taking the train to Boston a few times with my father to go into his office, a big building. Buildings sort of awed you at that age. You stand at the corner and look up and you wonder why they built them so tall."

Caveat

The limitations of this material must be obvious to the reader: the small size and unbalanced nature of the sample, the use of memories lying at the "surface" of the subject's mind, the fact that they refer to conditions ten or fifteen years ago. One would not conclude, for example, that cities should be built of trees, floor textures, spaces and streetcars, leaving out telephone poles or buildings because they are rarely mentioned in the interviews. Nor, to be somewhat less ridiculous, should we stop building playgrounds because children "do not like them." This material, rather, particularly if more broadly and firmly based on extensive and systematic research, might become one part of the background against which design decisions are reached: in the detailed layout of a playground, for instance, or in the attitude toward "waste" spaces in the city plan.

The reliance on memories, used here, should now be checked by direct interviews with children.

It is equally clear that these interviews have dealt with memories of certain years of childhood, and thus speak only of the way in which a rather restricted age group views its city. That cities cannot be built only for children is obvious enough. It would be most interesting to extend this method to the memories of years spent as adults in various urban settings.

Summary

Knowledge of how people react to their physical environment, and how they invest it with emotional qualities, is quite as important as knowing the technical or economic or sociological resultants of a given form. It may be extremely useful, simply to know something of the features which seem to be most significant to people, so that these features may receive special design attention.

The feelings and key elements that run through all the interviews on childhood memories have strong similarities. The remembered children were sharply aware of lawns and floor surfaces; they delighted in foliage, woods and green. There is a strong and pleasant memory for hills and for water in the landscape. A somewhat ambiguous fascination with the big transportation vehicles is equally clear. There was conscious alertness to spatial qualities, a definite preference for openness and spaciousness, and distaste for crowdedness. Even in childhood, perception is strongly colored by associations of social status: by "niceness," by cleanliness, by upkeep, and by money.

All of these must be connected with more spontaneous aspects to be satisfying. The child wants variety with a chance for some adventure; he has a strong need to act upon the physical environment, to be stimulated by it, and to realize his imaginative fantasies through it.

The majority of people interviewed preferred suburban living. They hate "the city," but when pressed express a fondness for a few central areas that have some of the virtues put forth above. For most people, the sense of the urban area as a total pattern is largely undeveloped, and they rarely conceive of the city as something that might give pleasure in itself. They hardly expect to have an *enjoyable* city environment, as if a mild civic nausea were a normal burden of man's existence.

Growing Up in Cities (1976)

with Tridib Banerjee

photographs by
Dennis Kirshner and
Edward Johnson

Research teams in Argentina, Australia, Mexico, and Poland have recently looked at the way young adolescents use and value their home territory. Boys and girls, aged 13 to 15 years, spoke about what they did there, drew maps and took the investigators on local tours. Their outdoor activities were recorded, and their habitats described.

The places where they lived differed sharply in landscape and culture. Villa Las Rosas, in the Argentine, is a suburb of Salta—a historic, provincial city of moderate size, in a depressed region in the far northwest of the country. Colonia Universidad is near Toluca in Mexico. It is also a provincial city and much smaller than Salta, but has had an economic boom. Colonia San Augustin sits on an old lake bed—harsh, arid, and alkaline—and is part of recent explosive growth at a distant edge of Mexico City. Braybrooke, in Australia, is part of an extensive area of single-family bungalows on the west side of Melbourne. Kleparski and Powisle, in Poland, are inner city neighborhoods of crowded, prewar flats in Cracow and Warsaw. Zatrasie (in Warsaw) and Kozlowka (in Cracow) are large apartment house projects built on the urban fringe of those cities within the last few years. A final study in Poland was made in the village of Bystra Podhalanska, in the foothills of Tatra Mountains.

The Australians in Braybrooke are working class people, with incomes well below the national average. Many of them are refugees from the last war, transplanted from Europe a generation ago. The Tolucans in Mexico are also mainly working class, and on the lower end of the income scale. However, they are a more stable group who have lived in the area for generations. The residents of San Augustin in Mexico are poor rural migrants, drawn from a wide radius by the glamour and work opportunities of the big city. The families in Argentina's Villa Las Rosas are lower middle class, rather mixed in occupation and status, often employed in local government. In the Polish examples, the city residents are of all classes. They have only recently moved to the housing projects, while the villagers have deep roots in their locality. In strictly material terms, all these people have quite different levels of resources, ranging from the Australians (even if they see themselves at the bottom) down to the residents of San Augustin, who are decidedly at the level of poverty, even by Third World standards.

Home, for most of these adolescents, is limited in space and often without basic facilities. Only the more fortunate children (more commonly from Salta, Melbourne, or Toluca) had their own rooms. About a third of all the village children from Bystra and half of those in Kleparski share their rooms with the entire family; this number is probably even higher in the

Reprinted, with permission, from *New Society* 37, no. 722, pp. 281–284. Children's maps reprinted, with permission, from *Town Planning Review* 48 (1977), no. 2, pp. 105–115.

The "corridor world" of blank walls and doors,
in the Colonia Universidad of
Toluca, Mexico.

Colonia San Augustin. In the case of children from Cracow, personal
ownership may be limited to a bookshelf, a desk, an armchair, or part of a
room.

But home is where the children spend most of their waking hours.
Over a third of this time is spent in homework, meals, washing-up, and
other chores. Watching television (except in San Augustin, which has no
television) takes up the remainder of their indoor free time. Only in areas
where the home is not so crowded do more home-based activities take
place, such as reading, sewing, or family get-togethers. Those fortunate
enough to have their own room considered it as one of the best places to
be. Many others did not talk much about home when asked about their
favorite places. Home means security, but not privacy or control.

They liked to use the "unprogrammed" spaces—the local streets,
the courtyards between apartment blocks, the apartment staircases, or the
spaces between buildings. This is where they talk and meet and walk
about together, play marbles or informal games. Streets are immediately at
hand, and they can do what they like there—unlike the home, where the
claims of adults take priority.

The range of their action varies. The Salta children play within part of
a circle which is only half a kilometer across. Children in the Polish housing projects keep consistently within their project bounds, which are only
slightly larger than the Salta territory (a quarter to a half a square kilometer). The Cracow and Warsaw children, on the other hand, roam the

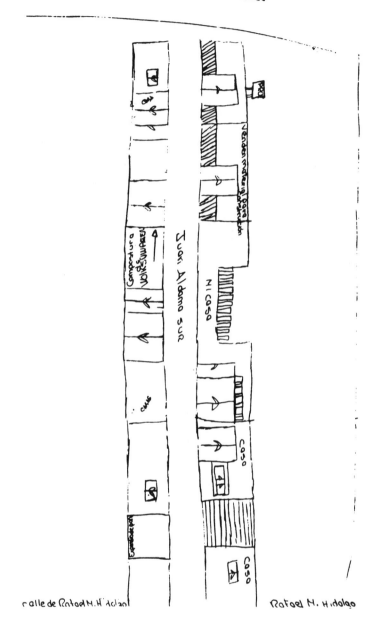

*A child's sketch of his neghborhood
reflecting that "corridor world."*

densely active central district. Their territories are more individual and confident. Tolucan children are also limited to the boundaries of their colonia (roughly half a square kilometer), but they often go outside this area: to the city center two kilometers away, for example, at least once a week. The San Augustin children are confined to the nearby streets, the playgrounds, and their school. The Australians are the most mobile of all, ranging over a ground of five kilometers on a side or more.

But the Melbourne region seemed empty to the children. They constantly spoke of boredom and the lack of things to do. Even in Salta, where children are included in some of the community activities, there were similar, though more muted feelings. They also suffered from lack of things to do, and were attracted to the sights of the city center or waited around for something to happen. A similar need for activity and stimulus was felt by children in the outlying residential districts of Cracow and Warsaw. But the situation was reversed in the Polish inner city neighborhoods. These children were not bored: they were quite aware of their luck in being near to city excitements. Their environment is more dangerous and challenging, and they have learned to cope with traffic and potential violence. But they missed the outdoor space where they could play.

In all these settlements, there is little for the children to be responsible for, no places they control or manage. The landscape is divided into ownerships (public or private), and the children are not the owners—even though the wastelands, the vacant lots, and yards may not be actively used by anyone else. In Melbourne, the children were finally driven off the mini-bike track, the one bit of ground in all that area that they had changed to suit their own purposes. Only in the Polish village do the children have some sense of ownership and control over space. Because they commonly share in the management of farms and yards, they are the most connected to community and place. Nevertheless, where unused and uncontrolled wastelands lay close to the settlement—the deforested hill above La Rosas, for example, or the polluted Maribyrnong valley in Melbourne, or the woods of Bystra—they were important places for free play and dreams.

The way the children saw their community also varied. Asked to "draw a map of the area they live in," the Salta children all sketched the same place: an area of similar houses, sharply bounded, with an entrance and a little central square. Every year the community organizes a ten-day Christmas pageant which draws visitors from all over Salta. This is one of the most memorable events in the lives of the children, and they repeatedly mentioned taking part in the tableaux. The small standard houses have decorated facades, elaborate front walls, and patterned pavements. So Las Rosas looks like a hopeful and active community, however poor its means. The children talked about neighborhood friends [and] emphasized the villa's trees (there are not really too many), its square, and its paved streets

The plaza of Toluca is an important reference point in the children's image of the city.

(of which there are few). They said they prefer their own area to others in the city.

The drawings of the young Polish villagers were equally consistent: a main road paralleled a stream; the institutions and activities of the village were located along the main spine; woods and hills defined the village. The maps were crowded with outdoor activities and vividly drawn houses of friends. They gave the strong impression of a well-known and well-used territory.

Maps of the two new Polish suburban housing projects in Zatrasie and Kozlowka, on the other hand, were neither coherent nor clear, despite the modern architecture and planned siting. These images were dominated by confused numbers of large apartment blocks, drawn without detail. The maps focused on the places where the children go—the outdoor play spaces between the apartment blocks—and passed over the adult locations.

The Polish central city children produced much more systematic and accurate maps, based on rather elaborate street networks and full of shops, institutions, places of entertainment, and historical buildings. These children have a place of their own, but it lies at the edge of an active city. They constantly discover new places in medieval Cracow, or modern Warsaw.

Colonia Universidad in Toluca is almost solidly residential—a regular, rectangular grid bounded by arterial streets and a huge athletic field. The boundary walls and unbroken facades of the buildings draw a sharp

*Two views of Colonia San Augustin in
Ecatepec on the outskirts of Mexico City: barren, but changing. The empty lots and the
paved streets are the province of the children.*

line between the private and public worlds. The children's maps were accurate street maps with few pictures. They showed the church, the school, and scattered shops in a relatively featureless setting. There was a sense of a corridor world, where doors were all-important.

In Colonia San Augustin, the houses are in different stages of development—typical of many squatter settlements. The older ones have outside plaster work and painting, some even have private gardens and gates. Further out, houses are nothing more than shacks, streets are unpaved, and the open spaces are littered with trash. The colonia is surrounded by dusty, open fields, without vegetation of any kind. The maps of San Augustin showed an interesting difference. One group (mostly boys) drew the environment as a simple diagram of streets and blocks. The other group (mostly girls) drew pictures of shops, parks, and green areas, full of details, and embellished with textures, ornaments, and splashes of color. These drawings had a romantic, almost escapist, quality—accomplished by putting in color, or trees where none existed, or sloping roofs where all were flat.

The Melbourne home region has no definite boundaries, no center in the physical sense. The children's maps varied widely, from the surroundings of a single house to an extended region. Even though every map was basically a street map, the children had difficulty in integrating the rectangular, but frequently interrupted, layout. The main activities were shown: schools, a park, a soccer pitch, some shopping centers. Everyone showed his own house on his map; most showed the houses of their

This patch of dirt is colored green in maps drawn by the children.

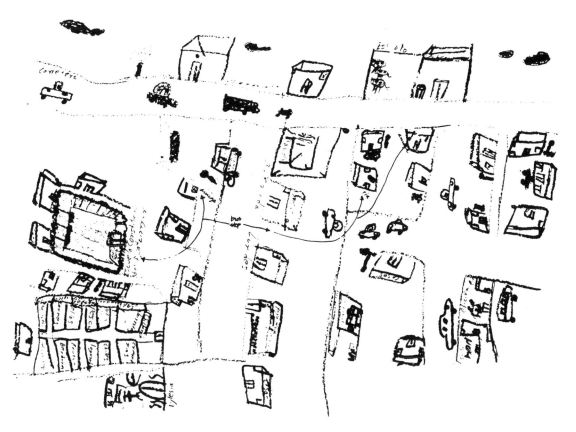

A child of San Augustin describes this world. Cars on every street, the houses have sloping roofs, and what is important are their doors and what goes on inside them. The school (middle left) is shown in particular detail, and all the shops are enumerated.

friends. But the playgrounds were featureless and the asphalted streets were bare, without trees. Formal rules prevent the children from digging, building, or bike riding on this public land. While the Australians are the most mobile—judging from the numbers of cars, bikes, motor bikes, boats, and horses shown in the photographs of their streets—they seem to be more restricted in the people they meet, their activities and places. They are less familiar with the city center and less at ease in parts unlike their own.

The important barriers to movement do not seem to be distance. Instead, they are personal fear, a lack of spatial knowledge, the cost of public transport, social barriers, or, in the case of the girls, parental controls. The boys are free to roam, at least in theory. Some of the Melbourne boys do so, but mostly within the western working class suburbs. The Tolucans and Saltese, who are within walking range, visit the city center or the large parks but rarely do more, despite their expressed freedom to do

Three maps of their neighborhood, the Barrio Las Rosas in Salta, Argentina, by 11–13-year-old children. Although each map has a quite different shape (indeed the top left one has a notation on the back: "has great difficulty in reading plans"), they show the same familiar, closed neighborhood, with the same major features: the bounding canal with its bridge (puente), the little church at the entrance (capilla or iglesia), the main street leading past the plaza (also simply p) and the school (escuela or just e), up to the grotto (gruta) on the flank of the surrounding hills (cerro, or a crenellated form). The great prison (carcel) is on the left, looking over their neighborhood. The cross marks their own house.

so. The children of Zatrasie and Kozlowka have quite good public transport to the center, but complain of being cut off. The Colonia San Augustin is truly isolated, save for one bus line to the center—a long, crowded, and relatively expensive ride. Opening the city up to these children—by transport, encouragement, or example—might be one way of educating them, of strengthening their independence, and answering their need for stimulus.

When asked where they like best to be, the children of Melbourne (and, to a lesser extent, [those] of Salta and Toluca) mention their own rooms, their own homes, or the homes of friends. These were the settings where dwelling space was most adequate, and the children had some control over their own private space. In addition, the children of Salta talked about the neighborhood square, the local street corners, and the hills. The Polish village children also talked about the streets, parks, and woods; while the children of Toluca emphasized the playgrounds rather than the streets, which they see as patently dangerous.

Several Australian and Polish children said their home was the place they least liked to be. In this connection, most children also mentioned the school, or where they are under control, or where there are no friends. In sharp contrast, the San Augustin children consistently named their school as a favorite place. For them the school is a welcome relief in an oppressive world.

When the children were asked to describe the ideal place to live in, most of their utopias had some consistent themes: trees, friends, quiet, lack of traffic, small size, cleanliness. The Saltese, Tolucans, and Bystrans most often pictured a village or residential area much like their own; the urban Polish children often described a center city, but those in housing projects at city outskirts always preferred another situation. The Melbournites talked of Europe, or of cities and seasides far away. The San Augustin children spoke of living somewhere on the ocean, or in southern California.

Beautiful places for the Australians meant all the gardens, parks, and trees somewhere else. Ugliness was a mixture of their own factories, "old" houses, impersonal public buildings, pollution, and rubbish. For many children of San Augustin there were no beautiful places in their colonia, although a few mentioned one small garden in front of the market. The Tolucan children, on the other hand, named a great number of beautiful places. The Argentines also named long lists of places they thought beautiful, consisting mostly of squares, monuments, and parks. They mainly defined beauty as cleanliness and modernity. When the Polish village children drew pictures of the worst environment they could imagine, they showed shabby, traditional rural houses, heaps of litter, broken equipment, unsanitary conditions, and places selling alcohol. Most of the Salta children said there were no ugly places, but a few put the neighboring prison in this class, or certain poor city streets outside their community.

Some of the children welcomed the changes of the past and looked forward to the future; others were ambivalent about past changes and unsure about what is to come. The villagers of Bystra have experienced rapid modernization and are eager for more. Most Tolucan children were pleased about the new schools and playgrounds, paved streets, sidewalks, telephone lines, street lights, water, and drainage. The San Augustin children also welcomed changes: there is less dust now, houses that used to be shanties are fully constructed, they do not have to go outside the colonia for certain services. They tended to think of the whole colonia and its people. They wanted more parks and playgrounds, more and better schools, and better basic necessities: drinking water, clinics, housing, and transportation. Their suggestions reflected a genuine concern for their families, as well as their own future. The Australians have seen many changes, too, but were less certain about their value. They have seen new ethnic groups coming in, more apartments, more noise, pollution, crowding, and traffic, and were quite divided as to whether that future will be better or worse. But it is the children from Polish Zatrasie and Kozlowka who have experienced the greatest amount of change. Like the Australians, they were not at all sure how well they like it. In any event, all these children believed they had little power to affect what happens.

It is clear that the area around home played a significant role in the children's lives. These children are in close contact with the physical environment; they depend on it for psychological stimulation. Since their action at home is restricted, they rely on the larger public setting for independent activity, for places to play, for opportunities to use space and enjoy new experiences. The public environment rarely responds to those demands. There is very little space that the children can control or change. Many parts of the landscape are dangerous, or inaccessible. The children lack an opportunity to participate in adult activity, or to be responsible for shaping and managing the environment.

A Walk Around the Block (1959)

with Malcolm Rivkin What does the ordinary individual perceive in his landscape? What makes the strongest impression on him and how does he react to it? In recent research at the Massachusetts Institute of Technology we have recorded the impressions of persons as they walked through the city streets. Other studies of urban perception have been made, but we believe this to be the first where responses have been recorded while actually moving through the city itself.

In this sample there were interesting agreements about what parts of the scene were most remarkable, and how these parts could be fitted together to make a whole. Spatial form seemed to be a fundamental impression. Spatially dominant buildings, of dominant use or association, also appear in the front rank. Of next importance was the quality of the city "floor," or pavement, and the contents and details of the various storefronts.

The Search for Order In the Environment

Most of these people felt strongly about their visual world, even if they found difficulty in being articulate about it. Emotions were associated with the spatial characteristics, in particular, and with the apparent coherence (or lack of it) in the whole scene. They seemed to search for, or try to create, a sense of order and continuity in what they saw. The look of the world about them did indeed make a difference in their lives.

The trip began at the corner of Berkeley and Boylston Streets in Boston, and each time the interviewer told his companion: "We are about to take a short walk. Don't look for anything in particular, but tell me about the things you see, hear, or smell; everything and anything you notice." A tiny microphone was attached to the subject's lapel, and the interviewer recorded his comments as they went around the block, through the alley, and into the park. (See figure 1.)

The block itself is not an extraordinary one. It has many typical features of an American shopping street, but with some touches of Boston tradition, and much physical contrast in small compass. Boylston Street, on one side, has a wide range of offices and middle-income specialty stores, while Newbury Street, on the opposite side, caters to a wealthier class, with its elegant dress shops, decorators, beauticians, and haberdashers. These shops occupy the ground floors of old, narrow-fronted business buildings, which vary markedly in height. Traffic on both streets is one-way, and that on Boylston is quite heavy.

Reprinted, with permission, from *Landscape* 8, no. 3, pp. 24–34.

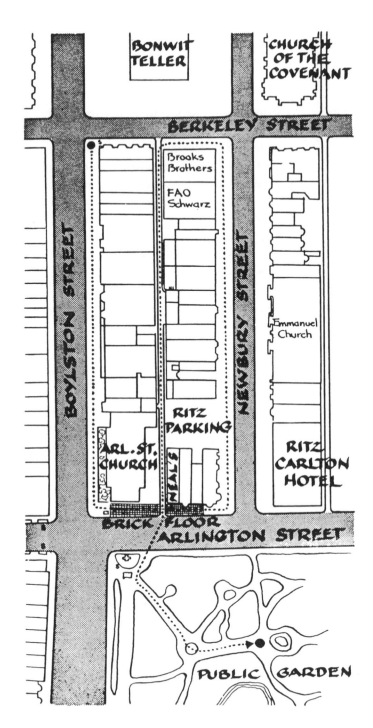

Figure 1 *The block itself. The dotted line shows the course of the walk, starting at the corner of Boylston and Berkeley Streets.*

Between the streets is a narrow alley, neither meaner nor dirtier than most. At the eastern end, across Arlington Street, lie the Public Gardens, planted in the romantic style. At the corner of Arlington and Boylston stands the old brownstone Arlington Street Church, completed in 1861, and one of the first buildings to occupy the newly filled Back Bay lands. At the western end of our block facing Berkeley Street is Bonwit Teller's, occupying the building built in 1864 for the Museum of Natural History. During the interviews the weather was cold, sometimes sunny. The trees were bare, and there were a few patches of old snow on the ground.

Twenty-seven subjects made this tour, which was an outgrowth of earlier tests along Copley Square, in Boston, and Brattle Street, in Cambridge. After the walk, the subjects were tested for their memories of the event, both verbally and through photographic recognition. Some of the subjects were very familiar with the area, and for others it was their first visit. They varied in age, sex, occupation, and national blackground, but the group was too small to be truly representative of American city-dwellers.

Since the process of perception is so rapid and complex, often so difficult to verbalize, the findings must be regarded only as the perceptions which were "at the top of the heap" in the whole conscious-unconscious sensing of the environment. Furthermore, a recorded tour in itself is sufficiently abnormal to intensify, and possibly distort, the usual day-by-day perception of the city.

Yet with all these qualifications, the results are a first clue as to how our cities affect us. Even aside from its value as a research tool, the method used has potential value in the training of designers, and as a device to make the layman more directly aware of the environment in which he lives.

The Walk Itself

The walk proceeded first along the wide Boylston Street sidewalk. Two-thirds remarked almost immediately on the spatial quality of the street—its breadth, the width of the sidewalk, the height of the flanking buildings, and the open vista at the Garden end.

I like the openness, I like the width of the sidewalks, I like the feeling of uncrowded space. You can never feel at the bottom of a well on this spot.

One or two referred to the heights of the buildings along the street, with the remark that they were not so high as to be uncomfortable. This same sense of scale is implied in the word "house," which several people used, even though few of these business buildings could have been residences in the past. Some subjects were conscious of the general architectural disunity:

Each individual building is almost ugly, and they don't seem to fit together at all.

A woman recalled after the walk:

There were all different styles of houses, they didn't seem to match, especially the heights of the houses varied so much, with some houses you could see the sides and you could see that they were not really meant to be exposed.

One walker summed it up briefly:

I think it is the hodge-podgeness of our streets, like down ahead of us, that is so sort of discouraging.

The majority of our walkers commented at one time or another on some sign they saw. However, there was little consensus of recognition of any particular one. Out of the vast number of signs strewn along the path, only a small minority were noticed at all, and some subjects referred to this welter of communication with irritation:

The first thing I notice are the signs along the street, a confusion of signs.

They sort of reach out and grab you by the throat.

A large clock on a standard in the center of the wide sidewalk excited the comment of a third of the subjects, as did a sidewalk book stall, both because of their intrinsic interest as well as their position in space. But a mid-sidewalk sign farther down the street was blissfully ignored. Alongside the Arlington Street Church a number of newly painted trash cans caught everyone's eye, no doubt because of their bright yellow and black colors, contrasting with the gray of the sidewalk and the brown of the facades.

All but one of the walkers commented at one time or another upon the stores themselves, and the contents of their windows. Window-shopping is undoubtedly a pleasant and absorbing occupation for many of them. Like the signs, the consensus of selection seemed weak, but the interest was real, and not marked by irritation.

At least half spoke of the parked cars along the sidewalk edge, most often in reference to the problem of parking itself. Almost as many remarked upon the moving traffic, although with little emotional connotation at this stage. But up to this point, of the multitude of other details to be seen or discussed, almost all were passed by in silence or with only scattered comment: street furniture, people, colors, smells, sounds, weather.

At the Arlington Street Church the subjects' animation once again matched that with which they first greeted Boylston Street. Only three failed to comment upon this church, which, by its associations, position, material, form, and landscaping, contrasts strongly with the remainder of the block. Their remarks conveyed pleasure as well as interest:

Seems to be the most exciting thing on the street, the church.

Every time I look up, I tend to look at our church steeple.

Being of sandstone, it has a much richer character, really, than most stone buildings.

As they approached this corner and remarked upon the church, they were struck even more forcibly by the space of the Public Gardens opening up across the street. Only one walker was so stubborn as not to mention it at all. The comments were precise and emphatic in their pleasure:

Well, the nicest part of this section is definitely the Public Gardens.

And the comments are often well-considered:

I often envy the people who are able to stay . . . [where] they can look out onto the Public Gardens, across the Common. . . . People don't realize what a beautiful thing, not only in the daytime, but at night. . . . Here you get the feeling of spaciousness and at the same time you don't feel lost.

Distant objects could now be appreciated:

Look at that dome on the State House. That certainly shines.

The space of the Public Gardens was one of the strongest experiences of the entire journey. It also called attention to details within itself: one-third of the subjects noticed the statue of Channing which faces the church, and several pointed out the old iron fence which encloses the Garden.

Around the corner on Arlington, the subway entrance, a low masonry box in the middle of the sidewalk, elicited diverse comments. To one women it was:

These ugly subway entrances—low, squat and dirty, black and cold-looking holes in the ground.

But to a little girl it held promise of adventure:

Why don't we go down there, and go out to another town?

Here the sidewalk material changed from patched cement slabs to brick. This drew a surprising amount of attention, mixing pleasure with the uneasiness of high-heeled women:

Brick sidewalks, hazardous, but very pleasant just to have a different texture for a sidewalk.

Over one-half spontaneously recalled the floor material in the post-walk interview:

I recall here the sidewalks seemed to be the major point of interest or the things that struck one most. It was a sidewalk which was in rather poor condition, extended for a great distance before the eye.

The mouth of the alley did not escape attention. Some were struck by its narrowness alone, others by a happy accident of the city—the view that opens up at the far end of the slot:

The spire of the New England Mutual Hall at the end of the alley—certainly dramatic—I've never noticed that before.

Particularly striking at night as you come along, to see the tower lighted as you glance up the alley.

Past the Arlington Church and across the mouth of the alley is one of the few stores in which there was common interest. "Neal's of California," with its gaudy display of women's apparel, stands in sharp feminine contrast to the church on one side and a dignified antique store on the other. Since the stores abut directly on the sidewalk, while the church is well set back, Neal's is also spatially prominent. Half of the observers seem impelled to pick it out.

A woman's shoe store with the whimsical address of "Zero Newbury" leads around the corner and into Newbury Street itself. Only one-third of the subjects referred to the Newbury space in comparison with the two-thirds who spoke up about Boylston Street, but among these there seemed to be a new enjoyment of the total composition:

I think looking down the street here, where the sun hits the buildings two blocks or so down, is a sort of unified loveliness. At least, all are approximately the same height, all built at approximately the same time, all have certain characteristics very definitely in common. . . . And I like the punctuation marks of church steeples here and there.

While another puts the feeling of harmony in a more prosaic way:

There aren't any old signs sticking out.

Three separate buildings draw comments from one-half to two-thirds of the walkers on Newbury: the Ritz-Carlton Hotel on the corner, with its connotations of luxury, its sheer cubical mass standing in contrast to the space of the Gardens; the Church of the Covenant at the Berkeley Street corner, whose tall spire is silhouetted against the sky; and the Emmanuel Church, which is also in architectural contrast to its surroundings, but which gets less mention, due probably to its more subordinate mid-block position. It is interesting to note that this is the only building in the entire walk to sustain any significant comment which is not spatially exposed on at least two sides.

One feature on Newbury Street aroused more comment than any building: the Ritz-Carlton parking lot, which separates the corner stores from those further up the street, and whose cars project forward over the sidewalk itself. The spontaneous remarks expressed annoyance:

An ugly little spot where they've cut out some buildings and provided parking . . . a gaping hole.

This parking lot here has always annoyed me. It separates the shopping. I always hate to walk across the lot from one store to the next.

Newbury Street was impressive particularly for its social connotations and personal associations. The non-familiar subjects immediately picked up its class character:

This seems to be the more fashionable sector. Seems to be more exclusive, since they don't have too much show and pomp in the windows, and no big signs.

The habitués found pleasure and many memories:

Dear old Newbury Street . . . it's just the epitome of the top aristocratic Boston.

I can walk in this area and never get tired of it. When I'm away, this is the only—not really the only place—but the place I think of most.

But some of the comments were uncomfortable:

In an area like this, I've always felt sort of like a stranger . . . sort of like this wasn't particularly your street . . . where the stores sell expensive things not particularly useful to myself.

The small, select stores with their carefully chosen, unpriced displays all came in for comment. But only two, F. A. O. Schwarz and Brooks Bros., caught nearly as much attention as Neal's of California. Schwarz has windows full of attractive toys, and Brooks Bros. is remarkable for its corner position and for its social standing. It might be noted here that throughout the walk only three stores drew the attention of more than half the observers, and all of these had spatial position in which at least two sides of the store were exposed.

At this point another of the strong impressions of the walk appears—the Bonwit Teller store across Berkeley Street, occupying the entire narrow end of the block from Boylston to Newbury. Spatially isolated on three sides, set among trees and grass in a stony environment, it is an obvious period piece of warm red brick and carved stone trim set against the massive smooth backdrop of the New England Mutual building. It is particularly remarkable for its contrast of contemporary commercial use in a building symbolizing institutional values of another time, and for its mannered additions of awnings and show windows. More people chose to comment on this single structure than any other in the total walk, except for the Arlington Street Church.

And I do like Mr. Bonwit. I like it largely because of space, the effect of non-crowding. I know it was an old MIT building at one time [it wasn't]. It's very distinguished, it's done with taste, and mainly it's space, I think, that makes it largely attractive. If the front steps were level with the sidewalk, and there was a new building on each side, it would just be something else, another rather homely spot.

The attention may be captured just as handily, even if the feelings are quite different:

I hate that monstrous awning coming out, it's so affected . . . like a worm coming out of a hole. . . . I've never heard anything so silly as converting a museum into a women's dress store and then showing it from the outside.

Two spontaneous post-walk memories of this building are interesting:

Bonwit's . . . was the dominant thing. It filled your eyes . . . set the mood for the whole place.

I have never realized that it was a museum until the other day [i.e., during the walk], when I looked at it from across the street at Brooks Bros. and noticed that these columns went up the front of it and gave it this museum or post-office-like type of atmosphere. Suddenly I saw the building as a whole though I had passed by it a million times. I had noticed its very obvious distinctive qualities but not the whole building.

Half of the walkers looked up along Berkeley long enough to catch a glimpse of the towering silhouette of the John Hancock building, two blocks away. The majority opinion was unfavorable:

You are suddenly faced with a very ugly mass, the John Hancock, which rises much too high, much too out of shape.

Just as the tour seemed about to end, we turned abruptly down into the alley, which, though not spotless, was reasonably neat by alley standards. In emotional vigor, the comments on this alley and on the Public Gardens stand alone. Three-quarters of the subjects reacted strongly, particularly to the spatial constriction of the alley and to its real or imagined dirt. The tone of voice, the facial expression conveyed the impact as well as the actual words:

Do we have to walk down here? There is no place to walk. Oh, this is awful . . . if they did have a fire people would come down here and land on the garbage, and they'd be killed for sure. . . . I'll bet its stinky in the summer.

Heaven knows what we're going to get into, in the way of rats and trash . . . it's back alleys and they should all be done away with . . . they're horrible eyesores.

Seems like the alley wants to make you look down not up. Seems as the walls are closing in.

As they proceeded down the alley they were preoccupied with the confinement of space, the lack of light, the dirt and water on the ground, the trash barrels which line the way. In this constricted volume their eyes no longer moved freely about but were turned downwards to the floor, or were fixed on the spot of light at the alley's end. Yards, breaks in the side-walls, or lighted windows caused them to turn their heads automatically. Smells were mentioned for the first time, not because the alley was actually very odorous, but because alleys are supposed to smell, and the subjects noticed the lack of them.

Little contrasts caught their attention, such as a small window with shelves of china displayed, or a "poor little weed tree" fighting for life in a storage yard. Their eyes went up to see such things as the tops of fire escapes, outlined against the sky.

But the principal impression, along with the space and the dirt, was the contrast between the backs of the shops lining the alley and the memory of their fashionable facades on Newbury Street. To the strong physical impression was added the dramatic and human one—of the wealthy shoppers in front and the poor workers behind. Almost half of the tourists were moved to speak when they passed the windows of a basement workroom:

Isn't it amazing—you walk down one street with ladies in furs, and you go down the alley . . . tailor shops down there. Miserable place to work. . . . You forget how many people there are working out of sight.

Ah, this is the true life of the city with the false facade!

Yet despite the sense of drama many of them felt, they were glad to get out again:

The one thing that really saves this alley is the fact that you look out and see that very broad space which gives relief to it. Pigeons flying there, and the sun silhouetted by the buildings.

The spatial release at the end of the alley was correspondingly strong. The Ritz-Carlton parking lot, which had been an irritation on Newbury Street, now became a window from the alley prison.

What a relief! This parking lot with the open space. . . . It feels so good coming out of that dark alley!

And when they came to the end of the alley itself, with the space of the Gardens before them, they were full of joy. These moments of relief were vividly remembered later:

When we finally came out into the Ritz parking lot, it was open, open space and the sunshine came in . . . everything looked so sunny and so clean and nice.

Crossing that street into the park was like . . . a sense of freedom, really.

In all of these reactions to space, it is notable how closely interwoven was the perception with the sense of potential movement on the one hand, and the sense of light or sun on the other.

Before reaching the Gardens, however, they had one more trial; they must cross the traffic of Arlington Street. Until this spot their reaction to traffic and parked cars had been mild, primarily sympathetic with the problems of the driver. There had been little consciousness of traffic noise, and some even managed to call a street a "quiet" one, in the midst of sounds of auto horns. But at this crossing they were faced with the problem of fording the traffic stream, and each one betrayed the anxiety and tense care that this required:

Cars keep coming around here. These cars keep coming around and I can't get by. They never stop—yes, here they come! Exactly what I'm talking about; they never stop going down the street!

During the crossing, there was no mention of any other feature of the environment.

It was with a sense of marked relaxation and pleasure that all entered the Public Gardens. The spatial liberation again came in for almost universal comment. For a second time a significant number of comments were made about other people in the scene: the moving, brightly dressed skaters, enjoying the last ice of the season. Half the walkers specifically mentioned the trees.

It seems like a very good idea to have a park in the middle of the city, if only for cars to go around as well as a place for a quiet walk in between the trees. . . . This is a place I'd like to explore more and look at in more detail. . . . The very idea of trees is pleasant, and there haven't been many on surrounding streets, if any at all.

Several people seemed to enjoy being able to see and hear the city from a little distance while in the park. They were particularly taken by the contrast of park and the city which visibly encloses it. Here they enjoyed two worlds simultaneously.

One man voiced his underlying anxiety that this open space may be one day swallowed up:

Tremendous real estate value this area must be ! I wonder if and when Boston will do away with it?

While another looked at it in terms of personal associations:

A park has always been for me a sort of quiet ground from the battle of the city. As you walk along any of the avenues that lead to Central Park, this one also, the battle crowds on, and when you finally get to the park, all of a sudden things are quiet and it's a different world.

The Walk Analyzed

After the trip, in some cases within a few hours and in others in two or three days, the subjects were interviewed again. First they were asked:

Try to put yourself back at the beginning of the walk, and describe to me in detail the sequences of things and events you noticed.

When they had completed this description they were then asked various questions; whether they remembered any particular buildings, features of buildings, people, sounds, smell, traffic signs, or pavements. They were asked how many definite areas they had passed by; if they felt the areas had any order or continuity and why; and whether this part of the city seemed to fit into their pictures of Boston. Some were asked to describe their feelings on the walk, and to say what made the greatest impression on them. All subjects were given a set of photographs of buildings, street views, pavements, details, etc. They were asked to say which objects they had seen on the journey. In general the items noted in the walk interview and in the spontaneous recall of the post-walk interview coincided very well, and a lapse of two or three days versus a lapse of one or two hours made surprisingly little difference in what was mentioned.

The fundamental impressions for almost all our observers came from certain individual buildings and open spaces. Moreover, there is agreement on particular buildings or spaces, and this is consistent between walk and recall. The buildings noticed are remarkable for singularities of style, material, use, or association, but particularly for their spatial quality. Only a few structures received significant mention which were not somehow prominent in space.

We might assert that open space is the most impressive feature of all in the cityscape. We might buttress this assertion by speculation that "building" is an expected element of city description, culturally what one "should" discuss; while space relations are seemingly more esoteric and more difficult to verbalize. Thus their frequency is all the more striking.

The spaces remembered afterwards seemed to be either those which were clearly defined in form, or [those] which made evident breaks in the general continuity. In certain earlier (and less systematic) interviews, for instance, the space of entering cross streets was ignored, except where heavy on-coming traffic forced recognition of the street as a break in continuity. There was a unanimous reaction of dislike to what was described as the "huge and formless" space of a railroad yard.

Somewhat less strong than spaces or structures, but still a dominant impression, was that of the city floor, the sidewalk pavement. Particularly evocative were the material and the state of repair. There was interest in variations of texture or color, but some irritation at rough surfaces, especially from women in high heels, As a footnote, it is surprising to find that 16 out of 27 people commented on the width of the Boylston Street sidewalk in their spontaneous recall. Four described it in their first sentence, four more in the second, and six in the next few sentences.

Next in interest was the impact of storefronts and their window contents. For most of our subjects these were a pleasant and absorbing feature of the stroll. But there was little unanimity as to which particular stores were singled out for comment. Much depended on the particular interests of the observer.

Signs were also important during the walk itself, but we found only one sign which drew common remark. Some sense of this scatter of attention may be gleaned from the fact that 78 different signs were noted by some one of the walkers; yet only six signs received the attention of more than two people, and only three the attention of more than three. Of these latter three signs, two were associated with buildings or stores which had received overwhelming attention for other reasons; the third was the clock in the Boylston Street sidewalk. Ninety-five percent of the people commented on signs while walking, but only 25 percent later recalled them. The subjects seemed highly conscious of the visual clamor, and often irritated by it, but particular signs seemed to make only a scattered and transitory impression.

Succeeding in frequency of mention were the two categories of street detail and people. The former includes such a miscellany of smaller objects as street furniture, fences, fire escapes, waste containers, subway entrances, and statues, and this makes generalization difficult. Specific reasons may usually be attached to the choice of specific items, such as the relation to the Gardens of the Channing statue and the iron fence; the spatial prominence of the book-stall, or the subway entrance; the association with dirt of the alley barrels and the Boylston waste paper container (although the latter was undoubtedly also characterized by its bright color); the spatial constriction of the alley, which forced an upward view and thus the silhouetting of the fire escapes. It is interesting to note that one type of detail which has been the subject of some recent design discussion—the street furniture (parking meters, light poles, etc.)—was only rarely mentioned.

There was somewhat greater unanimity in regard to the people selected for comment, and usually the remark seemed to involve a class or group: the dramatic contrast of the seamstresses in the alley basement; the well-dressed women on Newbury who symbolized the street; the skaters in the Gardens, bright moving objects in a peaceful setting. Some of the subjects indicated that during a more normal walk they would be much more observant of others than they seemed to be in these experiments. It may be that there was something in the test situation which implied that their attention should be upon the inanimate environment, and that the rest was not "the city."

Traffic came in for some comment, with somewhat more focus on the parked cars than on the moving ones, until the street had to be crossed. Up to this point, the emotional reaction was low, except where the parked car protruded onto the sidewalk. Feelings were intense and anxious while crossing, however, and all other perceptions were momentarily shut out. These pedestrians seem to accept, or at least to be hardened to, the car, until it threatens their safety, view, or freedom of movement.

Vegetation also played a role of some significance; not only its presence but its absence was expressed. Comments ran toward wishful replantings of street trees, or sadness at "pathetic" grass islands in the vortex of traffic. In fact, there was not much vegetation to notice, but where it occurred, as in the Public Gardens, there was a universal, and very positive, reaction of pleasure. Curiously enough, as with the signs, the recall of this part of the environment seemed to be quite low, in contrast to its relatively high mention during the walk. Why it should be forgotten so easily is a puzzle.

Few people talked about the weather, although there was perhaps a significant unconscious impression which was not verbalized. Sounds and smells were both equally low in conscious awareness. Some sounds were recalled after direct questioning, but even then smells could not be remembered. In both cases, we are probably dealing with a level of habituation, so that the signal rarely receives attention unless it varies significantly from the normal level. Thus, many of the "mentions" of sound or smell were actually the lack of it, i.e., a "quiet" street or an "odorless" alley.

Several obvious elements drew almost no comment at all: color, for example (which may nevertheless be important in making another object noticeable), or the sky; wall materials and textures, overhead wires, upper floor facades, or doorways.

The recognition of photographs also agreed with the interview results, since people tended to recognize easily photographs of items which were mentioned frequently, and vice versa. Unfortunately, since the photographs did not always cover what later proved to be some of the key visual features of the environment, this particular test was not so useful as it might have been.

The Need for Order

But how were these perceptions fitted together? This was a fundamental point. Take the way in which our particular block was mentally organized. It is interesting to note that interviewees did not hesitate to try to discover whether the area possessed any sense of order for them. Some broke it down into many sub-areas, and others felt it was all one thing. In the "average" case, it was organized somewhat as follows: the three fundamental parts were Boylston Street, Newbury Street, and the Public Gardens. Arlington and Berkeley Streets were considered as parts of one or the other of these. The alley was a puzzle, since it didn't "fit" well; usually it was considered either as a separate area or as something which occupied the "backs" of Boylston and Newbury and thus either sewed them together or belonged ambiguously to one or the other. In some cases it was simply forgotten; in one case [it was] even explicitly ignored as a part that was rarely seen and thus in a sense didn't exist. Here is a typical example from a foreign viewer:

I could make out three distinct, different impressions. There was the semi-gaudiness of Boylston Street and the sounds associated with that. There was the relative quiet, possibly even quaintness of the Gardens. Newbury Street was very distinctly on a different level than Boylston. . . . Then there was the alley, of course. . . . These areas stand off from each other, they don't go together. . . . Let's say, with any one of two impressions, Newbury or Boylston, the alley must be along with it; it's just necessary. So perhaps: the alley and Boylston; the alley and Newbury; and the Gardens.

This same agreement as to the organization of certain parts of the environment, coupled with indecision and disagreement as to other parts, could be detected in earlier exploratory studies. For example, the upper end of a certain street, with its large colonial houses, was easily organized as a distinct entity. This was contrasted to the lower end, a busy shopping district, by all observers. Between these two regions lies another piece of the street which corresponds neither in use nor in physical form to either end. On the other hand, it has no sharp character of its own, being a mixture of apartments, offices, houses, and irregular spaces. The observers found this to be a section that they could not easily attach to either the upper or the lower end, yet they were unwilling to give it a life of its own. Feeling compelled to organize their walk, and unable to leave their organization incomplete or to "forget" this section (as some were able to do with the Boylston alley), they responded by attaching it, half-heartedly, to one or the other of the strong "ends." The result was agreement on two classes into which the walk fell, separated by a weak, oscillating boundary.

Thus we have organizational consensus at one point, due to suggestions inherent in the physical form itself, coupled with disagreement in regard to the rest, where the unit into which a part is put depends primarily on past experience. Where this organizational indecision was strongest we found hints of feelings, not only of puzzlement, but of discomfort.

There was apparently a drive to organize the environmental impressions into meaningful patterns, which could be handled with economy. Since the city environment is complex and fluid, this is a difficult operation. Since the present environment so often does not suggest links by its physical shape, the process becomes all the more difficult. Yet it persists, and the resulting mental organization, while apparently quite loose, ambiguous, and even contradictory at points, is nevertheless clung to firmly. Certain elements seem particularly important in furnishing distinctions for area classifications in the city, such as people and activity; land use; and general physical form, spatial form in particular.

Native and newcomer agree surprisingly well as to *what* is worth their notice, but significant differences appear between them in the way they organize these things (see figures 2 and 3). The more familiar observer tends to establish more connections, and not to break his environment down into as many isolated parts. Thus a stranger might divide the walk into six parts: the four sides of the block, the alley, and the Gardens. For an old hand, however:

Brooks Bros. rounds the corner and Charles Antell rounds the other corner, and the Arlington Street Church rounds the third corner, and well, the fourth corner is a little bit broken up; there's two places there, but you sort of get this feeling like you never come to the end of the street and then make a sharp corner, you just sort of make a round corner there. This whole block therefore seems to be a very complete continuous compact tightly set-in block, and the stores such as Bonwit's, Peck and Peck, Schraffts, and so forth, which are on the outer periphery of this square belong to the square, definitely.

Not only is the block considered as one, but the facades facing the block are also drawn into the unit. Even the rectangular shape with its sharp corners cannot be allowed, and the form is distorted towards the seamless circle. (Compare the previous quotation from a stranger: "these areas stand off from each other, they don't go together.") Note also in this quotation that the corner of Boylston and Berkeley is resistant to the neat organization, which puts a key use to mark each corner from both directions; but that the resistant material is forced into place anyhow.

No, this is definitely all a piece of one material as far as I am concerned. There is a distinction between Boylston and Newbury. . . . But the whole area has always been very much one grouping, one place.

It is also true that these were the people who were less able to distinguish this block from its context in the larger Back Bay district. The streets are not boundaries for them. For the unfamiliar, however, this block seems to have no particular relation to the rest of the city.

These findings might be generalized in the following hypothesis: the individual must perceive his environment as an ordered pattern, and is constantly trying to inject order into his surroundings, so that all the relevant perceptions are jointed one to the other. Certain physical complexes facilitate this process through their own form, and are seen as ordered wholes by native and newcomer alike. Subsequent use and association simply strengthen this structure. Other complexes, however, do not encourage this fitting together, and they are seen as fundamentally disordered by the newcomer. For the native, this "disordered" complex may also seem to be an organized one, since habitual use and perception

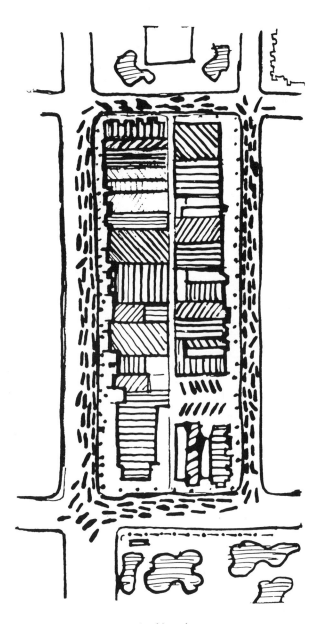

Figure 2 *The stranger organizes his environment: He sees no overall uniformity in the buildings or the types of business; signs and street furniture break the block up into small confused areas, heavy traffic isolates him from the other side of streets.*

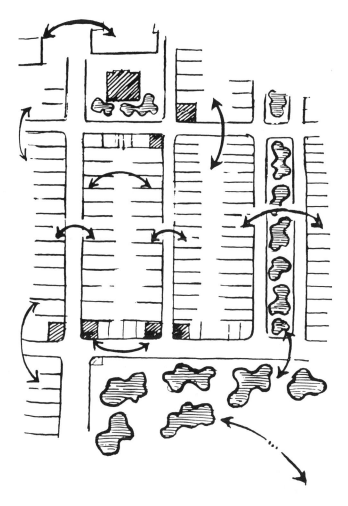

Figure 3   *The native organizes his environment: Familiarity with the area enables him to see similarities (often imaginary) between streets, blocks, buildings, and open spaces.*

have allowed him to put the collection together by means of associated meanings, or by selection, simplification, distortion, or even suppression of his perceptions. This progressive imputation of order is often alluded to, implicitly or explicitly:

I don't feel any sense of real order and yet I didn't feel that everything was jumbled and I suppose that is because I am familiar with the area. To me it didn't seem confused, it seemed right.

I've always liked this section, ever since I first became familiar with it about fourteen years ago. Although it has undergone some change, I feel the change has been a progressive one toward blending and uniformity of buildings rather than of strange contrasts and conflicts of colors, sizes and shapes.

Boylston Street.

Thus this sense of order can finally be achieved by familiarity despite physical chaos. Yet there is evidence that this organization is achieved only by real effort and by distortion of the pattern of reality, and that even after it is accomplished it is attended by emotions of insecurity where the required organization is particularly ruthless. Certainly it lacks the conviction and depth of a relationship which is backed up by physical pattern.

An "old hand" may recognize a shopping district as an organized entity where strangers say it is chaotic. Intensive use and association have satisfactorily overcome physical confusion, even if the satisfaction would be deeper were the spatial form more continuous. At least the physical continuities of land use and activity are there to back up the mental category.

But, even for the native, there is no satisfaction in the "fringe" of that shopping district. He can tell that it is more commercial than residential, and thus ought to go with the shopping, and he can hold it there in his mind when it is necessary for practical purposes, but the reality keeps wandering off, keeps contradicting him. It is like a restless animal which one must constantly correct. For the newcomer, moreover, the fringe makes no particular sense at all, and he is likely to recognize the fact, with some discomfort.

Some newcomers may ask for a very sweeping and rigid kind of physical organization:

I had no idea that the town would be built up as it is, just on cow paths and up little hills. . . . I just supposed that the city would be beautiful, quite modern, that the

Arlington Street.

Newbury Street.

stores would be in order, the dress shops together and the bridal shop with it and not off in a corner all by itself; the antiques would be together and the big business areas would be business areas.

Very possibly this observer might change her mind about such a "neat" city were she to live in it long, but the wish is indicative of the troubles she is facing. The native may be able to handle, and indeed find more pleasure in, a more intricate and complexly organized environment, but organized it must be, whether by city dwellers or by the sweat of his own brow.

Our study suggests one further remark. The method used may not only be useful for research purposes, but may be an educational tool as well. Such a recorded walk in itself tends to heighten the perception of the city. When combined with a discussion in the field of general interview results, along with the critique of the surrounding forms, it might prove to be an excellent way of awakening the citizen's interest in the form of his city, sharpening his critical abilities, and heightening his ultimate pleasure in a well-shaped environment.

The Urban Landscape of San Salvador: Environmental Quality in an Urbanizing Region (1968)

Environmental quality may appear secondary among the pressing issues of urbanization in a developing country. I will maintain the contrary by showing how environmental form and social function are repeatedly linked together. The resulting policy suggestions will therefore repeatedly mix visual and physical with social and functional recommendations.

The crucial question is how the landscape supports the activities, perceptions, and values of its daily users, and not how it appears to the casual observer. This report is suspect, as it is based on how things appear to an outsider after a brief visit, supplemented by a few conversations and some observations of behavior in the streets. This lack of information will often be referred to.

Environmental fitness and satisfying visual form relate to culture and customs of use. Designers in San Salvador are too often the uncritical copyists of European and United States forms, which arose in another context (and are often ugly or inappropriate in that context). The pages to follow will often comment on the values of those traditional or "spontaneous" forms which are most likely to be despised as "backward" and "lower class."

Most of my comments will be linked to two themes: 1. the relation of esthetics to social development, and 2. ways of providing for future demands while meeting urgent current necessities. The comments are grouped under three major headings: landscape use and conservation; the development of roads and roadsides; and the general process of management for environmental quality.

The Use of the Land

The natural landscape of San Salvador is the single most powerful visual impression that a visitor receives. It seems also (although this can only be my supposition) that it is the basis for the Salvadorean's sense of place. His attachment seems to apply more to natural features than to man-made ones; certainly the outstanding natural features are used for relaxation and enjoyment. To conserve this vivid and powerful landscape is an obvious way of increasing the present and future satisfactions of all classes of the people. To prospective tourists it is a strong attraction; for the citizens of El Salvador it is an even more important heritage.

The present urbanized area lies within a single visual unit, closed on the north by the range of small hills running out from the towering volcano. The city in this long hollow is surrounded by green ridges. Everywhere, one is conscious of the city in the land. The main highway, after distant views, plunges through the center. To the east is the wild surprise of Ilopango Lake deep in an ancient crater. The city is low and white—the surroundings (at least in the rainy season) are intensely green. The play of clouds overhead is magnificent and vast.

Urban growth is rapidly altering this visible landscape. Conserving it for present and future enjoyment seems to conflict with urgent requirements for housing, employment, and transportation. But to freeze extensive areas is simply impossible. Public policy must not withhold land, but open it up, insuring the future in some places by discouraging long commitments, or protecting sensitive terrain by developing it in harmless ways.

I would recommend some public agency for land settlement (*not* for land preservation), to open land for use as fast as it is needed, by providing access and utilities, and by purchasing and redistributing the land itself, wherever necessary to prevent speculation or lag. This agency would also be concerned with proper development, and with the conservation of key areas for future use.

To take a most pressing example, the tugurios, which seem to threaten the good order of the city, are in fact hopeful solutions to massive problems of low-cost housing and social mobility. Their difficulties lie in acquiring title to land, in poor layout, in crowding and lack of sanitation. Yet even in visual terms, there is a variety and [an] intimate scale, a sense of life and purpose, that is lacking in many other areas of the city. Compare them, for example, with the shabby neglect of the new IVU walk-ups. Public agencies should be concerned, not so much with regulating or suppressing these self-help developments, but with encouraging them, providing land title, access, water, power, bus service, schools, and social facilities. Environmental quality might be improved by supplying free surveying layout, or technical aid on design and construction, as well as construction materials, earth-moving machinery, free plants, or colored wall paint. The attitudes which encouraged the opening up of national agricultural regions might here be applied to the urban frontier. Environmental quality will be attained by positive aids which attract cooperation, rather than by punitive regulation which attracts illegal invention.

The land settlement agency would encourage less intensive uses, such as agriculture and recreation, where it was desirable to keep the land uncommitted, or to prevent its physical destruction. The need for food production is evident, that for recreation may seem less so. Yet Los Planes and Los Chorros are already overrun on weekends, and it may be expected that the great mass of the population, now with little margin of time or money, will in the near future, require extensive areas for cheap and accessible outdoor recreation.

Open uses may be induced or retained by many means: establishing national parks which guarantee life tenure to expropriated owners; public purchase and lease-back to new or previous owners for preferred uses; tax policies which progressively discourage conversions as time passes; the purchase of development rights; covenants between owners with a present interest in conservation. The policies to avoid are those that seek to prevent any increase in the intensity of use or, worse, to hold land without any use whatever.

Particular Terrain

In this light, there are some particular areas and points which will require special guidance:

1. The two natural water bodies: the Lago Ilopango and the Laguna Chanmico. Both are obvious targets for explosive recreational demand in the near future. The Lago already boasts one small and ill-kept beach, but most of its shores are still inaccessible. Ilopango is an astonishing national resource. Lying in a crater, with a small drainage area and a minor outlet, it is vulnerable to irreversible pollution. Any further unplanned development on the lake, its shores, or its drainage basin should be prevented, whether by creation of a national park or by the purchase of development rights. Until this is done, no further access should be built, nor utilities be extended. Once done, the lake can be developed, by public or private enterprise, as a major regional recreation area and tourist attraction. With caution, this can be done without causing water pollution or destroying the visual setting: the deep wild crater, the sparkling lake and bold islands at the very edge of the metropolitan region. Structures must be kept back from the shore, off the crater walls, and away from its visible rim. One misplaced "luxury hotel" will destroy the very scene which attracts the visitor. Given such caution, the lake can be used for intensive swimming and boating, provided some large arc of shore is left wild and inaccessible except by water. None of the shore should be held in any exclusive private use—it will in the future be in too short a supply. The lands back from the shore, and below the crater walls, can be used for sports and picnic grounds, for gardens, vacation cottages, and low hotels, all under the cover of the trees.

2. The furrowed upper slopes of the Volcan San Salvador dominate the land. The steep terrain would be expensive to develop and maintain. Any structures will only demean this striking form. In addition, this is the principal catchment area for the metropolitan water supply. There is a strong case for maintaining these slopes in agricultural use, preferably ones which do not encourage erosion. No excavations, quarries, scars, signs, or intrusive structures should be allowed there. The visible surface of this landmark should not be disturbed.

Future pressures for recreational use will develop: for a funicular, for panoramic viewing points on the peak and the crater, for a large tourist hotel. All these are legitimate uses, just as they are at Ilopango. Viewing platforms will do little harm, [and] a funicular with its moving cars may even sharpen the sense of dominating height. But a large building on the crest, or the visible forward slopes, will destroy the scale. It is quite possible to arrange a view for hotel guests without destroying the view of the future metropolis. A tall building may be sited between peak and crater, for example, looking out both south and north, or a well-planted terraced and slope-fitting structure may be used instead of a tower or slab. Approach roads must also be sited carefully, to prevent the scarring of the slopes.

3. On the other hand, the remaining slopes which surround the city as in a green bowl need not be so carefully controlled, nor could they be. As long as road access and water supply can economically be achieved, the surrounding slopes are attractive areas for residence, with magnificent views and a pleasant climate. Even for the man below, the buildings which rise up the slope, since they are not altering an important symbolic form like the Volcano, in fact heighten the visual unity of the city and express its relation to its site. There may be important technical reasons to discourage building on the slopes—cost, water pressure, erosion, or street gradients—but it is hard to find visual ones. The technical problems have technical solutions, although they are costly. Public policy should see that such costs do not fall on the general public.

It would be advantageous to keep buildings off the skyline itself, or at least to reserve it for special structures or important public symbols. I am not convinced that skyline control is feasible, and it may be better to rely on avoiding the building of skyline roads, or on encouraging preferred recreational uses there, particularly on such strategic peaks as San Jacinto, Cerro Nejapa, or Guaycume. Put principal emphasis on assuring that development of the slopes is orderly, that water and roads can be provided, and that deep cuts and quarrying, such as have scarred the San Jacinto slopes, are avoided. Even the extensive terracing for residential use, although it must be guided to prevent erosion, is in itself an interesting way of expressing the slope of the land.

4. In one case, however, the hills and their tops are particularly important. These are the range running out from the volcano behind Mejicanos, a set of five or six hills, including Carmen, Eremito, Colis, Milingo, and others unnamed, which I shall here call "the middle hills." This is a feature which occupies a strategic location in the region, dividing the buildable land into two distinct visual units, and overlooking both of them. At their eastern end lie the gorges of the Tamayate and the Acelhuate. While the slopes surrounding the metropolitan basin are elsewhere too big to be smothered, these hills can rather easily be obscured by urban growth. The present clear form of the metropolis will then disappear. Moreover,

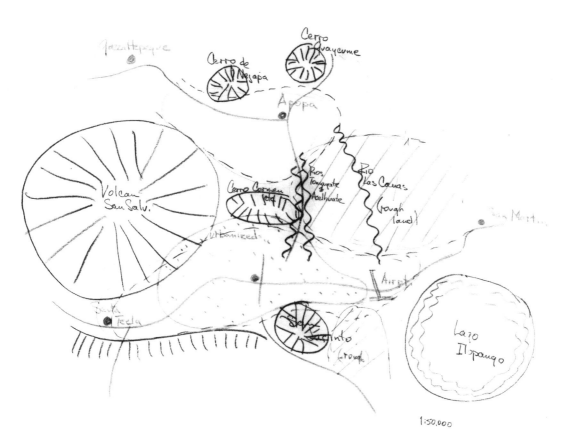

Visual structure of the region.

these hills present an opportunity to provide recreational space immediately accessible to what will be the center of the metropolitan population.

At the same time, they lie directly in the path of urbanization, and
settlement has already begun on their southern slopes. To hold most of
this land out of development is an unlikely mission, given its future central
position and good access. A preferable strategy would acquire a patchwork of public lands, inclusive of all the hill tops, the occasional level
bottoms, and the more dramatic "passes" between the hills, which overlook the basin below. These lands would be developed for intensive
regional recreation, a set of "people's parks" equipped to handle large
numbers in picnic and sports grounds, swimming or spray pools, places
for eating and drinking, dancing, music, movies, paseos, festivals, and
all kinds of popular entertainment. They should be interconnected, and
made accessible to the arterial roads that will pass through these hills—
easy to reach on foot, by bus, by bicycle or motorbike. Many of the facilities
could be run as private concessions. If the heights were kept open and a
regional concentration of recreation achieved, it would not be necessary to

defend the slopes of the entire range against the urban tide. A more detailed study of the necessary takings, and of the best organization of roads and activity in this vulnerable area, is therefore a high priority.

5. Another feature of the San Salvador landscape should receive particular attention: the deep rios and quebradas, which dissect the land in many places, most dramatically in the gorge of the Rio Cañas, or of the Acelhuate and Tamayate at the eastern end of the middle hills. At present the quebradas are an obstacle to development, an expense to bridge, but also serve as an open sewer system and a trench for trash. They are a resource for the future, since they provide an extensive and picturesque linear network. Their present use as trunk sewers at least keeps this polluted water well below the level of urbanized land. They act as storm drains with excess capacity for the torrential downpours. They will be invaluable as routes for future roads and main utilities, since they happen to run generally north-south or east-west. When their waters run clean again, they will provide a welcome green network throughout the region, to be used for recreational pathways, for chains of pools, for eating and resting places on the middle slopes, looking up and down the gorges. In the meantime, let them run as sewers, keep them open, provide for squatter settlements in healthier and more accessible locations, do not scar them unnecessarily with roads which cross in cut. Do not build in them and do not fill them, whether with earth or trash, since foundations will always be treacherous, and the blocked drainage a constant threat.

6. Within the middle hills, to the east of the Acelhuate, and in many other pockets in the region, the land is deeply dissected, a jumble of intersecting ridges. Visually, particularly with its patches of crops, this land is most interesting and delightful. Practically, it is very expensive to develop. Thus it is avoided by those who can afford to choose their place of residence, and left to the tugurios. The allocation of land is irrationally reversed. The gently sloping land, cheapest to develop and to supply with water and sewer, easiest of access on foot, is best suited to low-cost housing. It is reserved for the middle and upper classes, who cover it with their dull and exposed subdivisions. The rough land, most difficult to service and reach, but also the most promising of amenity given the necessary funds, is used by those without such funds, most vulnerable to the lack of service, and probably the least interested in the potential amenities.

Sufficient level land must be opened up to low income residents to relieve them from resorting to such difficult terrain. In the future, we may see a reversal of social conscience and power, but also of landscape taste, which will cause a corresponding reversal in the allocation of land.

7. Two other kinds of regional landscape deserve mention. In the eyes of a North American visitor, much of the land is wooded and therefore "wild." In fact, very little land is untended—these woods shade the valuable coffee plantations. If the coffee lands give way to urban use, it will

be possible to preserve this quality by building under the overstory of shade trees—thinning them, not clearing them. Given shade, the local climate is a very pleasant one. Although these shade trees are short-lived, they can carry over until more permanent ornamental trees are grown.

On the northwest of the volcano is a great frozen river of lava, dark, broken, turbulent and yet motionless. How best to use it is unclear. Undoubtedly it is a tourist attraction. Very likely it is under no present pressure for use, unless of quarrying, since it would be expensive and unpleasant to build upon. Should any such pressure arise, however, that lava stream deserves careful thought before it is committed.

The Visual Consequences of the Growth Alternatives

These considerations on the use and visual form of the regional landscape can lead to a specialized evaluation of the proposed metropolitan growth alternatives:

1. Considered solely from its effects on visual form and landscape amenity, a metropolis which grew into a linear concentration from Santa Teac to San Martin might be the preferable pattern. It would fit the visual unit of terrain, keep a clear northern boundary, and be surrounded everywhere by the recreational potential of open land and varied landscape. Its major roads, running generally east-west, could be given a strong relation to the city, and experience all the principal elements of the landscape in succession. The major disadvantage would be the additional pressure put on the development of Ilopango.

2. The alternative of concentration by growth to the north breaks the visual unit by spilling over the middle hills, which would be difficult to hold open, or to service without scarring. A formless fringe area will develop north of them. The pattern of present trends has the same effect.

3. If a new urban node [is] to be built to the north, between Apopa and Nejapa, the visual unit will also be broken, but in this case the visual division will be congruent with a functional division, and the northern area will have form and a visible center. The new center can be given an interesting relation to the Cerro Nejapa, and dramatic highways can be located around the northern and western rims of the visual unit. Like the previous alternative, however, this pattern also puts pressure on the middle hills, and it is questionable if the division into two urban areas can in fact be maintained. Despite this, the pattern may be the next most desirable one, looked at solely from this visual viewpoint.

4. The alternative of dispersion retains the unity of San Salvador proper, while developing a series of distinctive communities, each based on the form and traditions of an existing settlement. It seems extremely unlikely, however, that enough control can be exerted to maintain those

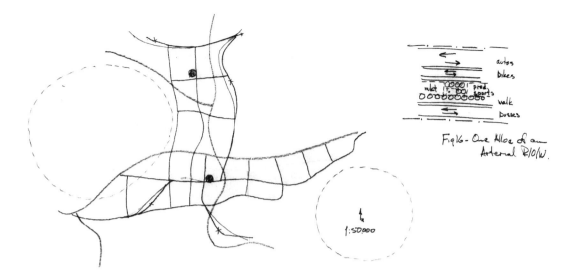

Fig 16 - One Alloe of an Arterial R/O/W.

Major road network.

identities. Local interests and national pressures will surely ride over and submerge the small existing centers, with their fragile traditions and semi-rural charm.

5. The remaining alternative is to build a new urban concentration to the West, near Quezaltepeque, or Chanmico. In addition to its social and economic disadvantages, which appear patent to me, and to its difficult implementation, it also has some landscape problems. It appropriates prime agricultural land; and it locates a large population in a micro-climate which is decidedly inferior to the San Salvador basin. The two urban areas would be widely separated, and have little visual relation to each other.

The Network of Major Roads

The major road system is a prime influence on environmental quality at the regional scale. As an instrument of access, a social link, and the viewpoint from which the urban area is actually seen and experienced, the road has a crucial functional, social, and esthetic impact, and these impacts are inter-linked. In addition, the road system is manageable at the regional scale, and already has an institution devoted to its management.

The space within the right-of-way should be used or usable for many different purposes—not only for the different modes of travel (car, bus, bicycle, cart, foot) but also for marketing, recreation, meeting, social ser-vices, agriculture, utilities, and many [other purposes]. The road can be used as a many sided device for regional development. This objective should have an institutional reflection: the road building agency would be concerned with the multiple development of road and roadside. I propose that a consistent system of rights-of-way be taken throughout the future metropolitan region—not to be retired from use, but to be brought into active exploitation. It would be managed as a public land reserve, a means of guiding regional growth and of providing services and activities where they are needed to support that growth.

There might be two basic types of right-of-way, within which development and road construction standards could vary as needed:

1. Rights-of-way intended eventually as limited-access expressways. These would be 250–300 feet wide, although varying with the terrain, and with widened takings at future intersections and at special terrain points, such as areas intended for major regional recreation. These strips should be taken through present open land, and not through urban areas. We have had bitter experience with the social damage and visual disruption caused by the urban expressway, and San Salvador is lucky to be able to construct a workable system without destroying its urban fabric.

Major roads of rural standard might be built in these rights of way, designed to allow progressive upgrading to an eventual grade-separated, divided-lane expressway. Road development would be paced to provide access as desired, but to prevent premature growth. No side access to the right-of-way would be permitted from the beginning, except on foot, and the intersections with future arterials would be pre-determined.

Access to the road from uses within the strip would be permitted, however. These encouraged uses would have the general characteristics of social usefulness, low structural density, and lack of permanent commitment. Many of them would be conducted by private individuals on a leasehold basis. Among them might be: the raising of crops and cattle, particularly demonstration agriculture (accessible and visible to all); regional recreation (sports fields, picnic grounds, race courses, dance floors, fair grounds, shelters for meetings and festivals, dining pavilions, swimming and spray pools, tree groves, look-outs); parking; open industrial facilities (storage, tile-making, timber fabrication); trunk utility lines; even airport approaches, should such coordination prove possible.

The road itself might at times be reserved for buses only, or heavy trucks, or motorbikes, or have separate lanes for these. The lanes would not cling to the centerline, but move flexibly with the terrain, within the broad strip. Opposing lanes can have separate alignments, to reduce earthwork and improve the visual fit.

2. Rights-of-way intended for arterial streets, 200 feet wide in many places, but varying with the situation, and spaced between one-half and one mile apart within the urban region. Lateral access would be allowed, although road entrances would be controlled. These arterial strips might also be brought through existing urban areas, at a reduced scale, or connected to widened city streets.

This width is not proposed to allow for broad and empty boulevards, but again to provide space for needed uses, as a device for opening the region to settlement as rapidly as necessary. Visually, the intent is not to impose a formal, controlled esthetic order, but to expose the life of the region to the traveler, to produce an interesting form deriving from active use, simple means, and fit of means to use. In general, separate lanes would be provided for buses, which are the backbone of the regional transportation system, and whose capacity must be maintained, as well as for pedestrians, and possibly for motorbikes or bicycles. Roads should provide for a whole range of transport modes beyond the car, which is now the vehicle of the upper class. A man can improve his transportation by moving up through bicycles and motorbikes, just as he can improve his housing in the tugurio.

Alongside and between the various transportation lanes, the land might be used for any of the activities mentioned under (1) above, plus others such as: open markets, water fountains, bus and sitting shelters, local recreation, temporary social services, eating stands, outdoor movies or television or bandstands, parking, vehicle repair, and so on. The intent is to provide an arterial movement system coupled with land for the future, the required parks and open public sites, and many of the necessary support activities. A right-of-way might be allocated, but this allocation could vary in many ways.

Existing Rights-of-Way

In addition to these basic types of right-of-way, to be taken principally in present open lands, there remains the problem of the existing system. I can make three comments at the regional scale:

1. If the railroads are gradually declining in importance and may in the future phase out, the nation should not commit the familiar error of allowing their rights-of-way to disappear. They are a continuous and consistent system; they are relatively level (however winding and narrow); they pass through some of the best scenery in the region. They should be retained for future public transportation routes, utility lines, bikeways, or recreational routes, paticularly where they pass through the gorges. With the addition of strips saved in the quebradas or along the utility lines, these old railroads may one day be the nucleus of an extensive recreational, walking, and bikeway system.

2. The original streets of the city center, and of the nearby towns—narrow, fronted by continuous ranks of one and two story buildings, with large entrances and prominent windows—have a very pleasant character, particularly when they are full of people. This is true even though there are no exceptionally fine buildings, that when empty they seem somewhat cramped and slabby. The intimate scale, the occasional brightly painted surfaces, the detail about the openings, the diverse bustle of activity, the traditional cast of these streets, are not to be discarded lightly. Very soon

the pressures of traffic and of new construction are likely to sweep these streets away, in favor of blank office towers and broad empty arteries.

Redevelopment of the present CBD is a matter of priority and requires special study. I would recommend that a sympathetic eye be cast on the present environment. Its scale might be preserved, and circulation improved, by excluding vehicles other than buses, bicycles, and motor bikes, or delivery vans at certain hours. Particular existing buildings need not be saved—most of them seem to have little architectural merit—but the continuity and height of the facades should be maintained by new development, while higher structures and patios could occupy the block interiors. The traditional device of arcades would add a great deal to the interest and comfort of the streets. The present scene can be improved by sign control, and by the fresh repainting of facades and trim in the bright combinations for which there is obviously a widespread talent. The manipulation of light will further enhance the evening aspect.

3. As to the newer residential building, there is less to say, except to be sorry for the use of exotic site planning models. Perhaps the most interesting new developments are the low row houses by IVU, which individuals have modified, decorated, and replanted in their own ways. Since these comments have less bearing on regional planning, I pass them by.

Location Rules

Given some prototypes for the right-of-way itself, there are guides to be set for their location at the regional scale. A number of these refer to traffic function: relation to load, interspacing, intersections, network continuity. But rules can also be set for some of the psychological or esthetic aspects of the location of the major road system:

1. The system should have some coherent large scale pattern, easy to remember and to operate within. In this case, there is a cultural tradition for the grid, which was intelligently used in the early growth of the city. The landscape itself has a grain which complies to this cardinal orientation: quebradas, slopes, and urban basins run east-west or north-south, and so do the strategic middle hills. Major features, like the volcano or the lake or the edge of the ocean ridges, can all conveniently be placed in one of the cardinal directions from the center. Since this system also corresponds to a good general pattern for moving dispersed traffic over a large region, it seems convenient to adopt it. Ideally, then, every major road, however it may curve in detail to fit local conditions, should have a consistent north-south or east-west direction, crossing routes of the other bearing in a consistent order. [See figure.]

2. North-south routes should be visibly differentiated from east-west ones, and arterials from expressways. Where possible, individual routes

Thus:

and not:

nor:

nor:

should be distinguished one from another. This may be done by such details as planting, paving, and signs, but is more clearly and permanently achieved by the location with respect to topography or major urban features, the activity along the way, or the typical cross-section. The principal intersections should be identified by similar means. There is an opportunity here for special planting, or the skillful use of rock and earth.

3. Take every opportunity to present good views from the road of major natural features and of urban development and urban centers, and make the traffic connection to the latter evident well before any decisions must be made. Fast roads may be confusing if they come close to or penetrate active centers—they work well if they pass at the side and above them. Exploit dramatic entrances into urban areas, making the visual entry congruent with actual entry. The approach from the airport is a successful example of this; the lack of visual contact with the Lago Ilopango from the main highway is a case of an opportunity missed.

4. Where possible, develop interesting sequences of motion, spatial variation, and areas traversed. A road which can pass from a great volcano to a narrow quebrada, to a view of the center and then of the lake, would be an example.

The present city has many good points of visual structure: its unity within the basin, surrounded by green ridges and mountains, the approach from Santa Tecla and the airport, and the dark spires of the old araucaria trees in the central area. The center itself, on the other hand, contains few tall buildings and is almost undistinguishable from a distance. The Italianate spire of the church is easily remarked, but the church is of secondary importance and at some distance from the center. The central cathedral is under construction, and has no strong sentiments attached to it. The major tall building in the center is a small hotel, although there are several rather bland institutional buildings farther west. A casual inquiry unearthed only three urban locales felt to be of any public symbolic value: the central Plaza Libertad with its arcades, the old hospital, and the zoological gardens. Now that tall buildings are permitted, the city is likely to develop a broad scattering of them. It seems unreasonable to insist on a concentration of tall buildings, primarily for visual reasons.

The basic city street system itself is logical and logically named, but this grid was allowed to disintegrate as the city expanded, making multiple discontinuities and confusions which seem to puzzle even the old inhabitant. Place location now relies on named "colonias," or individual subdivisions, each with its peculiar character and quite different street organization. I would judge that the visual structure of the future San Salvador region will hang primarily on three elements:

　　a.　the structure of the natural landscape;
　　b.　the visible structure of the road system;
　　　　and
　　c.　the identity of the named communities and
　　　　colonias, existing and to come.

I have not had the time or the information to deal with the third element. This listing of crucial elements is only a hypothesis, based on personal observation. It should be tested by an examination of how residents picture their region and orient themselves within it.

The entire system has a consistent north-south and east-west grain, except for one arterial which is constrained by previous development. The routes carry through in a consistent order. Routes are dead ended occasionally, but none are interrupted to resume again. The arterials attempt to reconnect the fragments of the existing city, and to carry out the original grid, at least on the arterial scale. All expressways together make a totally connected system, and so do all arterials together.

Second, each expressway would have a distinctive character, if for nothing else than the different land forms they traverse. Expressway 1 has a less vivid character, however. Some of the arterials have such character, but many would have to depend on urban detail for recognition. Expressways would be distinct from arterials by their intrinsic form, but there is no systematic way of telling north-south from east-west routes, unless by the sense of the landscape as a whole.

Many of the routes have potentially magnifient views of the city, lake, hills, and volcanoes. All the expressways make dramatic entrances into the urban basins, although certain points must be treated with care if this is to come off. Unfortunately, two are visually buried as they pass the city center, an important concession to the existing urban fabric. All the expressways contain good sequences of motion, space, and view.

Note that all these visual qualities are *intentions*, which depend on detailed design, horizontal alignments, lane elevations, and the clearing of views. Any proposed regional road network should be accompanied by a diagrammatic statement of its visual intentions, and these intentions must then be carried through, or explicitly modified, in the process of design and construction.

The Details of the Road Landscape

The visual quality of the roadscape depends on its detail, which must be considered at a sub-regional scale. But general comments can be made, and some rough prototypes indicated. Any visual amenity must be fitted to the way people actually use and perceive their environment—any formal esthetic imposition is meaningless, as well as difficult to maintain. To design an environment, one must pay attention to how similar areas are actually used, and learn what the users think about them. In a developing country, the means must be as simple as possible, employing underused local labor and materials. It is risky to copy the forms of other countries, however "advanced" they seem to be, and particularly then.

In this vein:

1. The man on foot is the most important user of the Salvadorean roadside. Yet sidewalks if they exist are narrow, close at the curb, and often blocked with poles, weeds, earth slides, and other lumber. Pedestrians, market sellers, and craftsmen fill the narrow space and spill into the street, to their danger and the drivers' annoyance. The pedestrian should receive the principal consideration in building roads. He should have a walkway which is adequate in size, well separated from the traffic way, shaded and sheltered by trees and arcades, with occasional widenings set with pavilions, simple blocks or benches, where he can sit, talk, work, and trade.

These provisions are not expensive ones. A very simple social facility could be located at intervals along the arterial routes combining some or all of the following activities: a bus stop, named and visibly identified; a water source; a place to sit and talk under shelter; a small market; an eating place; a sand pile or spray pool for small children; an outdoor classroom; a public TV or radio; a notice board with local announcements, bus routes and schedules, maps, emergency and other public information; a grove of trees; an area lighted at night. The physical facilities could be of the simplest kind; the area might be entrusted to local groups or market people to maintain and modify.

2. To a foreign eye, the region has a luxuriant variety of trees and other plants. These are an economical means of beautifying and diversifying the roads, and indeed there is already a strong tradition of the use of street trees. Unfortunately, the model is the line of standardized ornamental trees, on a narrow planting strip next to the road, or perhaps in a central divider. The trees shade the driver, who does not need them, and

endanger his life should he drive off the pavement. They interfere with utility lines overhead, and must be cut down whenever the street is to be widened. They will often obscure an important view, and while they produce a handsome effect when of good size, they are often monotonous.

It is better to relate the trees to the pedestrian rather than to the driver, whether planted in groves or along walks well separated from the roadway. For the driver, the roadsides should be open, with only occasional clumps of specimen trees, or planted to a low thick growth which will cut off the glare of approaching headlights and cushion the impact of a careening car.

A much greater diversity of trees and plants can probably be used, although I am ignorant of the local material. There is an apparent variety of form: pines, palms, araucarias, figs, bananas, and many kinds of flowering trees. The love of beautiful plants is evident in the flowers which are set out around the rural houses. Might it be possible, in a region in which food production is critical, to plant parts of the roadside to fruit trees and food crops, perhaps on lease to local residents? The visual effect, at least, would be far more interesting and meaningful.

The fine mature trees, in which the rural landscape abounds, should be conserved wherever possible. The local tradition of saving such a tree on a low elevated mound, surrounded by a stone curb to sit on, is an excellent model. The great spreading trees under which people gather in the village plazas would be dramatic in the urban setting.

3. Visible surfaces have an important bearing on the quality of the roadside: the pavements, embankments, and walls. Some of the old rural roads are cobbled, a pleasant visual texture (if not for the foot or the wheel). A return to hand-laid paving is improbable, but the modern pavement so overbears the scene that some experiments with varied aggregates for asphalt and concrete may be worth while.

For its retaining walls and embankments the region is lucky to have the handsome surfaces of volcanic ash and lava rock, and the skill to use them. These should be exploited wherever possible, in place of concrete. I have already commented on the handsome tradition of painted walls, which should also be encouraged. Might inexpensive paints, or painting advice, be provided? In a similar vein, why not promote the local ability for temporary decoration, so evident on roadside shrines and at festivals?

4. At present there are relatively few signs along the Salvadorean roads, save in the town centers, where they overhang the pavements in great disorder. A recent attempt to control them generated little political support. There are no existing sign regulations, thus the mattress advertisement on the volcano. What is about to happen is evident. Billboards are appearing along the major highway. Public street signs, on the other hand, are small, hard to find, often lacking. This is the moment to set a consistent policy on public and private signs.

The policy cannot begin with the idea that signs should be suppressed. They add to the visual interest of a scene. More important, they are a source of information, telling the observer many things in addition to identifying his destination. Public safety and general orientation should have primacy, but private signs are also important. The purpose of any policy should be to increase and clarify the information communicated.

There are two simple kinds of private sign controls which might be considered:

a. spatial zoning—private signs might be prohibited in certain locations , such as over the public right-of-way, within so many meters of a major intersection, over a certain height, or on, or in front of, key natural features, so as to maintain the visual primacy of traffic control and orientation, and of the great natural features.

b. sign content—prohibit, except in some compact designated areas, all private signs which do not refer to products or services available or manufactured at that same location. While relatively easy to administer, such a control enhances the information content of the sign system, and also successfully regulates the billboards, which turn out to be the principal visual annoyances along the road. If adequate and highly visible areas are designated for such billboards (or "non-rooted" signs) before the economic pressure to erect them builds up, the resistance to regulation may be small. Moreover, the billboards can be located to perform their proper function, informing the traveler of goods and services he wishes to find on the road ahead.

Sign controls may also regulate moving or flashing signs as distracting to the driver, but I would not recommend any complex controls on size, shape, design, or exact location. They require substantial administrative effort. Even the controls suggested may be too difficult to enforce, and it may be preferable to begin simply by requiring that all signs over the right-of-way, or above a given height, or "non-rooted" in content, be registered before erection, with an opportunity for advice and consultation. Or they might be permitted only on long, but revocable, leases.

The control of private signs is not the principal issue. The design and location of public signs is more crucial, since their information is vital, and they often cause greater visual clutter than the private system. They must be carefully made to be readable, and to inform the traveler of decisions and actions well before he must make them. For the driver, for example, intersections, routes, and their principal destinations should be signaled in advance, in some clear and systematic format. Information is particularly desirable at a change of mode—for example, a bus stop—where the observer has both the leisure and the motive to be informed. He should be able to learn where he is, where the principal destinations lie, what buses are routed here, where they go, and on what schedule.

Since many Salvadoreans are not literate, the words should be coupled with iconic symbols that would be understood by the typical observer. An intelligent public sign policy begins by learning what typical groups of city users want to know, and how this is most easily communicated to them. Inadvertently, most public signs are puzzling and obscure to the man on the street, however clear and obvious to the sign-maker.

The control and design of signs might be looked at in a much larger context, as part of a general public information policy, in a country where education of the great mass of the people is a crucial objective. Street signs might consciously be used to inform—to teach reading or arithmetic, to present current news or history, to describe the local ecology or the workings of the city in simple terms, to inform the new city resident where he can find employment, services, or emergency help. Tied in with public radios, television sets, and news sheets, the signs could be a general device for informing and educating the citizen. While sign control might normally be a function of the road development agency, it would in this case be given to an agency primarily concerned with education and communication: a radio and TV network, an education department.

The Process of Maintaining Environmental Quality

The suggestions above are rapid impressions, dealing with selected aspects of environmental quality. They are based on personal reconaissance, and a few informal discussions. Quality will not be achieved by such casual means, nor even by a single plan, however sophisticated. As in any other aspect of planning, it will require a continuous process of monitoring and guidance. Maintaining environmental quality and visual form should be a continuing charge of the urban planning agency, wherever it is located, as well as being the responsibility of the operating agencies concerned: public works, land settlement, public information, and so on.

To accomplish this, a central planning organization should be carrying on at least four kinds of studies:

a. analyses of the actual sensuous form of the environment;

b. studies of how various groups perceive, use, and value their surroundings;

c. development of the criteria for landscape quality;

d. preparation of public policy for various aspects of the environment.

It might be useful to list some of the principal studies under these heads:

1. Analyses of sensuous form

a. systematic photographic coverage of land form, visible activity, and development:

vertical and aerial obliques

panoramic views

photo grids (i.e. photos taken to show visible character at regular intervals over a region)

photo sequences or stop-frame movies along the major paths

ground photos chosen to illustrate typical development or form, or characteristic or special activity

photos taken at regular time intervals at important places, to show the sequence of activity.

b. mapping and analyzing the visual structure of the region:

location and description of major views, viewpoints, landmarks, skylines, approaches, visual units and visual divides, range of visibility, "blind" areas

location and description of principal visual districts, and their character

analysis of visual sequences along the main roads.

c. mapping and analysis of environmental danger points:

location and degree of erosion, water, air, and noise pollution, flooding, poor climate, recharge areas, solid waste disposal, prime agricultural land, and areas most sensitive to ecological and visual damage.

Sample efforts in many of these "objective" studies of the visual environment have already been made. However sketchy, they have already proved useful in making this brief report. Some of the material, particularly the panoramic views, will be of historic value as well.

2. Analyses of perception and use

Unfortunately, there was no time to conduct even the most sketchy examples of this type of study, which is crucial to any rational attempt to affect quality. Studies can include:

a. analyses of the image of San Salvador, as held by representatives of social groups of all levels, including both users and decision makers. Based primarily on sample interviews, dealing with:

the structure of the region and the identity of its parts

description of users' own neighborhoods

description of habitual trips

perceived environmental change

perceived environmental problems

what locales are most vivid or most valued
locales habitually used or journeys habitually taken and which are
used for pleasure.

b. a mapping of socially valued elements in the region:
historical or cultural locales
unusual or fine landscapes or objects
status and symbolic elements
visual dominants.

c. analyses of how particular important places are actually used and seen,
by the observation of overt behavior, plus interviews with users.

d. environmental descriptions in guidebooks and in historical, [literary]
and graphic references; anthropological data on the fit between environment and culture.

e. analyses of the training and attitudes of building and land developers
and designers, both professional and non-professional.

3. Evaluation of landscape quality

In this paper my evaluation is personal, and based upon untested and
implicit criteria. For public use, they must be explicit:

a. development of criteria for landscape quality, in a form which is testable
by the users and decision makers, derived originally both from the studies
in 2 above and from the general planning literature.

b. a general evaluation of present problems and potentials in the region.

c. monitoring and evaluation of planned changes which have actually
been executed.

4. Public policies

Studies to develop policies for the management of various aspects of the
environment, based on the above, plus creative solutions. Policies would
not be general, but would focus on particular problems, and would include
prototype solutions, necessary institutional changes, and how this is to be
communicated to those who implement the plans. I have only sketched
out some considerations in two of these areas. A more complete list might
include:

a. roadside development

b. land conservation and settlement

c. environmental possibilities of the tugurio and other low cost housing

d. landscapes for recreation

e. renewal of the CBD or other centers; the form of new centers

f. maintaining and building the identity and character of colonias

g. pollution: air, water, land, noise

h. ecological change

i. special visual elements, such as signs, lighting, planting, earthwork, tall buildings

j. training and use of professional and non-professional designers.

No planning agency should attempt to carry out all this list of possible studies, but would choose, and shift its efforts, according to current needs and resources. The purpose is to improve the real environment, via public policy. Thus the analytical studies (1, 2, and 3 above) would not attempt to be exhaustive, but would be pointed to illuminate the particular studies listed in 4. Some of this information will be of general use, and must be recorded and maintained to keep that usefulness. I especially recommend studies of the type described in 2a and c above: they will reveal many unsuspected gaps between user and designer.

Thought given to the training and employment of designers (4j above) will prove equally useful. Simply from observation, I would judge that the Salvadorean architect, like many of his counterparts over the world, is trained to be the skillful designer of a building, but not to think of that object in its context of use and other objects, and certainly not to be concerned with environmental design of the kind that has been at issue above. An exhibit at the airport of work in the school of architecture confirms this view: the exercises were competent, but preoccupied with formal order. No building was shown in its context nor in use. Moreover, by the nature of the clients who pay him, the principal objects that the architect designs are government buildings, office and commercial buildings, churches, and expensive single family houses.

The urgent (and also the most interesting) problems are somewhere else: in low cost self-help housing, in the treatment of the land, the development of the roads, in creating total environments for active use. The professional designer is unable to get at those urgent problems. Despite his high status in society, he is consigned to the fringes, while the real difficulties are dealt with by builders, engineers, and the user himself.

If this is so, then efforts will have to be made in three different directions:

1. To create the clients for whom designers can work if they are to perform their proper function. Perhaps the institutions suggested above may be part of the answer: public agencies dealing with roadside development, land settlement, or public information. Undoubtedly others will be required, particularly ones which enable low income users to hire their own designers.

2. To educate young designers to be interested, and competent, in dealing with basic social tasks. With no knowledge of Salvadorean training, but based on U.S. experience, I would predict that young designers would respond with enthusiasm.

3. To enable the non-professional to create an adequate environment for himself. The number of designers required to tackle all the basic tasks would be staggering. Meanwhile the non-professional and the user are actually building the urban region. They have the advantage, at least, of being better informed as to requirements and resources. Ways must be found to bring them technical design aids, and to train them for the work they do. This means design extension services, and special vocational training, on the job or part-time.

There is a common misapprehension that design is a static extra, a luxury finish applied after functional decisions are made. It must in fact be an intimate part of the whole decision process, and its considerations connected to the basic concerns of the user. It is a misuse of designers to save them for the "finer" things, or to call them in to sketch out a "nice form." The quality of life suffers thereby.

Nanjing (1980)

with Tunney Lee

The city of Nanjing, some 200 miles upstream from the coast on the Yangtze River, is over 2,000 years old. Much of the built-up area is still enclosed within what may be the largest city wall remaining in the world. Nanjing has intermittently been the capital of China under ten different dynasties or political systems, the last as recently as the Kuomintang up to 1949. It is still a major metropolis of China, a center of production, education, and culture.

Nanjing makes machines, vehicles, farm equipment, electronics, instruments, chemicals, and textiles, as well as processing food, mining coal, and refining oil. It includes a rich agricultural region. It contains over twenty important colleges, universities, and technical institutes, of which Nanjing University and the Nanjing Technical Institute are preeminent in the country.

Three surrounding suburban counties are under the jurisdiction of the city: city and counties together comprise 4,700 square kilometers and a population of 3.3 million people. The city proper contains 800 square kilometers and 2 million people, of whom 300,000 are engaged in agriculture, outside the densely built-up area itself (about 120 square kilometers). The climate is sub-tropical, and the terrain is varied, with mountains comprising some ⅓ of the land.

Before liberation, ⅓ of the land within the wall was still open, primarily in the northern sector. Now most of this is built upon, and development has spread somewhat beyond the walls, except to the east, where lie the large parks and historic conservation areas around Hsuan-wu Lake and the Tzu-shin Chan (Purple Gold Mountain). To the north, moreover, expansion is limited by the broad, swift Yangtze River, only recently (1968) spanned by the famous four mile bridge. The built-up area now comprises about 26 million square meters of floor space, a figure which has essentially doubled since liberation. All new residential units have been built as 5 or 6 story masonry walkups, and no further expansion of the central city is planned. (Nanjing is in the earthquake zone and the construction of tall brick apartments may be dangerous. We were told, however, that quakes are "light" in this region.)

The shortage of housing is very severe, exacerbated by the return of many citizens who had been sent out to the countryside during the Cultural Revolution. Many streets and open or waste areas in the city are now lined with dense one-story self-built houses, typically one or two-room structures in attached rows, made of brick and about ten to fifteen feet deep. These differ from typical squatter settlements only in their cleanliness, their relatively orderly arrangement (since they are "squatting" by official permission and direction—taking up a strip in front of the old building lines on the broader streets, for example), and because they are somewhat better built (since the work unit typically assists the family in their construction). General residential densities were reported to be in the range of 300–400 persons per hectare.

Present plans focus on the construction of new satellite cities, to stem the further growth of the city proper, and there was little discussion of rehabilitating the existing housing stock. The plan calls for five "rings" of land development:

1. the built-up city proper (120 sq. km)

2. a "greenbelt" reserved for growing vegetables and for scenic areas

3. a ring of satellite cities, 10–20 km out, including 3 major centers of about 150,000 population, along the Yangtze, and 4 secondary centers of about 30–50,000 people, mostly to the south

4. an outer zone of agriculture and forestry

5. another ring of small towns within the far suburban counties.

The satellite cities are presently under construction, and contain roughly half their planned population. The planners hope for a close relation of city and country, and it is a fixed policy that large cities will be fed (at least for vegetables and fresh meat) by the countryside immediately surrounding them. We had the impression that the rural communes immediately surrounding the city, with their ready market for produce and their ability to engage in small industrial enterprises, were better housed and had better income than most other groups in the society.

The locations of the large planned satellite towns were determined largely by the limited Yangtze frontages which are suitable for wharfage or for drawing process water. The Yangtze is deep and fast-flowing, 3–4,000 feet wide, with a normal flow in the range of 90,000 cubic meters per second. It is used for waste disposal (much of it as yet untreated) and also for drinking water. These conflicts are obvious and recognized. There is a Yangtze Valley Commission, charged with planning the coordinated use of the river water, but it has little power. Pollution of water and air continued to be a serious problem.

The city lies between two mountain clusters and the hills are being reforested. There are several remarkable large parks and historic green areas, especially to the east, but small parks within the dense residential areas are almost totally lacking.

The trunk highways go through the center of the city, the major traffic flow being north-south. Truck traffic became quite heavy after the opening of the Yangtze Bridge. Peak flows on the central street, which other than bicycles consist almost entirely of trucks and buses, are about

2,000 vehicles per hour. Two by-pass roads are planned, one on the east and one on the west. That to the west is partially complete. Cycle flows are very heavy, but cycle accidents, while frequent, are somewhat lower than in other Chinese cities.

Now that it is no longer necessary to ferry rail cars across the Yangtze, Nanjing has become a major rail junction, with heavily used connections to Shanghai, Anhwei, and Beijing, and future connections to Hangzhou, Hupeh, and northern Jiangsu.

The Nanjing City Planning Institute plans the physical development of the city and its infrastructure, but they do not build housing, nor even seem to be well informed about it. While they initiate detailed plans, they are dominated by the national economic plans, and detailed city plans must be approved by provincial or national agencies, depending on their level of importance. We were told that such approvals were relatively routine in most cases, requiring two to three months.

Nanjing was originally settled, before 300 B.C., at several locations along the Chinhuai River, near its junction with the Yangtze, but far enough upstream to gain a protected anchorage for river traffic, free from floods. The merchant city is thus at the southern end of the present city, along the Chinhuai, and survives today as the oldest portion. The Han capital and palace was established to the east of this merchant city and this pattern was followed by the Ming, the Ching, the Taiping revolutionaries, and the Kuomintang. The city walls enclosed both centers, and were pushed out to the natural limits—the Yangtze, the Chinhuai, and the lakes and mountains to the east. Even in the 20th century, the area to the northwest within the walls was empty. Thus the northern and eastern portions of the city were always administrative, and the south merchant and artisan. The governmental areas have been alternately rebuilt and laid waste, while the merchant city has endured. The villas of Western colonialists were built in the open, northern areas, and these now house the top cadres, or include major institutions and agencies (and our hotel). The Kuomintang cut major boulevards through the city, in the north, east, and center—producing serveral huge, empty traffic circles—but never completed this scheme in the south. Thus the city consists of two major zones, enclosed within a huge wall, with some overspill to the south and southwest, but backed against the lake and mountains to the east, the Yangtze to the north, and the Chinhuai to the west. Major shopping lies along the main north-south avenue at the center, north of the old city, but the traditional shops and crafts are still located in the latter.

The major streets cut the city into very large "blocks," which makes the city appear deceptively small on a map, at least to a Western eye. Within those broad streets, lined with pruned sycamore trees—along which pass great streams of pedestrians and cyclists—is a maze of narrow lanes, solidly lined with one-story dwellings, both old and new. Here the streets belong to their residents, and tourists are surprising intruders, openly commented upon. But the comments are usually friendly, and the maze, however indirect, preserves its orientation to the cardinal directions.

The bike lanes and the anarchy at the intersections makes street crossing an adventure. Trucks and buses drive wildly along opposing lanes to pass each other and the incessant sound of their horns, along with the jangle of bicycle bells, fills the air. A sea of white shirts advances toward one along the sidewalks, and curious crowds gather whenever the foreigner stops to talk or to do something peculiar. Walks are the setting for every kind of activity: barbers, welding, sewing, shoes, cooking and eating, weaving beds, cabinet making, selling chicken or vegetables, reading, wood-turning, beating cotton, weaving steel reinforcing. Small industries occupy the premises just off the street, and so the everyday work is open to view. But the edges of streets and lanes are uniformly walled-off, and gateways have an important symbolic function.

The long articulated buses are unbelievably crowded, and the people force their way in as intensely as any New Yorker, if with greater good humor. Seats are often offered to foreigners, which brings on complex discussions, but not to Chinese women loaded with packages. However crowded, noisy, and smoking, the buses are cheap, run frequently, and cover the entire city. They successfully move incredible numbers of people. There are many trucks and few draft animals, but many loads are still carried or pulled by human beings. The multitudes of cyclists are dangerous free spirits, and some motor bikes are beginning to appear. To walk to one's destination is still a normal thing.

In the evening, under the sycamores and the occasional street lights, the avenues are full of strollers. In the morning before the traffic horns drown out all other sounds one hears the bells of street vendors and garbage collectors, drums, voices, and the sounds of sweeping and flushing the streets. People brush their teeth at the gutter, and buy their breakfast at street stalls: fried bread on a stick or rolled in a pancake, flat bread, rice gruel, bean curd, noodles, or cakes. The stores are dense with customers, especially for all the less expensive products of industrial technology, while the foreigner is attracted to all the traditional products now beginning to be despised as "backward": the wooden buckets and tubs, baskets, rough cloth and tools, brushes, straw pillows, tin boxes, great clay jars, or matting. Meals are quite inexpensive by our standards: a dish of meat and vegetables, plus rice and a bowl of warm beer for 0.78 yuan, or lunch in a village shop for 0.48 (U.S. $0.55 and 0.34). Everyone appears well fed and in clean clothes. Housing, however, is desperately short. New apartments provide about 500 sq. ft. per family, with electricity, running water, and a small gas stove. But many families live in a single room, or less, carry their water, cook on soft coal or charcoal, and use public baths and privies, which may be a block or two away. Extended families are crowded together in one unit, nuclear families may be divided, or marriages be long postponed, for want of space.

Some quick thoughts and superficial judgments

Planning (including much economic planning) is more decentralized than we had thought. City planning bureaus follow very general national directives, but develop their own plans, subject to rather nominal national review, and compete with many other public agencies and economic units. We felt right at home.

Economic and physical planning are separated from each other, with the former dominant, while social planning receives surprisingly little overt comment. Thus the physical planners are concerned with the facilities and location of tourism, which is also being promoted for economic ends, but there is not discussion of the social or political impact of foreign tourists, nor of the pros and cons of wealthy vs. moderate income tourists. As another example, the planners are deeply engaged with laying out satellite cities, which are based on economic decisions to promote this or that industry, while there was little talk of the impact of these cities on the way of life of the people involved. We caught rumors of resistance to satellite life. Once more, we felt at home.

The planners are looking for definite standards and fixed answers: the optimum size of a city, the proper distance of a satellite from its parent city, the best residential site plan, the proper amount of park or apartment space per capita. We were evasive, which disappointed our hosts.

Despite the wide differences among cities, each one is focusing on the construction of a ring of new satellite cities around itself. This seems to make good sense, but the uniformity of the answer, especially in such a relatively decentralized planning system and among cities so varied in character, was a little surprising. The future linkages between these towns and their parent cities did not seem well considered. Moreover, little attention was apparently being paid to the existing old housing stock, which houses and must for some time continue to house the bulk of the population.

In building new housing beyond the city limits, the planners are under pressure to save as much good agricultural land as possible, since the crop land close to the cities is essential to feeding city people. Thus they build dense apartment housing, typically in the form of five and six story walkups with open stairs and balcony access. This seems very rational for reasons of cost as well for saving cropland. They are wise to avoid taller high-rise apartments, which require elevators, are more expensive, and are more difficult for family life.

But we had some indication—perhaps just guessed—that the population would prefer one and two story houses, with closer access to the ground, more like the traditional Chinese courtyard house. Thus the planner might think of developing models for high-density low-rise housing (as the students at Tsing Hua University are attempting to do) or of mixing some lower units with the tall walkups. In any case, the site planning of the apartments is monotonous and unimaginative, although they are always well landscaped, which makes the long lines of apartments more human than might be imagined. Moreover, would it be wise to look forward to a time when families will decline to occupy the upper stories, or will demand more internal space? How will these standardized walkups be modified in that case?

If quite small and simple, the apartments are solid and well laid out, except for the kitchens, which are cramped and sometimes double as entrance halls to the other rooms. This defect in the standard plan should be rethought. In the cramped living quarters much of the furniture is heavy and poorly arranged. Storage space is lacking. Studies of cheap, light furniture, efficient storage devices of typical apartment use, and good furniture arrangement might be very useful, and as important as housing design itself. Trained interior designers might be made available, to help people buy household equipment and arrange their tight living quarters.

Local open spaces are lacking despite some magnificent historic parks. Sidewalks and scraps of open ground are used intensely. Eating, washing, and economic activity spills into the street. While that is picturesque for the tourist, it may be less than comfortable for the inhabitant. Given the inevitable shortage of built space, inventive site design might provide more private or semi-private open space near at hand. Roofs might be made usable, for example, or the linear spaces along walkways or between ranks of apartments be better used.

We were disturbed by the first blossoms of western advertising, as have appeared on the terrace of Beijing's Temple of Heaven, or in the illuminated billboards of Shanghai, advertising the services of U.S. advertisers (to whom? and why?), which now form the most brightly lit spot in that city. On the other hand, some of the new neon shop signs in Nanjing add to the color of the street. Should a policy on sign control be developed, before the problem becomes intractable?

The ubiquitous street trees, many of them recently planted, are a great asset of these Chinese cities. It might be well to plant other varieties than the sycamore, handsome and suitable as that tree may be. Should there be a sycamore blight, all the streets would be denuded at once. The modest level of street light, filtering through the sycamore branches, is a great relief to one accustomed to the yellow glare of the American arterial. We hope that this sign of "backwardness" will persist, along with the habit of using the street for an evening stroll.

As planners we were impressed by the thought taken to control population growth to direct internal migration. Severe measures are being taken to check the growth of China's huge population (at least in the cities, among the people we talked with), and the devastating urban floods in which most developing nations are drowning seem in China to be contained or redirected. Where unavoidable, as in Nanjing, squatter housing is dealt with in a very effective way.

What the future effect will be of the present one-child-per-family rule is hard to foresee. Stubbornly pursued, it may later produce a strangely unbalanced age distribution in addition. The national restrictions on job and residence mobility develop great stresses among individuals and families. Without such determined measures, however, cities like Shanghai, Nanjing, and Beijing might swell out of control. We heard discussions of national policies for building large new cities, or encouraging the growth of present small towns, in the interior of the country, near the bulk of the relatively improverished rural population. But we were unable to form a clear picture of that policy, nor to learn of it as being effectively pursued.

Foreword to *Environmental Knowing* (1976)

What interchange between people and their environment encourages them to grow into fully realized persons? This book makes some illuminating responses to that question. Cognition is an individual process but its concepts are social creations. We learn to see as we communicate with other people. The most interesting unit of study for environmental perception may therefore be small, intimate social groups who are learning to see together, exchanging their feelings, values, categories, memories, hopes, and observations, as they go about their everyday affairs. The material on social images of the environment is one of the most interesting parts of this collection. It is unfortunate that as yet they are static analyses.

The studies of the development of environmental cognition in children, on the other hand, while still restricted to individuals, are admirable because they portray an unfolding process. Patterns analyzed at one moment fail to tell us where perceptions come from, or how they may change. They even fail to convey the flavor of the momentary experience, which is changing into something else. Even more, they prevent us from making a just evaluation, since the quality of a life is not dependent on a single event, nor even on the finale, but on its form as a realized process. The triumphs of maturity may give meaning to a troubled adolescence, and the wonders of childhood complete a crippled old age.

In place of studying the learning process alone, we could use our studies and methods to help others to learn to see for themselves. This is the most rewarding feature of personal construct theory and method, which tries to surface a person's own way of viewing the world, and to help him to clarify and extend his own concepts. (Although as a universal way of thinking, I am less impressed, considering its overpowering emphasis on verbal constructs,[1] distinct categories, and bipolar scales defined by opposites. This is one way of thinking, very logical, very common, very "scientific," culturally much approved. (Lord help us if that were the only way that we could make sense of the world!)

Wood and Beck give a clear example of that fusion of research and action in a learning process. When they taught their collaborators a mapping language, they taught them how to see and relate new things. Thinking and communicating are the same, as they say. No wonder that their trained mappers mapped more than the untrained ones. The effect, I should think, was not superficial. Of course it muddied up the research. Still another example, not reported here, is the work of Stephen Carr and Philip Herr in their Ecologue project in Cambridge.[2] They used many of the same familiar research techniques of analyzing environmental cognition, but not to elicit the views of "subjects," for scientific study. The methods were taught to residents to help them understand themselves in relation to their world, and thence to organize to improve that world.

Speaking of mapping, I cannot resist saying something in defense of pictures. Numerous contributors refer to the difficulties in the open-ended mapping techniques once used in "The Image of the City." Some go further, and seem to assume that all graphic techniques lack credit. In that view, since graphic representations are an alien language to most people, to force their use distorts a person's knowledge of the world. (Thus assuming that thoughts are independent of languages, and are only filtered through them.) Wood and Beck show that teenagers can be taught mapping literacy with ease, and that their maps are then a rich source for understanding more about their images. Of course their images are changed in the process (I would assume, enriched and extended). It would have been interesting to watch their graphic progress while in London. But all images are dependent on some acquired language skill, including the verbal skill we so much take for granted. For example, in applying personal construct theory, Harrison and Sarre must teach their interviewees to improve their use of general verbal concepts and polar opposites. They are helping them to form a view of the world. They could hardly do otherwise.

People will ask a painter what his painting "means," that is, they want it translated into words. But they are not permitted to ask that a scholar draw what his essay pictures. In some instances, such drawings could be made and might reveal difficulties. In other ways, the two languages are incompatible, and have different powers. The graphic languages are excellent for communicating multiple relations between things at one glance, in a single complex pattern. That pattern can be clear or ambiguous. Graphic expressions are obviously apt for describing simultaneous relations in space, but also for other tasks.

Any attempt to elicit mental images should use every means and language it can, to check interrelated findings, and to bring out aspects which are incommunicable in one tongue or another. Our original work used an array of methods—verbal environmental descriptions, imaginary trips in memory, mappings, photo recognition and sorting, interviews while way-finding in the field, requests for directions from passers-by, and so on. There are better techniques today, but I remain convinced that an array of languages must be used, and that the graphic language is just as central as the verbal one. Not just maps, incidentally (however dear those may be to the hearts of geographers, however sacred to imagery), but all kinds of graphic expressions: eye-level sketches, photographs, video tapes, diagrams, models.

I hold a lingering suspicion that many investigators in social science reject graphic means more because of their own difficulties with graphic products, rather than because of those that their interviewees might have. The suspicion darkens as I see how few writers in this volume use even maps to describe their settings, and that only one uses a set of pictures! Once you have a drawing, what can you do with it? A map or sketch, however naively drawn, and often just because naively drawn, is eloquent in many ways beyond a mere counting of its named parts (which is a technique imported from verbal analysis). A sketch can be looked at for the sequence in which it was made, its connectivities and gaps, its style, the particular things graphically emphasized and those left out, the evidence of indifference or emotion, the variance in detail, the confidence or timidity with which different parts are drawn, the total structure, and even to some extent for its scale distortions (although the *purposeful* communication of distance and direction in a map is a special skill, which usually requires explicit teaching). Moreover, drawings have that valuable quality of being permanent records, easy to store and to recall, which communicate a great deal beyond their overt content. They are improved, of course, if accompanied by what the person *said* while drawing them, or by other evidence. But, in their permanent registration of overtones, they are like those emotional modulations of a voice heard on tape, which are so often lost in written transcriptions.

"Unstructured" drawings (that is, ones which were structured by the person responding, rather than by the interviewer) have the further advantage, despite all their difficulties, of allowing the person to express something of his own way of viewing the world, just as personal construct methods allow for the appearance of idiosyncratic verbal concepts. Similarities and convergences are then all the more useful and emphatic. To use printed maps, on which the person is asked to indicate what is important to him, or where a boundary is, is to lose that quality. You force a conventional view of the world on him, just as when you use a semantic differential test, or interrogate by check list.

In employing any language, it is well to begin by teaching its use, so that your interviewees can use it freely. One may teach the use of a video camera, or a tape recorder, or how to make a map, or how to tell a good story. In the process, one should maintain a record of how the image develops during the teaching, and the language being taught should be as broad and flexible as one can manage. Personal construct categorizing is a very partial language. So is Wood and Beck's "Environmental A"—not simply because it is a mapping, but because it is a particular kind of mapping. It is the traverse strategy of the surveyor, which is a powerful way of achieving a "true" map, accurate in scale and direction. But there are other ways to draw a city—topological sketches, or symbolic diagrams, or illustrative views—which may be appropriate to other concepts. Had there been time, a whole range of techniques could have been taught. Nevertheless, "Environmental A" is better than being inarticulate, and clearly superior to being dependent on words alone.

Naive "image maps" have been particularly criticized because most people *are* so ill-trained graphically, so befuddled by our verbal civilization that they think that anyone who can draw must have been born with a special genius. If one dose not have the time or means to teach good mapping, should one ever ask people to make one? The trained draftsman will tell you more, but the native one will tell you much, as long as you realize that there is far more that he knows in other languages that he will not communicate on his map. A disconnected or distorted map does not indicate a defective mental image. But the very unfamiliarity of the task—like the unexpected question—releases impressions that might otherwise have been suppressed. The elements recorded with difficulty are even more likely to be important ones. See the drawings of children, or the Venezuelan maps collected by Appleyard, some of them made by people who had actually never seen a map before.

We have even asked people to draw eye-level views of places. Perspective sketching is more difficult than mapping, and while most Western people will consider a request for a map as within the bounds of reason, they are sure that sketches are only made by artists, or by children who are too young and innocent to recognize their lack of ability. Yet we have found striking information in such drawings made by untrained draftsmen, when we could induce them. Most difficult of all, perhaps, have been the rapid sketches made while driving along a highway, as reported in "The View from the Road." Even a skilled draftsman cannot do that well. And still, these apparent scribbles tell an interesting, coherent story.

Curiously enough, few investigators are aware of the difficulty that most people have in communicating verbally. People are assumed to be able to talk well. But university students (and professors, alas!) are notoriously poor writers, poor speakers even. Asking someone about their environment often elicits a set of disconnected verbal cliches, until one takes the time to go deeper, or somehow helps the person to communicate verbally. With the advent of photography, and now TV, graphic literacy is very possibly rising relative to verbal literacy, although the skill is passive rather than productive.

The diverse ways in which different groups see the same place are important for public policy. So are the fascinating similarities, arising from features of the environment itself, or from our common biological heritage, or, as the Duncans so nicely illustrate, from similarities in the nature of the social relations within groups which at first glance may seem wildly dissimilar. Similarities of cognition are particularly useful in making city policy. They are essential if people are to communicate and cooperate with one another. Then why not teach each other how to see the world, both to build those social bridges and also to enrich our common experience?

Yi-Fu Tuan's article is a shining example of how to enlarge and vivify the perception of the world in that way. Literature (and also painting and photography, of course) is a mine of compelling perceptions of perceiving.

Still another "perspective" could have been added to this book[:] the perception of design, which has always been concerned with manipulating things in order to enhance cognition of them. The designer's craft is a storehouse of principles and practical examples on how to shape things so they seize our attention, organize our perception, and convey meaning. True enough, many design principles are contradictory. For the most part, they treat only the object itself, as if that object had some magical, sentient existence all its own. But this traditional knowledge contains important insights. By linking it with cognitive research, we would also help designers themselves to see the process whole.

A number of contributors note the lack of theoretical connections between image and behavior. For the most part, they mean predicted behavior, that is, "think x and you will do y." This is of natural interest for policy, which is always anxious to predict the results of some action. (Incidentally, how about the prediction of a feeling, given a behavior?) But these longed-for predictions continue to separate thought and action. Why not study persons in their environment as they act and feel together? Feelings and ideas are not merely troublesome intervening variables which must be passed through in order to understand visible behavior. Good behavior is by no means a reasonable motive for improving the environment. Feelings and ideas, and the actions and sensations which are part of them, are what it is like to be alive, and the goodness or badness of that experience is the why of policy. Most studies look at behavior *or* cognition, rarely the two together.

This is a book which centers on theory. Theory is a necessity: it links and explains our observations, and tells us what to look for, predict, and test. All too often, theoretical discussions are stupefying to read, despite all their underlinings, Capitalizing, and lengthy lists of concepts in hierarchical order. It might be a matter of style, but more often it is because these abstractions are too remote from how people actually experience the world. The theories that keep us awake are those that arise and are tested in the midst of life. Planning action, for its own part, is crippled without theory and reflection, since if action is free of any intellectual framework, then if it fails (or seems to fail, since one has no sure way of knowing) it can only be abandoned, and no one the wiser for it. Theory and action require each other.

In the final essay, Wohlwill notes how often environment disappears in environmental cognition research. Studies seem to be concerned with pure thinking. How infrequently one finds any analysis—even a description—of the setting whose cognition is being investigated, or any thought as to how environmental features might be involved in the process!

Most designers and planners, on the other hand, as they take notice of environmental cognition, simply acquire a new verbal style, add a novel field survey to their repertoire (a survey done, as always, by themselves), and continue to ignore the city as experienced by their inarticulate clients. They are trained to look at place, not at people. Each profession looks along its own nose, and to see perceiver and perceived whole is a difficult business. To link that understanding to public policy is an even more difficult business.

This book is stimulating because it shows, here and there throughout, how the process of environmental cognition can be seen as a developing creative interchange between the person, his intimate social group, and their spatial environment. It is one of those strategic domains where we fuse theoretical research and normative action.

Notes

1. Lynch's original manuscript contained this note, which was deleted in the published version: "If a foreword is allowed a footnote, I will call it, 'In Defense of Pictures.'"

2. Phillip Herr, Stephen Carr, William Cavellini, and Phillip Dowds, "Ecologue/Cambridgeport Project," Final Report, December 1972, Office of Environmental Education, U.S. Department of Health, Education and Welfare, Washington, D.C.

Environmental Perception: Research and Public Policy

Research into environmental perception began about 1960. Its original purpose was to change the way in which urban areas were being designed. These first efforts have had continuing consequences in research in many fields, but only a superficial effect on public planning, at least until rather recently. It is interesting to follow the evolution of that connection.

We began to inquire into the way people perceived their city surroundings in the late 1950s. The aim was to clarify some vague notions about the visual qualities of large environments, and particularly to show that you cannot evaluate a place, and should not plan for it, until you know how its residents see it and how they value it. The very first trials were concerned with how people locate themselves in a city, and find their way through it, but these experiments quickly escalated to considering the entire mental image of a place.

This early work is reported in *The Image of the City*. In essence, it consisted of lengthy interviews with individuals, beginning with open-ended questions such as "What first comes to your mind when you think of Boston (or wherever)?" and "Please draw me a map of Boston." It then went on to ask the person to describe how he or she would walk or drive from some given location to another, and what they would see along the way. Further, they were asked to name the "most distinctive" elements of the city in question, and to describe a few of these in some detail. In addition, some of the interviewees were asked to identify a set of photographs of the city, and say how they were able to make those identifications. A few others were taken into the city itself. They were adorned with a portable microphone, and asked to find their way from here to there, while talking about how they did it. As a final check, interviewers fanned out over the streets of the city, stopped pedestrians at random, and asked them how to get to certain key locations, and then how to recognize those places when one got there. All these tests were performed, on small samples of people, in the central areas of Boston, Jersey City, and Los Angeles—cities chosen for their presumed differences of visual quality.

These experiments produced a rich array of data, some of it scarcely analyzable in any systematic way. Yet as one listened to the tapes, looked at the amateurish but expressive maps, and then walked in the real streets, one had a vivid impression of being, in some degree, "inside the heads" of these people as they moved about their city, or as they imagined it in quietness. Connections were made that did not appear on official maps; elements became prominent that designers thought beneath their notice;

No date. Courtesy of Institute Archives and Special Collections, MIT Libraries.

things were suffused with strong feeling. Simple analyses could be made of how often particular elements were mentioned or drawn; common distortions, breaks, and linkages could be found; the temporal order in which parts were drawn or spoken of could be investigated. It was possible to compare the visible reality with verbal recollections, with drawings, with photographic recognitions, with recognitions in the field, and with the hurried replies of those we button-holed in the streets—and thus to uncover some broad regularities or discrepancies. Common strategies of mentally conceiving a large and complex environment were discovered, and the foundations of a technique for analyzing them was laid down.

There were a number of faults with these data. The samples were quite small, and were largely made up of middle-class professionals (not professionals concerned with the environment, however). The analysis tended to focus purely on visual elements, and very much, at that time, on way-finding and orientation. It emphasized recognition and structure, and explicitly set aside the other meanings of places to their users. It was a momentary insight, which neglected the rhythm of time, or the way in which the image was changing, or how it had developed.

With all these faults, it set off or reinforced research efforts in many fields: cognitive psychology and geography in particular. It helped to direct a latent interest in the visual qualities of cities. Similar studies of the city image have since been replicated in scores of cities, in many countries of the world. The research techniques have thus been substantially developed and improved.

At the same time, the work has had very little effect on public policy, which had been its original aim. To begin with, the chosen issue—the visual quality of place—was a latent issue rather than a focused, political one. An early application of the technique to public planning in the Town of Brookline, Mass., for example, done by the same authors, simply fell into silence. The selectmen of the town did not see that it affected their concerns, and the authors made no effort to make that connection. A much more ambitious study, of the new town of Ciudad Guayana in Venezuela, which used a truly representative sample of the population and was carried out by people who knew the realistic issues of development, was simply dismissed by the planners in charge. It demonstrated the gulf that lay between the planners and the planned, and this was an uncomfortable lesson.

Most often, wherever offical planners tried out the method, they would simply skip the citizen interviews as a nuisance, and use the bright new terminology (nodes, edges, landmarks, . . .) to describe their own image of the city, thus giving a show of respectability to the particular pattern they were bent on imposing. The research techniques were found to be too time-consuming, the data too difficult to analyze, and the results either too remote from the pressing issues that confronted them, or too upsetting to their professional prejudices.

Thus the early work had important consequences for research, and few (or even negative) consequences for public action. Yet, as this kind of research persisted and grew, it kept reappearing on the public scene. Gradually, it was modified to make the studies easier to accomplish, or more relevant, or both. Let us review a few of these more recent attempts in the U.S.

In a part of the central ghetto in Baltimore, there had been an extensive rehabilitation program, beginning in the 1950s, which consisted of clearing the old structures on the interior lots of the large square blocks, while conserving the substantial three and four story brick row houses on the block perimeters. The cleared inner areas were then converted into landscaped parks, and equipped for children's play. These new parks were widely applauded in the professional press at the time, and strongly supported by local residents. Nevertheless, they quickly deteriorated, and today stand largely unused, except by teenagers, who are in constant conflict with the surrouding householders. If one walks down these streets, it is clear that the life and activity is on the street front, and not in the inner parks. The street fronts are clean, often furnished and decorated, while the inner blocks are heaped with trash. The city, and local community organizations, however, were committed to the extension of this inner block park system. How could they be designed or managed to make them useful additions to the landscape, rather than eyesores?

In this case, the planning department of the city, in cooperation with the local university, has designed a program of research into perception and behavior which is directly linked to those dilemmas. To inquiries as to how the residents think of their neighborhood, it has added an extensive and systematic observation of how they actually use the local outdoor space, including sample counts, photography, studies of children's games, and diaries kept by local people. Some especially interesting studies were accomplished with local children, who played out the way they used the local space, using life-like dolls and a large model of a street and block. This action, often quite dramatic, was recorded on videotape.

In addition, various experiments with possible improvements were made, and the results evaluated: a local park manager was installed, a local newspaper established, special park activities were initiated, minor physical changes achieved, new arrangements for collecting trash concluded. These experiments were modified or dropped as they succeeded, failed, or met local participation or resistance. The research is not simply policy-oriented, it is completely entangled in policy and action. While the results may therefore lack classic rigor, their relevance is unquestionable. Much is being learned about perception, behavior, and the possibility of action, all at once. The local conflicts, and also the official rigidities and misperceptions, that lie behind the mis-use of the inner parks have become fairly clear. Some reasonably successful uses for the parks have been found, and ways to encourage local care and management. At the same time, the basic intractability of the problem has also been laid bare, under current ghetto conditions. The city may be asking the wrong question—very likely it should not continue to build these inner parks. Possibly it should focus its ameliorative efforts on the socially more important street fronts, while finding ways to return the inner blocks to private, or to local block, control, as well to deal decisively with trash and teen removal (not by extermination, we hasten to add, but by finding a legitimate and constructive outlet for these adolescent energies). However difficult the problem, the work in Baltimore is nevertheless a good example of how research can be conducted in order to be of direct value in resolving serious public issues. In doing so, moreover, the Baltimore staff has elaborated important new research techniques.

A somewhat different, but equally instructive research attempt was undertaken in the city of Cambridge, Mass. In this case, a number of academics and professionals became convinced that research into perception could be more than a way for outsiders to learn about the thoughts of insiders. It might play a political role, by being converted into a technique by which local people might make clear to themselves how they used the world and how the world used them, and thence make explicit to each other their common problems. Instead of being a professional research method, it would become one of self-study. Ultimately, it would be a step to effective local political organization.

A part of the city was chosen that was relatively poor and shabby, but also changing and quite complex: a mix of black and white, working class and professional, young students and the elderly. The same familiar methods were employed: mapping, trip descriptions, behavior observation, the taking and discussion of photographs, verbal evaluations of the existing environment, the drawing of utopias, and so on. But they were used in quite a different way, and for a different purpose. To begin with, small groups of local people were formed, by local convenors, to whom a research assistant was assigned, simply as a technical guide and aide. Each group was a homogeneous representation of some segment of the local society deemed important in the initial survey: black male adolescents, widowed elderly white women, young unmarried white female professionals, white working class male heads of households, and so on. These groups went through a systematic course of study of their own perceptions of their world, which, via long discussions, culminated in group agreements about their environmental problems, priorities, and desires. Once sure of their own interests, one group began to talk to another, in order to uncover agreements and conflicts. They began to face up to those conflicts, and to advance to common positions by making trade-offs and accommodations. The twelve-month process culminated in meetings of the whole group of citizens, in which perceptions were shared, common needs outlined, and agreements made about common projects to pursue.

Since things must have a name to be visible, the whole process was called Ecologue. Its fundamental aim was to convert academic research into a local political organization. Organization would not be achieved by the classic device of polarization around a fighting issue, but by encouraging a complex community to surface the issues implicit in its own life experience, rather than those imposed on it by outside forces.

The actual process was a lengthy one, which required extraordinary energy and self-effacement from the researchers. At the same time, it elicited commitment, and strong interest, from the local participants. Groups discussed in earnest, and a sharp picture of the local life experience emerged. In the end, a stable local political organization did not survive the study, although one flickered for a year, and several individual participants moved into active political work.

Despite that failure, the Ecologue study makes it apparent that these research techniques can be used by ordinary citizens for self-examination, and that it is an excellent, if time-consuming, way of raising local consciousness and surfacing the important local issues, issues which otherwise may easily be obscured by the current sounds of battle. Some of the professionals originally engaged in Ecologue, now working in architectural and planning consultancy, have subsequently used these techniques to give voice to users of proposed facilities, and thus to let them influence their form. College dormitories were fitted to the needs of their student residents, and the planning for a downtown mall for Washington, D.C.—a plan which included changes in management as well as in physical form—made heavy use of consultant panels of downtown shoppers.

Lastly, in this brief list of examples, the Applied Social Science Section of UNESCO has been supporting an international series of studies on the use and perception of residential neighborhoods by young adolescents. This work has so far been carried out in nine different localities in Argentina, Australia, Mexico, and Poland. Adolescents were chosen as being a group for whom the quality of the neighborhood might be particularly important. Another intent, not always realized, has been to focus on lower income groups in the developing countries, where the stresses of the residential environment may be especially severe. While using a set of common research guidelines, and billed as "comparative study," it is difficult to make true comparative conclusions, since the studies were done by a great variety of local researchers, with very little financial support and no opportunity for joint discussion or training.

Yet a number of fascinating hints do come forth about how these boys and girls make the best of their surroundings—in different ways from country to country, but apparently in relation to some basic common needs. More important for the moment, studies show that it is possible to devise a research process that can be used in a relatively brief time by investigators new to perception studies, and that their results can have definite policy implications. Stimulating local interest in this kind of research, and showing its importance for public policy, was indeed the primary aim of the UNESCO effort.

In summary, the protocol calls for a rapid reconnaissance of the physical form of the neighborhood (recording it on existing maps and via systematic photography), followed by an interview with the children, followed by a systematic observation of their actual behavior outdoors (recorded by means of photographs and activity diagrams). The interview asks for a map, a listing and description of important places, a typical day's activity, and some questions about change, problems, future intentions, and how various places are valued. The usefulness of these questions is by now fairly well established, although they clearly must be modified to fit different cultural situations. Finally, there are a number of optional procedures which can be added to this core, including group discussions, guided tours led by the children, and interviews with parents and local officials.

These investigations are eloquent about the importance (and the dangers) of the local streets to these children, as well as the role of the sense of community. "Waste" grounds are highly valued, as places where one can act on one's own, and so is a private space within the home, if the children are lucky enough to have it. These children are quite sensitive to the rapid physcial changes occurring around them, and have some surprisingly widespread ideas about what an "ideal" environment would be like. Perhaps most striking is the hunger for stimulus, for engagement and responsibility, i.e., for the means by which they can grow, and through which they can enter adult society.

Some of these general findings are summarized in "Growing Up in Cities." Perhaps more important is the extract from a lengthier report, which describes the technique of data collection, as modified by experience. The research method has proven to be flexible, easy to learn, relatively undemanding of time and resources, and quite rich in the information it supplies about use and behavior. Naturally, it must be tailored to the chosen age group, and to some degree be rewritten for each culture in which it is applied.

What effects have these brief studies actually had on public action? It is clear enough that they *could* have a salutary influence, since the findings touch on such questions as the design of local streets and play areas, the type of housing to be provided, the distribution of open space, the access to the city center, the leaving of "waste" remnants, policies on access to land and its control, the content of school work, the provision of social facilities, tree planting, traffic control, the rate of physical change, the mixture of workplace and residence, and so on—indeed a long list.

Whether in fact a policy connection is established depends on the way in which these studies were initiated. Policy makers and planners are oppressed with what appear to them to be urgent immediate questions. They must be convinced that these peculiar studies are worth the effort— that they can be accomplished within the time limits of realistic planning and decision, and that they produce information that will actually improve those decisions. Thus, the Melbourne studies, since they involved officials, and also because they occurred in an information vacuum, just as public policy was ready for a change, have had some influence on public decisions about the replanning of the area. The Argentine studies will most likely have no effect on the planning of housing, but some influence on plans for the city center, since one of the investigators is consulting on those particular plans. The Polish studies, however illuminating, were carried out by educational psychologists, who had little contact with planners and architects. The results may have an influence in the Polish schools, but are not likely to effect physical planning. The Mexican studies were done by outsiders, and while they have stimulated new directions for research in that country (as they were intended to do), they leave untouched the public decisions that shape the fate of the squatter settlements.

Useful techniques are those that can be conducted and their data be analyzed within a reasonable time, by relatively untrained observers. The results must link up with practical issues of public policy. We think that the UNESCO surveys have begun to meet those tests. Whether they are so used depends on the process by which they are initiated and the questions to which they are addressed. Given that, they can be valuable in a wide range of circumstances.

References

Appleyard, Donald, *Planning A Pluralist City*. Cambridge: MIT Press, 1976.

Appleyard, Donald, M. Sue Gerson, and Mark Lintell, "Traffic in Neighborhoods: Policies for More Livable Streets." Monograph 24, Institute of Urban and Regional Development, University of California, Berkeley.

Brower, Sidney, and Penelope Williamson, "Outdoor Recreation as a Function of the Urban Housing Environment." *Environment and Behavior* 6: 3 (September 1974).

Carr, Stephen, William Cavellini, Phillip Dowds, and Phillip Herr, *Ecologue/Cambridgeport Project*, final report to the U.S. Department of Health, Education and Welfare. Department of Urban Studies and Planning, MIT, December 1972.

Donelly, Dennis, Brian Goodey, and Michael Menzies, "Perception Related Survey for Local Authorities: A Pilot Study in Sunderland." Research Memo 20, Center for Urban and Regional Studies, University of Birmingham, 1973.

Goodey, Brian, "A Checklist of Sources on Environmental Perception." Research Memo 11, Center for Urban and Regional Studies, University of Birmingham, March 1972.

Hack, Gary, "Environmental Programming: Creating Responsive Settings." Ph.D. dissertation, Department of Urban Studies and Planning, MIT, 1976.

Lynch, Kevin, *An Analysis of the Visual Form of Brookline*. Community Renewal Program, Brookline, Mass., September 1965.

Lynch, Kevin, *Growing Up in Cities*. Cambridge: MIT Press, 1977.

Lynch, Kevin, *The Image of the City*. Cambridge: MIT Press, 1960.

Sims, William, "Neighborhoods: Columbus Neighborhood Definition Study." Department of Development, Columbus, Ohio, 1973.

Reconsidering *The Image of the City* (1985)

The Image of the City was published over 20 years ago, and it is still listed in bibliographies. It is time to wonder what it led to. The research was done by a small group with no training in the methods they used, and no literature to guide them. Several motives led them to the study:

1. An interest in the possible connection between psychology and the urban environment, at a time when most psychologists—at least, those in the field of perception—preferred controlled experiments in the laboratory to the wandering variables of the complicated, real environment. We hoped to tempt some of them out into the light of day.

2. Fascination with the aesthetics of the city landscape, at a time when most U.S. planners shied away from the subject, because it was "a matter of taste" and had a low priority.

3. Persistent wonder about how to evaluate a city, as architects do so automatically when presented with a building design. Shown a city plan, planners would look for technical flaws, estimate quantities, or analyze trends, as if they were contractors about to bid on the job. We hoped to think about what a city should be, and we were looking for possibilities of designing directly at that scale.

4. Hope of influencing planners to pay more attention to those who live in a place—to the actual human experience of a city, and how it should affect city policy.

These motives found an early outlet in an erratic seminar on the aesthetics of the city in 1952, which considered, among several other similar themes, the question of how people actually found their way about the streets of big cities. Various other unconnected ideas sprouted during a subsequent fellowship year spent walking the streets of Florence, which were recorded in some brief and unpublished "Notes on City Satisfactions." These ideas matured during 1954, when I had the opportunity of working with Gyorgy Kepes on a Rockefeller grant devoted to the "perceptual form of the city." As we walked the Boston streets and wrote notes to each other, and as I listened to his torrent of ideas on perception and daily experience, the minor theme of city orientation grew into the major theme of the mental image of the environment.

Undoubtedly, there were many other less explicit influences: from John Dewey, with his emphasis on experience, to ideas of the "transactional" psychologists, with their view of perception as an active transaction between person and place. I had done fairly extensive reading in psychology, without finding much that was helpful. I had always learned much

Reprinted, with permission, from *Cities of the Mind*, ed. Lloyd Rodwin and Robert Hollister (New York: Plenum, 1984).

more from stories, memoirs, and the accounts of anthropologists. We were not then aware of K. E. Boulding's key study, *The Image*,[1] which was published at the same time as our own work and became an important theoretical underpinning of it. The role of the environmental image was an idea in the air, however.

The first study was too simple to be quite respectable. We interviewed 30 people about their mental picture of the inner city of Boston, and then we repeated the exercise in Jersey City (which we guessed might be characterless) and Los Angeles (booked as the motorized city). We took Boston because it was there, and we knew it and liked it. We asked people what came to their mind about the city, and to make a sketch map of it, and to take imaginary trips through it. We asked them to describe its distinctive elements, to recognize and place various photographs, and (with a small sample) to go on actual walks with us. Later, we stopped people in the streets and asked for directions to places. Meanwhile, other members of the team, uncontaminated by all this interview work, surveyed the town, in order to make some guesses about what a typical image would be, given the physical form.

This small group of informants produced an astonishing flood of perceptions. At times, as we listened to their tapes and studied their drawings, we seemed to be moving down the same imaginary street with them, watching the pavements rise and turn, the buildings and open spaces appear, feeling the same pleasant shock of recognition, or being puzzled by some mental gray hole, where there should have been some piece of the city. Our conclusion—or perhaps the hardening of our preconceived notion—was that people had a relatively coherent and detailed mental image of their city, which had been created in an interaction between self and place, and that this image was both essential to their actual function, and also important to their emotional well-being. These individual images had many common features—similarities that arose from common human strategies of cognition, common culture and experience, and the particular physical form of the place that they live in. Thus, an observer, familiar with the local culture and with the general nature of city images, could, after a careful study of the town, make predictions about likely common features and patterns of organization in the mental images of that place. We developed methods for eliciting these mental images from people, as well as a way of classifying and presenting them. We asserted that the quality of that city image was important to well-being and should be considered in designing or modifying any locality. Thus, orientation had been expanded into a general method of analyzing place, and a vivid and coherent mental image had been elevated to a general principle of city design. Later, this idea was expanded further, to include a vivid image of time as well as place.[2]

All of this from talking to 30 people! It was not surprising that there were sharp criticisms. The obvious remark was that the sample of people was far too small, and too biased, to permit of such sweeping assertions. Our handful of interviewees were all young, middle-class people, and most of them were professionals. The attack was well mounted; and yet it failed. The original work has by now been replicated in many communities, large and small, in North and South America, Europe, and Asia, because the method is cheap and rather fun to do. In every case, the basic ideas have held, with the important proviso that images are much modified by culture and familiarity, as was predicted in our original speculations. But the existence and role of the place image, its basic elements, and the techniques of eliciting and analyzing it seem astonishingly similar in some very diverse cultures and places. We were lucky.

A second criticism was that the techniques of office and field interview, of photo recognition, and of map drawing were inadequate to get at the true mental image, so deeply lodged in the mind. Map drawing, in particular, is too difficult for most people, and thus it is a very misleading index of what they know. Even just talking may be an exercise in pleasing the interviewer more than a revelation of inner patterns, many of which may be inaccessible to the person.

In principle, the comment is just. What is in the mind is an elusive thing. Environmental psychologists are busy debating the relative merits of various tricks for entering that fascinating realm. But one can reply that, although each method may elicit only a piece of the internal picture, and that may be distorted as well as partial, yet, if a sufficient array of probes is employed, a composite picture develops that is not very far from the truth. Of course, it may only be the tip of the iceberg, whose base is hidden far below, but the tip is the tip of a real iceberg, nonetheless. Luckily for us, the environmental image is usually not a painful subject for most people, something to be defended by unconscious barriers. People like to talk about it.

The possibility remains that the image brought forth for discussion in an interview is not the same one that is used in actually operating in a city. This possibility can be checked only by working with people as they actually move about, as we did in our street interviews. But even if the two images were disjunctive (which does not seem to be the case), the interview image can still have an important social and emotional role.

A method war erupted over map drawing, which was one of the techniques we used that seemed at first to take everyone's fancy. Drawing is indeed an unfamiliar act, as compared with talking, not only for most interviewees, but also (which may be the real problem) for most interviewers as well. Yet I cling to the value of drawing as a means of expression, especially of spatial ideas, despite our cultural downgrading of visual communication (a downgrading that may now be reversed, at least in a passive sense, for the current TV generation). Much can be read from amateur maps, in supplement to verbal comments, if one allows for common drafting difficulties. Drawings convey emotional tone as well as substance, just as actual speech does.

Whereas researchers worried over our methods, designers were fearful that these same methods might usurp their central creative skill—that a "science of design" might suddenly seize their territory. Image analysis would then lead automatically to form decisions, untouched by the free imagination. But their fears were quite unfounded. Analysis can describe a present situation and its consequences, and even—much more uncertainly—predict the consequences of some altered arrangement, but it is powerless to generate new possibilities. This is the irreplaceable power of the creative mind. Image studies, although they may threaten designer pretenses about how other people feel about places, are no more threatening to the central act of design than is an analysis of structure or of climate. On the contrary, perception studies could support and enrich design.

The most critical attack of all was that the study was overblown, if it meant to identify a basic principle of place quality. It focused on way finding, which was surely a secondary problem for most people. If lost in a city, one can always ask the way or consult a map. The study may have analyzed the nature of the way-finding image accurately enough. But it only assumed its importance and never demonstrated it. What do people care if they have a vivid image of their locality? And aren't they delighted by surprise and mystery?

This was a more direct hit. The study never proved its basic assumption, except indirectly, via the emotional tone of the interviews: the repeated remarks about the pleasure of recognition and knowledge, the satisfaction of identification with a distinctive home place, and the displeasure of being lost or of being consigned to a drab environment. Succeeding studies have continued to collect this indirect evidence. The idea can be linked to the role of self-identity in psychological development, in the belief that self-identity is reinforced by a strong identity of place and time. A powerful place image can be presumed to buttress group identity. The pleasures of perceiving a complex, vivid landscape are frequently experienced and recorded. Mature, self-confident people can cope with drab or confused surroundings, but such places are crucial difficulties for those internally disoriented, or for those at some critical stage of their development.[3] It is reasonable to think that a featureless environment deprives us of some very important emotional satisfactions. These convictions have been reinforced by many expressions of popular culture, as well as findings in psychology, art, and the sociology of small groups. (As to the role of surprise and disorder, I return to that below.) Nevertheless, it is true that this central assumption remains an assumption, however it may be shored up by anecdote, personal experience, or its connection to the structure of other ideas.

If these four criticisms—of sample size, method, design usurpation, and basic relevance—were the important ones made at the time, there were also other unremarked cracks in our structure, which only opened up later. The first, and most immediately dangerous, was the neglect of observer variation, which we passed over in order to show the effect of physical variation. This neglect was deliberate and explicit, as the role of visual form had been widely ignored, and it was also important to show that a given physical reality produces some common images of place, at least within one culture. Image variation among observers—due to class, age, gender, familiarity, role, and other such factors—was expected to be a finding of subsequent studies. Indeed, it was. Broader samples, such as those interviewed by Appleyard in Ciudad Guayana,[4] made clear how social class and habitual use cause people to see a city with very different eyes.

What was not foreseen, however, was that this study, whose principal aim was to urge on designers the necessity of consulting those who live in a place, had at first a diametrically opposite result. It seemed to many planners that here was a new technique—complete with the magical classifications of node, landmark, district, edge, and path—that allowed a designer to predict the public image of any existing city or new proposal. For a time, plans were fashionably decked out with nodes and all the rest. There was no attempt to reach out to actual inhabitants, because that effort would waste time and might be upsetting. As before, professionals were imposing their own views and values on those they served. The new jargon was appropriated to that old end, and its moral was stood on its head. Instead of opening a channel by which citizens might influence design, the new words became another means of distancing them from it. Indeed, the words were dangerous precisely because they were useful. They afforded a new way of talking about the qualities of large-scale form, for which designers had previously had only inarticulate feelings. Thus, the words seemed true in themselves.

Fortunately, designers have gone on to other fashions, and accumulating studies have made it evident how differently a low-income teenager thinks of a city from a middle-class professional (just as both see a compact, labyrinthine city very differently from one that sprawls over an extensive grid). The perception of a city is a transaction between person and place, which varies with variations in each factor, but which has stable rules and strategies. Armed with a sense of those strategies, and a set of analytical methods, a designer can help citizens to understand what they see and value and can thus help them to judge proposed changes. In their work in Cambridgeport, Carr and Herr[5] showed how these same image techniques could be used as a means of participation. In a few cases, image studies are now used in that way, but the first effect on city design was often pernicious.

Our second omission, less easy to repair, was that we elicited a static image, a momentary pattern. There was no sense of *development* in it—of how that pattern came to be, nor of how it might change in the future, as the person matured, her or his function changed, her or his experience enlarged, or the city itself was modified. The dynamic nature of perception was denied. Once again, the study unwittingly fed a designer illusion: that a building or a city is something that is created in one act, then to endure forever.

It is far more exhausting to analyze how an image develops, because this requires a longitudinal analysis. Yet that will be a necessity, if we mean to get a true understanding of this dynamic process and to link these studies to fundamental research in developmental and cognitive psychology. Some starts have been made: Denis Wood on the growth of the image of London among teenage visitors,[6] Banerjee's comparison of the images of newcomers and old inhabitants,[7] and Smith's replication of the original Boston studies,[8] which showed how 10 years of physical change had affected the public image of that place. The track of image development in the maturing person and also the path of change as one becomes familiar with a place are both progressions (or regressions) that stand in need of close analysis.

The static view is mistaken not only as a matter of understanding, but also as a matter of value. We are pattern makers, not pattern worshipers. Unless we are mentally at risk, our great pleasure is to *create* order, in an ascending scale of complexity as we mature. This is the pleasure that designers so enjoy—and so often deny to others. The valuable city is not an ordered one, but one that can be ordered—a complexity whose pattern unfolds the more one experiences it. Some overarching, patent order is necessary for the bewildered newcomer. Beyond that, the order of a city should be an unfolding order, a pattern that one progressively grasps, making deeper and richer connections. Hence our delight (if we are internally secure) in ambiguity, mystery, and surprise, as long as they are contained within a basic order, and as long as we can be confident of weaving the puzzle into some new, more intricate pattern. Unfortunately, we do not have any models for an unfolding order.

Third, the original study set the meaning of places aside and dealt only with their identity and their structuring into larger wholes. It did not succeed, of course. Meaning always crept in, in every sketch and comment. People could not help connecting their surroundings with the rest of their lives. But wherever possible, those meanings were brushed off the replies, because we thought that a study of meaning would be far more complicated than a study of mere identity. This original renunciation is now itself being renounced, particularly in the studies of environmental semiotics, in which the technical analysis of meaning in language is applied to the meaning of place. Interesting as this work is, it labors under the difficulty that places are not languages: their primary function is not the communication of meaning, nor can their elements be so neatly parsed into discrete signifiers. Nevertheless, if it can free itself of that analogy—if places can be considered in their own nature, and not as silent speech—the study of environmental meaning will undoubtedly bring rich results for city designers. Some promising advances have been made, by Appleyard just before his death,[9] Rapoport,[10] and others. If only it were not so difficult!

Last, perhaps, I would criticize our original studies because they have proved so difficult to apply to actual public policy. This difficulty is strange, because the principal motive of the whole affair was to change the way in which cities were shaped: to make them more responsive to their inhabitants. To my chagrin, the work seems to have had very little real effect of that kind, except for the first flurry of misuse, now so happily faded away.

To my surprise, on the contrary, the work led to a long line of research in other fields: in anthropology and sociology to some extent, and to a larger degree in geography and environmental psychology. Golledge and Moore's *Environmental Knowing*,[11] and Evans' review article, "Environmental Cognition,"[12] summarize this extensive work and lay out the current debates and preoccupations. The original findings have been extended, corrected, built upon, and superseded. In that sense, the work has fulfilled its function. That function was largely unforeseen, except for our hope of attracting perceptual psychologists to an interest in the urban environment. The work has become a small part of a much larger, and intellectually more fascinating, study of the nature of human cognition. Environmental psychology and cognitive geography are now well-established areas of concern in their general fields. Cognitive anthropology is maturing. The function of the human brain is the central mystery, and the study of humankind's perception of its environment has a valid place in it.

On the other hand—ironically—the early work has had only a minor impact on actual city design. Although researchers were quick to take up the idea, and many amateur city-lovers as well, fewer professionals have done so, saving only that early spurt, cited above. Those that have tried it in real situations report that the results are interesting, but hard to put to use. A soil survey or an analysis of a housing market leads quite easily into city design. Why should an analysis of the image of place, first motivated by design preoccupations, fail to do so?

One reason is that there are many mental images of the city. If one is concerned with an area used by many diverse people, it may be difficult to set out the common problems, and these problems may not be central to the concerns of any one group. Therefore, these techniques are more telling in smaller, more homogeneous communities, or in dealing with tourists, who are more dependent on overt visible clues. Yet, even in complex metropolitan areas, certain images are apparently very widely held.

I think that a deeper reason for this lack of application lies in the special place of esthetics in our culture. Esthetics is thought to be something separate from the rest of life (which it is not), and the perceptual form of something is believed to be solely an aesthetic issue (which it is not, either). Esthetics can be considered a sacred issue—the highest goal of human activity once basic wants are satisfied. Or it may seem to be a secondary affair, subordinate to more fundamental needs. In either case, it is thought special, idiosyncratic, and not subject to rational debate. Thus, it is not an appropriate concern for public policy, or at least, it must be dealt with separately, gingerly, and at late stage of decision. Urban design, which tries to deal with public aesthetic issues in conjunction with other "functional" issues (as if seeing were not functional!), holds only an uneasy position in this country. By custom and by institution, public policy at larger scales deals with economic and social ends, whereas perceptual questions are addressed at the level of small territories, or of single buildings. Decision makers often base their choices on a strong personal image of the environment, but this image is implicit and is not tested against others. Politicians do not base their campaigns on explicit sensuous issues, although such questions are often hidden motives in political battle, and even though there is the pervasive, inarticulate public response to the way localities look. What is usually called *urban design* today is more often large-scale architecture, which aims to make an object in one sustained operation, according to the will of a gifted professional. It may even be no more than a visible gloss, applied to a development "package" to help it glide along the rails of decision. True city design—dealing directly with the ongoing sensed environment of the city, in collaboration with the people who sense it—hardly exists today.

This quirk in our view of the world limits what we do. A public agency is unlikely to support a costly piece of analysis that deals with "mere aesthetics," and it is also unlikely to see how the results might fit into its decisions. The agency will be cautious about deciding anything on what seem to be such arbitrary grounds. The professional, in his or her turn, may prefer to cloak aesthetic judgments in the more dignified mantle of other criteria, and so keep his or her aesthetic underbody as safe as possible from defiling amateur hands.

Some attempts have been made to apply image surveys to city policy in this country, notably in San Francisco,[13] Dallas,[14] and Minneapolis.[15] These attempts are dissected in Yata's "City Wide Urban Design Policies."[16] They are not convincing examples of the effectiveness of this particular technique. More work has been done in other countries, notably in Japan, in Israel, and in Scandinavia. In this country, again, there is some application of the method in tourist areas, where images may equate with dollars, or at the local neighborhood level, where a settled and vocal group have an explicit stake in the quality of their surroundings.

But decision makers—and many professionals—still find the technique peculiar. Despite the continuing notoriety of the early study, it has been an enthusiasm of researchers in other fields, or of amateurs and contemplatives, or of beginners in the profession. I tried, in *Managing the Sense of a Region*,[17] to show how such studies and issues could actually be applied to public management decisions in complicated urban regions. For the most part, however, these were speculations, rather than actual experiences.

It may be that there is some characteristic of the analysis that adapts it for research, but not for policy. This characteristic is not yet apparent to me. It is ironic that a study launched with the primary aim of affecting policy seems to have missed its target and hit another one. I remain in hope that the flight is not yet over.

References

1. Ann Arbor: University of Michigan Press, 1956.

2. Kevin Lynch, *What Time Is This Place?* Cambridge: MIT Press, 1972.

3. H. F. Searles, *The Non-Human Environment*. New York: International University Press, 1960.

4. Donald Appleyard, *Planning a Pluralist City: Conflicting Realites in Ciudad Guyana*. Cambridge: MIT Press, 1976.

5. Phillip B. Herr et al., *Ecologue/Cambridgeport Project*. MIT Department of Urban Studies and Planning, 1972.

6. D. Wood and R. Beck, "Talking with Environmental A, an Experimental Mapping Language." In *Environmental Knowing: Theories, Research, and Methods*, ed. G. T. Moore and R. G. Golledge (Stroudsburg: Dowden, Hutchinson and Ross, 1976).

7. Tridib Banerjee, "Urban Experience and the Development of the City Image." Ph.D. dissertation, Department of Urban Studies and Planning, MIT, 1971.

8. B. A. Smith, "The Image of the City 10 Years Later." Master's thesis, Department of Urban Studies and Planning, MIT, 1971.

9. In his incomplete and unpublished manuscript "Identity, Power, and Place."

10. Amos Rapoport, *The Meaning of the Built Environment: A Nonverbal Communication Approach*. Beverly Hills: Sage, 1982.

11. G. T. Moore and R. G. Golledge (eds.), *Environmental Knowing: Theories, Research, and Methods*. Stroudsburg: Dowden, Hutchinson and Ross, 1976.

12. G. Evans, "Environmental Cognition." *Psychological Bulletin* 88, no. 2 (1980): 259–287.

13. San Francisco Department of City Planning, *San Francisco Urban Design Study* (8 vols.) and *Urban Design Plan* (1969–1971).

14. Dallas Department of Urban Planning, *The Visual Form of Dallas* (1974).

15. Minneapolis Planning Commission, *Toward a New City* (1965).

16. Tsutomo Yata, "City-Wide Urban Design Polices." Ph.D. dissertation, Department of Urban Studies and Planning, MIT, 1979.

17. MIT Press, 1976.

III Analysis of Visual Form

Before Kevin Lynch began his work on the analysis of visual from, appearance and design were considered matters of aesthetic judgment and personal taste—things for the experts to decide, and therefore not particularly amenable to public debate. Consequently, issues of visual quality rarely influenced public policy. Lynch tried to change that through his research and writings. He wanted to bring visual quality out into the domain of public discourse by documenting those qualities of the everyday environment that are commonly experienced by the public. He believed that such "public transcripts" of shared visual experience could ultimately influence public debates about the future form of the community.

The term "aesthetics" seldom appeared in Lynch's writings or works. Although he was gifted with aesthetic sense and design talents, and always emphasized strong relations between appearance and function in his writing, he preferred to use such words as "appearance," "look," and "sense" to refer to matters of visual quality. He considered the term "aesthetics" too vague, and talked about it as the "unanalyzed residuum"—what is left after objective analysis of the built form. He also considered it peculiar and paradoxical that the "intellectual isolation of design and aesthetics" still underlay the concept of planning for large environments.

We also believe that Lynch was not at ease with the notion that all matters of aesthetics are to be decided by a select few. Although he accepted the role of expert judgment, he felt quite strongly that such judgment must not be arbitrary, and that it ought to be based on a thorough understanding of what people like and dislike about their environments and why. Furthermore, he felt that the subjective polemics of aestheticians led nowhere—the arguments could not be defended. An intellectual rebel of sorts, a heretic, he always questioned conventional wisdom of authoritative nature, especially if it did not square with his personal intuitions about life and about the quality of places. Thus, while the tradition of design aesthetics has remained profoundly authoritarian and elitist, Lynch believed in a democratic basis for design decisions.

In his attempts to systematically describe and document the visual form of cities, Lynch began with a clean slate. There were no previous methods, no languages or lexicons, no notation systems on which such work could be based. Lynch was curious about several things: How to represent large-scale visual environments? What are the important visual qualities? What can be measured objectively? Clearly the techniques of architectural drawing—plans, sections, elevations, perspectives—were not sufficient. Conventional land-use maps were also totally inadequate. In the days of Camillo Sitte, Daniel Burnham, and Frederick Law Olmsted, civic and landscape design had been based largely on architectural representations. Objective documentation of the visual quality of the natural or built landscapes was not required in that tradition. So this was indeed a new frontier to be explored in the field of environmental design arts.

The first selection in this part of the volume is a previously unpublished piece, written in the late 1970s, in which Lynch tried to summarize the process involved in a community visual survey. Obviously this was written with some introspection; Lynch had conducted many such studies, and had seen others attempt to do so, and he was aware of pitfalls and lessons. The illustrations we have added to this article are based largely on the suggestions for illustrations that Lynch noted in the margin of the original manuscript. We believe that this piece should serve as a general model for community visual surveys.

The second and third selections are examples of practical applications of visual form analysis at a local community scale. The visual analysis of Brookline is based on a study conducted by Lynch in the mid-1960s as part of the federally funded Community Renewal Program for that Boston-area community. We have included the study almost in its entirety, for it represents a complete step-by-step demonstration of how concerns about visual quality can be identified, analyzed, and ultimately incorporated into policies for community conservation and change.

"Development and Landscape: Martha's Vineyard" is a chapter from a larger report, *Looking at the Vineyard*, prepared for the Vineyard Open Land Foundation in 1973. This study is truly a remarkable one, as it looks at the natural landscape and the visual form of an island ecology threatened by irresponsible development. As a long-time vacation resident of Martha's Vineyard, Lynch was familiar with the history, the development, and the human uses of the island; he understood the natural processes that endowed the island with an enormously varied landscape. Lynch wrote this report in simple yet vivid language, so that the public could understand and appreciate the fragile and unique quality of the island landscape. In it he reveals his love for the island, here worrying about its uncertain future, there admonishing against reckless and inconsiderate uses of land and water but at the same time suggesting creative ways of achieving greater social equity in the enjoyment of visual and physical resources. This study presents a methodology for analyzing and understanding the visual quality of predominantly natural landscapes, and for formulating policies for their preservation and management.

The last selection in this part is a review paper Lynch wrote for a conference in Stuttgart summarizing past and current efforts— including his own and those inspired by his work—to analyze the visual quality of large areas. This piece is reflective in nature and somewhat critical in content. What troubled Lynch was that many of these studies conducted as parts of larger urban design projects, despite their promising beginnings, had failed to lead to meaningful policies and to make any real impact on the visual quality of the communities. He ended this article by underscoring where we had failed, and why, and what was needed to make these studies more successful.

Despite his own disappointment, Lynch's legacy of visual studies has demonstrated that the "look" of the aggregate environment can matter, and that it can be understood and analyzed in a systematic way. We hope that these examples will continue to inspire visual studies and to influence the appearance of community environments.

This process is intended to be a relatively simple visual survey that a local community might conduct for itself within a period of a few months to perhaps a year, using non-specialized staff, volunteer community labor, and the occasional advice of a specialist. It should be the base for local visual policy. It will serve to convey an objective picture of the general visual character of the area, but, above all, it is directed toward identifying:

those visual qualities thought valuable and worth conserving;

those qualities thought undesirable, which should be changed;

those qualities which are changing, and whether that is for better or worse; and

those qualities which are most vulnerable to change.

The method, while "objective" in recording what can be and is seen, is involved in change and values from the start, and so leads directly to policy.

While this is a survey of *visual* character, it would logically be linked to studies of all the other sensory qualities of a place—sound and climate in particular, but also touch, smell, and other senses. This broader (and logically continuous) field is not further pursued here, however. Visual character includes esthetic issues, but goes well beyond them. A more thorough discussion of these issues, with elaborations, details, and examples, is given in *Managing the Sense of a Region*.

The survey may most simply be divided into two aspects: the character of the visible environment itself (i.e., what can be seen), and the particular places in which its inhabitants see it. Perceivable and perceived are analyzed together. Studies of the visible environment itself can further be divided into its character as a set of *places* which people live in and use, and a set of *journeys*, by which those people move through the area, and so experience it.

The Area as a Set of Places

In this case, the essential task is to divide the community into a mosaic of places classified by their visual character. A preliminary reconnaissance of the entire area is made, to see how typical visual characters vary within it, with regard to such elements as typical building mass and density, the character of wall and ground surfaces, topography, natural features and planting, visible activity, maintenance, details, characteristic views, and spatial texture. A broad classification of places must then be agreed upon,

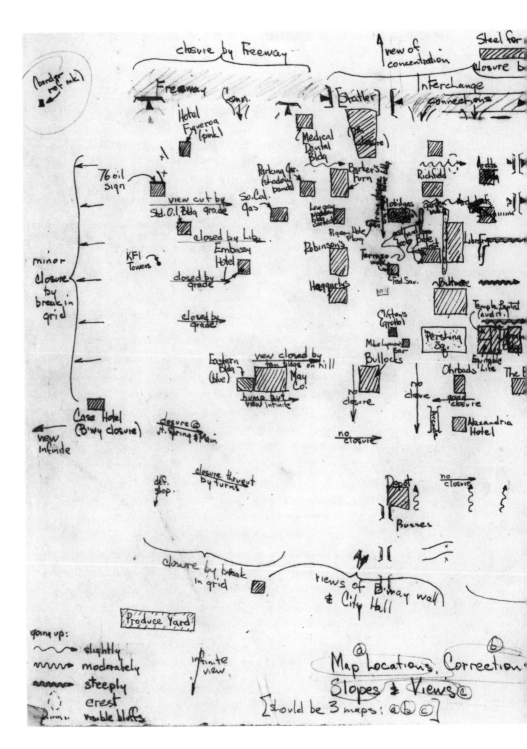

The area as a set of places, Los Angeles.

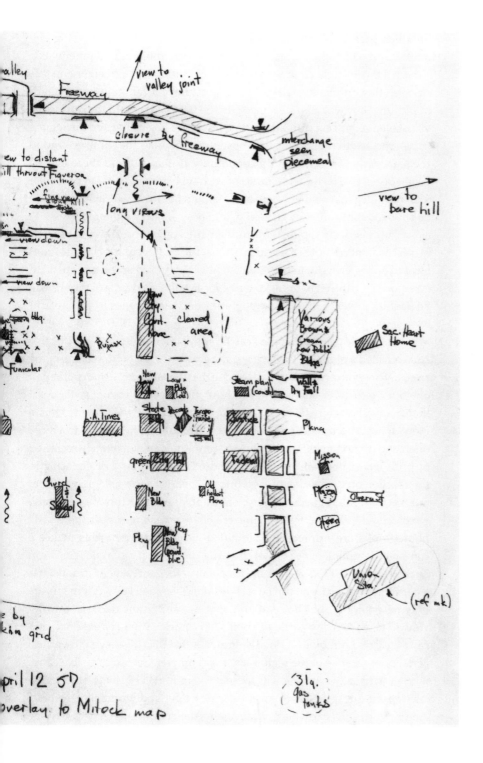

alley

Freeway

view to
valley joint

Closure by Freeway

interchange
seen
piecemeal

ew to distant
ill throout Figueroa

fine view

view to
bare hill

long views

view down

view down

green bldg

Ruins

Funicular

New
City
Court
House

cleared
area

Various
Brown &
Cream
New Public
Bldgs.

Sac. Heart
Home

New
Law

Law
Bldg
(old)

Steam plant
(constr)

Walls
Dry Fall

L.A. Times

State Records
Bldg

Tempo
tanks

Justice

Pkng

green City Hall

Federal

Mission

Church
&
School

New
Bldg

Old
Halbut
Pkng

Plaza

Olvera St

Guard

Pkng

New
Bldg
(round,
blue)

Pkng

Union
Sta.

(ref mk)

e by
kin grid

3 lg.
gas
tanks

in which each type of place is a typical composite of these varying elements, and which thus brings out the principal problems and potentials.

All those engaged in the survey must come to an agreement on this classification and its usefulness. They must have a common understanding of how they will map such places in the field, and record their principal visual elements. Test runs are made, both at the beginning and during the survey, to see that different field observers will map the same ground in the same way. Then the entire community is mapped into these chosen visual districts. The basic character of each type is analyzed—in particular to determine what elements and areas should be conserved, which should be changed, how are they changing, and how are they vulnerable.

This district mapping is the fundamental operation of a visual survey of place. It need not be detailed. A useful and accurate classification, located on the ground, and a careful analysis of typical problems, are what is required. Intricate mapping or bulky form-filling is a waste of time. It will be useful, however, to take photographs of typical scenes in the areas of each class.

This basic district mapping can be supplemented by a more objective survey called a photogrid, which is quite easy to do. Over a base map of the area, lay an arbitrary grid, of such a scale that it has no more than perhaps a few hundred intersections, and yet those intersections are not so far apart that many characteristic places would be missed between them. Thus a more densely occupied or intricate area will require a finer grid than a more open and homogeneous one. Many communities are adequately recorded by grids whose lines are one to two hundred meters apart. Locate each grid intersection on the base map, and find the nearest accessible point to that intersection. In the field, take a photograph at each such point, choosing what seems to be the most characteristic or revealing aspect there. The photographs are printed and identified by grid location. This makes a complete sampling of the visual character of the area, a sample which can be filed and consulted later, either for detail or for general verifications. It is a permanent record, and can be retaken at regular intervals. Judgments are only necessary in the choice of grid spacing, and in the decision of what view to take from any particular point. It is quickly done, easily filed, and can be carried out by untrained volunteers. Ideally, it is keyed to vertical aerial photographs of the region, giving a complete record of visible form.

It is usual to supplement these basic inquiries by some other more specialized ones. One is to inventory, describe, and locate all visual elements which are particularly valuable to the community. These may be buildings, sets of buildings, views, areas, or natural features, and can be valuable because of their beauty, their history, their social or ecological meaning, or perhaps just their fragility. Such an inventory is always important in developing a conservation plan.

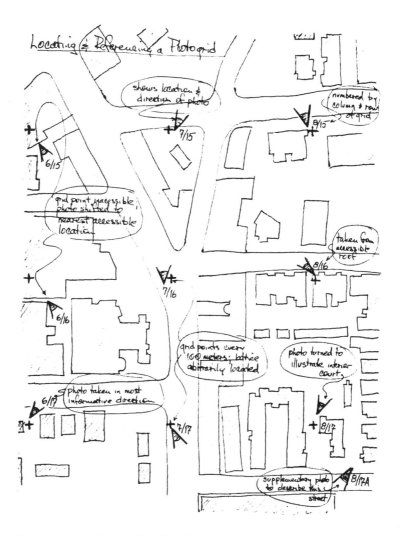

How to generate a photogrid. From Growing
Up in Cities, *copyright UNESCO, 1977;*
reproduced with permission of MIT
Press and UNESCO.

Secondly, it is customary to map the principal views of an area, since
the preservation and extension of views is a common element of a visual
plan. Thus, the important viewing stations are located, panoramic photos
are taken from them, the areas that can be seen from them are mapped,
and existing or potential blocks to good views are identified. Mapping the
"viewshed" of prominent features is the same operation in reverse. Potential views may be identified, and areas which have plentiful views or which
are shut in may also be noted. These analyses of views, and of valuable
elements, can be accomplished at the same time that the visual district map
is made in the field.

These are usually the principal elements of an analysis by place.
Other studies are occasionally made, depending on current issues of the

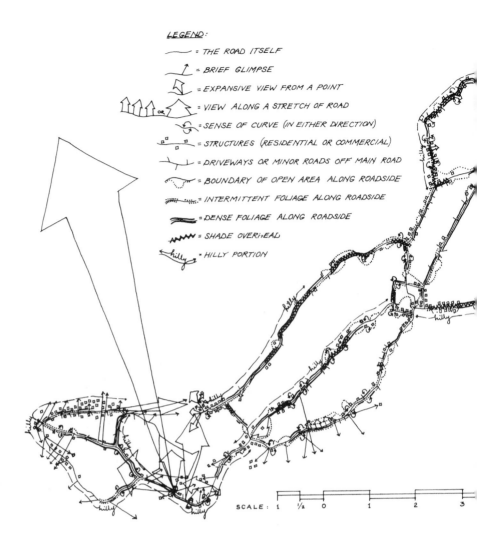

LEGEND:

⁓ = THE ROAD ITSELF

= BRIEF GLIMPSE

= EXPANSIVE VIEW FROM A POINT

= VIEW ALONG A STRETCH OF ROAD

= SENSE OF CURVE (IN EITHER DIRECTION)

= STRUCTURES (RESIDENTIAL OR COMMERCIAL)

= DRIVEWAYS OR MINOR ROADS OFF MAIN ROAD

= BOUNDARY OF OPEN AREA ALONG ROADSIDE

= INTERMITTENT FOLIAGE ALONG ROADSIDE

= DENSE FOLIAGE ALONG ROADSIDE

= SHADE OVERHEAD

= HILLY PORTION

SCALE: 1   ½   0   1   2   3

The road experience: Martha's Vineyard. (Reprinted with permission of Vineyard Open Land Foundation.)

5   MILES   NORTH

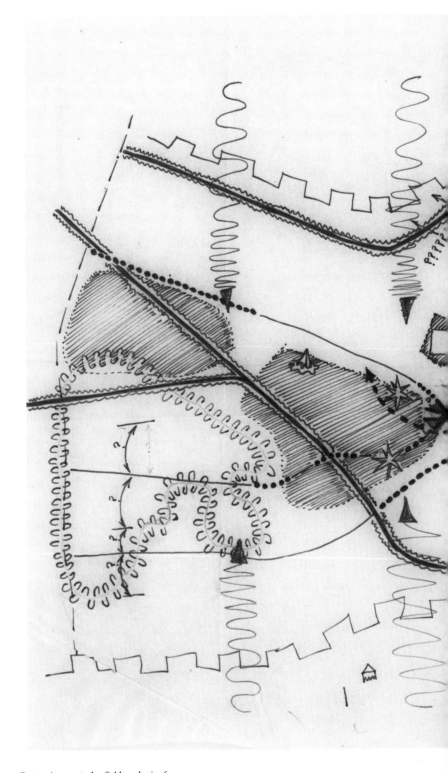

Boston image study: field analysis of major problems.

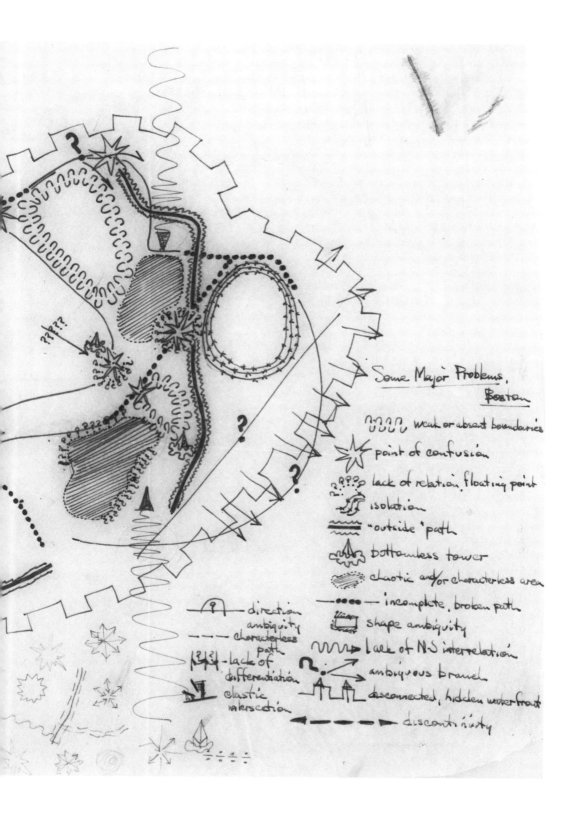

Some Major Problems,
Boston

ᴗᴗᴗᴗ weak or absent boundaries

☆ point of confusion

᠈᠈᠈᠈᠈ lack of relation. floating point

isolation

"outside" path

bottomless tower

chaotic and/or characterless area

—•••• incomplete, broken path

shape ambiguity

ᴗᴗᴗ lack of N-S interrelation

direction ambiguity

characterless path

lack of differentiation

chaotic intersection

ambiguous branch

disconnected, hidden waterfront

discontinuity

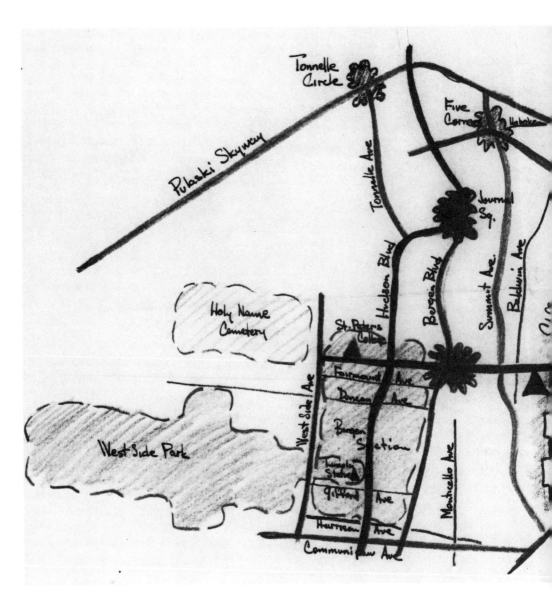

Jersey City image study: summation of interview and sketch maps.

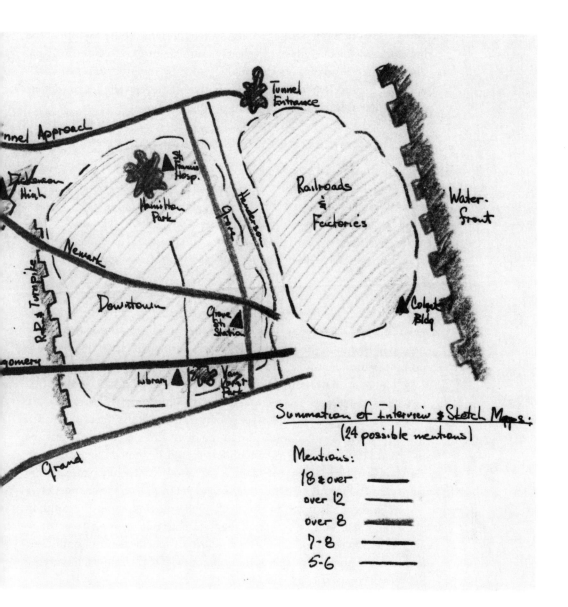

Tunnel Approach

Dickerson High

RR & Turnpike

gomery

Grand

Tunnel Entrance

St Francis Hosp.

Hamilton Park

Newark

Downtown

Henderson

Grove

Grove St Station

library

Van Vorst Park

Railroads & Factories

Water Front

Colgate Bldg

Summation of Interview & Sketch Maps.
(24 possible mentions)
Mentions:
18 & over ————
over 12 ————
over 8 ————
7-8 ————
5-6 ————

area: studies of night lighting, of the system of signs, of the rhythm of the important visible activities, of special natural features, etc. But the visual districting and the photogrid, supplemented by the inventories of views and of valuable elements, lay the groundwork. Special studies, or details of particular areas, can come later as needed.

The Area as a Set of Journeys

A community is also seen while passing through it, whether as a tourist or on habitual trips. This may be the principal way of experiencing larger areas. The basic survey required here is a description of the visual character of the major routes—highways, waterways, footways, bikeways, railroads, bus routes, or whatever—as seen by those traveling along them. This is a somewhat less familiar analysis than those given above, but equally vital.

The basic document required is a map of each principal route, showing what areas can be seen while traveling along it in either direction (its "viewshed," or "visual corridor"), and some characterization of the varying nature of that viewshed: major landmarks, principal visual districts, important natural features, and the sense of motion experienced along the way, and of spatial confinement or release. Entry points can be identified as well as visual approaches, and decision points, and whether they are clear or confusing. The general sense of orientation along the route, and of its connection to other routes or to major features of the area, can be recorded. Problems and potentialities should be noted: landmarks or views obscured, unpleasant features revealed, confusing places, route landscapes which are particularly fine and yet most likely to change, etc.

The record is made in the field, while moving along the route in question. It may simply be a set of diagrammatic notations on a base map, and refer to major important features. Or they may be a more continuous and detailed analysis of space, motion, and view. Techniques of varying degrees of complexity are available.

The more detailed field notation can be abstracted into a set of special presentations, such as the pattern of entry, approach, and arrival—or the portions of the route along which certain major features can be seen—or the general orientation structure of the system of routes—or the classification of routes into stretches of similar visual character (which is analogous to the visual districting of place described above).

While this field survey is the basic operation, it is also possible to make a more objective photographic analysis, as with the photogrid above. One may take a series of slides at regular intervals along the route, which can be studied individually later, or shown sequentially to simulate the real trip.

The stop-frame motion picture is still another technique, useful for more extended journeys. A motion-picture camera is set to take one frame

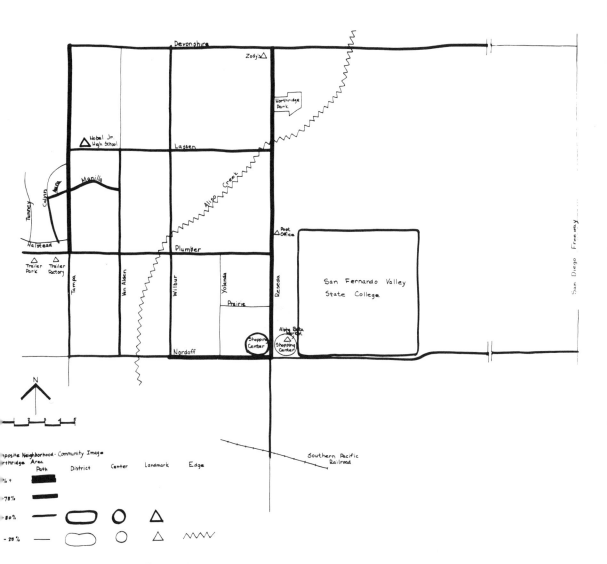

Los Angeles community image study: Northridge.

The following labels appear on the map:

Devonshire
Zody's △
Northridge Park
Nobel Jr. High School △
Lassen
Manilla
Culynn
Turney
Halstead
Post Office △
Trailer Park △   Trailer Factory △
Tampa
Van Alden
Wilbur
Yolanda
Prairie
Plumber
Reseda
Aliso Creek
San Fernando Valley State College
Shopping Center
Alpha Beta Market △
Shopping Center
Nordoff
Southern Pacific Railroad
San Diego Freeway

N

Composite Neighborhood - Community Image
Northridge Area

	Path	District	Center	Landmark	Edge
% +					
> 75%					
> 50%			○	△	
- 25%			○	△	ᴧᴧᴧᴧ

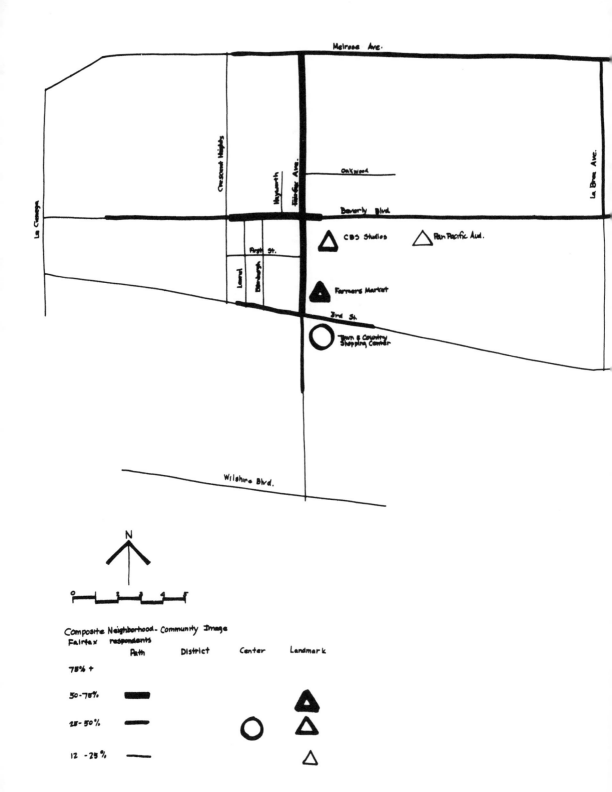

Melrose Ave.

Crescent Heights

Oakwood

Hayworth

Fairfax Ave.

Beverly Blvd.

La Cienega

△ CBS Studios   △ Pan Pacific Aud.

First St.

Laurel

Edinburgh

▲ Farmers Market

3rd St.

○ Town & Country
Shopping Center

La Brea Ave.

Wilshire Blvd.

N

0   1   2   3   4   5

Composite Neighborhood- Community Image
Fairfax respondents
                    Path   District   Center   Landmark

75% +

50-75%   ▬▬▬   ▲

25-50%   ▬▬   ○   △

12 -25% ——   △

Los Angeles community image study: Fairfax.

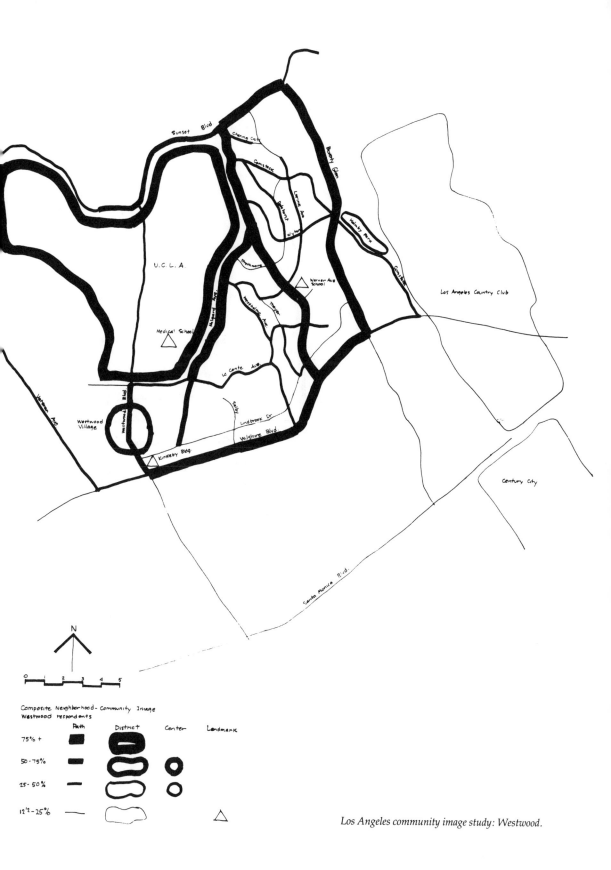

Los Angeles community image study: Westwood.

Composite Neighborhood- Community Image
Westwood respondents

	Path	District	Center	Landmark
75% +				
50-75%				
25-50%				
12½-25%				

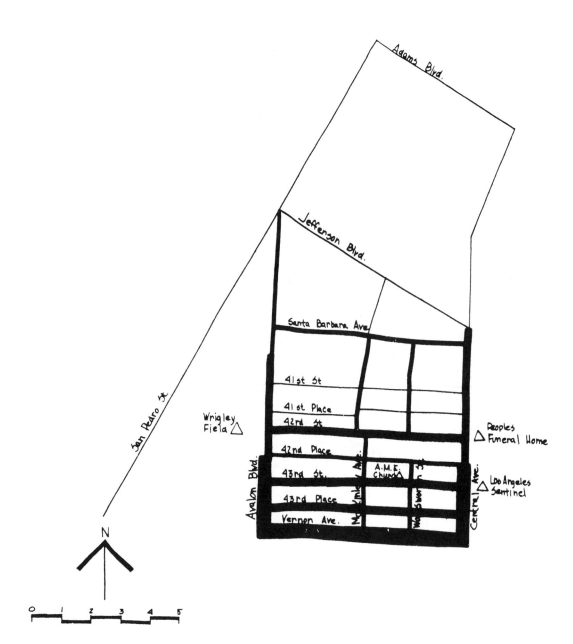

Adams Blvd.

Jefferson Blvd.

San Pedro St.

Santa Barbara Ave.

41st St

41st Place

Wrigley
Field △

42nd St

Peoples
△ Funeral Home

42nd Place

Avalon Blvd.

43rd St.

A.M.E.
Church △

Central Ave.

Los Angeles
△ Sentinel

43rd Place

Vernon Ave.

N

0   1   2   3   4   5

Composite Neighborhood - Community Image

Path   District   Center   Landmark

75% +

50-75%

25-50%

12 -25%

△

Los Angeles community image study: Avalon.

each second, and is hand-held in the front of the vehicle, while also hanging from a strap to ease the strain on the operator who simply keeps the camera level and pointed in a consistent direction. The result is a movie which rushes at terrifying speed, makes dizzying turns, and focuses straight ahead. But a viewer quickly adjusts to this, and can then read the result either frame by frame (which is a regular sampling analogous to the photogrid), or as a continuous whole, which compresses the visual variations of a long route into a summary form. The technique, at any rate, is easy to carry out with simple equipment and untrained surveyors.

The Area as Imaged by its Users

It is equally important to analyze the way in which the area is perceived by its people, since perception is a two-way process. The visual character of a place, and its evaluations, is impossible to analyze if divorced from the people who see it. These analyses of the mental image, are, at least apparently, more difficult to make than an "objective" recording of what can be seen (although the latter is always based on habits of perception, as well). But image studies are absolutely essential, and lead easily into policy recommendations.

The most direct method for gathering these mental perceptions is to interview a sample of the area's people. It is not necessary that a large number [be] interviewed—careful discussions with twenty or forty or sixty persons is worth far more than brief standard questions which are asked of hundreds.

The first task is to decide on the several kinds of people that are critical to the area: residents, workers, visitors, elderly, young, male, female, income class, or ethnic group. Since it is usually not feasible to interview a complete, balanced sample, it is better to choose two or three composite groups (i.e., young female middle-income secretaries, or poor white elderly long-term male residents) whose views of the area are likely to be most important in judging its quality, or are most likely to be neglected, or, on the contrary, will have the greatest effect on decisions. Additional groups can be interviewed, or can interview themselves, as visual policies are debated, or as new issues arise.

Having decided on the population groups to be sampled, a number (perhaps 20) of individuals of each group should be approached, whether by "random" sampling at homes or on the street, or by passing along networks of acquaintance. In an informal, open-ended way, each individual should be asked a series of questions to elicit how they perceive, remember, and evaluate the area. A simple series of questions might run as follows:

1. Please draw me a map of_____(the area). I don't want a finished drawing, just something to show me what you think are its main features. Now, would you show

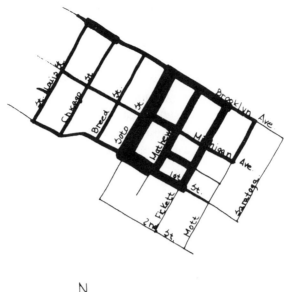

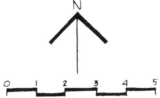

Composite Neighborhood - Community Image
Boyle Heights Area

	Path	District	Center	Landmark
75% +	▬			
50 - 75%	▬			
25 - 50%	▬			
12 - 25%	─			

Los Angeles community image study: Boyle Heights.

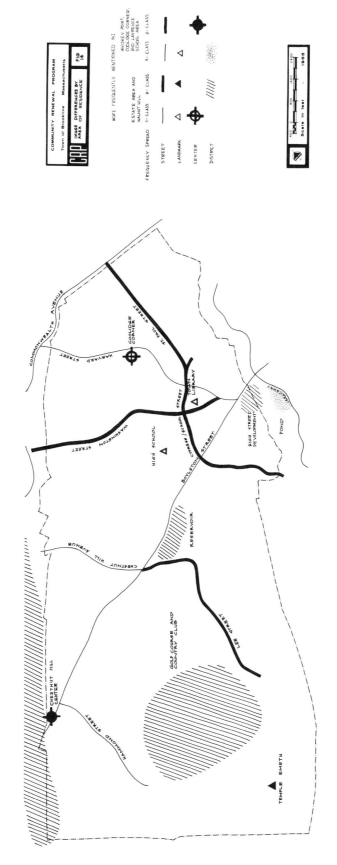

Composite image maps of Brookline residents from two different neighborhoods.

me on your map the places and routes you most often use or visit?" [This map is an excellent permanent record of what is salient in the area to the person, what is familiar, how he/she organizes it in his/her mind. The sequence of drawing, the character of the drawing, and the remarks made while drawing—all of which should be noted—are also valuable evidence.]

2. [Turning the map aside:] "Could you give me a list of all the most important places in this area?" [and, after perhaps two minutes, or when the listing has tailed off:] "In which of these places do you best like to be? Which are most beautiful to you? Why? Which are the most unpleasant, and why? Are there any other particularly pleasant or unpleasant places you forgot to list?" [This is the verbal analogue of the mapping procedure. Although it fails to get at structure, it will catch places difficult to draw, and it also goes on to evaluate these places specifically.]

3. "How has the look of this area changed in the past, and how is it changing now? Is this for better or for worse?"

4. "What do you think are the major visual problems in the landscape of this area today? Do you foresee any new ones which are coming up?"

This is a simple, basic interview, and might take a half-hour to accomplish. There are many variations that can be made on it. Persons may be shown photographs of key places in the area and asked to identify them and to comment on them. These photos can be those previously made of the typical visual districts or the main views or the principal routes.

Or, given more time, people can be furnished a camera, and asked to photograph places that they enjoy or think are critical, as a basis for further discussions. They may be asked how they would go from one location to another, and to describe what they would see on the way (which can be correlated with the analysis of the set of journeys). They can be asked what views they enjoy. They may be queried on particular visual issues before the community, as about new developments, natural features, signs, lights, or whatever. Subsequent to individual interviews, homegeneous groups may be brought together to discuss local visual issues. Or persons may be asked to give the interviewer a guided tour. While the four questions given cover the basic ground, they will always have to be modified to fit the particular circumstance, and there will always be particular questions to add.

The interviews are informal and open-ended, but the interviewers must be trained and tested to administer them without biasing the answers, and in a strictly comparative manner. It is useful to tape the interview, if the interviewees agree, as a more detailed and subtle permanent record. Transcribing the tapes, except for selected pieces, is normally not worth the cost, however. When concluded the interview data can be analyzed in several ways:

1. By maps or lists of places, classified by their frequency of mention.

2. Maps of typical home territories, or the areas of frequent use.

3. Lists or maps of elements judged to be of high value, and those of low value, with summaries of the reasons giver.

4. Diagrams of imaginary routes, and of what was described as seen along the way.

5. Diagrams of the principal way or ways in which people structure the area in their minds, where they seem to be confused, and what they leave out or suppress.

6. Diagrams which emphasize the principal agreements and disagreements between the perceptions of different groups.

7. "Speaking landscapes": maps or sketches of parts of the visual landscape with the comments of inhabitants appended. A similar device, very useful for public meetings, is to construct slide sequences which are coordinated with taped comments.

There are many elaborations possible in the conduct and analysis of such interviews. Communities, particularly in the beginning, will be well advised to keep them simple and to shape them to their own particular purposes. Complex questionnaires, and large samples, are not only tedious to conduct, but produce for more data than can be used.

Conclusions

These surveys will now have consisted of at least the following:

1. A mapping and analysis of the principal visual districts of the area, with a photographic record with typical scenes in them;

2. Diagrams of the visual corridors along the principal routes, with typical views; and

3. An analysis of the major elements, patterns of mental organization, evaluations, and perceptions of change by small samples of two or three key local groups.

In addition, it is likely that one or more of the following has also been prepared:

1. A photogrid;

2. An inventory and description of visual elements;

3. An analysis of major views and landmarks;

4. An analysis of the clarity of orientation, and the sense of entry and approach along the principal routes;

COMMUNITY RENEWAL PROGRAM

Town of Brookline · Massachusetts

CRP

BOUNDARIES OF
OWN NEIGHBORHOODS

FIG
15

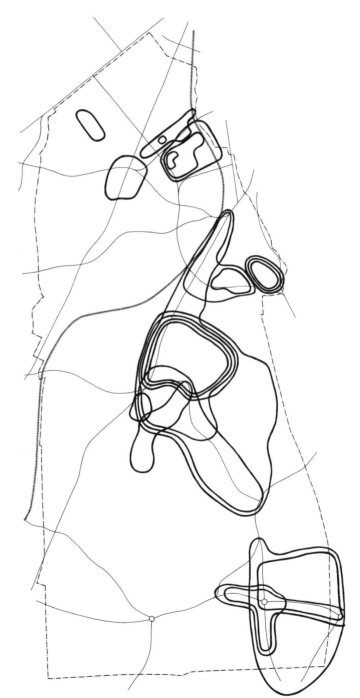

Neighborhood boundaries drawn by individuals: Brookline.

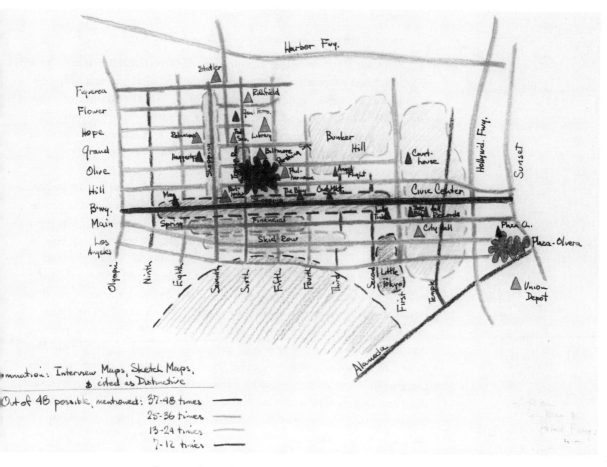

Consensus image: downtown Los Angeles.

5. Slide sequences, or a stopframe movie along these routes;

6. Diagrams of imagined routes;

7. Diagrams comparing typical group images; and

8. A set of "speaking landscapes."

In addition, a host of specialized analyses are possible, depending on local interest. The range of group interviews can easily be expanded. But the aim is *policy*, not data, and all this material must be condensed into a *diagnosis* of the area, covering the elements listed at the very beginning of this paper, i.e.;

what is valuable and should be conserved?

what is not, and should be changed?

what is now changing or liable to change, why, and is that good or bad?

what are the potentials for improvement?

where are we agreed, and where do we disagree?

The survey then leads, through an open community debate, to a recommended set of actions for conservation and change, including new regulations, policies, guidelines, procedures, incentives, investments, education, and public and private actions. Clearly, these recommendations will depend on the entire political, social, and economic context in which the visual quality is being reviewed. We do not go into [a] complex process of judgment here.

It is important to note, however, that visual surveys (like any other) should not be one-shot efforts, but must be continually updated as conditions shift and new issues arise. Moreover, the effectiveness of recommended policy must continually be tested by the review of actual results and of shifts in public perceptions. The survey should also be planned to develop field procedures which will be usable for project review: showing how the character of a proposal will or will not fit the character of existing visual districts, how it will modify existing or potential views, how it affects valued elements, how it will change the view from the road or typical features of the public image, and so on. Survey diagrams should be drawn to allow likely changes to be shown on copies of them; scenes of place or journey, or photogrid or panorama photos in the files can have diagrams of new landscapes and structures drawn directly over them on transparencies. Policy, survey, and action are continuous and interdependent. The visual diagnosis must continually be updated.

An Analysis of the Visual Form of Brookline, Massachusetts (1965)

Summary

An extensive field survey was made of the visual form of the Town, supplemented by a small interview sample of the citizen image. Specific criteria for the look of Brookline's centers, districts, streets, and general structure were derived from general objectives of comfort, diversity, identity, relatedness, and meaning.

These criteria were applied to uncover the basic problems and potentialities of the Town: the satisfying diversity, and yet the serious visual failures of its major centers; the chaos and ugliness of many of its main streets; the fine character of its residential areas, except for the defects of the growing apartment zone; the fundamental confusions in the basic structure of the Town and its relations to its neighbors. Future changes, and the potentialities of the natural setting, are also discussed.

The visual content of a comprehensive plan is elaborated, and priority areas for public action are outlined: standards and design review procedures for apartment development, public buildings, and special landmark areas; visual criteria to guide renewal; the design of the key centers; the design of main streets and entrance points; the location and design of parks and water areas; and policies for signs, lighting, landscaping, paving, and shelter.

There is a concluding discussion of implementation and staff requirements. The appendices describe the method of field survey, the method, and results of the survey of the citizen image, and close with a general critique of the analysis as a whole.

Purpose and Scope

We now think that the look of an entire city can be changed by design. The delightful cities of the past are usually happy accidents: their form was not consciously guided, except along infrequent public squares and avenues. We have long believed that the apearance of the daily environment affects well-being and efficiency. The new idea is that it may be possible to plan for the look of a large urban area.

This report will describe and evaluate the visual form of Brookline, as a basis for planning or future changes. It does not go on to make a "visual plan." Plans and designs must deal with a thing as a whole: its looks, its technical function, its politics, its economy, and its social basis. Our purpose is to point out the existing visual problems and possibilities (and

From "Visual Analysis: Community Renewal Program, Brookline, Massachusetts." Reprinted by permission of Town of Brookline, Massachusetts.

perhaps some of the predictable future ones) and thereby to indicate a part of the universe with which a comprehensive plan must deal.

Evaluation is the meat of this report, but we will go on to indicate how a general plan might operate on the look of the Town: what type of controls, criteria, or designs could be developed, and how they would bear on real decisions. The report will conclude by recommending how the process of planning for the visual form of Brookline should fit into the general planning process: what kinds of actions are needed; what it would require in terms of staff, data, controls or procedure.

What this report sets out to do has only rarely been attempted, and that rather recently.[1] To the author's knowledge, this may be the most systematic attempt to date. Therefore, many of the procedures are untried, and must be tested over a period of planning and construction. We have also been constrained by time and budget, but, considering the present state of the art, this may not have been altogether unfortunate.

Surveys Conducted

During the summer of 1964, a detailed visual survey of the Town was performed. This included a reconnaissance on foot of the entire Town, making notes on the visual characteristics of each small area and center, and taking representative photographs. Panoramic points and the visibility of major Town elements were noted. An analysis of the sequence of visual impressions on all the principal roads and transit routes was also prepared, based on repeated traverses in the field in both directions. Finally, with substantial aid from the League of Women Voters of Brookline, a sample survey was conducted of the mental image of the Town, as held by inhabitants residing in various sections. Figures 1–7 summarize some sallent features uncovered by these surveys.

[Figure 1] is a diagram of the principal objective visual characteristics of the Town and its immediate setting: the interplay of building density, tree cover, hills, activity centers, and main roads. Most apparent is the complexity with which these factors overlap each other, resulting in a rich texture, but also in a somewhat confused pattern. The major break in character between north and south Brookline, and the lack of relation to areas and features outside the Town, is also visible.

Figure 2 shows the location of the principal centers and visual districts. The latter are the areas of recognizable and relatively homogeneous character, which can be remembered as continuous regions: the estate district, for example; Pill Hill; or Cottage Farm. The centers are the focal points of activity (primarily of shopping and civic functions in this case), toward which people can orient themselves and which they frequently enter: Coolidge Corner, Brookline Village, Cleveland Circle. The general character of these districts and centers is also indicated. Thus the diagram

COMMUNITY RENEWAL PROGRAM
Town of Brookline , Massachusetts

CRP THE PHYSICAL FORM
OF BROOKLINE

FIG
1

BUILDING MASS

TREES

HILL

WATER

Scale in feet
400   0   800   1600   2400
1965

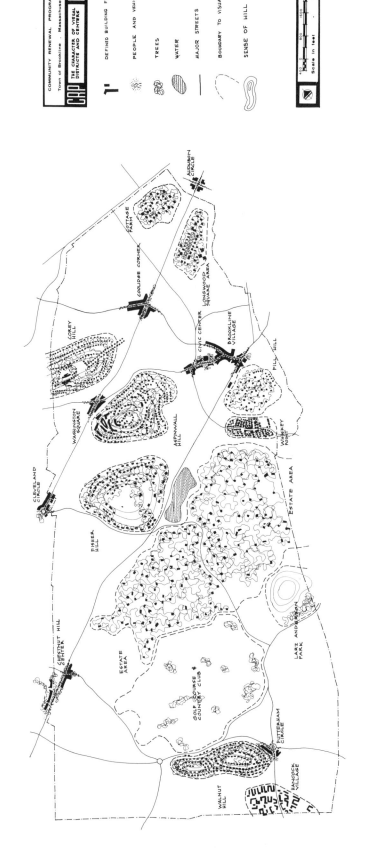

Figure 2 The character of visual districts and centers.

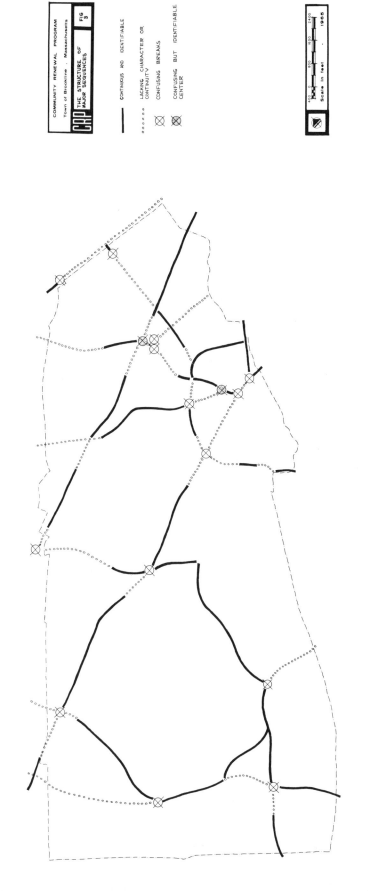

COMMUNITY RENEWAL PROGRAM
Town of Brookline , Massachusetts
CRP THE STRUCTURE OF
MAJOR SEQUENCES
FIG
3

CONTINUOUS AND IDENTIFIABLE

LACKING CHARACTER OR
CONTINUITY

CONFUSING BREAKS

CONFUSING BUT IDENTIFIABLE
CENTER

Scale in feet   1965

Figure 3 *The structure of major sequences.*

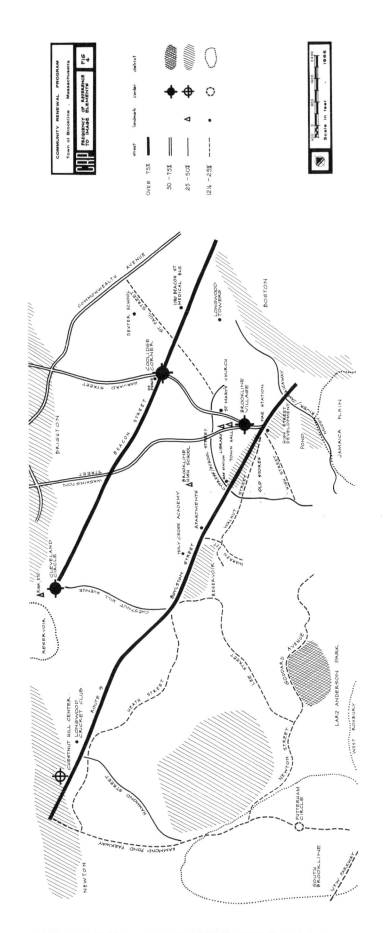

Figure 4 Frequency of reference to image elements.

is a first step in abstracting the relevant information from reconnaissance and the kind of data represented in Figure 1.

Figure 3, finally, is a similar summary of the character and structure of the path system, the moving view of the Town. What is the nature of main roads and transit lines, and how do they appear to relate to each other? This is the visual skeleton of the community, and the diagram indicates the breaks and connections. All these aspects will be further analyzed in the discussion of visual problems.

The Public Image

Figures 4 and 5 convey a different aspect of the Town: how it is imagined by its citizens, rather than how it appears to an objective observer in the field. These are based on the results of interviews with 28 residents of the Town, ably conducted by volunteers from the Brookline League of Women Voters. These interviews included requests for a mental recall of Town features, and for various maps and accounts of imaginary trips, according to methods which have been tested in several other cities. The results are interesting, suggestive, but unfortunately unreliable, since limitations of time and staff resulted in a small and unbalanced sample, with some inconsistencies in the interview procedure. Nevertheless, the results may often come close to evoking the public image of Brookline, and at least indicate what might be learned if such a survey were done more systematically.

Figure 4 shows the frequency with which various elements of the Town were spontaneously referred to by the interviewees, the frequencies being classified by quartiles. It may be taken as an index of the general public image of the Town. The network of Beacon, Boylston, Commonwealth, Washington, and Harvard Streets are the paramount features, along with the associated focal points: Cleveland Circle, Coolidge Corner, and Brookline Village. One isolated area also stands out in the minds of these people: Larz Anderson Park. The memorable landmarks, minor foci and areas, are generally those which lie along the two "great roads": Beacon and Boylston, or around the Brookline Village focus. The Muddy River is remembered, but the Charles is forgotten, although it is equally close. Except for Larz Anderson Park, South Brookline tends to fade out, and to be disconnected from the remainder of the Town.

Figure 5 shows the typical structure of these memories, judging from the maps that interviewees produced. Beacon, Boylston, and Commonwealth are thought of as three parallel roads, intersected by perpendicular connectors, such as Harvard Street or Chestnut Hill Avenue, to form a grid. Major foci, such as Brookline Village or Cleveland Circle, occur at the intersections of this grid. But the grid breaks down in many places: connectors fail to go through, memorable foci are absent at important intersec-

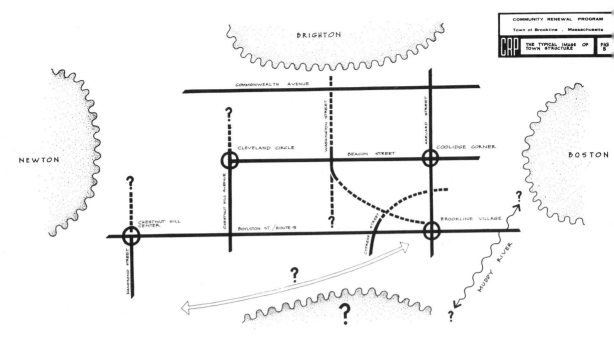

Figure 5 *The typical image of town structure.*

tions, Washington Street and Cypress Street do not act reasonably. Beacon Street seems to dead end at Cleveland Circle; there is no connection from Brookline Village to the south; the Muddy River is present at Boylston, but mysteriously absent elsewhere. Boston is east, Brighton is north, and Newton is west; but what is south? Brookline is a bounded place, quite different from nearby towns (many subjects drew schematic boundary lines), but few know where the boundaries are. The true diagonal relation to Boston is rarely understood, nor is the superposition of the main arterials on the old radial system which focused on Brookline Village.

Visual Objectives

All these data are of no value unless we are able to evaluate them. What are the problems of the Town? Where should action be taken? To decide this, we must know what we want.

Some of the criteria for a fine visual environment are highly intangible, very difficult to set forth in words or in any other systematic way. They will be diversely applied by different people in different circumstances. To that extent, however important they may be, they cannot be used as a commonly accepted basis for public decisions. Other criteria can be more clearly defined, can be shown to have widespread effects, and are likely to be accepted by substantial numbers of people in the Town. They will be subjective, since this is the nature of the phenomenon we are dealing with, but many subjective judgments will roughly coincide, once they are informed and directed to the same object. These are the criteria we seek as a basis for public action.

Known criteria of this kind can be summarized in a very general way as follows:

1. *Comfort:* Visual and other sensations should be within the comfort range: not too hot, too noisy, too bright, too cold, too silent, too loaded or empty of information, too steep, too flat, too dirty, too clean. The comfort range will vary for different people, but in any one cultural group, such as among the inhabitants of Brookline, there will be large areas of agreement as to what features in the public domain are intolerable, or at least unpleasant.

2. *Diversity:* There should be a reasonable variety of sensations and environments in the Town: calm or stimulating, peopled or empty, dense or open, restrictive or free, and these various environmental types should all be easily accessible. This is necessary to give the inhabitants a choice of the surroundings they prefer, and to provide a very widely felt need for variety and change. What is a "reasonable" variety is more difficult to define, but in a crude way certain contrasting types of visual environment can be defined, and their presence required within a given range of access.

3. *Identity:* Places in the Town should have a strong visual identity: be visually differentiated from other places, recognizable, memorable, vivid. This means that one street should not look like a hundred other streets, nor a residential district be indistinguishable from the square miles of housing round about. Every place cannot be radically different from every other: important centers and avenues may be unqiue; but most places will vary only subtly. This quality of identity, or as it is often called "a sense of place," is the cornerstone of a handsome environment. Without it, an observer can make no sense of the world, since he cannot distinguish or remember its parts. With it, he can begin to make relations; he has the visible basis for a sense of belonging; he can savor the uniqueness of places and people.

4. *Relatedness:* These identifiable parts must be so arranged that a normal observer can relate them together, and understand their pattern in space. This is not a universal rule, since there are times when it is desirable that parts of an environment be hidden, mysterious, or ambiguous. But in the general framework of the Town, and its public places, the linkage of one place to another must be legible. It must be legible to the man in the street as he goes about his daily routine, and also be legible in memory. The structure will have to be a rather simple and adaptable one, since various people use the city in different ways, they have different preferences for organizing what they see, and the city itself is constantly changing. Legible structure has an obvious value in the practical task

of way-finding, but it has more fundamental values as well: emotional security, a basis for civic pride or cohesion, or a means for extending one's knowledge of the world. It gives people the esthetic pleasure of sensing the relatedness of a complex thing. Again, what is "sufficient" structure may be impossible to make precise. Yet it is relatively easy to point out major flaws in the visual structure of a place, and to back it up by tests and interviews.

Up to this point we are on relatively firm ground. These criteria, however subjective, are likely to be shared by large numbers of people, although at times unconsciously, and by their use we can point out gross deviations from the desirable. From this point on, the ground gets softer. We can cite at least one more criterion, however:

5. *Meaning*: The visual environment should be meaningful to its observers; that is, its visible character should relate to other aspects of life: the functions and activities of places, their history, their future, the structure of society, human values and aspirations. People will "read" a city landscape; they are looking for practical information; they are curious; they are moved by what they see. The great cities of the world are expressive in this sense. Unfortunately, the significant meanings and values tend to be very diverse in our society, and the symbolic role of the city landscape is as yet little understood. For immediate planning purposes, we are limited to those aspects of meaning, which are clearly of interest to large groups of people: the clarity of public directional and control signals; the expression of basic function and history; the exposure of the natural site; making visible the most important social institutions.

There is more to a fine visual environment than this, but it is difficult to define. Moreover, if we have a landscape that is comfortable, diverse, vividly identified, well structured, and meaningful, in the senses we have given these words, we have the basis, and indeed much of the essence, of a beautiful landscape. Needless to say, there are many other non-esthetic criteria to be considered in designing a city: fitness to purpose, economy, social impact, and so on. Many of these are in their turn related back to visual questions: visual legibility may, for example, increase the efficiency of circulation, widen the range of choice, facilitate a sense of civic cohesion, or help a child to understand the world he is growing up in. The visual quality of the Town is clearly related to its offical goals of citizen well-being, excellent residential character, and social and physical variety. But we will speak primarily about immediate preceptual aspects in this report, with only occasional references to other purposes.

Specific Criteria for the Town

These very general criteria must be put in a more specific form, applicable to the Town of Brookline. For this purpose, they may be written as questions to be asked about parts of the Town or about the visual system of the Town as a whole. It will be apparent that while these questions have been organized and made concrete for better application, they all refer to the same five principles which have been stated above.

A. In each small district in the Town we may ask:

1. Are the sensations comfortable, particularly in regard to noise, dirt, glare, micro-climate, and perceptual overload?

2. Is there an adequate choice of visual environment within easy walk, particularly in regard to areas of high and low perceptual stimulus (open woods vs. shopping centers, for example)?

3. Is there a sense of special identity of place here, and a sense of general location with respect to the Town?

4. Do the residential areas, in particular, convey a sense of quiet, calm, and comfort?

B. In the major centers, the main public places, we will ask additional questions:

5. Is there adequate provision for shelter and rest?

6. Is each center clearly differentiated from the others? Does it have a vivid character, and well-formed public open spaces?

7. Is each center visually related to its surroundings? Are its entrances visually legible?

8. Are the signs readable without interference or overload? Do they fit their premises and their meanings? In particular, is the essential public information efficiently communicated; are emergency services and street equipment easy to locate and use, street names and numbers easy to find?

C. On the major pathways (streets, walks, transit lines), we ask:

9. Are the visual characters of these major routes clearly differentiated one from another, and their backward and forward directions distinguishable? Is there a distinction between radial and circumferential movement, and between local and arterial streets?

10. Is visual continuity maintained while traveling on the path—that is, can the moving observer sense the continuation of the path ahead of him, or is he subject to puzzling breaks and other uncertainties? Does each path have a good sense of direction, of where it is going? Are cluttered spaces and ambiguous movements avoided?

11. Is the viewer presented with a memorable sequence? That is, is there a succession of views, or a rhythm of spatial contrast, motion, and visible activity, or a recurrent sighting and approach to visible goals, so that he has a sense of forward progression, and can remember the road as a vivid succession of events?

12. Are the intersections clearly identified, with the intersecting path exposed, and the necessary maneuvers clearly evident? Are other confusing decision points avoided?

13. Are transit routes and arrival times clearly communicated?

14. Does the view from the main routes expose the major Town elements, activities, and institutions in a recognizable way, and does it make clear how to reach them?

15. Are visual connections made to major features just outside the Town, or to key metropolitan destinations? Is the Town, or a visual symbol of it, visible from the main paths outside the Town boundaries? Are entrances and exits to the Town clearly marked?

D. Finally, we can ask some questions about the visual structure of the Town as a whole:

16. Is there a coherent public image of the Town as a whole? Can the major paths, centers, and districts be remembered as a map or sequence pattern? What are the common confusions or blank spots in this public image, and what future difficulties can be foreseen due to predictable changes in the Town?

17. Is the significant history and the predictable future of the Town visible to the general observer? Is the basic natural setting exposed to him?

18. Can this observer, from the major routes and public places, develop an image of the Town which matches its basic social, functional, and physical character? Are there points accessible to him from which he can, at least symbolically, see the Town as a whole?

All of these questions ask for subjective judgements, but they can be answered in a rough qualitative way from the data at hand, and with a reasonably high degree of consensus between trained observers. The following evaluation of the visual character of the Town is based on them.

The Criteria Applied

Figures 6–9 express the results of this evaluation in detail, by locating and graphically symbolizing the problems revealed as these questions were systematically applied throughout the Town. Figure 6 indicates the problems that appear in various districts and centers (criteria 1–8 above), noting the areas that lack identity or choice of environment, those which lack a sense of location, or have a poor micro-climate or lack a sense of quiet and comfort. Places where noise and fumes are excessive, where there is perceptual overload, or difficult pedestrian movement, are given. Centers which have no well-formed public space, or clear entry, or sense of connection to their surroundings, or adequate shelter or resting-places for the public are also shown. Figure 7 diagrams the problems in the individual paths and intersections (criteria 9–13), locating failures of identity, visual continuity, sense of direction, memorable sequence, or distinction between local and arterial streets, as well as confusing intersections, cluttered spaces, hidden transit stops, and areas where the minor streets are generally confusing. Figure 8 is concerned with deficiencies in the visible

COMMUNITY RENEWAL PROGRAM

Town of Brookline . Massachusetts

CRP   THE PROBLEMS OF EXISTING
       CENTERS AND DISTRICTS

FIG 6

PERCEPTUAL OVERLOAD

NOISE AND FUMES

AREA LACKS SENSE OF CALM
OR HAS MICRO-CLIMATE PROBLEMS

LITTLE CHOICE IN ENVIRONMENT

AREA OR CENTER LACKS IDENTITY

NO SENSE OF LOCATION

INADEQUATE REST AND SHELTER

LACKS WELL FORMED PUBLIC
OPEN SPACE

POOR CONNECTION TO SURROUNDINGS

NO CLEAR ENTRY

DIFFICULT PEDESTRIAN MOVEME

Scale in feet   1965

Figure 6   *The problems of existing centers and districts.*

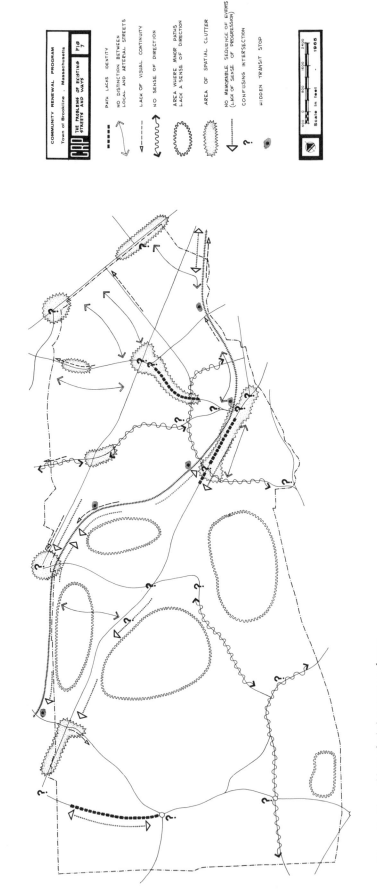

Figure 7 The problems of existing streets and ways.

COMMUNITY RENEWAL PROGRAM
Town of Brookline · Massachusetts

CRP THE PROBLEMS OF VISUAL CONNECTION

FIG 8

AREA OR CENTER NOT VISIBLE FROM THE MAJOR PATH SYSTEM

AREA PARTLY VISIBLE FROM THE MAJOR PATH SYSTEM

INSTITUTION OR LANDMARK NOT VISIBLE FROM THE MAJOR PATH SYSTEM

EXCEPTIONAL VIEW OF AN OTHERWISE INVISIBLE LANDMARK

LACK OF DIRECT VIEW OR VISUAL EXPOSURE

POOR CONNECTION TO SURROUNDINGS

LACK OF SENSE OF ENTRY OR EXIT

LACK OF CLEAR ENTRY

400   0   800   1600   2400
Scale in feet   1965

Figure 8 *The problems of visual connection.*

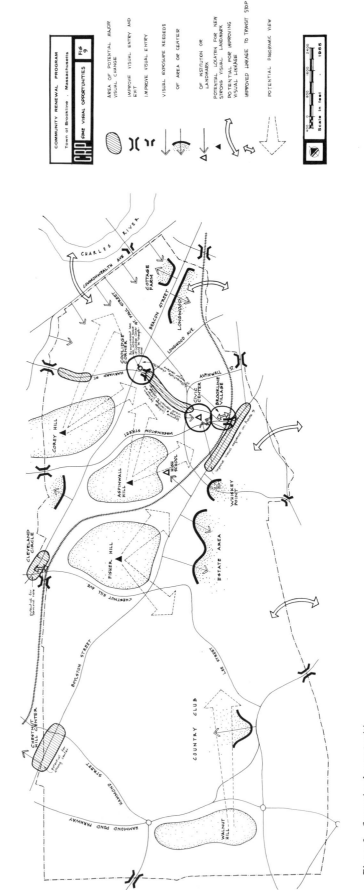

Figure 9 Some visual opportunitie

connections between elements (criteria 14–18), including important landmarks and areas which are hidden from the main roads, failures of orientation to points outside the Town, poor entries into the Town, and missing
connections between parts of the Town. Figure 9 points out some of the
visual possibilities that might be seized upon, a list necessarily incomplete
since no attempt to prepare a design for the Town has been made. But
possibilities already evident include visual exposure, dramatic entry
points, possible connections, new or improved centers, areas ripe for
reshaping, landmark locations, and panoramic points. Clearly, none of
these actions could be advocated except as part of a considered comprehensive plan, which will be based on many other non-visual criteria. In
general, the maps are only graphic summaries of the problems, which also
indicate their general locations. To understand the exact nature of the
difficulty, one must go back to the detailed survey data, on file in the
planning office. Other problems and possibilities have no particular location, and are therefore dealt with in the text below. The diagrams speak for
themselves, but it may be useful to generalize the results, as well as to
discuss them briefly.

Problems of the Center

A town is characterized primarily by the look of its centers, its major roads,
and its principal open spaces, and by the quality of its residential districts,
as the background against which these principal features are set off. The
visual quality of the centers of activity is perhaps the most crucial, since
these are used or seen by the greatest numbers of people, and publicly
"stand for" the Town.

Brookline has a number of centers of recognizable identity: the visibly dense activity of Coolidge Corner in its prominent position on Beacon
Street, Chestnut Hill as prototype of the new shopping center, the shabby
enclosed spaces of Brookline Village, the special topographical position of
Washington Square. Yet they all bear the marks of the typical American
shopping area: ill-formed spaces congested with empty parked cars;
noise, fumes, and a poor climate in summer and winter; danger to pedestrians; and a lack of any public places of shelter or rest. The public signs
and the important private signs locating shops and other activities are
engaged in visual warfare. They are dominated by billboards which have
no connection to nor meaning in the place. References to the centers by
interviewees are frequent—often appreciative of the range of services
available, but as often critical of the physical and visual conditions.

Approaches are confused, such as into Brookline Village from Route
9, or Coolidge Corner from the south, or Washington Square from Washington Street. Rarely does a center have any visible connection to its surroundings, except when it lies up against a prominent hill, as Washington

Square happens to relate to Corey Hill, or Putterham Circle to Walnut Hill. The juxtaposition of an active center and a contrasting activity or natural feature is a powerful way of conveying a strong sense of place, yet the Chestnut Hill Shopping Center turns its back on Hammond Pond, and one is unaware of the Town adminstrative center from the heart of Brookline Village.

Not one of the shopping centers has a well-formed public open space.[2] Most of the minor shopping centers are nondescript: they cannot be distinguished one from the other. A trip along Beacon Street is a dramatic revelation of some of these points. The street itself has strong character, as it rolls over the terrain between its massive apartment walls. Interviewees frequently refer to the handsome or memorable character of this street. But at each shopping center, where activity comes to a climax, the visual landscape falls to anticlimax—low irregular buildings, forecourts of empty cars.

The Town is fortunate to have an array of centers of various size, function, and history. If their visible characteristics were strengthened and differentiated, their entries and connections clarified, if they were given strong internal open spaces, these centers would be the visual foci of the Town, just as they are now its functional foci. Brookline Village is an important opportunity if it is to be rebuilt in the near future: it can be visibly connected to its topography, the pattern of converging streets, the civic center, Route 9, the transit station, and the Muddy River at the Jamaicaway, as well as given a strong new character of its own. It is still felt to be the principal focus of the Town, but a shabby one, and the citizens are prepared for change.

The Chestnut Hill center, since it is rapidly building up, offers a similar if less easily controlled opportunity to establish a strong visual character. Something might be done to make Hammond Pond visible, or to improve the highway facade, now given over to parking, or to link development on both sides of the road. Changes in Coolidge Corner will have to be of a more conservative nature, but even here there are opportunities for improving the points of entry, clarifying the spatial form, increasing the pedestrian domain, or codifying the gabble of signs. While Cleveland Circle is just beyond the Town boundary (as is part of Chestnut Hill), it is an integral part of the visual image of Brookline—the terminus of Beacon Street, and the focus of important recreational activities. Visually, it is an anticlimax stop to a handsome street. Willy nilly, the Town must cooperate with its neighbors to improve its environment, at this as at many other points. If these primary centers can be made pleasant and unique, the Town will have the foundations of a strong visual form. At other points, it will be important to clarify or even to develop new minor centers, as the junction of Boylston Street and Chestnut Hill Avenue, which is not only a confusing intersection but an unutilized strategic point. This could be local shopping, or devoted to office, civic, or religious use—so designed as to be visible and accessible from both streets, and allowing an open view of the Reservoir.

Problems of Visual Sequence

A town is presented to stranger and to citizen as a moving view from the principal roads, and this is the second crucial aspect of its appearance. Brookline has one handsome avenue in Beacon Street, now being eroded at many points. Its distinctive features are its breadth, its trees, and its movement over the terrain in its western reach, but particularly the wall of apartments which define it and makes it an avenue. Any new development which breaks that wall, such as a low commercial building fronted by parked cars, or an apartment set back or perpendicular to the street, begins to destroy the continuity and proportions of the avenue.

There are many pleasant minor streets. Portions of Route 9, especially as it passes the reservoir, have intimations of a remarkable approach to Boston. Farther east, below Cypress Street, that same road is indistinguishable from a hundred other cluttered roads in the Boston region. For the most part a rapid tour of the main streets gives an impression of confusion and ugliness, as well as a surprisingly poor knowledge of the actual character of the Town. To watch a speeded-up movie of a journey along the streets of Brookline is an eloquent demonstration of this.[3]

There are many confusing, cluttered intersections, particularly on Route 9, and there are places where the driver is threatened with perceptual overload. The intersections with Chestnut Hill Avenue and Lee Street, or Harvard and High Streets, are eloquent examples of this.[4] Parts of Route 9, as well as parts of Harvard Street, have no particular identity (see criterion 3); they might be a street in any town. The spatial form is often chaotic. Many of the major elements of the Town cannot be seen from its principal ways: the hills, for example, or Brookline Village and the civic center, the high school, as well as many memorable residential areas such as Longwood or the estate area. Beacon Street gives an impression of solid apartment development, and lower Route 9 of marginal commerce. Proposals for a Town garage and other industrial uses in this highly visible area will unfortunately only perpetuate the latter impression. The Riverside transit line runs blind, and stops out of sight: its visual isolation is complete. Very few interviewees mention it, despite its functional importance and the official policy of encouraging transit use.

Most entries into the Town are undistinguished, the destruction of the planted circle at Brookline Avenue being an example of medicority accomplished by public action. How will the wide cut of the Inner Belt[5] affect the entry at Audubon Circle? While residents are sharply aware of the uniqueness of Brookline, they are often confused as to its boundaries.

On very few roads is there any memorable sequence of visual events. Beacon Street, as a positive example, runs rhythmically from Audubon Circle to Coolidge Corner to Washington Square to Cleveland Circle, and the eastern approach to Washington Square is quite dramatic. There are points where the distinction between through streets and local streets is not visually expressed, on the north side of Beacon Street in particular. This contributes to the pressure of traffic on residential streets. In general, throughout the Town, while the radials to Boston are clear, the means of cross-Town movement are obscure. The future growth of traffic may increase the pressure on local streets, and thus intensify these ambiguities in the image of the Town, unless better throughways are developed. Commonwealth Avenue, Beacon Street, and Route 9 are clearly connected only by Harvard Street, which is itself disconnected from High Street. The by-pass at Coolidge Corner, proposed in the comprehensive plan, may disrupt even this one line. There is no easily imaginable route to the south corner of the Town. Washington Street is ambiguous: is it perpendicular or parallel to Beacon and Boylston? Where does Cypress Street go? or Grove? In part these system confusions arise out of the diagonal relation of Brookline to the orientation of the major Boston roads, in part from the imposition of an arterial system on an older pattern of local ways converging at the Village.

The public streets are a strategic opportunity, since their form is the result of public decisions, and so are most of their details: paving, signs, light, landscaping, even fencing and street furniture. At the same time, they are a visual foreground experienced by almost every citizen several times each day. Street form and details can be manipulated to confer identity (as Beacon Street has identity), to clarify movement, to point out the major features of the Town, or to create memorable sequences of light, space, and motion. Entry points into the Town could be made visible and symbolic of the Town's character. Transit stops could be visibly connected to nearby centers. The character of Beacon Street can be preserved from further erosion and perhaps rehabilitated, and those of Harvard Street and Route 9 might be revolutionized. The existing isolated pedestrian paths might be linked into a general walking system, or it might be possible to build a network of equestrian or bicycle paths. All of these actions, which are traditionally in public hands, will set the visual character of the Town, clarify its image (see criterion 4), and make moving through it a pleasure instead of an irritation.

Problems of the Residential Areas

The residential areas of the Town are in general of good character: well-kept, pleasant, and yet highly varied. Trees are everywhere and in summer they are one of the most memorable characteristics, even though they tend to blur the identity of various parts. Indeed, throughout much of the Town, public policy for the visual form of residential areas should primarily be aimed at preserving and enriching varied character, particularly by such means as choice of tree species and types of lighting, or by encouraging the better expression of topograhical character. As an imaginary example, the slopes of Corey Hill might be made visible from Washington Street and from Beacon Street eastbound; it could have some landmark on its crest, the Summit Path be clearly marked, and designed to make the most of its approach to a panoramic view; it could be planted to a particular tree species, particularly on the skyline and along the public ways; it could have a unique type of street lighting, which could distinguish it at night both from outside and from within.

Brookline's principal visual problem among the residential areas is its apartment zone growing out from Coolidge Corner. In contrast to the rest of the Town, these are nondescript places: crowded, relatively noisy and uncomfortable, hard-faced. Even the apartment dwellers seem to oppose the growth of this kind of development. Public policy must concentrate on the control and guidance of apartment development—not its proscription, since it satisfies a legitimate need—but the insurance of adequate open space, a better visual order, a comfortable climate, acoustic insulation, and some room for individual expression and area identity. Multi-family development can by design be made as pleasant as areas of single houses.

Change is threatening another area which to many people is a unique expression of the Town: the residential estates south of Boylston Street. This is a zone whose heavy planting, large but hidden houses, and narrow winding roads like country lanes all evoke seclusion and high social status. It is an example of an area where locational confusion and a maze-like road network are part of the very character of the place. It is also, interestingly enough, one of the few places in the Town where environmental contrast is lacking, where, for example, there is no nearby point of high activity. Although this may suit its inhabitants, it appears to the outside observer to be delightful yet oppressive.

However the outside observer may react, this is a unique area in Boston, and it will be important to preserve this special character, which to so many Town residents is a source of pleasure, identity, and prestige. From the viewpoint of visual form, the new institutional uses which are beginning to occupy this territory may in fact be a principal means of preserving it in the face of change, if close controls can be placed on their location and design. Visual character does not depend on wealth. An area such as The Point has its own strong identity, and is a valuable part of the visual landscape of the Town.

Problems of the General Visual System

In a more general sense, Brookline has some difficulties as a visual whole, however rich the texture of its parts. Its diagonal relation to the Boston region, and the formlessness of its major street pattern, have already been mentioned. In many other ways it is unrelated to the great city around it: approaches are obscure except on the main radials, views in or out are infrequent. This may be desired by the townspeople, but when they are visually cut off from such nearby amenities as the Charles River or the Jamaicaway, Hammond Pond or the Chestnut Hill Reservoir, the result is surely unfortunate. Much might be done to make these features psychologically accessible: by the location of roads or walkways, the siting of tall buildings, or the management of views.

A similar break within the Town occurs south of Boylston Street, where the street system, the social and land use barriers, and the lack of activity centers all conspire to detach the southern corner. Its location is politically and visually ambiguous, as is readily apparent even from the small number of interviews we have performed (is it part of Brookline or West Roxbury? and where are West Roxbury and Jamaica Plain?). Some means to bridge this break will have to be found if a unified sense of community is wanted. Clarifying the Lee Street–Chestnut Hill link, unifying the Goddard Avenue–Cottage Street–Perkins Street line, and even bringing High Street into it as a clear extension of Harvard Street might all be possibilities. The pressure for cross-Town movement is bound to increase, and visual difficulties will accompany the problems of circulation.

Brookline has a magnificent natural endowment of water and hills. There are ample open spaces in many parts of the Town, and individual houses often make good use of views and ground form. At the community scale, however, the natural setting has been buried: the hills and waters are largely invisible (the old Reservoir and Weld Hill are exceptions), major panoramas are neglected, and the parks often shabby and poorly exploited. Interviewees often seemed to be unaware of the hills that surround them. On the other hand, they are keenly aware of a well-developed park and visible hill such as at Larz Anderson Park. Unquestionably, any policy concerned with visual form would make the watersides and hilltops accessible, and open up the panoramic views from them. In reverse, it would make sure that those hills and streams were visible from the principal roads and centers.

In particular, there are three distinctive hills which stride across the northwest edge of the Town: Fisher, Aspinwall, and Corey. Just as the three major activity centers might be visually differentiated and conceptually linked as basic symbols of the Town, so might these three distinctive hills be made visible and inter-visible, and each given a distinctive character, to be islands of identity rising out of the mass of urban development.

Separate character might be conferred by planting, names, the control of new development, or the use of tall landmarks. From these hills spectacular views of Brookline and Boston can be had.

Not only is the natural setting obscure, but also the historical setting. The Boylston house on Route 9, and the Devotion house on Harvard Street (symbolically overwhelmed by the school which envelops it!) are the only visibly historic structures which are apparent from the major road system. No references to history were made in the interviews, except to old houses in the estate area by those living close by, plus frequent references to the Kennedys. (History is not just what happened a century ago—the environment can also be used to heighten our sense of the present, or the recent past!)

It may be possible to develop an historic district in the Cottage–Warren Street area, and to make other significant points visually accessible by road improvements, signs, and the control of surrounding form. As a more outlandish suggestion, would it be possible to give the citizens of the Town a sense of the present and future as well? Signs and symbolic markets might be used to show planned changes, or the thrust of new development. Citizens might be oriented in the time as well as in space.

These points represent only a selection among the visual problems of the Town, which are noted in a more systematic fashion in Figures 6–9 and for whose detailed character one must return to the original survey material. The potentialities mentioned above are only a few of the more obvious ones which have occurred to us in the course of analysis. Creative design would uncover many more.

The Visual Content of a Comprehensive Plan

An evaluation of visual character is only useful if it leads to action for visual improvement. This report will not propose a plan, but it must indicate how the evaluation could be brought to bear. With what sorts of visual issues might a general plan concern itself? What would be the visual component of such a plan?

Without making any recommendation or trying to construct a coherent proposal, we will simply make an illustrative list of the types of proposals that a general plan for Brookline might deal with, as suggested by the problems uncovered:

1. Recommended general standards for the design and siting of new development, apartments in particular—partly advisory, partly controlling.

2. Special controls in areas of particular quality which are to be preserved. Suggestions to maintain or sharpen the identifiable character of different residential districts.

3. Advisory visual criteria for new buildings in landmark locations. Design review procedures for such structures, or for any structures larger than a certain size.

4. Recommendations for the location, design, and design review of public buildings.

5. Visual criteria to aid in the selection of areas for redevelopment or renewal. Visual objectives to guide the redesign of those areas.

6. Policies for the location and design of public parks, plazas, wild lands, and other places of retreat and quiet. Recommendations for the design of water areas and their shores. Plans for the use of decorative water.

7. Designs for important focal points (shopping or civic centers), their approaches and internal spaces.

8. Policies, standards, and prototype designs for public signs, lighting, landscaping, paving, shelter, benches, fences, and other street furniture, with indications of how they might vary from area to area. Controls and standards for private signs and lighting.

9. Provisions for the control of noise, or of the micro-climate, including the use of planting or of shielding devices, the control of noise at the source, the orientation and spacing of buildings, the design of ground surfaces in regard to the way they reflect or absorb radiation, the introduction of desirable sounds or "acoustic perfume."

10. Proposed locations of new streets and highways, and designs for the sequence of spaces, views, and motion along the major ways. Policies for route marking and identification, and for maintaining the visibility of natural or man-made elements.

11. Designs for the crucial intersections and the major entrance points.

12. Policies for the alignment, signing, and station design of transit lines. Suggestions for communicating arrivals, destinations, or current loadings of the vehicles.

13. Proposals for opening up access (by foot, car, or lift) to rivers, parks, panoramic points, or other places of public interest. Plans for circulation networks for pedestrians, equestrians, or cyclists.

14. Policies for improving visibility of or from the hills: landscaping, height and character of new development, sight lines, etc.

15. Recommendations for expressing the history of the Town, and perhaps for communicating events to come: historical preservation and reconstruction, signs, access, visibility, etc.

All of these are areas in which definite proposals could be prepared, proposals which could be implemented and which would bear on the significant problems and objectives of the Town. Clearly, they could not all be dealt with simultaneously. Choices of where to concentrate attention would have to be made, choices based on the urgency or importance of a problem, its place in the strategic succession of actions, the probability of its being implemented, the resources available, and so on. At this juncture, the most strategic areas seem to be:

a. General standards for apartment development, and for the design review of large or landmark buildings, public and private.

b. Visual criteria to guide the design of renewal areas.

c. Designs for the key focal points: Brookline Village, Coolidge Corner, and Chestnut Hill.

d. Sequence designs on the major ways, with special attention to the intersections and entrances.

e. Location and design of parks and water areas.

f. Policies for public signs, lighting, landscaping, paving, and shelter.

This is not a thoroughly considered choice. Even this abbreviated list is beyond the work-load capability of the present planning staff.

Planning for the Visual Form of the Town

How, then, will it be done? What is required if the Town is to control and improve these critical areas of visual form? The required actions are continuing ones, which must be an intimate part of the entire planning process.

The Town now possesses a comprehensive visual survey, one of the first of its kind. It will, however, shortly have only historical value unless it is maintained as an up-to-date body of information. This means that major visual changes must be inserted as they occur, and that there must be periodic, if rather summary, re-surveys of the major routes, areas, and centers. This might be required once every two years.

More critical will be the continuing visual intelligence required for the preparation of specific policies as they arise: detailed analyses of a single route or a single center, a comprehensive survey of the sign system, and so on. The work to date provides only a general framework of information. It would be useful if this material were available in a form that citizens might easily study and comment on it: a public room equipped with models, air and ground photographs, and diagrams and descriptions of existing and proposed environments.

In one area, at least, the current survey is quite inadequate: the analysis of the image of the Town as held by its residents. This is an important complement to observation in the field, and techniques for this type of survey are already developed. Within our limitations of time and staff, the sample survey which was conducted was far too small and too uneven for any confidence to be put in it, however interesting the indications. The methods are so time-consuming as to permit no more than a sample survey in any case, but the present sample could easily and usefully be extended, and should be renewed from time to time, to check image change or to probe more deeply into special areas on which policy is being prepared.

At a later date, it may also be useful to analyze the actual behavior of people using crucial areas (in shopping centers, at intersections, in the parks). The techniques are not yet as well developed, but are rapidly becoming so. All these methods of getting at how people use, or react to, or think of their environment are obviously at the center of our concern: providing an environment which is a good setting for human life.

Many of these methods will be of particular value used as a feedback, that is, when they are employed to test how people actually use and enjoy some new design. Did the new square in fact achieve what it was designed to do? How can it be modified to avoid the unforeseen difficulties that arose, and what do we learn for the next time? Not only will this continuing visual intelligence improve the stock of knowledge on which designs can be based, but it will have effects in the other direction: the inhabitants of Brookline, in becoming more conscious of the effect of the visual environment, will inevitably become more critical and demanding of the product they receive.

Along with this intelligence function, there must be a continual reassessment and development of the visual objectives of the Town. The set proposed above is simply our recommendation, based on brief acquaintance. Surely the Town will want to modify and sharpen the set in many ways. This will be found to be a never-ending process, for not only does the Town and its people and its problems change, but the objectives themselves are only understood as they are applied to real situations. Thus each new problem will cause a revision and extension of these statements.

Finally, a continuing process of design will be required, as various projects, standards, and policies are developed, and as strategies shift. Just as the comprehensive plan for a community is always undergoing development, so are its visual components. A special initial effort may be required to set up framework visual policies for the Town as a whole, just as a special effort has been needed to initiate the process of visual intelligence. But it would be a mistake to think that there is something called a "visual plan" which is distinct from other kinds of plans for the physical environment, or that, once established, such a plan is complete and can be used as an unchanging future guide.

There are many ways in which visual policies may be carried out, and many of them are implicit in the suggested list of policies described above. We have emphasized the critical importance of the design of public facilities: road alignments and surfacing, signs, lights, parks, landscaping.

They may be designed directly by designers on the planning staff, or detailed recommendations can be made to the public agencies in control. Preferably there would be competent designers working on the staff of the operating agency—the parks or highway department, for example—who are in touch with the general policies evolving in the planning staff. This talent is often difficult to attract to a small operating agency, and these agencies may more easily borrow the services of a designer from the planning staff, or engage a consultant. Roads, parks, and utilities are traditionally designed by public staff, and they happen to be strategic for the visual impression of the Town.

Public buildings, which are not customarily designed by public staff, should be subjected to a careful review process. This does not mean a formal review after detailed plans are complete, since at that time changes are extremely difficult to make. Nor does it necessarily require binding legal control. The critical item is the program, the original instructions given to the architect, which should include how his structure is to relate to surrounding buildings, streets, and open spaces, and what its visual role will be in the context of the whole. Equally important are very early discussions between the public agency and its architect, on the one hand, and some public authority which is concerned with the quality of the entire Town environment, on the other. The Planning Board itself is probably the proper agency to take on this task. If this would cause an overload it might be possible to set up a special Design Advisory Board, which reports to the Planning Board and is supported by planning staff.

While program and design concept are still being formulated, it is comparatively easy for a review authority to influence the design by pointing out the public objectives which go beyond the function of the building itself. Acceptance of these objectives by the architect is relatively painless, and may be received with interest. Once the first meeting has been held, there must be continuing liaison between the architect and the planning staff as the design develops. Sketches and models which show the building in its setting should be required. Any final review will then become far less agonizing.

This review process might well be extended to private buildings built on certain designated landmark sites, or to structures which are of large scale. This would not require any further controls beyond the normal zoning and building codes. Its effectiveness would lie in the aptness and timeliness of the advice given. These review procedures, of course, would require some additional planning-staff support to make them effective, and they should not be extended over more than a limited number of strategic buildings, lest they become perfunctory.

It is possible that the planning agency might go further in this process of communication with private developers. It might offer reasonably priced design advisory services to private individuals or agencies who are not now using such talent in their building decisions—people engaged in house or store remodeling, for example. In this case, the private individual has the benefit of talented advice, while the public agency can influence the form of the city environment directly, and in the process become better acquainted with the motives and problems of its constituents.

This is, of course, a proposal that could generate large demands on the public design staff, even though in part or in whole it was supported by fees. It has been tried with promising results in a few areas in this country, but the experience is limited. All this would indicate a cautious and experimental approach to this particular idea.

The planning design staff may also be used to prepare illustrative or prototype designs, with the intent of stimulating public interest, guiding the decisions of private developers, or communicating new possibilities to them. It can refine and apply the visual objectives to particular areas, as a general guide to development.

In certain critical places, such as renewal areas or Town centers, the public designers should intervene more directly: preparing general site plans, standards, controls, or detailed visual objectives which will be used to guide the total development of the site. This is now becoming a familiar and effective way of improving the visual environment. This requires design competence on the staff of the Redevelopment Authority, or the borrowing of design time from the planning staff. A continuous process of design, revision, and review must be instituted. "One shot" plans will not be carried out.

Finally, there are existing controls, zoning in particular, which have an extensive influence on the general visual environment, particularly through the controls on bulk, setback, parking, signs, and use. The requirement for off-street parking, for example, which is rationally based on circulation efficiency, may have disastrous visual effects unless parking locations are carefully controlled. Vast parking lots, and the interruption or masking of store fronts by parked cars, are a prime cause of the prevalent emptiness and chaos of the American townscape. They clearly should be reviewed when visual criteria have been firmly established. Provisions might be modified in places, to help in achieving these criteria. As the framework of visual policies evolve, it may be advisable to place special design controls on particular places: unique districts or landmark locations, for example.

What is the magnitude of the costs involved in all these suggestions? Some shifts in legal controls may be required, but probably not substantial ones for the present. Major new review and liaison procedures will certainly be needed. New planning staff must be added, to gather the required visual intelligence, to make direct and prototype designs, to prepare detailed objectives, policies, and standards, and to perform design review and liaison. Some of these additions are recommended to be made to the staffs of the Redevelopment Authority and (if obtainable) to the park and highway departments. Even with these additions, one more full-time planning designer, in addition to the one presently on the staff, may be needed to carry out these new duties.

Above all, it will require a commitment of interest and conviction by the planning agency and the Town, and a major public debate on objectives and types of solutions. The importance of these issues for the quality of life in Brookline, and its long-run desirability as a place to live in, would seem to warrant the cost.

Notes

1. See Paul Spreiregen (for the Urban Design Committee of the AIA), "Guide Lines for the Visual Survey," *AIA Journal*, April 1963: 80; "Urban Design Study," City Planning Department, City of Minneapolis (background reports: (1) Livability Study; (2) Imageability Survey; (3) Historical Survey); "Visual Analysis—New Bedford Central Area," Blair and Stein Associates, Providence, May 1962.

2. It is interesting that the junction of Washington and Harvard Streets in Brookline Village (for all its shabbiness and confusion of traffic), and the block on Harvard Street north of Coolidge Corner (for all its gaudiness and congestion), are the only public places in the Town in which there is any sense of spatial enclosure or definition. Both of these may be hidden potentialities in the re-design of these places.

3. A copy of such a movie, made by exposing film at one frame per second while driving up and down each major street, which film can then be projected at normal speed, is on file at the planning office.

4. Proposals in the comprehensive plan to improve these intersections with overpasses must be followed up with detailed design attention. The normal result of such a change is to make the intersection even more bewildering, as well as cold and detached from its surroundings.

5. Editors' note: A proposal for building a freeway loop (called the Inner Belt) within central Boston was being seriously considered in the 1960s, but the idea was dropped after strong protests from local communities and institutions.

Development and Landscape: Martha's Vineyard (1973)

with Sasaki, Dawson & Demay Associates

It is possible to classify the visible Island scenery into major groups, based primarily on topography and vegetation. Each of these scenery groups, while containing variations, has a readily recognizable character upon which recommendations for future development can be built. While constant in topography, in most cases their vegetation has been influenced by man's activities, and is in a state of change. These groups can be called:

1. the salt lands
2. the bluffs
3. the moors
4. the hilly thickets
5. the wooded moraines
6. the open plains
7. the flat thickets
8. the wooded plains.

Figure 1 shows the distribution of these scenery types on the Island, as well as compact and linear settlements. The map defines those scenic areas which are in excess of 40 acres. Since the landscape can be a mixture of types and also occurs in patches smaller than 40 acres, the boundaries indicated are only approximate. For any particular area, an in-the-field survey is necessary to determine the landscape class. Places of compact settlement and the occasional overlay of linear settlement along the main roads are not discussed in this analysis, since the aim of this report is to discuss the future of the relatively undeveloped regions.

This map shows the distribution of these landscapes as they are today. Fifty, even ten, years ago a similar map would have shown a different pattern. And so it will in the future, as men clear or abandon their fields, build structures or move them, or as trees and brush grow quickly here and very slowly elsewhere. The moor land, for example, is much less frequently found now than it has been for centuries, but vigorous clearance could restore large areas to that condition.

The following text discusses the eight landscape types one by one. Each section describes the type's visual character, analyzes the impact of development, and recommends guidelines for development. These recommendations are summarized very briefly in figure 2. More detailed

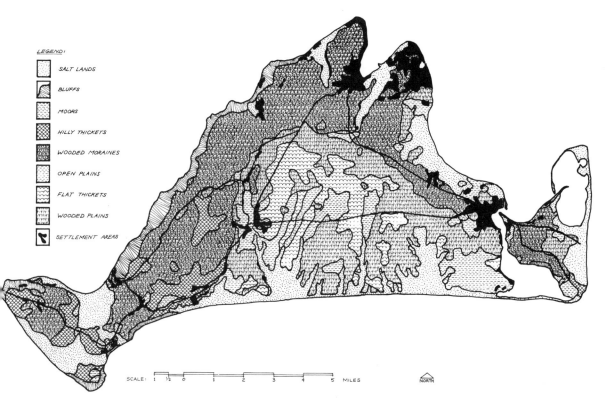

LEGEND:

- SALT LANDS
- BLUFFS
- MOORS
- HILLY THICKETS
- WOODED MORAINES
- OPEN PLAINS
- FLAT THICKETS
- WOODED PLAINS
- SETTLEMENT AREAS

SCALE: 1 ½ 0 1 2 3 4 5 MILES   NORTH

Figure 1 *Landscape districts*

explanation and reasoning behind the proposals are included in the discussion of each type.

The discussions of landscape types focus primarily on rules for developing within the various kinds of land, based on visual criteria only. It should be understood that additional limits to development will be set by such factors as water supply, land cost, town finances, ecological stability, and transporation, to name only a few. The discussion cites the limits to development set by visual factors, assuming a decision to develop has been made. These limits, quite proper for any small piece of terrain, would be disastrous if applied generally, even from a visual viewpoint alone. The charm of the Island lies in the variety of its landscapes, and the alternation between occupied and unoccupied is an important element in that variety. Moreover, the areas of unoccupied land must be large enough to give a sense of retreat and calm.

On the other hand, this analysis does show that the attraction of the Island lies in *how* it is settled, and that a truly "wild" Vineyard would hardly be very attractive. This is true not simply because an uninhabited island could not service its visitors, but because it would in fact be

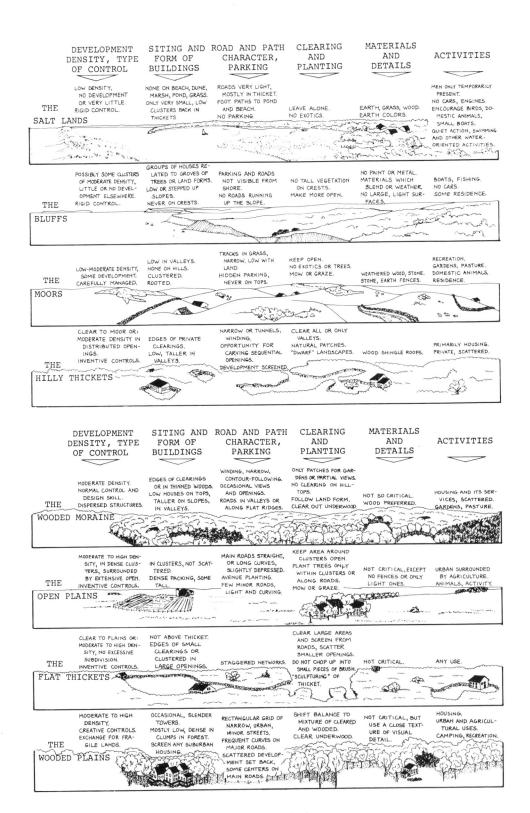

Figure 2 *Development guidelines by land-scape types*

rather uninteresting and unpleasant, save for a few wilderness campers and hunters. Moreover, certain kinds of land can profit from greater human use if it is done properly. Much of the thicketed land, and some of the flat plains and woods, are in this category.

Following the analyses of landscape types, the report draws some broader conclusions regarding development and the Island as a whole, and discusses effective policies for public regulation.

The Salt Lands

Characteristics

Particularly on the South Shore, there are extensive areas of salt pond and dune. It is the world of brackish ponds and tidal inlets, salt marsh, dune and beach, low grassland, and the open thickets that border them. It is an intimate interlacing of sea and land, created where the barrier beaches have cut across the mouths and points of old inlets and promontories.

The ponds, linked to the sea yet separated from its constant motion, are fertile nurseries for birds and fish, and still reflectors of the changing sky. Where this stillness is preserved there is a rare opportunity to feel part of the rhythm of life. The cycles of seasons and weather are clearly articulated in the changing vegetation and animal life, and the dunes of the barrier beach seem to grow and subside in the varying light. In moonlight the ponds are spectacular. The beach itself is of enormous visual scale, dominated by the sight and sound of the sea [and] seemingly absolutely cut off from the land behind by the bluff or barrier dune.

Development of the salt lands

These are special places, visually very powerful. Under light use, this landscape is almost self-maintaining, yet also very fragile when built upon or heavily used. So far the salt lands have received rather modest attention from the builder, but the signs of coming extensive settlement are now painfully apparent.

Preserving the power of the beach experience means there should never be any permanent man-made structure put on beach or dune, or even nearby, where its visible presence will destroy the rare sense of infinite space and natural order. Even the wheel tracks of beach vehicles leave a scar. Here there must be a simple iron rule: let the beach alone.

The pond edge of the barrier dunes should also be avoided altogether. This juncture of these two connected but powerfully contrasting types of scenery is a highly sensitive visual zone.

Recommending guidelines for development near ponds is more complex. There is great variety among the ponds, and the degree to which surrounding land, grassland, thicket, or woods are visually related to the look of the ponds varies also. The term "salt land" refers to that combination of land and water which forms a visual unit. The salt land character extends only for a short distance beyond the pond edge around Nashaquitsa, Stonewall, Tashmoo, or James. Here land rises quickly and shares few characteristics with beach and salt marsh. In contrast, where salt marsh merges gently into grass, and grass slowly into thicket, a broad band of land is visually part of the pond, and development within that band has strong impact on the look of the pond, and particularly to the sense of expanse so vital to the South Shore ponds.

Structures should never be built in the salt marsh, and pond and marsh should never be filled. The only structures directly on the pond edge should be those with a functional tie to the water, such as boat houses, and these should be small and low and few in number. In all cases, an even peppering of structures should be avoided: small clusters are better, with long stretches of the salt land left untouched.

Structures are less disruptive if they are sited at the edge of the bordering wood, or deep enough within the thicket so that their size is masked. Small clusters are possible, but buildings should be extremely low. The apparent large scale of these landscapes is due to the small height of all the objects in them. Buildings can be partially sunk into the ground, and might even use sod roofs. Near ponds, as well as anywhere that water views are dominant, the landscape has a "front side" and a "back side." Everyone is focused on the sea and the ponds, and one building should not upstage another by creeping forward into the other's line of view.

Muted color and soft form are other important characteristics of the landscape here. Bright colors, hard surfaces, and sharp forms are to be avoided. Wood, sod, thatch, and earth are preferable materials, and weathered silvers, greys, and browns are preferable colors. Metal, painted wood, and finished masonry are out of place. Automobile and pedestrian access should be as unobtrusive as possible. Roads should be narrow, single-track, unpaved, or paved or graveled only in the wheel tracks, keeping within the thicket or wood, and in slight folds in the land. Foot, horse, or bicycle paths are to be preferred in the open ground. A narrow wheel track might come down to the water only where essential, as where needed to put in a boat. Cars, by their form and shape, are a shock in this fragile landscape. They should not be parked in the open, or on the pond shore, beach, or dune, but always back in the thicket, and then in small numbers. The native plants and birds are an important part of the scene. Large trees and other exotic plants should not be imported; mowed lawns do not belong. The shore bird habitat should be preserved so that we see them and hear their cries. The stillness of the place is accentuated by these calls, by the wind, and [by] the distant sound of surf. The sound of cars, motorboats, airplanes, power mowers, radios, and other domestic engines is disruptive. But small sailboats and rowboats, domestic animals, [and] people in moderation and doing watery things all add to the effect.

Guidelines in brief for the salt lands

Never build on the beach or where visible from it. It is safest to leave the entire salt land unbuilt. If any building is done, it must be done with great care. Structures should be low, merging with the land, set back in the thickets or occasionally in small groups at the pond edge if that edge is hilly. Human activity is acceptable if kept moderate. The beach should be accessible on foot but not by car or other powered vehicles. The degree of control needed here goes well beyond normal public regulations.

The Bluffs

Characteristics

The steep edges of the eroding moraines create the second distinct type of shoreline: the bluffs. Here the effects of wind and water reveal an ever-changing face of sand or clay or rock strewn soil. Great boulders in the water mark the land's retreat, and provide a measure of the tide and shifting sand. Where the land behind the high cliffs is flat or receding, that land has very little to do visually with the beach itself, and development set back from the cliff edge is not visible from the beach below. Yet any development or tall vegetation which is visible above the bluff face both diminishes the apparent size of the cliffs and creates an alien note in the rugged landscape of land and water.

The shore effect extends further where the land continues to rise behind the bluff, as it does for a long portion of the North Shore, than it does when the land is level behind the cliff. The upper flanks of the hill as well as the cliff edge are dominated by the sights, sounds, and weather of the sea. Passing boats, though mere flecks, are important parts of the scene, as are distant islands and shorelines—sometimes clear and close, at other times vague or disappearing altogether for days on end. Vegetation is patterned by the winds, often high in the leeside gullies, but shorn low to windward. These shorelines and the development upon them are visible from passing boats and ferries, and so have a particularly wide impact.

Development of the bluffs

The small bluffs at Vineyard Haven and Oak Bluffs are now built up, but elsewhere the bluff lands are still for the most part empty. Now is surely the time to consider whether, and under what conditions, building should ever be allowed in them.

The broad outward view will inevitably tempt future builders, if they are free to choose their ground. Development here can actually enhance the view of the bluffs, but only if it is done with great care. A broad, bright, or reflective facade or roof will diminish the slopes, and so will a tall structure, or anything on the crest. On the other hand, low complex structures which step back up the mid-slopes or clusters of houses related to tree clumps or minor folds in the land can help to articulate the topography. Evenly spaced houses, or a continuous development of the bluffs, would inevitably destroy the image of the Island.

Roads are difficult to site, since anything running straight down from the top makes a demeaning scar (as well as causing erosion). Paths should move up a natural valley, or along the contour, or no more than diagonal to the slope. These bluffs and the slopes above them are, like the roadsides, the public face of the Vineyard.

Guidelines in brief for the bluffs

The bluffs, up to their visible crests, should be kept free of development, unless that development can be limited to carefully selected and widely separated points. If the latter, the permitted structures should be slope-following groups of buildings which maintain the visual scale and break no skyline. Since these would be highly privileged buildings, they should be open to public use, such as inns, rental units, restaurants, or public recreation facilities. The entire beach should be open to public foot access, in any case.

The Moors

Characteristics

The Up-Island "moors" are that part of the rolling, rocky terminal moraine which is open grassland with occasional low thickets. Some of this land will naturally remain in this state, due to its exposure and the quality of its soil, but most of it will grow back to thicket and forest if left uncut. This is the characteristic Up-Island ground which once extended shore to shore when sheep farming was the islanders' principal occupation. Little of it is left today, but it might be extended once again. It is now very attractive to summer residents, and much of it is peppered or peppering with small houses. But the old flavor lingers, and there is ground yet relatively untouched.

It is a soft, flowing landscape, quiet, rather old and worn— sometimes almost mournful. Stone is very much a part of it, as are erratic boulders, old stone fences, old foundations. The land does not change so much with the seasons as with the light. It has a special character at night, or in the mist. The rolling of the ground is one of its strongest visual characteristics, yet the hills are not actually very high.

Development of the Moors

A house which sits directly on top of one of the moors' low hills (and this is where many houses are mindlessly set) inflates its own presence and makes the hill seem to shrink. A large boulder or a clump of bushes belongs on such a hilltop, but not a house or a car, or even a large tree. On the other hand, houses in the small valleys, or at mid-slope where their roofs do not break the skyline, do not disturb the flow of the land. Indeed, they seem to "animate" it and give it interest. They must not be scattered everywhere, but are better clustered together. They are preferably low and firmly rooted to the ground. Earth, wood, and stone are harmonious materials here; weathered shingle and white trim are traditional. The form and material of the roof is very visible.

Although densities must be kept moderate, these landscapes can absorb a number of structures if the buildings are of modest size, low and well sited, and not surrounded by large-growing trees. This land should not be forested or allowed to grow into thicket: it is important to keep the skin of the earth visible, and to preserve the views of nearby water. Indeed, the old moor lands should be restored by clearance, where possible. While some of this land is self-maintaining, most must be mowed or grazed.

The sense of flow in the land should be conserved: lot lines can be left undefined when they do not coincide with old walls and hedgerows. Old stone walls dramatize the slope of the land, but high fences, or wire fences, or ones which are very regular in form tend to disrupt it. It may be possible to duplicate the character of stone fences without their cost, as by using low planted earth berms and occasional boulders, or low hedgerows, or even with open work concrete blocks, rough laid and planted. The character that is wanted is a low, solid, rough, permanent wall which by its alignment emphasizes the form of the land.

The minor roads should run with the land, in the valleys or mid-slopes, with only foot paths to the tops. The roads should be winding, unpaved, preferably one lane with turnouts, tracks in the grass. Cars should be kept off the tops, and never parked in large numbers. Parking can often be hidden in a valley or behind a hill, or dropped slightly into the ground or behind low clumps of bushes. These parking areas can be unpaved, or graveled, or covered with crushed shell.

Guidelines in brief for the Moors

The moor lands should be kept open, and extended by clearance. They can take moderate development if buildings are low and skillfully sited in the folds and low places. But as a general policy, brakes must be applied to the current rate of development in this highly attractive terrain. Public land regulations will be useful, but sensitive site design and cooperative efforts by landowners will be essential. The very special moorland quality must be conserved and increased.

The Hilly Thickets

Characteristics

The hilly thickets are land predominantly in scrub, brier, or small trees, higher than a man's chest but not too far above his head. Scrub oak and briers prevent movement, unless a path is cut, and the foliage is dense enough to block vision within a few feet. Frequently the vegetation varies, and low bearberry-covered hills, or clumps of oak or beetlebung, will rise above the general vegetation. In other places, patches of sand create clearings amidst surrounding growth. Frequently there is a close mix of all of these. The bald peaks rising above the thicket are notable landmarks, often appearing far larger than their actual size.

Development of the Hilly Thicket

If widely cleared, the land becomes a moor again, and should be so treated. Very often, this is the best action to take. If not cleared, the thicket has some peculiar properties of its own. It has not yet attracted extensive development, but will do so as land prices rise. When it does, it is usually cleared out in geometric patches.

Development near the notable bald peaks should be avoided, particularly when they are miniature ridgelines. But structures on overgrown hilltops do not destroy the scale quite so much, if they rise but little above the foliage and are not on any major skyline seen from a distance. The roof silhouette on a shrubby hill may even add interest to a rather shapeless landscape. Upland thicket frequently grows higher in hollows between hills than on them, thereby masking the subtle land contour and obscuring the variety which animates the moors, or the lands where farm and forest alternate. Variety can be introduced through careful site planning, and imagination may well produce a rather unique and novel type of settled landscape here. Clearing the valleys while leaving thicket or planting trees on the tops will emphasize the shape of the ground. The common practice of locating house and clearing above the thicketed valleys has the reverse effect: it flattens the land. In any case, unless clearance is total, the edges of clearings should not follow geometric lines, but rather the curving contours of the land and vegetation.

Thus a landscape of selectively distributed open spaces can be created: larger open areas for recreation or for small pastures or gardens, smaller ones for parking and housing sites. Buildings can be placed on the edges of these clearings, looking into them. Two-story buildings are acceptable in the valleys, while structures on the tops and the mid-slopes should be low, with dark shingle roofs. Substantial privacy can be had within a few feet, since the thicket is so impenetrable. However, the mutual siting of elevated buildings must be considered. Remote from each other on the ground, they may find themselves eye-to-eye at upper levels.

Roads are shallow canyons, or even tunnels, out in the brush. If they are moderately narrow and wind with the ground, they are easily hidden and convey a strong sense of motion to the driver. To prevent claustrophobia, they must pass occasional clearings, or openings to views. The thicket is a neutral solid which can be sculptured by hollowing out. Mazes can be made, or sequences of openings, or rather charming dwarf landscapes which are created by selecting and retaining an occasional bush or stunted tree. Beach plum, blueberry, and winterberry are only a few of the native shurbs which achieve striking form with age.

Guidelines in brief for the Hilly Thickets

Clear the hilly thickets to re-establish the moor. If not, emphasize the ground by clearing the valleys and planting the tops. Keep buildings low, or in the valleys, and away from open tops. The thickets may be hollowed out into small spaces. Moderate density and innovative controls are required.

The Wooded Moraine

Characteristics

Much of the terminal moraine and therefore much of the land on the Island is now in forest again, and this rolling, wooded land is one of the most pleasant features of the Vineyard, standing in vivid contrast to its moors and seaside lands. Although the woods seen from a road frequently appear uniform, there is in fact great variety within them. On much of the rocky moraine the dominant forest is oak, interspersed with occasional pine, and this is often a low wood, with trees stunted by wind or poor soil. Thus dramatic contrast is offered by wet pockets or stream courses where beech, maple, sassafras, and beetlebung grow tall and vigorous. This difference is especially notable in fall, when oaks turn russet and gold while the wetland trees blaze bright reds and yellow. The variations within the wooded moraine are finely distributed, and those who know the woods soon recognize its different aspects: where special mushrooms grow, or where a lovely beech has taken root.

Development of the Wooded Moraine

While (like the thicket) some of the rolling, wooded land might be cleared to moor again, and certainly some open glades are likely to be made in it, it would be most unfortunate if much of this land were to lose its character. Moreover, it can absorb [either] moderate, scattered development of a conventional type or dense clusters with little damage to its visual quality. Many summer homes are already secluded within it, but great areas remain unbroken.

Low houses on the very tops of the hills are often invisible from below, but on a major skyline they may be visible from a great distance if substantial clearing has been done. Another sensitive location is the military crest, that point somewhat below the gently sloping top where the hillside abruptly steepens as it descends to the valley. Here any building is part of the local skyline, but not necessarily the distant one. It is often an excellent place for a building, especially if the large trees can be retained, but wholesale clearance of the tops to get a wide view from every window damages the landscape. Narrow view openings are better, or clearances *below* a house which is on the military crest or at mid-slope, especially if a few trees are retained just in front of the house so that the view is seen through their limbs and branches. A broad view from every window is not desirable in any case.

Small openings can be cleared near the house for gardens and recreation. Structures site most naturally at the edge of these artificial glades, rather than in the middle of them. The clearings should not be too large, and particularly fine trees can be preserved within them. Their boundaries should curve with the ground or reveal old fences. Within the woods, cleaning out the undergrowth to leave the mature trees produces a landscape very pleasant to the human eye, although it may hamper the future maintenance of the forest.

Roads straight down a slope open up long views but scar the landscape. Winding tracks which follow the contour or run diagonally to them are better. At every turn a new view can be revealed by clearing a small lane or opening. The road can be paved or graveled, but the shoulders should be very narrow so that tree branches can close overhead. Minor roads can branch off from each other at staggered intersections and loop back in the valleys, rather than being arranged in a regular grid. But they may also run along the ridges if well back from the military crest: then they enjoy views without themselves being seen. Houses, however, will normally stay back some distance from the roads, especially if these are main roads.

All this is a familiar and pleasant type of forest development, rather easily achieved if encouraged by public regulations and supported by the intentions of developers and owners. There is no need to solicit development in these areas, yet on visual grounds it can be permitted under proper control. In doing so, the basic character of the wooded moraine must be conserved.

Allow development to continue at moderate densities under good public controls. Conserve the landscape character by careful siting of dispersed houses and roads, and by thoughtful planning of openings in the forest. Maintain some wooded areas free from development.

The Open Plains

Characteristics

The plains, which fall gently from the moraines' edge to the South Shore, are now predominantly in forest or thicket, but the open plains which remain have a striking character. Once these outwash plains were deforested and used for berrying or grazing. Today, Katama is the largest plains region still in grass, apparently a huge expanse, stretching to the shore. In contrast to the small scale and great variety elsewhere on the Vineyard it is most remarkable. Along some pond edges the plain is also in grass, but elsewhere, notably in the State Forest, the unforested areas are uniformly low scrub oak and shurb. Here the uniformity of the height of the vegetation reveals the grooves of the ancient glacial stream beds, the bottoms, which are filled on the seaward end by the ponds.

In distinction to these areas, some of the open flat land is in small fields, the remnants of larger agricultural enterprises. Most of these lie at the edge of the moraine, and tend to show a gentle undulation. Many are in the first stages of forest growth, and punctuated with small cedars. These invaded fields make a very particular, small, soft landscape, haunting by moonlight, a special quality to be preserved if at all possible.

Development of the Open Plains

Unfortunately the Katama plains is now sadly disfigured by a rash of widely visible new development. Like any open ground, its character is defeated by a widespread sprinkling of development. It is better either to keep such land clear, with buildings only on its edge where it borders woods or hills, or to convert it to something new by concentrated settlement. Since it is flat, it is relatively easy to produce a new urban character, and just as easy to make a formless suburbia.

The preferred development strategy may be to keep open the bulk of the land, but to site within it occasional clusters of structures. These clusters could be associated with plantings of large trees, and contain many dwelling units, if these were in two or three story buildings sited close together. The extended, rather featureless plain can also accept a limited number of relatively large structures, to add a note of strong form, as do barns. The materials used are not so crucial, although it may still be well to keep within the general Vineyard tradition.

Outside the clusters, it is important to maintain the open sweep of the land, avoiding trees and scattered structures, or any fences except where necessary for agricultural purposes. The openness is for the most part not self-maintaining, and the land must be continually cultivated, mowed, or grazed. Some thicketed flat land might well be returned to this plains character, and used for agriculture or developed in village clusters. The Island once again deforested would seem sadly barren to us (as well as once again destructive of the soil), yet if the balance in the flat lands were to be swung toward agriculture and open development, the resulting mix of wooded and clear would make the Island a more interesting place.

Roads can hardly be made to disappear in this landscape, but they can follow minor folds in the ground or even be depressed one or two feet below grade. Main roads are inevitably visible features, and they will run straight or take very long curves, since they have no reason to wander. They may even be made deliberately noticeable by planting them with avenues of trees. A rectilinear network of minor ways is quite fitting in the settled clusters. In the open ground, when applied over large areas, such a grid will be rigid and monotonous. Small roads should be kept out of these open areas, or if needed, curve as they follow minor irregularities in the ground, or even swing around small artificial hills or planted clumps of vegetation.

Things in motion make a plain interesting to look at: cattle, horses, sheep, grain and grass in the wind, temporary encampments and fairs, banners, vehicles, walkers and riders. The parked, "dead" vehicle is another story. Parking should be associated with the dense settlements, but not as a metallic fringe. Parking can be inserted within the settlements, divided into smaller pieces, and its impact reduced by sinking it into the earth a few feet. If there are tall buildings, however, the view downward onto a large paved parking lot will be unpleasant even if it is masked on the ground. Overhead planting and dispersal can overcome this.

The plains area, precisely because of its less decisive character, is a region which can take moderate development and occasional high densities, not only without harm but even with marked scenic improvement. But development must be managed carefully. A way must be found to encourage clustered settlements set in enveloping open fields. Otherwise the plains are in danger of being transformed into a shapeless suburbia, as is now occurring in Katama.

High acreage requirements in zoning are not the solution. If successful, they will simply scatter development even further and prevent the building of those houses of more modest cost and upkeep which are sorely needed on the Island. On the other hand, if the plains can be used for agriculture or for compact settlement, they will turn into a substantial asset. They may well be expanded by judicious clearance of the flat thickets or even the central woodlands.

Since the small, cedar-dotted areas are landscapes in transition from farm to forest, their preservation means a constant cutting out if the half-grown trees. These fields are more like the small clearings in the flat woods or thickets, and should be treated as described below. A building set carelessly in this land of young cedars is likely to look as if it were trying to hide among misplaced foundation plantings. It is better to withdraw to the edge and so to enjoy the view of the exclamations in the grass.

Guidelines in Brief for the Open Plains

Develop high-density clusters of buildings separated by large open fields. This will require innovations in public regulations and incentives. If this is not possible, keep the plains open. Maintain or encourage agricultural use.

The Flat Thickets

Characteristics

In places, the former flat fields are growing back to wood, passing through a thicket stage. Much of the interior of the State Forest is like this, and some of the borders of the salt ponds. Many of the characteristics of the thicketed moraine apply here: impenetrability of the brush, blockage of vision, the ease of gaining privacy and isolation. Even more than in the hills, this is a featureless, unpleasant, "useless" ground. The shallow "bottoms" that run back through the interior are the strongest feature of this relatively monotonous ground.

Development and the Flat Thickets

The clearance of the flat thicket to re-establish a plain may be very justifiable if the plain will be properly developed and if the clearance will not border on some more sensitive area. But if it remains in thicket, it can be sculptured like the other thicketed land to make a sequence of openings and small private landscapes.

Structures which appear above the flat thicket have wider impact than those amidst the rolling moraine. More depends on the designer's art, since there is so little given character. The sense of undulation of the bottoms may easily be obliterated. But they can also be emphasized by the careful siting of roads and structures. If the thicket mass is too frequently broken by roads and small openings, it begins to disintegrate as a visual background. Large openings can be made, and can be screened from the roads by relatively thin borders of untouched growth. Tall structures which peer over the tops will seem incongruous in this flat low land. The thicket, if not totally cleared, can be used for small private houses or campsites in scattered clearings, or also for relatively large areas of development which it is desirable to screen from the main roads: large parking areas, service industries, extensive camps, or disposal areas. Obviously, these should occur in extensive areas of interior thicket, not in the vicinity of the salt ponds, and must be kept low. Within these secluded clearings, it may be possible to create landscapes of special character by selective clearance, or the use of exotic plants, or the compact siting of buildings and walls.

Guidelines in Brief for the Flat Thicket

Return to open plains, if proper development can be assured. Or build low buildings for activity which it is desirable to screen from view. It is also usable for scattered development of moderate density, accompanied by small openings, if the thicket is not excessively subdivided.

The Wooded Plains

Characteristics

A substantial portion of the Island is wooded and flat, the old outwash plain. Some of it is pine forest, but most of it is oak, or mixed woods. Each of these has its own qualities: the dark pine groves with their soft carpet of needles, erect trunks, and shafts of light; the oaks with their rough bark, their pointed leaves fluttering in a diffused light. But the similarities of density and height of foliage, and the flatness of the ground, make it possible to speak of similar visual development rules. The ground is not really flat, of course, for in addition to its persistent general slope and minor irregularities it is also marked by the long "bottoms," the former course of glacial streams, which lead into the extremities of the salt ponds. These open furrows are marked features in the flat woods, and the main roads pass over them like gentle roller coasters.

Development of the Wooded Plains

The present character of the woodlands is rather mild and monotonous, without incident except for the bottoms. They can accept considerable development, and be improved by it. But, as always, that development must be done well, or we will substitute an aggressively dreary landscape for one that is now only mildly so. Until recently, this land has been largely neglected. Now suddenly there has been an explosive subdivision of this type of ground. Very likely substantial acreage will shortly be converted into standard tracts of suburban housing.

Moderate densities are possible in these woods, and even high densities where structures are clustered, as described in the section on the open plains, and surrounding woodland is left unbuilt. An infrequent lookout tower might provide a view that is otherwise impossible in this terrain, and can act as a distinct landmark as well. Spires and other tall structures can co-exist with trees, but they must be slender and not numerous. An apartment slab would, in contrast, be a visual shock. Clusters of lower, compactly sited apartments and row houses can create interesting small landscapes. A close, varied, visual density with intimate complex spaces, strong colors and textures, and attractive detail could be a relief in this forest. But these clusters should be nestled in the trees, and not have large peripheral parking lots. They must be incidents in the forest. Continuous development, even of single houses on large lots, would erase any sense of the Island character.

A minor network of straight and narrow streets, using staggered intersections and other devices to preserve the close visual spaces, are a rational way of laying out these compact places. On the other hand, if the main roads between settlements are straight, they reinforce the inherent monotony of the forest, and break its continuity by clearly dividing one side from another. We see only the road itself, and this is all the more true when it is given wide empty shoulders. In flat land, without the incidents of thriving farms or towns to enliven it, a road is not an interesting thing to watch. Thus main roads should be as narrow as is feasible and have frequent curves, so that we look into their wooded edges. The unexplained curves which might be exasperating in open country are quite acceptable here. Scattered development should be drawn back from the main roads and screened by intervening trees. (This will require a greater depth than in the thicketed areas, however.) Major development and parking should also be screened. But interest on the road will be increased if occasional centers of activity are sited on its verge, particularly at some change in road direction. A roadside clearing, or meadow, or garden will also relieve the scene. Some of the land may be cleared more extensively for agriculture or recreation, but not so much as to destroy the balance of wood and open. Near the clearings, structures should be kept in the trees, or the edge of the trees. These woodlands make fine camping areas, which can be developed simply by clearing the undergrowth while leaving a brushy screen between individual sites

The danger in these woodlands is not that they may be built upon, but that they may be converted into standard subdivisions, with straight wide streets, individual ranch houses, smooth lawns, trim fences, and foundation planting. The woodland is gone, and in its place is a landscape which is common to much of the United States. However functional these developments might be, the special character of the Island is thereby diluted. Yet housing of moderate cost is urgently needed, not only for the Island residents, but also for summer visitors of moderate means. Not everyone can afford fine houses spaced out in ample countryside, nor can the Island take much of this kind of extended growth without damage. However, costs can actually be reduced and densities increased if the model we suggest is followed instead of the conventional suburban one.

Developers and the construction industry, catering to conventional taste, may find it hard to change their style from a suburban form to one of compact housing clusters. If suburban districts continue to be built on the Island, they should at least be placed in the wooded or thicketed flat lands, and be well screened from the public roads.

Guidelines in Brief for the Wooded Plains

Develop moderate to high density clusters, well separated in the forest. Creative public controls and incentives are required. Some slender tall structures are allowable. Restricted portions of the land may be opened up. Encourage development to take place here instead of in the more visually fragile areas.

Settlement Areas

This report will not deal with the present settlement areas on the Island. Some of these areas have important and varied characteristics of their own that need study, conservation, and in some cases special regulation, as in an historic district. Edgartown, Oak Bluffs, Vineyard Haven, West Tisbury, and Menemsha all have important lessons for new development. For the most part, these are modest houses at close densities, and yet they are a pleasure to live in. Narrow streets, often one-way, pedestrian enclosures, plantings of large trees and bushes, painted fences, good detail, vernacular architecture, [and] scattered parking all contribute to the effect. The places work well for all their age, and despite the heavy pressures now put upon them. New areas of dense settlement should function just as pleasantly.

An Overview of Development

There are three principle conclusions to be drawn about development on the Island, speaking as always purely from a visual standpoint.

1. The Island landscape would be enhanced by being more open, to give a better sense of the land and a more widespread view of the water. Open land ideally would be used for agriculture or other extensive use, if this were economical, but it could also be occupied by structures, under the guidelines given above. More openness is wanted both on the moraine and on the outwash plain, although one would hesitate to clear more than small pieces of the wooded moraine, or even the wooded plain. No one would want to see the Island restored to the treelessness of colonial times, nor should land be cleared unless there is a promise of using it handsomely. A balance of wood and field should be preserved. Thickets, on the other hand, can be opened up almost everywhere.

2. In addition, these analyses indicate that efforts should be made to shift the balance of where development is going on. In some areas, development should be practically excluded—as near the salt ponds. In others, brakes should be set and strong controls employed—as on the moors and along the bluff shores. In still other—the wooded moraines—development can proceed under good normal controls, although substantial areas should be kept free, and there is no need to encourage it. In others again—some of the thickets and the open plains—development may well be encouraged, but innovative controls must be used. Finally, the flat woods would be able to take substantial growth without visual damage, if normal care is used and some creative controls applied.

3. The Island can absorb further development but it must be at a moderate rate, so that planning skill and good control can be applied, and so that visual continuity and harmony will be maintained. Moreover, development should not be brought up to permissible levels everywhere, but grouped so that substantial portions of open land remain. While the rate of building development must be kept moderate, it is possible in many areas to increase human activity and use without visual damage, if that activity does not imply many permanent roads and buildings.

Landscape guidelines of the kind we have proposed should be of direct value to the Open Land Foundation as it advises builders or develops particular areas. They may also have more general implication for VOLF policy. If VOLF's intent is to guide the development process in ways that are beyond the power of public regulations, then it need not be operating in areas where development should and can be prohibited, or in those others where normal good public regulations can be effective. This indicates a strategic concentration on those areas of the Island which are either delicate, and so need very skillful site planning—the moors, for example—or on those places where there is a need for innovative control, and where if that is forthcoming some of the development pressure may most easily be absorbed. The thickets and open plains are in this category, and may indeed be the visually most strategic places for VOLF to operate. Patterns of land ownership, ecology, water supply, or market operation, of course, may dictate other strategic areas. Furthermore VOLF could promote many of the above recommendations by other means, such as by encouraging variety, openness, and clustering by an innovative use of conservation restrictions.

The Public Regulation of Private Development

It is somewhat more difficult to draw conclusions for zoning or subdivision control from these analyses, except to show how often normal public controls fail to meet visual criteria. Minimum lot sizes may diffuse development monotonously. Strict standards for street layout (minimum widths, finish and paving) may produce suburban roads that erode the Island character. Normal mainland rules can only be followed at peril.

Some ideas do emerge, however. Building height and bulk can often be usefully controlled. Development can be prohibited on marsh and dune and pond. Some of the recommended opening up of Island views can be accomplished by town purchase of view easements, or by accepting conservation restriction. Screening setbacks can be used in wooded or thicketed land. But standardized, Island-wide setback rules would be wasteful and ineffective. In thicket a small setback is sufficient (until and unless it grows into woods!); in woods more is required; in open land a setback is worse than useless. Screening *performance* is what is sought, and the nature of planting between house and road and the alignment of the approach driveways are just as critical as the setback itself.

Although difficult, it may be possible to develop rules preventing the occupation of major skylines and exposed tops. There may also be ways of granting tax incentives for land clearance, for agricultural use, or for the maintenance of open land. In addition, use and density zoning would naturally be influenced by the development capabilities recommended above.

More detailed controls regarding exact siting, or wall or roof material, would be difficult to administer except in very special places (see below) and are not customary in our regulatory tradition. More than anything, the analyses point up warnings about what not to require, and suggest we use very flexible controls, supplemented perhaps by public design review boards whose function is advisory, not regulatory.

It is apparent that these analyses call for distinct *variations* of density over the Island, according to the nature of the landscape, and often point to a greater concentration of development, to be set off by more truly open land. Any regulatory or tax devices which will encourage clustering should certainly be employed. Indeed, from a landscape viewpoint, this variation of density is more important than standardization or the regulation of the particular *use* of a piece of land.

"Cluster zoning" is some help, but only when large areas are being developed as a single unit. Then, development which might ordinarily be spread evenly over the land is concentrated on a small percentage of the acreage and the rest is left open.

Would it also be possible to encourage clustering where ownership is scattered? One possible technique is the following: An analysis would be made of a region to reveal which land would be best for concentrated development, and which land would best be left open. All land owners within the region would be given "development rights," but these rights could be used only in the designated "zones of concentration." Owners in these zones could then build densely, but only in so far as they bought up development rights from owners of surrounding land. This is only one example of a procedure that might prevent environmental quality from falling prey to the legitimate economic interests of individuals. In any case, here is a prime area for developing some innovative concepts of land control.

Finally, the analyses have something to say about special state or federal legislation, such as the proposed Islands Trust. Local zoning is severely limited by the provisions of the state enabling legislation. Zoning by-laws cannot simply prohibit development on certain lands, for example, nor can they control the *rate* of development, which is as critical as its location. They cannot subject development to complex and subtle design rules whose applications must rely on skilled judgment. But controls of this kind may be necessary in selected places to protect the visually fragile areas, as well as the land which has a desirable intrinsic character. On the other hand, if development is prohibited indiscriminately, use of the Island will be denied to many people who would otherwise enjoy it. There is a need for powerful controls which can be used selectively to deal with rate and quality, and which are backed with the ability to buy out development or access rights on occasion. Towns do not have these financial or legal powers. The Commonwealth does, however, and uses them in the wetlands (the Hatch and Jones acts, for example). Legislation to make all beaches public has also been proposed at the State level and enactment would permit further use of these powers. The pending Islands Trust Bill is an example of the potential of the federal government's powers.

The visual analysis, therefore, supports the enactment of some state or federal legislation which will control development in special ways. The Islands Trust Bill is one current example. Speaking solely in visual terms, there are improvements that might be made in the present Bill. First, the Bill as proposed as of July 27, 1972, relies almost entirely on a division of the Island into three zones of increasing development control. Blanket controls by sharply bounded zones are not sufficient. The *nature* of development everywhere is critical. Flexible performance standards should be used, and guidance given to site design and site maintenance. Although the Bill allows for some administrative regulations of this kind, the time within which the regulations are to be drawn up is too brief, and the process too remote from public debate. Second, zoning, local or federal, is simply not enough. It must be supported by tax and transportation policies. Third, if one looks at the actual mapping of the zones proposed in the Bill, it is evident that they are not very closely related to the visual qualities of the land, at least as this report has analyzed them. The boundaries were apparently often located for ease of legal description. [Figure 4] shows an alternate verson of how these boundaries might be drawn. This illustrative map is constructed *solely* from scenic data. Other versions could be based on ecology, water supply, land value, use, or other single factors. But although it cannot be the sole basis for public policy, scenic quality

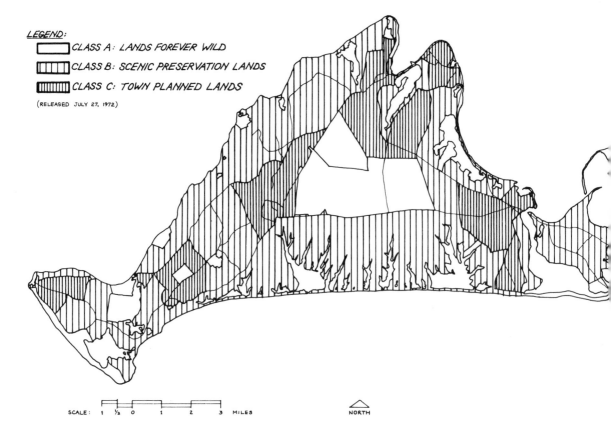

SCALE: 1 ½ 0   1   2   3   MILES   NORTH

Figure 3 *Proposed Islands Trust
boundaries.*

deals with an important aspect of the Vineyard which should not be
excluded from any map.

The alternate map is based on the idea that development in *all* areas
of the Island must be carefully regulated, a viewpoint reflected throughout
this report. The map shows those lands on which, according to the visual
analysis, all development should probably be excluded. Secondly, it
shows those on which it should be controlled in ways that go well beyond
the powers or concepts of present public regulations. The balance of land
will also need close development controls, but might not require extraordinary or innovative ones. Nevertheless, local zoning should be carefully
amended, and other scenic regulations and transportation policies be implemented Island-wide. Thus this map does not have quite the same
meaning as the official proposal. (For example, it does not propose to
abandon large areas to uncontrolled development just because they are
not shown in the two most restrictive categories.)

Even so, it is striking how far this hypothetical map varies from the
proposed Islands Trust boundaries. Since the new boundaries are drawn

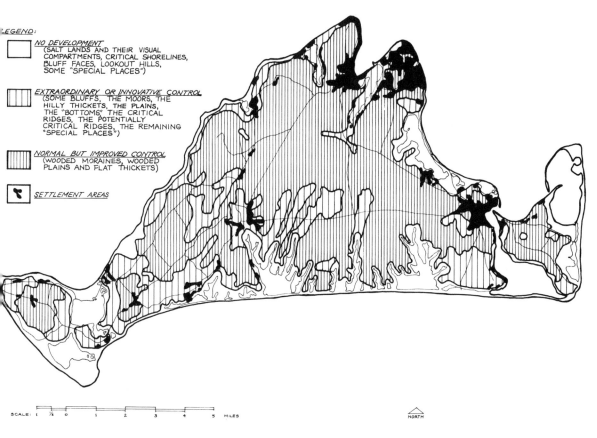

SCALE: 1 ½ 0 1 2 3 4 5 MILES   △ NORTH

Figure 4   *Illustrative modification of Islands
Trust boundaries.*

to follow natural characteristics, they are never geometrical. Since both sides of any road are in the same visual compartment, the new boundaries never follow centerlines. If they parallel the roads at all, they do so at a distance. This alternative map is *not* proposed as the correct substitute for the present one, but as one indication of how that document should be rethought.

Analyzing the Look of Large Areas:
Some Current Examples in
the United States (1974)

A surprising number of "urban design" studies—sometimes called "visual analyses"—have been made for major cities of the United States in the last few years. They are attempts to make explicit what have usually been considered to be intangible qualities of the visual landscape, "matters of taste," so that these qualities may now play an acknowledged role in public decisions. By reviewing some of these studies, I would like to see whether we are beginning to manage the large scale sensory environment successfully. Now, by that term I mean those qualities of the things and activities that surround us every day which are immediately perceptible to our senses and which affect our function, our pleasure, and our well-being: the look, feel, smell, sound of our world, and what that means to us. I refer to the analysis and control of such qualities at the scale of large districts, whole cities, or even entire regions. If we are not yet managing these things successfully—and I think we are not—I would like to speculate on what the necessary conditions might be for their successful management.

There have been perhaps a dozen "urban design" studies made in the last few years for major U.S. cities. They are concerned with such things as strengthening the identity and character of various districts of the town, or of particular streets or highways, with the provision of open space and "natural" areas (but is the remainder of city unnatural?), with the preservation of historic and esthetic landmarks, with a clarification of the basic visible form and structure of the city, with avoiding noise and air pollution, or with conveying a sense of "activity," "life," or "excitement." They deal with entries and skylines, with topography, views, and spatial enclosure, with pedestrian ways, street furniture, street trees, lighting, signs, building textures and styles. They even deal with images—supposedly the environmental conceptions of citizens—but more often those of the designers who are investigating the town.

The visual analysis of the town of Brookline, Massachusetts, done by us on a shoestring basis in 1964, was one of the earliest systematic attempts at describing the visual quality of an urban region. Brookline is a well-to-do residential and still partially suburban enclave surrounded by the city of

Courtesy of Institute Archives and Special Collections, MIT Libraries. Published in German in *Mensch und Stadtgestalt*, ed. A. Markelin and M. Trieb (Deutsche Verlags-Anstalt, 1974); reprinted with permission. This paper draws much of its substance from a detailed study made by Michael and Susan Southworth of the current states of city-wide urban design studies in the United States: "Environmental Quality in Cities and Regions: A Review of Analysis and Management of Environmental Quality in the United States," *Town Planning Review* 44, no. 3 (1973): 231–253.

Boston. It is concerned with preserving its character as the urban tide advances on it. We made a thorough description of the visual character of the place by small districts, and documented this with a large collection of photographs. We described the sequence of visual experiences as one passes along the major thoroughfares in both directions, and developed a notation for symbolizing it. We observed the quality of the various centers, as well as the visual structure of the town and its relation to the city around it. We analyzed the sensory problems and potentialities of these districts, centers, and movement lines. The problems and potentials, and the criteria lying behind them, were for the most part *our* criteria, problems, and potentials. But we also made a small sample survey of the image of Brookline as held by various citizens. All of this was intended, not as a plan for the visual form of the town, but as a body of data on the quality of the town landscape that would be useful in future public decisions.

To my knowledge, this information has never been used, although Brookline now has a design review process which applies to one of the streets of unique character that we surveyed. Most of our data just puzzled the town officials. It had been for us a first experiment. We were all wrapped up in methods. We made the very obvious mistake of not finding out what the townspeople were concerned about in the first place. The best part of the report is a self-criticism in the appendix, something usually thought risky in a professional report, but a good way of learning.

Visual analyses began to be popular shortly thereafter, but perhaps the first well-financed, systematic attempt was that made in Minneapolis, Minnesota, under the direction of Wei-Ming Lu, during the years 1965 to 1970. A preliminary study called "Toward a New City" was prepared, followed by a series of special pamphlets, and then a full scale plan for the central area entitled "Metro Center 1985." This series was completed by a consultant's report on the design process called "Organizing for Better Urban Design in Minneapolis."

These reports cover a wide range—from analyses of the basic visual framework of the city, and the citizen image of it, to case studies and plans for particular areas and streets, and a discussion of design possibilities for street furniture, planting, and enclosed pedestrian ways. The material is rich, but often disconnected. The citizen image survey is particularly interesting, but seems to have had little bearing on proposed policy. In fact, the plan is mostly concerned with supporting certain actions that had already begun in the central area, such as the Nicollet Mall and the enclosed pedestrian ways at second story level (the "skyways"). In part, it supplies interesting but disconnected data, or puts forth a long list of *possible* policies among which choices could be made. Perhaps the most important result of this study—and it is not negligible—has been the institution of a design review process for certain areas and functions in the city.

Quite a number of city-wide urban design studies followed these pioneers. The most elaborate to date has been the one recently completed for San Francisco, a city with a special quality of landscape which the citizens are determined to preserve. The "Urban Design Plan" came out in 1971, and was preceded by eight preliminary reports, dealing with background data, existing plans, design goals, an analysis of the existing form and image, design principles, a social and economic survey, a discussion of implementation, and a set of preliminary plans. Some of these preliminary reports are of substantial size.

The analysis of the existing form and image is elaborate and thorough. It discusses the visible setting block by block, the road environment, the "internal" form of the city as seen by the pedestrian, and the "external" form, or distant skylines and views which are so important in San Francisco. The "image," however, is the image of the experts, the designers who made the study. The problems come out of their heads. Nowhere are you aware of the fantastic variety of San Francisco's inhabitants, who have such different conceptions of the city they live in. A survey of residents was conducted, but it deals with local neighborhood deficiencies in traditional fashion. The answers ("safety," "cleanliness," "more parks," etc.) might have been predicted without the effort.

There is a small case study by Donald Appleyard contained within the larger studies, which deals with the impact of increased traffic on attitudes toward the street. It is a model of simplicity, clarity, and the coherent connection between analysis and policy. But in general the urban design principles which finally emerge seem to rise out of nowhere—or, more exactly, not out of nowhere but from among the familiar vague concepts of architectural criticism: variety, amenity, visual interest, harmony, scale, character, spatial definition, etc. When we come to the plan, it is mostly concerned with the preservation and design of open space and street space, and with the height and bulk of buildings. Only in the latter case does the plan produce a fully operational recommendation for the control of private building, a rule designed to protect the fine views from the hills. This particular proposal was finally carried after a heated political struggle. Thus the plan has had two definite outcomes to date: the bulk ordinance and the increased funds for residential protection. It has also raised citizen interest in the subject, but has had no influence on other public agencies.

A first report from the city of Seattle, Washington, called "The Determinants of City Form," is an interesting recent example of the analysis of city quality. It is a quickly done inventory of the general morphology of the city, based on its topography, its history, its pattern of transportation and activity. This is a familiar theme, and it is illustrated by diagrammatic maps. There is no reference to the perceptions of Seattle people. But there are some ingenious analyses of barriers and links, of activity timing, of

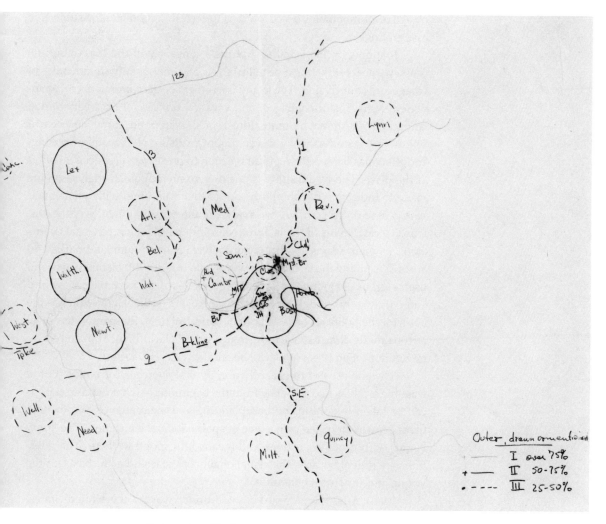

Boston metropolitan image: summary map.

special pedestrian and vehicular districts and routes. One evocative diagram is a map-like collage of descriptive words. These are further attempts to record sensory form at this extensive scale.

While most analyses have been urban ones, there have also been some attempts to describe the sensory form of rural areas. "Landscape assessment" studies have been done for the national forests and parks, using a quantitative index for the quality of visual scenery. Data of this type can then be combined with data on soils, land values, forest type and maturity, climate, accessibility, etc. in order to make forest management decisions. Professional foresters are evidently adjusting to the shift of forest use from tree growing to recreation. A Vermont study on "scenery classification" is one good example. Such attempts to systematize the evaluation of visual quality is certainly interesting, but the seemingly objective numbers are based on very uncertain, class-biased, subjective assumptions.

Just now on the island of Martha's Vineyard off the Massachusetts coast, we are conducting a visual analysis of some seventy square miles of village and countryside. The island is a rather special combination of abandoned farms, historic villages, and vacation houses set on a very varied landscape of terminal moraine, forest, moor, salt pond, dune, and beach. The island is under heavy development pressure for vacation housing, and there has been a strong local reaction to preserve the special qualities of the place. The visual study is one of a number of quick analyses being made to indicate what should be done. In a brief time, with a small and hastily assembled staff, we are analyzing the sensory qualities of the various typical regions of the island, recording the sequence of visual events along its main roads, locating and analyzing the unique landmarks and areas, describing the structure of views, and interviewing a range of island users—from old natives to "day trippers"—to see how they view and value it. It is this very variety among the users of the island which is the basis for the political conflict about it. Unfortunately, these interviews will be too rapidly done to have more than a superficial influence on our recommendations. Sad to say, this will be another "expert" report.

The analyses of the island are only first sketches for policy. But at least the study is tied to policy from the beginning—what definite actions can be taken in zoning, in road planning and maintenance, in development control, or in the provisions of special federal legislation. The study begins with urgent questions and means to respond to them. The questions are urgent because the visual quality of the island is the basis for the strong attachments it generates.

Many other similar surveys are under way in the United States. Environmental quality, or visual quality, is now a respectable and reasonably weighty public issue. Attempts are also being made to improve quality by intervening directly in investment decisions, notably in Boston and in New York City, without making any prior general plan or analysis. But I report here only on the general plans for quality and those plans have some characteristic drawbacks.

To begin with, there is a great confusion of terms. Meanings shift from one report to another, or even within the same report: design, quality, amenity, esthetics, form. . . . There is great uncertainty about what a study should concern itself with: visual aspects? esthetic questions? architectural qualities? matters of comfort? amenities? (a usefully ambiguous term which seems to refer to any desirable characteristic that escapes a direct definition). Without a solid intellectual base, the studies, however interesting, tend to be descriptive and fragmented, dealing with disconnected elements, many of them elements which are neither controllable nor significant at a regional scale. Important aspects of environmental quality, for example the characteristics of workplaces or of the public transit system or the quality of city sound, are quite neglected, while garage doors, shrubbery, and overhead wires may be treated in some detail.

The linkage between analysis and design is commonly weak. Most recommendations could have been made without the analyses that precede them, and most analyses seem to have been conducted without thinking of how they would affect policy. The strongest links occur when the issue is one of preserving a landscape which already has a fine quality—central San Francisco, or Martha's Vineyard—and where an inventory of generally accepted good features leads rather directly to a set of actions to conserve those features. Thus urban design studies tend to have a conservative tone and are most persuasive when they argue for conservation. They seem less pointed, even unimaginative, whenever they propose environmental change at city scale, although frequent suggestions are made at the more conventional site planning scale—such as for pedestrian malls, plazas, small parks, and so on.

Behind all this lies our lingering uncertainties as to what produces good quality in an environment, and for whom. Many of the standards and criteria are either very obvious, such as keeping the streets clean, or very dubious, such as avoiding visible garage doors. The reports have an elite tone; the operating criteria are the standards of the design-oriented professionals who are making the analysis. There is talk of the "city image," but it is the professionals' image. While a sample of the public is occasionally interviewed, the results are not applied to the policy recommendations. The client is allowed to speak, but no one listens. His variety and the way he actually uses a city [are] largely ignored. It is curious and chastening to see that our original work on the image of the city, which was done less for motives of pure research than to find new ways of attacking practical problems of city design, has had a reverse influence. It has stimulated widespread research, but has only been applied superficially to actual problems in city design.

In addition to all these internal problems—but undoubtedly connected to them—these urban design studies have had little effect in action. Minneapolis gained a new administrative process. San Francisco failed to implement its one clear-cut recommendation. The effect of the Vineyard study remains to be seen. Preservation actions have resulted, and also some small public projects, such as a mall. Admittedly, disconnection from action is a common feature of American city planning, but it is especially marked in these urban design studies. They describe and prescribe, but do not often link their proposals to the way American cities are actually made, nor even to such common regulatory devices as the zoning or building codes. Since the studies are not often converted into workable policy, their principal function is to educate the staff and the public, or even simply to reassure the public that the planning agency is somehow dealing with these questions.

Public education is not a useless function, of course. But these plans respond to some serious unexpressed deficiencies in our environment. They are first attempts to make those requirements explicit in a way that can affect public decisions. They contain much that is interesting, but they are far from being useful policy studies.

Their recommendations are not usually refuted directly in any public debate. Everyone agrees about the goodness of better design and then puts it in a secondary place in relation to whatever else is being advanced as a basis for decision, whether it be traffic, or property values, or jobs, or the elimination of poverty, or the suppression of crime. Until the issues of quality of place are made clear, and are securely grounded on the needs and hopes of the people who are using the environment, this will probably continue to be so.

You may object that we have been considering a branch of technical studies, and that a better test is whether we make good environments—not whether we talk about them correctly. Do we in fact build cities well? Or even parts of them?

From my own point of view the answer is yes—in a few cases—and clearly no in most. Without stopping to explain my criteria, which would be a lengthy affair (and surely not in the urban design tradition!) I can cite some typical areas of success and failure with which many listeners may agree. I only remind you that I am talking in the terms I set out at the beginning: the qualities of things and activities in the environment which are immediately perceptible to our senses.

I think that some of our best suburban residential areas, built for the upper middle class, are pleasant places to be in—not for the adolescent perhaps, but for the young child and for his parents. We have built some fine parks and a number of handsome rural freeways. There are some charming historic urban areas, and a small handful of good central-city malls or public plazas. The numerous regional shopping centers are pleasant places, but they are isolated and full of artifice. There are also some fine vacation regions—along the sea, in the mountains, or mixed with declining farms—which are happy landscapes.

But I am at the end of my list. It has no workplaces on it, no housing projects (barring a few done a generation ago), no renewal or rehabilitation areas other than the center city places mentioned above, no new towns (perhaps the center of Reston? but it is so contrived!). We cannot cite anything in those vast intermediate regions which make up the bulk of our cities. Indeed, it only touches a few spots, even at the center or the fringe. It does not include the vast outdoor factory landscapes which produce our energy, minerals, food, and fiber. The basic landscape of our country is magnificent and diverse. It may be that at last we are beginning to conserve it, but we have done precious little to enhance it.

So our record of achievement is not impressive. I daresay the situation is not much better in most regions of the world today. Why should this be so? Is there any connection between these real failures and the inadequacies of the technical studies we have been looking at?

One can always plead for time in reviewing the record. The fine cities of history achieved their quality gradually, as city-building actions accumulated over long periods of time. Most agricultural landscapes were quite raw in their early stages. The photographs which show Boston's now prized Back Bay district just after it was finished seem shockingly barren to us. The center of imperial Rome must have been a pretentious and repellently monumental piece of scenery in its day. Yet it makes a charming ruin. But while "in good time" is a comforting defense, it is dispiriting to think that only in future centuries may someone admire the mess we live in today. We are creating, and will in the near future create, new environments at a far more rapid pace than ever before. We would like to do it well, not for posterity, but for ourselves.

There are basic social issues underneath the technical ones: who owns the land? who develops it? what are their motives? The private ownership of land in the United States, the fragmentation of that ownership, and the motives of owners to exploit and maintain land values are patent and fundamental obstacles to rational management of our environment. Public control of the act of land development, public acquisition of any economic return arising from that act, and the use of criteria for development beyond mere dollar return are all necessities for us. Indeed, since land ownership is not the strategic center of economic power in a developed country, and since our environmental problems are so pressing, it may be that we will see much more public control of development rights in the critical growth areas of the United States. Not tomorrow, of course.

But public land ownership, exercised through large public entities, is not a sufficient condition for a well-made environment. We can cite many cases of barren public environments, not only in the U.S., but also in other countries where social control of the land is accomplished and accepted. More accurately, I think what we want is *community* control—i.e. that the actual users of an environment should decide how it will be shaped. Thus it is exactly in upper middle-class single family housing, where the user is in most direct control of his environment, that we find the most frequent examples of well fitted places. So many workplaces and housing projects, both in the capitalist and the socialist countries, are barren because the worker and the resident had no part in planning them.

User control is a straightforward idea when applied to permanent residential areas. Difficulties arise in the workplaces, where there are conflicting goals of production and economic control. Others crop up at the city scale, since many city systems are used by a transient and seemingly anonymous mass. Besides the political task of putting the control of environment into the hands of its users, there is also the intellectual one of finding ways of bringing him in when he is one of many, or just passing by.

Indeed, our difficulties in making good places are not only social but also intellectual. We think of esthetics as being something quite special and apart from other living concerns. We believe that esthetics has only to do with the way things look and whether they are pleasant to the eye, and that this is the central preoccupation of design. Thus the look of things, their "design," may either be their supreme quality—to which "mere function" is in civilized eyes clearly subordinate—or on the contrary design is "mere esthetics." In both cases, it is a separate subject, divorced from the way things work. While this intellectual isolation of design and esthetics may seem old-fashioned in certain fields, it is still very much alive when large environments are being planned. Until it is clear that seeing (and touching, hearing, and smelling) is a vital life process fundamental to any kind of action, and that the sensory qualities of things are functional and interrelated with all the other functional characteristics of things, we can hardly hope to create wholly pleasurable and well-working places.

When considering environmental quality we must deal with the whole set of attitudes, events, and objects that give a place its peculiar sensory characteristics and cause us to interpret them as we do. It is already clear that this means we are not restricted to architecture, but must deal with the entire realm of objects in space. It also means that we must consider the sight and sound of people and their activities in that spatial setting, since other people are an observer's prime concern. It means that we must deal with time as well as with space, since actions and even things vary in time, and that variation makes a fundamental impression on us. Nor can we avoid considering the institutions that control and maintain that space. Our impressions of a hospital, for example, are due to the nature of the hospital institution as well as to the hospital building and the actions of the hospital people. So one cannot recommend a design for a housing project without recommending a design for how that housing will be managed. We must also consider the images and attitudes of the users of a place, since quality is an interaction between user and place. We find that we are involved with activity as well as with object, with temporal as well as with spatial patterns, with institutions, with image and attitude. Bringing these together in the analysis of a place, and doing so within any realistic bounds of time, effort, and usefulness, requires a better intellectual scaffold than we have.

It will require still further work to apply these ideas at the city scale, since we are most accustomed to analyze and design at the level of buildings or groups of buildings. Knowing what is both controllable and significant at the scale of a district, city, or region, while well enough defined in a study of traffic or of an economic base, is still puzzling in the study of sensory quality.

Down at bottom, we find those old annoying questions: What for? For whom? What are the criteria for a good environment? How do we derive them? How do we validate them? How do we apply them? I think that we have begun to build up some of this knowledge. Teams are studying the physiological effects of the sensory environment on well-being and well-functioning (but too often, unfortunately, under isolated laboratory conditions). We can observe how a place actually supports people in doing what they intend to do. To some extent, we can analyze the image of a place, that is, the way it enhances our understanding of it and of ourselves in relation to it, and the way it acts as a ground for meaning and emotion. We can even talk, a very little, of how a place contributes to the development of a person. These are criteria for sensory characteristics that derive from basic human values, and that have distinctly different yet specific implications as they refer to different people. They can be shown to have operational consequences for city building decisions.

But we still have far to go. The value assumptions of large scale design are still marvelously doubtful. Even when we state them explicitly, we can't often show where we got them, nor demonstrate how they connect to what we propose.

Seen in this light, the faults of the current crop of U.S. urban design studies seem, if not inevitable, at least understandable. We can do substantially better work in the next round if we pay attention to our previous faults. But for fundamental improvements, we must look to social changes on the one hand, and to basic intellectual advances on the other.

IV City Design: Theory

Lynch spoke of three kinds of theories that address the city as a phenomenon. He called the first type "planning" or "decision" theories; these are about complex decision-making that affects city development. He called the theories that attempt to explain the spatial structure and organization of cities and their dynamics "functional" theories. Finally, he characterized theories that articulate and interpret connections between human values and settlement forms as "normative." If the first two are about how the modern city works, the latter is about how the city should work as a human environment.

Kevin Lynch began his career inquiring about the physical city, its forms, its structure, and its organization. The articles in part I of this volume reflect his early attempts to describe, categorize, and capture the essence of the physical forms of urban and metropolitan areas. These were early steps toward building a "functional" theory of city form. But as his intellectual career matured, Lynch seemed to become less interested in these matters. Increasingly he asked questions about what a good city *should be*, rather than how it works. He found conventional "functional" theories (also known as "positive" among some academics) somewhat disappointing and dull. He wrote:

It is a peculiar fact that much of the literature on the theory of city form is outstanding for its stupefying dullness. Moreover, it is elusive in memory: it is difficult to recall the principal line of a theoretical argument. Theory is not written for entertainment, yet when it is a successful and succinct explanation of the inner workings of a formerly confusing phenomenon, it is by its nature absorbing to read—difficult, perhaps, but unforgettable once grasped. Think only of Darwin's central ideas, or the fundamental laws of mechanics. That urban theory is so boring is more than discouraging. It must be a sign of deeper difficulties. (Good City Form, pp. 342–343)

There were other reasons for rejecting these positive theories as well. They did not seem to help much in explaining why contemporary cities do not serve basic human purposes and values well, or why there is so much inequity and injustice in the qualities of life experience, or why they fail to nurture individual growth and development, or why they have to be so resistant to spontaneity of life and social change. Most important, they offered little guidance for design and planning. Lynch was clearly most interested in developing "normative" theories of cities, a branch which he thought was "spindly and starved for light" and obviously needed more attention.

The articles included in this part of the volume represent that "what should be" side of Lynch's theoretical thinking. These essays are about performance characteristics of good city form, with ideas about how city design should be conducted to achieve such ends. We believe that these essays are fundamentally *normative* theories of city form and city design, even though Lynch himself might not have made that claim when he wrote them. We also believe that, as normative theories, they represent a very special facet of Lynch's unique contribution to the literature on cities.

Lynch himself discussed the difficulties of formulating normative theories—the problem of linking values to city form—in *Good City Form*, and he argued that ultimately it is the performance characteristics or standards at the city scale that should be used as building blocks for formulating normative theories:

The linkages of very general aims to city form are usually incalculable. Low-level goals and solutions, on the other hand, are too restrictive in their means and too unthinking of their purposes. In this dilemma, it seems appropriate to emphasize the aims in between, that is, those goals which are as general as possible, and thus do not dictate particular physical solutions, and yet whose achievement can be detected and explicitly linked to physical solutions. . . . performance characteristics of this kind might be a foundation on which to build a general normative theory about cities. Developing a limited and yet general set of them, which as far as possible embraces all the important issues of form, will now be our aim. This will be our alternative to the dogmatic norms that customarily guide discussions about the goodness of cities." (Good City Form, p.108)

Lynch's interest in linking human values to city form was apparent even in his earlier work. The article he wrote with Lloyd Rodwin, "A Theory of Urban Form," reveals this early interest. Much of this article is devoted to developing analytical categories of urban form and a theoretical model of how goals can be translated into elements of form. It focuses on basic values such as health, survival, continuity, adaptability, meaning, development, growth, stimulus, choice, participation, and comfort.

Soon Lynch wrote separate articles focusing on different themes of these basic values and demonstrated how they can be translated into specific performance characteristics of city form.

"Environmental Adaptability" was published in the same volume of the *Journal of the American Institute of Planners* in which "A Theory of Urban Form" appeared. Here Lynch addressed the fundamental enigma of physical planning and design: how to accommodate future contingencies and uncertainties in the face of the rather long half-life of the built environment. He showed how, through various creative strategies (some inspired by examples in nature), environmental form can be made adaptable to future demands.

The theme of adaptability remained in Lynch's thoughts for some time. Animated discussions were to follow in his graduate seminars on city design, taught to several generations of students. In the late 1960s, when he was invited to serve as an advisor to the programming of the new town of Columbia, Maryland, he would often reflect on how it is really too bad that new towns become instantly old as soon as the first road network is paved and lots are plotted.

"The Openness of Open Space" is somewhat different from other articles in that it focuses on a very specific aspect of urban form—open spaces. Initially written as part of a national task force report on open-space policy, the essay was an attempt to revolutionize the scope of open-space planning by redefining the very concept of open space and emphasizing the human meaning and purposes of such space. Kevin Lynch did not want to restrict the notion of open space to the system of conventional parks and playgrounds, but chose to define it as "the negative, extensive, loose, uncommitted complement to the system of land uses that make up a city region." He went on to elaborate on the social and human values of open space so defined, and how its performance should be judged accordingly.

The values of open space he felt quite strongly about were reiterated in "Open Space: Freedom and Control," a short article written almost a decade later with Stephen Carr. This piece reflects on the contradictions and tensions inevitable in the provision of open space. It argues nevertheless that the fundamental values, especially possibilities for uninhibited and spontaneous human actions, must never be compromised.

More comprehensive in scope is the essay "Quality in City Design." Written in the mid-1960s, this article deals extensively with the nature of the performance characteristics of city form, and with relevant strategies for city design. In two accompanying appendixes, Lynch outlines the current and past goals of city planning and enumerates what he considered then the basic performance characteristics of good city form. In a way these are precursors to the performance criteria he defines as the core of his normative theory in *Good City Form*. Readers familiar with that book will recognize some of the criteria described in this article.

"Where Learning Happens" (also written with Stephen Carr) captures another lifelong interest of Lynch: the city as an environment for learning, development, and stimulation. Here the theme is parallel to the writings of other scholars who also have empasized the potentials of the city as a communication and information network. (See, for example, John Dyckman, "The Changing Uses of the City," *Daedalus* 90 (winter 1961): 111–131.) But the tenet of this article includes a good bit of social policy, complementing ideas about how the physical city can be made more accessible and available to all groups—especially those who are historically isolated, underprivileged, and often lacking physical mobility.

Collectively, these six articles represent various stages of Lynch's normative thinking, leading ultimately to *Good City Form*.

A Theory of Urban Form (1958)

with Lloyd Rodwin

The principal concern of the physical planner is to understand the physical environment and to help shape it to serve the community's purposes. An outsider from some other discipline would ordinarily assume that such a profession had developed some ideas concerning the diverse effects of different forms of the physical environment (not to mention the reverse effects of nonphysical forces on the environment itself). And he might be equally justified in expecting that intellectual leaders in the profession had been assiduously gathering evidence to check and reformulate these ideas so that they might better serve the practitioners in the field. A systematic consideration of the interrelations between urban forms and human objectives would seem to lie at the theoretical heart of city planning work.

But the expectation would bring a wry smile to the face of anyone familiar with the actual state of the theory of the physical environment. Where has there been any systematic evaluation of the possible range of urban forms in relation to the objectives men might have? Although most attempts at shaping or reshaping cities have been accompanied by protestations of the ends toward which the shapers are striving, yet in fact there is usually only the most nebulous connection between act and protestation. Not only are goals put in a confused or even conflicting form, but also the physical forms decided upon have very little to do with these goals. Choice of form is most often based on custom, or [on] intuition, or on the superficial attraction of simplicity. Once constructed, forms are rarely later analyzed for their effectiveness in achieving the objectives originally set.

What does exist is some palliative knowledge and rules of thumb for designing street intersections, neighborhoods, and industrial areas, for separating different land uses, distinguishing different traffic functions, or controlling urban growth. Analysis of urban design is largely at the level of city parts, not of the whole. The prevailing views are static and fragmentary. When ideal models are considered, they take the form of utopias These serve to free the imagination, but are not substitutes for adequate analysis.

There are some reasons for this unsatisfactory situation. The profession is still quite young, and most of its energies are concentrated in professional practice. The men in the field are far too preoccupied with practical problems to fashion new concepts. The profession itself developed from fields, like architecture and civil engineering, which have not been research minded. The professionals in the universities have

Reprinted, with permission, from *Journal of the American Institute of Planners* 24, no. 4, pp. 201–214.

taught practical courses and spent much of their time in outside practice. Research and theory under these circumstances were expendable. In the rough and tumble of daily operations, preliminary notions such as economic base studies, land use master plans, neighborhood design, or zoning and subdivision controls serve a reasonably useful function.

But the planner's situation is changing rapidly. Most of our population now lives in metropolitan regions, and the metropolitan trend is still continuing. There is not only increasing dissatisfaction with our cities, but also an awareness that it is possible to make them more delightful and more efficient places in which to live and work. Tremendous public support has been generated by organizations like The American Council to Improve Our Neighborhoods. Housing, road building, and urban renewal programs are also providing powerful instruments for the transformation of our metropolitan environment. These changing circumstances and values are interesting symptoms of the age of leisure.

The planner's tools and concepts are being subjected to a severe test by this growing demand for action. Something better than rule of thumb and shrewd improvisation is required if his services are to warrant public appreciation. In short, we need better ideas, better theory. Formulated operationally, such theory can be tested, revised, and ultimately verified. Even if initially inadequate, theories can help to develop and extend our ideas, to make them more precise, embracing, and effective. Unless planners can devise more powerful ideas for understanding and controlling the physical environment, they are not likely, and perhaps do not deserve, to be treated as more than lackeys for the performance of routine chores.

Possible Analytical Approaches

It is not easy to create theories "full blown." Effective theories, as a rule, are products of many men's efforts constantly reworked into a more general and more systematic form. It is also hard to locate the best starting place. In tackling the problems of the physical environment one can employ a number of approaches, ranging from the descriptive to the genetic, from problem-solving to process and function analyses. All have certain advantages and disadvantages.

Description is the most obvious approach, and perhaps the weakest, standing alone. To describe the physical environment more accurately is an important aim; but since these descriptive possibilities are endless, it is difficult to be sure what is and what is not crucial or relevant. Description works best when there is enough familiarity with significance to permit vividness and terse accuracy. Too little is known about the form of the physical environment, or even about the appropriate analytical categories for analyzing these forms, to handle effective description. Description alone, moreover, yields little insight as to the underlying mechanism of operation.

Studying how the physical environment is transformed might be another approach. The nature of the changes can be recorded, the difficulties and directions in transition, the conditions associated with the changes, and the various social, economic, and political processes by which the alteration takes place. Often the historical, comparative, and genetic approaches are the best ways of following the dynamics of the physical environment. But there are limitations too; these lie in the difficulty of disentangling the strategic variables which should be examined and of understanding the mechanism of change.

Another approach, now most current, is pragmatic. Each case can be considered more or less unique. The emphasis is on problem solving, or on shaping or reshaping the physical environment to eliminate specific difficulties or to achieve specific effects. Limited generalizations or rules can be formulated, but the tendency is to emphasize the uniqueness of each problem and the inapplicability of "stratospheric generalizations." The advantage here is the "realism"; the weakness is the handicap implicit in the assumption that general ideas and theories are of almost no value as guides for dealing with specific cases or classes of cases.

A more abstract variant of problem solving might be a study of the goal-form relationship. This approach is concerned with how alternative physical arrangements facilitate or inhibit various individual and social objectives. It is an approach directly keyed to action; it would, if perfected, suggest optimum forms or a range of them, once aspirations had been clarified and decided upon. Its weakness is its static nature; its strength lies in the emphasis on the clear formulation of goals and on the probable effects of various forms of physical organization. The more that is learned about these effects, the more light will be shed on the process and perhaps even on the mechanism of change. Similarly, descriptive techniques and genetic and historical approaches might prove more effective if the emphasis were on objectives and if the evidence sought were related to the effectiveness of the environment in serving these ends. Problem solving, too, might be more systematic, less haphazard and subject to rules of thumb, if it were grounded on more solid knowledge of goal-form relationships.

This paper proposes to set forth an approach to such a theory. It will therefore necessarily deal first with the problem of analyzing urban form, secondly with the formulation of goals, and thirdly with the techniques of studying the interrelations between such forms and goals.

Criteria for Analytical Categories of Urban Form

Since the work on urban form has been negligible, the first task is to decide what it is and to find ways of classifying and describing it that will turn out to be useful both for the analysis of the impact on objectives and for the practical manipulation of form. Without a clear analytical system for examining the physical form of a city, it is hardly possible to assess the effect of form or even to change it in any rational way. The seemingly elementary step of formulating an analytical system is the most crucial. Upon it hangs all the rest; and while other questions, such as the statement of objectives or the analysis of effects, may be partly the task of other disciplines, the question of city form cannot be passed off.

There are a number of criteria which a workable system must meet. First, it must apply to cities and metropolitan areas and be significant at that scale. This is simply an arbitrary definition of our particular sphere of interest, but it conceals an important distinction. There are many environmental effects which operate at larger scales (such as the influence of climate or the distribution of settlement on a national level), and even more which are effective at a smaller scale (such as the decoration of a room or the siting of a group of houses). Cities are too often regarded simply as collections of smaller environments. Most traditional design ideas (shopping centers, neighborhoods, traffic intersections, play spaces, etc.) reflect this tendency. It is usually assumed that well-designed neighborhoods, with good roads and sufficient shopping and industry, automatically produce an optimum settlement. As another example, many planners are likely to think that a beautiful city is simply the sum of a large series of small areas which are beautiful in themselves.

But this may be no more true than that a great building is a random collection of handsome rooms. Every physical whole is affected not only by the quality of its parts, but also by their total organization and arrangement. Therefore, the first criterion for form analysis is that it identify form qualities which are significant at the city or metropolitan scale, that is, which can be controlled at that scale and which also have different effects when arranged in different patterns that are describable at that scale. This criterion excludes, without in any way denying their importance, such features as intercity spacing (describable only beyond the city level) or the relation of the front door of a house to the street (which is hard to describe on the city scale unless uniform, difficult to control at that level, and whose city-wide pattern of distribution would seem to be of no importance).

The second criterion is that categories must deal solely with the physical form of the city or with the distribution of activities within it; and that these two aspects must be clearly and sharply separated. City and regional planners operate primarily upon the physical environment, although mindful of its complex social, economic, or psychological effects. They are not experts in all the planning for the future that a society engages in, but only in planning for the future development of the physical and spatial city: streets, buildings, utilities, activity distributions, spaces, and their interrelations. Although cries of dismay may greet such a reactionary and "narrow" view, the currently fashionable broader definitions lead in our judgment only to integrated, comprehensive incompetence.

A planner in this sense is aware that the final motive of his work is its human effect, and he should be well grounded, for example, in the interrelation between density and the development of children in our society. He must be quite clear that the physical or locational effects may often be the least important ones, or operate only in conjunction with other circumstances. Above all, he has to understand that the very process of achieving his proposed form, the way in which the group decides and organizes itself to carry it out, may turn out to be the most decisive effect of all. Nevertheless, he takes the spatial environment as the focus of his work, and does not pretend to be a sociologist, an economist, an administrator, or some megalomaniacal supercombination of these.

Physical form and the spatial distribution of activities in the city are partly contained in the traditional "land use" categories of the planning field. Unfortunately, these categories are analytically treacherous.

It is true that their very ambiguity is often useful in field operation, where they can be made to mean what the user wants them to mean. But for theoretical study these categories thoroughly confound two distinct spatial distributions: that of human activity, or "use" proper, and that of physical shape. The traditional concept of "single-family residential use," for example, unites a certain kind of activity: family residence (and its concomitant features of eating, sleeping, children-rearing, etc.) with a type of isolated physical structure, called a "house," which is traditionally allied with this activity. This works tolerably well in a homogeneous society, as long as people behave with docility and continue to reside in families in these houses. But if they should choose to sleep in buildings we call factories, then the whole system would be in danger. Even under present circumstances, "mixed uses," or structures used now for storage, now for selling, now for religious meetings, cause trouble.

The pattern of activities and the physical pattern are often surprisingly independent of each other and they must be separated analytically if we are to understand the effect of either. In practice, planners operate primarily upon the physical pattern, while often aiming to change the activity pattern via the physical change. Only in the negative prohibitions of some parts of the zoning ordinance do planners operate directly upon the activity pattern itself. By sharp distinction of the two, it is possible to explore how activity pattern and physical pattern interact, and which (if either) has significant effects in achieving any given objective.

This paper, however, will develop primarily the notion of the urban physical pattern, leaving the question of the activity pattern for another effort. This is done not to prejudge the relative importance of the two, but for clarity of analysis and because at present most planners operate primarily upon the physical rather than the activity patterns. The time may come, of course, when city planners may manipulate the distribution of activities in an equally direct manner. Even should this time not come, and should our influence on activities continue to be indirect, it would be important to know the consequences of activity distribution.

Such nonspatial factors as the range of family income, political organization, or the social type of a city are excluded by this second criterion. This paper will also exclude factors such as the distribution of work place versus sleeping place or the quantity of flow on city streets. These latter are activity categories, properly considered under their own heading.

A third criterion of our analytical system, which adds to the problems of constructing it, is that it must be applicable to all types of urban settlement, used by any human culture. An American city, a Sumerian settlement, or a future Martian metropolis must all be capable of being subsumed under it. The categories must reach a level of generality that might be unnecessary in simply considering present-day cities in the United States. Not only is this necessary for complete analysis, but also by making our categories truly general we may uncover new form possibilities not now suspected. For example, dwelling-units-per-acre cannot be used as a basic descriptive measure, since some settlements may not have sleeping areas organized into dwelling units. (The fact of having such an organization, of course, may be part of a physical description.)

A fourth criterion is that the categories must eventually be such that they can be discovered or measured in the field, recorded, communicated, and tested. Lastly, the crucial test: all the factors chosen for analysis must have significant effect on whatever goals are important to the group using the facilities and must encompass all physical features significant for such goals.

Our aim is to uncover the important factors that influence the achievement of certain human objectives. Therefore the categories allowable here will depend upon the objectives chosen and on the threshold of effect considered significant. The categories used might shift with each new study. It is necessary, however, to set up one system of form categories so that comparisons may be made from one study to another. Therefore one must begin by considering the familiar human purposes and by guessing what physical features might be significant for those purposes. Subsequent analysis and testing will undoubtedly modify the categories based on this criterion.

In summary, the criteria for an analytic system of city form are that the categories of analysis must:

1) Have significance at the city-wide scale, that is, be controllable and describable at that level.

2) Involve either the physical shape or the activity distribution and not confuse the two.

3) Apply to all urban settlements.

4) Be capable of being recorded, communicated, and tested.

5) Have significance for their effect on the achievement of human objectives and include all physical features that are significant.

Proposed Analytical System

While several types of analytical systems might be considered, we have attempted to develop a set of abstract descriptions of the quality, quantity, or spatial distribution of various features, of types that are present in some form in all settlements. The abstractness of this system makes it difficult to conceptualize. It also divides up the total form of city, although not spatially, and it therefore raises the problem of keeping in mind the interrelations among categories. But for generality, clarity, and conciseness—and perhaps even for fresh insights—it seems to be the preferable method and will be followed in the rest of this paper.

A system for activity pattern would probably require a description of two basic aspects: flows of men and goods, on the one hand, and, on the other, the spatial pattern of more localized activities such as exchange, recreation, sleeping, or production. Although this side of the analysis will be omitted in order to concentrate on physical pattern, a similar breakdown is feasible in the physical form description: (a) the flow *system*, excluding the flow itself; and (b) the distribution of adapted space, primarily sheltered space.

These are quite similar to the familiar duet of land use and circulation, with the content of activity removed. It may be remarked that an overtone of activity still remains, since the physical facilities are divided between those primarily used for flow and those accommodating more fixed activities. This is a very convenient division, however, and seems to be a regular feature of all settlements.

There are many cases, of course, in which a given physical space is used both for flow and for other activities. Usually the other activities are alongside the flow, or sometimes intermixed with it, and here the space must be subdivided, or simply counted in both categories. Occasionally there may be a cyclical shift in use, as when a road is shut off for a street dance. Then, if this is important, a temporal shift of the facility from one category to another must be made. It is even conceivable that a city could contain mobile facilities in which both circulation and other activities are performed simultaneously, on the analogy of the ocean liner. But perhaps that can be faced when it happens on a scale that would be significant in a city.

Except for these difficulties, then, the division into flow system and adapted space is a convenient one. The former is usually easy to identify, and includes all the roads, paths, tubes, wires, canals, and rail lines, which are designed to facilitate the flow of people, goods, wastes, or information. The latter category, that of adapted spaces, although it seems tremendously broad, has sufficient basic similarity to be treated as an entity. It consists of all spaces that have been adapted in some way to be useful for some one or several significant noncirculatory activities.

In this country's climate, the key spaces of this nature are those enclosed and with a modified climate, that is, the city's "floor space." Elsewhere enclosure may be less important. Almost everywhere, however, the adaptation includes some modification of the ground plane, even to the cultivation of a field; and the key activities are often likely to take place in at least sheltered, if not enclosed, spaces. But in any case, the fundamental thing done to our physical environment, besides providing means for communication, is to provide spaces for various activities, to adapt the quality of those spaces, and to distribute them in an over-all pattern.

Since many of the primary adaptations of a space, such as enclosure or the provision of a smooth, level, hard, dry ground plane, are useful for many different activities, spaces are often used interchangeably. A "storefront" may be used as a store, an office, a church, a warehouse, or even a family residence. This interchangeability argues for the usefulness and necessity of generalizing adapted space into one category. Within it, one may dissect as much as necessary, dividing enclosed floor space from open space, picking out tall structures from the floor space category, or hard-surfaced lots from total open space. Occasionally, purely for convenience, it may be necessary to use activity-oriented names, such as "office structure" or "parking lot." But, whenever this is done, reference is being made solely to a physical type and not to its use.

Each one of these two general categories, flow system and adapted space, could also be broken down in a parallel way for more exact analysis.

1) *Element Types*: The basic types of spaces and of flow facilities can be described qualitatively in their most significant aspects, including the extent to which the different types are differentiated in character, or to which they grade into each other.

2) *Quantity*: The quantities of houses or streets, in length or capacity or size, can then be enumerated, to give total capacity and scale.

3) *Density*: Next the intensity with which spaces or channels are packed into a given unit area can be stated; as a single quantity, if uniform, but more likely as ranges of intensity and as average and typical intensities. This is a familiar idea when applied to adapted space, particularly enclosed space, as is exemplified in the concept of the floor-area ratio. The same idea could be applied to the circulation system, calculating intensity as the flow capacity which passes in any direction through a small unit area and mapping the variation of this ratio (as in potential vehicles per hour-acre).

4) *Grain*: The extent to which these typical elements and densities are differentiated and separated in space can be defined as coarse or fine in

terms of the quantity of a given type that is separated out in one cluster, and sharp or blurred in terms of the manner of separation at the boundary. Thus, house and factory building types might typically be separated in one city into large pure clusters, sharply differentiated at the edges; while in another town the grain might be very fine and the transitions generally blurred. Again, the outdoor spaces might be blurred and undifferentiated or, in the circulation system, footpaths and vehicular pavements might be sharply and coarsely separated. Essentially, this quality refers to the typical local interrelations between similar or dissimilar elements, but without reference as yet to total pattern.

5) *Focal Organization*: The spatial arrangement and interrelation of the key points in the total environment can be examined. These might be the density peaks, the concentrations of certain dominant building types, the key open spaces, or the termini or basic intersections of the circulation systems. Consideration of the arrangement of such key points is often a shorthand method of expressing total pattern.

6) *Generalized Spatial Distribution*: This could be taken as a catchall which included the entire analysis. What is meant here is the gross pattern in two- (or three-) dimensional space, as might be expressed on a greatly simplified map or model. It would include such items as outline (or the shape of the city with reference to the noncity) and the broad pattern of zones occupied by the basic element and density types. One city might have a single central density peak; another a circle cut by pie-shaped zones of "factory" buildings; another a flow system on a rectangular grid; still another might have a uniform pattern of small interconnecting enclosed outdoor spaces surrounded by a deep belt of free-flowing space punctuated by tall masses. Such a description would be needed whenever the notation of type, quantity, density, grain, and pattern of key points was insufficient to describe the significant total pattern.

Finally, of course, it would be necessary to interrelate the two basic categories, to show where the flow termini came with reference to the density peaks, for example, or to relate the pattern of the flow system to the general open space pattern.

The method given above is proposed as a basic system of analyzing a city's form in accordance with the original criteria. It does not try to cover all the physical features of a city, which are endless, but concentrates on those considered significant at that scale. Only systematic testing in real cities will indicate whether all the important features are included.

An Example of the Analytical System

Since this system may be difficult to follow in the abstract, it will perhaps clarify the proposal to use it in describing an imaginary settlement named Pone. Like any town, Pone is best described by the use of both words and precise drawings, but here words and a simple sketch must suffice.

a) Pone is made up of six types of adapted space: dirt-floored rooms, 20 by 20 feet, roofed with thatch and enclosed by adobe, each structure being free standing; concrete-floored shed spaces, 75 feet by up to 300 feet, in corrugated iron, sometimes single and sometimes in series horizontally; multistory concrete structures containing from fifty to two hundred 10 by 10 foot rooms; walled-in cultivated spaces of rectangular shape, varying from $\frac{1}{2}$ to 3 acres; walled, stone-paved spaces pierced by paths; [and] irregular bare dust-covered spaces, which take up the remainder of the area. Pone has four types of flow channels: four-foot dirt paths, unenclosed; thirty-foot cobbled roads, enclosed in semicircular tubes of corrugated iron; an interconnecting waterproof system of four-inch pipes; and some telegraph wires.

b) There are ten thousand adobe rooms, totaling 4,000,000 square feet; fifty shed spaces, totaling 1,000,000 square feet; and four multistory structures, with 40,000 square feet of floor space. The are five thousand cultivated spaces occupying 5,000 acres, two walled and paved open spaces of 10 acres each; and the leftover dust covers 1,200 acres. There are three miles of cobbled road, each with a capacity of 400 mulecarts per hour in both directions; and 60 miles of dirt path, each able to carry 2,000 persons per hour in either direction. There are 20 miles of pipe and 2 miles of wire.

c) Density of adobe rooms varies continuously from a floor-area ratio of 0.003 to 0.3; that of the sheds from 0.3 to 0.9 (with a tendency to group at the two extremes), while the tall structures are uniformly at 5.0. Road-capacity density varies from a peak of 1,600 carts per hour-acre to a low of 20; path-capacity density varies from 4,000 persons per hour-acre to 50.

d) The three types of enclosed spaces are sharply differentiated and separated in plan. Cultivated spaces are mixed coarsely with the adobe rooms, while the irregular dusty areas are finely distributed throughout. Roads and paths are sharply separated and do not interconnect except at the shed spaces. Any intersections are at separated grades. They are also coarsely separated, since the roads are associated with the shed spaces.

Wires and pipes follow along paths. Pipes are dispersed, but wires serve only sheds and the multistory structures.

e) Focal points in this organization are the two rectangular paved open spaces. The first is central to the area of adobe rooms, and is the focus of converging paths. It corresponds to the peak of room density and to one of the peaks of path density. The other focal point is flanked by the multistory structures, occurs at another convergence and density peak of the path system, and is touched upon by the road system. Here occurs the major terminus and interchange point of that road system. The wire lines all pass through a central switchboard in one of the multistoried structures. The pipe lines have a single source just beyond the town boundary.

f) The settlement is round and compact, with no holes. The multi-storied structures and second focus occur at the center, with the sheds occupying a narrow pie-shaped sector outwards from this. The focus of room density is slightly off center. The road system is a rectangular grid of irregular spacing, tying to the sheds, to the second focal point, and, by a single line, to the outside. The path system is irregular and capillary, but converges and intensifies at the two focal points, as noted above.

In theory (and particularly if we could use more drawings) we now know enough of the physical form to judge its value for various basic purposes at the city level of significance. One is tempted to object: Isn't this meaningless, if one knows nothing of the life that is going on within that form? Lifeless, yes, and saying little or nothing about the society of Pone (though one may make some guesses); but yet adequate, if you want to test its cost, or productive efficiency (given some productive system), or comfort (given some standards). Certainly it is the first step in trying to disentangle the effects of physical form per se, and the first step even if one wants to study the results of physical form in relation to activity pattern, or social organization, or politics. (To describe New York City in this way would, of course, take a few more pages.)

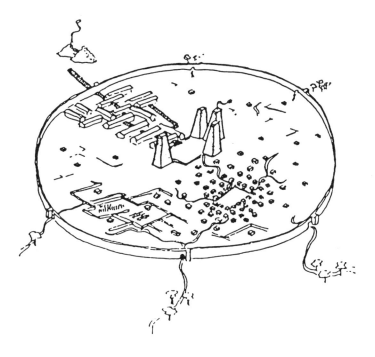

Figure 1 *A hypothetical settlement form: Pone.*

Problems of Goal Formulation

What will be the goals against which we will test this city? Unfortunately for a neat and workmanlike job, they might be almost anything. One group inhabiting Pone might find it highly satisfactory, another might find it useless or even dangerous, all depending on their several purposes and the variations in their cultures. Is there any method by which relevant goals might be set out and related to these environmental shapes? Unhappily for the reader, we now find that we must digress to consider the problems of setting up a goal system. Only after this is done will it be possible to return to the implications of the forms themselves.

The possible goals must first be considered. This may cause some confusion, since such a collection is not likely to be consistent or unified. It must be distinguished from a goal *system*, i.e., a set of selected objectives which are coherent, unified, and capable of guiding action. Construction of such a system is the desirable result of considering goal possibilities, but it can only be brought to completion by a particular group in a particular situation. Thus the possible range of goals might include both the preservation of individual life at all costs and also the maximization of human sacrifice. A particular system would have to choose, or, more probably, settle upon some intermediate stand; and this stand should be related to its other objectives.

Probably the most confusing aspect of this question is not the infinite number of goal possibilities, but rather their range of generality. Some objectives, such as "goodness," may seem to regulate almost every action, but to do so in such a vague and generalized way as to be of little help in choice. Others, such as the goal of having all children say "please" when asking for things at the table, are very clear in their implications for action, but quite limited in their application and their consequences. These two goals are interconnected only by a long chain of explanations, situations, and interactions. It is difficult to be sure that one follows from the other and hard to weight their relative importance in relation to other goals.

To avoid such confusions, it is important that any one goal system should contain only objectives which are at approximately the same level of generality. We may smile when someone admonishes a child to "be good, and keep your fingernails clean!" But we are also exhorted to build city additions that will be good places to live in and will keep valuations high. In many cases, of course, there may be no real confusion, as when the second point is the true objective and the first is only a verbal blind.

Similarly, it is meaningless to consider beauty and fresh paint as alternative objectives: they do not operate at the same level. Each objective may in its turn be looked upon as a means of attaining some objective higher up the scale of generality. Shouting at recruits may be considered a means of overawing them, with the goal of developing obedience, which is itself directed to the building of a disciplined military force, having as its objective the winning of wars, which may be thought of as a way to gain security. When constructing a rational system for guidance in any particular situation, what must be built up is a connected hierarchy of goals, considering possible alternatives only at the same level of generality and checking lower levels for their relevance to upper levels of the system.

The more general objectives have the advantage of relative stability: they are applicable to more situations for larger groups over longer spans of time. They have the corresponding disadvantages of lack of precision and difficulty of application in any specific problem. Very often, in goal systems of real life, such general objectives may have very little connection with objectives farther down the list, being, rather, top-level show pieces, or covers for hidden motives. The operating goals are then the intermediate ones, those which actually regulate action. To develop a rational set of goals, however, the connection must be sought out, or the motives that are the true generalized goals must be revealed. The aim is to produce a system that is as coherent as possible, although this again is rare in reality.

Since reference back to very general goals is a painful one intellectually, most actions must be guided by intermediate, more concrete, objectives, which can be referred to more quickly. Only the most serious steps warrant reference to fundamentals, while everyday decisions depend on customs and precepts that are actually low-level goals. City building is important enough to be referred back to more than simple precepts; but even here decisions cannot always be brought up to the highest level of generality, since the analysis is so complex. Therefore reliance must be placed upon goals of an intermediate level. But these intermediate goals should be periodically checked for their relevance to more general objectives and to the changing situation, as well as for consistency among themselves.

It is a besetting sin to "freeze" upon rather specific goals and thus risk action irrelevant to a new situation. If it is observed, for example, that growing cities have been prosperous ones, attention may focus upon increase of population size as an objective. Actions will be directed toward stimulating growth, regardless of any consequences of dislocation, instability, or cost. Industries may be brought in which will depress the wage level and the general prosperity, because no one has stopped to examine the objectives that lie behind the growth objective, i.e., to ask the simple question: "Why do we want to grow?" Because of this continuous tendency to fix upon goals at too specific a level, it is a wise habit to challenge current goals by always pushing them back at least one step up the ladder of generality.

Criteria for the Choice of Goals

What will be the criteria for the choice of goals in our case? If they are rational, they should be internally consistent. There should, moreover, be some possibility of moving toward their realization, now or in the future. Otherwise they are simply frustrating. To have operational meaning, they must be capable of being contradicted, thus permitting a real choice. And finally, the goals must be relevant to city form, since there are many human objectives which are little affected by environmental shape. Therefore, given one's basic values and the values of the culture in which one is operating, it is necessary to develop a set of useful intermediate objectives which are consistent, possible, operational, and relevant to the task in hand.

Devising such objectives is difficult; and it is not made easier by the fact that a planner is an individual responsible for actions or recommendations in an environment used by large numbers of people. He is not concerned simply with his own values, nor even with their interaction with the values of another individual with whom he can communicate, which is the situation of the architect with a single client. The planner's client is a large group, a difficult client to talk to, often incoherent, and usually in some conflict with itself.

To some extent the planner can rely on democratic processes to establish group objectives; to some extent he must use sociological techniques to uncover them. Often he is forced, or thinks he is forced, to rely upon his own intuition as to group objectives—a most hazardous method, since the planner is himself likely to be a member of a rather small class of that society. In any event, he must make every effort to understand his own values, as well as to uncover and clarify the goals of the society he is working for.

His troubles do not stop here. Even if he had perfect knowledge of group goals, and they proved to form a completely consistent system, he is still faced with the issue of relating them to his own personal values. He cannot be solely the handmaiden of the group, but has some responsibility (should he differ) to urge upon them a modification of their goal system or to acquaint them with new alternatives. He has a complicated role of leader and follower combined and must resolve this for himself. This is true of many other professional groups.

And should the public goals, as is most likely, prove to be internally inconsistent or in transition, then the planner must mediate these conflicts and changes. He must find the means of striking a balance and the way of preparing for the new value to come without destroying the old value still present.

But to all these everyday woes we can at the moment simply shrug our theoretical shoulders. Give us a consistent and operational system of objectives, a system possible and relevant and organized properly by levels, and we will show you the environmental forms to achieve these objectives. If your goals are superficial or shortsighted, so much the worse. That is your concern, not ours.

In Western culture, general and accepted goals would probably cluster around the worth of the individual human being, around the idea of man as the measure, with an emphasis on future results and yet on the importance of process as well as final achievement. Basic values for the individual might include such things as:

a) Health, equilibrium, survival, continuity, adaptability.

b) Coherence, meaning, response.

c) Development, growth, stimulus, choice, freedom.

d) Participation, active use of powers, efficiency, skill, control.

e) Pleasure, comfort.

Upon the basis of such generalities, one can make for himself (or for his group) a set of broad goals. One way of conveniently organizing such goals may be the following:

a) Regarding the relation of men and objects: Those goals

1) having to do with direct functioning: biological or technical goals, such as the achievement of an environment which sustains and prolongs life;

2) having to do with sensuous interactions: psychological or esthetic goals, such as the creation of an environment which is meaningful to the inhabitant.

b) Regarding the relation of men and men: Those goals

1) having to do with interpersonal relations: sociological and psychological goals, such as constructing surroundings which maximize interpersonal communications:

2) or having to do with group functioning: social goals such as survival and continuity of the group.

It is important to see that a mere listing of objectives is insufficient, even at this generalized level, if a policy of relative emphasis is not also included. Any real action may work for one goal and against the other, or be more or less helpful in relation to another action. Yet the choice must be made. Therefore a statement of objectives must be accompanied by a statement of relative importance: that, for example, group survival is valued. More precisely, it will have to be said that, in such-and-such a circumstance, group survival is more valued.

Since attainment of human objectives almost always entails the use of scarce resources, the next level of objective are the economic. In their most general form, they can be described as the attainment of ends with the maximum economy of means, while keeping or making the resource level as high as possible. In all these general objectives, moreover, there is an intertwining of means and ends, of process and final achievement. Particularly where "final" achievement may be as long delayed or even as illusory as it is in city development, the attainment of objectives may be affected more by the process itself than by the final form that is being sought.

But the goal system at this level, however consistent and relevant, is still too general for effective application to city-form decisions. Moving down to low levels for specific guidance, how can one define a "meaningful environment," for example, or the limits within which interpersonal communication is to be maximized?

It would be possible to move down the ladder step by step, ending with some such rule as "all buildings should by their exterior form reveal to any adult inhabitant of average education and intelligence their principal internal use," or even ". . . to accomplish this, the following building types shall have the following shapes. . . ." The latter is undoubtedly an example of "misplaced concreteness", but even the former poses problems in relating it back to the general descriptive categories of city form that were developed above. How does the "meaningfulness" of structure relate to density, or grain, or focal organization? In coming down the ladder of specificity we may find we have slipped away from relevance to form at the city scale, or have developed precepts which have multiple and complex effects on the various categories of city form.

Since the formulation of specific objectives is unavoidable, it would be preferable that they be reorganized by being grouped in terms of their relevance to the descriptive categories. Such organization is simply a tactical move, but a crucial one. It involves running through the list of descriptive categories of city form, and choosing (by intuition or prior experience) those general objectives that seem most relevant to the aspect of form.

For example, the following general goals are probably affected in some important way by the "grain" of adapted spaces in an urban settlement:

    a) Optimum interpersonal communication.
    b) Maximum choice of environment for the individual.
    c) Maximum individual freedom in construction.
    d) Optimum esthetic stimulus.
    e) Maximum productive efficiency.
    f) Maximum productive flexibility.
    g) Minimum first cost.
    h) Minimum operating cost.

By thus selecting and grouping our general goals, a hypothesis is being asserted, that, for example, "the grain of city facilities has significant (if unknown) effect on the first cost of constructing them." Such hypotheses may prove untrue, in which case the group of goals must be revised or, equally likely, it may indicate that some other objective not originally listed is also significantly affected and must be added to the list.

One objective may be significantly affected by more than one form quality and will thus appear in more than one group. Another objective may be little influenced by any one quality alone, but rather by the nature of the combination of two or more, such as the total effect of grain and density together. This is a separate point, to which we will later return.

The critical nature of the form categories previously selected now becomes apparent, since they impose their pattern upon the entire investigation. If they are not in themselves highly significant, or if they are inconsistent or poorly organized, the work must be redone. Nevertheless, by bringing in the relation to form thus early in our consideration of objectives, a much more economical and systematic attack is possible. The objectives not only contain hypotheses of relevancy, but are really turning into action questions, for example: "What grain of spaces gives a minimum first cost?"

It must be made clear that, if physical forms are considered in isolation, such action questions are not answerable. No relation between grain and first cost can be established until a construction process is postulated. Or, for another example, the impact of the grain of spaces on interpersonal communication depends also on the activity occupying those spaces. Nevertheless, once given a construction process or an activity distribution which is held constant during the test, then the differential impact of various grain alternatives can be analyzed. Thus, in a given activity context, the results of various physical patterns might be studied. Often, a principal result of a given physical pattern may occur via the manner in which it changes an activity distribution, given an assumption as to a fixed association between certain forms and certain activities.

The same limitations apply to the study of activity patterns in isolation, which are meaningless without reference to the facilities available for communication, insulation, and so on. Eventually, there would be a more complex level of analysis, in which both activity distribution and form might be allowed to vary simultaneously. Even here, however, a general cultural context is still required.

Once the general goals are arranged in terms of the type, quantity, density, grain, focal organization, and pattern of the adapted spaces and the flow system (and in the process just those objectives have been selected out which may be most critically affected by these qualities), and once a general context of culture and activity has been chosen, a more concrete level of analysis is possible. The level should be specific enough to say that "city A is closer to this objective than city B." The meaning of terms must be put in an operational, and often quantitative, way. For example, "what density of spaces allows a reasonable journey from home to work?" might become: "what density (or densities) allows 75 percent of the population to be within 30 minutes' time distance of their place of work, providing no more than 10 percent are less than 5 minutes away from their work place?" Different city models could now be tested by this criterion.

Not all goals could be put in this quantitative form, of course. But they would at least have a testable wording, such as: "what is the density at which there is maximum opportunity for interpersonal communication within the local group, without destroying the ability of the individual to achieve privacy when desired?" Such formulations are likely to contain the words maximum, or minimum, or optimum.

The caution must be repeated that, while satisfyingly specific, such goals require continuous rechecking for relevance to the general goals and the changing situation. The home-to-work objective, for example, is simply a definition of the original word "reasonable." Next year, or in India, it might be different.

Goal-Form Interaction

Having established an analytical system of urban form and groups of objectives cast in relevant operational terms, the next problem we have is the interaction of form with goal. One might begin either by considering the grain of adapted space and the objectives significantly related to it or, alternatively, a fundamental objective and the form aspects related to it. If one of the goals is minimum first cost, for example, are the shed spaces of Pone cheaper to build when concentrated as they are in a coarse grain than if they were dispersed throughout the adobe spaces in a fine grain? Or, perhaps, does the grain of dispersion make no difference whatever? Undoubtedly, the effect of grain on cost may differ for different types of space. For example, while the grain of shed spaces was critical because they were built by mass site fabrication methods, the grain of adobe spaces might be indifferent, since they were put up singly by hand in any case. Or it might be found that dispersion of the multistory spaces among the shed spaces did not affect their cost, but dispersion among the adobe spaces did. Only in certain cases could generalizations as to grain, per se, be made. More often, the grain of a certain type of adapted space would have to be the subject of a conclusion.

The grain of the shed spaces may also affect productive efficiency. To test this, one may assume a type of activity, a given productive system, similar to the assumption of construction methods to test the cost implications. To do so does not mean that activity distribution slips in by the back door; we are still testing the impact of one or another physical quality upon the functioning of an activity which is held constant during the test. That is, given a factory system of production, which operates more easily in the wide-span shed spaces of Pone than anywhere else in the city, is that productive system more efficient if all the sheds are close together or if they are dispersed?

In this manner, the goal implications of grain could be analyzed, testing each for relevance and effect, and ending by a search to see if significant goals have been left out. If this system is successful, one should be able to say that, given such-and-such a culture, this particular grain gives best results if your goal system has these particular elements and emphases, and another grain would be better for another system. Alternatively, the objective of minimum first cost could be explored throughout all its ramifications, resulting in a statement that, given a certain culture, this particular total urban form can be constructed at a minimum first cost.

These are final stage results, difficult to attain. Partial, and still useful, conclusions are more likely, such as: if this is the contemporary American society, and if the *only* goal is productive efficiency, then here is the grain to use for this type of adapted space (or: there are several equally good distributions or, perhaps, the grain is of no consequence). Of course, the answer is likely to be still more qualified. One may have to add that this grain is best in a city of small size, another in the larger city; or that optimum grain cannot be separated from density or pattern.

One further note must be made. The *process* of achieving goals or of reshaping form is, in cities, as important as the long-range goal or form. Building a new city of a specific shape may have vital side-effects on the administrative acts and organization required; sequence of development has as much to do with cost as final density. Moreover, one may have important goals which have to do mainly with the process itself, for example, that development decisions be arrived at democratically, or that people be allowed to participate in planning their dwellings, regardless of the final result.

The goal-form method, then, consists in ordering form analysis and definition of objectives so that their interrelation can be considered in a systematic and rational manner. It helps to pose the problem. There it blesses the investigator, and drops him in the mud. It has no further bearing on the analysis of any given interrelation. Each such analysis is likely to be unique and to demand its own method of solution. One might be amenable to mathematical methods; another, to sociological tools; a third, solvable only by subjective analysis; a fourth, by full-scale field tests. There is no guarantee, of course, that the fifth may be solvable at all. What is proposed is merely a way of attacking the central problems of cities in a methodical way.

This "merely," however, may in time open up new possibilities, simply because the problems are more precisely put. If the important physical properties of cities can be clearly defined, and if an operational standard can be set, such as one regarding commuting times, we may be able to study the implications of complex forms by means of new mathematical methods or with such aids as the high-speed computers.

If form qualities and goals could be analyzed and disposed of one by one, then in time a complete structure could be built with relative ease. Unfortunately (and this is perhaps the most vulnerable point of the system) physical patterns and goals have a habit of complex interaction. There is not one goal, but many; and the presence of other goals influences the force of the original one. The city forms, which we have herded into arbitrary categories to make our analysis possible, in truth make one pattern. It is not always easy to discuss the impact of grain without specifying density or size. The consequences of the distribution of adapted spaces rests partly on the flow system allied with it.

Thus there are frequently situations where a given goal may not only be influenced by more than one form aspect, but also may at times be affected by such an intimate interaction of aspects that there is no separable cause. A convenient system of notation for such a situation might be [as shown in figure 2], imagining that we are concerned with five goals, A, B, C, D, and E, which have the following relationships with form:

Achievement of goal is influenced by:

A—(1) space type; (2) flow system size.

B—(1) space, density, and grain combined; (2) focal organization of space and flow system combined.

C—(1) space, size, and flow system pattern combined.

D—(1) grain of flow system; (2) density of space and flow system combined.

E—(1) grain of space, and density and focal organization of flow system all combined.

Here the appearance of a goal in the top diagonal (shaded squares) indicates that it relates to a single form quality at a time. Elsewhere its appearance shows that it is influenced by a pair of form qualities that must be considered together. One goal is shown (E) which is effected by an inseparable combination of three, and must therefore be shown as a connected triangle. If a three-dimensional notation system were used, it could occupy a single solid cube. Higher interactions would require more complicated notations.

This figure would change, of course, as the system of descriptive categories was modified. It is simply a convenient way of reminding ourselves what must be taken into account in studying goal-form interaction. It indicates, incidentally, that in this particular case two aspects of form (space pattern and flow system type) happen to be the ones that have no bearing on any goal. All the rest are involved in one way or another.

Probably these analytical methods could handle situations where pairs of qualities were involved. Triads of qualities become much more

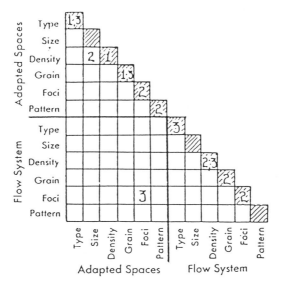

Figure 2 *Goal-form matrix 1.*

difficult, and many more are likely to make analysis impossible. Some questions may therefore be answerable, and others may resist our best efforts.

To complete the example, consider the city of Pone again. The people of Pone are simple-minded; they have few wants. They have only three goals relevant to city form:

1) Maximum individual privacy, when not producing.
2) Maximum defensibility in war.
3) Maximum productive efficiency.

In case of conflict, goal 2 takes precedence, then goal 3. The Ponians are a simple and a rather grim people.

These goals are set in the following situation: the town produces various kinds of simple consumer goods, which it exports to the surrounding countryside in return for raw materials. This production is most easily carried out in the shed spaces, directed by control functions in the multistory spaces. But the town also produces a large part of its food supply in the cultivated spaces within its limits. Other life functions, beyond production and distribution, are traditionally carried out in the adobe rooms or in the paved open spaces. Wars are fought by ground action, with simple short-range weapons, and may occur suddenly.

[Figure 3] indicates the probable relevance of various form aspects to the three goals. That is, objective 1 is affected by the type, density, and grain of adapted spaces, all acting singly. Objective 2 is influenced by the pattern of spaces and by the density, grain, and focal organization of the flow system, acting singly. It is also the prey of the combined action of

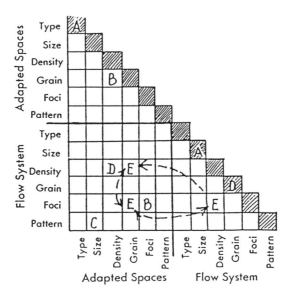

Figure 3 *Goal-form matrix 2.*

the size and density of the adapted spaces. This is true because, although the larger the city the greater the defensive army that could be raised for war and the higher the density the more compact the defensive perimeter, yet in combination they may work in another way. A large, very dense city might quickly succumb to food shortages, owing to the lack of adequate internal cultivated spaces. Therefore the optimum solution is likely to be a function of size in relation to density. Finally, objective 3 is related to the type and grain of spaces and the type and density of the flow system, acting singly, plus the combined effect of the spatial and flow-system focal organizations. The matrix indicates that the size and pattern of the flow system are meaningless to the Ponians.

The anaylsis on all these separate points could then be carried through and the total balance struck, comparing the actual form of Pone with any other forms within the reach of this people. One might come out with some such conclusion as: given these goals, the actual form is probably the optimum available, with the following modifications:

a) For the privacy objective, a new type of space should be substituted for the single-room adobe space.

b) For the defense objective, a better balance of size and density could be struck, particularly if the unused dust spaces were eliminated. Furthermore, if the capacity density of the flow system were stepped up and the system dispersed at finer grain throughout the settlement, then defense would be simplified.

c) For the production objective, an increase in flow capacity-density would also facilitate efficiency.

As was stated at the beginning, the high planners of Pone would also have gone on to a study of the consequences of the activity distribution in the city, and they would have ended with a higher level study of the interrelation of activity and form. But probably the reader has had enough.

Evaluation

Application of this method to a modern metropolis would obviously be far more complicated and, necessarily, more fragmentary. But the basic technique should still be applicable, though it would call for descriptions at a larger scale and goals less precisely formulated. Since the whole technique is analytical, a study of isolated parts, it will tend to give first approximations, rather coarse conclusions bristling with "ifs." It would nevertheless be the elementary knowledge upon which much more refined, and in particular much more fluid and integrated methods could be constructed.

To the student of the physical environment, perhaps the most attractive features of goal-form studies are the new possibilities for research and theory. Regardless of the inadequacy of our present formulations, there is a need to test and explore both the range and [the] appropriateness of form categories. Hardly anything is known of how they interact and what the possibilities are for substitution. And instead of fragmentary notions, such as the differentiation of traffic networks, the separation or mixing of land uses, and the organization of neighborhood units, there is the prospect of a general theory of urban form for the city as a whole. If some measure of success is achieved in developing such a general theory, it should not prove too difficult to fit these miscellaneous doctrines into this broader framework, especially since these doctrines purport to modify city form in line with some more or less definite objectives.

Goal-form studies also suggest a new lead for examining city planning history. Instead of the traditional historical survey of civic design accomplishments, the adequacy of urban forms might be examined in the light of some of the major goals of different cultures. The same approach might be applied with profit to current history. Significant contemporary plans for communities might be studied to see how adequately the goals are formulated and how explicitly they are related to the physical forms proposed.

The essence of progress for most disciplines lies in finding ways of systematizing as well as extending present knowledge. Goal-form studies offer a springboard for city and regional planning to achieve this extension and synthesis.

But aside from the elegance or logic of the theoretical framework, such an analytical system may find its ultimate usefulness in providing the raw material for planning decisions. Eventually it should tell the planner: "If your only aim is productive efficiency, and if other elements are like this, and if your society does not change, then this form is the best one yet found to do the job." This is the underpinning for what in part must remain a complex art, an art yet beyond the determinability of scientific knowledge in three ways. First, in that the more complex interactions are most likely to elude rigorous theory and depend on personal judgment. Second, because the method is indifferent to the choice of values, and the choice or clarification of objectives is a fundamental part of the art of planning. And thirdly, because the method can do no more than test form alternatives previously proposed. The creative task of imagining new form possibilities, as in all other realms of art and science, lies beyond it, although the analytical system may be suggestive in this work.

Environmental Adaptability (1958)

Planners impress each other with the notion that environments must be designed to be flexible in regard to future change. All of us are to one degree or another cramped by the survival of obsolete environmental forms: narrow streets, awkward rooms, vertical factories, crowded tenements. Elaborate constructions have been abandoned because of their inability to accommodate new activity. The structure erected to facilitate life has often become its strait jacket.

Moreover, we see that the tempo of change is increasing, and fear that what we are planning today will be tomorrow's incubus. Structures housing the activities in most rapid flux (laboratories or hospitals for example) are in a constant turmoil of destruction and change. In our cities we have launched on a desperate program of razing and rebuilding that gives promise of being endless. And so each day we murmur the magic word: "flexibility!"

It proves to be a difficult thing to accomplish, however. This is not the problem of choosing a form that, while serving one purpose today, will serve a different, but definitely known, purpose tomorrow. Preparation for a known change to come may have its complications, but can be approached and solved in a straightforward manner. The more adequate our predictions of the future become, the more will our anxiety for flexibility be transmuted into such tangible problems.

But as long as our environmental patterns outlive our original guesses, we face the rather harrowing problem of providing for *unspecified* future change, of providing generalized flexibility.

Among biological populations, the ability to adjust to new situations plays a vital role, both for the individual and for the species. The adaptable populations survive, and the inflexible succumb. This adaptability is often bought at a heavy price of constant destruction and renewal, both of individuals and of parts within the individual. Now we reverse the inquiry to discuss, not the adaptability of the organism to his environment, but that of the environment to the changing purposes of the organism.

Flexibility in an environment may be taken to mean several things, and confusion results if they are not distinguished. There is the flexibility which operates in the present, giving the individual a maximum of choice, a great array of potential activities or habitats. A large house with numerous rooms widens choice—so does a city with many types of living areas, so does a department store or a highway network. But they may not be particularly suited to future change.

Another meaning of flexibility is that it is that quality that allows the individual to take as active a part in shaping his own world as may be

Reprinted, with permission, from *Journal of the American Institute of Planners* 24, no. 1, pp. 16–24.

possible. This goes beyond choice to allow active participation. A large piece of blank paper, set before a child, has this quality; and so for an adult does a small house, which is within his scope of personal repair or remodeling. Such an environment might be called a plastic one.

Both of these are important objectives but it is necessary to keep them distinct from the kind of flexibility discussed here: the generalized adjustability of an environment or artifact, with minimum effort, to future changes of use. This might best be called adaptability. Means that further one kind of flexibility may or may not further another.

The distinction can be illustrated by two examples: If your objective were wide choice, you would present your subject with a roomful of pottery, of all shapes and styles. If plasticity is the aim, give him the wet clay to make his own. For adaptability, give him a simple, average-sized pot, suitable for many uses. Or leave the clay in the ground, for the disposition of future generations. If your problem is housing, build a great variety of dwelling types for the first objective; put everyone in low isolated dwellings for the second; but for adaptability put them in tents.

Assuming that adaptability is in many situations a valid objective, by what means may it be achieved in a physical setting?

Unspecialized Forms

From an analogy with biology, it might be suspected that highly specialized forms would be relatively inadaptable, while forms of little differentiation and low structure would be the ones from which future development will most easily proceed.[1] Thus a simple square house of one room would be more adaptable than the intricate design fitted about the special habits of a particular client.

But Simpson[2] points out the fallacy of this notion even in the course of biological evolution. We are accustomed to associate unadapted, and therefore extinct, species with "over-specialized" ones. We await the forthcoming fall of man and rise of the amoeba. But "specialization" has, ambiguously, two meanings. It may mean narrowly adapted, as of an organism to a very special and circumscribed environment. Such an organism might indeed be expected to perish with relatively small shifts in his situation. But specialization also means complexity, organization at a more advanced level. Such complexity implies neither adaptability nor inadaptability.

That complex and very specialized organism, man, has so far proved himself to be the most adaptable creature going. A complicated modern house is much more adaptable, both as to climate and as to internal function, than the simple sod shanty. Thus it is not the complexity or the degree of differentiation that matters, but rather whether the environment is specialized in the sense of "narrowly adapted."

The latter explains why a simple house may be more flexible than an intricate one: not because of its simplicity relative to the other's intricacy, but because the intricate one also happened to be built to serve the very particular whims of a special client. In this sense, city environments may be more inflexible if designed for special purposes. Blumenfeld[3] cites the long-term usefulness of the neutral Roman gridiron, versus the short life and painful destruction of Vauban's carefully designed defensive polygons. In the same way, our narrowly specialized cloverleaf interchanges may have a short life and an ignoble end.

"Multipurpose" spaces, large clear span areas with movable partitions, are often cited for their flexibility. The Peckham Center in London based its whole philosophy of construction on this point. But although such unspecialized, "non-directed" forms may be of great value in maximizing present choice, they are not necessarily more adaptable. Once occupied and in use, with partitions established, they may be as resistant to change as any other. Their only advantage lies, not in the lack of structure, but in the fact that by wide spans major structure is concentrated at certain few points. Changes in other zones are therefore less vital. This is a separate question, and will be treated below.

Most often, when a designer says to himself that he is being "flexible," in reality he is only being vague. By failing to define structure or allocation, he is simply shifting the responsibility for decision to other individuals, or to the play of circumstance. This may enhance immediate choice for first users, but not future flexibility. As often as not, the failure to decide opens the door to the multitude of small decisions, to a scattered exploitation of resource, that leads to inflexibility rather than the reverse. An environment of low differentiation, such as an area where uses are highly mixed, is often more resistant to change than otherwise. A shift at any one point necessarily brings ruin upon the adjacent uses, which may have no interest in the change. Modification becomes an all-or-nothing proposition. Chaos, or lack of structure, is not flexible per se.

The first suggestion, then, has not been very helpful. It warns against forms which are too narrowly specialized, but fails to indicate how to distinguish "too narrow" from "sufficiently broad." To shun "narrow specialization" may result in losing the more highly organized forms which often liberate and give power. Complexity of organization does not necessarily entail inflexibility: perhaps even the reverse, if the complexity has a purpose. A complexity like an arterial highway network may release new potentialities of function that markedly enhance the adaptability of the whole.

Zoning and Concentration of Structure

The Peckham Center, and many other structures, point to another way of achieving adaptability, however: concentration of structure and the zoning of fixed and fluid regions. It has a biological analogy in the way in which certain cells of the human body, having specialized functions of support or communication or chemical action, are relatively fixed in form, while to others are relegated the job of growth and change.

This trick may be carried off in a building by concentrating structural support at a few widely separated points, leaving wide spans where future changes will not affect the fabric of the building. Or, similarly, the relatively rigid and complex utility apparatus may be concentrated in "cores," such that other partitions may in the future be rearranged without disturbing them.

In direct analogy to these building devices, a city plan might concentrate its major structure (major highways, transit lines, utility mains) in a sharply differentiated network zone, such that other changes need not disrupt this common structure, and structural changes will have mimimum effect on adjacent uses.

In a city or large site plan, advantage might be taken of the fact that certain features of the environment are inherently soon likely to become obsolete, and others not. Where both narrowly specialized and also unspecialized units are needed, and these two types are kept apart, then the necessary remodeling in the specialized zones can occur without disturbance to the unspecialized units. Or the unspecialized spaces may be housed in tall or otherwise rigid but efficient structures, while the "temporary" specialized uses are put in low buildings, easy to change. This might refer to the housing of offices relative to laboratories, for example.

Other uses may be classified as more or less likely to change, whether specialized or not. From experience, for example, residential requirements seem to change less rapidly and radically than production requirements. Separation of these two allows production changes to be made with minimum total disruption.

A city may be zoned, not only on the basis of likelihood to change, but as to ease of change. Separating permanent from temporary structures, or lightly- from heavily-built areas, we allow future change with minimum effort. Uses in the "permanent" zones may have a higher ability to survive because of the adaptability of the "temporary" zones—an adaptability that would not exist were these same light structures intermixed with the heavy ones. As another example, if houses are clustered tightly along roads, and their usual attendant open space concentrated in a block interior, then the use and even ownership of the interior land is easily modified.

Thus where a city or an institution needs both environmental features which allow easy change and growth, coupled with efficiency and permanency for major activities, it may be useful to set up semi-derelict experimental areas, where new activities can be born and try themselves out, before demanding addition to the permanent plant.

These devices would seem to work even where the "likely-to-change" or the "easy-to-change" cannot now be distinguished from its future opposite. Assume that there is no basis for judging if use area A in a city will in the future be any easier, or more likely, to change than use area B. Nevertheless, the separation of A and B will ensure that changes in either one will leave the other unperturbed.

Thus a coarse grain (i.e., a texture in which relatively large "pure" use areas are separated out) has an adaptability advantage, but only as long as the changes occur within the use classes set down. Should it happen, for example, that the future tendency is to carry on functions A and B in the same structure, then their separation will prove most inflexible. Similarly, if the grain has been made extremely coarse, and the distinct use areas very large with small boundaries relative to their areas, then the system is inflexible if one use should tend to increase at the expense of the other. For if uses A should tend to grow, while uses B contract, the transition is much easier if they are interspersed than if they can shift only at their peripheries.

We conclude, then, by saying that in general adaptability in an environment seems to be enhanced where major structure is concentrated, and where functional areas are separated in a rather coarse grain, particularly where the likely-to-change or easy-to-change features can be distinguished. But where the categories of functional areas may shift, or there may be expansion of many units of one type at the expense of many units of another type, then a very coarse grain may be an inflexible feature.

Additive Structure

There is another type of structure which seems to have value for this purpose: the additive one. While the previous solution might be characterized as a fixed general framework, within which minor features are changeable, here, on the contrary, the details are fixed, while the total pattern is unspecified. Such are the bricks that can make infinite house shapes, the cage construction of a skyscraper, a child's set of blocks, or Japanese floor mats. The basic unit is rigidly standardized, inflexible. The flexibility lies in the myriad ways in which the constellation of units may be patterned, and in the interchangeability of parts. The total pattern is not highly organized, but is rather additive in nature: growth of units at the periphery does not change the structure at the center.

The additive system is probably more advantageous in enhancing present choice in a period of mass production than in favoring future flexibility. It does simplify the process if adding new structure, since joints are guaranteed to fit. On the other hand, as a physical form becomes very large, the necessary differentiation between center and periphery, between major structure and connective tissue, becomes difficult to accomplish. The parts repeat themselves everywhere, inside and out; while exterior additions go smoothly, internal stresses build up. Thus large gridiron cities must tear out their central areas to put in new, more intensive structure, or must superimpose radials on the gridiron ground.

If we look more closely, we may distinguish two different kinds of additive structure: modules and lattices. The former refers to standardized parts of one of more sizes, which may be linked together in a set way, but can in sum form very irregular total patterns. A set of dominoes can be used this way, or a varied collection of wall panels. The lattice, on the other hand, is a repeating plane or solid regular grid of dimensions, within which parts must fit.

The modular system has a particular advantage in its interchangeability of parts, allowing pattern rearrangement with minimum effort. This is not true of the street gridiron, since streets are not picked up and moved about, but is true of any system whose parts are not only modular but movable as well. A child's Mechano set, or a community of standardized trailers, [has] these qualities. In this case, however, the design of the inflexible module is the key. If the standard trailer continues to meet future demands, one has a highly adaptable system. But if change is required within the module itself, if the trailer becomes obsolete, then the system is a dead loss.

To succeed in this case, therefore, the module used must be a highly generalized one, neutral in quality, or performing a very simple function which is highly likely to persist. Most of the complex units typically standardized in designs, such as total houses, or central utility cores, or neighborhoods, are very unlikely to survive without substantial change. On the other hand, such a very simple unit as an electric plug can continue to meet different demands for decades.

In a city, the lattice is exemplified in the gridiron pattern of streets, first used either for magical reasons or for its ease in layout and allocation of land. The gridiron has other advantages (and disadvantages), but its value for adaptability lies in the ease with which new additions can be made, and, to some extent, in the interchangeability of locations, such that if one street corner is suitable for a drug store, then all corners are potentially so. This lattice is often applied as far as the lot, but rarely beyond it. Structures are not usually built to any common grid.

A lattice, a system of dimensions, is more likely than a module to have survival value, but even here it must not be too specialized, too "complete," or too inconsistent with other customary dimensions. The simple Roman gridiron has survived two milleniums in European cities; the American gridiron might do the same. But a hexagonal or triangular grid, although equally simple mathematically, may prove to be too inconsistent with customary building methods, if used at the local street scale.

It is proper to hesitate, therefore, before proposals to institute elaborate modular structures whose units are in themselves rigid, complex, and specialized. Modular parts at the urban scale are likely to be large and complicated. But there is a possibility, worth exploration at least, that adaptability might be gained if an urban area were built to fit some very generalized, rather coarse, three dimensional lattice. This would facilitate both additions and the interchange of movable parts. The principal problems, however, will be: first, how to keep the lattice sufficiently neutral; and second, how to allow for the specialization and concentration of structure that inevitably accompanies a large form.

Variety

Simpson[4] shows how the distribution of genetic variations in a population may affect its survival chances. A group whose variability is small may be best adapted to present conditions, but be wiped out by an environmental shift. Another group whose variability is very wide may be so poorly adapted to present conditions as to succumb immediately. The optimum condition for present and future survival is a distribution which peaks very closely about the characteristics ideally suited to present demands, but with a small percentage of individuals who vary widely from the norm. These individuals are sacrificed when conditions are stable, but are the potential forebears of a new adjusted population, should there be an external change.

By analogy, one might conclude that a certain amount of variation in an environment would enhance its future adaptability. There is a flaw in the analogy, however. Environmental features do not breed and multiply of themselves, and thus the minority, who can save the biological group, cannot perform the same function in an environmental system. If single-family houses are the preferred environment today, but there is a sudden shift to apartment living tomorrow, then a small percentage of apartments in the original system will do no more in the future than satisfy an equally small percentage of future inhabitants. And since this future satisfaction is paid for by an equal present dissatisfaction, and since there must be many present variations which will never pay off when the unknown future change arrives, then the solution becomes a very wasteful one.

A high level of environmental variety is undoubtedly an important means of maximizing present choice, but has no value for adaptability. However, the grain of distribution of such variation as may be needed for other reasons may have a bearing on adaptability, as discussed above. A coarse grain gives flexibility where future changes occur within the categories differentiated, and fails to do so if changes occur across the categories. Presumably, therefore, a fine grain of variations has adaptability where it is expected that the principal changes to occur will be in the shifting of categories, or in their relative growth (at the scale of small individual units within the category).

Over-Capacity

To put extra capacity into the initial design is almost infallible for our purpose. Again and again, in past experience, it has been proved that the roomy Victorian house (with many "wasteful" spaces), the large lot, [and] the low density development are always the kinds of features which are easiest to remodel for new circusmstances. Extra space or over-capacity leaves room for future growth and change. An overdesigned sewer can take an increase in the birth rate, a wasteful bridge will support the new monster vehicle. There is a future advantage, in this sense, in waste and inefficiency.

Furthermore, where the extra capacity is in the form of low intensity of development, then modifications can be made to one unit without serious detriment to other units. An owner can more easily remodel his house, and with less harm to his neighbors, if it is on a large lot rather than a small one. A laboratory housed in a single-story building is much easier to rebuild to a new shape than if it were a cell in a tall building. At low density, the interrelations, the connective structure, is much looser and more widely spread.

Unfortunately, these advantages of adaptability must usually be paid for by present loss. Over-capacity usually means the waste of scarce resources, or at least a denial of present use. More concrete or steel is consumed, or costly land may be required. Equally as important as the increased first cost are the enlarged operating costs incurred by extra capacity. There may be more rooms to dust, more miles to travel to work (as in Canberra), more square feet of siding to paint.

Thus a balance must continually be struck between increased present costs and decreased future adaptability. This is a conflict that a designer frequently mediates as he decides on his "factor of safety," or ponders how to give a shopping center room to grow in without surrounding it with large tracts of unused land.

The solution is most successful where two conditions occur: First, the unused capacity [is] of low or zero first cost in its unused state, as is true of undeveloped raw land, mineral resources left in the ground, water supplies, extensive forests, etc. Second, forms can be used that minimize or wipe out any increase in operating costs due to the unused resource. In the case of linear or open network developments, for example, open space off the highway, or interior block land, can be preserved without increasing the maintenance charges on streets or utilities, since the length of street per developed dwelling remains approximately the same as in a denser settlement. Similarly, a shopping center likely to grow might be connected to other uses by rays of developed street, but with internal wedges left for expansion. Unfortunately, however, there is an increased charge even in these solutions: individuals must travel farther in carrying out present interactions. These forms, incidentally, are additional examples of the zoning technique, where the open, or flexible, land is segregated from connective structure and more permanent development.

In its role of diluting the disturbance due to change, low density can presumably enhance adaptability indefinitely. But its capacity to permit change by allowing room for growth must inevitably disappear. In time the capacious structure fills up and is no longer capacious. The Victorian house converted to small apartments has now lost its adaptability; the medieval new town, once open and flexible, chokes within its walls over the centuries, and becomes a narrow prison.

Not only does open space gradually silt up, but there is often a further problem of preserving extra capacity until new development is desired. Thus, if large city open spaces are reserved in rapidly urbanizing regions, there is a powerful tendency for them to fill up with squatter settlements, impairing future flexibility. Unused forest lands, of no present use or concern, may be set fire or left to burn; unused space makes homes for rats. This is the problem of preserving resources for future generations; the issue of how much present effort can be diverted to such preservation. Sometimes administrative means alone can be used to achieve it; sometimes substantial economic value must be applied. Occasionally, there are physical arrangements which help, such as the ringing of open space with development such that a concerted effort is needed to begin to use such open space; or the spacing of houses so that it would be difficult to sandwich new houses between them; or the isolation of reservations from the customary routes of would-be trespassers.

Any wise designer leaves some extra capacity in his design, for the sake of future stress and change. He leaves as much as he can, but must strike a balance with present cost. Where unused capacity is expensive, in first or running cost, a society can hardly be expected to allow very generously for the future. But where it can afford it, it may count on the fact that low density is adaptable per se. And where the extra capacity may be of little first or running cost, or where it can be made so by zoning techniques, then that society will be well advised to put aside what it can.

Growth Forms

We seek the ability to grow and change without jarring disruption, or the loss of continuity and basic structure. Biological organisms have this ability to a high degree. Are there any particular shapes which permit growth without loss of structure?

The form that accomplishes this to some degree is one which keeps an open axis for each major type of activity. A large mass of development, in which many activities are imbedded, will almost certainly see a future choking out of the growth of some of these activities, unless they have the good luck to be immediately next to other activities which are contracting at the required rates. But if, for example, this same large mass is so organized that each major activity occupies a wedge from center to periphery, then the growth of one is not blocked by the presence of the other. Alternatively, the mass may be strung out so that each activity has a place along the chain, and can grow sidewise without running over other uses.

The same end is accomplished if, in zoning the intensive from the extensive uses, the pattern is arranged so that each use most liable to grow has in at least one direction a substantial low intensity buffer zone between it and the next important activity. This preserves an internal axis of growth, ensuring that no element which may grow in the future will in the future be boxed in.

This form generalizes as a series of intensive strips of foci, each devoted to one major activity (or divided chain- or wedge-fashion into several), with each strip or focus separated from the next by a transition zone of less intensive, more mobile use. If more than one growth axis is directed into the same transition zone, then advantage can be taken of the probability that all intensive uses will not expand as much as is theoretically possible, and the "vacuum" areas can be scaled down to accommodate only the probable total growth of all sectors combined.

Any environment whose differentiation is accomplished, not by division into sharply defined boxes, but by the establishment of intensive foci, or axes, from which the differentiated use grades out into a less differentiated, less intensive transition zone, is also an environment which is likely to be adaptable. At the same time, it can preserve its basic structure by the fixity of its major axes and foci, from which growth and change pulse in and out. In our existing city centers, we often find semi-derelict transition zones which are performing just this function of preventing intolerable conflicts between major uses. Where major activities are close neighbors, new development can often only be achieved by a convulsive process of abandonment and re-establishment in a new location. In a mammalian example of boundary organization, the bone-defined brain case, growth is only achieved by the exhausting process of bone dissolution on the inner surface of the skull and bone deposition on the outside.

Often, however, it is the very intensive center which most requires renewal, and yet it is the point where maintenance of structure is most vital. One way this can be accomplished is exemplified by the historic shifts in our downtown centers, which gradually move in a consistent direction. The central focus can be planned to roll along, with new development occurring on one side and obsolete structure steadily being abandoned on the other. There can be a continuous consumption of physical facilities, a persistent replacement, and yet the whole maintains its proper form, the desired internal interrelations. Like the candle flame, like the living organism, the form endures while the material flows by.

If it were not desirable that a rolling center move too far from its original location, it might be arranged to roll on a circular track, eventually returning on its traces. In theory, too, an activity zone might be arranged in a ring shape, which could renew itself by perpetual outward movement, like the growth of certain molds. The ring shape would be retained, but the increasing length of the circumference might in the end prove disfunctional.

Other growth forms may be thought of. Essentially they are the more detailed patterns by which one tries to achieve adaptability, once a certain amount of low intensity has been provided, and once this has been differentiated by zoning.

Temporary Structures

Future flexibility has often been sought after by the use of temporary facilities. If the structures have short life, they are not long obsolete. Not only when time or capital is short, but also when uncertain of the future, the temporary solution is attractive: to live in a tent, to erect a "portable" schoolroom, to amortize rapidly. This is the organic answer to adaptability, par excellence. The internal parts of organisms are continuously being torn down and rebuilt to meet changing stress. Life is willing to pay a tremendous energy price to achieve this flexibility.

In the case of temporary facilities, which are desired for adaptability, the price incurred can be found by comparing yearly costs with the more permanent solution. Given equal present quality, then the yearly costs are related:

$$\frac{\text{yearly cost of facility (1)}}{\text{yearly cost of facility (2)}} \quad \frac{bx}{ay} \times \frac{2 + i(a + 1)}{2 + i(b + 1)}$$

where facility (1) costs x and lasts a years, facility (2) costs y and lasts b years, and the annual interest rate is i. Where the interest rate is zero, this reduces to bx/ay, the cross ratio of years and costs. As the interest rate rises, the temporary solution becomes more and more favorable, and may remain so even if its original cost per year of service is markedly higher than that of the more permanent facility. Where $bx/ay = 1$, or nearly so, the temporary solution is always cheapest in cost per year.

Disregarding social cost, which will be referred to at the end of this paper, the choice of the relative life rests principally upon yearly costs, although there may also be additional side effects on the economy, where temporary facilities insure a steady flow of production. In the poorest economies, temporary solutions may be the only possible ones, due to the difficulty of collecting any surplus. This is particularly true in poor economies undergoing change: witness the shacks surrounding the growing cities of underdeveloped areas.

Yet where small surpluses are possible and where conditions are more stable, temporary solutions may not be used, despite high interest rates. Since annual capital surpluses are small, facilities are created by slow increments, and thus they must have long life. The room-by-room construction of a peasant house, built to last for centuries, is a case in point. The setbacks caused by great city fires and the relative cheapness of rentals in older structures are two other examples of our tendency to live, at least as far as our urban environment goes, upon capital accumulated in times long past. It may be that only a relatively wealthy system, with substantial mobile capital, can afford to consider the possible economies of temporary solutions, to speculate about disposable cities and Kleenex neighborhoods.

There may be hidden economic costs in temporary facilities, of course. The rapid exhaustion of material or energy resources involved in production for quick disposal may not appear as a cost on today's budget, but be a heavy liability in future ledgers.

There are difficult administrative problems involved in the use of temporary structures, primarily that of ensuring that the use is indeed temporary and not prolonged. It has never been necessary to police the use of soiled Kleenex (except among small children), but larger facilities have a tendency to be used beyond their time, perpetuating substandard conditions and consuming heavy maintenance charges. The last "temporary" house thrown up in London after the Great Fire of 1666 was demolished in 1936. A policy of using short-life elements must be accompanied by some means of regulating their demise. The mammalian body has an elaborate apparatus of specialized cells which see to the dissolution of unneeded structure.

Not only is it necessary to prevent prolonged use, if adaptability is to be achieved, but it is likewise necessary to arrange that all adjacent parts are replaceable at the same time. A house whose frame is temporary, but [whose] heating system [is] permanent, is impossible to manage. Similarly, if in a city only scattered elements are removable at any one time, the resulting adaptability is only marginal.

DeBeers[5] mentions that some Polyzoa regenerate themselves by periodic dissolution of their structure, by return of the organism to an undifferentiated slime, or "brown body." We may find that we can keep our environments "youthful" by a similar process of systematic destruction and dedifferentiation. But only if the process is somehow controlled, and somehow zoned to furnish continuous areas for new growth. Future implications of heavy resource use must also be carefully studied, as must the social and psychological costs (which will be mentioned below).

Communication Substitutes

Environmental adaptability may be achieved by quite another means, which does not cause permanent shifts in the visible pattern. This refers to the survival ability of systems possessing highly developed communication networks. If internal communication is good, then resources can quickly be mobilized and shifted to meet emergencies. More important, perhaps, a good communication system allows changes in patterns of interaction without corresponding changes in physical setting. A man may shift his place of work without shifting his residence; a factory may use new techniques in dispersed satellite plants, and still keep them keyed into an undisturbed main plant; new social groups or recreational habits may form with a minimum of necessary remodeling; retail distribution may be revolutionized by closed-circuit television, and cause no ripple on the architectural scene.

Although it may seem that complexity, interdependence, and high communication are signs of a fragile organism, while a simple, independent one is tough and adaptable, in fact the reverse is usually true. The groups of wide range and survival value are the interrelated, communicating ones. The isolated peasant village perishes in a famine; the dependent modern farmer survives. The most persistent of human settlements have been the large and complex ones, not the little hamlets. Despite all our forebodings over these "unnatural" groupings, once [they have] arrived at a certain size they seem able to survive repeated shocks. This adaptability that comes from high communication and interrelation is undoubtedly the basic factor behind the power and viability of our metropolitan areas.

The communication system will be most useful for our purpose if it is a neutral one, i.e., [one that] favors and interconnects most localities relatively equally. Then various interaction patterns can be set up without distortion by the communication arrangement, and can shift as easily. One future location is theoretically as good as another. This would seem to indicate some kind of a regular grid system, and to argue against highly concentrated, fixed communication systems. It also implies a rather finely netted circulation pattern, so that all locations are interconnected.

This may conflict with other aims, of course. Efficiency is likely to call for concentrated systems, such as rail lines. Therefore we may have to be contented with the reservation of future ways in a regular grid, while allowing efficient concentration of facilities within that grid. Or a transport system might be sought out which can alternately concentrate and break up according to need, such as the "piggy-back" combination of rail and truck.

There is some conflict even within our own set objective. If a fine net, fine grain communication system aids the interchangeability of location, where it occupies physical space it also works against the technique of concentrating structure, and to that extent [it] causes inflexibility. Undoubtedly a balance must be struck here, probably a differentiation of the communication facilities themselves, such that some are fine capillaries, easily moved, leading through a hierarchical grid to the fixed, concentrated major structural lines.

Therefore this constitutes still another means of gaining adaptability: the construction of a high-level, neutral, and perhaps finely-netted circulation and communication system, so that interaction changes may be accommodated without the agony of environmental ones.

Application

To pull together this discussion by an example, assume that we are about to design a large shopping center, and that adaptability to future unknown change will be an important objective. We would not be likely to turn to a vague "flexible" or "multipurpose" undifferentiated space, even if it would otherwise work. Nor would we strive to develop variety of facilities for their own sake.

But we would certainly keep the intensity as low as we could, without hampering present function. We would build extra capacities into the various structures, within our means. We would employ structures with as short a life as was economically feasible, *if* we had developed a way of controlling and timing their scrapping, and did not fear any future drain on resources.

Furthermore, we would attempt in the layout to zone temporary and low density facilities in concentrated areas, and to separate other likely-to-(or easy-to-) change uses from their opposites. We would concentrate major structure (here the mains of communication and utilities) in sharply defined bands, as widely separated as possible.We would see that all major activities had axes of growth into relatively "passive" regions, arranging these major areas like beads on a string, or as centers of activity grading out into a less differentiated matrix. Our plan might be such as to encourage a "rolling" growth of the center, and we would recommend that future re-adaptation of the center be in the hands of a continuing body who understood these same principles. We would certainly insist that we have as good a communication system as possible: highly developed, rather neutral, and, in its minor features, of fine grain. We might even, with due caution, look into the possible advantages of a three-dimensional modular system for all structures, but of a rather coarse and neutral character. We would avoid (if we could identify them) highly specialized features which are narrowly adapted to present processes, but would not necessarily shy at complicated, precise, or developed forms.

Qualifications

The reader must remember that we are discussing simply the physical means of attaining adaptability. There may be many other ways of gaining this end: administrative techniques in particular. Of such nature are flexible rules governing new development; or systems of carrying on scrapping and renewal as a smooth, perpetual process; or the institution of agencies which periodically check the present and future adjustment of structure to function, and recommend changes to meet this constantly shifting situation. These are important means, but we have here arbitrarily limited ourselves to the adaptability of physical environment, per se. In some cases, physical features are so important as to be the key to future adaptability; in most cases, they are at least one of the several important considerations.

It should also be made clear that adaptability is not the same as growth or development, but simply is a permissive quality which *allows* growth or development. The dangers of biological analogy are always waiting in the wings: the physical environment (at least in its urban aspect) does not grow of itself. We have no particular interest in the growth or change of the environment for its own sake. In fact quite the reverse, since every change exacts some price. We are only interested that, when it is desirable that life patterns should change, they can do so with minimum effort, and, were it possible, with no environmental change whatsoever.

If it is our objective to *promote* the growth or change of people and their activities, then we may not want environmental adaptability. Biological development probably requires some framework, some direction within which growth can proceed, and also some challenge to which response can be made. An adaptable environment is simply a highly permissive one, and this may be far from optimum for the stimulation of individual growth.

It should also have been noticed, throughout the previous discussion, how often it was necessary to qualify the conclusions with "if economically feasible," or "as far as present function will allow." There seems to be a continuous conflict between future adaptability and present efficiency. Low intensity, over-capacity, highly temporary structure, intense concentration of structure, modular standardization, separation of centers, avoidance of specialization: all are likely to exact a price in terms of immediate function of first cost. Present efficiency seems to prefer a high degree of structure, close fitting, fixity, [and] specialization in the sense of narrow adaptation to the immediate situation. When it comes to an all-out showdown, present efficiency will always take the pot, but usually the problem is one of striking a reasonable balance, with many unknowns and much looseness of fit. In our rapidly changing world, adaptability can usually justify a reasonable increase of present cost. Very often there are adaptability features which cost little or nothing in the immediate situation. And new, more complex forms may at once improve *both* efficiency and adaptability.

In all this preceding discussion, human implications of a highly adaptable environment have been consistently dodged. Here again there is a significant conflict, and this perhaps the most serious one of all. A loose, shifting, temporary world may be ideal for meeting major changes in man's circumstances, and for allowing his development without hindrance. But not only may it not be most suitable for the active promotion of development, and not only may it be relatively inefficient for present function, it may simply not be a very happy place for human existence.

We have psychological requirements for some continuity and stability in our world, for structure, coherence, and imageability. Without them, the organism breaks down. If they are weak, there is stress, dissatisfaction, uncertainty; and growth may be hindered. (If they are too pervasive, of course, we may have opposite effects of growth cessation, atrophy, or boredom.) Adaptable forms are likely to be ambiguous, unclear, shifting, discontinuous. Thus there is likely to be a conflict of basic objectives.

Within the limits of this analysis, we can do little more than to point out the conflict, which is indeed the basic problem of any system, and particularly of any human society: how to provide continuity and clarity of form and of aspiration, without hindering the flexible adjustment of function to the constantly changing situation. Undoubtedly there are ways to approach this ideal in the physical environment, and they are worthy of careful analysis. Zoning, the concentration of fixed structure, the provision of stable intense centers, the maintenance of form despite a rolling progression, communications which obviate the need to shift locations: all these can potentially provide emotional and perceptual continuity in the midst of flux.

Visual symbols are very useful in this regard, since they can denote continuity and similarity of general aspirations without referring to precise meanings or impeding new functions. An historic center, or a space preserved throughout long vicissitudes, may act as [a symbol] on a city scale. If it proves advantageous to rebuild a man's house every few years, then siting by a great stone or tree may symbolize its continuity of location and function with past generations.

The problem of adaptability, therefore, turns out to be more complicated than at first look, as to just what the objective is, how it can be attained, and how it relates to other human ends. This study has discussed it primarily as an end in itself, and entirely in relation to the physical means of attaining it. Certainly, in any real situation, adaptability must be considered only in context with many other objectives.

Nevertheless, it appears that adaptability to future change unspecified is a significant goal in city planning, and that there are some physical means of attaining it. These are primarily those of zoning and concentration of structure; avoidance of narrow adaptation; low intensity and over-capacity; use of growth forms; and a good, neutral, well-distributed communication system. In addition, it may sometimes be useful to employ a lattice structure, or facilities of short life. Systematic investigation of these means when used at the city scale, and a thinking through of their relation to other human objectives, would prove useful.

References

1. Gavin Rylands de Beers, *Growth* (London: E. Arnold and Co., 1924), chapter 13.

2. George Gaylord Simpson, *The Major Features of Evolution* (New York: Columbia University Press, 1953).

3. Hans Blumenfeld, "Form and Function in Urban Communities," *Journal of American Society of Architectural Historians* 20 (1943): 17.

4. Blumenfeld, p. 72.

5. de Beers.

The Openness of Open Space (1965)

Open space has many meanings in the planning of cities. It refers to grounds for sports and games, or to large areas in public or quasi-public ownership, or to un-built-on land, or to "natural" areas, or to voids which are open to view, or to places of outdoor assembly. To this ambiguous cluster of places is attached a similar cluster of purposes: conservation, recreation, contact with nature, social or mental health. Such areas are usually shown in green on a city plan, and the plan is judged by the size and continuity of the green areas which it exhibits.

The purposes are laudable. Many of these "green" areas afford unmistakable pleasure and satisfaction. However, to discuss the design of open spaces we must choose a more precise definition and a clearer set of purposes.

We proceed directly from the meaning of "open": free to be entered or used, unobstructed, unrestricted, accessible, available, exposed, extended, candid, undetermined, loose, disengaged, responsive, ready to hear or see as in open heart, open eyes, open hand, open mind, open house, open city. Open spaces in this sense are all those regions in the environment which are open to the freely chosen and spontaneous actions of people: public meadows and parks, but also unfenced vacant lots and abandoned waterfronts. These areas may be open to many kinds of activity, as a sandbank or a grassy slope; or kinds of movement, as a prairie or unobstructed wood; or to the roving eye, as a vista or the open sky.

This is a behavioral definition: a space is open if it allows people to act freely. It has no necessary relation to ownership, size, type of use, or landscape character. Moreover, a region can become an open space by minor physical changes, or by administrative action, as when underbrush is cleared out, a view is opened up, or public access is first allowed within a water reservation.

Certain other arbitrary omissions will keep us within practical bounds: we are talking about outdoor open space, or at least about regions predominantly un-built-on. We speak only of urban open spaces—those lying within a metropolitan region—and therefore of spaces with which city people are in frequent contact. Finally, since even a private yard or an obscure back alley can be open space in this sense, we will restrict ourselves to places normally accessible and able to be used by a significant number of city people. They may still be small, as a small urban square, or little frequented, as a lonely shore.

In our sense "open space" then is an outdoor area in the metropolitan region which is open to the freely chosen and spontaneous activity, movement, or visual exploration of a significant number of city people.

Reprinted, with permission, from *The Arts of Environment*, ed. G. Kepes (New York: Braziller, 1972).

This is a peculiar definition, too unstable to be of much use in law, and not automatically and easily related to ownership, use, or form. Moreover. this kind of open space may be rather finely intermixed with other areas. It includes places which are not green on planners' maps, such as vacant lots, and excludes others they color so beautifully: large estates, inaccessible water reservations, or special institutions, even baseball diamonds and tennis courts. Important as the latter may be for recreation, they are specialized facilities usable only in a particular formalized way, and therefore not open.

Obviously, we have no intention of denying the value of water reservoirs, hospitals, stadiums, and tennis courts. Yet through this definition we hope to bring out the design implications of certain purposes, disentangled from others with which they are often confused.

Open space is the negative, extensive, loose, uncommitted complement to the system of committed land uses that make up a city region. It performs important functions in the human environment, and we would like to consider those functions which arise from its immediate apprehension and use: the sight of it, the feel of it, the way it responds to action.

We assume that open space in a city is valuable for the following reasons:

1.) As uncommitted land susceptible of many uses, it extends the individual's range of choice and allows him to pursue his satisfactions directly, with a minimum of social or economic constraint. Private purpose can be pursued without elaborate prior planning or community intervention.

2.) Where open space is not highly manicured, and the social investment is low, the individual has a chance to demonstrate mastery, to meet challenges, and participate actively in a way usually denied him in the protected and expensive city environment.

3.) Since open space has a lower intensity of human use, and appears less structured to the human eye, it is a place of relaxation, of stimulus release in contrast to the intense and meaning-loaded communications encountered in the remainder of the city. Moreover, the perceptual signs do not fit so easily into socially determined stereotypes. People are confronted with new sights more directly, without the mediation of social norms and clues: experience is widened by the sight of a predator at his kill, or by a piece of trash appearing as a form in its own right, its social meaning stripped away or inverted.

4.) Open space is a convenient location in which to meet new acquaintances, whether it be boy meets girl or a convergence of people of particular interests. In a relaxed and temporary situation, removed from the guidelines of "serious" life, there is an opportunity to break through some social barriers, to make unspecialized contacts, to mingle in another social world. The camp and the outing allow a tryout of new roles, to experiment with being an adult or an athlete without serious risk.

5.) Open space extends the understanding of self and of environment. Engaged in unaccustomed actions, one can feel a new and more direct relation of self to the world. Open spaces can convey a sense of the larger landscape and of the great web of life. Orientation to the city itself can be improved by contrast, and by the views which are opened up.[1]

6.) As an extension of these ideas on a longer time scale, open spaces contribute to community control, since they make room for growth and change. Strictly speaking, this is beyond our scope since we are concerned with the immediate effects of open space. But such spaces confer an important degree of future adaptability on a community.[2]

Choice, mastery, stimulus, contrast, social experiment, orientation, and flexibility are important values. At least we will assume them to be so. We will concentrate on seeing how design can improve the ability of open space to achieve them. By now it must be obvious that our definition of open space was chosen to clarify this connection.

All these objectives have two common characteristics. First, they are meaningful only if open space is considered in context with the total urban setting. Freedom and challenge exist by contrast to a lack of choice or risk elsewhere. Stimulus release relates to the surrounding stimulus level, and perceptual orientation cannot be analyzed except by dealing with the total city form. None of these qualities exist in open space by itself.

Similarly, none of these effects can be understood without reference to the individuals and groups expected to use these spaces. Desirable, even possible, choices of activity will vary from class to class; a stimulating challenge to one person may be a terrifying danger to another; experiments in social role are permissible here and unpermissible there.

Choice

Consider choice as an objective in designing open space. One begins by looking at the choices that people seem to want, as indicated by the ways in which they now prefer to spend leisure time outdoors: swimming, picnicking, driving, walking, sightseeing, sports, fishing, boating, and so on. The designer must be careful to look at these choices as objectively as he can and not to load them with his own preferences and prejudices: not to attempt to discourage driving because it is "passive" or "mechanical," for example. Choices should be blocked where they can be shown to be harmful (the recreational smoking of opium, for example), or where they may interfere with the choices of others (motorboating on a small lake devoted to swimming and camping, for example, but not motorboating in general). The instinct of recreation planners for dividing recreation activities into "good" and "bad" is suspicious if we are serious about using open space to extend choice.

Even so, such a list of desired activities is inadequate. First, because it is "recreation," and there are many leisure-time activities not customarily ennobled by that title: gambling, making love, washing the car. We must observe the total spectrum of actions that people choose to do in their leisure outdoors, regardless of the conventional label.

Second, such lists are gross averages, in which the particular choices of groups and individuals dwindle and disappear. It is less useful to know what the "average family" wants to do than to learn about the desires of elderly working class men of Italian background, who live in this area and may be expected to use this particular open space. Individual differences are even wider than class differences, and a good open-space system would include a great range of possibilities for action, keyed to the range and frequency of freely chosen outdoor activities of the population, and in which minority tastes were not submerged.

The physical types of open space presently designed are astonishingly limited: the swimming beach, the roadside picnic area, the woodland with "nature trails," the grassed park dotted with trees and shrubbery, comprise the conventional range. But activities are not that stereotyped. In fact, many other physical forms can be imagined: pits, mazes, raceways, heaths, bluffs, canyons, allotments, terraces, hobby yards, caves, marshes, water networks, dirt piles, junkyards, space frames, aerial runways.

Special groups within the population should be specifically considered: ethnic minorities, teen-agers, single men and women, the old. What would they prefer to do and what physical form will give them that opportunity? Even within a "typical family," how may all its members be provided for? Must an excursion to the park be an exercise in outdoor baby-sitting for the adults?

Third, one cannot rely solely on present patterns, since these are constantly shifting, and occur only within present possibilities and constraints. In what ways are leisure-time activities changing, and how might they change if different facilities were provided? In this respect the designer is obliged to experiment, inventing new devices and new environments which suggest new activities. Suppliers of commercial recreation are perhaps more accustomed to this innovating role than are public recreation agencies.

The designer's work is still incomplete, even if he provides a variety of facilities for a carefully analyzed range of new and existing activities. Since he is providing open space, his principal task remains: to devise forms which are uncommitted and plastic, which adapt themselves easily to a great variety of behaviors, and which provide neutral but suggestive material for spontaneous action. Water edges and banks of earth or sand have this character; so do open meadows, woods, junkyards, abandoned buildings, and smooth white walls. These may differ from the socially approved formal garden or manicured park. The role of derelict and waste land in an open-space system must not be underestimated. Order and exquisite harmony affords one type of satisfaction. If it is insisted on everywhere, however, it will inhibit other equally important satisfactions.

All of these qualities of variety and plasticity are to no avail unless the open space is accessible. Choice must be within reach. Open spaces, particularly those for daily or weekly use, should be physically proximate to their users, and connected to them by visible easy paths. Thus a network of relatively small spaces, well distributed within the urban system, may be more useful than the large tracts which look so well on land-use maps. This is true as long as an open space is large enough to establish its own special character (a size which may often be astonishingly small). The access may be by foot or wheel, but should seem short and direct.

A space's relation to the general circulation system will be important, and so will the pattern of paths which enter it, and open it up internally. Since spaces are reached, and often used, through movement, an organization of linear sequences or networks will often give an impression of great extent and pervasiveness, despite actual small dimensions. Indeed, some of the favorite American recreation has to do with motion: driving, walking, boating, cycling, horseback riding. A good open space system will not only be generally accessible, but will provide extensive networks designed just for such pleasure in motion.[3]

The importance of access explains the critical role of the edge or border between open and non-open space (highway, housing, commercial area, and others). Although penetration in depth must also be possible, it is the border region which is most visible and accessible, and which is thus the most useful portion of the open space. Careful manipulation of the edge and the access system is the key to design. In a metropolitan open-space system, a system designed for frequent use and part of a region whose major characteristic is accessibility, location is more usually influenced by access than by any unique characteristics of the land, as might be the case in a major national park. Special character can be manufactured at the appropriate location.

Existing public and semi-public reservations, now closed, might be opened up as a matter of policy. At times this may be done on a selective licensed basis, to reduce numbers and potential damage, but also as a means of education for open space use. Roads and paths may be designed primarily as open spaces, so that a metropolis contains a whole network of recreational channels. These need not be developed to the same standard as ordinary city roads, and should certainly be differentiated as to vehicle and character. For example, it would be possible to develop an urban network of bicycle or riding trails, using bits of undeveloped land, old rights of way, waterways, or institutional areas.

New techniques may even open up new regions previously thought to be inaccessible without very special and expensive equipment. The underwater world has recently become a recreational region, so have "impassable" swamps, so has the air. All of these may be exploited as part of the open-space system.

The variety of facilities and spatial characteristics within any one open space should also be closely linked to one another. Choice is enhanced; members of a mixed group can enjoy a range of chosen activities; one individual can vary his actions over time. Deep woods and open meadows can be juxtaposed, dance halls and lonely outlooks, building yards and formal gardens.

Access is a matter of psychological, as well as physical, connection. An open space must *seem* to be close and easily reached, which is very much a matter of design. Moreover, access can be denied by social rather than physical barriers, and here social action is required to break through. The entire open-space system in a metropolis should be open to all its citizens. It can be one lever for the equalization of opportunity.

A person may be self-limited, as well as subject to physical or social barriers; he may be unaware of leisure-time opportunities, or be without the skill or the means to indulge in them. Advertisement, perhaps a general program of recreational guidance and training, might open up many of these unavailable possibilities. A generation of scouting and children's camps has undoubtedly been one reason for the present widespread interest in family camping vacations.

Clearly it is not necessary to open an infinite, or even a very large, number of immediate leisure choices for people. The cost would be overwhelming, and the effect on the citizen might be confusion, anxiety, and rejection. What is more to the point is to arrange the environment so that each differing person has some measure of leisure choice, inclusive of his existing preferences but also of some hitherto untried actions. These choices should be significant and not trivial, that is, they should imply experiences of substantially different nature. Preferably, these choices should extend with time: they should be so arranged that someone could try an ever-unfolding range, if he chose to apply sufficient time and energy. While immediate choices would necessarily be limited, there would be fewer ultimate barriers.

As a matter of public priority the system should first be designed to open up choices for groups now most deprived of choice. The opposite often occurs in city park systems, where the wealthier, less dense areas get the lion's share of public open space. Of course these areas are most influential, and also most vocal and consciously aware of the advantages to be gained.

Mastery

The open-space system can provide for a kind of experience which is often difficult to find in the intimate interdependent city (or which can be found only with adverse social consequences): the opportunity to manipulate material directly, to exhibit mastery, to meet a challenge or run a risk. There is profound satisfaction to be had in proving oneself, in seeing the results of one's own efforts, and these experiences are an important part of the process of growing into a human being.

It may seem perverse to manufacture danger and challenge in a world as dangerous and challenging as our own, and perhaps it is. And yet the chances for mastery and trial that are available to many city adults and children may be too costly to indulge in, or too overwhelming to be met, while the more fundamental challenges of this world, whose resolution would be socially constructive, are too difficult to confront in any meaningful way. Artificial dangers and creative opportunities can be justified as a siphoning of energies away from destructive action, as a preparation for more fundamental work, and simply for the satisfaction it will give. In addition, these energies can sometimes be turned to direct social account.

The open-space system is a favorable place to provide these challenges and opportunities, although the urban system may not be suitable for some of the traditional wilderness challenges of individual survival. There can be tests of individuals or groups graduated in all levels of skill and risk: rock-climbing, gang-fighting, underwater swimming, sky-diving, sports and gymnastics of all kinds, logging, mining, earthwork, construction, animal taming, group leadership, and so on and on. They can occur in the city open space without disturbing other parts of the social fabric or destroying important physical resources.

It is not simply a matter of providing danger. The challenge must be kept within the person's ability to meet it, and prevented from escalating. Therefore a whole range of risk must be established, and people be guided to, and often trained for, their own level. Adolescents might be coached, for example, in the art of group fighting in thick woods, with a set of rules imposed to keep injuries and the theater of war within bounds. Other areas might be retained, or even "improved," in dangerous condition, and entrance allowed only to those who passed qualifying tests.

Challenges are not restricted to risk of limb or to competition with others. The mastery of an art or technique; the chance to make something of one's own, or to leave an individual mark; the sense of group accomplishment, are all equally satisfying and often more useful socially. Therefore the open spaces should provide places where people can make something of their own: the victory gardens of the Boston Fenway, the famous junk playgrounds of Scandinavia, the rock dams that have been built by generations of children in small streams and tidal inlets. In some tracts, it might be policy to allow people to build summer or weekend cottages of their own, returnable to the public after some years, and built with technical guidance. Allotment gardens are a satisfying activity, and so is boat-building, which might be done in publicly equipped yards. Children want a place to make tree houses and caves, adolescents a place to tinker with a machine, and try it out. Too great an emphasis on neatness will prohibit these pleasures.

These energies can be put to coordinated use in work camps, perhaps quartered in or near the open-space system, which are occupied in reconstructing that system, or perhaps in operating on the surrounding urban fabric. The act of building a new playground by cooperative neighborhood effort, for example, may be more important than the playground itself, as is being demonstrated in Philadelphia and Washington today. The open-space plan should allow for this kind of local development of its facilities. All of these are ways of managing the useful, or at least the harmless and satisfying, release of energies now either perverted or suppressed.

New Stimuli

The open spaces afford us an ideal oportunity to substitute a new set of sensuous stimuli for those normally encountered. City perceptions are relatively intense, highly structured, and symbolic. The individual will experience a pleasant sense of release and relaxation when he begins to receive a set of messages which are less intense and less demanding of his response. He escapes the threat of communication overload, and can react in a more spontaneous way. Birdsong may be highly meaningful to a bird (it is most often a repeated cry of "no trespassing"), but to a human being it is pleasant rather than threatening, delightful in its liquid repetition, able to be disregarded with safety. The human observer releases his attention, receiving chance impressions or attending to inner stimuli of thoughts and reveries, or he attends to the song as an esthetic object, a fascinating pattern of sound with vague symbolic connections to human emotions or human speech.

This change in the stimulus pattern must not be too abrupt, or the individual may feel bewildered or even endangered. The cicada's call is loud and ominous to someone used to city traffic. One must either train the city-born to be at ease in the outdoor world or design the open space so that it exhibits continuities with the urban environment: perhaps it may have paved walks, or signs, or clipped and ordered trees. Once more, the design of the space depends on the expectations and temperaments of the users.

A complete absence of stimuli is not desirable, however much people may dwell on "quiet" or "calm." A stimulus vacuum is better achieved in a controlled indoor space, and is completely demoralizing to most people if long continued. What we want is often a lower intensity of stimulus, but particularly a set which is not so highly structured or loaded with meaning in a socially determined way. New kinds of perceptual organization should await discovery. In this regard, open space can serve two separate, almost paradoxical, ends: it can release a person from the pressure of demand on his attention, so that he can attend to himself and order his previous experience. Alternatively, it can present him with new stimuli, less explainable by social stereotype and thus serving to widen his experience and his repertory of actions. This new experience can be the sight of some stupendous natural phenomenon, or the inspection of a small colony of ants, or just the act of stumbling down a narrow woods path, crossed by roots and barred by branches. These new experiences need not all be "natural" ones: an artificial world may also be manipulated to produce new confrontations or to reduce stimulus intensity.

The usefulness of plant material for this effect is well known. The value of some of the more basic natural materials is more often neglected. Earth, water, and rock are the primary materials of this planet, and while they are sometimes appreciated in situ, they are rarely exploited as planting is, and as our technical means allow. Today it is possible to build artificial topography, to manufacture bodies of water, to shape and place rock, to build systems of caves, galleries, levels—in general to exploit and modify the earth's surface in three-dimensional depth. Coupled with our ability to introduce and manipulate plant species (and even to some extent animal species), we are capable of creating urban open spaces of a wide range of perceptual character.

Light and fire can be employed to diversify the scene at night, and so to extend the usefulness and safety of open spaces. Noises, smells, even local climate, may also be introduced or modified to enrich the scene. These are all presently available ways of diversifying the open-space system and its range of stimulus intensity and organization. New, even "shocking," stimuli may consciously be employed to increase the chances of direct confrontation and spontaneous reaction.

These patterns cannot be evaluated in themselves, but only in relation to their perceptual context. It is the entire system of intense *vs.* quiet areas, urban *vs.* rural, dense *vs.* open, that produces the desired rhythm of stimulus and relaxation, familiarity and strangeness. This effect is heightened by contrast, by close coupling of different areas, and by some measure of surprise. Thus a quiet leafy ravine seems even quieter and more secluded if the distant hum of traffic may be heard, or if one enters the ravine through a narrow door opening directly off a busy street. In the same way, a brightly lit, active waterfront seems more feverish by contrast to the dark and silent ocean. The confrontation may also be symbolic: a gaslight in a forest, or a window box on an apartment wall.

For these reasons of contrast, we again find that the edge or boundary, and the nature of the approach, are both critical to the usefulness of open space. It also means that very large areas are often not required to attain the desired rhythm of tension and release. Small pieces of ground of intense and special character, with carefully designed edges and approaches, may be quite satisfactory.

Social Contact

Open spaces may serve as a locus for certain new, unspecialized, or unusual social contacts, free from many of the restraints of routine living. On the one hand, people of similar tastes, whether it be kite-flying or anarchism, can convene temporarily. On the other, where broadly popular activities such as swimming, boating, or walking are concerned, there is an opportunity for the venturesome to break through some social barriers, even if only temporarily and superficially. They may at least observe other kinds of people, and engage in similar activities side by side with them.

Therefore, since we value social mobility and are disturbed by segregation, it should be our policy to place actively used open spaces between or equally accessible to different social groups. Smaller places of relaxation and recreation may be brought close to major lines of circulation, and the access from several directions made inviting, so that chance meetings and mutual observation become possible.

In this case, we are primarily concerned with the focal points of activity in the open space, in relation to the lines of access. A large open space, void of activity, will usually act as a barrier between different social groups, rather than as a common meeting ground.

Open spaces might be used in a conscious program of changing the tastes or opportunities of minority groups with more rigid or isolated patterns of behavior. Such groups might be encouraged to enter unfamiliar territory or to engage in new activities by devices like guided tours, group outings, and recreational training, or by the provision of familiar facilities —dance halls, amusement parks, picnic areas with full conveniences— which are set close by other areas of more varied character.

Open spaces may also be suitable places for adolescents, in particular, to try out new social roles, without risking permanent commitment. There might be camps or gathering places where for brief periods they could experiment with various occupations or skills, or with sex or child rearing, or with different styles of life. Uncommitted open spaces, which were an intimate part of the large city and all its diversity, could be an ideal location for such trial runs.

We may find that in the long run the prime use for much of our inner, obsolescent urban land will be for such activities of recreation, meeting, and education. Going to live in the inner city, with its full complement of intense urban use and diverse open space, might become a favorite mode of spending vacation time.

The Environmental Image

Open spaces play still another major role. Because of their openness to sight, their contrast to the most characteristic regions of a city, and the grand scale continuities they can provide, they are very effective in visibly explaining the organization and nature of the city environment.

They are most directly useful where they permit vistas and panoramas that allow the observer to see important relationships. These may be large-scale organizations, as the view of Manhattan from the Upper Bay, or the sight of central Boston over the Charles. The visual opening may also be small, but equally valuable: the setting for a public building, or a city square or a curving mall which allows one to take in a shopping area in one glance. Such effects are gained by manipulating the open sight lines, and may often be parsimoniously achieved by small gaps and minor spaces. The critical locations relate to the major approaches and static viewpoints, and wholesale clearings are not required. Airports and industrial yards may be as effective as meadows or water surfaces, and more effective than wooded parks. Clearance of obstructions to sight, or the change in viewing elevation, are the crucial actions. An immediate and powerful sense of the city and its relation to oneself can thereby be conferred.[4]

The city may also be palpable by exposure and contrast along a long boundary between it and an open space: a city wall in a rural landscape, a waterfront facade. Or, as noted above, the urban character may become manifest through symbolic contrast: placing a fountain and a tree in an office district, for example.

City areas may be given recognizable and unique character by the design of the open spaces scattered through them, as central Washington is known for its green avenues, and Charleston for its little squares. These effects may be further exploited by concentrating particular types of plants, floor or spatial form in the open spaces associated with particular city districts.

Planners have often advocated the use of open space as a general container, or background setting, in which would be placed relatively small, compact urban settlements, which would take their identity in contrast to their "green" surround. This is a lavish use of open land to separate the functional parts of an interdependent region. Unless such an open setting can be justified on other grounds—water or food supply, cost of development, or conservation—it is difficult to justify in terms of the objectives discussed here. Identification of city parts, and making open space accessible to its users, can be achieved much more economically.

The open-space system not only makes the city visible, but also the larger natural universe. It can give the observer a sense of the more permanent system of which he and the city are only parts. The geographic setting can be displayed directly, by exposure of ocean or river or mountains, by enhancing particular features such as the fall line in Washington, by revealing characteristic topography. The underlying rocks may be laid bare, or the sweep of sky with its clouds and celestial bodies made visible from open viewpoints.

To convey a sense of the web of life, of the intricate interdependent system of living things, will be even more important. Areas could be arranged as open-air ecological museums, with explicit explanations of the ways in which living creatures depend on one another. It would not be necessary to manufacture an artificial wilderness for this. It would in fact be more informative to illustrate the ecological system in the city environment, including all the weeds, insects, and rodents which live together with men. The normal city park is too specialized an environment for this purpose, while the neglected and vacant lands are difficult of access, and not explained.

These intuitions of life and the larger universe can also be conveyed symbolically, by small devices which recall the large: a fountain for the sea, a dwarf tree for the forest, a moving ray of light for the sun. Such messages can be spoken in very small spaces.

The open-space system, then, can be used as a powerful means of extending the citizen's intellectual and emotional reach, helping him to understand his physical and social environment, and how it relates to him. Motor and walking trails can be planned to give guided tours of the city and its setting, not unlike the present-day "historic trails." These trails should explain the form of the city, the kinds of people that live in it and how they work, as well as the larger setting of the city and its ecology. Such open-space sequences should penetrate into working areas, pass along key geological features, and come into contact with typical constellations of living things. Change can also be illustrated, whether it is the secular change of human or geological history, the rhythmical change of seasons and days, or the predicted changes of the future. (Here we return to the function of open space which we have willfully disregarded: its role as reserve for future development. This role can be visibly explained, instead of leaving the land seemingly inert.)

A sophisticated use of signs and symbols, going far beyond their present employment for sales or prohibitions, would be extremely useful in this regard.[5] There are, indeed, many design devices that may be used in and through the open spaces to make the city an intellectually open system.[6]

General Criteria for Open-Space Design

We have followed out the design implications of our original definition of open space, and of the purposes that we attached to it. These implications are numerous, and capable of much refinement in the course of actual design and testing. But they are an interdependent set, and it is possible to summarize many of them under a few main heads, in the form of a set of criteria for the design of an urban open-space system, given the validity of our original purposes and the accuracy of our discussion.

To begin with, an open-apace plan of our type would necessarily be pervaded by the general concept of "openness": open to choice, open to active use and manipulation, open to view and understanding, open of access, open to new perceptions and experiences.

It would be a system which was intimately connected with the total environment and the daily life—not a specialized antithesis to the city but a functional part of it. It would be designed in the context of the whole: the pattern of other city uses and circulations, the regional setting, the constellations of living systems. Therefore it could not simply be a map showing the location of land acquisitions, to be inserted into a general plan for the city.

It would be a complete *design*, even if a large-scale and abstract one: a set of drawings and text showing the pattern of use, form, and character of all open space as a complete subsystem, in relation to the same pattern of the city as a whole. All open spaces and their use and form would have to be taken into account, not just the publicly owned ones specifically designed for recreation. It would show the pattern of major views, the distribution and use of vacant lots, and so on. It would necessarily be based on a comprehensive visual and behavioral analysis of the region, among other surveys.

Furthermore, it is implicit in all these discussions that the spaces themselves are meaningless except in relation to their use, and to the characteristics and aspirations of their users. It would be necessary to show who would use these open spaces and how, how they would reach them, and how this use relates to present or future desires or to ways in which hoped-for changes in those desires could be brought about. Alongside the plan for the form of the spaces would be a plan for their use and administration, and for training those who will use and administer them.

In regard to the design of the open spaces themselves, certain recurrent themes have appeared. One is the emphasis on variety, and the avoidance of complete reliance on the normal park stereotypes: that the vast spread of user requirements and technical possibilities should evoke an equally wide spread of kinds of open space in a city. Allied with that is the emphasis on access and approach, the meeting edge, contrast, immediacy, and close coupling. Stimulus, rhythm, and confrontation by new experiences is another facet of the same idea.

The discussion has turned several times on the idea of movement and sequence design: its great potential for enjoyment in itself, its ability to communicate the meaning of large environments, and its obvious relation to access and to the fundamental nature of the city. This has been accompanied by suggestions about linear open spaces, specialized routes, and general organizing networks.

This essay has continuously stressed the ideas of plasticity and flexibility: the value of spaces which can be actively used or manipulated, and which are amenable to change of function. Along with that has gone a predilection for experiment, change, and innovation. The tremendous technical possibilities for shaping open space have been emphasized, as well as its many unexploited dimensions and materials: underwater and underground, artificial light, three-dimensional sequence, and so on. Our city parks occupy only one small niche of the universe of open-space forms. We do not propose to abandon that niche. Formal gardens and handsome parks give great joy to the exploring eye and mind. We simply propose to extend the system, to carve out new niches, to look for beauty and meaning in unaccustomed places.

Prejudices have also developed for certain styles of open-space distribution in preference to others, on grounds of access, efficiency, effectiveness in exposing environmental form, and ability to satisfy the wide range of demand. In general this prejudice has been for open spaces distributed in a finer grain, with emphasis on focal points, immediacy, meeting edges, and movement sequences, rather than on large remote areas of green, although these latter may be justified on other grounds not examined in this paper: conservation or water supply, for example. The tendency to judge open spaces as large-scale map patterns leads to the misapplication of resources.

In this same way, this essay has shown the importance of the detailed design of areas, and therefore that a plan at the large scale must deal, not only with acquisition boundaries, but also with the distribution of design characteristics throughout the open-space system.

All these are very general statements which can only be understood by reference to the discussion which preceded them. They will take on concrete meaning when applied to real situations—to a particular city with all its idiosyncrasies of form, setting, function, climate, social pattern, and cultural aspirations. As in any good design, an open-space plan should be instinct with a sense of special place, so that it seems that it could never have arisen except in that particular location.

Developing an Open-Space Plan

Beyond these general concepts of design, this essay suggests some modifications in the accepted procedure for designing an open-space system. The present method begins with a study of existing and projected future population, and perhaps with an analysis of the present patterns of recreation activity. By applying recognized standards of quantities of certain common types of recreation facility per unit population, a present and future "demand" for these facilities is calculated. Meanwhile, a survey has been made of existing public open space and recreation facilities, and this is compared to demand to give a present and future deficit. Independently, a survey is made of the region to identify the lands which are lightly developed and which have potential for use in one of the standard ways. These potential open spaces are compared to future demand, costs, and access to using population computed; and a "best fit" is found between location of demand and location of supply, within cost limits. This is the recommended plan, expressed as a staged program of land acquisition and open-space development.

This procedure is perhaps sound enough (with the likely exception of the use of stereotyped standards to generate "demand"), but from our viewpoint it is inadequate on many counts. It fails to deal with the total urban pattern of which the open spaces are a reciprocal part (except as it takes cognizance of the distribution of population, general time-distances, and the pattern of existing open land). It confines itself to some rather stereotyped categories of open space: beaches, regional parks, playfields and playgrounds, urban parks. Through its use of standards, it makes gross assumptions about the open-space behavior and desires of very large aggregates of the population, without much regard for class and individual differences. It plays down the possibilities of future change and innovation. It largely ignores both the possibilities of large-scale design (except for generalized map patterns), and also the vast number of potential site planning devices and characteristics. The use and administration of these open spaces are only superficially dealt with. It concerns itself only with publicly owned open spaces of a particular type. It does not contain a clear statement of objectives, and how they connect with proposals.

It is easier to attack an old concept than create a new one. It is by no means clear that we can suggest a new procedure which will overcome all these faults. Some additions to the usual process can be mentioned, however:

1. An operational statement of goals should be made, perhaps differentiated between different groups of the population, or undergoing changes in emphasis over the period of the plan. Proposals should be continuously tied back to these goals, even if only by explicit assumption.

2. A detailed study must be made of the existing open-space behavior and aspirations of the population, differentiated at least by economic, ethnic, and age groups. Estimates must be made of probable future changes in this behavior, and of ways it may be modified in desirable directions. Since we are now dealing with a broader, more ill-defined and shifting set of behavior than formal recreation, it will be more difficult to make quantitative estimates of land and facility requirements. Computations of front feet of beach, or the numbers of picnic tables, can still be made, but how many tree-house sites are needed? In some cases, quantitative estimates are not necessary, as in designing the positions from which the central city can be seen along an approach. In others, quantitative rules may crystallize as experimental activities become more standardized and common. But since we are dealing with open behavior, presumably partly free and idiosyncratic, we will always have to live with a penumbra of uncertainty, to be dealt with by feel, by experiment, and by a wide degree of physical flexibility. Facilities for formalized recreation, conducted according to fixed rules and requiring the commitment of specially designed outdoor spaces (our tennis courts, for example) would be programmed and located according to need, but not considered as part of the open-space system.

3. The entire existing system of open space, in the broad sense of the word that we have used, must be surveyed, including its physical character, use, and control. The potentialities for future open space must be analyzed in the same broad way.

4. Prototype facilities of a very wide range should be designed which exploit new technical and design possibilities, abandoning former stereotypes as to "proper" or "good" parks. These prototypes will be the basis for determining the potentialities of the total system. Flexibility, multiple use, plasticity, innovation—all need emphasis. These prototypes should include proposals for use and administration as well as physical form.

5. Alternative patterns for evaluation should be designed as total systems—as an intimate part of general urban form proposals, and not as independent aggregates of land purchases. These patterns must be large scale *designs*, indicating the distribution of use and physical character and their integral relation to similar characteristics of the remainder of the city. They would deal with, and be based upon, large-scale visual form.

6. It must be kept in mind that spaces are used only if they are accessible, that the view in motion is the most important way of seeing a city, and that many recreational activities are themselves types of movement. Thus the plan must include analyses and proposals for the moving view.

The above does not propose to be a complete discussion of the process of planning for open space, since we are only considering the design implications of open space defined in a particular way, and in the light of particular purposes. As has been stated above, other uses of undeveloped land have not been discussed, nor have problems which are primarily economic or administrative.[7]

References

1. Kevin Lynch, *The Image of the City* (Cambridge, Mass.: MIT Press, 1960)

2. Kevin Lynch, "Environmental Adaptability" [included in this volume].

3. Donald Appleyard, Kevin Lynch and John Myer, *The View from the Road* (Cambridge, Mass.: MIT Press, 1964).

4. *The Image of the City*, op. cit.

5. Ashley, Myer, Smith, *City Signs and Lights* (Boston Redevelopment Authority, 1971).

6. Richard Wurman, *Making the City Observable* (Cambridge, Mass.: MIT Press, 1971).

7. This essay was written in 1963: parts of it were published in modified form in Marcou, O'Leary and Associates, *Open Space for Human Needs* (Washington, D.C., 1970).

Open Space: Freedom and Control (1979)

with Stephen Carr

Open space, like an open society, must be free and yet controlled. Freedom of action in public spaces is defined and redefined in each shift of power and custom.

In those small, interdependent communities, in which we have lived for most of our human history, the use of the shared space was an integral part of the social order, like the obligations of kinship. Sanctions that enforced these rules were immediate and unwavering, for maintaining spatial order was essential to the social order. Conflicts occurred, if at all, at the territorial boundaries, where one group faced another.

As larger towns developed, residents at first maintained these settled ways. In the medieval Islamic city, for example, the residential quarters were walled enclaves. Those within were closely related, and the use of the common space was regulated as in the village. Even the main streets, as they passed through these enclaves, were closed off at night by pairs of gates. The market spaces were likewise shut off, divided between the separate merchant guilds. Paths between quarters, other spaces, and the ground outside the city walls were no-man's-lands, places for inter-group battles, the territory of misfits and criminals, that growing under-class caught between village, guild, and army. Here also flourished the storytellers and other entertainers. In other cities, some of this space was shaped to accommodate the rituals of institutionalized religion or government: those processions, executions, and displays of armed men necessary to uphold the temple and the throne. In St. Petersburg, Tsar Alexander built a gigantic chain of squares, one kilometer long, through which his human machines might march. Along with such places, however, there also came the possibility of mass protest and riot.

Like the anti-matter of physics, open space has been the opposing complement of the committed uses of any settlement, and, like anti-matter, it may have explosive consequences. It is the common ground for movement and communication, and likewise the place for deviance and crime. What is felt to be threatening in public differs from place to place, and time to time. The line constantly shifts between freedom and riot, and the struggle for control has sharpened as cities have grown larger and more diverse.

Battersea Park, in London, was built to provide "wholesome recreation" in place of the rowdy joys of the Battersea Field, once described by *The City Mission* magazine, in September, 1870, as if it were a program for downtown revitalization today: "Surely if ever there was a place out of

From *Urban Open Spaces*, ed. L. Taylor. Reprinted by permission of Cooper-Hewitt Museum.

hell that surpassed Sodom and Gomorrah in ungodliness and abomination, this was it . . . horses and donkeys racing, footracing, walking matches, flying boats, flying horses, roundabouts, theaters, comic actors, shameless dancers, conjurers, fortune tellers, gamblers of every description, drinking booths, stalls, hawkers, and vendors of all kinds of articles. . . ."

Sproul Plaza in Berkeley, California, was a decorative, rather empty entrance to the university when first built. Now, after the tumults of the 60s, it is vibrant with activity. Yet a regulation of this diversity is also evident. Rallies on those famous steps are now confined to certain hours and to certain decibel levels. The tables promoting various activities are lined up in a decorous row. The food vendors and the "street people" in their bizarre clothes are held, as if by an invisible barrier, to that end where the plaza meets the street. The freedom of use is greater than it once was, and it has been established through a process of testing, riot, repression, and, finally, more subtle and differentiated controls.

A humane mix of freedom and control may flow directly from the ways of a dominant culture. The English parks are known for their tolerance of eccentric or "private" behavior, but they are ruled by an unspoken agreement as to proprieties that are never to be violated. In more pluralistic cultures, public space becomes a battleground over appropriate behavior. It was feared that the opening of New York's Central Park would attract crowds of dangerous ruffians. Olmsted thought that his success in creating a park police, trained to correct public manners unobtrusively, was more important than the design of the park itself. Today, some street improvers worry that their outdoor comforts will attract unseemly vagrants, and so they contrive water sprays, spikes, hard surfaces, backless benches, and seats too short to sleep on.

Popular revolutions have always shown their strength in the central open spaces of great cities and have there been suppressed. The wool workers and small craftsmen of Florence rallied in the Piazza Signoria in the summer of 1378 to protest their exploitation by the great guilds. There, in control of the center, they created the first democracy of Europe. There, too, some months later, they were put to flight. The *place* before the Hôtel de Ville in Paris has been the focus of action each time the people arose: 1789, 1830, 1848, 1871, 1944, 1968. The tumultuous events in Tehran demonstrate once more the power of an aroused populace unleashed in the streets and open spaces of a city.

More often, we are threatened by the muggings, rapes, and knife assaults that have become so common in U.S. cities. In the memories of the urban middle class, reaching no further back than the 20s or 30s, this is a marked deterioratioin of public conduct. Yet, it is only a partial return to earlier behavior. The streets of 18th century London, for example, were far more dangerous for unarmed pedestrians. In medieval Florence, anyone caught on the streets at night without a special written pass was a proven criminal.

The free use of open space may offend us, endanger us, or even threaten the seat of power. Yet that freedom is one of our essential values. We prize the right to speak and act as we wish. When others act more freely, we learn about them, and thus about ourselves. The pleasure of an urban space freely used is the spectacle of those peculiar ways, and the chance of interesting encounter. It is an opportunity for the expression of self and group, unfettered by routine constraints of workplace and family. Watch the joy of both spectators and performers at Mardi Gras in New Orleans.

Except in final, violent confrontations, politics is waged with symbols. It is a struggle for minds and must be allowed full play. The citizens of 16th century Rome attacked their papal government in "pasquinades" or satiric verses attached to "talking" statues. The murals and wall posters of Lisbon and Peking are well known. Speakers mount soap boxes in the streets—never in public places indoors. Open spaces should allow for communication, peaceful protest, and demonstration in ways that will not disrupt the ongoing function of the city. There must be locations where a demonstration will be visible and have symbolic weight, where access is easy and panic or entrapment unlikely. The crowd must be able to sense itself and its leaders, have ample room and yet not be dwarfed. It needs skillful management to keep the expression of one group from inhibiting that of others.

Far more frequent contradictions occur when individuals are threatened or offended by some free behavior. Most of us agree on suppressing assault, theft, and damage to property, but what will be judged offensive will vary. The necessary management is accordingly complicated: to distinguish the harmful from the harmless, controlling the one without constraining the latter; to increase the general tolerance toward free use, while stabilizing a broad consensus of what is permissible; to separate—in time and in space—the activities of groups that have a low tolerance for each other; to provide marginal places where extremely free behavior can go on with little damage. Freedoms flourish as the system of regulation becomes more differentiated and the regulators more skilled in their art.

In open-space design, we seek a balance between openness and the articulations that allow mixed occupancy and use. We want spaces that reflect the complexities of our social life. This challenges our ingenuity, since the subdivisions and supports that smaller-scale activities require are in conflict with the use by crowds. Present central squares have gone to one extreme or the other. The new City Hall Plaza in Boston, designed with Siena in mind, functions well for occasional Stanley Cup rejoicings. At other times, activity clings precariously to its windswept edges. More often, central squares are designed like parks, filled with trees and fountains that prevent effective use as a stage for great public events.

In larger parks, the solution is again one of partitioning in time and space, and, above all, one of sensitive management. Design and management go hand in hand. Negotiating acceptable divisions of ground, providing the subtle markers that allow groups to find their places, teaching tolerance to those who operate the space, and controlling unobtrusively are keys to free use.

Wastelands

Freer than parks, the wastelands are places on the margins. They are eddies in the city stream, out of sight and out of mind: the vacant lots, back alleys, dumps, and abandoned rights-of-way, the province of the young and the derelict. Here children have a chance for risk and adventure, in the company of their peers and away from adult supervision. Here they can dig a cave, throw up a fortress, hoist sticks to build a high nest. Yet even these wastelands are not rule free. Games have their own rules; repeated use builds territory and traditions; and society is anxious over bodily harm.

In remodeling any open space, one begins with the rule system. What is legal and customary here? Does that fit with the ideas of those who use the space, or is it imposed on them? Who safeguards the system? What will be the repercussions if the place is liberated, and how may those repercussions be contained? Who manages and enforces the system? What are their own feelings toward their work, and toward those whom they control?

Opening a place to new activities can extend the realm of freedom too. Allowing cyclists and joggers to use the drives of Central Park, or people to walk on Memorial Drive, along the Charles River in Cambridge, is an entering wedge for other free uses. Importing entertainers and seasonal celebrations into shopping streets changes those atmospheres. As the streets become warmer, more relaxed, and greater fun to be in, the sense of public life is refreshed. Again, this takes careful management, since these changes can easily be seen as out of place or threatening. Boston's inventive "First Night," a public New Year's Eve festival staged in the central streets and public places, was clumsily damped down this year, due to a few bottle-throwing incidents that occurred on its first run.

The use of open space is an indicator of social growth and change. Here one first senses some shift in social relations, or an evolution of dress and manners. Here is the public place for free commentary and artistic expression. To design open space well, one must understand how the social order is developing—no small task. Not only must one know the people one is designing for—they should themselves be involved in the design, along with those who will manage and maintain the place. This involvement leads to a better place, but also to that investment that makes more likely its future care.

Each using group should find some reflection of itself there, be able to lay partial claim to some territory. Management should include users, to keep managemant open to shifting values. The controls and shapes that make space free are difficult to achieve and precarious to maintain. Spatial freedom is sufficiently precious to make that effort worthwhile.

Where Learning Happens (1968)

with Stephen Carr

The best learning happens by surprise; it is very different from the normal process of deliberate education. By watching young children happening to learn, it is still possible to sense what learning might be.

Surprising things happen in cities, although frequently their people, places, and events are predictable. The routine business of life demands some regularity and enforces it through selective attention to what supports our efforts. But often, when we have "nothing better to do," when we are waiting, in transit, on vacation, just hanging around—or even occasionally when we are busy with our tasks—cities surprise us. A particular scene—a place, the people in it, what they are up to—suddenly comes into focus. We see it as if for the first time.

When a "new" scene is related to our interests, we may learn something. When it is compelling, we may enter it to change it by our actions or to join with others. At such times, we teach ourselves: The learning is integral with the experience, a by-product of some perception or activity engaging in itself. Most likely this informal learning will be relevant to our needs, to finding or making our place in the world. The occasions for such incidents can be dramatically increased by urban policy.

Ideally, learning begins when we awake and ends when we go to sleep. If we are fortunate enough to learn how to learn from our experiences, education extends over a lifetime. Schools, on the other hand, are conservative institutions normally closed to the world around them and obsessed with the training of "skills." Formal education looks to the filling of career slots, certifying performance by a succession of numbers, grades, and diplomas. For the poor, and especially the black poor, schools fail to do even this much. For many, as Peter Drucker points out ["Worker and Work in the Metropolis," *Daedalus* 97 (1968): 1243–1262], schooling has become a way of filling time, sometimes a way of staying alive, more often a way of postponing entry into work. In a more reasonable society, time has other uses.

Our failure to help people to learn how to learn is not only due to the resistance of the educational establishment; the environment itself is growth-denying in the suburb as well as the slum. Too often the city fences us away from other kinds of people. By the scale, impersonality, and even hostility of its places and institutions, the city tends to discourage independence of action and to encourage fear and feelings of powerlessness. The white mother and child in the suburb are kept from new experiences almost as effectively as their black counterparts in a ghetto housing project.

Reprinted, with permission, from *Daedalus* 97, no. 4, pp. 1277–1291.

The growth of individuals into rich and competent human beings is a fundamental value, directly satisfying in itself. It is also instrumental to other social goals, such as survival and economic development. Development of the individual will be a future focus of social action in this country, both by choice and by necessity. Education is shifting from being preparation for work to being a continuing part of life. When more routine work becomes automated, learning and working may become indistinguishable in the same way that the boundaries between education and play are dissolving as leisure is devoted to learning. Education is already an expensive public concern, but only in the context of traditional institutions and conventional measures of academic performance. The development of the individual other than in these stereotyped ways has never been a matter of conscious public policy, neither in our society nor in any other.

By development, we mean that an individual becomes more competent in some way, more highly organized yet more responsive, more engaged in a significant interchange with the environment and yet more independent of it. We think of growth in its broadest senses: physical, emotional, intellectual, and social. We include development both to known and unknown ends; creating a new poetic style as well as learning to read. Development is whatever increases the individual's involvement in self-motivated choice and action, whatever increases his power to formulate and execute personal intentions, whether delighting in the moment or planning a course of life. In our view, development is not limited to the forms sanctioned by culture and class (by which weight-lifting is vulgar, and the growth of Black Power bad). The aim is not to produce well-adjusted people who will operate competently without making waves. Development in this radical sense is a disturbing and dangerous pursuit, one that sometimes must be subject to constraints to assure the stability of society and the continued development of others. What is developmental depends on the individual's unrealized potentialities, his situation, and his purposes. We refer to the process—growing well— rather than to any specific ends for growth.

If development is to be an aim of public policy, some criteria for selection will be needed. We choose to favor developmental experiences that are self-motivating and self-rewarding, absorbing and committing rather than momentary and whimsical. This kind of experience gives the most promise of further development. We would emphasize development that aids the development of others: for example, skill in teaching rather than in the art of domination. Finally, we would encourage development that has socially useful by-products, even if such a judgment may be hard to make.

Vague as they are, even these criteria may be too narrowly focused on the individual. In many cases, society will (or should) give higher priority to group development: the growth of community identity, pride, purpose, and competence. This may be the case for the poor nations of the world as well as the critical issue for the Negro American. Perhaps in a saner society, individuals would naturally develop best as members of a developing community. As things are, individual development and group development will often be in conflict.

How can the urban environment promote development? The city has been a center for acculturation in the past—even if it has not been the melting pot once assumed. For the present rural migrants, however, urban society is not performing well. Any improvement in this performance will involve the urban school and urban politics, as well as patterns of work and leisure. We will confine our speculations to the influence of city form—the distribution in space and the scheduling in time of people, their activities, and the spaces that contain them.

The urban environment, in this specific sense, already serves many functions in supporting the development of individuals. It is a medium for transmitting the form and content of contemporary society, a territory to be explored, and a setting for the testing of identity. With the attrition of family function and the waning influence of tradition and authority, the individual seeks identity through his own experience. He must make himself in choice and action, and he must do so, by and large, in the urban environment.

Growing Up in the Future City

The present city offers a wide range of opportunity and stimulus, if mostly for the mobile and well-to-do. The trend of city growth, however, is toward increasing the apparent standardization and masking the available choices. Although physical mobility is increasing, exposure to diversity is sharply decreasing, especially for women and children. The decentralization of cities is bringing about a coarser spatial segregation of life styles and environmental qualities, although over-all variety continues to increase. There has been a general shift from participation to observation, which increasing electronic communications will most likely accelerate. There are "do it yourself" compensations (if that is what they are), but the processes of production, distribution, government, and even daily servicing become more impersonal, invisible, and remote.

A substantial minority is shut out or disaffected by urban society. Many people go from exclusion to disaffection without any transitional engagement. Given the fear and blindness of the majority, there is little reason to suppose that frustrated and disaffected people will disappear in the near future. Such minorities will increase, along with those who simply find affluence boring. There will no doubt be a corresponding increase in such "counterinsurgency" efforts as the Peace Corps and Vista. For those fortunate young people who have not lost the faith, these experiences can have great educational depth, despite re-entry problems. Reports of the death of the hippie, however, are probably premature—at least in the sense that young people, whatever they may call themselves, will continue their search for involving experiences "outside the system."

The *laissez-faire* alternative to societal support for individual growth does not mean disaster (except for a minority). It does, however, represent a serious loss of potential. No set of policies dealing with city form can be a panacea for such problems. Yet cities are where we live. Their form shapes our experience and consequent growth. To our minds, the single most important endeavor for city planning and design is to understand the developmental function of environment and to find ways to improve it.

Access and Diversity

An urban region is an immense storehouse of information. Its stimuli, diverse ways of life, events, and facilities are a prime occasion for learning. Developmental policy should aim at making this information accessible. One straightforward way is to provide a free public-transportation system, bringing all parts of a metropolitan region within some reasonable time-distance. The system must be workable at low densities, so that nondrivers are not caught within suburban areas nor central city residents excluded. Young children, as well as handicapped persons, should be able to use it with safety. If it proved impossible for an affluent country to provide basic transportation as a free public utility, then public transit might be subsidized so that children and adults of low income ride free. A more limited policy would subsidize educational trips where the destination was a school, museum, or another specifically educational locale. It might even be possible to subsidize "first-time" trips by distributing free tickets to random destinations.

The transportation system should be easy to use, as well as cheap and ubiquitous. It should be designed to be completely legible—the system of routes and transfers easy to follow and the destinations clear. Symbolic maps should be displayed, and direction-giving devices installed at all critical points. Public transit vehicles and routes should visually correlate with their destinations not only by using route and destination symbols, but by giving a circumferential route or vehicle a typically different form than a radial route or vehicle. The location of moving vehicles in the system and especially their imminent arrival should be displayed at waiting points. There should also be a network of paths along which young children can move safely by the means under their control: by foot, bicycle, cart, pony, or otherwise. Even the prosaic walk to school might be an educational device.

All vehicles and routes should give a clear view of the region being traversed—of its most important activities and particularly of its changes.

The environment itself might be designed to be "transparent," wherever possible without intruding on individual privacy. The form of structures and of land, as well as signs and electronic devices, can communicate the activity and function of a place, express its history or ecology, reveal the flow and presence of people, or signal the social and environmental changes that are occurring. In an industrial area, factories would be encouraged to let their machines be seen in action, to label raw materials and their origin, to distinguish the different kinds of operatives and explain what they do, to exhibit finished products, to make their transportation containers transparent. Thus the city, like a good museum, would be designed to increase the physical and perceptual accessibility of its contents.

To some extent, city trips are already used for educational purposes: sight-seeing buses, historic trails, and the rather stereotyped excursions of schoolchildren to museums. The environment could be exploited much more systematically and imaginatively. A complete network of educational tours, clearly marked and adequately manned, would explain the city's history, its technical functioning, its system of production, its politics, its ecology, its diversity of social groups. Tours would be organized particularly for the young, the physically handicapped, or the socially disadvantaged. They would be available within the tourist's own region, in other cities or rural areas, or abroad. The promotion and subsidy of travel for those now unable to do so would be a matter of public policy. Temporary exchanges of groups of children between families or different institutions might insure that these new experiences were not superficial. In Boston's METCO, children from inner Roxbury attend suburban schools; in summer travel camps in Europe, children live temporarily with foreign families.

There are also ways to amplify environmental information. One step would be to prevent and reverse the growing spatial segregation of the population by socio-economic status. As larger areas of our cities are occupied by similar groups of people or shelter similar productive activities, the child and the housewife have fewer opportunities to see at least the outward show of other ways of life. To have diverse people and different ways of making a living within walking distance is a basis for a young child's education. In our ideal city, no one would be constrained to live or work in any very large and substantially homogeneous area. Each activity requires a certain threshold of extent to maintain its special character, but these thresholds are far smaller than the gross separations that our cities exhibit. The fine-grain diversity and interlude to be found in some of the more favored old inner suburbs would be characteristic of the metropolitan area as a whole.

In a similar vein, every intense center of urban activity would be easily accessible. The outward extension of metropolitan regions requires a well-distributed constellation of points of intense economic, institutional, and residential activity, each of sufficient size to offer a diversity of people and action, chance encounters and unsought information. Some of these centers must be small enough or be controllable on a small enough scale to be responsive to the individual, as town centers often are and regional shopping centers are not. Temporal diversity can also be encouraged: Opportunities can be provided for celebration and for the rescheduling of the daily and weekly routine of urban events.

Since growth thrives on the alternation between intake and meditation, these centers might be associated with places and facilities that are completely calm, safe, and quiet—gardens, cloisters, public cells. The withdrawal available in wilderness and institutionalized in some cultures might thus be introduced into the heart of the city.

Openness and Responsiveness

Making people and information accessible is one way of using the environment for learning. Another is to see that environmental form is responsive to individual and small group effort. To act experimentally and to see the results of that action are the most effective ways to learn. This can be done in the spatial environment in a way often denied us in our social world of complex and remote institutions. High-density housing, for example, could be designed to provide the relative autonomy of the single-family dwelling. Allotment gardens and sites for owner-built vacation homes might be provided. A new technology of house maintenance and rehabilitation would increase the ability of the tenant to "do it himself." Features in the environment could be responsive to individual manipulation: arrangeable lighting, "pop-out" shelters, controllable micro-climate. The present trend toward homeostatic constancy—the caretaker environment—might be superseded by sensing and control devices by which environments would react visually, aurally, or tangibly to manipulation, or to the motion of the observer—just as artists are now inviting the active engagement of the spectator in their works. We might train for environmental management—for development, building, gardening, interior and exterior decorating, and other socially useful skills that allow unlimited use of individual sensibilities.

As experiments in radical decentralization, it should be possible for the inhabitants of small city areas to shape and maintain them themselves. Communal institutions might assume some functions of planning, building, repairing, servicing, and policing in their own environments. Neighborhood teenagers, for example, might install and manage their own recreation facilities. Long-term changes in environment through new development or renewal can be growth enhancing, if effective roles can be found for individuals in shaping such change. Greater decentralization of change management will also be more productive of diversity. Our developmental city must include responsive local institutions for environmental control, as well as responsive physical features. Widespread political engagement would be its characteristic.

We would provide an ubiquitous network of open space throughout the urban region—"open" not always because it is free of buildings and covered with plants, but in the sense that it is uncommitted to prescribed users. Dumps and vacant lands would be in this inventory, as well as woods, fields, waterways, and marshes. In these open areas, actions and explorations are permissible that would be intolerable on developed sites. Anything might be constructed from the materials available—temporary sculptures (as on the mudflats of San Francisco Bay) or tree houses. Open lands would be widely distributed so that some are safely accessible to the young child exploring on his own. Open space could be interior space as well—for instance, large barn-like structures, whose volume would be temporarily allotted for spontaneously organized projects and constructions. Raw materials and technical advice might be available on call, much as in the junk playgrounds of Scandinavia. But since these uncommitted open areas are vulnerable to abuse and neglect, we must either provide enough of them to keep the density of use low or be prepared to police them regularly.

Environment as a Base for Special Programs

The environment may also be a base for special educational actions. We would, for example, attempt to increase the availability of symbolic information. Our policies would include a wide regional distribution of computer consoles (probably with reproduction capabilities drawing on large central libraries), museums, tutors, directories, local newspapers, local TV and radio programs, and other such information outlets. Moreover, this flow of information would be made responsive to the user in many ways: Observers would be able to shut off or turn on environmental displays, make simple inquiries of visible signs, or find places to put up their own public signs. Local newspapers and broadcasts should be open to the announcements, plays, and stories of their listeners, so that groups can speak to one another, rather than be spoken to. Community TV will facilitate this. Would ham TV be a future possibility?

Particular areas in the city would be devoted to self-testing. Adolescents or adults might try themselves against a graded series of challenges and difficulties—cognitive, physical, or artistic. Teenagers might scale buildings or drive in obstacle races. Others might compete in the skill with which they rearrange a landscape. Many of these activities can emphasize mutual dependence and trust on the model of Outward Bound. Areas of this kind would have ambiguous border zones, where the unsure could watch and consider whether to take the plunge.

Other temporary communities might be places where it was permissible to break the habitual mold of action and to try out new roles: child-rearing or marriage, different kinds of productive work, or new and unfamiliar ways of life. These groups would be like participatory theater or continuous happenings, the tentative gesture would for a time be the substitute for the competent committed act. Such a policy implies our judgment that vicarious experience—watching others, reading novels, seeing movies, learning by identification, processes already institutionalized in our culture—is no substitute for real experience. Obsolete parts of central cities will be apt locations because of their accessible, cheap, and anonymous space. These temporary communities could also be used for special celebrations or for the coming-together of strangers for some common purpose or interest like surfing, socialism, or yoga. They would be ephemeral, voluntary ghettos. This will be a touchy policy to implement since many of the strange activities in such places will be seen as threats to society. They will have to be monitored, yet the monitoring must not be impatient interference.

The school, the institution formally devoted to education, could make much greater use of the city environment not simply by field trips, but by dispersing its scholarly activities more widely in time and space. Children would then be drawn into contact with other kinds of children and adults, and learning would not be sealed off, but intimately mixed with other activities. The best teaching is mutual. Parents and local specialists can be drawn into the educative process—simultaneously being the teacher and the taught. Anyone may drop in, even if only to observe. Informal classes and workshops might be organized wherever people do not have other overriding purposes (while in transit, in open areas, vacation spots, in bars and hangouts, for example). There might be brief apprenticeships in work processes, recreation skills, politics, or the use of the city. Working and learning might be combined, as they sometimes are in research institutions or cooperative colleges, and not be a series of irrelevant lessons interspersed with drudgery. The school would be affirmed as a crucial institution, whereas it is likely to wither away as a separate physical plant.

Implementation

Since we are not recommending a single coordinated strategy, we can only indicate some means of implementing our main policy suggestions. The policies for accessibility and for encouragement of travel could be carried out by present transport agencies with new criteria that go beyond optimizing economy of use. Such performance standards can be built into the federal program on which local transport is increasingly dependent. Educational agencies devoted to exposing and amplifying environmental information and increasing the outlets for information could be established on a regional basis. To avoid creating a new monopoly with concomitant distortion and suppression, the function of opening additional channels must be kept apart from any attempt at over-all regulation of environmental information.

We will also need new institutions to increase environmental openness and responsiveness. One possibility might be to establish an agency charged with assuring that various city regions are open to access, that the kind of open space we have described and the means to use it are widely distributed. Such an agency might evolve from existing open-space programs. It would most certainly encourage experimental uses and responsive environments. Due to the failures of urban renewal, new attitudes toward city building are already in the wind. New criteria are needed for the design and management of urban development. Block grants for local self-help and for new community institutions can emphasize local control and decision-making. Such programs aready exist for farmers' cooperatives. Activities like Head Start, Upward Bound, and More Effective Schools may possibly presage developments *within* the schools (within in the sense of Trojan Horses) that will bring children out of the institutional shell into the kind of environment we have described. The new Leicestershire schools in England already demonstrate how a rich environment within the school may be used to stimulate freely chosen learning. Nevertheless, the educational establishment in the United States is well organized to resist such innovation in the near future, and thus we face the necessity of increasing educational opportunity outside the school.

Where might support be generated for these porgrams? John Seeley foresees a broad social movement, at least partially in this direction, for which the hippies are the early martyrs. Less optimistically, we can point to excluded and disaffected minorities. Others are left out as well—housewives, the elderly—for whom a more engaging environment might prove attractive indeed. There are the enlightened conservatives, for whom the individual is already the cause. Finally, a large group on the fringe of the education coalition is concerned with the growing problems of youth and may find such policies more compelling than the present one of suppression.

Difficulties and Issues

An environment for growth would be more exposed, accessible, and diverse, more open both physically and psychologically, more responsive to individual initiative and control. It would invite exploration and reward it; it would encourage manipulation, renovation, and self-initiated changes of many kinds. It would contain surprises and novel experiences, challenges to cognition and action. It would not be the most efficient and safe environment. Nor would it offer maximum stability and security. It would certainly not be extremely comfortable, nor even very beautiful, unless we look for beauty in the process of interaction rather than in static form.

We know a good deal about the developmental effects of environment in extreme situations, but less about the more normal case. Deprivation in environmental stimulus is particularly serious for early growth. Human babies brought up under sensorily deprived conditions do not flower so quickly or so fully as those growing under enriched conditions. In later life, sensory deprivation has negative consequences even for short periods. The McGill experiments have demonstrated that emotional discomfort and hallucinations follow quickly after the the sensory isolation of human subjects. At the other extreme, there is considerable evidence to show that overload causes breakdowns in normal functioning. Besides experiencing confusion and stress, the individual becomes closed to all but the essential perceptions. In between, there is some optimum condition where the individual is stimulated sufficiently to maintain interest and alertness, but is not overloaded.

Most environments, however, no matter how sitmulating initially, become dull and even "invisible" with repeated experience. Either the environment must continually change to maintain interest, or the individual must be motivated to search for new levels of experience and meaning in an environment that offers successive levels of complexity. Only when aspects of the familiar environment seem relevant to him will he attend to them, be they other people, indications of status, occupancy, or territory, signs of human activity, or symbols of strong cultural significance. Individuals may become sensitive to the aesthetic significance of the environment, because of its vivid, sensuous form or because they have been instructed by artists to see certain characteristics. (The romantic landscape painters once taught people to see the previously utilitarian or hostile countryside, and Pop artists are now doing the same with the utilitarian or hostile products of our urban society.) The organization of the environment can facilitate or inhibit a person in experiencing these several levels of meaning and the learning by discovery that accompanies it.

By current evidence, the preschool years are the most critical. Young children are still learning about the environment as a matter of necessity, organizing their impressions of it through direct action and sharp, vivid perceptual imagery. Less word-bound than adults, their sensibilities are not so attenuated by the categories and concepts of conventional wisdom. If brought up in a stimulating environment, the child is naturally a poet, painter, sculptor, builder, storyteller, and actor of great expressiveness, if limited skill. Such interests are not fostered by our schools

The years of adolescence are another critical period for growth. The teenager begins to explore the wider city. What does he know of the opportunities it offers? Where does he go and what does he do there? Does he find places where he can feel "at home"? The city is a stage for testing his identity and for playing various roles. How does it function? Beyond childhood and adolescence, there are specific moments in the individual's life when he is most open to new possibilities. These are not task-oriented periods, but times of leisure, holidays, commuting, waiting. They are opportunities for providing access to information or chances to engage one's self.

This is the dilemma of developmental policy. Simply because new activities disturb custom or are similar to real dangers, they often seem dangerous without being so. Marihuana is classified with heroin rather than alcohol; sexual experimentation seems to undermine the family and the raising of children. In some cases, the implication of new development may be highly uncertain. In others, a new way of doing things will run against the interest of a special group or threaten them psychologically without being of serious concern to society as a whole. More developed, participating individuals may make surprising changes, not always benign. If we encourage a developmental world, we must exercise greater social control and also be able to restrain that control, pending the appearance of real dangers. There will be protests and reactions. Education, except for limited and sanctioned ends, is a controversial affair.

In a world oriented to learning and development, we must allow for an escape from it. There must be retreats to which people can retire temporarily to digest what they have learned or permanently if they do not wish to change. If our policies are successful, it will be necessary to conserve places of stable, even archaic, ways of life. Many people may become increasingly impatient and dissatisfied with the mundane work of the world. Such a reaction would cause serious reverberations throughout the economy. The emphasis on an integrated life runs counter to the view that Western man has developed precisely because he has been able to abstract experience, reducing it to bare symbols. Some would suggest that the "highest values of man" are best developed in a judiciously impoverished environment. Although we disagree, there is no doubt that an environment as rich as we have envisioned would put a heavy load on the individual's ability to select and discard.

If we focus our efforts on individual development, we risk encouraging a wholly self-regarding attitude, a belief that the growth of self is the single central value or that the world is made for "fun" and novel experience. We intend, rather, that environmental novelty be primarily a device for encouraging long-term committed development. Growth of this kind is not always fun; it can be hard and protracted, exhausting and sometimes agonizing, even if deeply satisfying.

We would like to encourage skills that advance the development of others or require group interaction. Just how these features of commitment and a regard for others might be encouraged in each case is not always clear. Many side effects of the policies we advocate cannot be foreseen. Society will have to reappraise what is permissible. We see the city as a purposefully designed "school," a place for learning and growing throughout life. In our eyes, that is the brightest possibility for the future city, and there are definite public actions that might bring it about.

Quality in City Design (1966)

Can city designs be good? Few would doubt that they can, yet an honest answer must be tentative. It must pry into city planning objectives, and the relations between objectives, reality, decisions, designs, and achievements.

Utopias are out of fashion. They were not useful as guides for action: they were unreal, they were static, they dealt with a very narrow range of objectives. Yet it was those very qualities that made the connection between city form[1] and city purpose seem comprehensible. Now we must allow for constant change, for complexity in the city and in the way decisions are made about it, for shifts and conflicts in values, for irrationality itself.

In these circumstances, we would wish for a variable that explains everything. If we have a magic clue, all the rest can be ignored. Explanations become patent and actions decisive. The key may be climate, or culture, or the economic base, or our parents. But it is clear that the physical and spatial environment does not reveal this kind of singular influence.

We can also relax if we think that the spatial environment cannot be rationally controlled at the city scale, whatever its importance: that we cannot conceive of the existing set of interrelations or propose comprehensive new ones; cannot keep up with the rate of city change; or cannot carry out the grandiose interventions required, or only at an unacceptable cost. Therefore city planning is impossible, ineffectual, or at least irrational.

The real world seems to be more complicated, interesting, and hopeful than either of these notions suggests. The spatial environment has significant effects, but only as part of an interacting system of organism and environment, social and physical. Such effects can be demonstrated in extreme situations (the absolute sensuous isolation that brings on mental disorganization), or in obvious and less important circumstances (the discomfort of lack of shade under a hot sun). Less is known about spatial influences that are crucial at the city scale, and also fall within the range of conditions usually encountered.

We do control the city environment to some degree: most city streets, for example, are continuous, and connect into a complete network. The great majority of urban dwellings in this country have a safe water supply. Trivial and obvious, but not after an experience with discontinuous roads or contaminated water. It is clear that we are both rational and irrational in dealing with our cities, in command and helpless. Dirges about civilization get attention, but the interesting and useful problem is to see how far we can extend our rational command, and how significant are the values we can deal with.

However, there are ways in which a planner can avoid serious concern with values, and still do useful work: one method is to focus on present adjustment and coordination. For example, he arbitrates between the demands of two different activities for the same piece of land, he redesigns a road system to serve an increased flow of traffic, he points out that a tract about to be sold by the water department is wanted as a park.

Adjustment and coordination may be done on a more comprehensive and future-oriented basis: by making a survey of all existing spatially located activities, with their physical requirements and linkages, which is supplemented by a forecast of the future set of activities, with their proper needs and connections. The physical plant of the city is modified to accommodate those present and future activities, according to some general standards of reasonableness in regard to accommodation and linkage. The activity pattern is "outside" the design process—it is assumed to be dominant, changing irresistibly for reasons of its own. There is no consideration of general alternatives, no explicit reference to objectives (despite any polished words at the front of the report). The plan may be consistent within itself and satisfy its own standards of reasonableness. A hastily planned, temporary, industrial shed is designed with the same degree of forethought. Many current city plans are of this type. They are neither useless nor contemptible, but they inspire us very little.

Other plans use another type of design decision (and I include most so-called "bold" or "radical" proposals), which might be called design by model or stereotype. Ways of shaping city form arise by custom or, more rarely, by creative innovation. These models include not only large-scale ideas (satellite towns, greenbelts, or radio-concentric street patterns), but also many smaller elements: superblocks, gridirons, or U-shaped bays of row houses. Once applied and shown to work reasonably well, and sometimes even if never successfully applied, they exert a compelling force on future plans, by virtue of their very simplicity and decisiveness in the face of uncertainty. Their power lies in their usefulness to the designer more than in their effectiveness in the real world. We hear the injunction to make a city plan a noble, simple diagram; or we notice that the plan for a new port city in Africa looks suspiciously like a student scheme for an American "new town."

We cannot do without these stereotypes. The process of city design would become impossibly tedious for lack of such crutches, and the power of a clear form to seize the imagination of a designer is not a negligible effect. It is the use of such models without reference to purpose that is defective, as well as the poverty of our stock and the tendency to apply it repetitively, as if unaware of the vast range of potential city form. Plan clarity and plan effectiveness are not identical.

Other planners, retreating more decisively from an attempt at purposeful action, will advocate an information role for themselves. In their mind, their key function is to collect, store, interpret, and publish data on the existing system of activities and facilities, and to make forecasts of the future system. By continuously communicating this comprehensive, up-to-date information, the planning office serves to inform the decisions and actions of *others*: government agencies, private firms, households. Each agency, having a better picture of the present and the probable future, can act more intelligently to accomplish its own ends, and the total set of decisions will be better coordinated.

This is a valuable function. It goes even further than our first strategy in passing decisions about the city on to special-purpose agencies; in large degree, the planner is acting to support and improve the workings of the market.[2] But one is left, as in all liberal proposals, with the problems of imperfect markets, ignorant or deprived actors, value conflicts, and community goods that do not arise automatically from the sum of individual strivings. While it is a useful supplementary program for a planning agency to engage in, it is not a fundamental technique for improving our cities.

A planner may use one more method, instead of facing up to the demanding task of systematically matching recommendations to purposes. He will develop a set of form alternatives, generated at random from a prior stock of models, or by some unspecified creative process. Once they are developed, he makes an intuitive choice between them, or passes them on to someone else for a similar choice. Here at last we are dealing with better or worse, with choice and values. But objectives can be left implicit, and the choice made by a subconscious process of balancing the presumed consequences, with alternatives generated at random. If there is no systematic analysis of why one alternative is preferred (that is, if objectives are not extracted from intuitive preferences), there is no rational way of finding better alternatives, and decisions are trapped within the previously chosen possibilities.

This is a technique we all use every day, when there is little need for consensus or communication and small concern for comprehensive effect. The technique underlies much architectural design. It avoids the demanding task of defining and balancing objectives, and of seeking their connection with form. It may also be a good way of engaging democratic participation in city decisions, since most people are far better at choosing between sets of concrete consequences than at criticizing abstract goals. It is often a way of uncovering previously hidden values ("Why do you like that?") and can be used to advantage by a planner in an early stage of his work.

Planning Objectives

Planners' reports are full of talk about objectives and goals. But a careful reading of most of them will prove how imperfect a set they are. Very often it is Pollyanna talk—so general and high-minded that no one could object, much less use them to discriminate among real alternatives: "a fine living environment for all our citizens," for example, or "general welfare," or "best use of the land." But what is "best" or "fine"? The function of a goal is to be a rule for choice among possibilities, unless it is designed merely to keep people's spirits up.

By an opposite error, the objective will be set at too low a level, easily connected to form decisions, but only because the goal is itself a form decision, i.e., "all streets to be sixty feet wide," or "all new growth to be in the form of satellite towns." These decisions are legitimate enough, but by failing to ask if there is a more general reason lying behind the decision, the range of form possibilities has been unnecessarily narrowed. Why sixty-foot streets? If we wish to allow for parking, how about off-street lots, or what if we substitute smaller cars?

Other objectives may be unrealizable, still others essentially irrelevant to city form. Some will be very narrowly motivated, the values of an individual or a small group being imputed to the whole community (as often happens in urban renewal or suburban zoning). Or the motives may be narrow in time, dealing only with the immediate present and its problems, so that the plan can do no more than react to immediate difficulties, and is unable to make choices for the future. Or if the goals are future-oriented, they may be rigidly fixed, without room for change as situation and aspiration change.

In many plans, the set of objectives is far from comprehensive; it includes few of the crucial values significantly affected by city form. The plan therefore may be rational but sub-optimal: it may ensure a fast highway system but a poor living environment. Thus we find solutions which are irrational, or sub-optimal, or vague, or determined by a few unspoken criteria for which the stated objectives are simply camouflaged.

We may therefore list a series of criteria to be met by any set of objectives for a city plan:

1. City form must be significantly relevant to the attainment of the objectives.

2. The objectives must be realizable within present and foreseeable resources.

3. They must be operational: explicit and connectible to city form, clearly stating what is desired, according to what performance indices. A crude test is: will the goal help to discriminate between possible choices?

4. Subject to the above, the objectives should be as general as possible, as far back from actual form decision as is still connectible to that decision. In other words, the goals should be capable of regulating action while affording a choice of means.

5. Since they refer to a dynamic and complex situation, the goals should have a similar form: they will refer to rates of change rather than to final states; they will be expressed as an interconnected set; and very likely they will themselves vary over time.

These goals may be set in an optimizing form ("lowest cost," "optimum climate"), or as satisficing statements ("at least 100 square feet per child"), or as simple incremental ones ("increase the available housing supply"). They may be in a positive or negative form ("prevent epidemics"). The latter are often easier to state, since problems are usually more obvious than possibilities.

These are the general rules, but because of my professional bias, I would add two more:

6. The objectives will be weighted toward those that affect the community as a whole, or large groups within the community, with emphasis on groups that are normally *less* vocal in community decisions. There will be a similar weighting toward longer periods of time and unborn generations: the future will be discounted less than by other advisers or decision-makers. Short-run or narrow objectives are quite important in studying actual city behavior and will tend to control the planning of special groups. They are less appropriate for the work of public agencies of long life.

7. Where possible, the scope of the goals will be expanded to be more nearly inclusive of all the major relevant values and problems of the community, in order to prevent sub-optimizing. Since expansion will always complicate the balancing problem, it cannot be pushed beyond the capacity of the decision process to handle complexity.

Now, if a set of objectives is to be usable, we need an indication of how its elements are to be weighed against each other, since conflicts are certain. There are many ways that this can be done in practice: by priority ranking (I want this first, then that, then that other); by relative weights (ranging from quantitative and precise, which is most rare, to customary and fuzzy); by reference to the existing situation (some gain permitted in every direction, but no existing area to be disadvantaged too much in relation to others); or by choosing to optimize one goal while all the others are set as constraints at some minimum level. All the goals may be set as desirable minimums, and any alternative accepted that satisfies them all. As a final and most common resort, the objectives are conceived as a check list of desires to be used in the review of alternatives, where the weighting decisions are made implicitly in the final choice.

This limits what city objectives may be, but it is far from determining them; nor have we said anything about how objectives are, might, or should be decided upon. It must be clear from the way the criteria are formulated that objectives do not spring out fullblown at the beginning of the planning process. There is a continuing interplay among objectives, possibilities, models, and plans. Attractive solutions, present conditions, and likely future developments suggest new objectives, and the working out of consequences will modify others. We need not proceed from objectives to solutions; it is equally reasonable to reverse the process. The intent is to establish an explicit connection between the two. Even then, we are leaving out of consideration the political process by which objectives are set.

Nevertheless, we have a first test by which to judge any statement of goals, a test which sets the conditions under which such a set can be applied to the evaluation of a solution. Very few sets that we could construct today would pass the test, particularly with regard to a comprehensive and weighted system. But we can begin.

Motives for City Building

Our first step is to look at the objectives that have motivated past and current city plans and that seem to meet our rules—ones that are relevant, realizable, operational and yet general, as well as community-oriented and fairly long-range. A summary of these, and of the effectiveness of solutions for them, is one way of describing the present state of the city-planning art. Here are the cases in which planners have tried to go beyond accommodation, prediction, or intuitive choice in order to achieve a city that was "better" for some particular reason. I have made a general list of them in Appendix A.

One group of these objectives has less relevance today, either because the objectives are no longer felt to be critical or because they no longer seem to be realizable by means of city form: military defense, magical protection, symbolic expression, the maintenance of supplies. Others are clearly important today, but we find either that they are not clearly expressed or that we do not know how to achieve them: minimum cost, amenity, visual orderliness, mental health, enhancing the sense of community, efficient production, economic and individual growth, flexibility, participation, choice. A third set of objectives does not fit within our rules; that is, it is not long-range or oriented to the whole community, and is thus not capable of generalization: strengthening the tax base, for example; resisting change or maintaining local values, in most cases; separating activities in many cases; maximizing individual profit; the creation and protection of political power. No one could pretend that these are not ruling motives in contemporary plans, or even that they are not at times effectively applied. Yet they do not fall within the family of general objectives which we seek.

We are left with a small group of current planning objectives, which abide by our rules and about whose connection to city form we have at least some knowledge. Foremost perhaps is the objective of accommodating required activities and linkages at some reasonable physical standard, on which there is a fair amount of empirical information. To this may be added the principle of equity. Another prime motive is the avoidance of catastrophe, nuisance, or friction. A third is to provide a rapid and convenient transport system, although we have yet much to learn about this. A fourth is to protect physical health, insofar as we understand its relation to environment. Finally, there is an attempt to reduce construction cost, but on a very crude basis. The list is brief, not world-shaking, and yet it has social importance.

Planning Achievement

Next we may ask how effective city plans have been in attaining such objectives. The question is ambiguous, since we speak of objectives in general versus achievements in general, but the comparison is informative. We have little systematic evidence of the actual effects of city-planning efforts, but it appears that planning achievements today are probably as limited as planning goals.

If we were to generalize on scanty evidence, we might say that in this country various short-run, limited effects have frequently been produced: a small shift in the tax base, a slowing or diversion of change, a realization of profit to a particular development. In addition, it is probable (if not proven) that planning efforts have often increased the coordination of development and speeded the accommodation of physical change to activity change. It is likely that plans have helped us to avoid some of the worst threats to health and the more obvious wastes of building resources, or the nuisances and uncertainties that may be generated by certain mixtures of use or by unpredictable change. Plans have been successfully applied to the control of new, rapid development, such as in the new towns, and in this case facility standards have been notably improved. Transportation times have been decreased on a piecemeal basis, if not over a whole city system. We have been able to increase the level of service in some areas, even if we are far from doing it systematically. Major park systems and the widespread provision of basic utilities have been achieved.

The general level of living has risen, including the quality of housing, but one cannot credit much of that to planning. Substantial areas of substandard environment remain largely untouched by public effort. We have no evidence of having had significant effect on social or mental health, or choice, or economic growth or efficiency, or flexibility.

Planning has often had side effects not specifically cited as governing motives: it has occasionally raised the level of political participation, brought conflicting agencies into coordinated action, enhanced a sense of community, or increased the interchange of information and the rationality of decision. To be equally truthful, it has often served to obstruct action, to camouflage it, or to decrease the flexibility of the system.

The gains, like the motives, are not spectacular. Neither are they contemptible. They are simply short of what might be hoped for from rational public action. By no means is all of this due to a lack of professional knowledge and skill: the planner is only a small part of a much larger system of decisions. But the lack of technical knowledge has some bearing on this.

A Case in Point: Philadelphia

To illustrate the objectives normally used and how they are connected to proposals, we might look at an example of current planning work in this country. I prefer to take an example that is recent, in the mainstream of planning practice, and good of its kind. One which meets these standards is the 1960 comprehensive plan for Philadelphia[3] prepared by one of the outstanding planning agencies in the country. Since I have no close knowledge of the city and no acquaintance with the constraints and motives that actually determined the various decisions, I will rely entirely on this single published report, the written document itself. This simplifies my problem, but would be a severe deficiency if I intended any final criticism of the plan or the planning process as they actually affect Philadelphia.

The report begins with a bow to the city's history, then goes directly to a cost analysis of the final recommendations: how much, when, for what, from what source. Next it covers a survey of the city's population, and makes a twenty-year forecast by age and sex (but without reference to class or ethnic composition). There is a similar forecast for the city's economy, and then a set of "general concepts," or basic objectives and assumptions. This general statement is followed by sections which give the recommended shape of future development, by broad functional classes, in the following order: industry, commerce, recreation and community facilities, residence, and transportation. Each section contains written text supplemented by various diagrams. The plan concludes with two large maps, one of existing land use, the other summarizing all the spatial features of the plan as a whole.

The order of presentation is normal, except that the cost consequences of the plan have been put first. Population and economy are the usual outside forces considered to be determining in a planning study.

There are no discussions of existing or future technology as it might affect the city, nor of the present or possible future pattern of political power (although it is likely that the technicians knew something of this), nor of the current aspirations of different groups. The economic forecast is a bald statement of inevitable events. The population forecast is more carefully hedged and, interestingly enough, has been modified by provisions of the plan itself.

The section on "general concepts" briefly discusses why a city grows as it does, and, half concealed within this, contains the principal motives of the plan. The most general one is to improve the access of people to facilities. Another is to bring these accessible facilities up to some standard of adequacy. Two others are to acquiesce in, or to clarify, or at least not to disturb, two "natural" principles of city form: that density of land occupation is a function of access, and that service areas and centers tend to have a hierarchical distribution.

In general, planning is considered to have a facilitating function: clarifying, sharpening, and making consistent some fundamental characteristics of normal city development, as well as compensating for the stresses of growth occurring in a relatively fixed environment.

Most of the succeeding sections of the plan follow this motif. The chapters on industry and commerce are predictions of probable future location and density, with some attempt to "smooth out" these future map patterns. The smoothing out of the commercial centers is influenced by the preference for hierarchical form. The industrial plan includes provisions for the renewal of obsolete industrial territories.

The plan for recreation is the first that is guided by overt objectives: primarily a set of minimum standards for the size and accessibility of various areas. The future location of community facilities (except schools, which are not discussed!) is guided by a preference for clustering them in hierarchical centers.

The plan for residence is the most radical. Based on density standards, quality standards, and ideas regarding the proper relation between density and access, it proposes a striking change: a sharp reduction in over-all density, and a radical rearrangement of the density pattern. This will be carried out principally by selective clearance. The proposal was powerful enough to cause the readjustment of the population forecast noted above. The proposed shifts in housing type, however, are reflections of forecasted changes in population composition. There is no mention of the problems of racial or income segregation.

Finally, the transportation plan follows the future use locations. Using some simple standards as to continuity, spacing, and capacity, assuming a street hierarchy and a typical street pattern, and within a bias toward public transit, a system is developed that is reasonable, consistent, and presumably capable of carrying the required loads.

From our standpoint, the interesting features of this plan are the relative modesty of its objectives and their lack of comprehensiveness (although many standards of safety, market demand, etc., have been used implicitly in the proposals). There is no mention of social problems, for example, or of political ones, or of the visual form of the city, or of future flexibility. Second, a single future target date has been used, without reference to staging, future direction, or possible future choices for the city. (The cost section, however, *is* process-oriented, since it considers the rate of expenditure. This reflects one of the strong features of current planning in Philadelphia: its systematic capital-budgeting system.) Third, explicit alternatives have not been prepared and evaluated—the plan seems to be inevitable. Fourth, some parts of the plan propose to cause important changes, while others are simply smoothed-out forecasts. Finally, while the plan is programmatically adequate, there is little to show that this is a plan for Philadelphia, which is in fact a very distinctive city.

I chose this plan as a good example of its type. Considering the complexity of the task, it is far from incompetent. Other plans would have other drawbacks, and usually more of them. I could, in fact, cite some of my own work in this respect. The report is an illustration of the state of the field, insofar as it is apparent from the study of a single publication, rather than of the ongoing planning process.

We could press further to discuss the function of published general plans in such an ongoing process: whether printed plans do or should reflect the real system of planning, whether they may have only a superficial and propagandistic role, and so on. Without going farther, I simply state my conviction that published general plans can play an important part in informing community decision, although they must in the future be presented in a more time-oriented, radical, and yet choiceful and comparative form. In any case, if such plans are published, they must reflect the ideas of the men that made them, or else they are fraudulent.

Planning Objectives Reconsidered

What can we do to increase the comprehensiveness and rationality of our planning? One natural step is to restate the objectives previously mentioned as a consistent primary set, that is, a set that meets all our rules and whose elements are primary because they are considered to be good in themselves, as well as mutually self-supporting. I would think of such concepts as survival, health, choice, development, meaning, engagement, equality, social efficiency.

There are a number of problems in operating with such a set. First, they are a shopping list, rather than a system. They appear because a substantial number of people would argue for them in a substantial number of cases. But each group in each concrete situation would have to construct a set appropriate for itself. The elements recur, but not in identical combinations. They may act as a useful checklist, or as a guide to research ("How is city form related to health?" for example), but not as a universal set of principles.

It is impossible to weight one element against another, at this abstract level. How is "personal choice in general" to be valued relative to "personal development in general," for example? In a particular case, people can make rapid decisions of this kind, and call the truant officer without hesitation.

As single words, these headings are meaningless. Each one must be much more carefully defined: choice of what? for whom? to what degree and at what rate? under what conditions? in what priority? how will it be recognized and measured? and so on. Indeed, the full meaning of such a general goal cannot be developed until we are confronted with a specific choice, with its limitations and concrete consequences.

There is also a real danger that such general objectives may be verbal and not design categories. That is, they may lump together sub-objectives that have verbal similarities but that do not refer to similar behavior or to similar physical means of satisfaction. Generalization of the goal-form relation will then be meaningless or impossible.

The intellectual obstacles to making tested connections between city form and such general goals are formidable. Nevertheless, some useful research may be made: in particular we want systematic studies of how our cities perform, and how people behave in them—a continuous feedback on how well we are achieving our general purposes. But there is a strong temptation in practice to sound these high notes as a beginning flourish, and then to get right down to the practical business of street widths and acreages. What may be more useful for some time is an *intermediate* level of objectives, general enough to give us some choice of means and a sense of the importance of what is being done and yet concrete enough to give us a way of testing the consequences in plan.

I suggest that the objectives I would call "formal" are the strategic ones. They refer directly to the characteristics of the desired city form rather than being couched purely in human terms, yet they are broad enough to allow a wide choice of means. For example, we might cite the goal of accessibility, a city form that optimizes the access of urban activities and locations to one another, a goal that was central to the Philadelphia plan. As one crude index of accessibility, we might measure and sum the time distance of all locations to all other locations in the given city and divide this sum by some index of size, such as the total number of activity locations. The city with the lowest quotient would have the highest internal accessibility. Such a quality is desirable because it presumably facilitates a number of primary objectives: choice, efficient production, least cost, stimulus, survival, development, and so on.

Therefore, we now look for formal correlates of the primary goals, preferably the correlates of several primary ones. An illustrative list of my own, with brief definitions and indications of how they are assumed to relate to the primary objectives, is given in Appendix B: accessibility, efficiency, adaptability, safety, stress, legibility, diversity, congruence, adequacy.

Such a list, incomplete and unstudied though it may be, avoids many of the problems connected with the primary goals. What is wanted can be more clearly stated, and the connection to form alternatives can be more easily analyzed. Real cities or models may be tested for performance, and the quality of proposals evaluated. While this is still a mere list, there will be more general agreement on the desirability of its elements, because they tend to support several primary objectives. It should prove easier to weight these desirable characteristics against each other, or to state them as minimums, optimums, or rates of change.

A considered statement of formal goals or performance characteristics might be a partial answer, then, to our original question. This is how we define a good city, for our time and place. The definition can be given in a way that includes how the characteristic is to be recognized or measured. It would be fascinating, but beyond our present scope, to compare real cities, as well as plans, for their performance under these headings. We have some understanding about congruence, levels of service, legibility, and safety, and these seem susceptible of more systematic study. Accessibility, resilience, and some aspects of comfort could also be analyzed rather directly. Other questions, like diversity, adaptability, and efficiency are equally interesting but much more difficult to manage.

Research into these formal, secondary objectives seems to be one of the more hopeful ways in which we can make our planning technically effective. We can study how these characteristics can be operationally defined, or how the list might be extended or revised. We can perform tests on models, or make comparative analyses of real cities to relate the achievement of these goals to various city patterns. We can innovate new patterns to facilitate them. We can study actual attitudes and behavior to see how far these characteristics correspond to desired city qualities or how they connect to more general objectives. This is not to say that continuing thought should not be given to the primary goals, more difficult but more fundamental. Nor will planning objectives be entirely included within these general categories: real cases will partly be decided by lesser objectives of tax base, power, or preservation. These must also be made open and explicit, with rational connections to form decisions. But work on the formal list may be extremely profitable, since these are likely to be sought-after qualities in great numbers of proposals.

Design Technique

We are not out of the woods yet. Even in a technical sense, we must be able to show that city-form alternatives can be generated and evaluated in terms of such a set of objectives. Assume that we have marshaled our knowledge about goal-form relations in as systematic a way as we can, and that, in a real case, we have developed a system of formal objectives. This system has some crude weights or rankings, it deals with rates of change, it is operational, fairly comprehensive, long-range, community-oriented. It has not appeared suddenly, but has developed through a long interplay among general values, surveys, public discussions, theoretical models, power struggles, tentative plans, past experience in execution, and so on. Since I am not dealing with the total planning process, but only with one step—a single run of the creation and evaluation of alternatives—I can neglect how these objectives arose. The designer has very often been involved in developing them—particularly in clarifying, suggesting, or reducing them to an operational statement—but it is less likely that he will have chosen them.

If this is a real case, these goals will be imprecise, and their interrelation and weighting will be vague and crude. My problem is: how do I proceed from this to a recommendation? I have already discussed the techniques planners use when they avoid the explicit use of objectives. What methods are available when objectives *are* given? Deterministic methods will not serve, since we are not optimizing one clearly defined variable within a set of definite constraints (although such studies may be of great use in exploring the consequences of single goals). Nor are we able to construct a single function that shows the interrelation of all values within a common unit of measure. We face the typical situation in large-scale design: objectives numerous, poorly related, and possibly shifting, constraints imperfectly known and changing, the range of alternatives limitless and not occurring along a single continuum; even the potential variables not certain.

The general method is to generate a finite series of alternatives and then to evaluate their differences in terms of the objectives. Perhaps the most commonly used technique is to pick up some comfortably finite number of alternatives (3 [and] 4 are magic numbers), by means that are essentially unconnected to the objectives themselves. The alternatives may be generated at random, or suggested by the existing situation, or developed by a subconscious creative process, or chosen from a stock of "type" solutions. Typically, some alternatives are quickly ruled out because they violate single objectives too markedly (fall below minimum standards). The remaining possibilities are than weighed "in balance," which means examining their relative ability to accomplish the given list of objectives, and then making an intuitive choice. Essentially, this last step consists in giving more accurate weights to the objectives, i.e., "now that I see it, I value the recreational possibilities here more than I do the added cost." However intuitive, the process is at least open to scrutiny. The alternatives may be used to give form to public discussion: sharpening, weighting, and perhaps helping to resolve conflicting goals.

In some cases it is possible to give precise form to the marginal differences in achievement between alternatives, particularly if achievement is judged in terms of performance characteristics. It may then be possible to weight the objectives quite explicitly for this particular conjunction of possibilities and thus to make a choice completely open to present and future testing. The marginal differences must include the financial, administrative, and social costs that must be paid to accomplish them (or the negative gains in other objectives). Most often, the analysis of implementation and its costs is done roughly, on the basis of experience and "reasonableness."

Further testing is left to a period of public debate and to the actual events that follow the beginning of action. The feedback from reality is usually quite slow, so that a city designer rarely learns from his own mistakes. Other designers may be able to make a sample device, try it out, and return to correct the original design. The city designer depends on hearsay, or his personal experience somewhere else.

New methods of checking the implementation of plans by simulating city growth are currently being developed. In such growth models, which use assumptions as to decision behavior and the changes in such factors as population and economy, a train of public actions can be tried out to see whether it leads to a hoped-for result. If the actions do not reach the expected results, either the proposed results or the proposed actions may be modified until they fit. The model may be used to generate a whole series of future alternatives, using alternative sets of likely public actions, or even of different assumptions about why cities change and grow. At this point, the marginal costs, benefits, and likelihoods of the alternatives may be weighed against each other. There may even be a time when we can run these models backward, from a future desired state through a set of actions in reverse, to see if we reach an existing situation! Since the models depend on whole trains of doubtful assumptions, they are at present unreliable, but their form can be successively improved. Their danger lies in their natural emphasis on quantifiable factors and the impression of massive inevitability they may convey to the unwary observer.

One difficulty encountered in generating alternatives is well known to the designer. The search for possibilities is arduous, and when one is found and elaborated, its creator has made a large personal investment in it. Having succeeded once, he is committed to his success and is unwilling to try again. Often he will believe that any other workable plan is impossible, and attack it if it is presented. This effect is particularly sharp in complex design. Severe self-discipline, or methods of speeding the design search, are required to escape it. One useful social device is the competition, or dispersed-team solution, in which each man is expected to come up with only one solution, and the total effort produces the set of alternatives.

A more systematic possibility is to use some mechanical device, perhaps a computer, to try out all the combinations of a set of variables. Having given the machine a group of constraints, a set of variables with their permissible ranges, and a set of sufficing objectives as minimum standards, you ask it to give you all the possibilities within those limits that meet the standards. Most of these possibilities will be monsters, because you have forgotten to instruct the helpful idiot about the more subtle rules of the game, but presumably you will have everything within the machine's limited field of vision. The complexity and subtlety of city form makes it unlikely that many useful new possibilities would appear from such a mechanical process, but it might be worth a try.

Is there any way of looking more directly for the desired alternatives? Many creative designers will use the technique of "seizing the essential." They simplify a complex problem by choosing one goal or characteristic as being the primary one and bend all their energies to a search for an optimum solution to this one characteristic, be it the "primary" function, the "essential" character of the terrain, or the "key" symbolic expression. Other factors are considered only insofar as they are "reasonably" satisfied. This is of course the intuitive correlate of the method to optimizing one variable within a set of constraints. It is a telling way of exploring the consequences of optimizing one thing, and produces plans that are admired for their force, clarity, and consistency. It is a technique often used in architecture, or other design fields where the function is not as complex as in a city. But there is no guarantee that it will optimize a total system of objectives, unless this system is in fact dominated by one overriding goal. This is a rare occurrence in city design.

Other designers will use an incremental process: once a possible form is stumbled upon, they will let it "grow of itself." That is, incremental changes will be tried out that are suggested by the latent features of the original form, exaggerating, developing, or systematically transforming them until an interesting possibility is uncovered. If no such possibility appears, that line of development will be abandoned, and a new starting point will be sought.

This incremental process may be extended outside the design process itself, particularly where the consequences of actions are as imperfectly known as they are in cities. In this case, incremental changes are tried out in the real world on an experimental basis, and, if they succeed, are enlarged upon and transformed in the search for better solutions.

Perhaps the most rational of the current methods of design is that eclectic one which begins by generating alternatives for single goals, plus partial solutions for small areas or for single functions of the whole, plus solutions suggested by the existing situation, plus known stereotypes, plus random formal play incrementally developed. This cloud of disconnected, partial alternatives is then gradually woven into a small number of comprehensive alternatives, which are gradually developed and refined, with much preliminary evaluation and recasting of parts, with many an anxious search for missed opportunities, and frequent returns to the beginning. When these alternatives are thought to be in preliminary form, they are evaluated for their marginal effects on the given objectives, and the chosen alternative or alternatives are further developed.[4]

This is a time-consuming process, but it pays off in the thoroughness of search, and in the form in which alternatives are presented for evaluation. It should be noted that this technique includes a great deal of detailed decision-making—evaluation, rejection, refitting—as an integral part of developing the basic alternatives, and long before a formal and explicit decision between possibilities is made. In fact, this is true of the design process in general—the designer limits the scope of the final decision by many quite personal and subjective prior decisions. Yet in so doing he has short circuited some of the problems involved in complex decisions. By his cyclical, tentative method of design search, he deals directly with the fluidity and ambiguity of objectives and conditions, and prepares the ground for explicit judgment.

In any of these methods, much depends on the personal abilities of those who are developing the alternatives. The creative process is in part a learned one, but it is traditionally learned by experience and emulation rather than by any formal, communicable steps. Some techniques for freeing the creative flow have recently been developed, including group brainstorming and the systematic use of unusual analogies.[5] The enlargement of our range of choice in city form, by means of form play and creative innovation, is of first importance. Here the skill of the designer is irreplaceable.

One possible new technique of design is the "decision tree."[6] In this case, all the ruling objectives and standards are listed exhaustively, instead of being confined to the major ones. They are broken down into as many sub-parts as possible, i.e., "cost of rough grading to be minimized," or "newly formed families of low income to have at least three types of housing to choose from." Single-valued solutions are then sought for each sub-objective, where that objective is optimized within some very low standard of reasonableness for other characteristics. Each solution is developed by the method of "seizing the essential," but even more heavily caricatured solutions are chosen.

Each ideal but partial design is then confronted with one other, and conflicts between the pairs resolved to establish a balanced compromise. Each solution that resolves a pair of solutions is now confronted with another partial solution, and they are in turn resolved. Thus the design proceeds step by step up a whole "tree" of decisions, beginning with a large number of partial solutions, and ending in a single resolution which in some way reflects all the numerous goals and standards. Yet each step of the way has been only a relatively easy resolution of a pair of forms. Members of the various parts can be weighted as desired, according to the relative importance of the goals.

This method depends on the assumption that a step-by-step solution is much better than one arising from a simultaneous consideration of several objectives. This may or may not be true; it is certainly easier. The order in which the pairs of solutions are confronted with each other is crucial, since a different order produces a different end product. The recommended strategy deals with the sharpest conflicts first; that is, subobjectives are grouped for initial compromise so that the resulting group solutions will be found to be relatively independent of each other when final syntheses are made. The crucial decisions are made early.

This is one interesting effort to clarify the process of generating and evaluating complex alternatives. It may be possible to conceive of still other strategies: perhaps there is a way of exploring a continuous system of alternatives that occurs once a set of interconnected variables and constraints is defined. Here we are not looking for single alternatives chosen more or less at random from the continuum, but for the breakpoints, the sudden changes in the rate of satisfaction that occur when this system of alternatives is considered in the light of a system of interconnected objectives. Once the breakpoints are known, one can look for the highest peak, or just any peak that rises above a certain level, in a more rational way. Strategies for directing goal-seeking systems presently being developed in other fields may one day be applicable to city design: rules for continuously modifying solutions in the direction of improvement, and for searching for disconnected peaks.

Another new aid on the horizon is the computer, which is already being used for routine tasks of data storage in city planning, and could undoubtedly be used to search mechanically for workable combinations of variables whose nature and range have been precisely defined. It will probably be used in much more important ways, however, as present capabilities for graphic input and output are refined. The planner can begin to design in direct conjunction with the computer, suggesting solutions whose consequences the machine rapidly develops, or asking for the possibilities of a certain kind, which the machine quickly presents for review and revision. He may even ask the device to evaluate partially certain solutions for him, according to those criteria which can be put in precise form. The designer is *not* being replaced, he is being freed from many detailed operations that presently limit the number of alternatives he can consider.

The direct coupling of man and computer will effectively broaden and deepen the cyclical, tentative, eclectic method.

Meanwhile, the eclectic technique of generating likely alternatives is already developed, however little used in city design today. It can be expanded or compressed according to the resources available—it can "learn," producing a richer and more effective set of alternatives as experience and possibilities develop. It is an important adjunct to a set of operational "formal" objectives, to the use of the growth model, and to the technique of evaluation of limited choices by considering marginal differences. It is partly because of the theoretical neglect of this step in the decision process—the possibilities and problems in generating alternatives—that complex decisions often become hopelessly irrational.

Even competent designers are often oppressed by the difficulties of the design process, and look hopefully for traditions, or fixed requirements, which limit their responsibility for search. But many restraints are transient or superficial (as in the city design which was partly based on the length of a standard fire hose!). Technical advance is constantly weakening the grip of such limitations, or shifts them from one factor to another. Cultural traditions, habitual ways of doing things, no longer furnish a powerful directive.

Restraints, like purposes, are not immutable; they refer to a particular situation. Within his limits of time and knowledge, the designer must not avoid the choice of purpose and the broad search for possibilities. Psychologically painful though it may be, I prefer to emphasize purpose while remembering restraints [rather] than to emphasize restraints while remembering purpose.

Fluidity

We are faced with still another technical problem, in addition to those of the multiplicity of objectives and alternatives. Plans have traditionally been conceived of as targets, that is, as states to be achieved after a given length of time. The normative words themselves—goal, objective, aim, end—connote fixation on an ultimate reward. This conception is appropriate to the architectural or project scale, where development is episodic: a revolutionary period of construction is followed by a longer period of physical conservation. However, it is not appropriate to the constant cyclical and secular change of a city.

In an unsophisticated city plan, the recommended solution is thought of as a final state, which is impossible. Even a designer who is aware of the continuous flux of the city must unfortunately use a static graphic device to indicate a momentary state, a slice of future time. Sometimes the plan will include several successive slices: it will be a staged plan. Even such staged plans are most often developed first as a plan for the "key" period (two, five, twenty years away), and then the preceding and succeeding stages are elaborated. Each stage will be thought of as suddenly frozen, somehow freed from rate and direction of change.

What we require instead is easy to describe but most difficult to develop: a technique of preparing and evaluating a set of continuous alternatives, presenting processes of development much as motion pictures might do it, judged for the way they satisfy a changing set of criteria throughout an entire time period. Even more, these plans should change their precision as they proceed further forward in time, as a result of the increasing uncertainty of prediction.

For the time being, lacking such a technique of dynamic planning, we use the substitute method of staging, making future stages more diagrammatic, and perhaps developing a limited number of possible future branches for each basic alternative. This requires constant reminders that these are approximations to reality. One corrective is to add to each stage symbols that describe the process of change going on at that moment. Another corrective is to generate the stages in many ways: not only from a key point outward, but also from the immediate present forward, and from the distant future backward. Solutions can also be visualized as a general "shape" of development process: crescendo, pulsation, cataclysm.

Here again the computer may prove useful: perhaps it will be able to put together and present motion pictures of diagrammatic development from rough indications, and help in evaluating them according to a system of objectives which is itself changing over time. If the underlying difficulty of planning in process terms is the sheer time consumed by it, then such mechanical aids will be of real value.

Planning Theory

We seek greater knowledge of how the form of a city relates to our objectives, and better techniques of design for utilizing this knowledge. Both of these are only parts of a more general body of potential knowledge: a comprehensive theory of city form on the one hand, and of the planning process on the other. We can only characterize them here in passing, to illustrate how our subject of discussion fits into a larger context.

A general theory of city form, today nonexistent, would deal with the interaction between city form and human behavior: how a city is shaped by social events and conditions, and how it in turn modifies them, in a constant interchange. There are contributing streams which have begun to prepare the way for such a theory: ecology and cultural anthropology, urban history, locational economics and the recent attempts at the simulation of urban growth, various ideas from utopian and innovative design, plus a scattered literature on the results of certain form changes or conditions (on such various topics as perception, mental health, social relations, climate, cost, and transport efficiency). Not only is this material scattered, but we lack organizing concepts with which to bring it into one structure.

Studies of the planning process are further advanced, since these are of interest to other fields intellectually more mature than city planning. Here we are dealing with such questions as how objectives are formulated, the role and limits of intelligence, the process of generating and evaluating alternatives, decision-making, implementation, the role of irrationality, the presence of multiple planning and decision systems, and how all these processes are interlocked in a constantly interacting whole.

For our purposes, both these lines of thought should be brought together in a single body of knowledge, explaining how the various imperfectly informed actors in the city seek to realize their objectives by using or changing city form, how city form changes as a result, how this affects the achievement of the various objectives, how both objectives and constraints shift accordingly, and how the process continues in constant cyclical interaction.

This is the theoretical base we would like to have. What we have been discussing is only one event in the process: the actions of the designer in a single planning system, a planning system that can bring considerable weight to bear and can afford to hold comparatively long-range, community-oriented goals. If this community-oriented planning system is to be effective, the planning designer must be engaged in what might be called "continuous design." Ideally, there will be continuous revision, an ever-developing basis for current decisions. Practically, because of the same technical limitations that constrain us to use the staged plan, the general set of alternatives is more likely to be overhauled episodically, part by part, or level by level.

The Planning Art

What a long way round from the original question, and no answer in sight! Perhaps no direct answer was needed. As in other design fields, the conception of an "ideal form" is a dead end. What counts is the artistic mastery that can be applied to each new situation. For city design is an art, and not a science, however heavy its intellectual apparatus. Its focus is creative innovation and subtle evaluation. For all our shortcomings in designing and judging cities, rough techniques already exist, and better are in sight. In time, city design may master its subject matter sufficiently to become a great art.

We can already talk of style in city design, arising from common goals and circumstances, and a common artistic technique. Even now we have some rules of thumb with which to confront a new city proposal:

Are the objectives clearly put, do they satisfy our original criteria? Do they deal with some of today's critical problems: segregation, poverty, congestion, growth, visual form, health? Were they applied to the choice of alternatives? Does the proposal have variety, choice, fine texture—a sense of city scale and complexity? Is there a mark of uniqueness, of special place? Is the plan part of a process in time, does it have direction and pace? Is it programmatically adequate: does it provide sufficient space and facilities for basic activities, for family living, recreation, and public services in particular? Is the transportation system fast, choiceful, adequate? Is there a sense of legible form at the city scale: visually vivid parts visually related to each in the ground-level view?

These are subjective rules, derived from the performance characteristics and the nature of planning design. They will not substitute for a systematic evaluation of the plan and the process that produced it. But they are often useful in that rapid evaluation which is so commonly used in judging other works of art, but which seems to be so baffling when one is presented with a city proposal.

It must be obvious that our inabilities in city design are not simply technical ones. There are social conditions, attitudes, and powers that frustrate us. Yet if our technical skill and knowledge were more comprehensive, we could see our path and define the social obstacles more clearly. Indeed if we really know how to build cities of high accessibility or great flexibility, ones which promoted mental health or individual development, or increased men's opportunities, we might be moved to change some of those social conditions.

We have evidence that reliance on the private market, with all its imperfections, inequities, and disregard for community goods, is a poor way of improving our cities. Existing problems are glaring; we are technically capable of ameliorating some of them. Despite the dispersion of values and decisions (and partly because of it), there are effective ways for public agencies with more general objectives to intervene in the city-building process.

Complex decisions in our society are fragmented, serial, are restricted in the final evaluation to a limited number of concrete choices. But our objectives do not have to be so pitifully restricted in scope. There are close limits to our ability to predict the consequences of our actions, but this need not confine us to proposing small incremental changes, since the future effects of an incremental series are at times as hard to predict as a jump. Continuous design, the marginal evaluation of finite choices, experimental and exploratory action, the use of predictive growth models, [and] theoretical analyses of city development or the consequences of city form are all useful ways of confronting uncertainty. In a doubtful situation, one can often prescribe more accurately than one can predict.

City planning is a little child, but little children learn fast. Indeed, this one will have to. For all its youth, it has occasionally done an adult job. At a comparable stage in its development, how well would any profession fare in a similar review of its methods, aims and accomplishments?

Effective goals for our cities can be set today, simplified versions of the general performance characteristics: minimum standards of accessibility, public service, housing choice, open land, pollution control, safety, visual legibility. It would be possible to measure our cities against them, and to develop public strategies to move toward their achievement. Similarly, a number of potential public actions or control devices await trial and analysis.

There are features of our economic and social system which prevent us from attaining even such simple goals, but these features are not eternally fastened on us. Technically, at any rate, we can say something pertinent about the value of a city design, although what we say will be inseparable from an analysis of the arts of planning and complex decision.

Appendix A: City Planning Objectives, Past and Present

Those primarily of historical relevance:

1. Military objectives are primarily those of defense, or the establishment of a base for attack. Among the prime motives in historical city building, they governed the founding of new settlements, the siting of cities, and the form of certain elements: city wall, density, street pattern. With our present capacities for mutual extermination, these considerations seem irrelevant.

2. The maintenance of essential supplies (food in particular) governed many decisions in the past as to city size or location, the provision of open space within the walls, etc. While starvation is still with us, city form now has little direct connection to it. It seems that huge metropolitan areas, many times the size of our largest, could easily be fed and watered.

3. Many historic cities were shaped for magical reasons: orientations and forms were used that were meant to protect society, maintain celestial harmony, or promote human fertility. We have no evidence of successful performance except in the reassurance it afforded the believer.

4. Many cities have taken their particular form for symbolic reasons: their visible shapes were meant to awe and remind: to stand for the government, the community, religious beliefs, or other dominant values. This has been a potent drive in city planning up to relatively recent times. It still affects the design of special governmental centers like Brasilia. However important this motive may be, we find it increasingly difficult, in a diverse

society, to decide whose values should be symbolized. Symbolism is left to the component parts of society, and the resulting visual clash is in its own way symbolic of our time.

Other planning motives have greater relevance today:

5. Housing the required activities at some satisfactory standard of accommodation and accessibility controls many contemporary city plans. Many studies have been made of linkages and standards of accommodation, and while some of this knowledge is static and empirical, it constitutes the largest body of information in the field. A critical addition to this statement is the principle of equity: that facilities be provided which are not only adequate but in some way justly distributed. Justice may mean material equality between individuals, or equality of opportunity, or distribution according to some scale of contribution, rank, or need. Major disputes develop over these conflicting notions of justice. Often enough, real distributions have little resemblance to professions on this score.

(a) A sub-category of this objective is to house activities under conditions of rapid growth or scanty administrative resources. Military camps and boom towns have met these conditions by standardizing parts and controlling a minimum of key factors: street lines, water lines, the survey grid. This had become a critical need in fast-growing cities in underdeveloped areas, where the data and technicians needed for effective control are almost nonexistent. We would like to know more about the crucial form elements that the community must control in this case.

6. The avoidance of nuisance, friction, or "incompatibility" may be in the general social interest ("keep through traffic off residential streets"), or more narrowly motivated ("keep that kind of people out"), but it is a powerful determinant of city plans. It contributes to the planner's vice of thinking in exclusive categories. Sometimes it is rational, sometimes less so (certain kinds of housing and manufacturing mix very well, for example). This type of motive appeals strongly to local planning groups, but requires careful analysis.

7. The prevention of catastrophe (fire, flood, epidemic, major accidents) is a clear motive when not stated as an absolute, but as a level of acceptable risk. We know something about achieving it through construction, density, siting, water supply, etc. It is the exceptional case, however, in which this is the crucial motive in choosing among city alternatives.

8. The minimization of transport costs in terms of money, time, and convenience is a dominant objective in current city plans, and has clear connections with other values, such as economic efficiency or choice. The difficulty is that we know something about minimizing time on single elements such as a highway, but we are still green about minimizing travel time in a total system serving a changing activity pattern. This is a surprising gap, but strenuous efforts are currently being made to close it.

Then we come to a number of relevant and often cited goals, about which our information is far from decisive:

9. The minimization of first or maintenance costs of the physical city as a whole is obviously desirable—the surprising thing is our ignorance about it. Something is known about costs of standard types of facilities, but practically nothing about how total city form affects cost. This is an obvious opening for research, but the analysis is tricky.

10. A major economic motive in planning is to build cities that are locales of efficient production, thereby raising the material level of society. There is a body of knowledge about the interregional location of production in its relation to efficiency. There is other data about site planning for efficient production or distribution. On the city level, there is an assumption that an efficient city transportation system (objective 8), plus the provision of adequate space, utilities, etc. (objective 5), will be conducive to efficient production. We have little further evidence of how the spatial pattern of the city relates to efficiency.

11. Another important goal is that of economic growth: providing an environment that attracts labor and capital and stimulates enterprise or the improvement of technology. This is a critical motive throughout the world, but particularly in the underdeveloped areas. It has long been valued; many medieval new towns were planned for just this purpose. Some interesting new information is beginning to appear on this subject: perhaps the city environment itself, or city size and location in particular, has something to do with growth stimulation.

12. Allied to the motive of growth, but more general, is the desire to make a plan flexible, to allow for future change with as little disruption as possible. This is often spoken of in planning reports, but with little comprehension of how to bring it about. Many of the techniques used to achieve it (making future proposals vague, for example) probably have nothing to do with it. While it is possible to provide for near-future changes of known direction, we can say rather little about general flexibility beyond a few broad assumptions about low density, growth zoning, good communications, or open form.[7] Here is an area wide open for study.

13. Another kind of growth, a more important one, is the development of the individual: intellectual, moral, artistic, emotional, physical, or in terms of specific skills. We build schools for one kind of growth but are far from understanding what aspects of the general environment are conducive to growth. The growth-facilitating environment is capable of partial study, at least, and this should prove productive.

14. Mental and physical health, which most people would agree is important, is often cited in reports. It is clearly interrelated with growth and development. We have some knowledge about maintaining gross physical health in cities, have exploded some old myths on the subject,

and are learning new things, such as the effect of air pollution. But these are not often decisive objectives in city design, because of our ignorance of some of the more subtle and probably more critical ways in which cities affect health. What is the relation between city form and mental health? We wish we knew. If work on the behavior of the mentally ill in architectural spaces can be expanded to the observation of normal behavior in the city, we may begin to hope.

15. Most planning reports will give choice as a major objective: increasing the citizen's choices of life style, facilities, work, or recreation. The objective is vaguely put and does not usually determine any major decisions in the plan, except as it is used to back up the provision of facilities to house activities at standards set by the market. That is, if people are buying suburban houses, let them exercise that choice by providing space for such houses in the plan. Choice for the population in general is at times confused with free choice for the real estate developer. With more careful definition, choice could become an operational criterion.

16. Engagement or participation is an allied motive: the democratic desire that an individual be actively engaged in society, that he participate in its decisions and activities. In regard to the physical environment, this can take two forms:

(a) an urban pattern consistent with a political and social organization in which it is easy and attractive for the individual to participate; or

(b) physical forms which because of their plasticity or small size are easy for the individual or a small group to change by their own efforts.

How to achieve the first (and more profound) motive is not clear; the latter is easier. The general motive may have a more critical bearing on the way city decisions are arrived at, rather than on the forms to be decided on.

17. Partly in support of participation, but also for its own sake, enhancing the sense of community is another valued goal: building stable, well-knit, intercommunicating social groups, with a sense of common identity. This has been a major driving force behind many city plans, which employ neighborhood units, satellite towns, greenbelts, greenways, and activity centers to accomplish this end. Following on a number of community studies, however, we are no longer so sure that these physical provisions are determining. The physical environment seems to play a minor facilitating role once certain social conditions have been set (homogeneity, social isolation, particular class or culture, stability). Questions have been raised as to whether strong local neighborhoods are possible in our big cities for any but minority groups, or even whether they are desirable.

(a) A sub-category of this objective is that these local communities be *balanced* ones, i.e., that they contain as wide a range of social groups and activities as possible. This qualification is inserted in the hope that the community will thereby become even more self-centered, since all needed activities can be found there, and also avoid the isolation of social classes that might otherwise occur. The designer is then confronted with a dilemma in that, to the extent there are a variety of social groups in a locality, the possibility of a strong intercommunicating community is weakened. Moreover, it seems highly unlikely in the modern urban economy that people will work, live, shop, and enjoy leisure time in the same area. The planner may then back off from the community idea, and simply try to ensure that activities and services are close at hand if wanted, and that different social groups are within sight of each other, allowing possible intercommunication.

18. A sense of orderliness, harmony, or visual control has been a common motive in city design and remains so. One is never sure whether harmony in the mind of the designer is what is wanted, or simple order on paper, or perceived order on the ground. Until this motive is clarified (see #6, Appendix B), it is a dubious one, however much it influences actual decisions.

19. Amenity is repeatedly referred to, a word whose usefulness resides in its vagueness. It refers to being pleasant, agreeable, comfortable, or convenient, usually in some conventional way. It may be taken as "avoidance of the inappropriate." It mixes a host of qualities, definable and elusive. The word is useful in debate, but hopeless in analysis.

Our original criteria excluded objectives not oriented to the whole community. If we relax them, we discover the following objectives, some open, some covert.

20. Strengthening the local tax base is often a goal, i.e., diverting new development from one locality to another, so that the locality to which it is diverted can maximize its tax revenue. This is normally a gain for one group at a corresponding loss for another, and arises because of a particular tax structure. It cannot be stated as a general objective. Nevertheless, it is a very real motive that determines many planning and renewal projects.

21. Another important motive is resistance to change, the maintenance of the existing character of a locality. This is described in many ways, but usually implies a policy of exclusion (discouraging development, keeping densities low and housing expensive, keeping out "undesirables"), or a policy of keeping existing activities from leaving an area (stabilizing the center, preventing industrial shifts). In some cases, when one is preserving some unique character that adds to the range of diversification (a historical district, an area of unique topography or use) or when one hopes to convert disruptive change into a smooth and orderly process, these motives may represent the interest of the general community. More often they favor small local groups at the expense of the whole. For all that, or because of that, they are important drives behind many plans. We have rarely been successful in preventing change, but have frequently succeeded in diverting or delaying it.

22. A proposal will be shaped to increase the profit possibilities for a given developer, land owner, or commercial entrepreneur. This may take the form of an attempt to maximize general profitability (see objective 10), or an unacknowledged set of decisions to increase densities in particular locations, to favor certain land areas, or to create monopoly locations.

23. The maintenance and increase of power or control has often been a motive in cities designed to regulate subject populations, facilitate policing or riot control, or increase royal power. This can be a major motive today, as in South Africa. Removal of the political capital from heavily populated cities may also be based on this consideration. It is quite common in any country for plans to be influenced for reasons of political power: voting populations to be maintained, development authorities created or resisted, and so on. It is not fashionable to acknowledge these considerations in a report.

Appendix B: Formal Goals, or Performance Characteristics

The following list is an attempt to indicate a series of criteria, relevant to city form today, which:

(a) may be stated quantitatively, or will in some other way allow the comparative evaluation of two particular city patterns:

(b) can be defined and tested in terms of the spatial pattern of physical form and activity, given assumptions as to technology, society, environmental setting, etc.;

(c) seem to correlate very frequently with more fundamental human goals;

(d) and, subject to the above, are as general as possible.

In a few cases, these criteria might be stated as optima, for particular conditions. More likely, they will be stated as minimum standards, or as desired rates of increase of a quality, or simply as the increase or maintenance of an existing level. Quite often, without making any general statement of desirable achievement, planning choices will be based on the marginal differences in performance characteristics occurring between concrete alternatives. In all these cases, a more general knowledge of how these qualities could be defined and what they imply for city form would be extremely useful.

1. *Accessibility*: the cost in time or effort to move or communicate between activity locations; the possibility of interaction, or choice of mode of communication. This could be defined in various ways, many of them quantitative. It seems to be a fundamental criterion of city form, which apparently facilitates many primary goals: survival, choice, development, economic efficiency, etc.

2. *Adequacy*: the amount and availability of facilities of an acceptable quality—housing, schools, recreation, shopping, etc. Here we are in-

volved with standards, many of which have been developed in fragmentary form, more or less reliably, and with more or less reference to the primary objectives on which they are based. The standards must deal, not only with global quantities, but with availability and choice on a local basis. Principles of equity must be included. Such standards necessarily shift from place to place, and time to time.

3. *Congruence*: the fit of the system, the coordination of parts in operation. This may include the correspondence of physical facilities to the activities housed within them, the fit of circulation capacity to flow, or the match between the visible form of a city and its functioning. There is fairly abundant data on the congruence of form and activity, but work on visual congruence is just beginning.

4. *Diversity*: the range of variation of facilities, qualities, and activities, and the spatial mix of this variation. There may be an optimum level of such range and mix which is conducive to choice, development, and perhaps other objectives. While it is often used as an intuitive criterion in judging the "richness" of a city, there is very little solid information as to how to measure this criterion, or what the optima are.

5. *Adaptability*: the ability of an environment to adapt to new functions at minimum cost. New functions may be foreseen, in which case the form may be designed specifically for that future transformation. If future changes are unpredictable, generalized adaptability is desirable, a quality much discussed but little understood. We can draw some analogies from experience, but this is a very difficult characteristic to recognize or measure.

(a) One special aspect of this is *resilience*: the ability of the city system to absorb sudden stress, avoid breakdown, or recover from it rapidly. In the technical sense, this is the "health" of the city. What city forms recover most easily from a major fire, explosion, flood, earthquake, epidemic, riot, traffic breakdown, or massive shift of function? We have little knowledge of this, but many interesting studies could be made, in actual cases or via models.

(b) An additional special aspect is *openness*: the degree to which the environment can be easily modified or used in alternate ways by the individual or by small groups.

6. *Legibility*, a perceptual characteristic: a sensuous form that is vividly differentiated and easily structured, making a pattern that is continuous in time and space, producing a strong image. Primarily, this is instrumental to the goal of meaning, but also has connections to such values as development, engagement, choice, perhaps to mental health and accessibility. We have lately been clarifying this goal and analyzing its form implications. It is a necessary (but not inclusive) component of a more fundamental value, *beauty*, which is notoriously difficult to define for large communities.

7. *Safety*: the degree to which the city form tends to reduce the incidence of accidents, disease, death, or other calamities. This is frequently cited, and we have some substantial if unorganized knowledge about various aspects of it, particularly in regard to traffic safety and epidemics. This knowledge can be broadened, but setting the acceptable level of risk is difficult.

8. *Stress*: an environment that places neither unduly much nor unduly little physiological or psychological stress on the individual, in regard to climate, effort, perceptual stimulus, etc. Some parts of this objective (such as standards in regard to climate) seem to be widely held values susceptible of definite analysis and prescription. Other aspects are much more difficult to define.

9. *Efficiency* of the city system itself, the balancing and limiting criterion: maximum benefit in terms of the other objectives at a given cost of building and operating the city, or minimum cost at a given level of achievement. It cannot be defined except in relation to other goals, but is of obvious importance. We know something about construction and maintenance costs for elements of the city system, almost nothing about comparative costs of whole systems. Our knowledge of the social and administrative costs of various patterns is also very incomplete. The problem of relating total costs to the entire complex of valued things is by no means easy.

Notes

1. By "city form" I mean the spatial arrangement of physical structures and spaces, and of localized activities and flows at the scale of the community or urban region.

2. Perhaps a more consistent laissez-faire position would require the suppression of other public agencies, such as highway authorities, which operate outside the private market.

3. *Comprehensive Plan: the Physical Development Plan for the City of Philadelphia* (City of Philadelphia, 1960).

4. For a description of this process at another scale, see Lynch, *Site Planning* (Cambridge, Mass.: MIT Press, 1961), chapter 8.

5. See William J. J. Gordon, *Synectics, the Development of Creative Capacity* (New York: Harper's, 1961).

6. See Christopher Alexander, *Notes on the Synthesis of Form* (Cambridge, Mass.: Harvard University Press, 1964).

7. For a generalized discussion of these, see K. Lynch, "Environmental Adaptability" [included in this volume].

Although Kevin Lynch had a strong interest in theory and the ideal environment, he had an equally strong commitment to applying his ideas to actual planning problems. Throughout his career he was engaged in professional practice, acting as a consultant to many public planning agencies and to private planning and design firms. This part of the volume presents some of his theoretical work that makes strong connections with practice. We also include a piece on city design education.

In the first article, "City Design and City Appearance," Lynch explains what he means by city design and then goes on to suggest how a public agency might conduct city design—how to organize for it, how to implement it, and what kinds of problems to address. Throughout he emphasizes that design should not and cannot be separate from other aspects of a problem, that it is not pure esthetics or cosmetics to be tacked on at the end. A later article, "The Immature Arts of City Design," asks whether city design can be an art and discusses its relations to architecture and landscape architecture.

Also included here are two rather comprehensive articles written for two different sources: the *Encyclopaedia Britannica* and the *Enciclopedia Italiana*. Although written as authoritative accounts, they are not necessarily encyclopedic in tone. The article on urban design, for example, begins with Lynch's personal views of where and why urban design has failed. But he then proceeds to discuss the scope, the objectives, the social context, the typical problems, and the historical visions of urban design. The article written for the Italian encyclopedia is even more of a personal view of city and regional planning, and perhaps one of the relatively rare occasions where Lynch specifically addressed himself to the problems of urbanization and the challenges for planning. This article has been abridged; the themes that have been covered elsewhere in Lynch's essays have been left out.

Highways have typically been designed according to engineering standards, with little or no consideration of their visual form or impact.

"Sensuous Criteria for Highway Design," written with Donald Appleyard, explores the possible positive experiences a highway might have for its users and abutters and suggests standards for its design that address their needs. This is an extension of an earlier work, *The View From The Road*, in which Lynch and his colleagues took the position that properly designed highways could be a positive element in the perceptual form of cities. Unfortunately, it seems that Lynch and Appleyard's work in this area has not yet had much influence, for highways continue to be built with little awareness of their environmental consequences and potentials.

In "Designing and Managing the Strip," Lynch and Southworth study another problematic element of the American urban landscape, the commercial strip. Like the highway, it is typically poorly planned— or totally unplanned—with little consideration of how it might be improved. The study examines the strip from the points of view of its various users and their needs, and then suggests standards and patterns for improving it.

Lynch was always uncomfortable with pure historic preservation, although he felt that the expression of time in the environment was at least as important as the spatial image. In "On Historic Preservation: Some Comments on the Polish-American Seminar" he reports on his mid-1970s visit to Poland, where preservation is a well-organized and significant public activity. Although impressed with the technical competence of the Polish preservationists, he questions what they have chosen to preserve and how meaningful it is to the people. These ideas are taken further in the concise and provocative article "The Image of Time and Place in Environmental Design," which draws on the Polish visit but then goes on to question the motives for preservation and what should be preserved, with specific suggestions for Boston's Copley Square. How can the past be made more relevant and meaningful to the public? Many of these ideas were extensions of Lynch's book *What Time Is This Place?* (1972).

Two of the items included here have to do with the design of new towns, which were much in vogue in the 1960s. Lynch was invited to visit Venezuela and comment on the Ciudad Guayana design and planning process then being undertaken by an interdisciplinary group of academics assembled by the Harvard-MIT Joint Center for Urban Studies for the Corporación Venezuela Guayana, an autonomous development authority set up by the national government. Although his visit was short, Lynch, with his uncanny ability to quickly get to the heart of the problem, made some insightful observations about the nature of the design and implementation process, as well as about the central design concept being pursued at that time. One of the things he found untenable about the process was that the designers were based in Caracas and physically removed from the site. Lynch's comments on "A Manual for Site Development: Columbia, Maryland" grew out of his consulting work with the Columbia new town planning team, headed at that time by Morton Hoppenfeld. Although Lynch was involved to some extent in the development of the design guidelines for site development, his comments are quite critical in tone, questioning underlying assumptions at some places and regretting lost opportunities in others.

"Controlling the Location and Timing of Development" is another article which was prompted by the more recent concerns of growth control and management. In this article Lynch considers the popular notion of managing development rights, addresses the tricky problems of allocation rules and fair share, and suggests that local governments can play a positive role in the process.

The last essay is about the pedagogy of urban design. The paper was prepared for presentation at an urban design colloquium organized by Donald Appleyard and Allan Jacobs at the University of California, Berkeley. Originally titled "Some Thoughts on Teaching City Design," it was later published in a slightly altered form in *Urban Design International.* In this significant treatise on urban design education Lynch articulates his views of how to educate future city designers.

Design is a confused word in environmental planning. Tautologies such as "design plan," or vague phrases such as "the design element," are symptoms of an oscillation between two equally incorrect conceptions: either that design is concerned solely with apparent finish, or that it is principally a matter of planning buildings. This paper will deal primarily with the appearance of cities, but it cannot avoid the broader issue of design.

Appearance and esthetic quality are not final touches; they are fundamental considerations that enter into the design of a thing from the beginning,[1] but they are only one consideration. Similarly, architectural design is only one kind of design—many others affect city form. For our purposes, we may usefully distinguish at least four:

Object design—of a single object, or a standardized series of them (a building, a chair, a bridge);

Project design—of a defined geographic area, however large, in which there is a definite client, a concrete program, a foreseeable time of completion, and effective control over the significant aspects of form (a housing project, a new campus, even a small new town);

System design—of a functionally connected set of objects, which may extend over large areas but do not make a complete environment (an arterial street system, a lighting system);

City or environmental design—of the general spatial arrangement of activities and objects over an extended area, where the client is multiple, the program indeterminate, control partial, and there is no state of completion.

These types of design are so diverse in their nature as to call for different techniques, attitudes, and criteria. The misapplication of project design techniques to problems of city design has resulted in such sterilities as the monumental axis of the past, or the "mega-form" of today. City design is so complex and fluid, so uncertain and beset with conflicting values, as to be thought an impossibility by many thoughtful critics.[2]

Yet in fact we *do* design our cities, however imperfectly, and it is even possible to analyze, and in some measure control, their sensuous qualities, as will be described below. There are serious gaps in the continuity and coherence of the design process, and substantial ignorance as to the consequences of city form. Our esthetic achievements are small: our past efforts have most often led to isolated monuments, or to patterns appreciable only on paper, or to pathetic applications of cosmetics. Yet the city is a great (if disordered and uncomfortable) sensuous spectacle, and could be manipulated for the joy of its inhabitants.

From *Principles and Practice of Urban Planning*, ed. William I. Goodman and Eric C. Freund. Reprinted with the permission of the International City Management Association, Washington, D.C. All rights reserved.

Design is the imaginative creation of possible forms and arrangements, together with the means of achieving them, which might be useful for human purposes: social, economic, esthetic, technical. One designs a possible piece of sculpture, but one also designs a possible gear, a possible crop layout, or a possible population distribution. City design is the technical core of the process of city planning, and its concerns are equally broad. Design does not focus solely on appearance, nor indeed on any single factor which is affected by form.

The immediate sensuous quality of an environment—the way it looks, smells, sounds, feels—is one consequence of the way it is put together, and of how and by whom it is being perceived. Occasionally, this is the most important characteristic of a form, as in an ornamental garden or a festival. Occasionally, it is of no importance, as in a sewer layout or an automated warehouse. In most cases, wherever men are acting in the environment, this quality is one of the several significant consequences of form. The city is such a case.

In the esthetic experience, the dialogue between perceiver and the sensuous environment is intense, and seemingly detached from other consequences. But environmental appearance also has other functions: comfort, orientation, or the communication of status, for example. These characteristics are not easy to disentangle from each other, nor is it always profitable to try.

Planning consists of three processes, all continuous, concurrent, and mutually linked: formulating objectives and criteria, obtaining and organizing information, and designing, or the creation of possible sets of actions. Whenever these processes come into a reasonable fit they lead to intermittent decisions to take action. Within this framework, this chapter will cover two subjects which are commonly confused with one another:

1. *Appearance*: the sensuous quality of the environment as one of the several major aspects of environmental form. It is analytically separable from these other aspects in the process of gathering information, and to some extent in formulating criteria. Except in special cases, it cannot be separated from them in the process of design.

2. *Design*: the role of design in local planning. Only passing reference can be made to the general subject of city design, which is dealt with at some length throughout this volume [*Principles and Practice*]. Somewhat more attention can be given to project and system design, particularly as they relate to city design in general, and to sensuous quality in particular.

What Is Good Appearance?

Our first question is whether the appearance of an environment is of any importance to its inhabitants, and how we can derive criteria for judging better or worse. Sensations which crowd the limits of our biological abilities—too much heat, cold, or noise—are obvious sources of discomfort, and some of these may have long-term, cumulative effects of which we are not fully aware.[3] Through our senses, we gather information which we organize and transform as a basis for action. If this information is ambiguous or false, we are unable to carry out our purposes effectively.[4] The environment serves as a medium of social communication, by which men transmit data, values, feelings, or desired behavior to each other. As such, its look and smell and sound support the fabric of society. We have some evidence that the form of the environment can encourage or frustrate individual growth.[5] The look of our surroundings is obviously crucial to the esthetic experience, the joy of sensing the world immediately and intensely, which is an experience not confined to the gifted few.

In all these ways, the appearance of the environment affects its users, and in many cases it can be substantially improved. As more desperate questions of survival or conflict are met, and as we have the courage to go beyond criteria which are easily quantified, these psychological attributes of cities may come to be the central concern of environmental designers. For the present, they are surely significant.

There are patent difficulties in developing and applying these criteria. Perception of the environment depends not only on its visible form, and its objective nature, but also on the nature of the individual, his history, his needs and purposes, and his social environment. The same object may be seen quite differently by two people of different class, or different visual acuity, or different upbringing, or different immediate tasks. The consequences of appearance are only partially predictable—there are some pervasive effects due to the nature of men as biological organisms; others which are common to large groups, based on class, culture, environmental history, or typical tasks or character traits; and others which vary widely, according to individual idiosyncrasies. The problem of providing for common, frequent, or large group needs, while minimizing intergroup conflict and tyranny over the individual, is a familiar one in environmental design. It is not unique to questions of appearance.

The taste or need of one group may too easily be taken to be the proper esthetic standard. Current campaigns for "beautification" are a reflection of middle and upper middle class taste, with its emphasis on tidiness, appropriateness, and camouflage. The junkyard, abhorrent to the garden club, is a rich mine of form for the sculptor. A lower class citizen may be attracted by visible signs of security, durability, newness, or upward mobility, and take pleasure in forms which to an upper class observer seem coarse, hard, and vulgar. A good environment provides satisfactions for both groups, while offering new possibilities to tempt each to enlarge their desires. Since the designer is usually a person of special class, as well as special temperament and training, his intuitive judgments of appearance, while sophisticated, may not be widely held. His value to society lies in his ability to create new possibilities, rather than to set criteria or to make final judgments.

Criteria must embrace the multiplicity of need and place even as general statements. In emphasis and concrete detail, they will necessarily vary with the particular situation. This relative emphasis will lie at the heart of any decisive evaluation. Criteria must be directly related to form, so that one proposal may be evaluated in comparison to another. The best source for such a set would be an environmental psychology. Lacking that for the time being, we may use hints from art criticism, or from professional consensus, or from individual experience. We may seek indications from current political decisions, or go to community organizations as sounding boards. Unfortunately, the public expression of sensuous criteria is often inarticulate, confused, and conventional, and unrepresentative as well. Our best source for the present may be the user himself, either by watching his market choices, asking for his preferences (which is a slippery affair), or observing his behavior (whether real, as on a shopping street, or simulated, as in an orientation test or a real-estate game). Yet all these methods only test reaction to the present environment. There is little indication of how users might value a setting that they have not yet experienced.

Some Perceptual Criteria

A general list of criteria can be useful as a checklist, and as a guide to applied or basic research. Some criteria are intangible and difficult to set forth in any systematic way. They cannot yet be used as a commonly accepted basis for public decision. Other criteria can be more clearly defined and are likely to enjoy substantial acceptance. Our knowledge regarding criteria of this latter kind can be summarized as follows:

1. Sensations should be within the range of comfort, and not interfere with the activities that people wish to pursue: not too hot, noisy, bright, cold, silent, loaded or empty of information, too steep, dirty, or clean. Climate, noise, pollution, and the level of visual input are perhaps the most critical factors. The acceptable range has a partly biological, partly cultural basis, and will vary for different people engaged in different tasks. But in any one group there will be large areas of agreement as to what is unpleasant or intolerable. We have some specific information on the effect of temperature or noise on health or efficiency, and these data could be expanded. The discomfort of our cities is a common complaint.

2. Within this range of toleration, a diversity of sensation and setting will give the inhabitant a choice of the environment he prefers, and correspond to his pleasure in variety and change. Diversity is an important support for human cognitive development, and, indeed, for the very

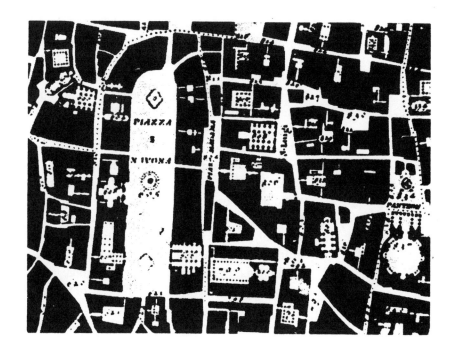

The intricate web of indoor and outdoor space in
18th-century Rome. Reprinted from L. Halprin,
Cities *(New York: Reinhold, 1963).*

maintenance of the perceptual and cognitive system.[6] Adequate diversity
is more difficult to define, as are the critical elements that should be diversified. To some extent, we may look to market behavior, and the expression of preferences, to find the kinds of diversity people presently seek. But
present choices are constrained by past experience and perceived possibilities. The effective designer opens up new choices.

Given the low level of environmental diversity in our cities and the
even lower visibility of such diversity as exists, given our evident appetite
for novelty and our human ability to cope with it, we are for the present
safe in striving to increase environmental diversity, to make it more
visible, and to broaden its spectrum by experimenting with novel environments. Experiments which involve human beings must always be
cautiously designed; novelty and diversity can sometimes be felt as a
threat. The safest tactic is to increase the availability of diverse environments, without forcing them on the user, and then to monitor the way in
which those users choose to operate in the new settings.

We can guess at some of the important variations which people may
seek: the range from lonely to gregarious places for example; or from
highly defined and structured surroundings to ones which are free and
loose; from calm, simple, slow worlds to rapid, complex and stimulating
ones. Diversity is not a matter of mixing together a large number of varied
sensations, but rather of constructing consistent and directly accessible

sub-environments of contrasting character. A secluded garden opening directly off a busy street is one example. Diversity must be not only present but accessible and be perceived as accessible. The door to the garden must open, and no one should fear to turn the handle.

3. Places in the environment should not only be diverse, but have a clear perceptual identity: recognizable, memorable, vivid. A street should not look like all other streets. Every place in a large environment cannot be radically different from all others; important centers may be unique, most places will vary only subtly. But this quality of identity, or a "sense of place," is the cornerstone of a handsome and meaningful environment.[7] Without it an observer cannot make sense of his world, since he cannot distinguish or remember its parts. Wide regions of the contemporary city are visibly faceless and gray, yet conceal much social differentiation. If the setting is vividly identifiable, the observer has a concrete basis for a sense of belonging. He can begin to make relations; he can savor the uniqueness of places and people; he can learn to *see* (or to listen or to smell).

Identity can be tested for, by recall or by identification in the field, and its presence can be predicted in planning proposals, if the user's viewpoint is simulated. A sense of identity also depends on the knowledge and past experience of the observer, and can be conveyed to him indirectly just by verbal symbols. But a unique set of perceptual characteristics is a powerful, concrete reinforcement of this symbolic identity. The designer will accentuate any special traits of form and activity that he can find, or invent and encourage new ones. The typical units within which people function or into which they mentally organize their environment, or the elements which can realistically be manipulated for identity of character, will set the strategic scale at which places should be given identity.

4. These identifiable parts should be so arranged that a normal observer can mentally relate them to one another, and understand their pattern in time and space. This is not a universal rule, since there are occasions when it is desirable that parts of the environment be hidden, mysterious, or ambiguous. But at least the general framework of a living space, and the linkages between its public places, must be legible—in the street and in memory. Legible structure has an obvious value in facilitating the practical tasks of way-finding and cognition, but it has other values as well. It can be a source of emotional security, and one basis for a sense of self-identity and of relation to society. It can support civic pride and social cohesion, and be a means of extending one's knowledge of the world. It confers the esthetic pleasure of sensing the relatedness of a complex thing, a pleasure vividly experienced by many people when they see a great city panorama before them. The structural chaos of our great urban regions is notorious, and lies behind some of our distaste for city life.

Legible structure will have to be simple and adaptable to maintain itself in a constantly changing city. It must also be flexible enough to facilitate different ways of organizing the environment (map organization, sequence organization, and schematic organization, in particular). It must be designed to work for the wide-eyed tourist, the old inhabitant intent on his practical task, and the relaxed and casual stroller. Different groups will search for different clues which they wish to link together: work places, historic spots, or specialty shops for example. Yet certain elements will be crucial to almost all of them: the main system of circulation, the basic functional and social areas, the principal centers of activity and of symbolic value, the historic points, the physical site, and the major open spaces.

Legibility of an existing environment can be tested by field reconnaissance and by interviews of the inhabitants.[8] We have some clues for designing for spatial legibility in large environments, particularly through shaping the circulation system as a comprehensible sequence and a comprehensible geometry, but also through the pattern of open space, centers, and important districts, and through such design techniques as form simplicity, perceptual dominance, articulation or clarity at the joints, and increasing visual range and exposure. Simply to make important elements and activities visible, for example, particularly those which carry high levels of potential information or are of common significance, may be a strategic way of increasing legibility. It can be heightened by keying other informational aids to the visible landscape: giving coded telephone exchanges a visible spatial reference, for example, or keying maps to real objects, or bestowing evocative and relatable place names.

Spatial legibility is the more obvious aspect of our subject, but temporal legibility is equally important—space and time together are the dimensions within which we live. We would like to know not only where but when we are, and how "now" relates to time past and to come. By emphasizing the clues of time and season, by exposing the scars of history and the signs of future intention, the visual environment may effectively be used to orient its observers to the past, to the present with its cyclical rhythms, and to the future with its hopes and dangers.

Historic preservation is a common way of preserving orientation to fragments of the past, but no one has yet paid much attention to clarifying cyclical time in the environment (day/night, winter/summer, holiday/workday), nor to smoothing or explaining current transitions (the visual shock of urban renewal, for example), nor to making the known future visible.

5. The environment should be perceived as meaningful—that is, not only should its visible and identifiable parts be related to each other in time and space, but they should seem to be related to other aspects of life: the natural site and its ecology, functional activity, social structure, economic and political patterns, human values and aspirations, even to individual idiosyncrasies and character. The city is an enormous communications device—people read its landscape, they seek practical

information, they are curious, they are moved by what they see. Great cities are expressive environments, but in ours the information is often redundant or trivial, false, suppressed, or unintelligible. Unfortunately, the symbolic role of the urban landscape is little understood, and to deal with meaning at the community scale is most difficult, since significant meanings and values differ widely between various groups in our society. The formal legibility discussed above is at least a common visible base on which all groups can erect their own meaningful structures.

It would be desirable, however, to make this visible structure at least congruent with functional and social structure, so that visual units correspond to social units, or a visually dominant tower occurs at a focus of intense activity, or at a point of high symbolic significance. As one effective example, the visible setting may be used to convey the structure of "territories," or "behavior settings," by which much normal behavior is regulated: the public, private and semi-public areas; the places in which one should be decorous, and those in which one can be free.[9] Proper behavior is socially learned; but the visible marking of territory can reduce the distress and conflict of inappropriate action. The environment can also express the temporal organization of behavior; light, or changeable forms, will convey when as well as where an action is proper. In general, congruence of the visible and social world, to the extent that it can be managed, will facilitate action and make both worlds more comprehensible. In the same vein, city forms can accent and be congruent to the basic features of the site—hills, rivers, escarpments.

The designer can deal more directly with the explicit communications in the city landscape; the signs and symbols by which people openly speak to each other, using established formal codes. Although city signs are generally damned on esthetic grounds, they perform an important function and add to the interest and liveliness of the scene. The designer's task is not to suppress but to clarify and regulate the flow of information, so that priority signs (such as public control messages) cannot be missed, but also so that a greater flow of other kinds of information is transmitted more easily to the observer, while still giving him the possibility of ignoring it. Signs in themselves are an effective and relatively inexpensive way of enhancing identity, legibility, or congruence.

Not only can they have the graphic clarity that we find in some European cities, but policies can be set about their location, their timing, and their relevance to the place to which they are attached.[10]

They may consciously be used to expand what a man can learn about his city: store locations and goods for sale (which are important), but also history, the site and its ecology, the presence of people and what they are doing, the flow of traffic and information, the weather, time, politics, or events to come. The individual or a small group should be able to transmit

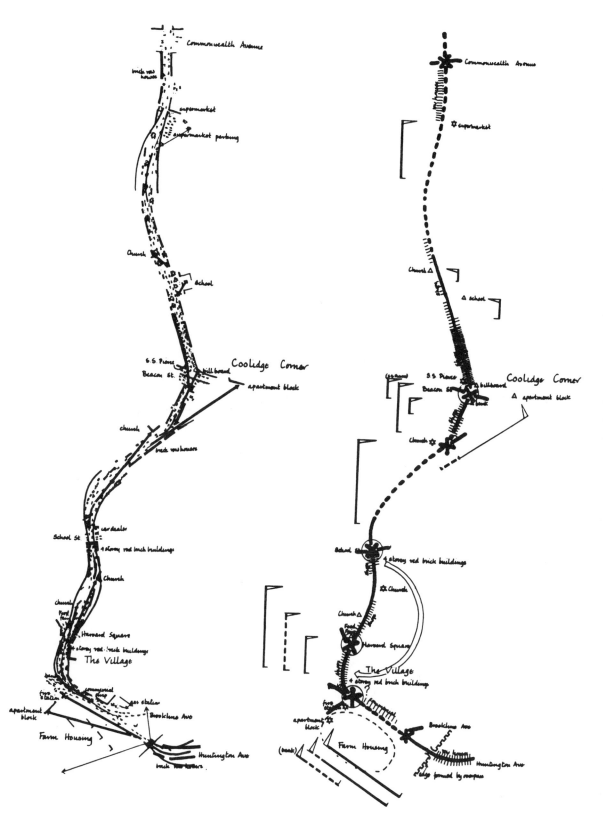

Analysis of the visual experience of Harvard Street in Brookline, and a diagram of its structure. From An Analysis of the Visual Form of Brookline.

messages when they so desire, and this can be kept in mind in the design and regulation of residential structures, for example.[11]

If we go beyond simple congruence and the regulation of explicit communications in an attempt to make the environment more meaningful, we strike numerous difficulties. It is sometimes desirable to increase the transparency of the urban landscape, for economic and social processes are increasingly hidden from sight. Building construction is fascinating because it is one of the few industrial processes left open to view, and city policy might well be directed to making transportation, industry, or meetings and celebrations visible.[12] Public places should be provided where people can congregate and parade—to see and be seen. On the other hand, we risk an intrusion on privacy, the exposure of persons or activities who choose to be hidden. Similarly, if we wish to make our cities symbolic of our society and its values, we are faced with such questions as the diversity of values, and the confusion and emptiness of much of our symbolic vocabulary (or even our embarrassment, should we reveal our society as it really is).

6. The environment plays a role in fostering the intellectual, emotional, and physical development of the individual, particularly in childhood, but also in later years.[13] Certainly, the negative effects of highly impoverished environments can be shown. We can speculate on the sensuous characteristics of cities that might facilitate human development.

Some of the characteristics noted above are valuable: perceptual diversity, legibility, and meaning, particularly if they are not immediately obvious but communicate a simple pattern which becomes more complex and subtle as the object is attended to more closely. This condition of "unfoldingness" is easy to specify in general, but difficult to identify or achieve at city scale. An educative city would visibly encourage attention and exploration, particularly at those times when the observer is not task-oriented, for example when he is at play, traveling, or just waiting. It would provide opportunities for children to manipulate the environment directly, whether by building, reshaping, or even destroying it. It would alternate between situations of high stimulus and times of quiet and privacy. It might even present visual shocks, puzzles, and ambiguities— challenging the observer to find a satisfactory organization for himself.

The use of the city environment as a teaching device is a fascinating topic going well beyond questions of sensuous form. We have done little careful thinking and fewer experiments on it. The subject warrants close attention, since many social problems and possibilities revolve about the subject of education. The criteria for city design which it can provide are as yet meager and uncertain.

There is more to a fine visual environment than can be compressed under the headings above, but it becomes progressively more difficult to define. Moreover, if we achieve a landscape which is comfortable, diverse, identifiable, legible, meaningful, and developmental, in the senses we have given those words, we have the basis, and indeed much of the essence, of a beautiful landscape.

In any application, these general criteria must be turned into specific statements. Where does background noise rise above a certain level more often than a given number of occasions per year, or which major routes cannot visually be differentiated one from another, or where is essential public information unreadable? The nature of these questions will vary from place to place, in relation to the environment, the needs and values of the people served, and the purposes of the planning operation. We lack the space here to discuss the difficult question of how such specific criteria (or any planning criteria) are decided upon in the course of the planning process. Sensuous criteria will interlock with other criteria at many points, and must be consistent with them. Visual legibility may be emphasized, for example, in order to increase circulation efficiency, or to develop a better sense of civic cohesion.

Gathering Information

Data on the appearance of the environment must be gathered in order to prepare designs and take action. Professional uncertainty as to what is relevant at the city scale, and how it may best be organized for analysis and manipulation, has made it difficult to include visual considerations in city designs. The nature of the data, and the language in which it is recorded, always have a profound impact on the nature of proposals. We tend to forget that many other arts (architecture, music, for example) have well-developed languages which can be used to describe, to manipulate form symbolically in design, to evaluate, and to transmit solutions and give directions for achieving them. They are economical and fluent, concentrating on essentials but allowing endless complexity and variation. Unfortunately, for us, architectural language is both too detailed and too limited to be very useful at the community scale.

Data on the sensuous characteristics of an environment may conveniently be classified into: (1) the pattern and quality of the relatively objective and separable sensuous elements; (2) syntheses of these elements into more compact and interdependent clusters of information; (3) descriptions of the system of observer and observed: the environment as perceived and remembered; (4) an appraisal of these characteristics in terms of the criteria.

Sensuous Elements

The sensuous elements are those particular characteristics of the city environment which seem significant to its perception, and which can be recorded with some objectivity by trained observers. The quality of the environment is founded on these raw materials. Diversity in particular can be measured from their distributions.

Spatial form: a central concern to man as a mobile animal. At the city scale, we must deal with the major publicly accessible spaces, both external (which is a traditional subject of city design) and also internal (lobbies, halls, arcades, and concourses). We are concerned with their location, their scale, their general form and clarity of definition, and the linkages between them. We may also wish to record the *texture* of spaces throughout a city district—their typical scale and form, without reference to exact location. All these qualities may be recorded in models, in two or three dimensional diagrams, in long sections, coverage plans, or in isometric views. This is a well-developed and much-discussed subject, and we have acquired a rich variety of form possibilities.[14] We are less prepared to consider these spaces as a linked, city-wide system, although the legibility of an environment is anchored here. Modern transportation and use have made it difficult to maintain well-defined external spaces of the classic type. Will it be possible to specify the characteristics of an area-wide spatial system, without controlling building form in detail?

Visible life and activity: the sight of other people in action, a constant fascination for all observers, which conveys much of the meaning and "warmth" of the city scene. Visible evidence of plant and animal life is similarly important. Diagrams, diagrammatic models, and selected photographs or sketches can be used to convey the location, apparent intensity, rhythm, and type of life and activity open to view. This is a fluctuating condition, and its diurnal and seasonal rhythm is important. Visible activity is distinct from the usual planning concept of objective use or activity: an intensely used place may *seem* quite empty or "dead." The disposition of objective activity, its exposure to view, the nature of the actors, and the proportioning of space to activity will determine the subjective sense. Many city designs are prepared without reference to this crucial quality.

Ambience: the set of encompassing conditions—light, noise, microclimate, smell. Light is the medium for visual perception, and the typical rhythms, intensity, and texture of both natural and artificial light will always be important. Artificial light, in particular, now offers largely unexploited resources of color, form, and sequential change. Prevailing microclimates, by small areas, and the intensity, character, and rhythm of city sound affect all observers. Both can now be recorded accurately, and to some degree be manipulated. Smell, while a more subtle sense, and one difficult to record, can also occasionally be crucial, and not only in a negative way.

Space, visible activity, and ambience will prove to be the key factors, but there are many others that are often worth recording.

Visibility: the general visible form of major landmarks, and the locations from which they can be seen—skylines, land forms, and building masses. To this may be added the key viewing positions. Manipulation of visibility is a well-known device of the environmental designer.

Surfaces: generalized descriptions of the visual and tactile texture of walls and floor, visible evidence of the surface we inhabit, or the material of which the environment is constructed: topography, earth, rock, water, paving, facade character. Much of the city floor, in particular, is already under public control, and it usually is a salient perceptual feature.

Communications: the location, intensity, clarity, type of information, and "rootedness" (relation of a sign to its locality) of explicit signs and symbols in the environment.[15] As noted in the discussion of meaning, these explicit symbols play a very important visual role, and they are amenable to control.

Syntheses

These studies will produce a mass of data which is difficult to use in the initial process of design, however useful for analysis or for detailed design. It is more efficient to coordinate this material into a set of sensuous characteristics which correspond to typical ways in which people organize their surroundings. The pattern and nature of these sets are the physical basis for the diversity, identity and legibility of the environment. Selection and judgment are required to make such descriptions, and thus they must already include some recognition of the nature of the observer.

Focal and district character: the environment as a pattern of regions and points: (1) The spatial form of the important focal points, their fill with light and activity, their climate and noise, the approaches to them and the views in and out of them, the ways in which they are linked together, and how they relate to their immediate environs. (2) The characteristic spatial and surface textures, activities, skyline, planting, detail, light, noise, and climate of the major city districts.

The analyses must indicate how the characteristics fluctuate according to cyclic rhythms of light, activity, and climate, and also how they are changing over the long run.

Sequence system: the environment as a pattern of journeys: the visual continuity, the rhythm of events, and the character of goals and decision points along the important individual pathways (auto, transit, pedestrian, etc.), as well as the sequence of space, view, and motion along them. In addition, the network of paths must also be analyzed as a complete system, including its general form, coherence, and rhythm, and the nature of transitions between its parts. This is a relatively new subject of attention, for which new diagrammatic languages are being developed.[16] Information may also be recorded in special models or in compressed-time movies. Cyclical and secular changes must be noted. As population becomes more mobile, the importance of these sequence systems increases.

Images

To understand the quality of the environment, we must consider the interaction between observer and observed. Here our techniques of analysis are much less secure, and more liable to revision in the near future. While such studies may begin with field surveys, which simply take observer characteristics into intuitive account, they must rely more and more on the sampling of opinion, or the observation of real or simulated behavior, to disclose how the environment is perceived and endowed with meaning. If not, the subjective bias of the typical designer will seriously distort the information. We may call this group *images*, or descriptions of the environment *as perceived*. They now bear directly on our criteria.

Significant objects: an inventory of those special objects or locales which are unique, or which are highly valued or meaningful to significant groups or people, including historic structures, elements of special design quality, sentimental or symbolic things, etc. This type of inventory is especially useful in conservation work.[17]

Territory: division of the environment into spatial or temporal regions symbolically controlled by various individuals or groups, or within which certain types of behavior are expected: private or public territories; prohibited, decorous, or free areas; wilderness; quiet zones. This is a particular (and particularly useful) subdivision of a more general topic:

Public image: the differentiation and structure of the general (or large group) image of the environment, as organized into districts, centers, pathways, edges and landmarks, all as determined from various field and memory interviews and tests. Here the criteria of identity and legibility may be tested.[18] To this may be added information on how this image is changing.

Value and meaning: by tests and interviews, or perusal of existing descriptions, or by watching behavior, information may be gathered as to the values and meanings that observers coming from various significant groups impute to their surroundings.[19] This is an important factor, but difficult to analyze, and little studied to date in any systematic way.

Appraisal

All this material is only brought to the point of usefulness if it results in a set of judgments, organized in some way congenial to design and decision. Any set of data must be reduced to text and diagrams which pick out the problems, strengths, and potentialities (for better or for worse) of the existing sensuous environment as perceived by its users, in the light of the chosen criteria. The nature of the data will affect the choice of criteria and vice versa. Appraisal may reveal certain goals to be improbable or untestable, or it may uncover previously unstated goals. When working with few resources or little time, it may be most efficient to begin by identifying

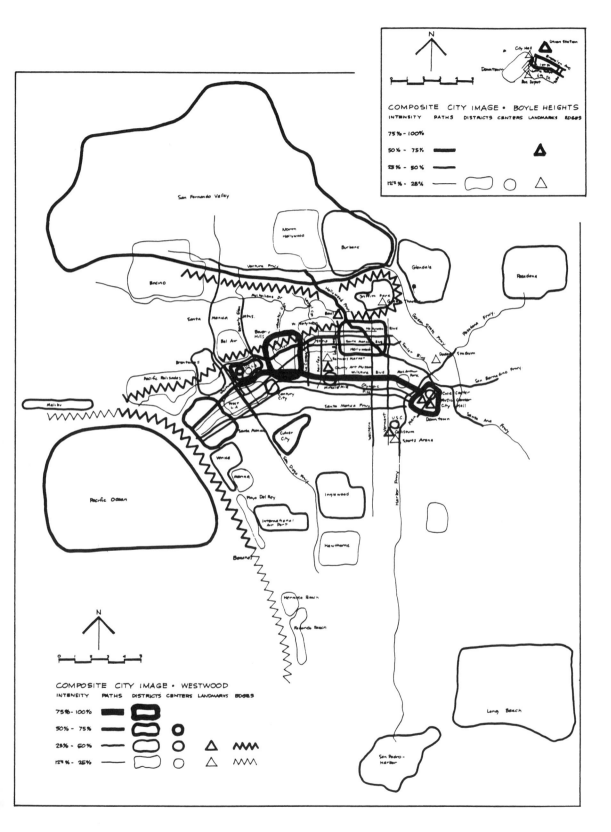

Two views of Los Angeles: the image of the Mexican-Americans of Boyle Heights compared with that of the upper-middle-class residents of Westwood. By Robert Dannenbrink.

problems and possibilities directly in the field, shortcutting any more systematic gathering of information.[20] Data on those sensuous elements which bear most directly on critical problems can then be gathered in a selective way. Evaluative judgments should be organized into forms suitable for design, pointing out problem clusters, major opportunities, latent form, pivotal points for manipulation, and so on.

One of the difficulties in dealing with the appearance of cities has been the lack of a developed and accepted language for noting sensuous conditions at that scale. While conventional means may do in certain cases (microclimate, visibility, significant objects) in others it is necessary to use newly evolved techniques (sequence, public image), and in still others an effective language has yet to be created (light, focal character, meaning). In most cases, we have yet to evolve a language which is useful for design as well as for description. The information itself is still typically gathered by field reconnaissance, but new techniques of interview, the observation of behavior, or the use of games in simulated situations, are all beginning to develop. In the future, we may be able to store these data, not simply in texts with illustrations, but in movies, constantly changing models or diagrams, or in visual data banks based on computer storage, which could maintain constantly updated records of sensuous conditions, including sequences or views at special or even at generally distributed points, so that it would be possible to call up a representation of any point in a city, or to simulate any trip.

What we have gone through is a content checklist. No agency in its right mind would gather all this information as a matter of routine. Although some evaluative statement is always needed, all the other items will be dealt with or neglected according to the situation. In general, surveys will focus on those items which are amenable to public policy, and which seem to be relevant to the scale, the problem, and the key criteria. (In return, designs and criteria will have to focus on items for which there is information.) The scale of the environment, as one example, will indicate whether floor texture is important. One survey may concentrate on signs, because these can realistically be controlled and are at the heart of a current controversy. A transportation study may focus on the sequence system, while a long-term analysis will be directed to the public image, and to the values people ascribe to these elements.

Sensuous intelligence will have to fit in with other data collection, so that questions must be found which can be employed in an origin and destination survey, or data compiled on an area basis compatible with other statistics. In the past, visual information has been gathered as though it were something special and remote from all other concerns, and the result is often that the information is in a form which cannot be applied in making comprehensive decisions. On the contrary, sensuous data are relevant to many other questions. The quality of visual sequences bears on traffic flow and safety; visual identity affects market value; stimulus load has a meaning for health; and so on.

There is a need for continuous intelligence about the appearance of the city, however simple or selective that intelligence may be. Since appearance depends heavily on dynamic conditions such as activity or light, and on the character and purposes of its observers, it is itself a constantly changing phenomenon, requiring constant re-analysis. The planning agency must know what perceptual changes are being introduced by other agents, and in particular it must look candidly at the results · of its own efforts. If a program has put potted trees on downtown streets, then what has been the resulting change in appearance, and how do users view it? The absence of feedback in city design is even more notorious than in building design.

Designing the Sensuous Form

Design is not normally confined to visual ends, nor indeed to any other single purpose. In two special cases, however, we may speak of "sensuous design." In the first case, the design may be dealing with a predominantly visual system, in which other factors are of lesser importance, or can easily be dealt with by solving their requirements in any reasonable manner. This will be true in a minority of cases at the city scale, but may occur in the design of a festival, or of planting, paving, or artificial lighting in an ornamental area, or in the provision of special viewing points. It can also occur even where other important interests are involved, but where the sensuous factors are felt to be the critical ones. Control of signs or of a city silhouette, the improvement of climate or pollution, the design of a re-creation area, are examples. In these cases, we are sometimes justified in designing for the sensuous characteristics first, and then checking to see that other factors are within reason, just as we so often (and often wrongly) design an environment from an economic or technical point of view, and then adjust to social or sensuous factors.

In the second case, a designer making a more comprehensive plan may deal with major factors one at a time, until he has a better feel for the whole problem. He may concentrate on certain cirteria (low cost, for example), or on certain elements (the transportation system), or at certain scales (the block), and develop sketch designs which deal with that element. It is a convenient way of exploring the implications of various factors, and of looking for interfits between them. In this way, the designer can develop a system of visual sequences through an area, even before he looks at circulation requirements, or may play with silhouette before he understands the requirements for enclosed space, or may work up a desirable image structure while still in a functional vacuum. Odd as this may seem, it is neither more nor less reprehensible than the other way around. The results will be revealing but exaggerated caricatures, useful as temporary steps in constructing an integrated design.

Except for these cases, design cannot deal with sensuous aspects alone. "Design plan" is an absurd tautology. "Beautification" is an ugly word, with overtones of fraud. Yet a good design deals with the sensuous qualities of its object, and only in special cases are these qualities of small importance. The best design language, therefore, is one which expresses all the relevant aspects of a thing, as an architectural drawing can simultaneously convey appearance, structure, and (to some extent) function.

Designs for large environments become too complex to be compressed into a single display, and thus diagrams of activity distribution or structural density or traffic flow may be accompanied by diagrams of spatial texture, lighting or focal character. None of these diagrams is a separate plan. All of them are particular aspects of a single integrated design, and they will change together.

Sensuous aspects need not be communicated solely by graphic means. They may be expressed in words, where words are most appropriate, as in setting general policy or describing sequential actions with various alternatives. Unfortunately our verbal (and as often our graphic) abstractions do not refer precisely to the concrete visual characteristics intended. The language is full of ambiguous generalities: "proper," "harmonious," "balanced," "suitable," "an orderly framework."

An environmental design need not include exact specifications of material and form. It is often more efficient and flexible to prepare a sensuous *program*. That is, the design can state that there be a landmark structure at an important junction, which shall be visibly full of activity, easily identifiable as distinct from its surroundings, continuously visible from a mile away up to the junction itself, and that it have a form which can be used to distinguish the various approaches to the junction. This visual program can be satisfied by many particular forms, according to the market and the abilities of the building designer. The design for a large environment may therefore contain a spatial pattern of visual performance characteristics, or programs, covering such items as space and form, visibility, texture, visible activity, apparent motion, signs, noise, light, and climate. These characteristics would be expressed verbally and diagrammatically—best of all, perhaps, in a diagrammatic model.

The design will also specify form, but in a very general way. Thus it will locate the major paths and the rhythm of views from them, the principal visual centers, the axes of view and the barriers to view, the landmarks, the districts of consistent visual character and the major boundaries between them, the form of the dominant open spaces, and the land and building masses. It is for these major elements, arranged in space as prescribed, that the visual programs will be specified. All this is part of a comprehensive design, which also deals with objective activity location, flow, and objective physical form.

Preferred sensuous form is as dependent on goals as any other aspect of design. Alternatives should be prepared for public evaluation. Different groups will have different interests, and designers should represent them. Visual form is also a subject for political debate. It is not holy ground.

At the moment, this appears to be a likely way of dealing with large-scale sensuous form. It is applicable from the project scale even up to the metropolitan region. However, we have produced very few examples of this technique, and have little concrete experience by which we can test its effectiveness.[21] Under pressure, we are thrown back on more familiar methods: the site plan, which specifies the shape of building exteriors; the illustrative sketch, or "artist's conception," which conveys mood or character by the use of selected detail (usually fraudulent); or the verbal statement of general policy, often ambiguous. These older methods are useful under certain conditions—the site plan in particular, when working at that scale and when in realistic command of building form. They are dubious when expanded to a larger scale—one cannot lay out a city as though it were a single subdivision, or model its three-dimensional form as if it were a piece of sculpture. But one might design an urban region as a constellation of distinctive focal points connected by a cobweb of identifiable paths; or as an organized mosaic of visual districts; or as a visible spine of mass and activity along a major topographic feature; or as a coordinated grid of visual sequences. Specificity of form necessarily decreases as the scale of design increases. A proposal at metropolitan scale will consist of visual programs, illustrative designs and standards for typical situations, and the general location of the fundamental visible elements. A community design may include site plans, the exact location and expected visual performance of elements, even the detail and finish at crucial points.

City Design

Design at the city scale, in its comprehensive sense, of which the above techniques are only aspects or partial approaches, is too large a subject to be treated here. City or environmental design deals with the spatial and temporal pattern of human activity and its physical setting, and considers both its economic-social and psychological effects (of which latter the sensuous aspect is one part). The concepts and techniques for manipulating this complex pattern are as yet half-formed. The ambiguity of our graphic notation system, and its lack of inclusiveness, is one symptom of this inadequacy. The goals for which this pattern are manipulated are not clearly stated, and their relation to pattern is imperfectly known. Our vocabulary of city form is impoverished: the need for innovative ideas is correspondingly strong. Yet it is clear that city form is a critical aspect of the human environment, and design it we must.[22]

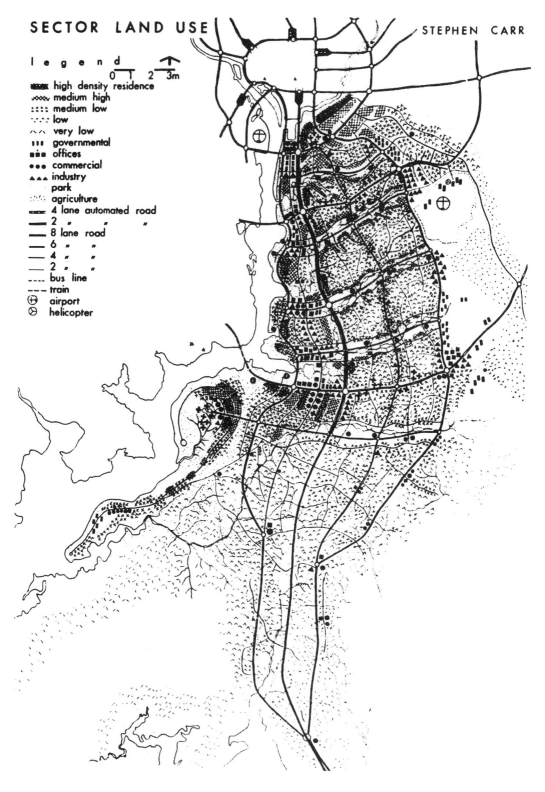

SECTOR LAND USE

STEPHEN CARR

l e g e n d

0 1 2 3m

- ⋙ high density residence
- ⋙ medium high
- ⁚⁚⁚ medium low
- ⌃⌃ low
- ⋀⋀ very low
- ⁝⁝⁝ governmental
- ▪▪▪ offices
- ●●● commercial
- ▲▲▲ industry
- park
- ⁚⁚⁚ agriculture
- ▬▬ 4 lane automated road
- ▬▬ 2 " "
- ▬▬ 8 lane road
- ▬▬ 6 " "
- ▬ 4 " "
- ▬ 2 " "
- ---- bus line
- --- train
- ⊕ airport
- ⊘ helicopter

Proposed visual texture for a sector of the
Washington metropolitan region: a design by
MIT students.

Project and System Design

Project design is usually what people refer to when they speak of "urban design" or of the "design input" in city plans. Project design is a better developed subject than city design. We have substantial experience with various aspects of it, a rich vocabulary of form, a history of success and failure, and a partial set of principles. We are accustomed to training professionals to deal with it.

System design is similar to project design in its concreteness of program and timing, but concerns a group of objects which may not all be in the same location, and do not make up the total environment in any area. This is a type of task to which the industrial designer is habituated. In this chapter, we can only point out typical examples of system and project design in the city environment, and briefly discuss their connection with city design.

The classic areas for project design in the city (with which chapters on design in former editions of [*Principles and Practices*] have largely been concerned) include such features as boulevards, parks, civic centers, cultural institutions, waterfronts, and garden cities. Most of these are settings for leisure, or for so-called "higher" activities: governments, museums, churches, schools.

This focus implies a hierarchical ranking of activity, a feeling that the remainder of the city must of necessity be unattractive, subject only to "practical" requirements. The garden city made an effort to include all aspects of life in a humane environment, but elsewhere the bias is obvious, and carries over today in the linkage of design with special events, or with upper middle-class taste. Some of these former design preoccupations have lost their importance for us, such as the boulevard and the civic center. Others are still live issues—parks, new towns, large institutions—although the forms are shifting.

The design of new towns and of large institutional campuses are two examples which lie on the border between project and city design. Typically, they are marked by well-established central control of form, by a definite area (however large), and by an explicit future program (however mistaken it may often be). But the time span embraced by the design, and the complexity of its elements, make them akin to city design. Some of our best design talent is currently engaged precisely in these hybrid areas, and new ideas for city design are evolving there, including the management of future flexibility, the use of activity location for visual effect, the establishment of a formal framework for individualized building design, a creative attention to circulation, and so on.[23]

Current project design in the stricter sense is concentrated on shopping centers, suburban or in-town housing developments, plazas and other special open spaces, and sites for natural or historical preservation.

The urban renewal program has opened up many opportunities for project design, particularly high or medium density housing, and partial replacement of the central business district. We are learning many new lessons about project design in the process.[24]

Inevitably, these design foci will shift, to some extent in response to shifts in design fashion, to a larger extent as social need and possibility evolves. We may guess at an increased role for system design, as in lighting or sign systems, mobile housing, open space networks, and systems of automobile, transit, and pedestrian movement. We may hope for attention to urgent environmental problems which have been considered beneath the notice of design, such as the slums and "gray areas," the strip commercial street, or the industrial complex. The concern for new towns and large suburban development may grow into the problem of designing new cities, which returns us to our original subject. We may begin to consider designs for the development of areas previously thought uninhabitable: mountains, deserts, water surfaces, wastelands, arctic tundra.

The joint between project and city design is always a crucial issue. City designers may be so remote from action that they recommend policies which cannot be carried out, or which have unanticipated or indefinable outcomes. Project designers may wreak havoc on other areas of the city. Urban renewal and campus design have by now furnished us with many bitter lessons on coordinating these two levels of attention. Until we have developed more skill, our only answer is that both concerns must overlap. That is, the city designer, in preparing his comprehensive framework, must test his ideas in the form of illustrative project designs or be to some extent involved in implementation. Vice versa (and this is rarely done), the project designer must see what consequences his particular scheme has for the general form of the city. Both professionals must therefore be at least familiar with the techniques of the other. Since city design is rarely taught, and many practicing city designers were originally project (architectural or landscape) designers, this linkage works somewhat better in the one direction than in the other. Even if mutual knowledge were improved, the institutional barriers between these two professionals, and the discrepant values they must work for, are formidable.

Public Policy and City Appearance

Many attempts have been made in history to control the look of a city. Most often they have failed. A few successful efforts have been carried out by strong central authorities, and many beautiful old cities were produced by the guidance of restricted technology or strong custom rather than by conscious design. Today those historic constraints have little controlling force. City design successes have typically been confined to the ceremonial areas: palaces, squares, religious compounds, parades. Few of these have direct relevance for us.

Our present achievements have been concentrated in planned suburban housing for the affluent, shopping centers, some campuses, and a few parks and squares. Many of our control systems have in reality gone wide of their mark, or broken down under the stress of the market and political conflict. Other attempts at control—"look-alike" ordinances, the specification of allowable style, powerful review boards—have often succeeded in stifling design innovation. "Design studies" which accompany city plans are usually done by separate specialists. They exhort, but do not often affect development decisions. Yet popular demand for a better environment is rising, and steam is collecting in the political boilers.

There are perhaps three general ways of managing city appearance: direct design, regulation, and influence. Let us take them in that order.

Direct Design

Direct design implies that a central authority specifies the form that the environment will take. Direct design of the entire environment is possible at the project scale. At the city scale it is a dubious affair, requiring immense power and superhuman foresight. The inner city in Peking was done in this way, Fatehpur Sikri in India, central Le Havre and Brasilia in our time. Many architects dream of designing cities as they would a single building. Even aside from the political power required, the technical demands—staff, ability, and information—are staggering. Breakdowns are normal.

More frequently, even in the past, design focused on the outward form of certain key elements, a public square or the flanking facades of a major street, while leaving internal design and the bulk of the city to private developers. This was the strategy of Sitte and Haussmann, and the key idea in the City Beautiful movement. It continues today in such projects as Pennsylvania Avenue (Washington, D.C.). Where the stakes are high, and authority is willing to exert its power, the strategy can be effective at the central focus of a city or along a major processional way. But to hope to control the entire appearance of a city by this means is unrealistic.

Design efforts may concentrate on those elements that are normally built by the public: post offices, city halls, hospitals, schools, streets and highways, transit lines, parks. They make up a large proportion of the city landscape, and must somehow be designed in any event. Unfortunately, separate government agencies may be more resistant to design improvements than are private builders (who have something to gain from cooperation), but it is true that good public design, particularly of such common elements as streets and open space, could make a strategic change in city appearance.[25]

The maintenance and constant renewal of these public elements is even more important than their orginal design. Money, energy, and skill

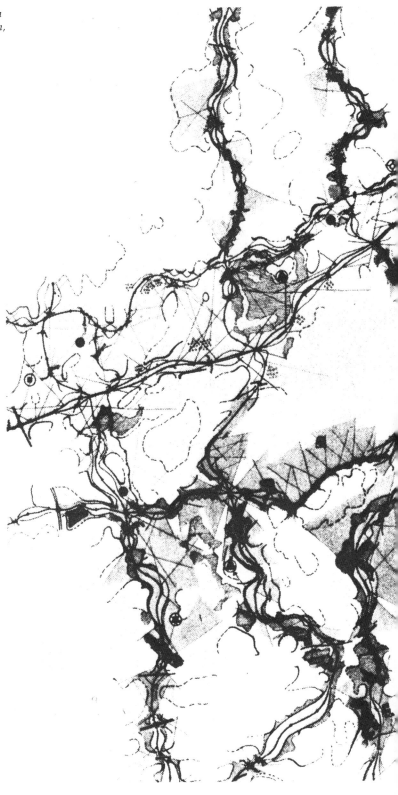

Proposed system of highway sequences in a sector of the Boston metropolitan region, showing horizontal and vertical alignment, space definition, views, and relation to landscape: a design by MIT students.

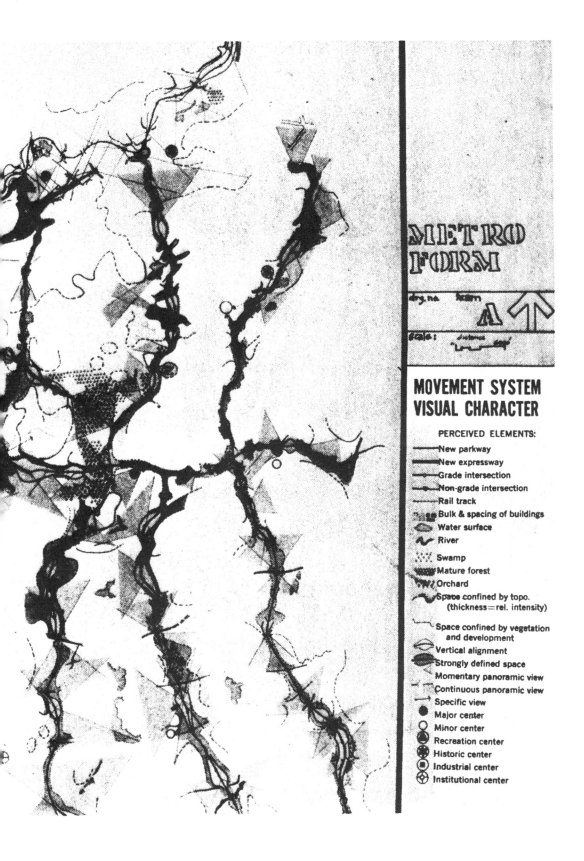

METRO
FORM

dwg. no. form A

scale:

MOVEMENT SYSTEM
VISUAL CHARACTER

PERCEIVED ELEMENTS:

New parkway
New expressway
Grade intersection
Non-grade intersection
Rail track
Bulk & spacing of buildings
Water surface
River
Swamp
Mature forest
Orchard
Space confined by topo.
(thickness=rel. intensity)
Space confined by vegetation
and development
Vertical alignment
Strongly defined space
Momentary panoramic view
Continuous panoramic view
Specific view
Major center
Minor center
Recreation center
Historic center
Industrial center
Institutional center

must be applied regularly. The public areas of many European cities, and the current revival of the New York City park system, are striking examples of what can be done by good housekeeping, imaginative remodeling, lighting, and decorating.

It is also possible to design particular areas directly, where these have been previously delimited and programmed. Urban renewal, in particular, has offered this possibility to us, and so does institutional growth. If the current results have been sterile or chaotic, we have some grounds for hoping for better as project designers learn their trade. Too often, they are designed as a collection of unrelated buildings. Unfortunately, even these projects are usually small, and their pattern a patchwork. Where areas are larger, as on the urban fringe, the potential is correspondingly greater.

Finally (and this is a technique as yet hardly used by public agencies) it is possible to design systems (highways, corridors, connected walkways or open spaces, night lighting), or to develop prototypes for frequently encountered problems (a local commercial intersection, a pocket park, a trailer park), or to innovate what Maki calls "group form": elements which can be repeated, although with detailed changes, and whose flexible agglomeration can produce harmonious variations of general form.[26] The row house is an example of the latter, and the visual character (and functional adequacy) of many old towns is due to the consistent use of some such well-developed form. Standardized forms still characterize the great bulk of building today. Innovations in group form, in systems, or in prototype designs may be one of the most effective ways in which a central agency can affect city appearance, and they will be of great future importance. For reasons that go far beyond those of appearance, there must be a massive increase in public control of land and development in this country. But even under these conditions, we will find that the strategies of selective design, visual programming, systems and prototype design, and coordination and control will still be fundamental techniques for managing the resulting complexities of site, function, and agency.

Public Regulation and Review

Visual form controls may be area-wide, similar in principle to zoning ordinances or even made part of them. The height limitations in Washington are an example, as are the specification of allowable materials in a housing development, setback lines along main ways, the regulation of signs, or the control of noise or light emission. These controls are applied to the entire city, or to large regions of it, or to all areas of a similar use.[27]

Almost all regulations of development—zoning ordinances, subdivision regulations, fire and building codes—have an impact on appearance. Density, building location, and open space requirements; rules as to street, block, and lot geometry; the regulation of parking, signs, land-scaping, fences, earth removal or noise, should all be reviewed for their sensuous implications. In particular, they should not be so worded as to prevent good visual results, as they so often and unwittingly do. Regulations have typically been directed to the single object: the building or lot. They will be more effective where they refer to the group of objects as in cluster zoning or rules for integrating building forms. Just as in direct design, the move from the object to the system scale may be especially strategic.

Area-wide controls must of necessity be simple, and have often been supported by nonvisual arguments, even when the motive was esthetic. They cannot produce a fine environment, but may prevent the worst or ensure consistency. Whether it is possible to control form indirectly, and thereby produce a visible harmony without interfering with the flexibility of individual design, is still a moot point. One strategy is to concentrate on specifying some salient element, such as the shape and material of the roof. Another is to develop a vocabulary of allowable forms, materials and colors, which can be combined at pleasure, but are calculated to sit well together. Both these devices are usable in strong control situations, such as renewal or a single-developer subdivision.

More recently, special controls have been used as strategic points—at landmark locations, for example, or to keep open important views. A visual easement may be purchased, or the immediate environs of a monument be protected, or unique regulations even be imposed on a single lot at a highly visible position. These entail compensation to the owners of the property affected.

Historic districts and landmark zones are by now familiar cases of special form controls, usable where a unique environment already exists, and the purpose is to preserve, rather than to create. Typically, a special commission is given veto control over all exterior changes within the district. It might indeed be desirable to vary visual regulations area by area, consistently over an entire city, to heighten area identity and make a closer fit between the form and meaning of each place. Such a sophisticated set of controls has not yet been attempted.

Controls may be applied more flexibly by the use of boards of review. These boards review development plans and make advisory suggestions, or they may have the power to prohibit undesirable form. In the latter case, the veto power may be more or less detailed. It may be guided by administrative rules or left to judgment on the spot. Discretion of the latter kind can take into account particular situations and integrated effects, playing a creative rather than a purely restrictive role. But the administrative energy consumed in each decision is large, and such a board may itself become mechanical and arbitrary.

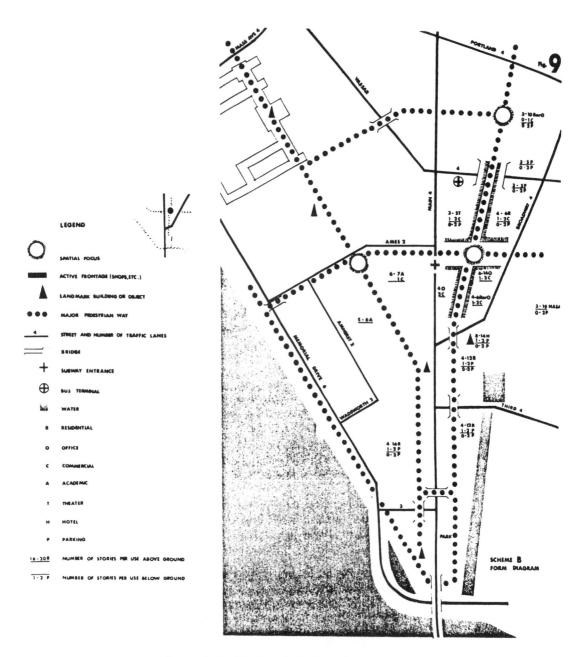

Program for the visible form of a development, and an illustrative sketch of one way of carrying out the program. From D. Appleyard and K. Lynch, Opportunities in Kendall Square.

For the former reason, it is impossible to review the detailed form of all development proposals in a city. The review process would break down under the load. Review must be confined to strategic points—historic areas, important centers, highly visible locations, or zones where strong control is easily achieved, as in public buildings and urban renewal. For the second reason, it is dangerous to give review boards powers of control which are based solely on their own judgment, except perhaps in cases of preservation, or when a board is temporarily created to pass on one unique site. Preferably, their work should be guided by a set of detailed criteria.

It is at this point that visual programming is particularly useful. If the general plan contains detailed statements of what the visual form should achieve in the various locations of the city, then the board's recommendations can be based on them. Even prior to review, they will act as persuasive guides to the developer and his designer.

Review has most often been applied at the moment of decision, when a design is complete. Changes are difficult and the confrontation may be savage. Review is much more effective if it enters into the initial stages of a design, when the program is being formulated and first sketches are being made. Changes involve fewer commitments, and new ideas may be received with interest. Frequent informal advice and persuasion, applied flexibly to design difficulties as they develop, is the correct tactic.

The review process is a useful way of controlling visual form. It should be confined to strategic locations and strategic types of development, and occur during the process of design, rather than at its terminus. It is preferably based on a well-developed visual program for the environment as a whole. It can be most effective as an advisory procedure, except in cases of preservation, or in some unique location of special public interest. The review function may be carried out by the regular staff of a planning or renewal agency, rather than by a separate board.[28]

A public agency can also affect environmental quality by influencing the selection of the designers who will plan it in detail. This influence may simply be informal, by recommendation and indirect pressure, or there may be a public list of recommended designers. Some European cities admit designers to practice in crucial areas only by special license. These are sensitive policies. An accepted means of controlling the selection of the designer is by the design competition, organized and judged by recognized procedures. This is a useful device for key landmark locations (and also a useful way of arousing public interest), but too unwieldy to be used often.

Influence

Controls and direct design are overt means of shaping sensuous form. What might be called sensuous information and design influence is an equally powerful tool. When people with visual design ability are present at a top decision level, or key staff points where development is being planned, there will be an obvious impact on the resulting form. An alert design staff may often exercise important leverage by "brush fire" work—intervening persuasively with suggestions and criticism at the moment of public or private decisions. This requires tact, and also the ability to recognize the correct moment: when decisions will soon be made, but are not yet fixed.

Influence may be formalized by offering design services to public agencies or small developers who do not have such capabilities. In return for supplying design service at a nominal fee, and for imparting its superior knowledge of the future setting of the design, the agency gains influence over decisions, and can inform itself of the motives and capabilities of those who actually construct the environment. The resulting feedback, in its turn, will modify the proposals of the agency. This act of design liaison is as important as the services being directly rendered. By assigning staff (or even volunteer) designers as area service and liaison, the quality of the environment may be sharply improved simply because of the improved flow of information between the public and private agencies, large and small, which are shaping that environment.[29]

The flow of information may be improved in other ways. Visual surveys and analyses of the existing environment, coupled with predictions of future change and its impact, will by themselves influence the actions of builders. Communicated to the general public, they may help to generate political demands for an improved environment, increase public interest or pleasure in the cityscape, or make necessary controls more acceptable. Illustrative designs (which are despised by many designers) are another source of information. Far from being mere window-dressing, they communicate new possibilities, and transmit the intentions of the public staff in a more concrete way than abstract criteria and generalized diagrams. But these illustrations must depict real possibilities. Too often, they are drawn to show unlikely or distorted scenes—they convey false information with the intent to deceive and "sell."

Organizing to Deal with Visual Form

Given the wide range of devices for influencing visual form, the multiplicity of situations in which this form can be a matter of concern, and the prevailing ambiguity between the concepts of design and appearance, it is difficult to generalize about best ways of organizing to manage environmental appearance. We can only note a few elements of organization which might be usable in a large public staff, concerned with continuous environmental planning for an extensive area:

1. The general "design" or "planning" section (meaning the staff which is preparing alternate possibilities for the general form of the area)

should regularly include the capability to deal with visual form, along with other implications of form. It would be best, of course, if all members of the team had some such capability, however they concentrate their efforts. But since many points of view are pressing for attention in a large staff, and since city planners trained to deal with visual form are rare, it will probably be necessary to include specialists, or a special group, in the design team. However, there should not be a separate "visual design" staff, producing a "visual plan" which is disconnected from other design decisions.

2. It may be legitimate, however, to provide for a separate visual intelligence section, since factors can often be separated analytically if not in design. The function of this intelligence section would be to conduct a continuing analysis of the present and future sensuous form of the environment, by means of field surveys and studies of attitude and behavior. It could also be used to evaluate proposals, to test accomplished plans, and to communicate all this information to the public, to staff, and other designers. Members of this section might be specialists in perception, or behavioral science, or visual form.

3. There could be a liaison and review section, dealing primarily with the project and system designs made by other agencies and individuals. Again, it would necessarily deal with the designs as wholes, and not simply with their visual aspects. Its functions could include process review and "brush fire" intervention, design liaison and service, and recommendations for the maintenance and treatment of existing public areas.

4. Finally, a large staff may have one or more design task forces, which are composite teams temporarily set up to do certain strategic project or system designs. Such task forces may also be used to develop prototype or illustrative designs, and in general to explore new possibilities. They will be composed of project or system designers, along with specialists peculiar to the particular problem.

While project design and project appearance are matters of long tradition, city design and city appearance are not. Techniques and criteria for dealing with the latter are still developing. Much of what has been said may be superseded. Certainly it will be expanded and clarified.

New powers, new public attitudes, new means of training professionals will all be required. But the key may be a better understanding of how the sensuous form of the environment affects us, a better knowledge of what we want, and a richer store of form possibilities. Given those, we can define and seek the power we need. Meanwhile, we know enough of some of the consequences and possibilities of the environment, and are backed by a sufficiently strong (if diffuse) public desire, to build, even now, a more comfortable, delightful, meaningful world.

Notes

1. Designers have a dirty word for the idea that appearances come last. They call it "cosmetics." They are unjust, of course: cosmetics is an honorable art, when you have decided you can do no more than change the visible surface of a thing.

2. See, for example, Jane Jacobs, *The Death and Life of Great American Cities* (New York: Random House, 1961), pp. 372–391, and Werner Hegemann and Elbert Peets, *The American Vitruvius* (New York: Architectural Book Publishing Co., 1922).

3. Rene Dubos, *Man Adapting* (New Haven: Yale University Press, 1965).

4. George Miller, Eugene Galanter, and K. H. Pribram, *Plans and the Structure of Behavior* (New York: Holt, 1960).

5. Harry Fowler, *Curiosity and Exploratory Behavior* (New York: Macmillan, 1965).

6. Donald W. Fiske and Salvatore R. Maddi, *The Functions of Varied Experience* (Homewood, Illinois: Dorsey Press, 1961).

7. Ian Nairn, *The American Landscape* (New York: Random House, 1965).

8. Kevin Lynch, *The Image of the City* (Cambridge: Technology Press, 1960).

9. Sidney N. Brower, "The Signs We Learn to Read," *Landscape* 15 (autumn, 1965), pp. 9–12

10. Massachusetts Institute of Technology, Department of City and Regional Planning, *Signs in the City* (monograph, 1963).

11. Julian Beinart, "The Pattern of the Street," *Architectural Forum* 125 (September 1966), pp. 58–62; Sidney Brower, "The Expressive Environment," *Architectural Forum* 126 (April 1966), pp. 38–39.

12. Stanley F. Moss, "A Policy for the Visual Form of Industrial Areas," master's thesis in City Planning, MIT, 1964.

13. Clarence J. Leuba, "The Concept of Optimal Stimulation," in Donald W. Fiske and Salvatore R. Maddi, *The Functions of Varied Experience* (Homewood, Illinois: Dorsey Press, 1961).

14. Hans Blumenfeld, "Scale in Civic Design," *Town Planning Review* 24 (April 1953), pp. 35–46; Gordon Cullen, *Townscape* (London: Architectural Press, 1961); Ivor DeWolfe, *The Italian Townscape* (London: Architectural Press, 1963); Camillo Sitte, *City Planning According to Artistic Principles*, tr. G. R. Collins and C. C. Collins (London: Phaidon, 1965).

15. *Signs in the City*.

16. Donald Appleyard, Kevin Lynch, and John R. Myer, *The View From the Road* (Cambridge: MIT Press, 1964); Mahmoud Yousry Hassan, *The Movement System As An Organizer of Visual Form* (MIT Ph.D. thesis, 1965); Philip Thiel, "A Sequence-Experience Notation," *Town Planning Review* 32 (April 1961), pp. 33–52.

17. Stephen W. Jacobs and Barclay Jones, "City Design Through Conservation" (unpublished); Oakland City Planning Department, *Design Resources in the Oakland Central District* (Oakland, 1963).

18. Lynch, *Image of the City*.

19. Gyorgy Kepes, "Notes on Expression and Communication in the Cityscape," *Daedalus* 40 (winter, 1961), pp. 147–165; R. Richard Wohl and Anselm L. Strauss, "Symbolic Representation and the Urban Milieu," *American Journal of Sociology* 63 (March 1958), pp. 523–532).

20. Kevin Lynch, *An Analysis of the Visual Form of Brookline* [included in this volume].

21. Donald Appleyard and Kevin Lynch, "Opportunities in Kendall Square" (unpublished); Okamoto and Liskamm, *Mission District Urban Design Study* (San Francisco, 1966).

22. Kevin Lynch, "Quality in City Design," in Holland, ed., *Who Designs America?* (Garden City, N.Y.: Anchor Books, 1966), pp. 120–171.

23. Oscar Newman, "The New Campus," *Architectural Forum* 124 (May 1966), pp. 30–55; Leslie Hugh Wilson, "New Town Design—Cumbernauld and After," *Royal Institute of British Architects Journal* 121 (May 1964), pp. 191–201.

24. Roger Montgomery, "Improving the Design Process in Urban Renewal," *Journal of the American Institute of Planners* 31 (February 9, 1965), pp. 7–20; Jack Lynn, "Sheffield," in *The Pedestrian in the City: Architect's Yearbook XI*, ed. David Lewis (London: Elek Books, 1965), pp. 53–97.

25. David A. Crane, "The Public Art of City Building," *Annals of the American Academy of Political and Social Science* 352 (March 1964), pp. 84–94.

26. Fumihiko Maki and Masato Ohtaka, "Some Thoughts on Collective Form," in Gyorgy Kepes, ed., *Structure in Art and Science* (New York: George Braziller, 1965), pp. 116–127.

27. Joint Committee on Design Control, *Planning and Community Appearance* (New York: Regional Plan Association, 1958).

28. Roger Montgomery, "Improving the Design Process."

29. Mary Hommann, *Wooster Square Design* (New Haven Redevelopment Agency, 1965).

The Immature Arts of City Design (1984)

Few Americans think that city-making is a fine art. Most professionals agree, if judged by their actions rather than by their words. We may at times enjoy a city, but only as a fact of nature—just there, like a mountain or the sea. But, of course, we are mistaken; cities are created objects, and at times in history they were managed and experienced as if they were works of art. However misshapen, a city is an *intended* landscape.

If we think of a fine landscape, we usually think of a rural one, or of some historic city center. Those places evolved gradually, and within the confines of custom, site, purpose, and technology, they emerged coherent. Or, when we remember some deliberate act of city design—Paris, Rome, or Beijing—we also remember it as a demonstration of dominant power. If we abhor tyranny, perhaps we should not look for an art of city design. If we live in a pluralistic, changing high-technology society, perhaps we cannot hope for one?

Art (or design: the two terms are confounded) is something "soft," irrational, concerned solely with appearance. At the scale of the city, it can only be a matter of decoration. It has no appreciable connection with the fundamental issues of city policy, which are economic and social. City planning is quantitative, rational, analytic. It speaks in words and numbers, not merely in pictures. It is oriented to policy, wrestles with administrative detail, skirts the political mine fields. Although it may appreciate the luxuries of design, it does not have time for them. Other things are too pressing.

This view of art as something isolated from other life concerns runs deep in our culture. "Arty" is a term of contempt, while "artless" means something genuine or natural. "Inartistic" and "unscientific" have very different connotations.

Even if we lay those prejudices aside, the judgment that modern cities cannot be works of art may be quite correct. There seems to be a universal division in the planning field, a division between those engaged with social, economic, and locational policy at the urban level, and those concerned with physical form at the project level. Schools, professional roles, clients, and institutions are all divided in that way. Those academic departments of urban design that try to throw a bridge across the gap are subject to the constant temptation to devote themselves to the architectural design of large-scale, unified development projects. Students with talents for the design of sensuous form drift to the established profession of architecture. Our schools of urban design depend primarily on foreign students, coming from countries in which there are greater opportunities

From *Places* 1, no. 3, pp. 10–21.

for the design of large-scale projects—whether because of the stage of the country's development, or the presence of a more authoritarian regime. This surge of foreign students will recede in time, as urban design begins to be taught in the schools abroad (or it *should* recede, since urban design is rightly tied to the particularity of place and society). Few U.S. cities have an urban design division. Is urban design un-American?

In any art, someone creates an object or event to convey meanings and feelings to a critical audience. The various arts may be more or less complex and ponderous, but they all involve an intentional creation, and the conveyance, intentional or not, of a personal experience through the sensuous form of the thing created. The artist has precedents, a trans-mitted skill, and works within a style. He makes inventions. In part, at least, his creations are enjoyed for themselves, and not solely as means to other ends.

If it exists, city design is thought to be a branch of architecture. But it must manipulate things and activities that are connected over extensive spans of space and time, and that are formed and managed by numbers of actors. It operates through intervening abstractions: policies, programs, guidelines, specifications, reviews, incentives, institutions, prototypes, regulation, spatial allotments, and the like. Through all this clutter, it seeks to influence the daily experience of a bewildering variety of people. As a process, it is as far removed from the immediacy of direct handwork as one could possibly imagine, but in its effects it is just as immediate, and far more encompassing and powerful.

City forms are more resistant to design than architectural forms, for the city has a ponderous inertia. It is the accumulated product of many historic actions, and will surely undergo as much again. Just to attain a well-known form—as axis, arcade, cluster, or greenbelt—can be a notable success. While innumerable precedents and images run through the head of any architectural designer (grand staircases, serpentine walls, tent structures, broken arcs—who could not go on and on?), the repertoire of the city designer is far more limited. City designers are piecemeal artists working within a persisting framework. Since they communicate only occasionally with each other, this persistent setting is an important link between them. Cities cannot be designed as comprehensive wholes in all their aspects. They must be dealt with in partial ways, whether as chosen groups of features, or via strategic abstractions. This combination of pro-tracted time, complex and extensive material, collective design, a plural audience, and a perpetually unfinished result, must be unique among the arts, if art this is.

Baroque architects were adept at large-scale work. They could use irregular sites and disordered buildings in complex contexts, because they focused on movement and sequence, emphasized details, used illusion and cosmetics, played with contrast and ambiguity. But since they spoke to a restricted, courtly clientele, their work was also simplified. Later, architectural theory felt a broader social responsibility, but it stressed clarity and integrity of form, and the composition of complete, extended areas. It called for clean sites and total control. More recently, architects talk once again of context and contradiction and seem more comfortable in a disordered world. But they are still object-oriented, still intent on innovation and personal expression, traders of historical spare parts and refined allusions around a closed professional circuit. Their products follow a recognizable international style, despite the welcome deference to context.

Until architects change these attitudes, the city designer must unlearn much of what they have to teach. Landscape architecture seems closer to city concerns, since landscape architects deal with large areas that grow and develop in time, that are only partially under the designer's control. Yet contemporary landscape architecture is not as intriguing or compelling as contemporary architecture. The fires that played behind the great French and English gardens seem to have gone out, along with the moral and political statements that those gardens made.

Three Accepted Modes

To begin, we can say that there are at least three ways of improving the sense of our cities, which most people who might stop to think would accept as reasonable. First, we can manipulate certain key *parts* of a city with aesthetic intent, wherever those parts are built new and at one time, under unified control—certain squares, principal streets, parks, or groups of buildings. Doing this well, and fitting those new parts smoothly into their context, is the task that "urban design"normally sets for itself. Such work draws on the skills and precedents of site planning, architecture, and landscape architecture, against a background knowledge of politics, sociology, and economics. The urban designer works with public or private clients who have the resources to achieve large projects of this kind. The traditions of such work lie in the achievements of kings and princes. Today it is based on redevelopment and big captial.

Indeed, it may rely on them too unreservedly. Many of these projects are alien intrusions in the city fabric, and unresponsive to their users. Critics can compare them with well-fitted small projects, and conclude that decentralized design is always a better way of achieving a humane and varied environment. Nevertheless, large project design can at times be quite legitimate, when the work is by its nature at that scale, as in a large new park, for example, or the refashioning of a major street. A lack of response to context or to user is not a necessary characteristic of large projects, even if it is a common one.

Large development projects occur at the city center or along the city margins, while the design of new towns or town extensions has become much less frequent in the United States. Elsewhere, much of the work at this scale is stiff and arid, even if there are exceptions, such as Tapiola in Finland. Turning to the past, we can cite the achievements of Amsterdam South, Boston's Back Bay, or Edinburgh's New Town. But these older extensions benefit from the incrustations of time.

Beyond this somewhat risky art of big parts, one may well deny that city design is possible. Perhaps a really fine urban landscape only results from some long and favorable historic development, an evolution beyond our ability to cause or direct. In that case, the best one can do is to protect those beautiful places, once they have evolved. Therefore, we should focus on conservation rather than on creation. In any new place, one can only construct a stable, practical framework, which will perhaps later become the stage for some eventual flowering. This is a defensible, but rather despairing, view of city quality. Some will even assert that an adequate provision for the more direct requirements of a place—its accessibility, its healthiness, its close fit to behavior—will *insure* its beauty. But that extension of the familiar functional theory seems even less likely to be true of a city than of a good machine, since cities have such contradictory purposes.

Even if we believe that city design is not an art, in the usual sense of a direct creative process, yet surely sensory quality is a legitimate and necessary concern of city planning. Criteria for the immediate, sensuous, psychological effects of the environment should certainly be added to all those other impacts that we consider in setting city policy. Area programs should deal with shape, sound, smell, climate, color, texture, symbols, space, and sequence, as well as with use, access, bulk, and the like. Programs and criteria are effective ways of improving the quality of everyday life, even if their composition is a rational exercise rather than a creative act. Creative artists work within them, and are supported by them. I am convinced of their importance, and city planning is at last beginning to move in this direction.[1]

And Six Possibilities

These three views of city design—that it is only a concern with big new parts, or an exercise in conservation, or a preparatory programming process—are reasonable but unsatisfying. I would like to think that an art or arts of city design (peculiar arts, to be sure) are at least possible, certainly desirable, and, in prospect, engaging. Clearly, they cannot be big architecture, that dream of pervasive, never-failing control. City design is, indeed, concerned with big places, but it must deal with continuous change, a plurality of clients, conflict, and participation, yet leave room for the creative act and the aesthetic response. It should be possible to create new forms and styles and to convey meanings and feelings worthy of critical judgment. What possibilities might we think of, that could sustain such development, judgment, and delight?

One would be a concern that focused on the basic *perceived structure* of a region. Such designs might deal with the character of key centers, landmarks, and districts and their connections, and propose a strategy of how those characters and connections should develop in successive stages. This mode of design fixes essentials and leaves openings; it is loose and tight at the same time. It is a proposal for developing the public image of a settlement, along with those physical interventions and guidelines necessary to create that image. "A line of towers and public plazas, following a suspended transit line, will be extended from the present cluster up that ridge, flanked by a close packing of low workshops and residences on either side. The line will begin at the new bridge, at the confluence of the streams which everyone thinks of as enclosing the town, and it should be possible to see this core in foreshortening as one approaches up the river valley." This is the way (if too simple an example) in which great cities are remembered. But intended frameworks are not solely appropriate to great cities. They can be used wherever an area or a project will undergo substantial development, by numerous actors, over an extended period. They can guide growth in a renewal area, for example, or on a large campus.

Such images are crossings of social meaning and recollected form that grow and elaborate in time. They link citizen and place, enhance the significance of everyday life, and reinforce the identity of group and self. "I am the citizen of no mean city." Just as topography is the basis of a site plan, present images are the basis for framework designs, and present hopes their guide. In daily converse, ordinary citizens participate in making those images, and yet they can also be conscious inventions, new forms. Images arise from changes in perception, as well as from physical changes. Newspaper critiques, "town trails," new viewpoints or entrances, painters' or designers' visions, or the enthusiasms of renovators, all remold a city's image.

There are powerful precedents for such structures. Analyses of existing city images have often been made. Image *designs*, on the other hand, have been rare. They require a fluent, diagrammatic language that can be interpreted and applied by a broad public, and can be followed or modified over a long period of time. Image design must be supported by concrete illustrations of the character implied by the diagrams, and by such familiar abstractions as a proposed network of public spaces, the locations and visibility of future focal points and landmarks, such as a tree-planting plan, and, surely, a scheme for the principal approaches. As an area develops, and these elements gain prominence and character, and as their popular image matures, the proposed structure is more easily apprehended, and its conservation and enhancement are more likely to be supported.

Image designs require the intuition of latent public perceptions and the application of this forecast to actual development decisions. But they do not require total control, since there are many ways of carrying out such general structures. They *do* demand sustained interest and continuity of application, however, which implies an agency concerned and competent at that scale, or at least a body of informed opinion that can exert effective influence. Framework designs are an appropriate way of dealing with something as large, as dynamic, and as persistent as a city. Sensory programs can be grounded in them. They would be works of art, lengthy social collaborations. They are not customary.

In a more concrete and realistic mode, city design can focus on the *journeys* by which people actually experience cities. City trips are enjoyed or suffered, but they are remembered. The pleasures of motion, and its connotations of energy and life, are, perhaps, especially meaningful to us today. Streets and vehicles are under public control, and this is accepted as normal and necessary. It is routine to design streets, bridges, tunnels, and sometimes street facades, but only occasionally are they treated as sequential experiences: as comings out and goings in, as arrivals, glimpses, risings, fallings, a winging around, a sudden view—as approaches, progressions, or foretellings. There are techniques for recording such temporal forms, although they may be unfamiliar to most designers.

There are precedents for this in modern highway design, which at its best has a well-developed style: the rural, long-curve, split-lane freeway, following the form of a rolling ground. Other styles can be imagined: ones that cut through, oppose, and so dramatize the ground, or which emphasize surprise and ambiguity, or exaggerate apparent speed, or open and close space rhythmically, or amble about and investigate oddities. We find rich examples of sequences in classic monumental approaches, or in the byways of old cities. Architects sometimes consider these spatial narratives within their buildings. Garden designers have created many marvelous outdoor sequences—the Wang Shih Yuan in Suzhou, the Sento Gosho in Kyoto, or great English gardens such as Stourhead.

But ordinary streets could also be designed that way, and as such could transit lines and cycleways and promenades: along a waterfront for example, or through a succession of neighborhoods. Such effects would seem natural to consider when making the initial layout of circulation, but they can also be considered in planting or lighting an established street, when opening a new connection or locating a major new roadside feature. Even the character of the vehicle is part of a sequence design. Wind and swooping motion makes almost any city ride memorable, when it is accomplished in an open-top, double-decker bus.

In the city, of course, one cannot remold the entire setting for the sake of serial vision, as one might do in a garden. One shapes the road—and perhaps also the vehicle—to reveal what is latent in the surrounding fabric, just as one would work with the topography of a highway corridor. While serial design is unfamiliar as a deliberate city intention, yet certain chance sequences are well known: approaching Pittsburgh by tunnel from the south, or New York on the Staten Island Ferry, or riding along New York's East River Drive or Chicago's Michigan Boulevard.

It is unlikely that anyone would specialize in sequence design (as one might specialize in some others of these possible modes). Sequence design should simply be a normal preoccupation of the engineers and site and city planners who arrange our public streets—an element normally considered and normally commented upon. If they are unfamiliar, the principles of sequence design are hardly new. See various garden texts, or Philip Thiel's work,[2] or "The View from the Road,"[3] or Cullen's "Concise Townscape."[4] The opportunity is there, if rarely exercised. Journeys are real entities, deliberately planned and directly experienced. But to propose designing a succession of visual experiences only raises eyebrows.

In its third mode, city design can be a conscious art of *renewal*, an art of refurbishment, tinkering, and redoing. This work may not sit so well with some designers, who want to make it new and all their own. But we commonly find pleasure in renewing an old house, and an artist can be absorbed in recombining found objects. By making one's mark on something old, by recovering selected features, one achieves a richness otherwise unobtainable.

This is the appropriate stance when working in almost any city area. It is especially appropriate in a plural, changing world, so full of ambiguity and contradiction. Our middle-aged suburbs cry out for such enrichment. Current achievements in "place making" (as described by Fleming, for example, in his book of that title) are good examples of the art. Renewal is creative design, not just preservation. New and old are contrasted to bring out the meaning of each, and so the depth of time is made visible. There can be different styles of selecting what will be presented: should we pick out an underlying pattern of function or condition, or emphasize an historic succession, or make a surprising contrast? To take another example, the color applied to old buildings need not be historically correct, as current conservation doctrine would have it. It can be used to glorify details, to create a disruptive pattern, or simply to be outrageous. We may deny that cosmetics is a fine art, but a tattooed face can blow the mind.

To paint add planting, lighting, graphics, shelters, and street detail, the insertion of "pocket" open spaces and public art, the placement of a modest monument or new building at just the right location, or the encouragement of street activity. Guides for any future construction can be part of the package. If most current examples of this art have been located in modest downtown areas or historic conservation districts, and have had a rather similar stylistic cast (we begin to have a sufficiency of Victorian main streets), yet refurbishment could also deal with newer areas and use different styles. Residents enjoy these accomplishments and can participate in them. The renewed neighborhood is reaffirmed as *home*, a place whose history and function has been made meaningful. There are institutional means for bringing this about, even if public budgets are slender.

Still another city art is the design of *events*, with which the artists of the Renaissance were quite familiar. The great aristocratic and religious festivals of the time required the collaboration of architects, painters, sculptors, poets, musicians, dancers, players, costume makers, cooks, and the confectioners of fireworks. Celebrations can be invented, streets decorated, sound and light shows composed, parades, fairs, carnivals, and dances organized. We all know successful examples: Boston's First Night, Macy's Thanksgiving Day Parade, Baltimore's ethnic fairs, New Orlean's Mardi Gras, the planned entertainments in shopping malls, neighborhood street dances, coronations, grand openings. Some are traditional, others consciously designed. They add meaning and sparkle to city life, and make us aware of our common humanity: we take joy together. Celebrations need not be confined to the special occasions. They can lighten and inform our daily routine. Of course they can also fall flat, like tired Christmas wreaths on the light poles along the street, and the jolly Santas at the corner.

Most city events are accepted as if they just happened. Event designers are unsung. Their professional role is precarious, their work ephemeral, and their next job uncertain. If these happenings had a more stable institutional base, and if their composers had more explicit recognition—perhaps if their works, like that of a composer or a dramatist, were repeatedly performed and thus attracted critical judgment—then event design might be a more compelling role.

Of course there is a danger here. The deliberate "animation" of a city street can rise to the level where we simply become the passive viewers of an encompassing spectacle or, worse, the manipulated participants in some false demonstration of loyalty or "fun." But if good event design makes use of showmanship, it does so not to compel the actions of its audience, but to give them opportunities for action. Moreover, in the human diversity of our streets (and except for the initial tourist experience), it is less than likely that any event will be long maintained without the assent and interest of those who attend it. Boredom, dissent, and disbelief are effective censors. While the freedom of the streets must be preserved, it is not so easy to subvert.

The fifth mode of city design is just routine: something unnoticed, of low order, a task for draftsmen, who are employed by towns or by equipment suppliers to shape those small repeating pieces of which the city is composed. Their work is everywhere: signs, paving materials, seats, fences, shelters, light standards, power poles, hydrants, trash cans, telephone and letter boxes, parking meters, curbs, and all the rest. Designed as isolated, standard objects, they coalesce into the commonplace jumbled scene. On the other hand, designing each piece afresh to respond to each particular situation (as one might design the special fitting for some exceptional building) would be enormously expensive. Design, production, installation and maintenance would then be unbearably complex. The customary process—piecemeal, standardized, and out of context as it may be—fits the way city furniture is actually produced and distributed, and the way its parts are stocked. At least this process ensures the technical adequacy of each piece.

City designers might intervene more effectively in this area if they were to engage in *system* design. By that I mean the design of constellations of things that will be used repeatedly: a typical bus shelter, along with its signs, lights, seats, and associated services; or a minor street, including its cross-section, walks, carriageway, curbs, planting, lighting, signs, fences, and system of maintenance; and the ways in which all these may be interrupted or modified to fit changes in use, topography, or local preference. A pattern and schedule of landscape materials could be prepared for typical public places, in a certain urban region, with rules for their location, grouping, planting, and upkeep. One can deal with the shape and finish of subway entrances, steps, and tunnels; with a cycleway in relation to other ways and fronting uses; with a fencing system; with the location, form, and information content of public signs; with typical pocket parks and playgrounds; and with many more features to be used in a general locale. The craft of the industrial designer is relevant here, and perhaps these designers might venture into the municipal realm, if they could bear the confusion. Recent trials have not always been so successful, however, since industrial designers are accustomed to clients who are in firm control of their products, who can see that they are made and delivered just as they are designed.

Where the institutional capability exists, system design can be highly effective. Much of the success of Haussmann's parks and boulevards hung on this attention to detail. Since system designs will be used repeatedly, they have significant influence and can justify substantial design attention and careful citizen consultation. Suitable parts must be found in supplier's catalogs or developed from local sources. Technical demands must be met, and maintenance procedures instituted. It must be determined where the system is relevant, as well as in what particular locations it should *not* be used. The operating departments must be satisfied.

This is where the city designer will be likely to find his stumbling block. Operating departments have long-standing ways of conducting their business, and, with some reason, are jealous of their control. System design is, therefore, best located directly within the operating departments, provided that they are open to new ideas, and have a unified responsibility for that system of objects. But in most cities the streets and their appurtenances, which are our primary public places, are managed by a great jumble of agencies. When the streets are under unified management, system design has been handsomely done: in parks, in shopping centers, in some new towns, and in renewal areas. Unfortunately, urban designers too often see this as lowly work.

System designs can be partial designs: intended, that is, to be completed or modified by other professionals or amateurs yet to appear on the scene. A basic bus shelter might be furnished, sited, and decorated according to the plans of a professional hired by a neighborhood association, or a pocket park of standard layout might be planted by those who will enjoy it. This has financial and administrative implications, as well. For example, instead of demanding that "one percent for art" be expended on works chosen by experts before a building is erected, let that sum be reserved for outdoor improvements one year after the building is occupied, as determined by the actual tenants of the building.

Design may also extend to features not under the control of the public or private agency for whom the designer is working. Designs then become illustrations, or *prototypes*: models to be followed by other builders, expositions of possibilities that other actors are neglecting. In that way, design services are brought to those who would normally not use them or could not afford them. Prototypes may even aim to inspire the formation of a new agency or client group in order to seize some newly revealed opportunity. Ideas for remodeling an ordinary storefront or for installing an engaging window display might be useful, as would models for self-built houses, designs for low-rise apartments to be put up by small builders, and schemes for a backyard community garden, a small workshop on a residential lot, or a street vendor's stall. Christopher Alexander's "patterns" are outstanding examples of this genre. Early pattern books guided much of the house design in this country, and popular magazines continue that work today—if in a slick and illusory way. Fantasy designs, such as for a sea-bottom landscape or a communal house, may spark the formation of a group that seeks to realize them.

Prototypes must be done in communication with the shopkeeper, house builder, gardener, or street vendor, and in response to their felt needs. Otherwise, the work is fantasy (although fantasy, if explicit, has its own usefulness). Built and furnished examples in use, like the developer's "model house," will be much more effective than a plan. Once accepted, a model can have an enormous influence. Most current models do not come from public sources, but rather from the media, or some source of supply, or as an imitation of an object owned by people of higher status.

These Uncertain Arts

So we find six possible and, for the most part, undeveloped modes of city design, in addition to the three accepted modes with which we began. These are different ways of thinking about our city environment. For the most part—except perhaps in the case of renewal—they refer to relations and actions for which no public or private bodies take public responsibility today. They are fitted to situations where actors and audiences are decentralized, and, in many cases, they imply some degree of redistribution of power, if they are to be successful. All of these modes have one thing in common: they are based on the ways in which we actually experience a place, rather than on some professional or administrative division—when we experience it as an event, as an image in the mind, as a journey, as a home place transformed, as a purposeful group of objects, or as a workable and familiar pattern. Here lies their potential power and, since they leap the institutional lines, their difficulties as well.

Each possible mode has its allurements and its difficulties. Structural designs for the underlying perceived form of a settlement match the sense of these places at their own scale, and deal openly with change and continuity. But communicating them requires an abstract language, and implementing them demands sustained concern. They must be firmly based on how the citizens see their settlement, and not simply on the perceptions of the single designer. To my knowledge, this mode is not taught or practiced anywhere in this country. Intentional precedents hardly exist, although a rich palette of structural form and element character is imaginable, or can be harvested from observation.

Sequence design is a more tangible possibility, since its material is normally under public control and its effects are consciously experienced. There are notations and simulations for manipulating this material, and a store of historic precedents. This could become a strong and attractive mode of design, although not a likely specialty. On the other hand, it is a rarely considered mode. It still seems an odd thing to think about when laying out a street, a highway, or a transit line.

The rehabilitation of individual buildings has often achieved attractive results, and we are beginning to see some success at the community level. For the moment, renewal design is tied to downtown renewal and to historic preservation, and to the doctrines of those endeavors. It is unusual to see renewal design practiced in those ordinary areas where it might be more broadly effective. It is considered merely cosmetic and not a fine art with its own traditions, styles, and talents. But renewal has all those possibilities, and perhaps the continuing evolution of historic preservation is leading us in the direction of those possibilities. For designers, it begins to take on some modest glamor, glamor being the lodestone that attracts talent. To be more effective, this mode must develop better methods for involving the ordinary residents and users of a place.

On occasion, event design has been done with great skill, and surely it has its historic precedents. Well done, it is a common pleasure. It could be extended from the great holidays to our daily experience. Its practitioners are unknown, however: their role unestablished, their budgets and their institutional base uncertain. If this art is to bloom, stable public or private agencies must take up the responsibility for happenings without sacrificing the freedom of the streets.

The design of city furniture, on the other hand, is commonly practiced, paid for, and implemented. These standard designs are uncoordinated, and respond primarily to technical demands. They focus on the "hard," manufactured things. Imaginative designs for clusters of these objects—as they will be managed and used in typical public situations, and which allow further adaptation—would go far to humanize our cities. The obstacles to this particular mode lie in the structure of the supply industries, the fragmentation of municipal operating departments, and the stubborn values of trained designers.

Last of all, while prototype design could be an efficient use of scarce design talent, it requires a more intimate response to the user than most public or private planning staffs are accustomed to. Without that response, the work remains on paper, a prospect that reduces the enthusiasm of designers. Moreover, agencies must become motivated to provide such indirect design serivces. Good prototypes could reshape our daily environment. Their generation would be a model of participatory design.

None of these six modes is a developed art; some are emerging. Each requires its own skill, models, languages, institutions, and practical experience. All six meet the criteria laid down at our beginning. They deal with the large environment in daily use; they are comfortable with continuous change, partial control, pluralism, and participation; and they are creative arts, eliciting an aesthetic response. The principal obstacles to their development lie in a lack of institutional support, in the attitudes and training of professionals, in the rarity of user participation, and perhaps, most of all, in the absence of any public or private responsibility for the way in which the sense of a city affects our daily lives.

Attitudes in the planning profession reinforce this lack of public support. Talented designers move into architecture, where they have some hope of seeing their dreams made flesh. Once there, they are socialized to value innovation, large and expensive projects, a fashionable surface, and strong personal expression. Planners, on the other hand, think of themselves as administrators and technicians, not as artists. The gulf between sense quality and public policy, between art and planning, widens and deepens.

All six modes could be taught, practiced, and critically appreciated. They could manipulate a rich variety of form, develop a style, and exhibit talent. They are possible but peculiar. Might our schools of planning and urban design lead off by demonstrating some of these potentials? Or must schools always waddle after practice?

Even if we fail to nurture these arts, and so fail to make cities that are intentional , collective works of art, nevertheless we *must* be concerned with the sensory form of what surrounds us, since it is critical to our survival as well as to our pleasure. So we at least must manage city sense in a programmatic way. A concern for sensory quality is an absolutely necessary part of environmental policy. Otherwise, our cities will remain alien to us.

But why not hope for an art as well as for a policy?

References

1. Kevin Lynch, *Managing the Sense of a Region* (Cambridge: MIT Press, 1976); The Boston Redevelopment Authority, "Boston Tomorrow" (1983); New York City Planning Commission, "Midtown Zoning" (1982); San Francisco Department of City Planning, "Downtown" (1984).

2. Philip Thiel, "A Sequence-Experience Notation," *Town Planning Review*, 32:1 (April, 1961).

3. Donald Appleyard, Kevin Lynch, and John R. Myer, *The View Form the Road* (Cambridge: MIT Press, 1964).

4. Gordon Cullen, *The Concise Townscape* (New York: Van Nostrand, 1971).

Urban Design (1974)

Design is the imaginative creation of possible form intended to achieve some human purpose: social, economic, aesthetic, or technical. One can design a garden, the layout of a book, fireworks display, a drainage channel. Urban design deals with the form of possible urban environments. Urban designers work on three different kinds of task: (1) Project design, which is concerned with the form of a definite geographic area in which there is a definite client, a concrete program, a foreseeable time of completion, and effective control over the significant aspects of the form; housing projects, shopping centers, and parks are examples. (2) System design, which considers the form of a functionally connected set of objects. These may be distributed over extensive areas, [and] are built or managed by one agency, but do not make a complete environment. A highway network, a lighting system, and a set of standardized signs provide examples. (3) City or regional design, in which there are multiple clients, indeterminate programs, partial control, and constant change. Regional land-use policies, the formation of new towns, and the rehabilitation of older urban districts are examples of this kind of design. In emphasizing the direct human impact of the environment, it must be noted that design is not solely concerned with any single influence of form.

Modern Practice

Failures of Urban Design

Many examples of magnificent buildings, gardens, or bridges may be cited. It is far harder to find cases of fine complete environments particularly in the modern world. There are a few residential areas of moderate scale that are comfortable, workable, and handsome. There is an equally small number of well-designed urban centers.

Large planned settlements of distinguished form are quite rare; Tapiola in Finland and Vällingby in Sweden are among the few. But planned, ugly and inhuman places, formless suburbs, gray city districts, and industrial wastelands are endless.

Distinguished historical, unplanned areas are much easier to find. Most texts on landscape or urban design are illustrated with views of historic cities, old farming regions, or primitive or wilderness areas. The apparently unplanned squatter settlement, or the old urban district, can have more visual warmth and interest than the newest designed suburb or apartment project.

There are a number of possible explanations. One is that a fine landscape will only develop in time, as historical meaning accumulates, and form and culture come to a close rubbed fit. If so, the best that can be done is to conserve the past, while producing technically workable settings today in the hope that they will acquire character for later generations. If true, it is discouraging for a generation committed to building more urban environment than already exists.

The difficulty may be one of scale and control: that good environments are the direct products of their users, or of professionals who have an exact knowledge of user requirements and values. Superb houses are designed, but not superb housing projects, which are designed for people en masse. Or the true reason may be more profound—that environments reflect the state of society. The crisis of environmental quality arose with the Industrial Revolution, which looked on space and people as resources to be used. That crisis can only be surmounted by a radical change in society, and technical innovations will be of small account.

A possible solution may be the resolve to spend greater resources on quality, but while it is true that such efforts are often starved for funds, some very expensive projects are equally inhuman. And many areas of the world are too hard pressed to be able to allocate economic resources specifically to fine environment.

A final explanation for failure is the technical one: that large-scale environmental design is simply very new, and that urban designers have yet to learn their trade. Good environments were made piecemeal, because that was the only way in which they could be produced in the past. Good ones are not made now, because no one has mastered the new scale of intervention. There have been some successes in planned environments and there may be some hope in increased technical skill. But it will not be effective on any substantial scale unless it is linked to changes in values and in society.

Urban design is effected by many kinds of professionals and decision makers, sometimes consciously, often inadvertently. Those who call themselves urban designers are most likely to be men with architectural or landscape backgrounds, working as parts of much larger teams. For the most part they do project design: shopping centers, housing projects, parks, expositions, universities, medical or government centres, urban renewal sites, and large suburbs. Their employers are large investors and real estate developers, or public development authorities.

Urban designers tend to be found in one of three kinds of organizations. One is the large architectural planning and consulting firm which develops complete projects for their clients from market studies, through programming, financial and legal planning, physical design and engineering, to working drawings and field supervision. They are also employed within public or private agencies that are actually building and managing a piece of the environment. Finally, urban designers may be found in area governments, particularly at the city level, where they regulate the design of public and private projects.

The professional urban designer is distant from the ultimate user, and often at odds with the other actors in the decision-making process. The designer may only implement decisions already made, or may wield substantial power, because of his personal prestige and his ability to frame the terms of debate about spatial alternatives. But his concerns are usually seen as skills to be applied after a basic program is fixed and are thus rarely well meshed into the web of decision. Many other professionals and decision makers shape the city environment, with far more aggregate effect, most often without conscious consideration for environmental quality. Engineers design roads, bridges, and other major features. Real estate developers create substantial districts. Economic planners set resource allocations. Lawyers and administrators frame tax regulations and municipal codes, or set the standards of eligibility for grants. Architects and builders erect single buildings; industrial designers create store fronts, signs, light fixtures, and street furniture. Government departments build and maintain the public ways and put up public buildings. Surveyors lay out subdivisions; utility companies design and install their systems. The manufacturers of standard products, such as light standards or wall panels, have a pervasive effect. Even in Socialist countries, the responsibility for developing and maintaining the city environment is widely fragmented. The man who ultimately suffers or enjoys the product is heard with difficulty.

Elements and Materials of Urban Design

The raw materials from which the urban designer creates his effects are numerous, but the more salient ones may be categorized as follows:

Space.   The voids in a landscape are of primary importance, since man is a mobile animal. The urban designer deals with the spaces accessible to the public, both external (streets, parks, squares) and also internal (lobbies, arcades, tunnels, concourses), with their location, scale, and form, as well as the linkages between them. Large spaces, outdoor ones in particular, are often loose in form, and subject to many optical illusions of distance, visual masking, level change, and geometry. Spaces may be enclosed by opaque barriers, or by intermittent walls, or even by visual suggestions: colonnades, bollards, changes in group pattern, breaks in grade, and imaginary extensions. Buildings have been the traditional enclosures of urban space, but outdoor places are rarely completely enclosed, and contemporary spaces are increasingly open and complex.

Spatial character is affected by proportion, or the size of parts relative to each other, and also by scale, or the size in relation to surrounding objects and to the observer. Spaces vary in effect by the way one moves through them, and by the spaces that precede or follow them. Appearance is modified by activity, by the color and texture of walls and floor, and by the objects with which they are furnished. A deserted square is quite different from a busy one. Light can be used effectively to emphasize texture, conceal or reveal a feature, contract or expand spatial dimensions.

Other senses than vision convey the shape of a space, hearing most notably, since echo location is an accurate cue. The smell of a place is part of its identity, and so is its microclimate: it will be remembered as cool and moist, or hot, bright, and windy. All of these can be modified by the design of a place. Spatial forms have symbolic connotations as well: the awesomeness of great size and the interest of diminutive scale; the protection of the cave and the freedom of the prairie.

There is a rich vocabulary of spatial types: the vista, the court, the slot, the maze, the tunnel, the avenue, the canopy, the glade, the meander, the park, the bowl, the crest, the valley, and many others. At a less abstract level, there are complex urban spatial types: the English residential square, the Italian piazza, the formal French place, the parkway, the avenue, the arcade, the waterfront promenade. New social requirements and the creative efforts of designers are evolving new types as well: freeway, subway station, shopping mall, superblock interior, and industrial estate.

Visible activity.   While designers traditionally focus on visible space, it is not as prominent to most observers as is the sight and sound of other human beings. Seeing and being seen—observing who is there, what they are doing, and what they intend are permanent attractions. The designer can make activity visible; [can] provide places for meetings, promenades, and celebrations: and can reinforce the conduct and mood of action. Light and distance determine whether faces can be read; sound levels make conversation easy or difficult. The movement of ships and trains, the workings of giant machinery, are as fascinating as fire and water.

Sequences.   A landscape is also a network of sequences along the streets, walkways, and transit lines. Any single view is less important than the cumulative effect of a series of views. Coming out of a narrow slot into a broad expanse, for example, is a sure-fire effect. Questions of orientation become significant: the apparent direction toward a goal, the marking of the distance traversed, the clarity of entrance and exit. Each event should prepare for the next. Great cities are known for their walks—a pleasure now often denied. A basic step in urban design is to analyze the consequences of a setting seen, not flatwise or instantaneously, but as a form through which one moves.

Communications.   A landscape communicates meanings to its users, whether by explicit symbols or by the observer's knowledge of the meaning of visible shapes and motions. These meanings are frequently embodied in intentional symbols: words, icons, or conventional referents like the barber pole or the marquee. These signs are necessary and interesting, a flow of information to be clarified and enhanced. They can be used, not simply to sell or command, but to speak of history, ecology, the presence of people, the flow of traffic, weather, time, events to come, and basic values.

Surfaces.   The texture of walls, roofs, and floors is a very noticeable characteristic of the urban scene. The city floor is most important: one touches it as well as sees it. Its cleanliness is an emotional symbol; changes of level force one's attention to it. Textural patterns guide and express action patterns: curbs, runnels, footpaths, tanbark, sand. Textures neutralize or dramatize form. Asphalt is a metaphor for urbanization, but the range of possible surfacing is much wider: cultivated and stabilized earth, low shrubs and ground covers, tall weeds and grass, thickets, tanbark, macadam, sand, gravel, concrete with jointing or surface aggregates, wood blocks and decking, terrazzos, mosaics, blocks, bricks, tiles, cobbles, setts, and slabs. Short-run cost and mechanical maintenance lead to the use of concrete or grass, but variety of use should lead to variety of material.

Rock, earth, and water.   Under the surface finish, the environmental base is rock and earth. Cuts and fills, pits and outcrops, cliffs, caves, and hills give one an intuition of the planet whose surface one inhabits. Underlying rock is hidden, and bare earth seems indecent, yet they are expressive, and often welcome, materials.

Water is also elemental—simple in its nature but extremely varied in effect. The range of common terms is an index of its potential—ocean, pool, sheet, jet, torrent, rill, drop, spray, cascade, film—as are the kinds of liquid motion—trickle, splash, foam, flood, pour, spout, surge, ripple, run. This range of form and motion, this changeableness in unity, the play of light and sound, the intimate connection with life, all make water a superb outdoor material. Moving water gives a sense of life, still water unity and rest. Water plays with light, reflecting the changing sky or sunlit objects nearby. Water is technically troublesome, but hypnotically attractive.

Plants.   Many great landscapes are treeless; there are handsome squares that do not include a visible plant of any description. Yet plants are one of the fundamental landscape materials, and the most widely enjoyed. But planting is the "extra" in development, the first item to be cut when the budget pinches.

Plant species are chosen for their hardiness, given the microclimate, soil condition, expected traffic, and level of maintenance. Texture and the general habit of growth are more predictable than individual shape, and more telling. Initial appearance, maturity, and decay must all be considered, since this is a living landscape. The aim is to so manage the landscape that it becomes a stable, self-replacing system as rapidly as possible.

Detail. A developed site includes many man-made details: fences, seats, signal boxes, poles, meters, trash cans, fireplugs, manholes, wires, lights, mailboxes, steps, curbs, and telephones. It is curious that most of this list evokes a sense of disharmony. This is the as yet unassimilated equipment of urban civilization whose presence cannot be banished. Alarms must be found; trash cans must be moved; tired people want to sit; fences mark off personal territory. Designers have often been concerned about site detail, but usually in order to hide it, or to "organize" it, or to give it stylish form. Less attention has been given to its actural use and the form appropriate to that use.

Criteria

Environmental stress. A place may be too hot, too noisy, too bright, too loaded with information, too odorous, too windy, too dirty or polluted, even too clean, too empty, or too silent. The physiological and perceptual stresses imposed by the physical environment are a common complaint of city life. Climate, noise, pollution, and the level of visual input are the factors most often referred to. Usually there is an acceptable range, with a threshold of tolerance at either end. The range has a biological basis, but it is affected by what is culturally acceptable, by the temperament of the person, and by the activity he is engaged in. For particular groups, engaged in similar behavior, one can usually find substantial agreement about what is unpleasant or intolerable. Thus there is a commonly accepted Western stantard for the maximum noise level in a sleeping area, while the standards for comfortable domestic indoor temperatures shift by as much as ten degress from one European country to another.

Somewhat more objective than the sense of comfort is the relation of environmental stress to health and efficiency. There is information that links air pollution to lung disease, and noise to work output or to the health of pregnant mothers, for example. But the human organism is notoriously adaptable, and survives, sometimes without conscious difficulty, under conditions of loud noise or heavy pollution. They key issue is whether these adaptations may not be exacting a severe but hidden price. In any event, the complaints about city noise, city pollution, and city climate are widespread. There are known ways of ameliorating those effects, and no place should be designed without thought for the microclimate it will produce, how clean its air or water will be, and whether it will be well shielded from intrusive noise.

Behavioral support. It may seem obvious that a place should support the actions that people want to undertake in it, but this is normally disregarded. Doors cannot easily be opened, packages must be carried up steep stairs, paths are slippery or do not lead where people want to go, there is no place to sit or to talk in comfort, public toilets are lacking, there is no place to wash the car, or to dig, or to leave the baby. Outdoor spaces are conceived of as volumes having a visual or formal character, rather than as settings for people doing things. If behavior is considered, it is usually of the most formal and stereotyped kind: playing baseball, admiring a view, or parking a car. The actions intended are reduced to a single class, to which the place is completely dedicated. Or the setting is used as a determinant to compel people to act in a certain way—an effort that normally and happily fails. No thought is given to the actual diversity and richness of human behavior, nor to how different groups and actions often overlap with each other. This can in part be overcome by a specific program; i.e., a careful and detailed statement of the human behavior that is expected and desired, an account of how the environment should facilitate it, and to what extent it should be open to variant behavior. This is quite different from the standard program, which is a simple list of spaces to be provided. The behavioral program must consider timing as well as location, so that conflicts and joint use can be provided for. Places can also be analyzed to see if they provide for the actions that men are always engaged in: the ability to move about easily, without confusion, and safely; the ability to use one's senses; the opportunity to communicate with others; the chance for privacy and security. A place should increase a user's competence in doing what he proposes to do and, even more, make it possible for him to act in new ways. Thus the designer must consider the management of a place, as well as its initial form.

Identity.   Particular places should have a clear perceptual identity: recognizable, memorable, vivid, engaging of attention, and differentiated from other locations. This is the objective basis for perception. It is a support for the sense of belonging to some place-attached group, as well as a way of marking a behavioral territory.

The test for site identity is not the novelty of its graphic presentation, but the degree to which it is vividly remembered and identified by its people. Thus an understanding of how a user looks at the world is critical to achieving identity. Since it is a function of the observer's mental image, identity can also be increased by educating the observer, and by training him to see significant differences that he never noticed before. If users are allowed to adapt a site to their particular purpose, and if these adaptations are allowed to accumulate over time, the identity of the site can be expected to increase.

Diversity.   One of the commonly recognized delights of of great cities is their diversity of people and places. A corresponding criticism of small towns, or suburbs, or central ghettoes, is the lack of access to varied opportunities. Diversity is an obvious prerequisite for choice, and corresponds to a widely felt pleasure in variety and change. Some variety of stimulus is an important condition for cognitive development, and indeed for the very maintenance of the human perceptual system, as experiments have demonstrated.

It is more difficult to determine what should be diversified, and the relative diversity between two different proposals is also difficult to measure. All objects are to some extent different from each other, and most differences are trivial. Equally puzzling is the measurement of "adequate" diversity. A range of choice exhilarating to one person may be threatening to another. One person may want choice of places in which to buy clothes, and another a choice of views.

An urban designer must therefore inquire into the diversity that people consider important. Much of the apparent variety in the environment—of commercial products, for example—is simply trivial and confusing. Some of the diversity that is desired will refer to the sensuous environment—to having choices between places that are calm or stimulating, lonely or crowded, artificial or natural, as well as some choice of behavior settings. There is a common fantasy, for example, of living in a secluded garden, from which one may pass onto a lively street.

Perceived diversity is a function of actual variety, but also of how accessible that variety is, and of how capable or interested the residents are in being aware of that objective variety. Perceived diversity can therefore be changed by increasing objective diversity, but also by improving the access to it, or by educating the person to be interested in it. Building on present choices, a good environment also opens up new ones.

Legibility.   There is a common, and more debatable, argument that the elements of an environment should be so arranged that the normal observer can understand their pattern in time and space. Under this rule, a city whose layout can be understood, or whose history is visible, is better than one that is chaotic or has destroyed its past.

Legible structure in the outside world has an obvious value in facilitating the practical tasks of way-finding and cognition. It improves access, and therefore opportunity. It can be a source of emotional security, and a basis for a sense of self in relation to society. It can support civic cohesion, and be a means of extending one's knowledge of the world. It also confers the aesthetic pleasure of perceiving the relatedness of a complex thing. There is a common pleasure in seeing a city from some high place. On the other hand, the structural chaos of the great urban regions is notorious.

Legibility must work for the anxious tourist, the knowledgeable inhabitant intent on his practical task, and the casual stroller. Different people look for different kinds of clues, yet most refer to certain basic elements, such as main circulation, basic functional areas, principal centers, the natural site, the big open spaces, perhaps the best-known "historic" points. Temporal legibility is as important as spatial legibility. The landscape can orient its inhabitants to the past, to the cyclical rhythms of the present, and even to the hopes and dangers of the future.

Meaning. The environment is an enormous communications device. People read it constantly—they seek practical information, they are curious, they are moved by what they see.

The symbolic role of landscape is interesting, but it is unfortunately little understood. Significance differs widely between various groups. Dominant values may be clearly expressed by the size of buildings devoted to large corporations and insurance companies, or by the multiplicity of signs that urge one to buy things. But these symbols are not correspondent to the values of the submerged groups, or to values newly rising into prominence.

Regardless of this divergence, the identity and legibility of places provide a common visible base to which all people can give their own interpretation. A cluster of skyscrapers may signify exhilarating power to one and cruel oppression to the other, but both have a visible object for their feelings. Visible structure should be congruent with functional and social structure. Visual units, for example, should correspond with social units, such as the family. Landmarks should correspond to actual foci of activity or of social significance. Physically defined territories fitted to behavioral territories is another example of congruence between the visible and the social world.

City signs are often damned on aesthetic grounds, but they perform an important function. The flow of information must be regulated, so that priority signs (public control messages, for example) cannot be missed. At the same time, the observer must be able to tune out, which argues against various obtrusive devices: public broadcasts, flashing lights, or the preemption of key locations in vistas or at decision points. Signs may be used to expand what a man can learn of his city. Public information centers could become highly attractive.

It may also be desirable to increase the "transparency" of the city landscape, for economic and social processes are today increasingly hidden from sight. Indeed, construction sites are so interesting because they are one of the few industrial processes still left open to view. It might be public policy to encourage visual exposure, partly directly, and partly by remote sensing. Cities might regain, without impairment of function, some of the vitality and immediacy of the pre-industrial city, with its open workshops and markets. On the other hand, there is also the risk of invading privacy. A policy of visual exposure is intriguing but senstive.

As one goes deeper into the subject, numerous difficulties are encountered: diversity of values, the efforts of special interests to capture and to falsify the communications system, and even the embarrassments of revealing some features of society as they really are. And yet places and buildings evoke strong feelings in their observers, and these feelings should be an important concern for the designer; the seeming aloofness and impenetrability of a city hall, for example, the awesome frigidity of an office lobby, or the calm invitingness of a public park.

Development.   Particularly in childhood, but to some extent in later years, environment plays its part in the intellectual, emotional, and physical growth of the individual. The negative effects of highly impoverished settings have been demonstrated. The role of rich sense perceptions in human maturation has some basis in laboratory experiment, but for the most part it remains speculative, although highly probable.

An educative environment would be full of available information, visibly encouraging attention and exploration, particularly when the observer is not task-oriented—as when he is at play, traveling, or just waiting. A learning environment alternates moments of high stimulus and quiet privacy. It would include opportunities to manipulate the world directly. The use of a city as a teaching device is a fascinating subject. Its connection to city design criteria is suggestive but uncertain.

Perceptual engagement.   Beyond all these, there is the sheer delight of sensing the world: the play of light, the feel and smell of the wind, touches, sounds, colors, forms. It is difficult to impose such things, but the designer can prevent the blotting-out of sensation (as by featureless noise, or a bland facade). He can keep the environment open to the sky or the presence of people. Dynamic elements never fail to catch attention: moving water, living creatures, clouds, light and fire, moving machinery, or pennants, which make visible the currents of air.

Constraints.   The power and purposes of clients and users will always be the key determinant in the urban design process. There are numerous other conditions, however, that also influence the outcome. One is the basic nature of the site itself: its topography, vegetative cover, climate, ecology. Seacoast and riverine sites, plains and mountains, marshes and deserts, each impose typical limitations and offer typical possibilities. Local accidents of ground, as well as basic site character, are also influential: a small rise of ground may determine a view, the orientation of a building, or the course of a street. The variations in the microclimate can be particularly important.

Natural site conditions are perhaps less determining than in the past, because of the power of modern technology to change them: to fill in the sea, cut off a hill, or air condition large interior spaces. But as this power is exercised, it is often found that the secondary consequences are surprising: the buried river floods, heat islands build up over the cities, tidal water becomes stagnant, and the land slips and erodes.

The power to override the particularities of natural site has had still another effect. Cities begin to look like one another all over the world. Airports, as an extreme case, are almost indistinguishable, but so are many central areas, suburbs, or apartment districts. Closer attention to site conditions would help to prevent this. But close support and expression of cultural differences would do even more.

Urban designers must cope not only with natural, but [also] with previous man-made conditions. There are existing structures, and an existing system of circulation. There is a network of utilities and of public services. Only occasionally can a society afford to sweep away all its previous environmental capital, and even then the unanticipated social and psychological costs are likely to be severe. Urban designs are most often complex remodelings, successive sets of changes that retain much of the previous pattern of development. An analysis of what previous elements must be retained and which can be cleared away is a typical early step.

Circulation patterns are particularly persistent, since they are reinforced by other patterns such as ownership lines and utility systems. The pattern of streets will last for centuries, while buildings come and go, and even the street itself is many times rebuilt. The invisible lot lines and buried utilities are extremely conservative in effect. There will be other legal or social rights, inclusive of mutually agreed-upon "territories" felt to be the proper domain of some special group. There will be persistent behavior settings: places where people are accustomed to doing certain things, and which resist disruption. There are sacred places, old market locations, and meeting grounds; and any plan that displaces them will meet resistance. Therefore, account must be taken of the images that people have about their environment: the territories they divide it into, how they link it up, what meanings they attach to it, what activities they are accustomed to carry out where. Like the ecological system, or the inherited physical setting, this existing social image must be understood before changes can be made. If not, the consequences may be unexpected: vandalism, bitterness, the failure of a new commercial facility, disorientation, or political opposition.

In planning, as in spatial economics, the environment is considered to be a set of activity locations and their linkages. Each activity has preferences for its site and for its connection to other activities. A plan seeks an optimum pattern of locations and linkages, considering the relative importance of each activity (which may be measured in social value, political power, or the ability to pay). This planned pattern, which includes a transportation network, can then become the framework of an urban design. How those activities were classified, linked, and weighted was critical in setting the pattern. Therefore, those assumptions cannot be accepted without demur. Circulation requirements, in particular, are a chief technical constraint in urban design. Requirements for moving and storing automobiles loom very large in most urban schemes: the demands of access, alignment, and sheer volume of space are substantial. That these demands are not iron laws, but rather the reflection of social decisions about the mode and speed of travel, is sometimes forgotten. But a high level of circulation and communication, whatever the mode, is likely to be a persistent feature of any new urban development, and so the techniques of arranging highways, vehicle storage, transit lines, airports, waterways, railways, and pedestrian paths turn out to be the most frequently used urban design skill. Utilities and communication nets are equally important features of the urban infrastructure, but their technical demands are less often determining in the spatial arrangement of a place.

Among other technical requirements, the demands of safety usually rank high; i.e., safety from fire or earthquake, and individual safety from moving traffic or personal assault. Traffic fatalities are numerous, and the incidence of theft and assault is rising. Thus there will be much attention given to the safety of intersection designs, the spacing of buildings for fire retardation, or the ability of an area to be surveyed and controlled by police or local neighbors. Elsewhere, the dominant fear may be the likelihood of organized assault: aerial bombardment, ground attack, or organized sabotage. Historically, one of the chief technical skills of a city designer was his knowledge of defense fortifications.

Health requirements are another set of technical constraints. The greatest success of 19th-century city planning were their improvements in local sanitation, improvements generally well assimilated into the urban design principles of today. The worst problems are now the large-scale pollution of ground, air, and water and its long-term consequences for human health. Preventing such pollution puts some special constraints on environmental design, of which planners are only now becoming aware. Of the effects of environmental form on mental health, however, there is still great ignorance.

Cost is a powerful constraint, as in any kind of capital investment, and urban designers must know how to make estimates of construction and maintenance costs. These costings are not only less detailed than typical architectural or engineering estimates, but are quite incomplete in other ways. The social and psychological costs of a change are often disregarded, a feature sadly so familiar in most economic decisions. But even the direct money costs of a proposal are incompletely analyzed due to the multiplicity of clients, the long time spans, and the way in which decisions are made. Political costs may dominate the outcome. Only the money costs to the initiating developer or agency may be computed, while the resulting costs to other actors—a transit agency, for example, or a dislocated business—are simply ignored. The effects of inflation over the long period of construction, or the costs of maintenance, are as often neglected. Urban developments thus typically cost substantially more to carry out than originally estimated. Since benefits are calculated even more carelessly, it sometimes happens that real benefits may inflate as rapidly as costs. Rational cost-benefit accounting of urban designs is just beginning and necessarily remains incomplete, since many costs and benefits are not to be translated into money units. More rational cost-benefit studies may, in fact, tend to submerge factors not easily quantifiable.

The Social Setting of Urban Design

The visible form of a city reflects the social and economic setting in which it was created and maintained. This is quite apparent during the normal design process. When the designer enters that process, the solution has long been evolving. A problem has been recognized, a client organized, the economic resources to be allotted to the task are usually determined, and the political and administrative rules are set. Even the act of turning to an urban designer implies that a new spatial pattern should be a part of the solution. More often than not, a complete schedule of space requirements has been prepared.

Even within these limits, the designer has some room in which to maneuver. He can raise questions about elements of the program. He can communicate with others who have a stake in the outcome, or even help them to maneuver into a client position. He can propose other values and criteria, such as those outlined above, and suggest possibilities that resolve old conflicts or that create new values to be exploited. He may also sway decisions by his personal prestige, or by the way he formulates the complicated alternatives for decision, alternatives that are difficult for the non-designer to pick apart and reformulate. Finally, he is often able to make decisions about form in areas independent of his client's major concerns, which may focus on profit, on a favorable political reaction, or on completion on time and within the budget. In this case, the client may be glad to leave to the designer features that do not compromise those central aims.

A number of groups are usually involved in any decision, and the designer is often motivated to bring in still more, so that ultimate users can also participate in the decision making. This implies complex and sometimes cumbersome communications, and causes frequent recycling of design. Usually it is necessary to impose arbitrary limits on the participating clients, if the decision process is to work at all. Deciding on the key clients—those with the greatest stake in the outcome or with the greatest real power to carry it out—and determining the balance between those clients is difficult. Enforcing it takes substantial political energy. The designer does not usually make such decisions, but he plays some role in the decision making, and is ethically implicated.

Since there are many decision makers, conflicts are to be expected. Progress is made by negotiation, and the negotiators who have a single functional goal in mind or are focused on a small area and can therefore be flexible on all other issues are those most likely to succeed. The private developer will accept all sorts of public rules that do not threaten his rate of profit. The transit agency is happy as long as it gets its routes and terminals. Quality, however, usually depends on the effect of a whole system. At the points of hard bargaining and over a long succession of decisions, quality gives ground to the thrust of quantifiable, bounded, functional goals or of narrow territorial interests.

On occasion, this typical situation is modified. Sometimes the designer is part of a constructing agency that has effective powers of decision and implementation—a new town authority, for example. The designer does not make the decisions, but he is linked directly to those who make and carry out decisions; and he is therefore in a much better position to help set up the problem and participate in its realization and management. In return, the decision makers and implementers penetrate more deeply into his own design process.

At other times, designers attach themselves directly to some client group, helping the group organize to influence the definition of the problem. Rather than creating some definite solution, the designer gathers technical information and sketches possibilities so that his group can influence a larger decision process. He is an advocate, whose loyalty is to his client group—which may be a comfortable position, or may entail sacrifices if the client is weak and poor.

The designer may become a champion rather than an advocate, attaching himself to some solution and pressing to assemble the client and the power to carry it through. This is uphill work, only rarely successful in the individual case, but often having a slow cumulative effect, as the possibilities of some new kind of design solution begin to enter the world of alternatives perceived by the decision makers. Thus new towns, parkways, adventure playgrounds, urban renewal, city parks, [and] downtown plazas have been successfully championed and picked up by other groups to carry through. In some cases, however, the motives of the implementing group may differ from those of the champion, and thus the nature of the solution will be distorted.

The form of the environment can be influenced in a number of ways. The most obvious, to a designer trained in architecture, is simply to specify the environment in a set of drawings. This is rarely possible. It may be possible, however, to design the key localities in detail (major squares, main avenues) or some special elements or systems (bikeways, lighting, prototype housing, highways). The design of repeatable systems is an opportunity often neglected in urban design. One may choose to design some demonstration project as a stimulus to other actors.

Most urban designs are diagrammatic. They refer, not so much to the exact form of things, as to the character or spatial effect intended, the clusters of behavior expected in the spaces provided, the image structure, the basic circulation and activity location, and the types of management of control. They may specify selected detail: lighting, signs, textures, sounds. A diagrammatic model, a control document, a series of slides, or a film may be better than a plan, section, or elevation. Showing how a place will develop over time is more effective than drawing what its final form will be. Illustrative sketches, showing one possible outcome according to the principles proposed, are frequently used in place of definitive plans. The "hard-line" drawings of engineering and architecture are too frequently used in circumstances in which there is no certainty, finality, or detailed control.

Without making specific designs, one may control the design process of others. This can be done by legal rules, or by specifying characteristics of the design process (imposing competitions or user consultation, for example), by design review, or by indirect economic controls (subsidies, tax rules). In the complexities of large-scale development, such indirect controls must be relied upon. Design review has often been successful, especially where it has been introduced early in the design process. Economic controls are a powerful means in an economy dependent upon private enterprise. Design controls, such as those that specify the character of facades or the shape of built volume, have had very uneven success, and are laborious to administer. All too often, they are a signal that urban designers are playing at designing a city as if it were a building.

Performance standards of environmental quality might be a more efficient and flexible means of control, although they are not often employed. They could be founded on a sensuous program that would specify desired visibility, spatial character, visible activity, texture, apparent motion, sign content, light, noise, or climate. Thus such a program might propose, at some particular junction, that there be a landmark identifiable day or night from a mile away, visibly displaying its internal activity, whose form distinguishes the various turns and approaches one from another. Such a program could be satisfied by many particular shapes, according to the motives of that structure's developer. In another case, the desired microclimate, noise level, sign content, and provision of seating and shelter along a public street might be the characteristics specified, just as one is as accustomed to specify lane width for traffic, or the allowable inflammability of building materials.

The principal aim of urban design is to improve the quality of the human spatial environment, and, by so doing, to improve the quality of human life. It does not directly attack underlying social problems, such as poverty, war, inequality, or alienation, nor is it usually a very efficient way of doing so. But since it deals with the setting of social life, it is necessarily influenced by those underlying problems, and in turn influences them. War can destroy a fine landscape, poverty can make it unbearable, and alienation can render it meaningless. The effect of a place cannot be judged without reference to social conditions; neither can the quality of life be deduced solely from social conditions without reference to the spatial setting. Environment can have specific effects of its own: its territorial division may serve to reinforce segregation; it may open up new opportunities to people; its form influences the personal growth of children. The process of building the environment may support self-reliance and new institutions among disadvantaged people. Environmental modification is always a possible element in any general strategy of social change. Most revolutionary societies devote some of their effort to the reorganization of their living space, even though purely perceptual effects may not have a high priority.

Typical Problems in Urban Design

A better understanding of urban design comes from looking at some of the typical situations in which it is involved, or might be involved.

Area policy. Only rarely has environmental quality been considered at the scale of the whole city or region, at which level recommendations have traditionally dealt with land use and open space patterns, housing supply, public facilities, and the technical systems of transport and utilities. Regional quality is the framework for local quality, however. Analyses of the visual form of a region or a city have been accomplished recently in the cities of Minneapolis, San Francisco, and Los Angeles in the United States. Large landscape elements have also been surveyed, such as the lower Thames and its banks in England and part of the valley of the Ticino in Italy. Regional plans have been made that incorporated visual criteria with ecological considerations, such as a plan for the Green Spring and Worthington valleys near Baltimore. The new agriculural greenbelt around Havana, the so-called Cordon, is a conscious attempt to create a new visual scene, as well as to remold the economy of the city and the ideology of its citizens. Existing areas of strong character have plans for their preservation, as in the vicinity of Florence. Studies of the ability of small areas to absorb new development without visual damage are being used as one input for regional growth policy, notably around Helsinki. But the technical and political effort that will be required to control regional landscape quality, and to think of humane conditions of existence at that reach of size, has still to be made.

New settlements. Where new settlements are being built by conscious plan, there is greater acceptance of the necessity for dealing with sensuous form, although the results have not been spectacular. The best work has been done in residential suburbs of moderate size, usually built for the well-to-do. Roland Park, Riverside, Chatham Village, and Radburn in the United States, and the earlier Bedford Park and Hampstead Garden Suburb in Great Britain, may be cited. Good suburbs are still being built, and the most recent phenomenon is the designed community of vacation homes, as at New Seabury, on Cape Cod. These are pleasant places, relying on a careful fit to the ground, ample space and greenery, good design of spatial form along the street, and close control of signs, lights, fences, street furniture, and other detail.

Designs for new towns have been more ambitious, and in general the earlier examples, such as England's Welwyn, seem to be the more successful ones. Reston, Virginia, has a handsome, if rather unreal, central area and lake; and the recent Tapiola in Finland is outstanding for its landscaping and the variety and finesse of its detailed site planning. Most of the new towns, however, have been no better than moderately pleasant suburbs, at least in visual terms, and many are quite monotonous or raw. Thamesmead, upriver of London, displays a sophisticated use of industrialized components and a fine use of river bottom land, but the housing is expensive, and some of its formal brilliance is of doubtful use. Cumbernauld (Scotland), Chandīgarh (India), and Brasília (Brazil) are now widely criticized for their imposition of an alien form on a living community.

The difficulties in dealing with the form of new towns are quite similar to those in evolving areawide policies: the large scale, the complexity, the distance between designer and user, the inability to control or diversify rapid mass development. Thus the plans for one of the newest and technically most advanced of the British new towns—Milton Keynes—passes over questions of visual form very lightly, except for policies on the retention of natural features. To these difficulties must be added the peculiar nature of the new towns—their rapid growth, their lack of a past, the dissociation of the planning from the future inhabitants. The visual richness deriving from a visible history, or from the diverse ways in which different people fit their environment to a local situation, are necessarily missing. Any successes have primarily depended on skillful local site planning. The vast mass of new urbanization throughout the world is monotonous and barren. Nor is this simply a matter of poverty, since some of the most interesting new places are the intricate self-help settlements of the underdeveloped nations.

The record in the denser housing project is equally poor, although the task is closer to the normal architectural one, and the techniques are better developed. It is quite possible to cite moderate- or high-density residential projects of good quality, but they are lost in a great wilderness of inhuman slabs and grim barracks. In Great Britain and Scandinavia, however, there are many more frequent examples of livable, pleasant housing projects.

Rehabilitation, redevelopment, conservation. Urban design received its strongest official impetus in the United States from the federally sponsored urban renewal program, in which moderately large sites were cleared for complex housing and commercial projects in the center of cities. Since this was a highly visible program under political attack and was backed by groups for whom visual quality was important, a substantial stress was put on good urban design. Opportunities for laying out complex projects were frequent, whereas previously they had been rare. Schools and firms specializing in this work appeared. The results were uneven. While some handsome projects resulted, mostly in central business districts, most work suffered from designer megalomania and administrative confusion. Operating agencies and large developers made the key decisions, while the future user (much less the existing one) was rarely consulted.

Even though these projects were concerned with city-center areas, they were usually treated as isolated designs. True renewal (i.e., a restoration of the existing fabric for the use of existing occupants) was not accomplished. Urban design has little skill in enhancing existing social and built values, as one might enhance a natural landscape. Improvements have occurred in older areas attractive to higher-income owners, but these improvements usually conceal social costs. In only a very few instances have public agencies been successful in helping local inhabitants to improve the appearance of their own local region, as in Wooster Square in New Haven. The key action has been the rendering of design services to the inhabitants, rather than designing for them. Rehabilitation and renewal remain among the most critical social tasks to be undertaken in urban design.

When the problem is not rehabilitation but the preservation of quality already achieved, the technical task is relatively simple and familiar: to analyze the existing visual quality of the place, and to draw up guidelines for any remodeling or new construction. These guidelines may require strict replacement or copying, especially of exterior facades, or may only entail careful attention to mass, scale, spacing, fenestration, and materials. There are numerous successful and admired examples of this type of action: Boston's Beacon Hill, New Orleans' Vieux Carré, [and] the heart of Charleston, South Carolina spring to mind. At times, preservation of this kind may have a high political priority, and may absorb significant capital in a hard-pressed nation, as did the Stare Miasto in Warsaw. Preserving existing values is easier than creating new ones, yet preservation can play no more than a minor role in the general task of urban design.

Lines of movement.   One perceives the city while walking or riding through it. Since roads, paths, and transit systems are normally built and maintained by public agencies, the design of these channels is an important branch of urban design. The design criteria focus on the functioning of the transportation line, the pleasure and information to be had while traveling along it, and the impact of the channel on the observer who is outside of it. The latter concern introduces goals partially in conflict with the formal ones.

Main avenues have been designed in the past, principally in terms of their cross section, and sometimes as slow monumental approaches. Designs that deal with sequence and dynamic experience are relatively new and scarce. A number of rural freeways in the United States are among the best examples of large-scale environmental design in the world today. The fit to ground, the use of landscaping, the variations of space and motion, are superb. On the other hand, although there are interesting urban highways whose form arose by exterior circumstance (the Schuylkill River Parkway in Philadelphia, for example), there are no examples of successful deliberate design, although there have been illustrative proposals.

While some thought has been given to highway visual design, almost no consideration has been given to mass transit design. Riding a bus or train is quite different in visibility and role from driving a car, and expectations are low. The view from the bus enters into no current designer calculations. The design of pedestrian ways in parks or tourist grounds is a more traditional concern, but the pedestrian on the ordinary city street is usually ignored. Bicycle paths are carefully designed in many European countries and are appearing in the United States, but again with little thought for the moving view. In Great Britain, some of the old industrial canals have been retained and refurbished for recreational voyages. The view from the airplane seems a ridiculous question and yet in the future may merit attention. Roads are often only one element of an entire linear environment. The highway commercial strip is notoriously ugly and confusing, but it has a strong functional justification. In order to create a handsome landscape, it might be feasible to combine a highway with linear uses in one integrated structure. The idea has been proposed intermittently, but never carried through, except in a few rather trivial uses of "air rights" by office or apartment buildings.

Commercial centers and central districts. Some of the most sophisticated work in urban design has occurred in commercial centers. This is hardly surprising, considering the large investments in those centers, the effective control of form that is possible, and the importance of attractive form for increasing profits. The urban renewal work most often admired for its quality has almost all occurred within central business districts. The projects are typically a mix of shops, offices, public buildings, and some luxury apartments. They are complex in form, using separate levels and specialized buildings to deal with use and traffic mixtures at high densities. Normally, they include a public plaza. Arcades, escalators, raised pedestrian decks and walkways, and underground parking are common features. They are expensive, handsome in detail, and often rather cold and inhuman in general effect because of the design focus on pure form and of economic pressures toward a narrow spectrum of high-paying uses. The complex sequences of interior public space set new problems for design. Artificial light and climate replace their natural counterparts. The public ways are the corridors and tunnels.

The regional shopping center is now a successful and much imitated model, more closely based on behavioral knowledge than any other type of environmental design. Now rather artificial, specialized, and physically isolated, they could, nonetheless, be integrated with other functions to become true social centers.

Special areas. Urban design has had some success in the layout of large institutions, where centralized control of form has also been possible. Large urban hospitals have usually been an exercise in complex technical form at high intensity. Campus planning for universities and colleges has provided frequent opportunities to establish an integrated landscape. Not only are the existing schools growing, but new campuses are being set out. Many of them are barren affairs, but it is quite possible to produce a pleasant environment. Some of the outstanding successes provide complete living environments, usually with enough space to allow for fine landscaping. Planning for rapid growth is a typical difficulty, as is maintaining a handsome landscape in the face of demands for parking and access. The traditional organization of higher education often results in some rather stereotyped buildings and unit organizations. The nature of an environment for learning has not yet been considered in any profound way. Yet university campuses are often, because of their visible life and landscaped setting, very attractive parts of cities. Too often, they are islands of culture, as shopping centers are islands of consumption.

Another special area that has received some design attention is the industrial park or estate. Extensive areas under single control are set aside for industry, often with accompanying services such as banks, restaurants, or maintenance and distribution facilities. Most often, the form of these estates has been determined by rail and road access, or by internal layout requirements. More recently, the visible aspect of these estates has come to be considered. Such estates or parks are regulated to keep factories simple in form, of good materials, and well set back and landscaped. At best, an innocuous green landscape of low buildings is the result. Little attention is given to making the work that goes on in these areas significant or pleasant, or to connect it with other life functions. Similarly, no advantage is taken of the potential drama of industry: there is no immediate vision of what goes on inside.

The great expositions are excellent occasions for innovation, and indeed many of the earlier ones were outstanding: the World's Columbian Exposition of 1893 in Chicago, the Paris Exposition of 1889, and the London Exposition of 1851. Recent fairs have produced little that is new amid much visual confusion. There have been innovations in structures, such as Montreal's Habitat, but not in the organization of the general environment. The modern fair is highly competitive, and the scattered developers, who are under extreme time pressure, are difficult to coordinate.

Large natural and man-made features. The design of large state and national parks has become a well-developed environmental specialty, closely related to landscape architecture and forestry. Handling big crowds, preventing ecological damage, preserving the appearance of a natural landscape, supplying a whole range of recreation for varied tastes without mutual interference—all of these are the central problems, and they are often competently handled. Details are simple, and maintenance is stressed. The landscape is used to teach the visitor about the structure of nature.

The smaller urban park was the problem on which landscape architecture cut its teeth, and some of the older city parks provide fine examples of environmental design. Recent city park design has been less successful, and suffers from a certain standardization and emptiness of appearance and function. New work in children's playgrounds has been more impressive: complex and challenging landscapes have been created, built of simple materials, and fitted to the actual behavior and interests of the child. The "adventure playgrounds" in which children use space and raw materials to build their own surroundings and equipment, have been particularly interesting. Hopefully, this will lead into the design of true "learning environments."

The enhancement of large natural features was an important aspect of earlier work in what was then called civic design. Seafronts, lakefronts, streams, and ponds were improved as promenades, or for boating, swimming, and picnicking. Waterfronts and river banks have been magnificently developed in many European cities. They have been generally neglected in the United States, although there are a few fine examples: the Chicago lakefront, the basin of the Charles River in Boston, the Golden Gate Park in San Francisco, and the river walk in San Antonio. But with the economic decline of the city waterfront as a port and industrial region, many cities in the United States are now slowly moving to reclaim those water edges: Boston, New York, Philadelphia, and St. Louis are but a few among the best-known American examples.

Mountains and great hills, less frequent within urban limits, are rarely used for their landscape qualities, although they may have a small park or panoramic view near their summit. A number of great cities have exceptional opportunities in the contrast of mountain and city: Caracas, San Salvador, Buenos Aires, and Los Angeles, to name a few. The great bridges are dramatic city elements, but few are designed as landscape to be walked over, climbed, passed under, and played upon. Dams and reservoirs are strong landscape elements, but the enormous spoil heaps of industry are classed as ugly and therefore ignored or camouflaged.

Special systems. Some work has been done on particular environmental systems: sets of things that are extended over large areas but do not make complete landscapes in themselves. In a time when urbanized areas will expand at unprecedented rates, using industrialized components in designing systems may be an excellent lever for the extensive improvement of quality. Planting plans are the most familiar example of environmental system design. Typical arrangements and species are prescribed for avenues, minor streets, walkways, paths, and front gardens. The designs are intended to ensure minimum quality and to fit tree types to typical demands and scales. They may also be used to give an identifiable character to particular districts or streets, or to mark out the main structure of the region. Although trees are not usually thought of as industrial products, in fact they are grown in quantity, on demand, by factory methods. Many fine urban areas are notable primarily for the way in which they are planted.

Signs have been given some attention. Most of the emphasis has been on immediate visual appearance, and very little on information content, which is a sign's reason for being. Public lighting has also been discussed, since many designers see the tremendous potentialities of artificial light. But lighting studies frequently come down to the form of the light pole, which is the least important aspect of the subject. Other products are rarely designed for their direct human impact. Various pieces of street furniture are obvious examples, as are the ubiquitous paving materials: asphalt, concrete, and the concrete curb.

System design might also be applied to larger chunks of the environment. One promising possibility is the design of mobile housing units and their immediate settings. While the houses themselves are meticulously designed as industrial products, the trailer settlements are not far from the quality of the original lots where they were first parked. Systematic design of typical units and their arrangement in housing neighborhoods would be a strategic way of affecting the quality of a large sector of the moderate-cost housing supply. The temporary settlements of the Tennessee Valley Authority were pioneer successes whose results have been forgotten.

Visions

Most often designers take no time to create new visions, in contrast to their reputations as imaginative men. Their visions are the historic plazas of Europe or the romantic site planning of Sir Raymond Unwin and Frederick Law Olmsted, or that combination of high density and high technology that is found in Le Corbusier's designs.

Perhaps the most famous recent demonstration of new environmental possibilities has been the Habitat of Expo 67, the Montreal World's Fair of 1967, in which residential units were piled one above the other in an irregular hill-like structure. The roofs of units below provided the open spaces for units above, and all parts were interconnected by pedestrian links at every level, as if the apartment building had become a three-dimensional village. Construction costs were high, but visitors were enchanted.

Recent visionary projects for large environments take up the theme of three-dimensional complexity and usually marry it with a very advanced technology of movement and climate control, coupled with an emphasis on rapid change, high density, and a display of startling, machine-made yet organic-looking forms. These ideas arise just at a time when most people in the world are hoping for lower densities and when there is a revulsion against high technology and centralized control. The visions seem to point where no one wants to go and ignore much of what has been learned about the impact of environment on behavior.

Another strong idealistic current has as yet had less direct effect on urban design, although the current comes from deep historical sources, and most urban designers have a sympathy for it. This is the theme of ecological balance which links up with the old ideas of a "return to nature," and to some extent with the Marxist ideal of the merging of city and country. The romantic, low-density suburb and the widespread American "second home in the country" have been a realistic working out of the same ideas. But while suburbs and vacation houses allow many people to enjoy a more pleasant and humane setting, they have also been one further step in the urbanization of the countryside. They make no true integration to rural pursuits.

In the United States the new "communes" are another expression of the longing for a rural return, as were many attempts at subsistence farming during the Great Depression. The communes combine radical social change with the old dream of agricultural simplicity and with a preference for handmade artifacts and environment. As yet all these currents have had little direct influence on the practice of urban design, except for the new use of ecological surveys to help determine the future use of undeveloped land. It is remarkable that no visions (with the exception of the "paradigms," which appeared in the 1940s in the Goodmans' "Communitas") deal with new social possibilities or with what we are learning about the interaction between man and environment.

The urban design field is in upheaval and conflict. Throughout the world, the architect is losing his unquestioned position of primacy and is becoming one member of a complex design team. Some attempts are being made to train men as designers able to analyze and deal with areawide spatial form, or with the coordinated management and design of environment, rather than as architects with an added knowledge of city problems. Research on the interaction of environment and behavior is developing, and its findings are challenging many cherished ideas about civic form. New methods for large-scale design are evolving, relying on the computer in particular. Urban design is under attack for its preoccupation with visual form, and is accused of remoteness from basic social issues. Designers themselves are bewildered by the complicated politics and economics of large-scale decisions. Clients are no longer passive and mute, but demand a part in the design process.

Urban design as a separate profession arose in response to certain gaps between the older arts of environment, disturbing gaps which appeared, for example, when it became necessary to design large building complexes for multiple clients. The new profession aspired to the design of entire cities, under the misapprehension that they might be detailed in the same way that buildings are, as if constructed rapidly for a single client. It tended to stress the psychological and sensuous aspects of form, because these factors were generally disregarded at the scale of the community, region, or large engineering work. It blossomed in the wake of the city planning field, which is moving from purely physical concerns to a focus on economic and social policy, and is probably on the verge of breaking into various subdisciplines. It is instructive to note the areas of environmental success: the affluent suburb, the shopping center, the historic district, the rural freeway, the campus, the large country park. It is even more instructive to see the areas of failure, or at least of nonperformance: the quality of large regions, the new towns and extensive new residential areas, localities in need of rehabilitation and renewal, the city streets, the working landscape of industry and agriculture, the mobile home park.

Where this turmoil may lead is hard to see. Hopefully, it would result in a profession competent to deal with community spatial form in all its social, political, economic, and psychological dimensions. This implies that the profession would focus its attention on those qualities in the environment that allow people to develop to their fullest potential. It would mean looking on the landscape as a changing, living system of which man is an integral part. Therefore, it would draw eagerly on knowledge from ecology, environmental psychology, and sociology. It would develop the design process into a recycling process of forethought, invention, experiment, and management, in which the ultimate user has an intimate role, so that the acts of planning and building and maintaining become joyful social arts. Its attention would turn to neglected areas: regions, rehabilitation, new settlements, environmental systems, and the small ordinary everyday places where people live and work and pass their lives. Necessarily, its course would parallel, and reinforce, changes in the organization of society.

The urbanization of the earth

New cities have been laid out, and old ones remodeled, since ancient times, but city and regional planning has become a recognized profession only in this century. Originally, the profession was solely concerned with regulating the use of urban land. Since then, it has progressively broadened its scope, and, as it does so, it becomes involved with progressively deeper issues.

The antecedents of the profession lie in the first shocked response to the horrors of city life during the Industrial Revolution. The profession itself was organized at a later time, on narrower and more technical grounds. Now it is swiftly changing, as the urban region changes. The profession remains unsure of itself, without a deep understanding of events, a clear view of its own role, or an array of effective solutions. To understand this situation, we must look first at the events occurring outside the profession itself.

We are witnessing the urbanization of the earth. Except in geologic cataclysm, and in the first spread of settled agriculture, the skin of the world has never been transformed so rapidly. In some places, this change is already profound; everywhere it is visible, for men are remaking their spatial circumstances. Farm and village are transmuted. There are new lakes and new deserts, vast tilled fields, continuous regions of houses and factories. Even mountains have been altered. We may possibly be destroying our habitat on a world-wide scale. But we are clearly building the geographic base for a different way of life.

The phenomenon is surprisingly similar even in very diverse societies, although regions are in different stages of the process, and some events are just now becoming visible which may cause that process to fork in new directions. Human populations are growing, supported by an increase in technical power. The new technology feeds the new mouths, and in some nations has permitted a great surge in the level of consumption. We are able to change the form of the land, alter its cover, mine its energy and its minerals, crop the plant and animals of entire regions, transport persons and goods in great number, modify the oceans and the atmosphere. Yet if all the world were to consume goods at the rate now current in the United States, a sixfold increase in the gross world product would be required, with probable catastrophic consequences for pollution and for the stock of resources.

Cities, once spatially insignificant events on the land (whatever their cultural importance), have now become one of the more remarkable com-

Reprinted by permission of *Enciclopedia Italiana* and Institute Archives and Special Collections, MIT Libraries.

ponents of the world landscape. Eighty-five percent of the Japanese people are urban people. Even in as extensive and thinly settled a nation as the United States, 75% of the population is already urbanized, and the proportion continues to increase. While yet far from these percentages, the developing countries are moving in this same direction. If some 600 million people in those countries are urban people today, that number is expected to be 3 billion by the year 2000. Moreover, modern history has recorded a constant acceleration of that trend. While it required four generations for Great Britain, the urban pioneer, to move from a population that was 10% urban to one that was 30% urban, the same shift occurred in Australia in little more than a single generation.

Past trends are not mysterious, irresistible forces. Official forecasts of population and economy have been notoriously unreliable. The principal determinants of change are the shifts in men's motives and values, and in their political and social institutions—and not in any iron laws of economics or in some glacial inevitability of technological development. An increasing urbanization of the earth may perhaps be confidently expected, if by urbanization we mean a turning from isolated rural subsistence to a more interdependent, industrialized, and complex way of life. But current trends in population growth, in resource consumption, or in the concentration of people into large metropolitan centers, while they will not be easy to reverse rapidly, are nevertheless not inevitable for the future. Indeed, we may hope they are not.

Industry has been freed from its ancient dependence on water power and water transportation, and concentrates in the urban areas, where the markets, labor, and services are. Even there, it is no longer tied to fixed rail transport at the center, and can disperse outwards within the urban region. The cities have become primarily producers and processors of information, rather than simple goods handlers. The new agricultural technology, using the earth like a factory floor, multiplies production per acre and drives the farm worker off the land. So driven, or attracted by the possibilities of urban life, the people of the world are pouring into the cities, or have already done so. A vast social uprooting has accompanied this disappearance of the neolithic village. Nations have attempted to check this flood, but, except to some extent in Cuba and in China today, those national policies have had little effect.

As the urban regions swell in size and importance, they also change internally. The density of occupation is falling as those who can choose move into more ample quarters, and those who cannot build shacks on the periphery. The older central areas receive the new immigrants, or are converted to other uses, or are even progressively abandoned. Workplaces move out in the wake of residences, so that the defined, compact city of the past is dissolving into an extensive many-centered network. Wheels replace feet, trips no longer converge on the center, and main-line transportation gives way to the small autobus, or to automobiles, bicycles, and other private vehicles.

The enormous growth in city populations, and its wider and wider dispersal, has been accompanied by a greater degree of segregation in space. Workplace and living place become separate. Diverse kinds of people, once within sight and sound of each other, may now live miles apart. Spatial segregation by income has become a marked feature of cities in wealthy countries such as Great Britain, the United States, and France, as well as in most cities of the Third World. In some fewer nations, however, such as Sweden and Poland, this segregation has been effectively prevented by government policy.

The generations have been separated: the old communities dissolved. Connections are more fluid, more specialized, less personal. Work has been detached from its previous cultural meanings. Society and its political organs seem to be of enormous size and almost uncontrollable. Indeed, they have long been beyond the control of most people, but now the disconnection is patent and is perceived as wrong.

Instead of periodic famine for most and scarce luxuries for the few, the city man sees before him an immense ladder stretching from poverty to affluence, from malnourishment, ragged clothes and no shelter all the way to domestic machines, plural cars, and dual houses. The visible ladder of affluence, set forth so concretely in the city and so vividly in the mass media, sharpens the ancient inequities of position and wealth. Moreover, the economic disparities which once were primarily internal to nations are now become external disparities. Ratios of per capita income between the rich and poor nations, which perhaps were 2:1 a century ago, now stand close to 15:1. Housing in particular has emerged as a critical problem. Once built from local materials for one's own use, or inherited from the slow capital accumulations of generations, the house is now an expensive and desirable manufactured object, in short supply in every city in the world. While the manufacture of clothing, formerly so difficult to acquire, has apparently been solved, supplying housing strains the resources of nations.

The increased extent of these urban regions, accompanied by the massive exploitation of energy and resources, has meant a serious increase in the extent of pollution, if not always in its local intensity. In the wealthy nations, the sanitary advances of the nineteenth century had already checked the heavy loss of life in recurrent city epidemics. But now it is not the small city streams but extensive water bodies that are foul. The air over most large cities hovers between the annoying and the dangerous. In Mexico City, where air pollution is at its most serious, there is some evidence that this condition contributes to one-half of the child mortality in the low-income areas. Ironically, that pollution is largely due to the automobiles operated by upper-income people. Even where the air has not reached that danger point, many citizens are now aware of the threat—they *see* the hazy air and the oily water.

While the congestion of cities and their transport systems is universally decried, it is probable that congestion has in fact decreased as densities have fallen. But people have become more aware of such discomforts, or are more prone to compare them with the remembered or imagined openness of the countryside. Commuting trips are longer, and the rising use of the private automobile makes the future of public transportation uncertain, which has the side effect of disadvantaging those unable to drive.

The rural countryside is now farther away, although for many people it may be more accessible, as their means of transportation improves. Basic attitudes toward nature are changing. From being seen as a threatening wilderness, or the setting for hard rural labor, the countryside has become a lost idyllic landscape, steadily receding before the urban tide.

In the cities of the richer nations, there has been an apparent decline in services: the streets are dirtier and more poorly patrolled, the schools are troubled, public transport is less convenient, utilities fail. In the Third World, the services are even more desperately hard pressed. For those coming from a rural background, on the other hand, the city may appear as a great improvement in public service. The city man enjoys schools, electricity, buses, and public water. The great strain on urban services is in part a revelation of previous inequities, evidence of a modest redistribution of the public goods previously commanded only by the minority.

Cities are also dangerous places. Where once one could walk safely at night it may now be foolhardy to do so. These dangers are another tangible result of the spatial concentration of poverty and the cracking of social molds.

All the super-cities feel the strain of this growth and change. Depending on their political economy, some city administrations are still abreast of their difficulties; others are floundering among political divisions, failing services, and financial incapacities. Social change accelerates, and citizens must learn new ways of life while struggling to survive.

At least until very recently, divergences among national urban patterns have seemed to be associated more with the rate and stage of economic development than with any formal political or social structure. The problems of Moscow and London are surprisingly alike, although they may be handled differently. Calcutta is another world. Even here, however, there is evidence that the cities of the Third World are in a stage which the cities of the developed world were in decades or a century before, although now that stage is more nearly desperate, and not as likely to be resolved by the same painful growth.

For all their difficulties and perils, the urban regions also release people to develop in ways previously unimaginable. And while the transformation of the earth is clearly the work of a vast social current, there is nothing inevitable about the particular channels it is following—the new urban landscape that is being created. It is only because those landscapes are so often alike, world-wide, that they seem inevitable.

Typical landscapes

"Landscape" is the visible physical character of a region and its associated human use and meaning. Just as geographers classify rural landscapes into groups which developed under similar influences of climate, geology, and human labor, so we may classify the far more intricate and fast-changing landscapes of the urban world. Generalized forces are now at work where once there was a greater diversity. And so tourists are brought to the historic sections of a city to see something "new"—that is, some-thing unfamiliar to them.

One typical landscape may be almost everywhere: massive slab-like apartment buildings set freely among broad pavements and grass. Inside these slabs, small families live in separate dwellings. Most other life-functions—activities beyond those of procreation, eating, rest, and nurture—go on elsewhere in more specialized buildings. The apartments are maintained by some corporate agency. There are not many people to be seen on the streets; this is an interior world.

This apartment landscape is the product of central decision, using a building technology which allows a high density of population without serious loss of light and air. An ideology which rejects private ownership, or the high land values of a capitalist economy, may lie behind these structures, or the desire to build mass housing quickly at moderate cost, or even a tenant desire to avoid the troubles of ownership and maintenance. However diverse the motive, these apartment landscapes are remarkably similar the world over: giant, barren, impersonal. Their inhabitants may be poor or moderately well to do, and still the landscapes look the same. Hardly ever do they correspond to any desired pattern of life of their inhabitants, except for brief periods in the family cycle. They are widely disliked.

In contrast to these apartment districts there are the extensive peripheral suburbs covered with small houses, houses which are most often quite new but may have been built even several generations ago. The suburbs are the favorite target of the urban critics and the favorite dream of many city people. To each house there is one family, perhaps an extended one or one amplified by lodgers. Each family maintains its own piece of ground. Single-house suburbs appear whenever governments or land values do not prevent them. We find square miles of them in the U.S. and Great Britain, and in the well-to-do sections of South American and Euro-pean cities. Subsidized housing has frequently been built in the suburban form, when land is in plentiful supply. Low-density suburbs also appear in the socialist nations wherever substantial percentages of new housing are supplied by private action. Suburbs are criticized for their cost, their consumption of land, their monotony, their lack of public transportation, and the presumed sameness of their people. They continue to grow wherever people build for themselves or developers cater to the wishes of those able to buy. In various countries they may be occupied by the affluent working class, by the middle class, or by high-income groups.

Zones of heavy industry, storage, and transportation occupy large blocks of land on the urban fringe, or belts along the railways, canals, and highways, or those internal tracts reclaimed from water or waste. Large low buildings, huge machines, vast yards encumbered with goods and vehicles, wire fences, smoking chimneys, [and] pavements congested with trucks and cars are the familiar visible features of these landscapes of power. Streets and buildings are in mechanical and orderly array, yet chaotic in detail. These lands are harsh and busy in the day, bleak and empty at night—powerful symbols of the application of non-human energies to vast new resources.

On the urban periphery, and sometimes where there are internal waste areas, we find the "squatter settlements"—owner-built shelters often erected on illegally occupied land. Small workplaces and shops are dispersed among the crudely fashioned residential shelters. Appearing now in the swollen cities of the developing countries, they were also a common feature of the urban centers of the U.S. and Europe in their earlier stages of growth. They are called barriadas, favelas, bustees, colonias proletarias, shantytowns, [or] bidonvilles, and they reappear whenever the urban influx cannot be met by housing action within the normal channels. One-third of the population of Mexico City is now so housed. Insanitary, makeshift, crowded, deprived of the simplest public services, they seem to be symbolic of despair and failure. On the contrary, closer inspection reveals that here the inhabitants are meeting their own problems with their own energies. Typically, the environment is steadily improved as occupation continues.

Elsewhere the poor live in the central slums, in rented huts, [in] old tenements, and [in] the former houses of the middle class or the wealthy. The buildings are decayed, the streets full of vitality and danger, the rooms overcrowded and dark. Some of these people are recent arrivals, seeking their way out. Other are caged there. Slums have been a feature of almost every large city of the world, although in a very few cases—Sweden, some British cities—they have largely been replaced. In the U.S., whose cities are more "advanced" in the sense of being farther out along a particular evolutionary branch, central living areas are rapidly being abandoned to the poor, and in some degree are even being abandoned by the poor themselves.

In other cities, more mature and less unsettled by the currents of change, extensive central areas may yet be occupied by the classic nineteenth-century landscape: apartments of moderate height, with shops at ground level, lining the streets without interruption. The streets are lively with people and traffic and commercial enterprise, and the apartments may be occupied by a broad mixture of social classes. Noisy, congested, deprived of light and air, these areas nevertheless have many cosmopolitan attractions. Mixed dense areas of this kind are rarely reproduced today, and those that remain often show signs of shifting to specialized use, class segregation, or obsolescence.

Between the single-family or apartment suburbs and the old centers are the extensive intermediate regions, the former growing edges now long passed by, or the old towns and villages engulfed in the process of growth. These are the regions so carelessly called the "gray areas," but the phrase is surely an outsider's term. They will often exhibit much more variety than other zones, due to their incremental growth and the successive modifications of generations of tenants. Modest houses and apartments, densely built, are mixed with many other public and commercial uses. These old fringes of the city, now occupied by the working class or lower middle class, are for the moment more stable than either [the] center or [the] periphery. Somewhat worn, they are still functional. Occasionally they are maintained and improved by piecemeal private effort, more often not. In a few countries, fragments of these intermediate regions are being rehabilitated by public action. But indeed we nowhere maintain our extensive urban environment in any ongoing systematic way. Governments focus on the critical slums, the disturbing shantytowns, or the green promise of the periphery. A massive debt of obsolescence develops in between.

Simple as this classification may be, it includes most of the more extensive urban territories which can be seen throughout the world. A traveler sees these features wherever he goes. Lives within these familiar places may have quite different qualities, according to the differences in culture and political economy, but the landscape images are as reliable as "alp" or "steppe" or "tropical beach." Indeed the similarities are much too strong. Evoked by a few pervasive motives, they fail to reflect the real diversity of place and culture. Moreover, this international standardization of the urban landscape is even now, inevitably, being overlaid by local differentiation as the diverse residents take command.

These similar areas have similar parts within them: the shopping street and its apotheosis in the U.S. commercial strip; the shopping center; the governmental or private office district (at times empty, at times thronged with office workers); the central business district, from whose crowded bed the glassy office towers are now sprouting up; the large institutional grounds; the monumental places; the city parks on the English model; the modern planned industrial estates with their sealed, imposing structures, flanked by lawns and parking lots; the airports which look so alike from one nation to another.

Urban-linked areas outside the metropolis are also internationally recognizable. Agro-industry has organized enormous tracts for the production of food, while the old marginal agricultural areas relapse to waste, or wait for development, or are replanted to forest. There are the extractive outposts: the mines and dams and chemical plants, marked by giant structures, smoke plumes, scarred earth, and small isolated settlement. We find extensive recreation zones: seacoasts, islands, mountainsides, lakeshores, and forests, with their tall hotels in ranks, or multitudes of cottages, approached by highways lined with tourist services. Indeed, as incomes rise, recreational regions of this kind have become one of the most extensive of all the urban uses. Cities no longer stop at their gates; they occupy far-flung regions, regions increasingly characterized by segregation: of workplace from living place, rich from poor, black from white, leisure from everydayness.

Within these contemporary urban landscapes are the encapsulated remnants of the past: fragments of historic city centers, old towns and villages (now stagnating or captured by bohemia), quiet suburbs or inner residential districts of old wealth, small farms. These fragments are more diverse in their landscape character, but the bulk of the world city is familiar to us. In some nations, of course, this world city is only now beginning to appear within the older landscape of village agriculture.

It is instructive that this recital should leave us feeling depressed. No one despairs when we say that most of the world's surface is occupied by oceans, mountains, deserts, tundra, steppe, fields, and forest. But when we recount the major urban landscapes—high rise or central apartments, suburbs, slums, "gray areas," shanties, factories, offices, mines, mechanized farms, airports, highways, vacation houses—it is as if we intend to convey a taste of monotony and oppression. That this is so is partly a result of our own ideological attitudes toward nature and the artificial, but they also surely reflect our real personal experience of those settings.

Admired places

Where are we at home? If the world will be fully urbanized—and it is on its way—can we imagine wanting to live in it? Indeed, some urban places are cited with approval. We think fondly of the home territory where we spent our childhood. (The memories of small-town North America, which up to now has been our nostalgic staple, are no longer being written. Present authors look back to the city tenements, and we can shortly expect happy memories of early suburbia.) Childhood memories are of great value in uncovering the deep springs of emotion that lie concealed beneath physical places. They speak of the importance of openness, of the stable home territory, of imagery and meaning, of many things to do and see. But just because of that automatic suffusion of feeling, these memories are less useful for making general judgments about landscapes. Therefore, what type of place is commonly approved by those who were not born there?

The great metropolitan centers are frequently cited, the urban foci of great size, known for their special environmental and social character. They are now, or have been, the centers of political and commercial decision, and the springs of cultural innovation. Even if no longer capitol, none are sunk to province—each remains a vital place, expressive of pride and power. Each has a valued history, each has had a large population for some period of time. If we set as an arbitrary criterion that a great center of that kind is one that has had more than half a million people for at least the last fifty years, we find 40 to 50 such centers in the world today. All are praised, at least as places to visit. Each has its fervent devotees who have lived there for years and will never leave.

These devotees are usually upper-middle-class or professional people, living in protected, small, intimate neighborhoods, yet easily accessible to the heart of the city, with all its diversity and turbulent action. This is a particular clientele: people of some means, with common tastes for high culture and for stimulation, often not engaged in raising children. Other people, of different status and with different interests, are fleeing these same intensive centers whenever they can. The worst examples of poverty and oppression can also be found there. Feelings are strongest close to the center; the intermediate zones and outskirts of these great cities are not invested with the same special attention. Nevertheless, here is one recurrent example of deep attachment between person and place.

Similar, if more muted and nostalgic, feelings are generated by some smaller towns, particularly those which have some special reason for being: academic, social, sacred, commercial, or topographic. Happily, they will be surrounded by open country, and enjoy their own specific spatial character and location. It is this sense of specialness that is valued, and the feeling of community, and perhaps of calm. But again, this is a special taste—other people escape from such places as from an airless tomb, while some are driven out for lack of livelihood. The feeling for the locality, even for those who love the place, is often tinged with sadness for a vanished past and for the emigration of the younger generations.

Both of these examples are not typical places, and they are attractive to restricted groups of persons. Good suburban housing is more widely appreciated. The dwellings are close to the ground, carefully sited, and of ample size, not of any distinctive style but showing care and attention. The grounds are well planted. The settlement has had time to mature. Typically, it was built for the middle class. It is a bedroom suburb, but the basic services are close at hand. The population is diverse in age, but socially rather homogeneous. This is a landscape close to the desires of many people: a good place to bring up young children within the nuclear family. But for the adolescent, seeking broader contacts, it may be an oppressive place. Non-resident critics point to its social exclusiveness, its waste of space and resources, Its dependence on the private vehicle. Yet this is the one urban landscape that we now produce which also corresponds to the wishes of a significant number of people.

In some countries, there are certain housing developments of higher density which are also approved by their residents. Most often, they contain a mixture of housing types, with a preponderance of row houses or low walkup apartments, carefully sited in ample open space and greenery. They will have some local facilities, such as nursery schools, clinics, or small shops on the ground floors. The automobile is strictly regulated, or banished to the periphery—not always to the pleasure of the residents. The individual architecture may not be distinctive, but the complex is coherently planned, and built as a unit. There were pioneer developments of this kind in the United States and Europe in the thirties, but it is Great Britain, Holland, and the Scandinavian countries that have gone on to build the bulk of these successful housing places. Even in those countries, they are uncommon relative to the entire housing supply, since they require unusual effort and coordination.

There are other agreeable regions. Productive rural landscapes are a pleasure to live in—not the vast fields of agro-technology but the more intricate fields, woods, and meadows of the small mixed farm. Unfortunately, its economic viability daily declines, and the rural inhabitants must turn to service work in the urban fringe, or become retired or commuting city man.

Deep attachments are also felt for some vacation places, to which many people now have a more permanent emotional connection than to any of their more temporary urban dwelling places. But until there are ways to earn a living there, or to commute regularly (this seems about to happen now at high levels of affluence) they remain the terrain of an occasional escape. The qualities for which vacation areas are admired— their informality, slow pace, and natural beauty—can teach us something about building a more humane environment. But large areas of land are now being absorbed by the rapid expansion of vacation cottages, and much of this cottage housing may eventually become obsolete.

We know how to make great parks, and we enjoy them. Some of our rural freeways are beautiful modern landscapes, despite the problems of the automobile. But here we are at the end of our list of admirations. It includes no workplaces—no factories or offices—no commercial zones (except the inside of a modern enclosed shopping center?—but how unreal that is!), no sacred places or monuments, no institutional areas (except a few new universities?), no transportation systems other than the rural freeway, and no residential areas beyond the middle-class suburbs, the few coherent mixed housing projects, and the sophisticated places for the professional elite. Of course there are exceptions—some uniquely handsome hospital or factory or low-cost housing structure—but not whole landscapes which are extensive or capable of being reproduced extensively—as could be said for the village, the family farm, or the town house and its square. Complaints about the worlds we build are almost universal. When we look at an ordinary new apartment area, factory, office building, shopping street, institution, or suburb, our hearts contract. It is true that as they mature these urban settings may acquire greater diversity and a better fit to use. But for the time being they are as raw as a new-cleared farm.

Problems and aims

Men are rebuilding the earth to fit a new way of life, but the result is discouraging. Communities are destroyed, people uprooted. The housing and services provided fall short of expectations, and inhabitants are unable to obtain those goods by their own efforts. The process of urbanization consumes vast resources, but the product is wasteful and monotonous. The spatial segregation of social groups and of activities is increasing. We may summarize these and many other difficulties under three main heads:

1. *Equity*—groups and individuals are being excluded from a just share of the use and control of the environment and its resources. The disadvantaged group may be an economic class, or a sex, or an age class, or a whole people.

2. *Ecology*—the previous ecological balance is being destroyed without creating a stable new balance. Species diversity is impoverished; relative stability gives way to sudden perturbations. Accumulated resources of energy, land, water, air, and genes are lost.

3. *Behavior and Development*—the environment does not support human behavior or human expression and development. Health is endangered and intentions are frustrated. Worst of all, the achievement of human potential is thwarted.

These three issues recur constantly. Planning though must understand them in their interaction with each other, seek their resolution (or their underlying unity), and thus imagine a world whose conditions will satisfy all three demands.

Again and again, the man-made environment fails its users. The residential suburb is the one extensive, existing example of a preferred environment being built today, and it has substantial flaws. Yet if we look at the more exceptional admired places, we find that people do indeed derive strong satisfaction from living in a well-made setting, and that the characteristics of that satisfaction are not obscure. While people of different temperament and situation will make diverse individual choices, and while different cultures will demand a special character in the preferred habitat, yet these preferences, taken in the gross, exhibit some very general themes.

A sound dwelling adequate to shelter the accepted functions of the family is one pervasive theme, although what is thought adequate will shift with culture, income, and expectations, and it is possible that even the family itself may be changing its structure and its role. A safe and healthy environment is another obvious desire, and there is a growing body of information on what this implies.

People want easy access to services, and to a diversity of people and of activities, although they may not want that access to be so close as to make contact unavoidable. Growing children, in particular, take pleasure in an abundance of things to do and see. An *open* environment is valued, one that can be entered and used according to desire.

There is widespread satisfaction in having a home territory, a defined place peculiar to oneself and one's own small group and so controlled. Most people—not all—wish to be part of some close social community which is clearly settled on its own ground.

As a result, one preferred locale is the small secluded community which is at the same time linked into an intense urban network. This contrast of stimulus and calm, of novelty and security, extends the range of choice and makes vivid the feeling for home and city.

The pleasure in living close to nature is also very general. By "nature" people do not mean wilderness, but rather that kind of diverse, productive rural scenery which is largely man-made (and thus artificial) but which displays and harmonizes the basic natural and productive processes and the array of living species. Sky, water, ground, living plants and animals are fundamentally attractive to us. Few people will give up urban advantages to live in a remote countryside, but easy access to both earth and city is widely appreciated.

We are happy to live in a place which has some particular character— a strong image of its own, some renown. That cities of marked character and diversity will often survive and grow over long periods, at the expense of more monotonous, single-function places, is some confirmation of this assertion. If physical and social character reinforce each other, the pleasure is deeper. Men speak to each other through their settings. The place must have a history, a sense of continuity with the past and with the future. Taking pride in our locale, we are inclined to be proud of our own place in the world.

These are extremely general statements. They do not tell us to use wood, or to build two-story houses around cul-de-sacs, or to make linear cities or radial ones, or that 50,000-person settlements are best. If such confined rules of form are universally applied (and rules of that kind have been applied), the result is dreary in the extreme. On the other hand, these general statements are not meaningless. They point to inadequacies in the new urbanization and, as we will see, they point toward a possible framework, toward urban regions which are conscious works of art.

Responses

How have the nations responded to the process of urbanization, with all its problems and its unsatisfied desires? There has been a flurry of action. The attempts to build cities directly and from the beginning, the "new towns," have been the most glamorous response. As in the thirteenth and fourteenth centuries in Europe, this is an age of deliberate city foundation—even in the U.S., one of the last major countries to join in the effort. But the character of the new towns is quite different in the different nations. In the U.S., they are built by large private corporations, mostly in the outer fringes of the metropolitan regions. They are planned residential suburbs, with complete shopping and institutional services and some employment, built for the middle class. These new towns are outgrowths of the normal operations of the large suburban house builder.

In Great Britain, the new towns arose out of a socialist reform movement of the nineteenth century, which led to two prototypes, and thence to a major effort by the Labor government after World War II. It was the government's aim to redirect the urban growth of the nation into healthier and more efficient patterns. British new towns are built by autonomous public corporations, and are deliberately designed to shift population and jobs out of the metropolitan centers. They house all classes of society except the poorest and the most wealthy. They are heavily subsidized, but now they are beginning to show a modest long-term profit. Many of the capitalist countries of Europe have followed the English lead, notably Sweden. France is beginning to try its hand. Holland has built new towns to service the new-made polder lands. Israel has settled the Negev desert with them.

Hundreds of new towns have been built in the USSR and other socialist countries, primarily to support national industrialization, or to exploit certain natural resources far from the existing cities. Cuba is building small rural towns to attract a work force for mechanized agriculture. The developing countries of the Third World are also building new towns—to exploit some new resource, or to create a new political center, or simply for prestige.

Despite the diversity of motive and means, these new towns have similar problems: the social disruption which attends on mass movements of people, the economic drain caused by heavy early investments in infrastructure, the rawness and lack of services in the early stage, the clash of central initiative (public or private) with growing local power, and the monotony of standardized large-scale design.

However numerous, the new towns are far from absorbing the current rate of urbanization, although they demonstrate how normal suburban growth could be better organized at a larger scale. They have proved indispensable for opening up new territories and new resources, but insufficient for retarding the growth of the great cities. Beginning on new ground to a coherent plan is naturally attractive, and the new towns have usually escaped the worst features of the old ones. But with few exceptions (the Finnish town of Tapiola is often cited), the results have not been much better than mediocre. Most new towns are characterless and rather monotonous; sometimes they are like a huge army encampment. They do not yet generate that local pride which is one mark of a city. They are built by some outside agency—whether large corporation or national authority—which is able to muster the land and the initial capital. Only much later does the local community gain any degree of control. Any values created by the act of urbanization are thus exported beyond its boundaries.

Public efforts have also been directed to rebuilding the old central city areas. Like the new towns, slum clearance is a nineteenth-century inheritance, with its associated belief that areas of dilapidated housing are like sores whose excision will restore the city to health. Experience shows (although not everyone may yet have taken notice) that slums are a product of poverty and social disorganization. Razing them forces poor people to find worse or more expensive quarters elsewhere. While replacing the slums with subsidized low-rent housing improves the physical condition, rehousing alone does not get at the root of the difficulty. Like the new town, rebuilding at the center is an "imported" action, remaining outside local community control.

Rebuilding of the central city has been systematically done in only a few nations. The Scandinavian nations are one group: there are few physically dilapidated housing areas left in those northern cities. Great Britain has done extensive and generally successful rebuilding—notably in London. Germany also furnishes numerous examples of central rebuilding. In both [Germany and Britain] it was wartime bombardment that cleared the ground. On the other hand, the program of "urban renewal" in the U.S. has been a source of sharp political conflict. It has been most effective where used for rebuilding the central areas for commercial use, or for pushing low-income groups out in favor of the well-to-do. In any case, it has affected very little of the total central area. The private abandonment of the worst housing, and the significant amount of private remodeling by individuals as their incomes rise, have been much more visible events. Most of the developing countries, and the socialist countries as well, have lacked the capital needed for central rebuilding, although an impressive new commercial avenue has recently been built in Moscow. The cost of rebuilding, in the face of other urgent priorities, as well as the problems of relocation, have been towering obstacles. When it occurs, much central rebuilding is cold and monumental.

Nowhere in the world has any attention been paid to the systematic improvement of those vast urban areas which are neither at the center nor at the fringe, and where the great majority of urban people live. We cannot yet maintain and improve extensive urban areas as we might maintain and improve a farming region or a forest. The public ways are kept up, the main streets and utilities may occasionally be rebuilt. In the affluent countries, significant improvements are made to single buildings on individual initiative. But no major restructuring occurs, except for the building of automotive expressways, or occasionally some new fixed rail transit lines.

In the United States, building new urban expressways has been an expensive and disruptive process, and it is slowing down as local community resistance stiffens. At times, automobile traffic will temporarily be immobilized in a central city, due to some block in one element of the system, which every day is very close to capacity. In this situation, additional highways or parking spaces in the center are solutions that simply renew the problem. Improved public transport is a more rational response, combined with a dispersion and mixing of regional activities. Thus traffic densities are lowered and people may live closer to their work if they choose. Serious proposals are also being made for the complete prohibition of private automobiles in the central areas of large cities like New York, Tokyo, or Rome, or for the power to reduce automobile traffic by gasoline rationing, progressive tolls, or a temporary withdrawal of the right to drive when air pollution reaches critical levels. It is notable, however, that some of the worst traffic jams in the United States now occur on the outer expressways on summer weekends, as the segregation between residence and leisure activity becomes as marked a feature as the separation between home and work.

In many countries, public agencies are turning to preservation as a significant way of improving the habitat, since planned urban growth seems to transform all space into the standard urban landscapes. There have been two types of preservation: of historic zones at the center, and of natural open spaces at the periphery. The preservation of entire urban districts as historic areas is a relatively new phenomenon, symbolically important and most interesting and diverse in character over the world. Yet these districts are microscopic in proportion to the whole of the urbanized region, and moreover their vitality is frequently undermined by the act of freezing their outward form. Sometimes, like urban renewal, they have been the cloak for a displacement of some low-income community.

Open space preservation may have a broader effect, although these reserved spaces are often too far out on the metropolitan fringe to be useful to many center city people. (But so were many of the great historic urban parks, when first created.) These large spaces are being preserved by various means: public purchase or seizure; voluntary deed restrictions by the owners; the purchase of development rights; or severe public regulation. A number of large cities have established encircling "greenbelts"—London, Toronto, Moscow, and Havana are examples. Others are trying to develop "green wedges" which would penetrate closer toward the city center. A vigorous effort to save land which has a fragile ecology has developed in the United States. These are hopeful actions, if still inadequate in contrast to the pace of metropolitan expansion, and difficult to sustain in the face of market pressures.

But the most visible action, all over the world, is neither in the separate new towns, nor at the center, nor in the intermediate zones, but at the metropolitan edge, where the city continues to grow by simple addition. This growth may be in the form of endless apartment buildings, as in the USSR, or of single-family suburbs, as in the U.S., or of shantytowns in the developing countries. Only occasionally, a well-planned and well-served mixed residential development may be sited in this peripheral zone, as we have noted earlier. Here on the fringe, governments are heavily involved in extending roads, utilities, and services, if not in constructing the complete urban fabric.

The widespread efforts to check this metropolitan growth have had only a very mild success. They seek to prevent an over-concentration of skill and resources in a single locality, and especially to halt the decline of lagging regions, with the consequent social disruption and waste of installed infrastructure. Due to sustained effort, the growth of greater London is now reduced below the average for the nation, but is not halted. Moreover, this reduction has brought on local problems of job loss and local finance. France has for some time sought to reduce the dominance of Paris, and it at last appears that net in-migration into that city (but not its natural increase) has virtually ceased. Yet the attraction of the capital remains, and professionals, at least, leave it only reluctantly. Even Moscow grows, despite severe controls on population movement. In Budapest, the forced relocation of industry out of the city brought on a drop in production, as workers chose to stay behind. In the United States, on the other hand, there are signs of a relative slowing in the growth of the very large metropolitan regions such as New York, in favor of regions whose population size is closer to one or two million. Newer, more diversified and more pleasant urban areas seem to be growing at the expense of earlier, single-function regions. Economic activity may now be following population movements induced by residential preference.

Cuba has achieved some success in diverting the flow to the cities: nontransferable food rationing and a decisive switch of public investment from city to countryside has slowed but not halted urban migration. China has acted even more drastically. Large agro-industrial communes have been created in the countryside, and there is forced out-migration from the cities back to these communes and to the frontier regions. As a result, the large cities of China have almost ceased to grow in the last decade. Short of such severe measures, and short of the deliberate foundation of entire new metropolitan regions, we may expect fringe growth to continue. But experience shows that we can vastly improve the quality of these urban additions.

The deliberate founding of new metropolitan regions, rather than modest new towns, has yet to be attempted. But many nations are consciously engaged in guiding urban growth at a national scale. Great Britain is planning for the long-term development of its southeastern region. France has designated eight provincial centers as "growth poles." Holland has a coordinated scheme for the expansion of its "Ringstad," or circle of major cities. The idea of a coordinated national policy for economic and spatial development is beginning to take hold.

While national economic planning has been practiced for some time, physical planning on a scale larger than the city has only a modest history, going back to the speculations of Patrick Geddes In Scotland and Benton MacKaye in the U.S., and to the ideas about the integration of town and country generated in the early years of the Soviet revolution. Since then, regional physical planning has been practiced only sporadically. The principal examples occur when nations are expoiting new territories (the Dutch polders or the Negev of Israel), or are dealing with backward areas whose economy is lagging (the TVA in the U.S.). For the most part, spatial planning at that scale has been crude. It accepts the growth of the economy and the population given in an economic projection, and then provides the necessary space and facilities for that growth according to accepted standards. A transportation network is laid down, and perhaps there is some consideration of preferred city size. In essence, the regional spatial plan is a mechanical accommodation of the national or regional economic plan. Moreover, like most economic plans to date, these spatial plans have been concerned only with growth, and give little thought to maintenance, adaptation, conservation, or stabilization, and certainly not to decline. Recently there have been some attempts to look for preferred spatial patterns at that large scale, that is, to *design*. Ideal city size has been analyzed, as well as the preferred spacing of cities in hierarchical systems. But the theoretical description of existing urban pattern is confused with preferred pattern.

Optimum city size is a concept much discussed but difficult to substantiate. It may not exist, or may be so variable as to have no general utility. The size generally thought ideal has within a generation steadily escalated from 20,000 people, to 60,000, to 250,000, and recently to one million or more. Identifying optimum growth *rates*, or the thresholds at which new costs or benefits appear, may be more useful exercises. Considering the continuing vitality and attractiveness of metropolitan regions, one may also wonder about the possibility of creating new regions of that kind deliberately, based on existing smaller centers.

Cuba recently prepared a detailed, comprehensive national spatial plan, based on soil capabilities, the transportation of export goods, and labor needs on the farms and rural industries. It proved too rigid to follow. Nevertheless, Cuba is transforming the rural landscape at an enormous scale, and the effect is often exhilarating, as on the Isle of Pines or in the greenbelt of Havana. Similar transformations have occurred elsewhere in the past, but rarely so rapidly and with such direct intention. It is precisely this creation of new landscape at a regional scale, inclusive of urban as well as rural uses, that we must master if we hope to divert the urbanization of the earth to humane ends.

Current thinking and effort in regional spatial planning has been focused on the conservation of open space and natural resources. This preoccupation had its antecedents in the U.S. national park system. Our attention has escalated to an awareness of the global threats of air and water pollution, and to studies of the ecological balance over very large areas. Indeed, the very word "environment" has lately been captured to mean simply a concern with threats to the natural ecological balance. The growing interest in preserving historic and cultural resources has paralleled this drive to conserve national resources. Both movements are alike in mood and outlook, and their adherents reinforce each other.

Vital as these concerns are, they are still negative ones, based on a desire to halt development, to keep regions "as they were." The preferred pattern is assumed to be the previous stable one. Human values beyond the biological or [the] nostalgic are discounted. However useful this awakening to the importance of the physical environment has been, it is yet only a step toward a comprehensive view. The emphasis is on limits and restraints—a sane reminder indeed. But we must also consider new opportunities. . . .

A profession in doubt

In all this turmoil, the profession of city planning is also changing and struggling to survive. The transformation of the world city and of the political-economic system it shelters, and the progressively articulate dissatisfaction with the world we are building, are forcing the field to come of age or to perish. Until recently city planning was concerned with street patterns, with parks and public buildings, and with the regulation of private construction by means of zoning and building codes and other legal devices. City planners typically worked for a city government, or for a private firm who advised it. Their concerns were the concerns of their clients, and were circumscribed by the client's powers. In many countries, city planning was not even a separate profession, being only a bureaucratic branch of architecture. The intellectual basis of the profession came from a mixed heritage: on the one hand from the concepts of the utopian socialists, the settlement house movement, and the housing reformers; on another from the civil engineers, with their knowledge of transportation, public utilities, and land subdivision planning; and on a third (if a profession may be allowed three hands) from the esthetic ideals of those architects and landscape architects who were concerned with parks, civic centers, planted avenues, and the City Beautiful. This mixed intellectual substance had been worked into a set of ideas useful for the limited regulatory planning available to a municipality.

Traditionally, one prepared an area plan according to a clear professional sequence. It began with some very general goals like economy, beauty, health, or "balance." Once the goals were set, a broad survey was made of certain prescribed aspects of the existing situation: population, economy, land use and transportation patterns, geography, and the like. These comprehensive data were analyzed to reveal the apparent problems of the area in the light of the stated goals. A long-range plan was prepared to respond to those problems, using a set of traditional form concepts: greenbelts, hierarchies of centers, radial patterns, residential neighborhoods, and others. After a review of the plan by city officials or other client representatives, a detailed plan for implementing the proposal was developed. A final check with the client, some detailed revisions, and it only remained to carry out the plan.

In reality, the sequence floundered as data changed, motives shifted, restraints lifted, and groups contended. A wide gulf appeared between general value statements and particular actions. The process has repeatedly been discredited for its assumptions of absolute knowledge, absolute control, explicit values, stable conditions, and an articulate community consensus.

New tasks appeared as new clients spoke out. Further, while there had already been a body of practitioners in economic planning, there was no such group engaged in social planning, and city planners were drawn toward that vacuum. Thus the definition of the field is in doubt. City planners are working for state and national governments as well as for cities, for public and private development agencies, for industry, for national interest groups, for local community groups, and as community organizers. They are involved in economic planning, in open space and resource planning, and in planning for education, recreation, welfare, and health. They have at times become advocate planners, opposing the official plans of various branches of government. They are involved in politics at all levels.

Planning is now more often considered to be a process of coping with urgent problems, or a particularistic one of making short-range, small-area proposals for special groups. Or at best it is plain grand strategy—the accomplishment of large but very simple and partial goals by the use of opportunistic tactics over a long period of time. Values and criteria are little thought of, or are reduced to simple statements about avoiding such immediate dangers as accidents, tax loss, or an influx of unwanted new people. The conventional time scale for planning has steadily fallen from fifty, to twenty, to ten, to five, and recently to one or two years. Thus the target period for physical planning has come to coincide with the conventional time horizons of economic planning.

The schools and scholars of planning are moving into "urban studies," that comprehensive non-field which takes as its province all the problems which can be found in urban areas. This brings them up against our civilization as a whole, but does not supply them with a correspondingly broad theoretical base. Urban studies faculties now include urban historians, urban economists, urban sociologists, anthropologists, lawyers, psychologists, ecologists, engineers, computer specialists, public health workers, political scientists, and political activists, as well as the traditional physical planners. A field which had its beginnings in the comprehensive outlook of the utopian socialists, and then progressively narrowed its focus to various technical issues of physical function or reforms, is now broadening out once more. But this time there is no comprehensive view. More likely, the profession is beginning a process of splitting into several pieces.

It is not yet clear what these pieces will be. One likely piece will be concerned with integrated economic and physical planning at the regional or national scale, another with natural resource and conservation planning ("environmental planning" in the now commonly accepted but narrow sense), another may merge into the budgetary and administrative planning of social programs such as education or health services.

The original concern with spatial planning is left as a remainder of the old "comprehensive" field. This remnant, which I would call environmental design, may merge again with those branches of architecture and landscape architecture which are themselves becoming engaged at a more ample and dynamic scale. It should be apparent that this essay is largely written from this particular viewpoint of environmental design.

Yet each piece of the planning field is still faced with the persistant problem of wholes and parts. Each place must deal with the interaction of social and technical issues, and with the content of many previously separate disciplines. Planning constantly threatens and is threatened by all the other established academic territories; planners suffer unending professional jeopardy.

"Interdisciplinary teams" are fashionable, yet it turns out to be extraordinarily difficult to mesh the language and thought patterns, the concerns and motives, of different disciplines as they deal with a common problem. A joint effort usually results in a series of parallel reports bound with a common cover. True interdisciplinary thinking still occurs within a single person's head, or, more rarely, between a very few persons who have long worked together. An effective style of joint attack on complex planning problems is badly needed. It requires a fluid team of specialists and clients who know enough of each other's work and values—and trust each other enough—so that information flows rapidly and accurately between them, and team leadership can shift from person to person as the problem shifts.

The issue arises in a more general form in the debate between holistic and analytical thinking. Is it better to begin with a view of the whole, however general and uninformed, and thence come systematically down to a study of the parts, seen in their general context, or is it better to understand thoroughly the working of a part, and thence to put together a picture of the whole by the synthesis of these well-known elements? Moreover, what is a whole, and what a part? With all its breadth and ambiguity, planning is peculiarly subject to such doubts, and most planners operate in a middle ground, shifting continuously from the more inclusive to the less and back again.

Planning has long suffered from the wars between the proponents of environment and those who plump for culture. One side once asserted that, given a particular genetic endowment, the physical environment determined the outcome. Geography and race were to be correlated with intelligence and civilization, as well as with skin color and house-building materials. Anthropologists and sociologists then demonstrated the importance of culture, emphasizing that "man makes himself." Architects who dreamed of reforming (or controlling) society via their buildings were exposed as dreamers, frauds, or worse. Now lately the environmentalists have hit upon the importance of pollution and resource limitations, and a new contest arises. It is the academic shadow partner of the world struggle between social justice and resource conservation.

Unfortunately, the battle may end in an armed truce at a false boundary—an agreement that environment is important as a limiting factor, particularly in large "natural" regions, while culture is the creative factor, predominate in ordinary urban settings. There is little sign of an understanding of environment, culture, and the individual as an interacting system. Sociologists pride themselves on their insensitivity to spatial surroundings, and environmental designers defiantly gloss over the "mere words" of social analysis.

The battle over "process" and "product" is an allied argument. Early planning focused on a final desirable outcome. Recent studies have shown the importance of the process of getting there—who decides and how, what conflicts arise, how rapidly events occur and at what cost. Now process is all—or, in the words of the old song: "it ain't what you do, but the way that you do it." Moreover, the proponents of process are intellectually allied to those who emphasize culture, while the product orientation has been assigned to the environmentalists. It is a peculiar assignment, a reflection of intellectual history and not of intellectual necessity.

Of course process (or culture) isn't all, and neither is its sparring partner. We evaluate a process and its recurrent outcomes together. The propensity of the human mind to deal in neat polar opposites—and not in triads or in interacting systems or in continuous flows, for example—is surely one of our biological liabilities.

Our way of looking at conflict, change, and time is another important ingredient in our planning method. We may think of environment as stable and enduring: designed and built in one brief heroic period, and then become a permanent good for everyone, requiring only a little care to remain like new. If it does decay or become obsolete, then a new cycle of planning and building must begin. Plans are a series of long-range jumps to a fixed goal. Similarly, utopias are an eternal future. The cost of reaching the future, and who pays the fare, is a negligible issue, since all will enjoy the future forever.

But change is continuous. The pleasure and pains felt along the way are the entire story, and who suffers them is the point. Plans should be conceived as continuous flows, structured to diverge as aims and constraints shift. Evaluating them means weighing the value to different groups of the succession of temporary future states. Since uncertainty is certain, diversity and adaptability of form and process are desirable. The future is preserved by saving basic resources, but also by flexibility and by the active exploration of the future (whether in imagination or in actual trials).

Not only is the concept of the technical process and subject matter shifting, but also the concept of the professional role. Is the planner an inspired artist, or is he a very knowledgeable spatial scientist? Should he prescribe what is best for his clients, or should be simply advocate their interests whenever they conflict with those of others? Or should he just lay out the possibilities and their technical implications in some neutral way? Is it possible to be neutral? But if he is neither neutral nor just a paid advocate, is the planner then responsible for the welfare of the entire community, and a valid spokesman for the future? If so, how are those general or future interests to be determined?

Some assert a planner can do no more than analyze the present situation and predict the possible near future, leaving policy and action to others. Others deny the existence of any legitimate professional role, believing that no one can truly understand any group's interests but that small group itself. Any group must therefore plan on its own behalf, and not be planned for. From that viewpoint, the specialist's role, if it exists at all, is either transitory or quite remote. He uses his knowledge to train ordinary people to analyze and plan for themselves, or perhaps he plans very large environmental systems (such as transport nets, or land allocations, or the housing supply) so that they impose as little as possible on small group decisions. Still others deny the very possibility of planning for anything but the most immediate future. To them, public planning is no more than an art of managing recurrent public crises.

All these conflicting conceptions of the professional role are based on different views of two fundamental issues; what is possible in complex decision making and what is ethical. For example, what is the public interest? Does it exist at all? How much can realistically be controlled? How far into the future can reasonable predictions be made? What (and whose) values should predominate? How can they be determined?

Looking forward to the urban countryside

Assume that we had that will to build. Can we see a way forward, or should we simply put our strength into halting and backing a runaway world? Could we imagine a world which was just, balanced, and developmental in the sense we have discussed above—one which fundamentally satisfied its users? Are there any paths that lead from here to there? Could the profession help to find them?

Barring some gigantic disaster, we can expect that very extensive areas of the habitable surface of the world will in time be urbanized. Even places now thought uninhabitable—under and on the sea, along mountain ranges, in deserts, undergound—will be invaded by urban uses. The possibility strikes us with loathing. We imagine endless pavements, a world-wide pall of smoke, billions of human beings sealed into great buildings like beehives.

These are vain imaginings. Population will not, indeed cannot, ascend to those levels, nor will world urbanization be an extension of the old central city, or even of today's suburbs. It will necessarily be a thinner occupation, far more diverse. In some form, vision or nightmare, it will be a realization of the old dream of fusion of city and country.

The shift to urban life now seems irreversible. The people of the world could no longer be fed or housed if they all lived in rural villages, nor would they allow themselves to be shipped back there. But are not the great metropolitan regions already unmanageable? If all the people of the world should enjoy an "advanced" standard of living, where will we find the space, the energy, the food, the minerals, and the wastebaskets?

The present metroplitan regions may not be managed well, but they are hardly unmanageable. There is no evidence that ill health or social disorder is more prevalent in them than among similar populations elsewhere, probably the reverse. Air pollution *is* increasing, and there is the same exploitation and poverty in the city that we see in the countryside. Financial management is poor. Yet urban life is inherently humanizing, and no metropolis has yet been abandoned, as small towns and villages and hardscrabble farms have so often been abandoned. A dispersed pattern of urbanization is not necessarily wasteful of resources. It has often been so, but that has been due to land speculation, chaotic growth, a dependence on the automobile, the use of lavishly equipped dwellings, the gross separation of functions. None of these are necessary features.

On the contrary, it is possible to imagine an urbanized countryside which would be a liberation, and there are features in the present process of decentralization that might be directed that way. An urbanized countryside could mean a network of low-density communities in which merge workshops, farms, offices, houses, and decentralized urban facilities. This would not be a simple extension of suburbia, although it might grow out of it. The integration of activities, the inclusion of open space, [and] the degree of community control would necessarily be quite different. Living would not be subjugated to the private automobile, nor require lengthy daily trips or ones which converge on massive terminal areas.

The urban countryside could enjoy the complementary advantages of city and country without their disadvantages: open fields and city services, work places in the presence of nature. One might enjoy a garden and a wood and still be close to friends and restaurants and theaters. Segregation from production and from diverse people has been the most dispiriting feature of the contemporary suburb, not its density. A good communications system will surely be necessary. Dispersed, integrated activities could permit ordinary movements to be relatively short range and omni-directional. A great diversity of transport modes must be used, emphasizing flexible, small-scale, public transport that leaves no age group immobilized. The urban countryside could be starred with intensive urban centers of specialized character, containing a range of services, where those who chose to do so could live at the center of the action. Still others might prefer a more mobile pattern of residence, living at times at close quarters in a center and at other times in a simple or temporary dwelling in some more remote location. The apparent wastefulness of an alternating domicile could be mitigated by rental or by joint tenure.

The region would contain factories, offices, farms, and forests. It would be threaded with continuous open space, taking advantage of water or hills to bring everyone into close contact with a sense of non-human life or even of wilderness. It would be the spatial setting and expression of a fusion of work and leisure, of learning and doing and being. Thus it would no longer be necessary to "escape" the city in order to enjoy the country, nor to import all food from great distances. The environmental aim would be a landscape open and accessible, but also highly diverse in its range of activities and intensities. Such a mixture, although at first blush the antithesis of orderly planning, in fact requires a deliberate creation. It will only rarely appear as the result of long history or a special topographic circumstance, and not by the chaotic workings of the speculative market in land.

This pattern can be brought about in the new regions, and on the fringe of established cities. But it can also be created by a progressive restructuring of the existing suburbs and intermediate zones. Wholesale clearance will rarely be possible or required. Local community must be strengthened, activities integrated, and open space introduced. The influence of the existing pattern will only add to the richness of the resulting fabric, but community control of the development rights in land is clearly required.

Even the central areas can be rebuilt, as they are partially abandoned. Local density and use mixture may occasionally be intensified, in order to build up strong, diverse urban centers. But the future adaptation of some of the more recent extensive, dense apartment zones will be a sore puzzle.

It is clear enough that the rate of consumption of world energy and material resources must not climb much further. Unfortunately, this limit seems to collide with the legitimate aspirations of ill-fed, ill-housed people. So an egalitarian world could become a burnt-out one, if the inequities in resource consumption are resolved by leveling upward. Learning how to reconcile conservation and social justice is a critical issue for us. Conservationists now ally with upper-class owners to restrict access to a sensitive landscape, or to prevent industrial growth. The developing countries suspect the environmental rules proposed by the advanced nations.

Social openness can be reconciled with habitat conservation, but not within the stable "climax" state of the ecologists, nor within an economy geared only to growth. Using the earth for human purposes, men impose states maintained by constant intervention, and those states continuously evolve. We strive to avoid catastrophic change, and irreversible change when we can, but cannot hope for stability.

Reduced consumption is clearly necessary. We can make artifacts of longer life, use less wasteful processes, re-use waste, and set prices which expose the costs of consumption and pollution, so that they are automatically considered in each small decision. But there are two much more fundamental reforms to be made: a redistribution of resources between rich and poor, and a rejection of the image of the good life as something defined primarily by material abundance. The affluent life style must be scaled to a level attainable by all without permanent damage. Many privileges will necessarily be surrendered, including that privilege so dear to conservationists: an exclusive access to the wilderness.

Values change slowly, and political changes must be fought for. The prerequisites to a reconciliation of social openness and environmental conservation will not be brought about by spatial planning, but the spatial environment will be its theater. Urban dispersion does not make the reconciliation more difficult; it supports it. Dispersed settlements could grow some of their own food, generate some of their own energy, and use local materials for construction, in a way that dense cities can never do. Relying less on imported goods and imported energy, we might shift our emphasis from the global exploitation and transport of material resources to the transfer of persons and information.

It seems clear that a dispersed urban countryside *could* evolve out of the world-wide process of urban concentration and suburban decentralization. But it will not happen spontaneously. Supporting the emergence of such a countryside implies vigorous national and international action. It means facilitating the growth of the metropolitan region, extending and improving public transport, services, and utilities, opening land for development without speculation, reserving open space, organizing the pattern of growth, supporting self-help housing and other low-cost building processes, breaking the pattern of segregation. To be effective, these actions demand a capable theory of environment.

It means initiating new metropolitan regions, rather than isolated new towns. In nations still largely rural, it means locating industry and services in the countryside where the people are, rather than forcing them through the historic migration cycle from farm to city slum. Indeed this is the policy that China has recently begun to follow. In the end, a humane urbanized earth means a planned international redistribution of urban settlement.

An international urban policy is perhaps a wild dream. But it would be a rational response to unequal access to world resources, to world-wide pollution, to the growth of metropolis in the wrong places and with inadequate capital, to hungry villagers and uprooted slum dwellers, to immigration driven by despair, and even in some measure to the threat of international conflict. A world urban policy would channel resources to rural and undeveloped areas, direct migration by incentives, create new international city regions, transfer skill and resources from nation to nation, [and] fund international development corporations. The political obstacles to these policies are as clear as the need for them.

There are intermediate steps which seem more possible now: joint analyses of world settlement and studies of how to optimize its distribution; the cooperative encouragement of migration to certain regions, plus actions taken to ease the pain of it; international action in the development of border cities; working alliances of cities which cut across national boundaries; international analyses and experiments in urban habitat; a better transfer of development technology. Large urban regions will develop in any event—they are the only settings within which our fundamental needs can be met. Guiding their growth into rational patterns at the national scale is now an accepted idea (if yet rarely practiced). An international structure of settlement is a logical extension of that idea, as our urban problems begin to emerge at that international level.

An international policy does not imply a superstate, but a series of agreements, joint actions, studies, and incentives. The basic units for the control of urban development should be the urban region and the local community, rather than individuals or corporations on the one hand or national or international agencies on the other. Residents should maintain control of their environment, and be assured that the values created by their activity are returned to their own benefit. Regional and national—even international—bodies can regulate the general pattern of settlement by incentives and guides, control the decisive act of initial development, and furnish the necessary infrastructure of distant transportation and utilities. Individuals and small groups can hold long leases or life tenures of the land, so they may enjoy a security and control of their own. But permanent ownership of the land should rest in the local community. Ghettoes, slums, stagnating villages, private hunting preserves, absentee landlords, [and] foreign-owned mines and plantations are environmental dominations. Any place should be open to the use and enjoyment of its own inhabitants, a permanent common resource. Only then will it be actively maintained and managed by them.

The ability to manage and maintain large urban areas on a continuing basis has so far escaped us. Systematic monitoring techniques, new technologies of structural maintenance and cleaning, [and] a design attitude that favors adaptable forms will all be useful. But the key to the problem is clearly that a territory be occupied by a stable community which has a vital stake in the continued functioning of that territory, and the power to protect it. Modern city areas often decay rapidly, but there are also numerous examples of older city areas still working well after centuries of occupation. Some settled farming lands have functioned for much longer periods.

The dispered urban countryside is a generic pattern that allows for a great array of particular solutions—patterns of agriculture, of industry, of housing clusters, of kinds of centers and types of open space. The variety of design solutions can match the real diversity of cultures, individuals, and geographic settings. New life patterns can be explored, new living territories be opened up, without disrupting the general framework. It is a generic pattern that could become as stable, as widely distributed, [and] as loved as was the hunting territory in its time, the village and its fields, or the city-state and its hinterland.

A development environment

In the end, our fundamental aim is the development of human beings as fully realized persons. What environmental setting best promotes human development? Just as we say that the primary role of the professional may in the future be as a teacher who shows other people how to design and manage environment for themselves, so we can speculate that the primary role of environment will in good time be its use as a place for learning. The first consideration in judging a place will then be whether it provides the physical support, the information, the challenges, [and] the chances for active manipulation that make it possible for users to reach their own potentialities. Whether a place enables one to become a skilled dancer, or a naturalist, or beautiful, or a community leader will then be more important than whether it pays, or is flat enough, or keeps off the rain.

Given our immediate pressing requirements, and the visible dangers of natural disaster and human oppression, the importance of environment as an educational setting may seem overblown. Yet preventing disaster, abolishing oppression, having enough food and houses and clothes, [and] living in security are only preparatory or incidental to the realization of human potential. The educative role may even excuse inequality (the condition of a child), a restriction of access, a lack of control, waste, or instability—but never in any way that stunts growth, or that threatens the long-run conditions of survival.

Cities have been the places where individuals and their cultures developed. Purposeful action—making and doing—and interactive stimulus have been the ground of that development. Thinking of a developmental environment, one dreams of places rich in information, places that require cooperation and endeavor, that challenge or respond. Not "all the world a school," since schools are far from being good learning places, but an urban landscape deliberately organized to match and foster the creative capabilities of men.

Indeed, these developmental characteristics are integral to those admired landscapes which we have described. They go far to describe the joy we experience in a vacation region or near a great city center, or during a childhood spent in open countryside. These are secure home territories which also have a wide access to the world, locations rich in history, character, and meaning, where we take pride in our time and place, where we build and explore, where we express ourselves to other people. The art of environmental design is properly directed to that end.

We could go further, and consider the effect of the man-made environment on the growth and development of other living species. We could think of a world managed to help dolphins to develop, for example, or cats, or plants. The ideal is enticing, but unfortunately its meaning is uncertain. For the time being, we must speak for ourselves. That requires us to think again about the values inherent in the material basis of our lives.

Sensuous Criteria for Highway Design (1966)

with Donald
Appleyard

Highways may be judged for their effects on the driver and his passengers, and also for their effects on the bystander: the nearby resident, worker, or man in the street. These two effects are not completely distinguishable, since the innocent bystander is often, a little later, the guilty driver, and the highway is part of the city as a whole. But the two are distinct enough to allow separate discussion, and they are sometimes in conflict with each other.

The View of the Road

To the bystander, the city expressway is a threat or at least a nuisance, and from his standpoint avoidance of problems should be the basis of many of the basic sensuous criteria. We will try to show, however, that highways might also play a more positive role for him, although concrete examples are rare.

Bystander criteria can be divided into several general sets:

1. avoiding undesirable sensuous effects of an immediate, objective kind;

2. avoiding damage to existing environmental assets, and possibly, creation of new ones;

3. making a good local fit with other elements of the urban landscape;

4. taking full advantage of the sensuous potential of the visible highway activities and structures themselves.

We will take them up under those heads.

1. The first criteria are the more easily defined. In general they are critical only for a rather narrow strip along the right-of-way, and their importance varies according to the nature of the activity in that strip. A first criterion is that the road must not produce an excessive level of noise in the areas adjacent to it. "Excessive" will have to be defined for several frequencies in the audible range, and will vary according to adjacent use. Quiet natural parks, or areas for outdoor conversation or music, will demand strict standards, while railroad yards, playgrounds, and sealed factories will tolerate a much lower standard. Noise standards will also have to be differentiated by time of day in some cases—in residential areas, in particular, it is essential that noise levels be low during hours of sleep. Some

Courtesy of Institute Archives and Special Collections, MIT Libraries.

studies have been made of existing levels of ambient noise in city environments (notably the recently completed survey of London), and inquiries have been conducted into levels felt tolerable or desirable by city residents. It should be possible to express these findings as maximum intensities, at given frequencies, allowable in areas just outside the right-of-way, depending on the nature of adjacent use, and in some cases on the hour of day.

Prediction of the noise level that will occur, given the location, design, and probable traffic load of a highway, will be more difficult, but surely not impossible. As a basis, studies can be made of noise production in many existing situations. Spatial isolation, the location of expressways through areas relatively insensitive to noise, and the avoidance of "gear-shifting" grades are perhaps the most effective means of satisfying the criterion. Other devices may be partially effective, however: the use of noise barriers, or the depression or high elevation of the roadbed. In critical cases, adjacent use might have to be modified to reduce noise sensitivity or the volume and mix of traffic restricted, perhaps at certain hours. The redesign of the noise source, the vehicle itself, is a more fundamental way of attacking the problem.

Highways can also produce unpleasant or unhealthy fumes. The pollution of city air by vehicle exhaust is a general and critical problem. In the broad sense, this is not a function of highway location and design, but of vehicle design, and of general public policies as to the transportation system or overall city form. We therefore do not treat it here. Locally excessive concentrations of fumes may be ameliorated by spatial isolation, by raising the roadbed, by exposure to wind, or by the design and location of ventilator outlets. They are less likely to be crucial, except for uses very close to or over the right-of-way. In a similar way, excessive vibration may be an undesirable effect for uses in or close to the right-of-way, but this is less likely to be an unpleasant sensuous effect than a structural danger, or a physical problem for certain sensitive processes.

Abutters must not be subjected to unpleasant light: too bright, too dark, too strongly contrasting. It would be unusual for abutting uses to be subjected to headlight beams from an expressway, nor is it likely that general illumination would be unpleasantly bright in sheer intensity, but lighting must be designed to prevent direct glare into nearby windows. Too dark is a more likely occurrence: elevated expressways may cut off sunlight and daylight from the ground below and beside them. At night areas may seem dark and dangerous by contrast with the brightly lit traffic surface. The high even lighting of this pavement, particularly when it is not in active use, is a depressing sight in itself. The unvarying, greenish illumination reinforces the eerie sense of emptiness. Perhaps it may be possible to vary the intensity or color without impairing safety, or even to allow the presence of traffic to actuate higher levels of illumination. Certainly it is possible to screen out glare and "cold" light, or to use illumination underneath or alongside roadways to create variety and warmth. These criteria bear principally on the detailed design of the highway and its illumination, rather than on its location or basic alignment.

It is possible that an expressway may have undesirable effects on the microclimate, principally in the obstruction of sunlight or the blocking of air movement. It is also possible that an elevated expressway might be designed to *improve* the local microclimate, by use as a wind baffle, sun reflector, or shading device. This is speculative, however.

2. Expressways disrupt the pre-existing structure of the areas through which they pass. The economic and social costs of such disruption are treated elsewhere in this study. Similar visual and symbolic losses occur, and though they may be more difficult to define than the direct sensuous effects noted above, they are likely to have more serious and widespread effects. The damage is done in two ways: valuable landscapes are directly confiscated or damaged, or important connections are destroyed. The blocking of cross movement, and the lack of activity frontage, tend to make the limited-access highway a major visual and symbolic barrier in any landscape. Many people not directly along the route will feel the losses caused by such barriers and takings.

To assess potential damage of this kind, it is necessary to identify the significant existing visual and symbolic elements and areas: historically or culturally meaningful buildings and places, buildings of high architectural quality, areas of strong visual character and identity, fine natural areas, or those of particular geological or ecological interest. Identification of these elements and areas, and their ranking on some general scale of significance, cannot be a mechanical process, but it can be done explicitly, in a form for which community or group agreement can be sought. A number of surveys of this type have already been carried out at the city scale. They have generally not been checked, however, with the values of other social groups than are represented by the surveyor. Sample interviews would be required to determine significant elements for which there is community consensus, or to identify elements about which consensus does not exist but which are significant in the minds of some one significant group: a geographic community, or people with common occupational interests, for example.

Once these elements and areas are identified, a highway location should be chosen which avoids taking them, dividing them, or damaging them by its close presence. A route which passes along the interstices of a mosaic of such areas is to be preferred. Where some significant element must be taken or damaged, it should be replaced or reconstituted as far as technically possible: a new park, a redirected stream, a relocated church or area of fine housing. This will usually prove to be an expensive and difficult undertaking, which is, indeed, a measure of the damage caused, and should be accounted as part of the cost of highway location.

Beyond direct damage to specific elements, an expressway may break off important visual and symbolic connections: destroy a fine view, or shut off psychological access between one section and another, as by visually disrupting a customary line of approach, or a continuous linkage of activity. Again, the first step is to identify the critical connections, by field survey and interview, and then to choose locations which minimize the cutting of these connections. Where locations must go across such links, various devices may be used to minimize the damage: manipulating the elevation of the roadway, or re-connecting structures, activities, and pathways over or under the roadway.

Sinking the highway into a tunnel or cut is usually advocated for this purpose, but no general rule is possible, not only because of technical or cost difficulties but for visual reasons as well. A tunnel breaks no surface connections, but is expensive and visually unpleasant for the driver. The tunnel roof must be returned to active use, and not left as an empty ribbon of grass and service roads. A cut is more reasonable in cost, and less oppressive for the driver, who can at least see the sky, if not the city around him. But the wide opening is still a psychological barrier for the man on the surface.

A low elevated road may be least desirable, since it blocks the view and produces dark undersurfaces as well. If on a solid berm, the break is absolute. And yet good design of such a berm may produce a pleasant backdrop for other uses, and even contribute useful terraces where a visual break is acceptable or desirable. But a high elevated road on open supports can often be the best solution, if it is high enough to open up the view both for man on the ground and [for] the driver [and if it is] designed to allow light, air, and active use to pass easily underneath, along the surface. Such a road may raise difficulties of ramp access, however, except where a varied topography can be exploited.

The psychological sense of connection may be restored, even where the view is blocked, by carrying pedestrian ways and local streets over or under the main traffic way, at flat or easy gradients, and by lining these crossings with activities normal to the area. The Ponte Vecchio in Florence, lined on both sides with jewelers' shops, is a psychological as well as a physical bridge across the River Arno. Such possibilities are rarely exploited.

The highway may also be designed not only to minimize disruption to valued places or connections but even to create new ones. The right-of-way and the land taken along its margins could be used to create new development which has values and purposes beyond the transport of vehicles. Some use has already been made of structures bridging highway rights-of-way, and highway margins have occasionally been designed for park purposes. One can go much farther, to imagine large structures which combine traffic and other functions in a complex whole, or linear redevelopment projects of which the road is only one interlinked portion, or the systematic use of road margins, berms, and interchange areas for recreation, or the employment of space under the roadway for commercial purposes. Since the highway is a continuous facility, its right-of-way is usable for other continuous activities: transit, utility lines, and particularly for mobile recreation: walking, bicycling, skating, horseback riding. On special occasions the structure, or parts of it, might be reserved for holiday uses: parades, races, dances. Viewpoints overlooking fine natural or urban scenes may be attached to it. Expressways need not be single-purpose structures, but most of these possibilities remain to be developed.

3. However well the expressway may fulfill the above criteria, there is still a satisfactory jointing to be made between it and the local landscape. The most crucial visual joint reflects the functional joint: the lanes and ramps of the highway must make an apparent fit with the local streets which feed into them. Intersection maneuvers must be clear; on-ramps should have legible entrances and seem to point to what they lead onto [and] off-ramps should fit into the street system with which they will merge. On- and off-ramps together must be imageable as a single coordinated entity, placeable at a definite point on the highway and in the city fabric as well. City streets and highways must seem to make one system. All too commonly, exit and entrance points are uncoordinated, ambiguous and complicated in form, and seemingly unrelated to the local streets. The criterion of visual fit between the two flow systems may be tested for by rehearsing (mentally, or via movies, models, or diagrams) the movements and decisions to be made by entering, exiting, and through drivers, as they will have to be made in the visual sequences which will be presented to them.

Other kinds of visual fit are also important, although they do not have the same direct functional relevance. The road should seem to fit into the general landscape: the flow of the land, for example, the planting and other natural features, the scale and geometry of buildings and open spaces, or the texture of artificial lighting. This is not to say that the road should look like its surroundings; it need not disguise itself as a country lane, a wood, a bank of earth, or a line of buildings. Such deceptions are disturbing, or at best amusing. The problem is to design the joint where the two unlike things come together, taking care that this joint is visually smooth, but also legible. Landscape designers have given thought to some of these joints: the form of the embankment which will visually connect a graded roadway with irregular natural contours, or the arrangement of planting which will connect road space into rural open space. Similar thought should be given to the question of tying road structure to surrounding building structure, or road lighting to surrounding city lighting.

This general criterion has a subjective and somewhat elusive test: it depends on the evaluation of a trained designer who imagines the final result, set in its context. The differences in quality between radically different levels of achievement are, however, apparant enough when the job is done, and current levels of achievement are sufficiently low that crude and subjective tests can be quite useful. Even to point out the need for designing the road as part of its total visual context is useful in itself.

The criterion of fit bears principally on detailed design, once major alignments are set: the nature of embankments, of exact levels, of ramps, of lighting, and so on. It has the important consequence that typical cross sections and details cannot be standardized for entire routes, since roads pass through territories of different character. A varied set of details must be developed, and applied judiciously according to the environment. The cost of designing will inevitably rise.

While general location is not often affected by this rule, it is also true that many rural or urban areas have a sort of "grain"—a pervasive geometry of streets and buildings, typical orientation of stream valleys, or a repetitive profile of ridges—that make it much easier to insert new roads which run in particular directions or have particular vertical alignments. If these general alignments are violated, numerous and repeated problems of local fit will arise. In congested central areas, or landscapes of very special value, it may be possible to reduce design speeds, to make it easier to bring about a fit between road and environment. Sometimes it is feasible to use existing roads as service drives for the highway, minimizing the paved ribbon and insuring a tighter interlocking.

A more objective symptom of a lack of fit will often appear: the repeated occurrence of waste areas and structures at the edge of the right-of-way. There are fragments of land under and along the road which have no function except to be fenced, grassed over, or asphalted, [and] pieces of buildings which can only with difficulty be put to economic use. A highway plan should concern itself with the use and character of *all* the spaces and structures in or near the right-of-way, and takings may at times have to be enlarged in order to solve these problems satisfactorily.

A highway, due to its very function of joining, must often come close to active or symbolically important areas: city centers or waterfronts, for example. The problem of fit becomes acute in such sensitive locations, and may justify special expenditures of design time and talent. The highway may be located to make only intermittent contact with a river or waterfront, so that the natural feature is not continuously sealed off from other users. The road can pass close to a center, but tangentially, or dive beneath it (although this can be puzzling). By manipulating levels, or by erecting symbolic barriers (such as arcades or screens), traffic may have a view of the center, without visually dominating it.

While visual domination should be avoided at sensitive points, it would be imprudent to attempt to mask the highway, or to reduce its visual scale, throughout its run. It is too large and functionally important a physical feature. Camouflage is expensive, technically improbable, and reduces the expressiveness of the cityscape, whose prime function is the flow of man, goods, and ideas. The highway need not be hidden. It should fit in.

4. The highway may not only be designed to avoid damage to its surroundings, it can be exploited for its own inherent beauty. Most of these possibilities will be covered in discussing criteria from the standpoint of the driver, but the road is also a visible event for the bystander. The general structure of the expressway system, and the nature of the activity occurring on it, should be legible from the outside. This is important not only for reasons of orientation, but also because the expressway is a key function, and its visible presence helps to explain the way a landscape works. There is a fascination in the sight of flowing traffic, as long as one is protected from its noise and fumes. The view of an expressway snaking across a city region can be an impressive one. This kind of visual exposure may be achieved without sacrificing any of the previous criteria.

The visible structure of the expressway system—its alignment and its interconnections—can also be used to clarify and strengthen the general visual structure of the city. As a wall, it can define an area; as a visible pointer or view opener, it can draw attention to areas formerly unseen; as a link, it makes possible the mental correlation of previously unrelated elements. Its interchanges can be effective landmarks. If the total highway system is understandable as a unified whole, it can be the basis for understanding a wide region. Expressways which have an unclear pattern for the nearby observer, which appear and disappear capriciously, are wasting their power to make our chaotic cities legible. The test, therefore, is whether the organization of the expressway system, once it is in itself clear to the viewer, can easily be related in the mind to other aspects of the visible structure of the region. This is to some extent predictable by the designer, and can be checked, after the fact, by various interview techniques.

Finally, the expressway is itself a portion of the visible landscape, a complex of physical forms: pavements, banks, retaining walls, ramps, trestles, bridges, signs, lights. Most of these are visible from the outside, as well as to the driver and his passengers. All these forms can be evaluated in their own right, by conventional standards of architectural and landscape design: coherence, differentiation, fitness, expressiveness, sensuous pleasure, and so on. Criteria for the driver may be quite distinct from criteria for the bystander, since the former is viewing these objects in sequence, from a special viewpoint and at a different speed. But for the latter, at least, it is possible to evaluate these objects as static forms, according to well-developed criteria of "good form" about which there is a fair measure of agreement among professional designers. Thus the bridges of Maillart are very generally acclaimed for their elegant fitness, and the substructure of the normal elevated highway is generally deplored for its clumsiness. The design potential of bridges has long been recognized; that of highway trestles is less often attended to; the possibilities of such elements as lighting, signs, or surface color have been almost entirely neglected.

Most of these considerations apply not only to the highway in place, but to the highway in process of construction. Excessive noise, glare, and vibration, the interruption of significant links, [and] intersection confusions all commonly occur during the building of a new road. While transient, such effects are not negligible, and must enter into the entire constellation of design decisions.

The View From the Road

The form of the highway must also serve the needs of those who travel on it. Design criteria for the traveler come under the following headings:

1. The form of the expressway should not subject him to excessive stress, domination, annoyance, or deprivation.

2. All decision points and interconnections should be visually distinct, clear and "expectable." Each expressway and its major segments should have visual identity, continuity, and directional clarity, and [should] be related to other expressways and different circulation systems on some systematic basis.

3. Each route should provide a coherent, rhythmic, vivid, pleasant, and progressive sequence of visual events.

4. The principal features, symbols and activities of the landscape should be visible and visibly related to the expressway.

1. The first criterion is negative: the avoidance of discomfort. Stress can be caused by prolonged conditions, or by sudden extreme changes. Fast-traveling or heavy traffic is clearly a stressful experience, but so are excessive glare, visual flicker, noise, and fumes. Travel over bridges, in cuttings, and through tunnels often suffers from some of these. Objective minimum standards for these conditions can rather easily be set, and attained by the detailed design of the roadway: planting, lane separations, lighting, ventilation, etc.

Acute contrasts and sudden surprises, tunnel entrances, confused decision points, unexpected off-ramps, views of high complexity, and other diversions of attention at critical decision points can all be dangerous. Problems of this kind can be predicted by visual simulations of the experience, or by mental rehearsals of the scene. It is not true, however, that anything which diverts the driver's attention from the road at any point is inherently dangerous. Evidence seems to indicate that long periods of low visual stimulus will, on the contrary, induce dangerous inattention. The prolongation of any quality, however "good" or "beautiful," can result in stimulus deprivation. Restricted views, straight roads of constant width and spatial cross-section, repetitive movements at similar curvatures, continuous landscaping, or uniform lighting can lull the traveler to sleep. Variations in curvature, differentiated lanes, separate levels and alignments, spatial contrast, the clumping of planting, climaxes of artificial lighting, [and] the exposure of interesting views all serve to enliven a journey.

Finally, much annoyance, fatigue and frustration result from the visual noise and clutter encountered. The expressway suffers too frequently from trivial movements in alignment, ragged spaces, half-seen views, [and] a random clutter of signs, poles, and wirescape. Direct control of some of these features is not within the power of the highway designer, but he can shape the features within the right-of-way, and guide or mask the outward view.

These criteria vary in their importance for different travelers. Problems of prolonged stress or boredom are more serious for the man who must travel the road daily. Shock and surprise are the concern of the occasional traveler, many of whom, especially women, express fear of travel on expressways. The driver is more acutely aware of decision-making problems, of distractions and domination, while the passenger may only experience general unpleasantness and ennui. The road must keep within the comfort range of everyone's experience.

2. Visual clarity of decision points is essential for the driver. These points must be immediately recognized on approach. Off-ramps marked only by signs often go unremembered, and some times unused, by road travelers. But if ramps occur at points which are distinctive in other ways, at a bend or transition in the road, at a bridge, if they are marked by a distinctive building, or if the ramp itself is unique, then the chances of recall become much stronger. Each decision point should be distinct from the next, but when there are many of them the traveler is unable to cope with the cognitive load unless they are clustered in groups of limited number. Thus "downtown" off-ramps can be distinguished from those "along the river," or those related to each town, by having similar forms, views, and landmarks, or by common names, or through the color coding of signs.

Movement through decision points, their approach, and the choices to be made within them require careful attention. Adequate time should be allowed for maneuvers. Preparatory cues can be an aid: the lettering on signs might grow in size, or change in color from green to red, as its particular off-ramp is approached. The form of the decision point or accompanying landmarks should also be visible from some distance away. Neither should there be distractions in the approach zone unless they aid in marking the destination or [the] choice of routes. A striking view unrelated to this choice will provoke unnccessary anxiety in the driver who is weaving towards his off-ramp. The intersection should have a clear visible form which fits the maneuvers that must be made within it. If possible, the intersection road should be seen from the highway.

Once at a point of decision, the choices should be clear and limited in number. Decisions must be simple on the expressway; they may be more numerous at the end of the ramp, and time on the ramp may even be prolonged, or its direction be shaped, to make those decisions easier. Those leaving the highway are searching for information about their destination. At present, from the destinations within range of any off ramp—be they local centers, important streets, or whole communities—only one or two names are signaled. Usually, these have no consistency, and refer to diverse elements of the urban scene. Simple maps on the signs, to accompany the key names, could be color coded by the destination type. A view of the destination area itself and of its major visual features is a most direct and efficient means.

While the clarity and identity of the decision point may be an obvious need, the same principle may be applied to larger parts of the movement system. The expressway must be a vividly identifiable, continuous unity, in which the driver senses his own position with security. It is not difficult for an expressway to achieve immediate continuity; there are no stops, and the channel is usually well defined. But attention must be paid to the forward view, in perspective, to assure that this seems continuous and clear.

Each expressway should be readily identifiable as a particular route. Usually, one expressway is very much like another, and traveling in one direction is like traveling in the opposite direction. This not only causes driver errors, but generates a prevailing sense of drabness and monotony. Expressways, or large segments of them, can develop an identity by their relation to the larger landscape—by traveling down a river valley, along a sea or lake shore, or by an industrial belt, a major center, or a renowned institution. Or they can be distinguished through particular motion or spatial qualities. If the character is asymmetrical, or graded in intensity in one direction, it will be easier to differentiate between opposing lanes. Occasional vertical or horizontal separation of the lanes can be equally effective. Using continuous-flow intersections, it is more difficult to distinguish where one expressway ends and the other begins. Contrast in character then becomes particularly important.

A clear sense of direction ranks as an important criterion by itself. The slow unseen curve of a circumferential highway can deceive even the most able travelers. Changes in direction should be relatively sharp and perceptible, and the directions of off-ramps and other inter-connections should be as simple as possible.

While expressways, interconnections, and major segments all require identity, this differentiation should ideally be accomplished in some systematic and meaningful way. Where possible, differences should arise out of some general factor such as location, direction, or transportation function, so that different highways may be easily grouped together in the mind. Map patterns—linear, ladder, grid, and radial—can be a good basis for the organization of systems, though further differentiation is necessary to distinguish between paths of similar direction, and in any non-rectangular grid directional problems are severe. The grouping of identities can also be achieved through alignment with or against the natural or urban landscape. The crescendo form of radials as they approach downtown can be contrasted with the oscillating rhythms of circumferential routes.

Where the landscape is featureless, more abstract methods of structuring may be necessary. All routes in one direction could pass over routes in the perpendicular direction. Routes in one direction could be planted, lit, signed, colored, surfaced, or named according to a set of rules different from those in the other direction.

3. The expressway should offer the traveler a stimulating, coherent, and developing experience. Motion, spatial enclosure, the view, goal attainment, activity, signs, surface character, and light are primary components; continuity and contrast, rhythm and progression are organizing factors.

Each component of the environment can be presented at a different intensity. The traveler's attention heightens on curves and rises, in confined spaces, in the presence of heavy vegetation, traffic, intense illumination, bright signs, or wide stretches of water, or when confronted with complex views. He then becomes acutely aware of visual character. At points of transition or contrast—the entry into a tunnel, the opening up of a view, the arrival of a dominant landmark—interest climbs to a peak. The temporal organization of intensity and transition is basic to sequential design.

The development of clear and simple rhythms can establish a sense of order. If the road moves regularly up and down or from side to side, if it moves back and forth in relation to a river, or [if it] passes through successive confined and open sections, attention is maintained. A poorly organized road is immediately noticeable, it begins to "fall apart" or "never gets going." Rhythmic sequences can also aid prediction, since the rhythmic occurrence of decision points makes them more expectable.

Coincidence of events can create a powerful beat. A highway can rise regularly over cross streets, opening up a view each time and using some vertical landmark, sign, or special lighting to mark the off-ramp. The simplicity of this kind of organization can be wearing, and variations are in order. The road may alternately rise above and drop below the cross streets, [or] the view might alternate from side to side or grow in complexity, [or] the signs could change, still within the same temporal pattern. The tempo could also be quickened in some sections, slowed in others.

As the length of an organized sequence increases, the rhythmic organization must jump to a higher scale. Short sequences may occur within larger ones to form a loosely hierarchical system. The aim is to present the traveler with a coherent and rhythmical succession of visual events. As for any work of art, the test is a highly subjective one, but it will be aided by the new means of simulation which are now developing: graphic notations, motion pictures of models, or computer graphics. This is a new art form with tremendous potential for the enjoyment of millions of observers.

The other essential aspect of the highway's sequential form is its sense of progression. The traveler wants to feel that he is on the move, that he will arrive at his destination. The design of foreground detail may be used to augment or diminish the psychological sense of speed. When the driver sees his goal, a view of downtown for example, his attention begins to pick up; he has a sense of purpose which is lost in travel through endless suburbia or featureless terrain. Rhythmic repetition alone will not solve this problem. A developing or unfolding structure is needed. Views of important features can act as goals to be sighted, approached, and achieved. Major entries can be marked. Basic themes, like views of a river, the form of cuttings or bridges, or the nature of the artificial lighting can be developed and gradually intensified. The classic approach to a climax is one basic model for this kind of organization.

If we consider the visual sequences produced by the real nature of extended expressway journeys, in which drivers enter at intermediate points and use parts of several routes, we raise the problem of organizing whole networks of intersecting visual sequences. For the present, the question is too speculative to warrant discussion here. More conservatively, we ask that single highways, and their segments between principal intersections, offer coherent, progressive visual sequences in both directions, and that the highway intersections themselves be visually legible and smooth.

4. Finally, the expressway should be designed as a meaningful and informative experience. What the traveler sees should be worth looking at. The significant features of the landscape should be sensed from the road. What are the significant features? On practical grounds, the major destinations qualify first: the downtown; the financial, government, shopping, and entertainment districts; widely used recreation areas; and local activity centers. Other places of symbolic importance, or those features which are an essential part of a city's personality—historic monuments and areas, places of architectural quality, cultural centers, key natural features—should also be visible from the highway system. The road may be used to expose the natural base on which the human landscape is

erected: the geology and ecology of the area. It should afford the sight of people and of their typical activities. This not only adds to the pleasure of a drive, but gives the highway a new, educative significance—one which is rarely realized today.

The most obvious way to communicate with the traveler is to put the message directly in front of him, or to put it near to the road and give him time enough to look at it. Billboards are frequently put at axial locations, where they are most dominant and damaging to the highway landscape. The control of axial highway views is critical to the image of our surroundings. Here the best views could be developed, the symbols and significance of the metropolis [could] be exposed. To reinforce his point, the designer may arrange a series of views from different angles and at different distances. The driver may be brought very close to a strong feature—the base of a tall building, the bustle of an open market, the edge of the sea. Clearly, all significant places cannot be seen from each expressway, but a few, like the downtown area or a harbor, might be seen from many routes.

Signs and local radio broadcasts may also be used to explain the roadside scene. Some experiments of this kind have already been made and, so long as listening is voluntary, [radio broadcasts] can be useful sources of information about the form of the landscape and the events taking place within it. Current information of particular interest to the driver, such as traffic and parking conditions ahead, time, weather, road conditions, or the imminence of public events and spectacles, can also be communicated. The driver wishes to retain contact with the landscape. He wants to see local streets and buildings, farms and quarries, the interesting activities and people, rather than being screened from them by a veneer of vegetation.

These considerations, as well as those of sequence, monotony, and visual coercion, tend to make it difficult to design a satisfying highway which runs for very long in a tunnel or [a] deep cut. We may well pause, for more than economic reasons, before putting our transport system underground. Nevertheless, since this is a recurring problem, there is interesting design research to be done on the amelioration of sensuous conditions on "blinded" roads: ways of producing interesting sequences by manipulating light and surface alone, and of avoiding hypnosis or visual coercion [; and] methods of relating surface activity to the underground world.

Summary

We may summarize these criteria in outline form:

A. *For the bystander*:

    1. To avoid undesirable sensuous effects of an immediate, objective kind:

a. Keep intensity of noise at certain frequencies below standard maximum levels in adjacent areas, dependent on time of day and the nature of the area traversed;

b. In special cases, avoid excessive local fumes or vibration;

c. Avoid glare, or excessively dark areas, or the blocking of sunlight and daylight for abutters; mitigate the cold, even pallor of "safe" highway lighting.

2. To avoid damage to existing environmental assets, and to create new ones:

a. Minimize taking or damage to visually or symbolically significant elements and areas, and replace them if damaged or taken;

b. Minimize the interruption of significant visual and symbolic connections, re-establish them, or reinforce breaks where desirable.

c. Create new areas of visual and symbolic significance, and new visual linkages, where possible.

3. To make a good local fit:

a. Form a clear joint between highway and local street system;

b. Arrange a visible fit between road and general landscape;

c. Avoid waste areas and structures at road margins;

d. Avoid visual domination by the highway at particularly sensitive and symbolically important points.

4. To exploit the visual potential of the highway itself:

a. Make legible the general structure of the expressway system, and the activity on it;

b. Relate this visible structure to the visible structure of the city as a whole, and use the former to reinforce the latter;

c. Give good form to the visible elements of the highway itself.

B. *For the traveler*:

1. To avoid undesirable sensuous conditions:

a. Prevent levels of glare, noise, fumes, and visual clutter which cause excessive stress;

b. Avoid sudden, extreme changes which startle or disorient;

c. Reduce the duration of stimulus deprivation and monotony;

d. Avoid visual domination or coercion, in which the traveler is unable to choose his field of view, or to control the motion of his vehicle.

2. To make the movement system legible:

a. Insure that all decision points have a clear form, which explains the necessary maneuvers as well as the connections to destinations; and insure that these forms are readily identifiable and predictable, and can be mentally grouped in systematic categories;

b. Give each expressway visual continuity and a vivid identity, such that both movement directions are visibly differentiated, and compass directions can be grasped, and so that these identities can be grouped in some systematic way for the entire system.

3. To provide a satisfying succession of visual events in both directions on individual roads:

a. Organize a coherent, rhythmical sequence of such elements as motion, space, view, light, and visible activity;

b. Give the traveler a sense of progression, development, and arrival.

4. To use the view from the road as an information device:

a. Expose characteristic views of the significant features of the landscape: important destinations and centers of activity, symbolic places, the sight of people and activity in progress, key natural features or those explanatory of local geology and ecology;

b. Convey current information of interest to the traveler: local events, driving conditions, time, weather, history, etc.

There are some latent conflicts between these various criteria, particularly between criteria for the bystander and for the traveler. These conflicts are sharper when the two groups are also distinct social groups, for example, when suburbanites ride the highways, and in-town dwellers must look at them. In particular, the visual conflicts arise because for one group the highway is a path of access, and for the other an alien barrier. Moreover, the view out and the view in are radically different, both in viewpoint and in dynamic quality. These differences lead to design quandaries, which can only be resolved by compromise or ingenuity in particular cases. They are made more difficult by the acute technical demands of the highway itself: continuity, inflexible alignment, and large size. But these technical demands are not absolute; they also rest on value judgments such as design speed. All values must be considered together when generating a compromise. In a tight spot, design speed may be as modifiable as visual form.

Conflicts between these criteria can often be resolved, as has been hinted several times in the discussion above. In particular, the authors are convinced that highways are not necessarily ugly, neither for driver nor abutter, that they need not be single-purpose structures, but can instead be used for many ends, and that they represent an important but unrealized source of delight as well as utility. Highways are used not by cars but by people, and the important conflicts are not between machines and pedestrians, as contemporary cant would have it, but between different sets of people, playing different roles.

We cannot, as yet, state these sensuous criteria with precision. But they point to areas of concern, and in many if not most design situations the presence of monotony, confusion, or excess, or the destruction of adjoining landscapes, can be generally agreed upon. Nevertheless, it is clear that much research and field trial is urgently needed, although to outline these requirements would require a separate memorandum. One major complication is the variations among the persons affected: drivers, passengers, abutters, young, old, of different social and temperamental character. To this extent, highway design shares the complexity of any public design for human use. We have mentioned the importance of interviews. Rather than waiting for a population to rise in protest, it would be more prudent, and more in the public interest, to incorporate interview and testing procedures into all major highway design decisions.

Since these criteria refer to the direct satisfactions achieved by road users, they rank in importance with more obvious criteria such as traffic capacity, safety, and cost. While some of these sensuous criteria can be achieved by manipulating road detail, in general they bear on fundamental decisions of location, alignment, and highway characteristics. It is a common mistake to defer the "looks" of a road to a final application of cosmetics, when damage and ugliness can only be ameliorated. The sensuous quality of a road, or of a system of roads, must be considered from the beginning.

Designing and Managing the Strip (1974)

with Michael
Southworth

sketches and
photographs by
Michael
Southworth

The arterial street is the skeletal system of the American city. When continuously lined with shops and services, it becomes the "strip," the street in its most uncomfortable form. This study investigates the possibilities for improving the environmental quality of these ubiquitous, always criticized, commercial strips. It looks at the impact these places have on their users, and it suggest standards of quality which might be applicable to them, as well as some patterns of use and form which could bring out their potential as a human environment.

By "commercial strips" we mean linear shopping developments along arterial streets or highways. They are sometimes called by other names: "roadside ribbon developments," "business ribbons," "string streets," or simply "strips." Activities along them are primarily commercial, but office, residential, and light industrial uses are commonly included. All these uses front directly onto the arterial, making the strip only one parcel deep on each side of the street. Strips are typically unrelated in function or form to the activities behind them, which are usually residential but are sometimes industrial or undeveloped.

The commercial strip has many deficiencies—its noise, its confusion, its harsh climate, its monotony, its inhospitality to man on foot, its overwhelming ugliness. Strips are among the most "polluted" man-made environment we have. They affect the quality of entire regions because of their extensiveness (figure 1). They are among the most visible elements of the American city. A product of the streetcar, the automobile, and private speculation in land, they are one of America's unique contributions to urban form. Now strips are found in cities throughout the world. They epitomize the irresponsible use of the public environment for private gain. These endless, formless, eventless, cluttered avenues saturate the urban experience. Every city has them; few cities want them. They are most prevalent in the areas of new growth. For example, Los Angeles conducts nearly all its work, travel, shopping, and recreation "on the strip." Sunset Strip has become almost a national monument, a symbol of Los Angeles and the golden age of film. Nearly every American city has at least one "Sunset Strip": Minneapolis [and] St. Paul are linked by a four-mile strip called the "Midway," Boston has its "Route One," and Dallas has its "Lemmon Avenue."

Shopping streets are an ancient urban feature, but strips in their present form first appeared with the advent of the streetcar. Typically, they grew in residential areas. The improved access created by the streetcar, which opened up new suburban land to residential use, sharply in-

Reprinted by permission of Harvard-MIT Joint Center for Urban Studies, Cambridge, Massachusetts.

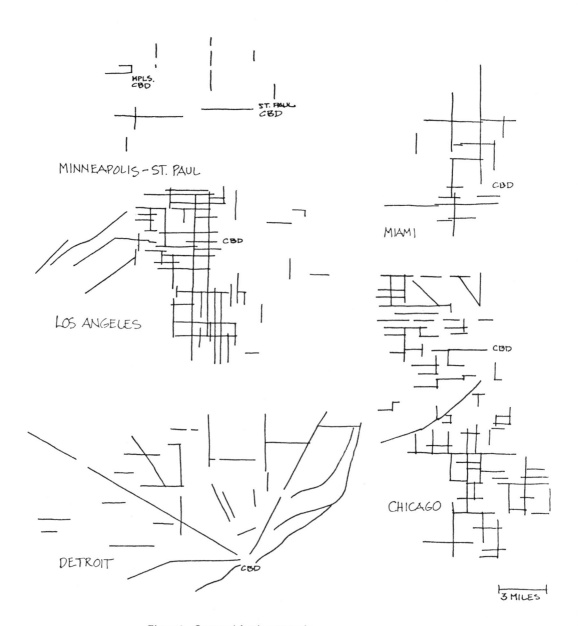

Figure 1 *Commercial strip patterns in American cities.*

creased the land values of property along the route itself. At the same time, the moderately dense population that lived along the streetcar line created a demand for commercial space. Residents fled from the street; their houses [were] converted to stores and offices or demolished to make way for new commercial construction. A few remaining houses were converted to rooming houses or apartments. Strips as they developed tended to be very shallow, at most 200 feet deep, and usually 100 feet or less. Frontage was continuous, with occasional breaks for free-standing houses. This type of strip development occurred between about 1890 and 1930.

The widespread use of the automobile after 1930 made for a drastic change in strip form. Not only was a route needed for the automobile but a parking space had to be provided for each shopper. Thus the form could no longer be compact. The depth of the strip was greatly increased, often to 400 or more feet on each side to allow on-site parking and servicing by large trucks. In the case of old strips, traffic lanes were widened and sidewalks were narrowed to accommodate the automobile. Sometimes sidewalks were simply deleted. Structures were no longer built directly adjacent to each other, but became free-standing, most often set in the midst of a parking lot. The speed of the automobile also caused a change in advertising: signs became far larger and more demanding of attention— the billboard and the revolving, flashing sign first appeared in the auto-mobile era. Some of the old streetcar strips have partially adapted to the automobile and are relatively successful, but most have suffered economi-cally. Because of the enormous space demands, the true automobile strip appears only in areas that have been developed more recently. But some are growing in older residential districts, following the same patterns as the earlier streetcar strips. Homes are converted to business uses or are torn down to make way for larger buildings. Well-to-do suburbs have resisted the process through zoning controls that confine the strip to some marginal location or to some other town. But purely residential use of the arterial frontage is difficult to maintain. Strips appear to grow wherever they find some foothold in the crevices of public regulation. Without in-tervention, we can expect the public face of the American city to become more and more like that of Los Angeles.

Arterial streets are an obvious necessity, and strip developments grow for good reason. Automobile-oriented businesses, in particular, have been attracted to the strip—automobile sales and service businesses, drive-in restaurants, banks, and motels. But many businesses of other types that cannot afford to locate in the urban centers have also chosen strip locations. These provide good automobile access (unlike many urban centers, the older ones in particular), and taxes, rents, and land values are typically lower. Each business on a strip has a good opportunity of being seen by motorists; moreover, shoppers are made to feel they are parking at the door (though they may walk 200 yards through parked cars to reach the entrance). Strip locations are made for impulse buying, for handling heavy consumer goods, and for single-purpose stops. Growth and change are easily accommodated: individual additions can be made at the side or rear, or the strip as a whole can extend lengthwise. The location of any particular establishment is no longer constrained—it has many choices. In addition, controls on site development are frequently very loose. There is usually no master plan or design review; signing ordinances are weak; zoning restrictions are few; and typically the few existing controls are poorly enforced. In short, the strip, along with the low-value industrial zone, permits the greatest entrepreneurial freedom of any large-scale urban environment in the United States.

These advantages have created corresponding problems. Strips have generated destructive levels of automobile pollution and congestion. Advertising has become garish and competitive, distracting to the point of endangering safety. Strips bear no relation to their context, and they blight any residential area through which they run. Natural or historic features of districts through which they pass are obliterated: strips look quite the same wherever they occur, distinguished only by the decade in which they were built. Strip businesses themselves are usually unorganized socially or politically; and few outsiders identify with such areas, thus making it difficult to gain the necessary support to improve them. Nevertheless, popular complaint about the quality of the strip environment is commonplace.[1]

Subjects of interviews have complained:

There is no place to park, yet the parked cars are ugly. The streets are congested; the cars turning in and out are dangerous and annoying. It is unsafe to cross the street, or to cycle along it. It is difficult to service the establishments without disturbing customers.

The strip is too noisy. The air is polluted with fumes. There are unpleasant smells. It is too wet, too cold, too windy, too hot. It lacks shade. There is too much dirt and litter. There is too little light at night and yet too much glare. There are no benches, no shelters, no public rest rooms, no telephones, there is no place to sit and talk at ease.

Foot pavements are wet, broken, or just missing. One cannot carry packages, or manage small children easily. There is no accommodation for the aged or the handicapped.

There is a lack of planting, of natural areas. There is a clutter of signs and overhead wires, ugly buildings and chaotic development. The street lacks identity and character. There is nothing interesting to look at. It is hard to identify things or to find one's way.

The fronting activities lack variety and interest. They are too crowded or too empty. There are gaps in the frontage and at times the strip is deserted.

The list may be imprecise and internally conflicting, but it is a strong condemnation. It is not surprising that the life span of businesses on most strips is relatively short. Real estate brokers who were interviewed in the course of this study said that they do not advise businesses to invest in strip property if they want long-term economic growth or value. Urban centers have proved to be far more stable for business. One realtor felt that the "people traffic" at a center was an essential ingredient to business success. Some large companies such as E. J. Korvette typically locate on strips but plan on a ten-year maximum life for each store. Drive-in eating establishments plan on a similarly short life span. The Massachusetts State Department of Commerce advises communities to control or prevent strip developments, because it has been shown that strips lead to the decline of the central shopping areas and at the same time disrupt the environment through which they run. Their unplanned nature causes many diseconomies. But they are ideal for many low-capital, new, or "short-life" businesses. And so they continue to grow.

Local planning agencies attempt to stop strip development by ceasing to create new strip zones or by rezoning existing strips to residential or institutional uses. For example, the Boston Redevelopment Authority has rezoned Blue Hill Avenue, an old and failing strip, into residential use, and it is attempting to consolidate the remaining commercial activity into centers. But this is a slow and painful process, and it is hard to find substitute uses. In planned new communities, where the commercial strip has usually been banned, the disposition of arterial frontage is notoriously difficult. It may be parceled out to large institutions, tall apartments, or civic buildings, but more often [it] must be devoted to costly, unused, and rather monotonous belts of trees and lawns. Meanwhile, the commercial strip reappears just over the city line. There has been much popular criticism of the strip, but little of that criticism explains how to improve it. Innovative modifications to the miles of existing strip are urgently needed. What is more, if the strip reappears so persistently, it may represent an important function that must somehow be given a more humane form.

The Venturis, in *Learning from Las Vegas*, proclaim that string of gambling casinos along Nevada's Route 66 as the Apotheosis of the Strip. This is a proclamation of love, but it is underlain with hate. The cultural elite may look down upon the strip, but the Venturis see a new landscape, faultlessly performing its function. Admittedly, the function is "basely commercial."

On the contrary, Las Vegas is no new function, no new landscape at all. It is the further extension of vehicle-dependent Main Street, a form now at least a century old. Since ordinary Main Streets are common enough, it is worth the effort to see how well this further extension works, and also to consider if its function (in this case the thrill of gambling, the brief extravaganza) could be better served in other ways.

The Venturis do not attempt the latter, nor do we, in most part. But how it really works for the people who use it is still a legitimate question. Behold! We find that Highway 66 is ill-made for the turning in and out of cars—that drivers can rely little on directional signs, but must use their sense of where a lot begins (and their stereotype of how one usually maneuvers in it) to carry them through. Are they not confused at night by all the moving lights, as many people are on other strips? In the day, the spindly light poles and painted parking lines are weak clues. The giant signs, and the buildings shaped as signs, must be relied upon. The signs and building-signs are interesting enough. They compensate for the direct contact with people and things that has been lost. The potentialities of the commercial sign have been well-argued before. Yet in Las Vegas those signs perform only moderately well. They are far short of their potential impact. Moreover, a landscape that depends on a single clue for its identity is surely at risk. "If you take the signs away, there is no place."

The transiton between inside and outside, between strip and desert, is brutal: "a zone of rusting beer cans," "ill-kempt backsides." "What gives poignance (to the interior patios) is the vivid, recent memory of the hostile cars poised in the asphalt desert beyond." The brilliant strip seems to lack some quality even for the people who pay to enjoy it. And how does it function for those that work there, or who drive by on the way to the airport? To look at a place with open eyes, in order to learn from it, is surely admirable. That does not require us to become ecstatic about it, however.

The arterial streets are the most traveled routes in the city. Their improvement could enhance the public image and the social and economic value of a much wider surrounding district. In some measure, these strips are the archetypal public places of vast regions. They also represent an opportunity for new development to take place without disturbing local settlement.

Strips can provide an important way to structure the cognitive image of city and region, since street networks are easier to conceptualize than other urban patterns. They are the entry ways to the important urban centers. The sequential street experience has grown steadily in importance, as daily trips have covered larger and larger territories. This does not apply solely to automobile drivers; arterials are also the natural channels for public transportation. And one must certainly consider that astonishingly persistent species, the pedestrian, and his reappearing cousin, the bicyclist. Moreover—and this may seem wildly utopian—certain locations along these arterials might become the places for public life, as city streets have served us in the past.

We possess hundreds of miles of these streets. What shall we do with them? If we had the power, would we abolish them and never allow another to be built? One way to look at these questions is to consider the effects of the spatial form of the strip on the people who actually use them.

It is probable that strips have continuing useful functions, since they constantly reappear when suppressed. More to the point, they are on our hands. So it is also useful to see how strips might be designed and managed to better satisfy the needs of all their users.

The purpose of this study has been to find a legitimate role for the strip, to extend its useful life where it now exists, and to prevent it from damaging the district through which it passes. In particular, we hope to apply the findings to areas of new growth, where a special opportunity exists to manage the strip from its birth. Emphasis will be placed on hitherto neglected qualities that have an immediate impact on the way arterial streets are experienced and used. These will range from safety and comfort to questions of information and sensuous delight. The focus is on arterial streets of mixed traffic, where there are mixed and relatively intensive uses, primarily commercial ones. In formulating recommendations, some unified control will be assumed of those aspects of fronting uses which directly affect street function: access points, the intensity of motor traffic or of pedestrians generated by an activity, parking, signs and views, and the activities taking place on sidewalks or in spaces directly abutting them. In some cases, the agency managing the right of way might also control (initially or even permanently) the fronting uses.

Case Study: Main Street, Waltham

To better understand a typical strip, its form, its use, and its management, it is useful to look at one. Main Street in Waltham, Massachusetts, offers a good case. The strip section of Main Street begins at the edge of the old town center on the village green and runs west for over three-quarters of a mile (figure 2), passing through the middle of an old residential area of multi-family homes. The commercial success of this strip is partly evidenced by the heavy traffic, both pedestrian and vehicular. People walk to the strip from within the neighborhood, and many more drive to it from throughout the community and even surrounding towns. A large amount of the traffic is not strip clientele, however, but is en route to Route 128, a circumferential regional highway. The first impression of congestion intensifies the longer one stays. The traffic noise and the polluted air become almost unbearable after an hour. The visual impression is one of chaos. There are structures of many types and eras: an old white frame church, a shiny six-story office building, a row of small stucco and brick shops dating from the 1920s, a new A&P supermarket, new aluminum and glass shop rows, a "Finnish chalet" church, a "Southern classic" library, several gas stations and drive-in restaurants, and even a colonial house of some historical significance. Besides this last, the only other expression of history is the single stone marker, somewhat obscured, which commemorates the delivery of artillery to General Washington during the revolutionary siege

Figure 2 *General character of Main Street.*

of Boston. This is the old main route to the West. In several structures the conversion from house to store is still evident. There are peaked, flat, round, spired, and barn roofs [and] buildings of stone, plastic, metal, glass, wood, or concrete in all colors.

The range of activities is also large: barber shops, fish market, electronics shop, supermarket, beauty salons, variety stores, taverns, gas stations, a drive-in hamburger stand, liquor stores, doughnut shop, dry cleaning, laundry, submarine and pizza shops, bank, handicrafts and art supplies, shower shop, drug stores, book and novelty shop, clothing store, hardware store, real estate office, printing shop, professional offices, boating and marine supplies, auto sales and repair, houses and apartments, post office, churches, school, library, political office, bicycle shop.

Activities have varied relations to the public street. Most structures run to the property line and provide a standard door entrance, often slightly inset, yet many are set back from the sidewalk. A drive-in restaurant provides a small eating area next to the sidewalk. Some provide parking directly in front of the establishment, often for only one row of cars. Others have vast parking areas between the building and [the] side-

Figure 3 *Signs dominate the typical strip.*

walk or are located in the middle of a parking lot. Still others provide a small space between building and sidewalk, apparently for "esthetic" reasons.

Signs of innumerable sizes, shapes, and colors rear up on cumbersome supporting structures. They project from buildings, stand on poles or roofs, hang from awnings, or occupy facades. Many paper signs hang behind windows announcing sales. Except for some window displays, few objects serve as their own sign—some sacks of potatoes, two church steeples, and a small tower identifying the old trolley yard that is no longer in use. Signs which locate distant features are present but infrequent, difficult to find amidst the clutter of other forms. Although the Charles River is a short distance away, there is no view of it, nor any other indication of its presence. Nor is the traveler oriented within the strip itself, for each block is similar to the last and the next. There are glimpses of housing behind the strip, but even this appears anonymous. Here, on this historic street, one might be anywhere. Only three elements provide orientation to the strip as a whole: the white church steeple, the single large tree remaining, and the old trolley station watch tower (since demolished). The visible activity and noise of the strip add further confusion to the scene—moving cars, trucks, buses, bicycles, motorcycles, and pedestrians.

The juxtaposition of the strip and the solid residential area immediately behind is jarring. Chain-link fences, parked cars, and the macadam of parking lots frame one's view of large old homes one block or less away. A gas station and its appurtenances mark the entry to one of the more commodious residential streets; the station presses against a large and dignified apartment house. From within the residential area one is also aware of the strip. Its untended backside reveals chimneys, air conditioners, garbage bins, and storage yards. The fumes and traffic noise penetrate even farther into the neigborhood—even when the strip itself cannot be seen, one can smell and hear it.

Attempts to alleviate the harshness of the strip are evident but ineffective. Small evergreen shrubs, often in pots, are a frequent remedy, set in small patches that have found no other use. Shriveled, dying, isolated, they only affirm the destructiveness of this environment. Elsewhere there are large imitation plants of plastic, which survive the fumes but are caked with dirt. The supermarket parking lot, with its fence, flag, [and] clusters of shrubs, tries to be beautiful and dignified but in fact only emphasizes its barrenness.

There are attempts to provide for the physical comfort and convenience of strip users. Canopies occur in a few locations. They provide some rain protection, but do little to shelter the pedestrian from wind and wind-driven rain; they are high for their overhang and give little side protection. Most of them make another visual intrusion on the street. The inset doorways provide much better protection from wind, cold, and rain, although they accommodate few users. The supermarket has provided the only bench on the strip at one of the bus stops. However, it is not well used. Typically, people waiting for the bus stand and put their groceries on the bench. At first glance this seems puzzling. But observation reveals that people must stand to see when the bus is coming. From a seated position the bus is not visible for more than a block because of the heavy traffic. Another convenience provided by the supermarket is a terra cotta bas-relief map of the city. But this contains little information. An inadvertent convenience is provided by the supermarket, since it is the common practice for shoppers to wheel loaded shopping carts out of the store to their parked cars and abandon them; these carts are then put to use not only by supermarket patrons but by anyone with packages. Other support facilities along Main Street are phone booths, mail boxes, and trash cans, all of which are well used. The ill-formed trash cans are paid for through the advertising of local merchants which appears on their sides.

A comparison of the present street with the way it was almost a hundred years ago (figure 4) is both shocking and saddening. It was a

Figure 4 Main Street in 1886. (Courtesy of Waltham Public Library.)

quieter street then, yet it accommodated a variety of activities. Signs were simple and modest. Overhead protection and porches with seating were common. The structures and spaces were varied yet related in material and form. Large old elms overhung parts of the street. There were also signs of change. A streetcar line runs unobtrusively down the middle of the uncovered, unpaved street. The elms are beginning to be cleared away, and the one in the foreground has a damaged trunk. A house has converted its first-floor front to a store. The transformation of a rural New England highway into a commercial strip has begun, but an easy air still lingers. A look at the same street today can only confirm our failure to improve the quality of our everyday environment.

Users of the Main Street Strip

As we watch the street, we see people—

Passing through in cars, trucks, bicycles, motorcycles, taxis, buses,
Walking, running, standing, climbing, sitting, lying down,
    in wheelchairs or on crutches.
Looking for destinations,
Getting in or out of vehicles, parking and deparking them,
Window shopping, buying, selling,
Using phones, mail boxes, trash cans,
Socializing, playing, "hanging out,"
Cleaning, repairing, constructing,
Policing,
Waiting, resting,
Taking care of children,
Carrying parcels, delivering.

How can we classify these users of Main Street, and how does this environment suit them?

The Passing Driver

To the passing driver, the strip is a place to drive through on his way to somewhere else. Hence his judgments are largely negative ones. The driver deals constantly with turning and entering traffic, with stop lights and signs, with jaywalkers, trucks, and buses. He is presented with sudden dangers and sudden decisions, and faces long waits of idling cars. The road surface may be pitted, or encumbered with ice and snow. He cannot easily see the traffic signals, or the name of the street, or be sure where he will make his next turn. He may like to know the time, or something about the traffic ahead, or even what the weather will be. Road repairs, unloading trucks, and people entering their cars all encroach on the traveled way.

The noise is incessant; the air is heavy with fumes; the numerous metallic reflections hurt his eyes.

The commercial activity along the way and the people on the walks may be interesting to watch but are difficult to see because of the crowding vehicles. There is much less expression of what is going on inside the buildings: the strident signs and the bright-colored buildings are actually quite standardized, for all their random arrangement. The goods and services available can hardly be seen from the passing car. The vital public utilities are invisible or, if visible, do not explain their function. Natural features—trees, rivers, rocks, hills—have been obliterated. The history and the future of the place are indecipherable.

There is no coherent sequence of space or motion or view, such as might be displayed to someone in a moving vehicle. There is rarely any long view, or only a formless one. One is isolated within a metal shell, which dulls sight and hearing. There is little chance to stop to talk to someone on the street, or in another car.

At night the unpleasantness mounts. There may be fewer entering cars and so less traffic interference. But the high street lights and the oncoming headlamps glare in the empty darkness, surrounded by a chaos of lighted signs, moving and flashing in odd ways. Most of them refer to absent activity. Some stores, internally lit but empty, reinforce the loneliness, as do the brightly illuminated gas pumps. Only the occasional entertainment spot, lunch counter, variety or liquor store is alive, and this activity is internal, largely unseen.

For the motorized sightseer, the scene is fearfully familiar. It is Anyplace—displaying the same signs, the same services, and the same chaotic forms he has seen on any commercial artery in the nation. Does anyone ever take a tourist out of his way to see a commercial strip, or fail to apologize if he must drive down it? It may seem ridiculous to consider that these workaday places could ever attract a sightseer. Yet tourists almost invariably use strips in entering the city; they stay in motels along them, they pass through them in taxis, buses, or cars, and then go elsewhere to see the sights. To imagine them as tourist attractions is one test of their quality.

The Motorized Shopper

One may insist that this is a working street, and that it cannot be made pleasant for passersby. Still, lives are spent here, and the street does not work even in its most "practical" sense. Strips are built for the shopper on wheels, and yet he suffers from the same disabilities that the through driver endures. Moreover, he has further difficulties.

He must locate his destination from some distance, see just where to turn in, and be able to do so easily. Commercial signs are designed for that purpose; however, they do their job inefficiently, and they face fierce competition. The actual motor entrance is often surprisingly obscure. In addition, the shopper would generally like to know whether his destination is open, whether it is crowded, where to park, and (particularly if he is a transient buyer) something about the quality, price, and type of its goods and services. Only some of this is visible.

He wants to park nearby, preferably in direct relation to the door. So the curbside is still the most favored location. But it is a scarce and wasteful commodity. Getting out of the car is a trick in itself it it has to be done in the midst of traffic or up against another car, or if one is crippled. Once out of the car, there are packages to carry, pets and children to manage— especially as one goes through doors, or across the street. Alternatively, one may leave the dog (or the children) shut up in the car, imprisoned in the midst of the noise and fumes.

It may be raining, cold or hot, windy or glaring, as one moves from car to building. The pavement may be wet, muddy, or icy. There may be steps or high curbs to be overcome. Can the now dismounted shopper walk to nearby establishments, or are the sidewalks discontinuous and the buildings scattered? Is there any provision for getting a heavy package to the car? Is it safe to cross the street? Is one safe from assault, especially at night, and the car safe from vandalism? Are toilets, alarms, telephones, mailboxes, drinking fountains, medical aid, storage lockers, and other essential public facilities within easy access and clearly marked? Even for the motorized shopper, the strip falls short of being a good setting for his activity, although convenient access by car remains its fundamental advantage.

Bus Passengers

Other shoppers come by bus, and have problems of their own. Like others, they must be able to identify their destination, but they have special disabilities. They can only see sideways; their destination may come after the nearest stop, as well as before it, and so they overshoot. Where is the bus taking them? How long before their stop should they begin moving to the door? For anyone but an habitual rider, getting off a bus is usually a matter of some anxiety. But for any elderly person, or someone crippled or burdened with children or packages, the act of moving in a lurching vehicle, and descending its steep steps, is patently difficult. Once off the bus, the passenger faces the same problems of obstacles and the weather that other pedestrians do.

When the transit shopper chooses to leave the strip, there are packages to carry, the bus step is high, and the curbside may be blocked with cars, water, snow, or mud. Waiting for the bus may be protracted, and there is no certain knowledge when the bus will come, nor any easy way to see if it is coming. There is usually no place to sit, or to find shelter from the wind or rain. Nor is there any clear information on the scheduling and routing of the buses—perhaps not even a clear marking of the bus stop itself. Looked at another way, the vacant minutes of waiting are a wasted resource—a time when people might be amused or informed, might meet each other or call a friend, hear some music or take a social drink, rest by a fountain or in a pleasant shade. Since people may spend considerable time waiting for buses, this might easily justify a shelter or other special facilities. What bus riders normally get is a patch of exposed sidewalk and a narrow passage between two parked cars.

Cyclists

There are other means of transportation, of course, although little attention is paid to them. Cyclists are dangerously exposed in moving traffic and are excluded from the sidewalks (figure 5). The suddenly opened door of a curbside car is an ever-present danger for them, and for their part they present a threat to the pedestrian and make driving more difficult. Riding in the open, they are exposed to all the natural inclemencies plus the noise, the fumes, the spattered mud. A sudden hole can be much more dangerous for them than for a driver or a man on foot. The parking of a bicycle where it will both be safe and not block the movement of others is no trivial question. Cycle tracks and cycle parking need to be a matter of conscious consideration in strip design.

Figure 5 *Cyclists are dangerously exposed in moving traffic.*

Figure 6 *The group of passing teenagers exclaim: "Spread out—I'm crowded!" "I am spread out—I'm practically in the street!"*

Walkers

Walking along the street, the pedestrian is assualted by all the adverse influences of heat, glare, rain, noise, fumes, wet or broken pavements, the threats of entering cars and bicycles, the danger (real or fancied) of assault (figure 6). Sidewalks are usually too narrow, and tree planters, utilities, and parked cars become annoying barriers, especially to people with carts or parcels or to mothers with strollers and buggies. In places the sidewalk simply disappears, giving way to a driveway, gas station, auto repair yard, or simply mud. Crosswalks are often unmarked and much too infrequent, and people jaywalk everywhere. For all this, there is some compensation in the intrinsic interest of the visible activity, the chance of dropping in to buy on impulse, or the opportunity of encountering a friend (if there is a place to talk and be heard). Many walkers are children coming or going from school who dart across the street. Pedestrians carry loads, or push carriages, or convoy infants, or struggle along on crutches. The curbs and puddles can become formidable obstacles. The strip is not very gracious to the person on foot, and it is forbidding to the blind or to a person in a wheelchair.

Street People

Not everyone is just moving through, or coming to shop. The strip is a preferred hangout for teenagers, a place where they can gather, talk, and watch the world pass. They need a place to be at the edge of the action and close to food, where they can see and be seen but not be directly in the public way. It should be a place that is securely their own territory, that they can mark out and decorate, a sheltered place, provided perhaps with telephones, food services, places to sit, lie, read, watch TV, play music or games. There could be computer printouts here, exhibitions, notices, and other sources of information. But what they usually get is a cramped street corner, or the narrow space in front of a store.

Even more neglected are the older men who stand on the street corners, or lean against the walks, in pairs and alone. Unemployed or retired, uneasy at home, there is little in the street to fill the emptiness of their time. The automobile has forced the strip to abandon many of the social functions of the old public street. Other people, also, might use the strip if it were not so uninviting: children for their play, housewives for their free hours.

Workers

People work along the strip, too. They need good access and parking just like the other users. Shop owners need inexpensive space, storage and delivery room, easy access for their customers, and a chance to be seen. These are the attributes that the strip realistically offers; these are the reasons for its existence. But, as individuals, workers might also prefer quiet and pleasant surroundings and many of the services described earlier. Here the strip fails them.

Public employees work along the strip—maintaining and repairing its pavements, utilities, and structures. They have too little room to work in, often impede traffic, or run the hazard of being struck down. There is usually no place to store materials or wastes or machines; no place to pile the snow. The noise and disruption caused by repairmen are the subject of constant complaint, and they must feel that social disapproval. The surfaces they deal with are hard to clean. Things are too high up or are buried underground or lie in the paths of others. It is difficult to find the utilities they seek to mend. New work is often quickly vandalized.

Still other service agents are patrolling the strip, or are charged with protecting it in an emergency. They must be able to reach any threatened point quickly, [and] to monitor the street from on foot, from a car, or from some more remote location. Traffic controls must respond quickly to traffic changes. Effective night-time surveillance must be possible. Ambulances, fire trucks, and patrol cars must be able to move with speed.

Neighbors

Sometimes the strip runs in splendid isolation through woods and fields. Wild creatures are its only neighbors. Then the rear lots stop and the trees begin in that completely inattentive way peculiar to the American landscape. More often, there are human neighbors behind the strip—workers in nearby industrial plants, families in residential neighborhoods. Both suffer from its presence: its noises, pulsing lights, and fumes. Neighbors see the "backside" of the strip, the service doors, the cheaply finished facades, the parking lots, the cyclone fences, and the deposits of solid waste that accumulate along the banks of the commercial stream. Merchants and customers attend to what fronts along the artery and they ignore the land behind. The strip is somewhat like a giant stage set, part of whose audience is unhappily seated behind the scenes.

When the strip is a major artery with side streets flowing into it, then neighbors suffer further difficulties. The heavily traveled artery is dangerous and annoying to cross; neighboring residents are caught in its congestion when they enter or leave their homes by car or bus. The convenience stores are located there; their children go to school along the strip, or use its hangouts. So neighbors, in their turn, become direct users.

One of the strip's advantages should be the way in which its linear form brings services within easy walking distance of many more local residents than any focused center could do. So a strip should be easy to reach along its entire length, have frequent services, meeting places, and convenience outlets, and be a route along which it is pleasant and informative to stroll. The strip need not pass through the city as if through an alien land.

Demonstrators and Celebrators

There is still another historic use of streets, now rarely seen on the modern strip. This is their use for demonstrations and celebrations: marches, street dances, street meetings, parades, funerals, fairs. These activities are now largely confined to the main streets of the city or town center. Processions need a continuous, traditional route, safe to traverse, with a place that can provide a symbolic destination, and room for an audience along the way. There should be places to gather to hear speeches or music, objects that can be decorated, a setting which lends impact to the event. A procession is dramatic if it can see itself (due to curves and slopes along the way, for example). Participants can sense the power of the day. Providing settings for public ceremonies may seem strangely remote from the contemporary strip; yet these commercial arterials are the principal public spaces of many urban regions, even if they presently provide no space in the sense of public "room."

Management of the Strip

In so many ways, then, the commercial strip fails its users. Some of these deficiencies are specific to particular kinds of people, but many (even most) of the faults are felt by almost everyone who ranges along them. They can be summarized under a few general headings. A good public street will:

1. *Support the Normal Behavior of People:* It will allow them to move and act with ease, to have access to what they need, and permit them to behave, if they wish, in a sociable (rather than a merely task-oriented) manner.

2. *Inform Them:* It will communicate time, locations, function, the presence of other people, history, local ecology, the future, public rules, and much else in some clear and interesting way.

3. *Promote Their Health, Comfort, and Safety:* It will protect them from an adverse climate, noise, pollution, danger, and other types of stress.

4. *Engage and Delight Them:* It will provide visual rhythm and continuity, express natural features, dramatize light, form, and view, create sequences, exploit the esthetic potential of common street elements (even of utilities, for example).

These general values take on concrete meaning only when one considers how specific people actually use, attempt to use, or might use the strip. We have attempted in the previous section to convey some of that meaning on Main Street. These values have implications for a wide range of street elements, but it appears from those earlier descriptions that there are some specific elements and issues (actual or potential) which are particularly rich in needs and possibilities. These include the following:

1. *Provision of Access for Non-Motorists,* such as pedestrians, dismounted motorists, public transit riders, cyclists, the handicapped, children, and mothers, through the design and management of the sidewalk, the cycle way, the doorway, and the curb to meet their needs.

2. *Control of Air Pollution, Noise, Heat, Cold, Wind, Rain, and Glare.*

3. *Creation of Convenience Clusters* that provide for basic human needs in some focused locality, such as a bus stop, and which might expand to become social meeting places.

4. *Communication of Function, Time, and Place,* creating an informative and pleasant sequence to pass through, in which destinations can easily be located and entered. Public and private signing, for example, can be designed as a total system.

Table 1

Street Element	Controlling Groups
Street location and pattern, width, posted speed, gradient, curves, access rules, parking, materials, drainage, construction details, metering	Dept. of Streets and Traffic, Planning Commission, Urban Renewal Authority, Dept. of Public Works, Dept. of Transportation (Fed.), State Highway Dept.
Utilities	Water Commission, Telephone Company, Gas Company, Electric Company, Fire Dept.
Height/bulk of structures, setbacks, spacing	Building Dept., Board of Appeals, Planning Commission
Quality and style of built form, building materials	Individual Builders, Owners, Developers, Historic Commissions, Municipal Building Dept., State and Federal Institutions, Design Review Boards, Manufacturers and Suppliers of Materials.
Street furniture, rest rooms, shelters, etc.	Dept. of Streets and Traffic, Parks Dept., Public Works Dept., Manufacturers
Curb design, walkways, crossings, bike paths	Dept. of Streets and Traffic, Individual Owners, Dept. of Public Works, Parks Dept.
Service and loading areas	Planning Commission, Dept. of Streets and Traffic, Building Dept.
View protection	Historical Associations, Planning Commission
Tourist information and services	Chamber of Commerce, Dept. of Streets and Traffic, Public and Private Travel Services
Public signs	Dept. of Streets and Traffic, State and Federal Highway Depts., Transit Agencies, Parks Dept., Building Dept., Fire Dept., Police
Private signs	Individual Businesses, Sign Companies, Building Dept., Board of Appeals.
Art objects	Parks Dept., Civic Associations, Owners, Institutions, Planning Commission

Street Element	Controlling Groups
Lighting	Lighting Commission, Parks Dept., Dept. of Streets and Traffic, Property Owners, Businesses.
Landscaping, natural elements	Parks Dept., Dept. of Streets and Traffic, Tree Commissions, Business Associations, Owners, Dept. of Natural Resources, Planning Commission
Transit access, waiting space	Transit Agencies, Dept. of Streets and Traffic, Dept. of Public Works
Activity, occupancy of fronting lots	Building Dept., Board of Appeals, Business Associations, Owners
Programmed activity (organized street activity)	Business Associations, Civic Associations, Institutions, Parks Dept., Licensing Bureau, Police
Spontaneous, unofficial activity	Police
Noise, air and water pollution, smell	Police, Pollution Commissions, Health Dept., Building Dept.
Safety	Police, Dept. of Streets and Traffic, Building Dept.
Maintenance, construction and repairs	Public Works Dept., Property Owners and Tenants, General Public, Building Dept., Police, Utility Companies

5. *Use of Street Space and Street Objects*, turning waste land and ordinary objects to useful and pleasant account.

6. *The General Form and Pattern of Strips*, going beyond the existing accidental form to consider the relation of parts to each other and to their context.

All these opportunities will be discussed at length below.

The quality of the strip cannot be radically improved without new institutional structures. Analysis of its current control and management reveals an exceedingly complex puzzle of actors. Sometimes they create a feature or maintain it; sometimes they administer a particular activity; sometimes they simply regulate someone else's activity. A partial list [is given in table 1].

On Main Street in Waltham the situation is considerably more simple than the [table] would imply, since Waltham is a small community and lacks the developed bureaucracy of a large city. Nevertheless, it is sufficiently complex and disjointed to prevent planned change (figure 7). Moreover, many qualities are not managed at all: noise, pollution, conservation of nature and history, and many more. The existing controls are poorly enforced. The city planner has almost no influence on the form of the strip or on its day-to-day management; his major impact has been in suggesting locations for planters. The Building Department enforces most of the existing building controls, but the Public Works Department is the real manager of the day-to-day quality of Main Street, since it is responsible for maintaining the public street and implementing most changes on it. Yet Public Works neither controls the private buildings that front on its streets, nor has any voice in the management of the traffic, parking utilities, and pedestrians that use those streets. Difficulties always arise when the development and the management of some facility are placed in different institutions. But here the problem is compounded by the numerous agencies that partially manage, and partially remodel, the facility throughout its useful life. The account of how street signs are designed, located, and maintained in Boston[2] illustrates only one small example of that confusion. It should be noted that the signing and building materials have considerable indirect influence over the quality of all strips. Within the low-price range, they offer a poor selection and quality of products. Even the standard signs provided to retailers, by manufacturers such as Coca-Cola, have a strong negative impact.

Wherever development and management are unified, and are somehow responsive to the needs of users, one finds a much better fitted environment. The inside of a regional shopping center is one such example, the individually designed upper-middle-class, single-family house another.

There is not a single well-managed, well-fitted contemporary commercial strip, although some are less offensive, due to planted medians, sign controls, or other measures. On the other hand, there are hundreds of pleasant shopping centers (once one gets beyond the paking lot!). There are also pleasant pedestrian-oriented downtown shopping streets, which grew up slowly under traditional limitations, and are sustained by custom, controls, and shared values. There are a few downtown pedestrian malls—humane environments converted from shabby streets—which have not resorted to a single public managing agency. Nicollet Mall in Minneapolis is one well-known example. In each of these latter cases one finds a strong association of fronting merchants, an association with the political strength and the financial capital sufficient to compel and entice inter-agency coordination and special public investment in one small local-

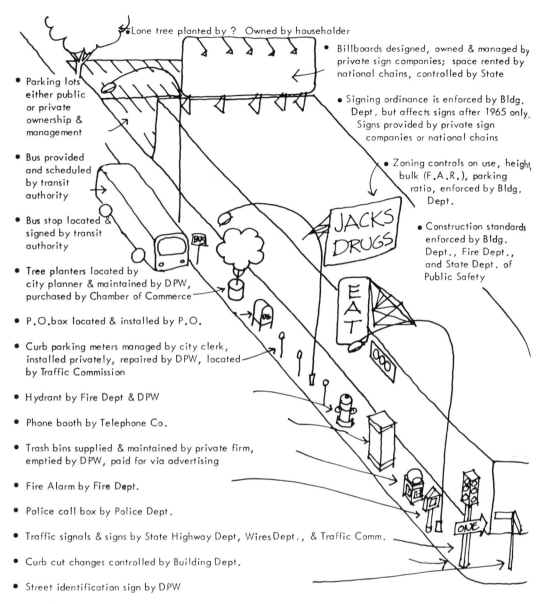

Lone tree planted by ? Owned by householder

• Billboards designed, owned & managed by private sign companies; space rented by national chains, controlled by State

• Signing ordinance is enforced by Bldg. Dept. but affects signs after 1965 only. Signs provided by private sign companies or national chains

• Zoning controls on use, height, bulk (F.A.R.), parking ratio, enforced by Bldg. Dept.

• Construction standards enforced by Bldg. Dept., Fire Dept., and State Dept. of Public Safety

• Parking lots either public or private ownership & management

• Bus provided and scheduled by transit authority

• Bus stop located & signed by transit authority

• Tree planters located by city planner & maintained by DPW, purchased by Chamber of Commerce

• P.O.box located & installed by P.O.

• Curb parking meters managed by city clerk, installed privately, repaired by DPW, located by Traffic Commission

• Hydrant by Fire Dept & DPW

• Phone booth by Telephone Co.

• Trash bins supplied & maintained by private firm, emptied by DPW, paid for via advertising

• Fire Alarm by Fire Dept.

• Police call box by Police Dept.

• Traffic signals & signs by State Highway Dept, Wires Dept., & Traffic Comm.

• Curb cut changes controlled by Building Dept.

• Street identification sign by DPW

• Installations & maintenance of sidewalk, curb, & street by DPW

• Sidewalks swept & shoveled by adjacent owners

• Traffic & behavior monitored by Police

JACKS DRUGS

EAT

ONE

Figure 7 *Management of Main Street.*

ity. Even here, though, one rarely finds the active management that is so evident in the regional shopping center, although recent plans in some cities are calling for such a continuing function. With its many overlapping, conflicting, uncoordinated, and necessarily short-sighted actors, one cannot expect the quality of the commercial strip to be similarly upgraded. A much more unified and effective management of this vital public resource is necessary. Street trees, new lighting standards, or inventive ways of displaying signs will by themselves be ineffective.

The institutional chaos of the strip prevents coordination and encourages self-seeking action. Only the crudest of rules can survive in such a fractionated world. Streets and driveways may be brought to the same level, or buildings be kept from collapse, but issues of quality are ignored. Indeed the strip is our most visible urban expression of the chaos of local government and of untrammeled free enterprise. Its improvement demands a new institutional base, just as the environmental qualities of regional shopping centers are founded on a new means of commercial management. Could such a new institutional base for the strip be created, short of a revolution in our ways of owning and exploiting land?

This report focuses on problems and standards, and not on issues of institutional policy. Nevertheless, certain assumptions about what is institutionally possible do lie behind our recommendations, and those recommendations will necessarily be compromised if no managerial improvements are possible. Two such possibilities come to mind:

1. Unified Street Agency

A unified public agency might manage all the public functions of the street. It would be in charge of the public right-of-way and all its equipment. It would build and repair the streets and paths; install and maintain lights, utilities, and signs; carry off solid wastes; plant and tend the trees; install the toilets, shelters, telephones, and other street furniture; regulate traffic; and provide the public transportation. All these are accepted public functions; what is proposed here is simply their consolidation.

"Simply" cloaks the substantial difficulties that accompany any governmental reorganization. Establishing street agencies may be a workable proposal only when a new local government is being organized (as in a new town), or when a rural locality takes on new functions before it has developed a set of entrenched public departments. However logical for the large, mature city, the unification of street functions may simply be impossible, except within selected zones.

Nevertheless, a street agency is well within our governmental traditions. Indeed, the typical public works department is already a consolidation of previously separate public engineering, construction, and utility functions. It would be the logical core of a street agency, since almost all its present work is in the street; but it must at least encompass the management of all traffic and parking and preferably the management of public transportation, pedestrian movement, and sidewalk activity as well. Thus its personnel, motives, and internal structure would necessarily be different. The advantages of a street agency are obvious; it coordinates functions and it identifies a single administration on which responsibility for the street may be fixed—an administration that may be expected to have a stake in environmental quality and that also has the power to create it. Its functions and territory would be clearly demarcated from other domains, such as education, police protection (as distinct from traffic management), health, or welfare.

We are not proposing one of those super-agencies which are so neat in the organization chart and so disastrous in practice. A street agency does not mass together functions that are only conceptually similar (like "Human Services"), but it links the development and management of a clearly marked spatial territory used by a related bundle of functions and requiring a similar group of operations. The agency would have identifiable clients to respond to and from which it might seek political support, although those clients would be of two kinds: the transient users of the street (the same as the clientele of a highway department, but minus the economic impetus of the large-scale road builders) and the stable commercial occupants of the street (similar to the merchants' association of a CBD but not so powerful or so concentrated). The client backing of a street agency, therefore, would not be as potent, stable, and unified as a school board's, but it could equal that of many other public agencies. Its principal difficulties would lie in resolving conflicts between its two sets of clients and in forming strong and responsive links with the transient users. The functions of the street agency would be reasonably broad and varied, yet they would be sufficiently similar to make their consolidation a gain in efficiency. A street agency would appear to be a workable unit rather than a mere super-agency.

A street agency would license and regulate the private use of rights-of-way and plazas—as by street vendors. It could prevent interference with street functions by setting rules for lighting, signs, planting, or the emission of noise and pollution. It might encourage desirable private activity or construction in the street through financial or administrative incentives. It could post signs of general educational interest, as well as regulatory signs, or provide space for personal communications, or sell space for commercial signs. It could regulate fronting uses in terms of the loads they put on the street. Different classes of street could be rated differently for their maximum load of cars (or persons or wastes) per day per unit of street front. Fees for maintaining the street could be charged on the basis of that permissible load. Thus the street agency might be financed, wholly or in part, by such an "access tax," plus betterments for capital improvements. Use, zoning, public services, and financing would then all be linked directly together.

2. A Frontage Association

Even where a unified public agency is out of reach, a private association of the fronting users might often be possible, as in a downtown mall. In a weak form, this could simply be a voluntary agreement among existing owners, such as the Fifth Avenue Association in Manhattan. In a stronger form, it could be the creature of the original developer or redeveloper of the strip, and so be built into the conditions of sale of the fronting lots and have the power of assessing and regulating its members.

A frontage association would not control the public right-of-way, but it could install, maintain, and control pedestrian ways, bikeways, and service drives; plant and maintain fronting strips and other small spaces; provide shelters and public services; install lights, signs, benches, trees, and other objects; control use, density, and building details via covenants; advise owners on development and maintenance; promote street activities and advertising; and even provide local transit or services such as patrols, waste disposal, or the maintenance of buildings and grounds.

A frontage association could be financed by assessments on the fronting owners. It might charge user fees, or sell licenses for the use of association space. It could not control the public street, but [it] could speak for its members, and its stake in the quality of the strip would be patent. It could stimulate, even compel, inter-agency coordination. The homeowner associations now routinely created by large-scale residential developers as a way to maintain future quality provide a direct model for what is proposed. So a commercial developer might leave a frontage association behind him; or it might be the creation of urban redevelopment that had cleared and rehabilitated a decaying strip. Dependence on a frontage association, of course, strengthens the voice of the merchant at the expense of other users (through traffic or bus riders, for example, or teenagers and the elderly who may use the street but who buy little).

The association would have an even clearer stake in quality if it owned the fronting land and leased it on extended terms to commercial tenants. This is the model of the shopping center applied to the more loosely organized strip. As owner of the land, the association would then have a direct economic interest in long-run quality and profit. However, long-term ownership of the extended, slow-growing, and relatively low-value strip, divided by a street in public hands, is less likely to be attractive to a profit-making corporation than is the compact, high-turnover regional center. But consolidated ownership might be possible in dense, active urban areas. It would also be possible for a short loop commercial street, in which everything, inclusive of the street, is under single ownership.

The unified street agency and the private frontage association (preferably in a strong form created through development or redevelopment) are desirable and possible in a significant number of cases. They can be used in combination or separately. The standards and patterns to be suggested below will sometimes be useful even when there is no unified control of the street and its frontage. The more common model is a simple coordination of existing public agencies, brought about by some group— such as a planning department—which is interested in overall environmental quality and has the political leverage, the persuasive power, and the disposable funds to initiate and maintain that coordination. It must look to diffuse public support to give it those levers. However, most often, this study will assume the support of one or the other of the two institutional devices described above. Not only will it be assumed that there is a unified managing agency, but also that that agency will be oriented toward identifying the users of the street and what they are trying to do. Thus, the agency will routinely specify the connection between qualities, standards, and the desired behavior of users. In other words, the agency will use explicit environmental programming and employ performance standards open to public scrutiny.

In addition, a national or regional environmental research agency might develop and maintain a detailed set of recommended street settings, qualities, and standards for typical situations. A large national or regional agency could afford to test its prototypes. They could become local law by reference, or could be used in local review. The larger agency might analyze the relative success of innovative arrangements, study user behavior, and create and test new settings. It could disseminate information on environmental standards. Admittedly, an applied environmental research function of this kind need not be confined solely to arterial streets, and the large-scale agency might have a larger functional scope.

Standards and Patterns for the Strip

[The study goes on to suggest possibilities for standards and guides for the strip, considering management and form together. These include standards for access, ambient quality, convenience clusters, information, street space and street objects, and strip form. Because of space limitations, we include here only the discussion of strip form. — the editors]

The Form of the Strip

The typical strip today mixes cars, buses, and bicycles in a central roadway, with curb parking at the edge, bordered by public walks. Stores may front on these walks, but are often set back behind further parking, so that

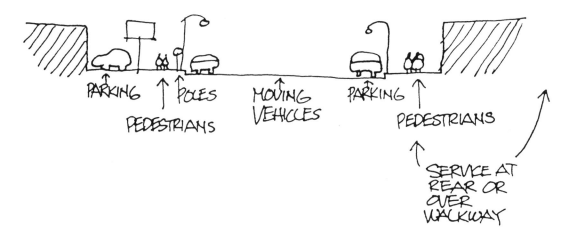

Figure 8 Typical strip cross-section.

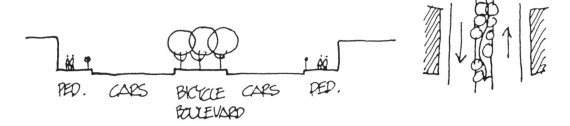

Figure 9 Boulevard pattern.

the walker is literally surrounded by cars, service is confused, bicycles compete with automobiles, and buses have to stop outside the ranks of parked vehicles. There is no room for trees (figure 8).

There are many other ways of relating automobiles, pedestrians, bicycles, public transit, and commercial space. The traditional answer (the boulevard) solves the problem with a very wide circulation channel, and the various modes of movement are separated out and interleaved with planted strips (figure 9). The boulevard can, for example, provide pedestrian and bicycle paths down a planted center strip. But walkers and cyclists are forced to cross traffic to reach the shops, the trees are misplaced because they are not where the people prefer to walk, and the shopping walks are still exposed to noise and fumes. The problems with parking and service are not solved, nor does transit have any advantage. Some utility poles are still needed at the edge of the walk.

If through traffic and local low-speed traffic are divided, cycle paths, utilities and trees can occur between them. In this pattern, the pedestrian is more protected from the presence of high-speed traffic while he is on the sidewalk, and cyclists do not have to cross heavy traffic to reach the shops.

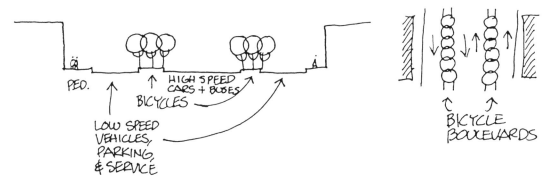

Figure 10 *Split boulevard pattern.*

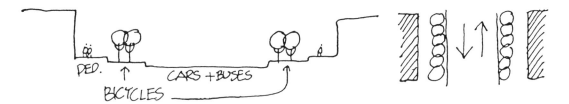

Figure 11 *Side boulevard pattern.*

Through traffic and transit are freed from the maneuvers of local traffic and service, but bus turnouts need to be provided in the planted strips as well as room for the bicycle paths. The street has become very wide, and the trees are still in the wrong place (figure 10).

If the planting strips are attached to the sidewalk, then cyclists can have a lane next to that, perhaps with different levels for the planted walk and the bicycle path. Pedestrians are now comfortably provided for, but bus stops become a problem, and the traffic is mixed once more (figure 11). All these traditional models, although handsome and lively if the fronting use is intense, seem wasteful and potentially "empty" at contemporary densities. Moreover, they can be applied only to new construction.

Given a congested existing strip, perhaps the most reasonable solution would be to ban curb parking and to give that space over to planting, utilities, and bus stops. Car parking could be subject to a setback, so that it would be put behind and between the commercial structures, which would then be encouraged to return to fronting directly on the walkway. Service would occur at the rear. Common parking lots would also be necessary, and any parking lots not behind buildings could be required to be shielded from the sidewalks. In addition, a cycle track might be opened along a strip of open space behind the ranks of commercial buildings. This open space could be allocated for other public uses, and could serve as an alternate route for pedestrians. It would also serve as a buffer to the resi-

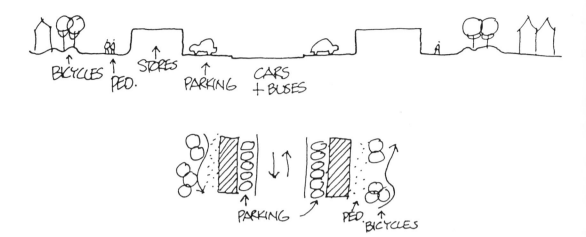

Figure 12   *Rear pedestrian/cycle path.*

dences behind. Pedestrians and transit riders and cyclists would now be better provided for, and traffic would be somewhat improved. However, cyclists would be removed from the lively face of the street (figure 12).

In new strips, the shops could be turned around to provide primary access at the rear for both pedestrians and cyclists. Automobile parking would be adjacent to the roadway, but pedestrian paths would be on the other side of the shops, adjacent to the bicycle paths. This would be possible in some old strips, but only if they were redeveloped. The solution is a pleasant one, and relates well to housing along the strip. But pedestrians and cyclists would be far removed from the stores on the other side. The street would be only half as "lively." Perhaps it would work best if there were only a single rank of commercial buildings.

A better solution in a new strip would be to split the road, placing pedestrians in the center between the shops, and the parking and service areas between the shops and the roads (figure 13). Bicycles or even slow transit could possibly be given a central lane within the pedestrian lane. Otherwise, cycle and transit lanes would occur just outside the shops. This plan would provide a protected enclave for the person on foot and place parking and service facilities in highly visible and accessible locations. Transit and cycle routes would also have an advantageous position. There would be a separation between opposite directions of traffic movement, but turnouts would have to be to the left, unless lanes could be reversed. Intensely used sections of the central space might be covered to provide protection from rain, cold, or sun; but this solution would also work with discontinuous structures at low densities. There must be a buffer between the traffic and the area "outside" the strip, however.

There are a number of ways to make a transition between the strip and any residential land behind it. Where possible one could put a band of

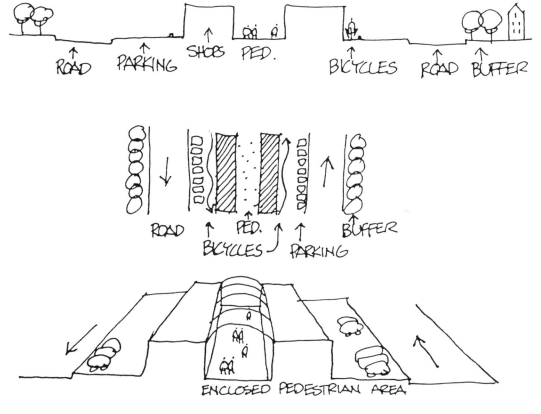

Figure 13 *Split road with central pedestrian path.*

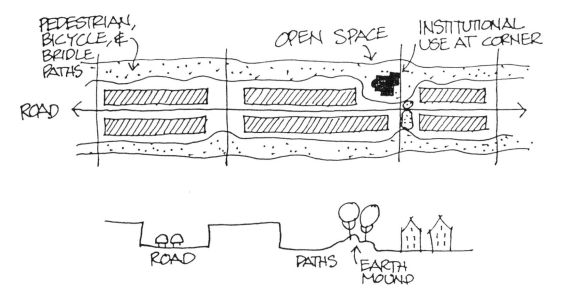

Figure 14 *Open space strips.*

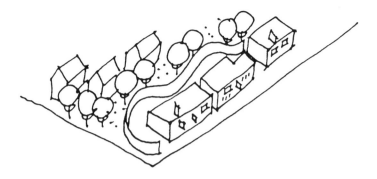

Figure 15 *Buffer walls.*

open space between the two uses, which could be used for bicycle or jogging paths, for bridle trails, for allotment gardens for the neighborhood residents, or as park land. At points, the strip might widen out to accommodate public buildings, to provide a deeper open space, or to include some natural feature (figure 14).

Where space of this kind is not available, a shield could be created by using a wall, an earth berm, or continuous planting. Landscaped pedestrian ways might lead back to the residences from the bus stops and convenience clusters on the strip (figure 15).

Gateways from the strip into the residential area behind could be created by carrying residential landscaping from the neighborhood out onto the strip at the intersections between the arterial and the residential streets (figure 16). These landscaped corners could also be the locations for personal service centers and bus stops. Such approaches might be adapted to existing strips but in many cases, as with Main Street in Waltham, the land area is too limited.

A change of levels can also be used to separate different uses. If the strip were put in a shallow linear depression, natural or man-made, its backside would run into the earth; noise would be deflected upward; and fumes would settle in the channel. The residential areas would be at a higher grade. In some cases, the rooftops of strip structures might even be used as public space (figure 17).

The strip should be well differentiated and legible for the person who moves along it. By structuring it around a few unique elements, a sequence of views or events can be created for the motorist or transit rider which will give an underlying rhythm to his experience. A general rule might be to provide a chain of landmarks or events, so that from each point along the strip, some identifiable form is in view; once that point comes into view, another then appears. The visual experience can also be made more vivid by the kinetic experience of road motion through bends, dips, and rises. Signing, lighting, and planting can also be varied along the route (figure 18).

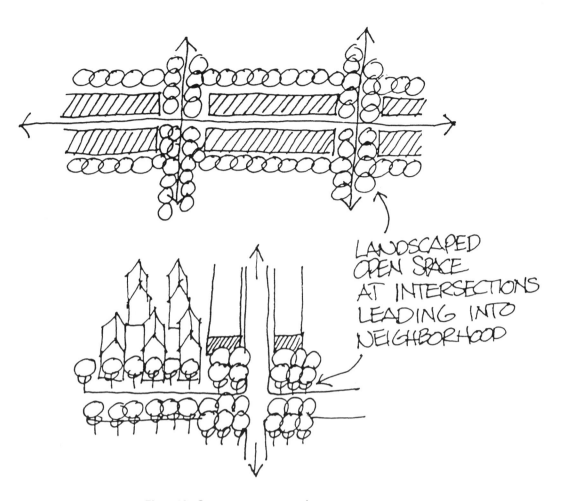

LANDSCAPED
OPEN SPACE
AT INTERSECTIONS
LEADING INTO
NEIGHBORHOOD

Figure 16 *Open space connectors to the neighborhood.*

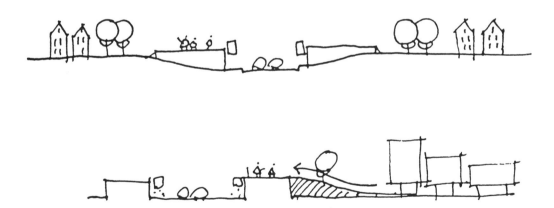

Figure 17 *Use of changes of grade.*

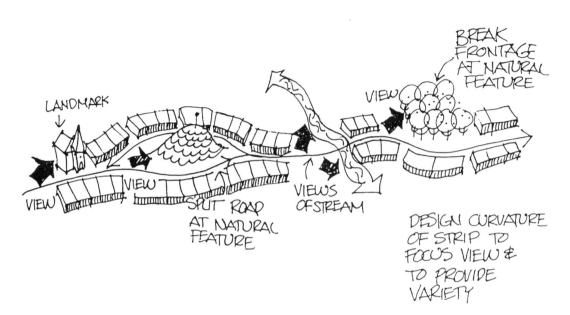

Figure 18 *Sequential form.*

General controls on heights, setbacks, bulk, and spacing of structures along the strip might also help create continuity and legibility. However, since densities and values are low, there is not the same pressure to "fill the envelope," and thus public limits would not automatically create a continuous form. At selected points, say at major intersections where values are higher, greater height and bulk might be allowed, thus encouraging the creation of "landmark" structures. The space envelope of the strip might also expand at these points.

A variant of this would be to allow the structure to pinch in at the intersection. Between intersections, structures would be set back to make room for parking and public services. Thus, the strip would be divided into a series of segments (figure 19).

Thus far the strip has been viewed as part of an arterial that follows a relatively straight path. However, this arterial strip affects long sections of major traffic, as well as enormous amounts of bordering land. It might be preferable, in new development, to lay out commercial strips as planned and concentrated, but still linear, developments, which would be entered from the main arterial but which through-travelers could bypass. They might even connect two arterials (figure 20).

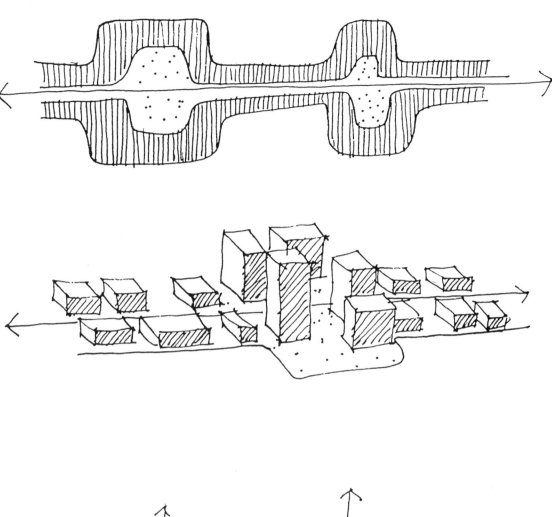

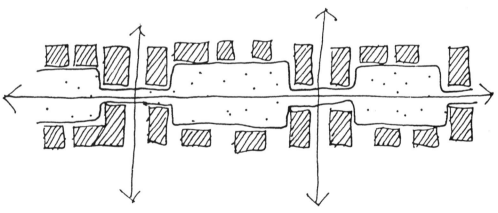

Figure 19 *Possible strip form: nodes.*

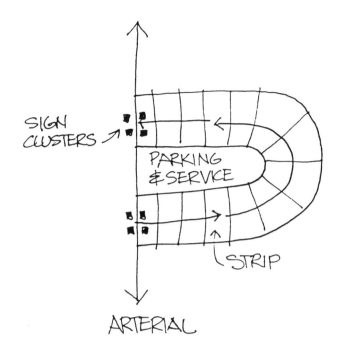

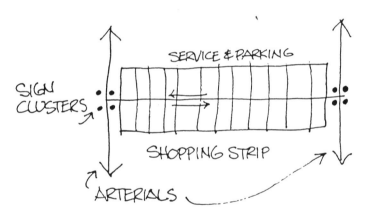

Figure 20 *Possible strip form: loops and arterial connectors.*

These loop and link patterns provide for auto- and transit-oriented commerce, but they contain it and minimize its impact on other traffic and the community. At the same time, they are easy to find from the highway, and quite accessible to the residences behind. Of course these patterns are appropriate only for new development, or where major redevelopment can displace the through-traffic system.

All of these suggested standards and patterns need development and testing in a real situation. Few specific environmental standards have universal applicability, and therefore few standards can be fully developed in the abstract. A good standard needs to be tailored to the nature of the environment, its users, and the management framework of the area. The suggestions offered here are a guide to the development of standards for a strip but do not specify the final form of that standard.

Conclusion

The reader may remain in doubt about the motives and conclusions of this paper. Does it advocate encouragement of the commercial strip in some improved form, or does it only accept the strip as unavoidable? Neither and both are true. Given our economy and our ways of holding land, given our reliance on the private car, the commercial strip is a likely and advantageous pattern, but one that is capable of great improvement. If the basic factors shift—our affluent private economy, the private exploitation of land, the heavy reliance on the private car—then the commercial strip itself will need to be reassessed. That reassessment has not been made here. Pollution and energy crises may greatly reduce the use of the private car. However, it seems likely that a more compact, but still linear, pattern of service—one based on public transport, walking, and bicycles or other light personal vehicles—would even then prove to be a persistently useful form. Meanwhile, the strip is a characteristic feature of the American city today. It cries out for improvement.

It is reasonable to think that the changes recommended here might actually occur? The strip represents a relatively low value use of land, and the level of investment proper to a downtown or a regional center is unlikely. Still, substantial public sums are regularly put into the arterial streets, and private investors put sizable amounts of money into signs, access systems, and other attractions for their customers. The dollar amounts demanded by the suggestions in this paper are not so different from these normal expenditures, although they may be applied in different ways. Expensive solutions have not been considered, such as continuous enclosed grade separations or coordinated facades. But some of the suggestions—the new patterns of strip layout, for example—would be feasible only in new development.

The heaviest costs are the institutional ones: the political and administrative battles that will occur in the creation of street agencies or frontage associations. Our institutional ideas may unfortunately have less significance for mature areas. But the benefits of institutional reorganization are clear, and surely worth application in new growth, or in redevelopment. These administrative issues undoubtedly need further study.

The standards and patterns proposed here are but an outline. To be credible and usable, each would require separate analysis. Each analysis will have to answer certain questions: What is the basis for the standard or pattern? How can achievement be measured? What levels are appropriate for different situations? What are the likely costs and benefits of achievement? Finally, they must be tested in practice. At least this paper may have suggested a useful agenda for research.

The focus of attention has been mostly on new strips, but many of the observations and suggestions in this paper also apply to "mature" ones. Old, declining strips are everywhere in the American city. How can these semi-abandoned frontages be restored to useful life. Has anyone given thought to what empty stores, vacant parking lots, or old gas stations could be good for? Could worn-down strips accommodate some community uses now cramped for space? Strong public management and relatively modest physical changes could rehabilitate these older arterials.

Perhaps urban redevelopment areas might sometimes be linear ones, taking a length of arterial street frontage for renewal and lease or resale. Benefits in traffic, service, environmental quality, and the urban economy might be realized at little social cost in relocation or community disruption. If purchase costs were high, resale values might more nearly equal them than they do in most renewals. Standards and patterns for the development of existing, declining strips will therefore be most useful.

Even the prosperous commercial strip can be improved without disruption. There are a number of reasonable actions, ripe to be taken today, which would make the strip a far more humane place to be. Thus its future abandonment might be prevented (or perhaps might even be provided for?). What will happen to the strip as automobile use declines or gasoline is rationed? These are not unlikely eventualities. Can the strip be converted to a form that will survive and even flourish if and when most people travel by public transportation, by bicycle, or on foot?

Notes

1. See Donald Appleyard, unpublished interviews on perception of the Boston street system; San Francisco Department of City Planning, *Urban Design Study*, 1970; and Signs/Lights/Boston (Boston Redevelopment Authority project), *City Signs and Lights*, 1971.

2. *City Sign and Lights*.

On Historic Preservation: Some Comments on the Polish-American Seminar (1974)

Our tour of preservation work in Poland was a most pleasant and instructive experience. What follows are some rather superficial and unorganized impressions. It is true that I learned little that could be directly applied in the U.S., but it would have been naive to expect that. The Polish context is too far removed from us, not only because Poland is a socialist country, with public control of the economy, but also because restoration work there has intense political meaning, in a country so often and so recently overrun, in which foreign conquerors have sought so deliberately to destroy the continuity of Polish culture. Restoration in Poland is a political and psychological necessity, a defiant assertion of continued existence. The U.S. has never had such an experience (despite the British raid on Washington), although particular groups have suffered in this way, e.g., the Navaho, the Cherokee. Nor do we have such national homogeneity, nor such centralized control (happily). Nevertheless, visiting another country is always instructive, and seeing how they tackle historic preservation makes one think again about one's own.

To a U.S. visitor, the most impressive thing is the scale of resources being applied to historic reconstruction, and the sheer quantity of remains worthy of reconstruction, despite the successive wars. In town after town, entire central areas are being rebuilt or restored to sound conditions and to their historic external form. Scattered buildings throughout the remainder of the cities, and in the rural areas, are subject to preservation orders or are being rebuilt. The resources being applied are substantial in proportion to the resources available: 40% of the total development budget of the nation went to the rebuilding of Warsaw in the early post-war years. Most of this was not historic restoration, of course, but rebuilding the Old Town "just as it was" was a significant part of the total.

Just how much historic restoration is costing the country we were never able to find out, perhaps for reasons of policy, but more likely that no one seemed to know, or even be much concerned. Public budgets are so unlike our own as to be difficult to compare. Restoration work received its funds from many sources, direct and indirect, and accounting seemed fuzzy. Some conservators in charge of local works estimated that restored dwellings in historic areas cost approximately three times as much as new dwellings of comparable size elsewhere, but they were uncertain.

We picked up some criticism of the cost of preservation work, when housing is so desperately short, but surprisingly little. Mostly we heard about the strong popular support and interest. Of course, we were talking primarily to conservators, but others repeated it. Undoubtedly there are struggles over the budget, but they were out of our hearing. The conflicts that we learned about were mostly of two other kinds: 1) the contests between Conservator and Architect in each administrative area; and 2) the resistance of local owners to historical designation.

The Polish system is interesting in the way that it institutionalizes the two opposing views of conservation and development. Each voivodship, and each major town, has its Conservator and its Architect. Both are in essence appointed and financed by their own separate central ministries. One is charged with saving, and the other with building. Naturally, they clash. The president of Gdansk said that he must resolve such conflicts "twice a day." Often the clash must be shunted up to higher levels, to be decided in a political context. The Architect has the bigger funds, the larger and better-paid staff, and most of the muscle; he seems likely to win in most cases, especially in areas of new development. The Conservator can entrench himself within his designated historic district, however, and unilaterally designate single buildings outside it. Thus there often seemed to be a sharp transition of environmental quality at the edge of each restored district, although greenbelts, on the site of old defense works, often mitigated the clash. In Gdansk, for example, in a set of maps in the planning office which recorded the major constraints to future development, there is one which shows the areas under the Conservator's control: the old center and the warehouse island opposite it, the site of a heroic defense when the Germans first attacked Poland, an area of old bourgeois summer villas, a long allee of trees, and a scatter of separate buildings.

Institutionalizing the conservation/development conflict has its usefulness, as long as conflicts can be resolved. There is a regular advocate for each side. The conservators still seemed to be concerned mostly with buildings, and less with total landscapes. However, control was imposed on the natural setting of Kasimiersz, after a new press club building dramatized what might happen there. So conservators are beginning to think in those terms. Yet they are still more concerned about the structure than about its use and access. Planned shifts in use and transportation around and in the historic areas obviously have profound effects on their quality. Moreover, the hard lines that are mapped to separate the two interests have disturbing effects at the margin, just as they do in our land-use zones and historic districts.

But the Polish system suggests that cities and regions in the U.S. might appoint public conservators, whose responsibility was not simply historic buildings, but the conservation of all the particularly valuable qualities in their areas: buildings, landscapes, activities, views, symbols, celebrations, clean air or waters, quietness, or whatever. A staggering task, yet a public advocate for conservation might be a useful counterpoise to our typical Office of Development.

The second struggle in Polish restoration is that of individuals or small groups against the State. Buildings are designated historic by an "expert committee." The owner or user is not consulted (but when an old church was so designated in the Nowa Huta new town area, a long battle erupted with the new town authority). There is strong popular support for designating *public* buildings to be preserved, but frequent resistance to the designation of *private* ones, since designation means expensive repairs, red tape, and the impossibility of replacement. We heard of complaints, appeals, informal political pressure, and even of cases of arson, in order to block designation. Appeals can only be made up the administrative line, and not to independent courts. In the Cracow voivodship, there had been numerous appeals, but none had ever been granted! Tenants of historic buildings are shifted out without much ado when major repairs are undertaken. They have a priority for replacement housing, but of course, the housing is somewhere else.

Each voivodship or major town is required to make a complete catalog of its historic monuments. Presumably, this list is good for eternity. The Cracow voivodship has a total of 3226 monuments, of which 2 are class 0 (extraordinary), some 100 are class I, and the rest II, III, or IV. Classes 0, I, and most of II must be maintained "unchanged."

Whatever the technical qualities of the restoration work, it is obviously done with much thought, care and affection. The contrast between these areas of environmental concern and the ordinary areas of new housing is as glaring as the contrasts between U.S. public housing and the well-to-do suburbs. The new housing in Poland, typically in long tall apartment slabs of heavy panel construction, seems overwhelmingly gray, confused, shoddy, and inhumane. Its quality cannot merely be a result of tight resources, since these elevator apartments are more costly than walkups or terraces. From casual conversations, it appeared that no one is glad to live in these new developments, but that for lack of anything else they are eagerly sought and long-awaited. (We also have some independent evidence from Polish children, studied under UNESCO sponsorship, of the disadvantages of these new projects.)

It is tragic that so much design care goes into the historic areas, and so little into the standard housing. One has the impression that the authorities are rapidly building the slums of the future, although at present there are no signs of the "slums" such as we are accustomed to. All housing, new and old, is used and apparently valued. The abandoned or completely neglected building is a rarity. But construction is poor, much work is unfinished, and ordinary maintenance is quite bad in the grounds and public hallways.

We did not see a single interesting or remarkable new building in Poland. (I was later told that there are a few, which we missed: a well-sited new stadium across the river in Warszawa, and the central underground railway station there, for example.) All the design talent in architecture appeared to be concentrated in historic restoration. Indeed this may occur even as early as in the schools, where students must make early decisions between conservation, urbanism, and ordinary building construction. In the latter, the emphasis is clearly on system, standards, directly accounted first costs, and speed. Conservation work may be the only legitimate outlet for careful design, even for fantasy.

We had some impression that the various conservators were designing their historic areas as if they were personal landscapes. Decisions as to style and epoch and details are personal ones. Individual conservators have their own strong views, and are able to impose them. Even new buildings may have to come down, if they do not "fit." Where there is no certain information as to the character of former buildings, then new old ones are created, or facade designs imported from other areas. There are extended expert discussions as to the technical details of restoration, or what is the "right" period to restore, etc. Apparently the users have no voice in this. The conservators seemed to be confident and opinionated, and at the top there are autocratic leaders like Lorentz and Majewski. There is a definite élan among them, a sense that they know best. Many women, incidentally, are attracted to this work. The people at the top are still male, however.

While the cities—outside the historic districts—seem gray and prematurely old, the countryside is changing rapidly, and was most interesting to see. New brick houses are going up, crops and cultivations are changing, [and] there are new farm machines and new rural or small-town industries. An afternoon's visit to the village of Bystra Podhalanska, near Jordanów about 40 km south of Cracow, was most revealing, since for once I was able to walk about, visit houses, and speak to local people. Since no one else in our party had an equal opportunity to visit a village, let me describe it at more length.

Bystra is a sprawling "street village" which extends for perhaps a mile along a narrow, local paved road between Osielec and Sidzina, in the foothills of the Tatras. Some research on children's perception of the environment has recently been done there, under UNESCO sponsorship. Bystra lies in a narrow valley, and its small fields lie up on the hill slopes, with forests beyond. It has a church, a school, an agricultural coop, a saw mill, a town hall and police and fire station, a kiosk, a new restaurant, a clinic, and a number of small shops (baker, butcher, four grocers, clothes, household goods). There are numerous new brick houses and new utilities going in. The population was 3090 in 1960, and is 3060 now. Yet 80% of the graduates from its primary school leave the village permanently. It has maintained its size because the birth rate has been high—6 to 8 children per family. But now there are more like 1 to 3 children in each family, and a sharp drop and an aging of the population is to be expected.

Some 40% of the people live by farming (perhaps half of them exclusively so) on some some 500 farms of $\frac{1}{2}$ to 4 hectares (when 10 hectares is considered necessary for a fair, but not good, living). Others commute to work in the nearby coal mines, on the railroad, in town industries, or services, do woodwork at home, or provide rooms for vacationers. The constant pressure to encourage conversion to state farms is steadily resisted, but farms are gradually enlarging as individuals give up and sell out to larger farmers.

The school is 20 years old, with old equipment, but clean and well cared for. There was scientific apparatus, devices for teaching mathematical concepts, and the children's drawings of "your friendly policeman" (shades of home!). Class sizes have by now been reduced to 30. Some 90% of the pupils go on to the agricultural technical school in Sidzina, or to the academic high school in Jordanów, whence some 30% may go on to higher levels. I was told that by 1975, only those who have graduated from an agricultural school will be allowed to farm, which will cut out some 20% of the existing farmers!

I was taken into the "parlor" room of one traditional log house, built by its present owner in the '20's. It was a spotless display piece: highly varnished peeled logs chinked with moss painted blue, weavings and ikons on the walls, electric lights, a room crowded with furniture and cushions, including a brand new display cabinet in the corner. The owner-builder, solidly built and cheerful, was obviously very proud of his house. He thought that log construction was much better and drier than the new brick houses, but that logs were now too expensive, and besides, wooden construction was now prohibited because of the fire danger.

I went into a new brick house, whose main floor had been occupied only within the last few months. The owner is a part-time farmer, bus driver, and jack-of-all-trades who built the house himself (with the help of five other men in erecting the shell). It contains 95 square meters (and thus is much larger than the urban norm for a family of four), and the materials were financed by a 300,000 zloty loan from the state bank (which I understand is a quite new program). The house is rough brick, to be stuccoed later when the walls dry out. It has a heavy tile roof on a timber frame. The work is amateur, with rough joints and a settlement crack in the brick. The interior plaster is still damp. The rooms were almost empty of furniture, but there were curtains on the windows, electricity, and TV. Living room, kitchen, and two bedrooms occupy the first floor, which is high above the ground and has a balcony. The second floor, yet unfinished, has four more rooms, and there is an attic above. The basement contains a motor bike, a new small washing machine, a garage all ready for the hoped-for car, a future workshop, and still another bedroom, a pig, chickens, coal, potatoes, and a large assortment of tools. The owner planned and built the house, laid the brick, did the carpentry, built a sidewalk, made the metal light fixtures and the iron balcony rail, made the picture frames and an ingenious Christmas tree holder. Every part of his house contains some dream about the future for this energetic man. All the extra rooms must be for eventual renting out. Indeed, some farmers in Zakopane now own 3 or 4 houses for rent. They are nascent capitalists.

As a comparison, a professor's new apartment in Warsaw contained 55 sq. meters, which is 7 sq. meters above the present norm for a family of four, because he is a professor. Tight but quite well furnished, it contains a living room, bedroom, study, and a narrow kitchen and bath as extensions of the hall. Elevators are locked ("to prevent danger to children"), halls are shabby and defaced, [and] buildings are unfinished outside and set in mud and confusion. It is hard to find the right building, or the right apartment.

Bystra is certainly changing fast. Nearly 20% of the houses have been built in the last two years. Building materials are being accumulated in people's yards. But the side lanes are still deep mud, the traditional barking village dogs are chained to the houses; half the houses have no water yet, and most of them lack toilets. The main road is pitch dark at night and full of people walking home, including the traditional singing drunk. As many of us did, I felt more hope and expectancy in the countryside than in the cities, and yet that countryside is being depopulated as Poland rapidly urbanizes.

Historic reconstruction is most active in the old city centers, rather than in the country, since Polish conservators are only now beginning to think of preserving historic landscapes. (I have heard of some exceptions: an historic battlefield, a prehistoric area, and some gardens.) Yet central city reconstruction must inevitably compete with the rapid changes in central activities. One common solution is to preserve the historic center and allow a new one to grow up on another location, as in Warsaw. But then the historic area becomes an empty stage set, a spectacle for tourists. This was certainly our impression of Warsaw's Old Town, despite its careful reconstruction, its resident population, and its strong political symbolism. Old Town is pleasant to visit, but seems unreal, and soon a little boring. One has only to compare this with Cracow, where the beautiful historic square is still the real city center, and old monuments are surrounded by life and activity. I think we all responded with delight to Cracow, and its sense of continuity. One must remember that Warszawa was destroyed in the war, [that it] was never a great city until relatively recently in history, and [that] its center had already moved south away from the old town, along Krakowskie Przedmiescie and Nowy Swiat. But the impression of lifelessness in the old town remains, while the restoration of Nowy Swiat, while less careful, is more successful.

The pedestrian streets of central Cracow, Gdansk, and Torun are still full of people. But will they remain so? Gdansk has no true service center now, and people are forced to use the old city, however inadequate it may be. A new center is now building alongside the old one, and the old city is deliberately being consigned more and more to foreign tourists, who will bring in hard currency. The population of old Gdansk was 40,000 before its destruction, and was restored to 40,000 people when reconstructed. But now it will be reduced to 25,000, with more museums, craft shops, restaurants, artists in residence, and other such tourist attractions. The population of central Torun is to fall from 23,000 to 7000 people, and there are signs of new central activities appearing to the east, just across the greenbelt. Suppression of the central tramways, as planned in Cracow and already accomplished in Torun and Gdansk, will accentuate the shift away from the center, especially as new highways are constructed. People now walk substantial distances from tram and bus to their workplaces in Torun, since there is no alternative. The crowds on that central mall may decrease noticeably when people can find work with more convenient access.

The plan in Cracow is to preserve the old center without disrupting it, by surrounding it closely with four new activity centers on all four sides. But new belt highways will also be built around it. My guess is that the relative timing of development between those new centers will cause one of them to "take off" before the others. If that happens, then it will be very hard, even in a centralized economy, to keep four centers growing evenly around the old city. The end result may be similar to Gdansk or Warsaw.

I don't think the Poles have solved the problem of how to remodel an historic urban area to serve intense new central functions without destroying its character, any more than we have. Moreover, the struggle of Conservator versus Architect, and the use of sharp district boundaries to mediate that dispute, seems to make the problem worse. If a center is to stay alive, it must change to meet its new functions, and this means a shift, but not an abrupt break, in activity, a mix of old, new, and in between, and the retention of a normal resident population. Even where the population is restored after rebuilding, it will be new people who return, as is happening in Sandomierz and Torun.

I most admired the original Polish policy of leasing restored housing to a normal spectrum of families, regardless of their income or occupation. I wish we were able to do as well. But we also saw some early signs of segregation: by policy in old Gdansk, which is being geared up for tourism, [and] by individual choice in Warsaw, where the Old Town is becoming fashionable for professional people. Quite often, we would be taken to an old building being remodeled as a museum or institutional quarters, and would learn that it had previously been low-income housing.

Talks with city planners in Warsaw, Cracow, and Gdansk echoed some of these tensions between conservation and development. The planners seemed to support the idea of reconstruction, but they unconsciously referred to conservators and conservation districts as obstacles or constraints; they feel that the conservators are concerned solely with saving buildings, and have no sense of the dynamics of urban activity.

In general, the problems of physical planning that I saw in Poland seem surprisingly similar to those in any locality where the emphasis is on rapid economic development. Major new industries come first, and have ample funds. Profits of operation go back to the central ministries, and not to the localities which must serve those industries. Housing and services lag far behind the growth of employment. Housing is desperately short, but norms are improving. The emphasis is on speed, crude standards, first cost, and central control. No one seems to like the gray apartment slabs that result, but everyone seems to think they are a sad necessity. I doubt it. They are probably more a result of monolithic planning, and implicit architectural theory, than they are a rational answer to providing humane housing at low cost. Warsaw planners admitted that the tall slabs cost about 50% more per square meter than do the lower buildings. There is some recent Polish experimentation with low-rise housing at close densities, as well as self-help housing (we saw some on the outskirts of Chelmno). But while the present average density of Warsaw is 3000 persons per sq. km., planned extensions will be 10,000 per sq. km., exclusive of greenbelts and large factories. Everyone we talked to would prefer a villa with a garden, but would also like to be close to the center!

Local planners give the same impression of intelligence, good will, and imperfect control of events that is familiar here. They operate under extreme pressure. Grand plans for linear metropolitan expansion seemed to be the universal fashion, although the ability to control growth in that way seemed dubious. The Poles are beginning to build a system of superhighways. They seem to be scrapping their network of trams in the central areas, although they are expanding transit lines at the periphery. They will soon turn out automobiles in quantity. Warsaw is also planning a new subway, although the size and density of that city may hardly justify it. We tried to convey some experience on these issues.

There is a national spatial plan, coordinated with the national economic plan, that allocates population territory, resources, and major facilities to the large cities or voivodships. Within this framework, cities and voivodships develop 5-year plans, which are discussed with the local communities and then sent to the central ministry for modification and approval. City boundaries can be extended as growth occurs, so that unified metropolitan planning is possible. Once approved, all building projects are passed on for conformity to these general plans. The planning staffs are extremely large by our standards (some 300 professionals in Warsaw alone), to cope with the complete detailed central planning and regulation that their system demands. Problems of coordination then show up within the planning organization, as well as between agencies. Most of the professional staff are architects, and architects are in the control positions, which biases the work they do. Cities battle the national plan for bigger growth and more resources. Warsaw is to be 2.8 million by 1990, according to the national plan. Warsaw planners think it more realistic (or desirable?) that the metropolitan area will be 3.5 million by that time. They lost their fight to revise the figure in the national plan, but their local plans are preparing for that higher figure anyhow. Cracow was to be 720,000 by 1990, but battled for 1,500,000, and apparently won its revision. These are presumably technical battles for resource allocation, but surely they must be largely political.

Under the central ministry of environmental affairs, newly consolidated, there is a central research institute of environmental development, also newly consolidated, and directed by Adolph Ciborowski.

We were shown many castles. I wondered whose history was being celebrated. For me, there was an underlying problem of continuity in the Polish restoration work, although the political meaning of its symbolic reassertion of nationhood was clear enough. One got a powerful sense of continuity in the active center of Cracow, and also in its university, where the ancient buildings were occupied by the same living institution. Another moving example of continuity was the sight of the old painted church of Orawka, still in active use (as, of course, are most of the Polish churches). I was similarly impressed by Professor Prüfferowa's talk in the Ethnographic Museum in Torun, where material remains are connected to a living tradition. Objects in the cases were made by people she knew personally, and the question was how these things fitted into a total functioning culture, and how some of those skills might be transformed for use today. The official conservators, on the other hand, often gave me an impression of being the guardians of a dead world.

To them, no buildings worth saving were built after the 17th century. Many structures of the 19th century are therefore not worthy of a second look. There are some fine Jugendstil buildings in Cracow (and in Torun), and I understand that there has been some public pressure to save them. In Cracow, unfortunately, Jugendstil is connected with the hated Austrian occupation. Or, as another example, the Austrian buildings in Wawel would be removed if possible, yet the Austrian occupation is part of the history of Cracow (surely as much as Malbork, which symbolizes a much crueler occupation?). History, it is clear, is no longer being made (not since 11:15 at least). There is no mechanism for commemorating what is happening now. Nor any way of communicating *whose* history is being symbolized. Gdansk is rebuilt, but the German merchants who built and occupied it have been moved away. Or, now that Malbork is rebuilt, could I see what life was like for those who lived under the rule of the Teutonic Knights?

The antiquarian principles used in restoring the royal castle in Warsaw are painfully scrupulous, with all their agonized considerations of surface imitation versus deep imitation (should one eschew concrete footings below ground, for example?). Yet the way of life expressed in the restored library seems—at least to an outsider, without strong Polish nationalist feelings—to be an extraordinarily trivial one. How did other kinds of people live under the kings? How did the kitchen work in Baranow castle? How can a setting convey a more complete sense of the social milieu, as it was for everyone concerned? The question may be more important than whether a brick vault is brick all the way through, or uses hidden concrete. Tourist money, nationalist feelings, the lack of a voice for local residents, and the professional conceptions of the conservators in charge may all be causing a narrow view of restoration in Poland.

There was great concern about the way in which local peasants were ruining the charming village of Chocholow, for example. Its old log houses are interesting indeed, but I for one would not care to live there. Were I a resident, I would try to rebuild them. On the drain pipes of the professionally despised new fire station were little tin figures which were the direct descendants of the ornamental gargoyles of the castle! Kitsch, I suppose, but couldn't this living creativity be encouraged? In the gray city environment, almost every apartment displays flower boxes. The lush, almost wild, allotment gardens were to me one of the most attractive and human features of the Polish landscape. The work of the Torun ethnographers was exciting because they were looking for ways to adapt features of the old rural culture to use today, ways to help country people to see where they had come from and where they could be going. Could urban conservation be a record of how city people live now and in the recent past, how that is changing, and how valuable elements of those ways of life could be projected into the future? How were city buildings built, and how were they used, a few generations ago? What memories do they have for the people living there now? The efforts of the Torun Ethnographic Museum seemed to me to be a good model for city conservation, and not just a matter for peasants.

This has been a wandering piece. I suspect there are many technical innovations, and much in regard to organizing the industrial support for renovation, that we can learn from Poland. I leave those to better-informed commentators. I was most impressed by:

1. The scale of the work, in relation to resources, and the apparent popular consensus about its value.

2. That when an historic area was rebuilt, the new occupants are generally not chosen by income or status. They comprise a relatively complete and normal mix of society.

3. The idea of a Conservator as an official advocate for saving and restoring things, equipped with a budget and legal powers. But I would pry him loose from his historic districts and his designated landmarks, put him to thinking about conserving activities, landscapes, qualities, natural resources, etc., and make him responsible for an entire region in which people live and work.

And in reaction to what we saw:

4. That restoration decisions should not be imposed by experts, but arise out of the values and memories of an area's actual inhabitants.

5. The crucial task, besides saving things and qualities that people value, is to explain their own past and their future to them.

The Image of Time and Place in Environmental Design (1975)

The achievements of historic preservation in Poland are very impressive. There is a national Ministry of Conservation, parallel to the Ministry of Development, and there are Conservators for each region and large city. These Conservators have broad powers to designate buildings and districts to be preserved and reconstructed, and substantial budgets to carry out the renovation work. The rebuilding of the old center of Warsaw, which was deliberately demolished by the German army, is world famous, and the similar reconstruction of the noble heart of Gdansk now draws hundreds of tourists from Poland and from Europe.

Meticulous, expensive efforts of this kind are being made throughout the nation, in small towns and in the countryside, as well as in the larger cities. It is the defiant answer of a people to the repeated attempts of neighboring states to erase the physical evidence of the Polish culture. It is a political—that is to say, psychological—necessity for a nation recovering from the shock of war and occupation.

Yet there is also a peculiar quality to much of the Polish restoration. Or rather, it is a quality peculiarly like the historical restorations which are carried out in the U.S. and in Europe, and, in a socialist country, this is what seems so peculiar. When on tour to learn from the Polish experience, for example, we were taken to see a handsome fortified feudal mansion at Baranow, and filed through all the elegant, carefully restored rooms around the central court: dining rooms, reception rooms, ball rooms, studies, dressing rooms, bedrooms. Our tour completed, we asked to see the kitchens. We learned that they had been somewhere in the basement, but that the space had been given to a sulphur museum, since the sulphur mines had paid for this particular restoration.

It seemed strange that a socialist country should so tenderly preserve its aristocratic past, and yet erase the memory of the working people who carried that aristocracy on their backs. The past had been neatly disemboweled. We were used to it at home, but hardly expected it here.

The physical environment is an embodiment of time. It is critical for our sense of identity and continuity, for our feelings of connection with the past and thus with the future. Yet, just as in Poland, the great bulk of the conscious, public conservation of environment in this country is being done in a way which narrows and distorts the past, which disrupts the sense of personal and group continuity. There is a groundswell of interest in historic preservation. If the past is a social creation, a product of the stories we tell each other, then, alas, our stories are so often untrue!

These distortions have a number of causes. Environmental conservation is an expensive business, concerned with bulky, awkward objects which almost always are either in daily use or stand in the way of some new use. It requires money and power to effect their preservation—or at least that is the current view of it—and so preservation is done by official agencies or by groups who have that wealth and power. Naturally, then, preservation in the U.S.—as elsewhere, and even in Poland, it seems—reflects the interests and values of the well-to-do and the viewpoints of official agencies. The people who actually live in or use a place may have quite different views or values. They must come to see the official view, or learn to ignore it. Or they can be removed, if necessary.

This emphasis is reinforced by a number of other ideas. Since we think that a thing must be old to be "historic," we are limited to structures which have survived a hundred years or so, and more often than not these are the expensive ones built for upper-class use. "Architectural value" and "uniqueness" are commonly accepted as further reasons for preservation, and they simply reinforce that same narrow focus. Not least, we seek to simplify and stabilize the past, and the neglect of conflict (or its stylization), the compression of the historic continuum into a few static, classic periods, and the golden light that is cast over those periods all help to reassure us that the past is safe and simple, in comparison to our own shabby and troubled times.

However understandable, these attitudes, as they work on the physical remains of our culture, have serious consequences, since those remains are such important symbols for our personal sense of time. Preserved by official selection, they convey a very distorted view of who made history, when, [and] with what values. History is reserved to special periods, special people, and even certain special localized areas: Williamsburg, the Vieux Carre, Nantucket town, Disneyland. Other times, other places, other people, our everyday lives, have then no past at all. They are left gray and characterless, disconnected. We enjoy a glimpse of the past on a special occasion, but it is not *our* history, and we make do with personal memories, or such minor souvenirs as we can keep.

But what could be a basis for the public act of conservation? Keep all ugly and ordinary things? At least we need not shy from the ugly and ordinary. Is everything historic? Yes, of course. Should we save everything then? No—not only because the cost would be beyond counting, but because creating the past is a work of selections—it includes forgetting and destroying as well as remembering. We can perish by total recall as easily as suffocate under saved objects.

So we must continue to create the past by selection, but we could use a different selection rule, instead of keeping what has lasted longest, or is most expensive, or most unique or irreplaceable, or belonged to approved people or approved periods. It could be our aim to conserve *and* to destroy the physical environment so as to support and to enrich the sense of time held by the very people that use it. By that I mean their understanding of the rhythmical ongoing present as a process of change from the past toward the future, in which they themselves have a firm place. While that rule may at first sound platitudinous, it would have a surprising impact if applied. It is a relative rule, not based on any presumed intrinsic values in buildings themselves. It would begin with the people who actually use a place, and with their own experience of time.

What we can learn from psychology, biology, social science, and philosophy about the human experience of time would be at the center: how time is a creation of the human mind, socially constructed, how it is stretched, shaped and patterned, is rhythmic, goes fast and slow. How past, present, and future are intertwined. How time seems to have its distinct regions, boundaries, and landmarks, just as does our image of space. How time is the basis of our sense of identity, and is a matter of deep emotional importance. How physical things outside of us reinforce or disturb, extend or dismember, that image.

If public policy were to be based on this kind of knowledge, then preservation would not begin with a survey of buildings by experts, who proceed to classify them by their "historic" importance or "architectural quality," but by a collaborative study with the users of a place, to expose their own image of time: how it is put together, what its critical foundations are, where there are gaps and disconnections, how it is changing.

Then we might begin to commemorate the histories of ordinary people in ordinary places. To commemorate means to remember together, for indeed this is the role that the physical environment can play so well: to be a stable visual (audible, olfactory, . . .) emblem which enables an intimate social group to remember together. Trees planted at a birth, gravestones, footprints in the sidewalk, personal carvings and decorations, favorite sitting places of well-remembered people, photographs and sketches, playhouses—such things humanize the landscape, and make us keenly aware of who we are and who we were. Local, intimate time has a much more powerful meaning for us than the illustrious time of national monuments. When it is physically commemorated, then the entire settlement comes alive, becomes engaging. The old should not be condemned to reliving the past within their own heads, or the young to be[ing] cut off from it. It should be made physically secure outside of us. History is then no longer coddled in a few official places. Historic districts and cemeteries—whatever their origins in sanitation, economics, or the elephantine ways of institutions—isolate and immobilize the past. Public policy might well turn more often to making people aware of their own rooted history, and to encourag[ing] them to make it visible. Under what circumstances could scattered burial be allowed again in cities or small groups be permitted to consecrate their own special memorials? Would historic societies study commonplace locations, connect oral history to physical place, protect local memories, place local markers? Our streets should remember us.

In central, public places, we would think less of freezing some idealized moment than of allowing the scars of time to accumulate visibly. By selective collage we would try to make everyone aware of the depth of time and its cross-current. Fragments of former structures would routinely be incorporated in new construction. Current use would be asked to signify previous use, or the activity from which it evolved. Conflicting views of the past should be exposed, traces be erased and redrawn as our views of the past shifted. In other words, in place of sanitizing the past by purifying and freezing it, we should contaminate the present with it.

Take Copley Square in Boston, with its rather handsome but also rather detached ring of notable public buildings, over whom peer the new office towers. Why is the Square? Why is there no history connected to it, that anyone can remember? What have all those office workers to do with Trinity Church, the Public Library, the old Copley Plaza Hotel? In such a place, one could visibly demonstrate that the Square was the casual by-product of a political negotiation, the unmarketable space left over where two street grids met, which gradually accumulated some institutional buildings about it. One could mark out the negotiated line between public and private development, and the street that once bisected the Square. One could signify the water still underneath, and how it rises and falls. There was a famous public taking of air rights here (which left caryatids mightily upholding empty air), just where John Hancock now rears above the Trinity Church and sheds its glass panels on the ground. There was a peace museum (whose ground plan might have been staked out while we dallied in Vietnam) and MIT, S. S. Pierce, and the Museum of Fine Arts. Quite as important, perhaps, there were other structures that did not happen—a federal building which was dragged, protesting, to help transform Scollay Square; the University of Massachusetts which now defies Columbia Point. There were great balls at the Copley Plaza. The sunny corner of the bench along the Library facade (which once, but no more, graced every discussion of the development of American architecture, while Trinity yet appears) has for decades been the preferred seat for idle old men.

Would not the Square be a more vital place if it expressed these things? if it displayed the rise and fall of the tides and thus the phases of the moon? if John Hancock yearly shed symbolic leaves? if all this were somehow contrasted with the events in the lives of the office workers who now pass through this space, or eat their lunches there? Preservation is not just saving buildings (although Trinity Church is surely worth saving) but the use of an entire landscape to symbolize the flow and eddy of events.

Commemoration is not simply a marking of the past, but, more precisely, a celebration of the present. Thus it is equally important to make great occasions vivid with ritual, decoration, and special arrangement. Those times when sealed doors are flung open, when we ceremoniously eat together, when cars are excluded, parades formed, flowers strewn, fireworks exploded, or bells ring in unison, are heightened moments of time, to be anticipated, enjoyed, and remembered. The time of day and the time of night can be signified, sunrise and sunset can be heralded, the passage of the seasons can be made as remarkable in the city as it is in the countryside.

Ways could also be found to display current change: the ebb and flow of traffic or of telephone messages, the movement of land values or of water to the sea, the passage of the winds and the fluctuations of air pollution. We are alive *now*, and want to feel our living presence. We wish to connect that presence to past events, but above all to know where we are, and how our present place is changing about us.

Significant environmental transitions should be celebrated as well. In the past, the inauguration of great public works—fountains, railroads, canals, bridges—have been memorable occasions. We are still accustomed to the cornerstone or "first shovelful" event, but it is a pallid affair. Moreover, why is nothing made of demolition and abandonment processes, which are equally important to construction and occupation, and often more dramatic? Forgetting, extinction, the cycle of return, is an essential part of remembering. We have yet to learn how to live with death and loss.

Moreover, it should be a public policy to preserve the future, that is, to permit, encourage, or even demand that the physical environment be eloquent about what is about to happen, to the extent that we can foresee. Relatively secure future trends—whether of development, reconstruction, or decline—can be marked out, as well as the physical consequences of official plans, which so often exasperate the citizen by their sudden appearance, after years of quiet maturing. Much of our distrust of the world, our sense of helplessness, comes from the suspicion—not ill-founded—that powerful institutions scheme in secret. How much more informed (as well as acrid, of course) would the public debate be if the proposed highway were traced out on the ground, or the corners of the new tall building were marked by cables strung from balloons!

Environmental alternatives might be directly displayed, conflicting proposals be demonstrated visibly. Smaller agencies or individuals might be allowed to express their hopes and intentions: the new addition, the future use. Clearly there are opportunities for confusion in such signings—they could not overlap each other endlessly. Moreover, since information is power, there will be a sharp political conflict over the necessity, or the truthfulness, of an environmental display of environmental intentions. Propaganda and fraud could have a field day. (Or do they have one now?) Yet there are many fairly certain and less controversial changes that could be displayed, as well as many non-threatening intentions. And the on-site display of large public or private projects might be mandated just as environmental impact statements are today.

What we are pleading for, in short, is that the physical environment as a whole be made a vivid emblem of time: past, present, and future. There is recent emphasis among environmental designers on the value of creating *place*, that is, giving a locality a memorable and specific character to which the user may attach himself and his thoughts and feelings. This concept can be expanded to include the image of time, so that we make time-places, which root us in both space and time, the great dimensions. The environment should convey to us that we live in a flowing, particular present, whose past and future [are] linked in our minds and [are] securely commemorated outside of us, so that we know where we come from and where we are going, and thus who we are and that change is part of us.

As you see, I am not interested in understanding the personal experience of time, simply so that a knowledge of it may be applied to make the environment more satisfying. That is important, surely. Beyond that, however, I want to learn how to use the physical environment to *change* the experience of time, to enrich it and to structure it in some valuable way.

Some Notes on the Design of
Ciudad Guayana (1964)

To begin with, the reader must be warned as to the basis for these notes: one day and a half inspection of the site, three days discussion with the design staff, and study of staff documents, ignorance of the country and its customs, and an inability to speak the language. The comments may be weighted accordingly.

The designers of this new city suffer from an acute case of a standard planning anxiety: the maintenance of control, the preservation of form and quality, in the face of rapid growth and a continuously shifting situation. The designer must concentrate on present decisions, but each decision must be considered for its long-run effect. This can only be accomplished if the staff is involved in a continuous process of information, of formulating purposes, and of the creation and evaluation of alternatives for action. To discuss these three briefly, in the Guayana situation:

1. If control is to be exercised, there must be a continuous feedback to the designer. How are his designs working? What do the users think of them and how do they behave in them? How are the designs being executed, and what problems of execution are appearing? The communications between designers, builders, and users in the Guayana seems to break down rather frequently. This communication is not a one-way system—a matter of the designer seeing that his ideas are being properly carried out—he must be equally alert to modify his designs if they fail to fit behavior or the process of construction. Specific and accurate information about the site is also needed—a careful check of strategic proposals on the ground on which they will be built. I am convinced that the design of a city of this size can only be done on the site itself, where the ground, the inhabitants, and the builders can be watched and interrogated continuously. I see no other way of establishing control, or of building a city that fits actual needs.

In addition to on-site design, the staff must engage in the systematic and continuous gathering of data: image, behavior, and opinion studies; detailed site analyses at critical points; investigations of the process of construction; continuous inventories of population and housing; market studies; etc.

2. The general objectives given in the plan report are only a beginning. They must be made much more specific if they are to have any bearing on decisions. For each portion of the design, they must be elaborated in depth, and checked against the motives of users, builders, and decision makers. Eventually, they must be developed into such a specific

and localized form that they can be used as an instrument of control and of inter-staff communication.

Furthermore, they must constantly be readapted as the city situation changes, or incomes and aspirations shift. At present there seems to be no provision for such elaboration and revision of objectives. Present goals are rather rigid, and yet very general.

3. Finally, continuous design is required, rather than the preparation of a single fixed design to be executed over a long period. Designing must be carried on on at least two levels: the preparation of detailed designs for immediate execution (a center, a road) and the constant reworking of general sequences for the development of the city. Both levels of design must deal in alternatives: a limited number of desirable and realistic possibilities, which represent open choices at the time. The long-run designs, in particular, must present alternatives, and show how development sequences might branch off, depending on likely shifts in such major factors as population, economy, transport technology, etc.

These long-run designs must be under continuous revision, both to show the effect of accumulating present actions and events, and the possible effects of new uncertainties, as they arise. What will happen to the plan if the northern bridge should not be feasible, for example? Obviously, only a small number of the infinite set of future shocks can be provided for, but those considered can be the most likely ones, and the process builds flexibility not only into the plan but also into the planners, which may be more important.

Designs must always be strategic ones, consisting of a timed sequence of limited moves calculated to have major effects. Initial stages are often the most crucial stages, the way it begins being of more effect than how it is supposed to end. Effort will have to be concentrated at successive points. The quality of the long-run future form must sometimes be sacrificed for present, or near-future, form. Areas must be expected to change: densities increasing, population shifting, facilities improving. Techniques of land reservation, but also of planned redevelopment, must be employed.

A continuous process of design, information, and formulation of objectives will require a substantial staff. It would therefore be foresighted now to set up a long-term system for collecting and training a design staff based on Venezuelan talent: internships, competitions, aggressive recruitment.

Given continuous design, how can it be implemented? How can a city of quality be insured? In this fluid situation, the most suitable techniques seem to be:

1. The direct design and construction of public works: streets, public buildings, public detail—the streets in particular, inclusive of grades, alignment, paving, sections, lighting, landscaping, signs. Not only are

these features directly controllable, but they are crucial in the visual quality of the city, and have important secondary effects.

2. By the use of detailed design programs for development done by other agencies or individuals—localized, specific programs which not only state desired bulk, use, access, etc., but also indicate the desired quality and visual role of the area. These programs can be used as instruments for guidance and for control by review, and are much more flexible and less demanding of administrative effort than direct regulations.

3. By design liaison: the temporary attachment of staff designers to construction agencies or to city areas which are building up, both to give design service and guidance on the spot and to maintain communications between the design staff, users, and builders.

4. By coöption: the involvement of local groups or other agencies in the preparation of plans as a means of committing them to their execution, and of training them to do improved design on their own account. This method is time-consuming, and requires the central design staff to be ready to modify their own ideas in a two-way accommodation, but may be much preferable to thwarted execution, or unskilled and resentful local agencies. The design of the Las Delicias Lagoon, for example, could be developed in conjunction with the San Felix community.

If the above is a general comment on the process of designing in a fluid situation, I also have a number of impressions about the form, particularly the visual form, of the city as now proposed:

1. I believe that the general decision—to construct a linear city based on the Avenida Guayana, and with a principal center on the Alta Vista— was a correct one, given the situation of site, industrial location, and previous settlement.

2. This decision having been made, the visual coherence of the city, and its principal visual impact, depend on the design of the Avenida Guayana, which must be considered as a sequence in both directions. There are a number of difficulties here: the ambiguous turns in featureless country west of the airport; the probable inability of the heavy machinery area to act as a visual dominant; the frequent large traffic circles; the remoteness of visual contact with the Alta Vista center; the unclear location of the avenue as it dives under the railroad and avoids the Dalla Costa ridge on its way to El Roble; the long and rather featureless climb up to Alta Vista from the Caroni crossing; the inconclusive termination east of San Felix. On the other hand, the road has some fine moments—particularly the panorama as one plunges off the Alta Vista ridge down toward the Caroni falls.

Many of the negative features are already under restudy and improvement—such as the alignment west of the airport and the contact with the activity of the Alta Vista center. In general, I would recommend a thorough reconnaissance of the entire line in both directions, with careful attention to alignment, grades, and what can in fact be seen from every point, and how this will build up into a sense of the whole. For quite a time, this trip will be the principal impression of Ciudad Guayana.

Special tree planting will be important to establish the line visually. But how well will trees be maintained on the arid upland? Would it be possible to supply water to them automatically, by some leaking underground aqueduct laid along the Avenue? Special lighting can also be used effectively, plus devices such as unique pavement, special details, and the encouragement and control of highway signs. Artificial topography—mounds which recall the peculiar domes of the neighboring hills—might also be used on the flat uplands as landmarks, goals, or space dividers.

I have some sense that it would be preferable at a later stage to shift the Avenue south on its western end, so as to occupy the military crest of the central ridge, and thus to overlook the dramatic topography of the Caroni valley, which will eventually be the principal town site. I am also inclined toward the use of the Punta Vista site north of the Avenue for housing instead of the technical school, so as to establish an immediate contact of activity between the two sides of the Caroni. This would be an example of sacrificing long-range form for an immediate strategic gain.

The general street pattern of the town site south of Alta Vista, as first presented to me, contained several confusions of geometry: parallel roads crossing each other, radials becoming circumferentials, and so on. I believe that these confusions are now clarified. The general strategy of successive bypassing of the main Avenue seems correct to me, provided that continuous feedback is maintained, to see how traffic actually develops.

I have some doubts about the northerly crossing of the Caroni: whether it will be easy, whether it will seem to diminish the dramatic narrows at the Caroni mouth, whether it will blur the linear form of the city by encouraging development and new centers north of Puerto Ordaz. At any rate, I would advise that other crossing possibilities be kept under review.

Incidentally, since traffic flow in the city will probably ebb and flow in a marked tidal fashion, would it be useful to investigate reversible flow devices?

3. The new center is correctly located on commanding ground which will be the most accessible position in the future city. It will be a difficult birth, however, due to its present off-center location, and to the competition of other flourishing centers, Puerto Ordaz in particular. Every effort must therefore be made to see that the new center begins strong and develops rapidly. I would suggest, in the first stage, a concentration of all new central uses here: not only middle-class but also lower-class retail, services, auto-oriented commerce, offices, transportation, the initial stages of the technical school, government, cultural institutions, hotels, entertainment, housing, etc., etc. All this should be grouped close to and

visible from the Avenue, and close to the commanding position on the nose of the Alta Vista ridge. Rather than spreading activities out by type, with room for all eventual growth and parking, which will result initially in a vast and empty center, let them be concentrated and mixed in the initial stages. Then, as growth occurs, specialization and outward movement can also occur. This is the "natural" sequence of center development. It incurs costs of redevelopment and rebuilding, but here the redevelopment can be foreseen and planned for: using techniques of land reservation for future specialization away from the center, a system of roads and utilities adequate for future loads, land tenure allowing easy re-assembly of plots, and the design of buildings adaptable to new uses.

Similarly the south side of the Avenue at Alta Vista should not be held open for future offices, service activities, high density housing, etc., but occupied soon for mixed commercial and housing use, particularly as a reception and temporary lodging area for new in-migrants, who will then be close to the services and opportunities for casual employment which are critical for them.

I would also recommend that the pedestrian system, at least initially, lead to and from the housing areas, and thus along the natural lines of movement. Early residential backup for the center will be critical: reserve spaces should be held open in more distant locations and the immediately accessible areas should be filled now. Residential contact on the north will be more difficult, however, without destroying the fine natural bluff on that side. Perhaps, if access roads are located in the natural indentations of that bluff, they will be less destructive of the landscape. The bluff is eroding rapidly in any case, and will have to be artificially stabilized.

Lastly, I am doubtful of the local street pattern, which is based on the "steady flow" system. This reduces intersection problems, but is a great nuisance for anyone engaged in local movement about the center.

The details of the Avenida Guayana will be crucial at the center. The impression should be one of activity, close contact, even congestion at first. Can the section be compressed, shopping be brought right to the roadside, signs, lights and special planting be used? Slight variations in alignment coupled with structures or artificial topography can be used to give visual closure, or a sense of entrance. The Avenue might be dropped a few feet to allow pedestrians to look over the cars, or walk on bridges over them, while still maintaining visual contact and access for the driver.

4. I have the impression that the present gross division of the city by income and class on the two sides of the Caroni may become fixed unless energetic measures are taken to counteract it. Such a split may have serious future consequences for social mobility and understanding, for just distribution of services and facilities, and for political effectiveness of the city administration. The efforts of the designers to put some of the lowest-income groups west of the river, and more substantial housing to the east, should be carried through vigorously.

In general, the new city, in contrast to the social mixture and visual interest of the "uncontrolled" growth in Dalla Costa and San Felix, may turn out to be huge in scale, coarse in grain, even blank and visually somewhat inhuman, like the Banco Obrero housing in Puerto Ordaz.

Efforts to variegate this by rules about variation in roof materials, or in the choice of architects, may turn out to be superficial and unavailing. More fundamental would be the construction or layout of housing areas in as small units as is economically feasible, coupled with a variation in the social group housed, and in the basic housing type. To this should be added provisions for individual expression and modification, so that over time the areas will develop as a rich landscape whose variation arises from real differences in history or use, and not from arbitrary rules. Finally, I would look particularly to the design of local centers to give sections of the city a strong sense of place in the early stages: these relatively small but intense areas can more easily be given some memorable and unique character, and thus can identify the surrounding zone.

I would recommend, therefore, the development of a general policy on the mix of social groups in housing areas—the scale of units, the range of variation between neighbors, the access and services required for each —and that the location of this mix be planned for, staged, and mapped just as housing density has been. I would provide for change and growth. I would develop and map a design program for the characteristics of local centers.

5. For the moment, at least, I am impressed by the problems of maintainance, in contrast to those of construction: public or reserve areas are neglected or invaded, road improvements decay, trees are left to die. The immediate solution would seem to be the minimization and concentration of public space; the massing of public planting in a few well-watered areas; the shelving of such imported ideas as pedestrian routes, greenways, or planted medians; [and] the reservation of needed future lands only in presently inaccessible locations. Public structures, plantings, and details should be of a "fail-safe" kind, visually and functionally hardy when neglected. It may also be possible to shift some amenities into private hands, where they will be conserved. For example, could trees be planted on a "self-help" basis, rather than on public land: parcels being brought right to the curb, and individuals being furnished advice, encouragement, tools, and seedlings to plant on their own property?

Undoubtedly the great future amenity of the site is its natural setting—the waterways in particular, which are so rich in recreational possibilities, and are self-maintaining (if not deliberately polluted!). The reservation of water edges and water access in public hands is amply justified, although the development of these amenities may not be an immediate priority.

6. A critical aspect of the new city will be its micro-climate, which to this casual visitor seemed so precariously poised between comfort and misery. It is possible that new construction will block the wind but not the sun, and so cause a substantial deterioration in local climate. I suggest that the staff should now be studying ways of modifying climate in developed areas, via shading, wind channels, and the use of water and particular ground or building surfaces.

At a more general level than this, it will be important to look at the public health aspect of this new city: climate, pollution, disease, nutrition, even mental health as far as we know anything about it. These things will be especially critical as the population jumps.

Ciudad Guayana is potentially a great city—continuous design, careful formulation of objectives, and the realistic evaluation of success or failure will help to make it so.

Comments: A Manual for Site Development for Columbia, Maryland (1969)

The manual contains both general and detailed rules. In developing them, a number of important issues have appeared which are worth management attention, and which usually correspond to current disagreements among the staff. They serve as a summary of the most important decisions which must be made in accepting, rejecting, or modifying the manual:

1. *Social Diversity*—One of Columbia's major problems, common to all U.S. new towns, is that it does not house a full range of the economic classes in our society. A broad cross section would be desirable, but serious economic and political obstacles stand in the way. The manual makes a pious statement to that effect, but addresses itself primarily to the way in which whatever diversity is achieved is to be distributed geographically within the town. The original Wilde Lake had a fine grain mix of class within a relatively restricted total mix. Subsequent development is tending to sort people out in coarser lumps, in the more usual suburban pattern.

The manual takes an intermediate position—that groups of 20 to 50 dwellings should be relatively homogeneous as to price, the timing of construction, and the life style accommodated, in order to make neighborly interactions natural and easy. Beyond these groups, there should be as much social diversity as can be achieved. Arguments may be made both for greater mixing and greater sorting, depending on one's judgment of purpose and possibility.

2. *Visual Diversity*—A second issue has to do with visual diversity, which is only partially related to social diversity. Here there are substantial disagreements among the staff. The manual calls for visual coherence (of spatial form, scale, texture and color, roof character) within small visible-at-a-glance units such as a short cul-de-sac or a length of concave street front. This coherence is not meant to prevent the mixture of compatible housing types or styles, nor to blur the identity of the individual dwelling. Beyond the visual unit, no rules are set for visual connections, except for those that have to do with the form of streets, or with the fit of development to the land.

A number of differing stands may be taken: a) that the issue is not important except to professional designers; b) that it may be important but there is no way to control it unless HRD does all the development itself; c) that visual diversity should be maximized by making every house unlike its neighbor; or d) that greater visual homogeneity is both desirable and inevitable, as residential development occurs in larger units.

3. *Circulation Hierarchy*—Along with the organization into neighborhoods and villages, there is an accepted hierarchy of arterials, village collectors, neighborhood collectors, and local streets. These various levels are to attach to one another in a series of loops built upon loops. Actual practice has followed this system for the most part, although it gets blurred as it grapples with the realities of topography and the existing road systems. The manual repeats this concept, while trying to make it more precise and clean.

It can be argued, however, that this pattern imposes a rigid solution, however convenient it may be for quick design, and that it often forces expensive or awkward layouts on the ground. The constantly curving streets, meeting at T intersections, baffle the easy flow of traffic and disorient the user. The rules might be changed to a simple classification of streets by expected traffic and required design, while leaving their pattern open for solution in the particular case. Nevertheless, the manual only suggests that local streets might make more use of small loops and interconnecting nets or of short one-way roads. Even these suggestions are a matter of disagreement, however.

4. *Public Transit*—The nature of Columbia's transit system is now under study, and in anticipation of this, the manual does little more than repeat the generalities of the past. I would guess that the optimum system for Columbia may prove to be a highly dispersed one, running over the street system itself as is appropriate for a low-density region. This remains to be seen.

Obviously, the character of the system is crucial to residential design, and many of the present rights-of-way may later prove to be useless for their purpose. A section on transit must be added to this manual when decisions have been made. Nevertheless, the manual does make some assertions: that transit routes should never run alongside roads, but should either use those roads, cut across them, shortcut them, or diverge to touch some important point. Furthermore, it sets a maximum distance of 1200 feet between multi-family units and transit stops (assuming that there will be "stops"), but states no rule for any other housing. This is a touchy number, and it can only be set in relation to a number of other policies. It tends to bunch the multi-family housing in extensive single-use tracts.

5. *Pedestrian Paths*—The manual repeats and tries to clarify the present rules, which assume that much normal traveling will be done along these paths, particularly by children. Since few collector paths are built, there is little experience to check this assertion. Experience elsewhere indicates that most people will in fact move about by car, or along the street sidewalks—even the children on their way to school—except where walks offer very substantial shortcuts in relation to the street. If this proves true, the design rules should be revised, perhaps to provide two kinds of walks:

a) fragmentary paths which connect up major sidewalks by shortcutting the streets or leading to critical underpasses; and b) long, continuous, but more infrequent routes designed for recreational walking, riding, or cycling.

As it stands, the manual discourages paths at rear lot lines if they will only receive minor use, and encourages the interconnection of local sidewalks. Grade separations are required at arterials and village collectors, but not at neighborhood collectors unless the pedestrian traffic will be substantial. In walking from house to neighborhood center the crossing of two streets is allowed, and a maximum distance of 3000 feet is set. These rules are a relaxation of the original concept, and are based on approximate present practice. Even these are questioned: are they in fact attainable? They have important design and economic consequences, and are tied up with other policies as to density and neighborhood population. The manual also proposes that paths should be lighted and built early, which fits their intended use, but is beyond present budget allocations.

6. *Schools and Centers*—The present rule ties elementary schools to neighborhood centers, and upper and middle schools to village centers. Matching school units to residential units seems too fundamental to the Columbia idea to be questioned here, but the issue of adjacent sites for schools and centers might be looked at again. The manual follows the present concept, which requires physical proximity as a means of encouraging adult use of school facilities, and the joint use of parking and of recreation grounds. On the other hand, since both school and center demand sizeable and relatively gently sloping sites, linking them severely limits the places where they can be put and encourages costly and unsightly grading. School sites, by their size and "emptiness," tend to act as isolating barriers next to the centers. Existing linkages between the Wilde Lake elementary school and the neighborhood center seem insignificant, although the high school students may make much more use of a village center. Future reshufflings of school districts as population changes will cause some future mismatching in any case. The present minimum elementary school size of 600 results in a neighborhood unit which is larger than designers prefer. In other words, the decision to match the school and the residential units, and particularly to put centers and schools together in space, has advantages, but also distinct social and economic costs.

7. *Other Center Linkages*—Some other center relationships are perhaps less crucial. One is the link between centers and multi-family housing. The manual expresses a preference, but not a rule, for the location of apartments near village or town centers. A case can be made for doubting this. The emphasis might be put only on good road access and special environmental amenity. I would argue for locating a substantial minority of apartments in or next to the *town* center, and allowing others to

be dispersed throughout Columbia. In any case, the rule linking transit with apartments and townhouses is the more demanding constraint.

The manual also encourages locating a village center near an employment center or an institution, to strengthen its market and to give it a special character. This proposal raises some doubts, as being dangerous for the intended social coherence of the village itself. In any case, some thought should be given to the services required by those working in Columbia, or living in its institutions. Not all of Columbia['s] clients will be village residents.

In general, the manual has skirted the edges of another basic issue: the relation of Columbia['s] residential units to the outside world. Should the design of the open spaces, centers, schools, and road systems assume that the residents of the outparcels will or will not be an integral part of Columbia? There are natural pressures to focus on serving and unifying the HRD land, and problems as to school districts and the use of open space are likely in the future. There are continuous difficulties in designing the edges of the HRD parcels. This manual suggests the location of active open space, schools, commercial land, or other jointly used areas along these edges, but there is an opposite opinion that the edges should be sealed off and masked where possible.

8. *Open Space*—Open space in Columbia has been conceived of as [a] ubiquitous "background" to other uses—a continuous network, often of rather narrow proportions, that provides the channels for pedestrian paths, and preserves the flood plains and wooded valleys. While agreeing that flood plains must be kept open, the manual puts greater emphasis on the active *use* of the open space, and on analysis of the possibilities for development and maintenance. It recommends more compact and usable parcels of land, accessible to streets, and continuously connected by paths, but not continuous in itself. Small valleys and flood plains would be incorporated into lots and protected by easements. The required minimum percent of open space would not be lowered, but the nature, distribution, design, and use of that space would be significantly altered. While reducing the responsibility of the Columbia Association for the maintenance of little-used space, the provisions of the manual as they stand imply a larger total budget, since they require detailed design and improvement of the open space.

9. *The Small House*—The conventional, broad-frontage, single-family house on the 6–8000 square foot (or smaller) lot is a key element in the housing market, since it corresponds to the dreams and the ability to pay of many American families. But it is difficult to design for, [it is] wasteful of land, streets, and utilities, and [it] saddles a family with land to maintain which is neither usable nor private. Some of the staff believe that the "ranch house" on the small lot should not be used in Columbia, and that much greater use should be made of townhouses, of singles on larger

lots, or of experimental types. Certainly the "townhouse," at least, is at long last being favorably received. The manual does not outlaw the small "ranch house," but simply encourages experiments with short row houses, patio units, narrow-front units, zero lot lines, and so on, and advocates the mixture of types in the same street. A more searching analysis of the proper mixture of types may be called for, especially since it so intimately affects overall densities and neighborhood sizes.

10. *Interrelations*—Most of these issues cannot be dealt with singly. Budget allocations affect them all. The nature of the open space, the path system, and the street hierarchy are all linked together. Perhaps most crucial of these linkages is that in which social diversity; the mix of housing types; the matching of schools, shops, and residences; minimum school size and shopping market areas; the maximum distances to center and transit; and the nature of the transit system itself are all locked together. The rules on these matters as they stand in the manual are a consistent set, but surely not an optimum one. In changing one provision, however, the effect on all the others must be accounted for. My own feeling is that there should be a coordinated shift toward greater social and housing diversity, with more use of new moderate-density housing types, as well as a wider spatial mixing of those housing types, based on a diffused transit system and a relative relaxation of the school and neighborhood and shopping center links. In any case, modifications should be studied for their system effects.

Controlling the Location and Timing of Development (1975)

Assuming that local control of the rate of development may be desirable in some situations, this essay proposes a mechanism for controlling that rate. After setting a desirable general rate, as well as the locations in which development is to be retarded or encouraged, a local government would issue the number of development rights each year which equals the rate of growth desired. These rights are distributed to landowners in proportion to their land holdings and may be transferred, bought, and sold. They may be used at any location in the region, subject to established density limits. The issuing agency may hold one block of rights to be used to encourage development in specified areas, or as a subsidy for low-income housing, or for other types of explicitly defined and socially desirable development.

The control of private land development in rapidly urbanizing areas suffers from certain well-known weaknesses, which zoning and subdivision regulations only partially overcome, or even accentuate. Chief among these weaknesses are the rigidity of comprehensive zoning; its inability to control rate in step with the provision of public services; the inequities inherent in zoning land at different densities, which also accentuates the imperfections inherent in the land market; the sudden profits to be made at a change of zoning, and thus the pressures of political influence and corruption; the inability to prevent development entirely in some area without outright and costly purchase of land, as well as the legal questions raised when densities are set very low; the use of land controls for social exclusion; and the focus on "ultimate" levels of development rather than the crucial rate of growth. Moreover, if a control over growth rate is actually attempted, there then arise some very stickly problems of rationing.

An equitable annual distribution of development rights to all landowners by a local government might circumvent *some* of these difficulties. We will not discuss the serious social and economic problems raised by growth-rate control in general. Our discussion is limited to the description and analysis of one particular mechanism which might be used to accomplish that control.

One development right would be a permission (subject to other normal development controls) to build so many square feet of structure on any location in the area, or perhaps to build one dwelling unit, if residential growth were the key problem. This right would be good for five (or ten or . . .) years from the date of issue. It could be bought or sold on the private market, and used at any location where building were permissible, but with some limits on the distance over which it could be transferred

From *The Transfer of Development Rights: A New Technique of Land Use Regulation*, ed. J. Rose. Reprinted by permission of Center for Urban Policy Research, Rutgers University.

(i.e., "good only in the Town of X," or "may be transferred to locations no more than y miles from the land to which originally issued").

A local government would make two political determinations: one as to the desired locations for development, and the other as to the rate of growth. The first would be a more stable decision, and would locate desirable densities and uses by zone, including areas where further development was prohibited and others where it was strongly encouraged. This is normal zoning, except that development can now be prohibited in certain areas without outright confiscation. Moreover, since development rights themselves are equitably shared, locational density can be manipulated more sharply with less political pressure, opportunity for corruption, or charges of inequity.

The desired rate of development would be reset on a more frequent basis, perhaps annually, perhaps for longer periods. Or, to combine public flexibility with private predictability, the rate might be set annually for that year which is three to five years in the future. For example, if it were a question of controlling residential growth, a local government might determine that it could reasonably handle N new dwellings per year in the coming three to five year period. There would necessarily be limits on this power to set the rate, particularly if it is to be exercised by a local authority. It would have to be shown (to a state authority, or to a court if challenged) that this proposed rate bore some reasonable relation to past growth and to public purpose, [and] to ecological and social constraints, and that it was tied to the planned and budgeted expansion of public services. Moreover, a supervisory body, like the state, might require that the rate include a certain number of rights assignable only to low-cost dwelling units, so that local rate control could not be used to exclude a fair share of the regional need for low-cost housing. Some portion of the total development rights (call it W) could be withheld in public hands, later to be given or sold to developers of low-cost housing, or to developers in locations where it is a stated public purpose to stimulate growth. All these hedges on the rate-setting power are not unlike the legal and state restraints imposed on local zoning today. Nevertheless, the locality retains a better chance to manage its growth from year to year.

Once the growth rate of N units per year is set, and the number of W units per year to be withheld in public hands, then the amount to be distributed, $N - W$, is divided by total number of acres, A, in the locality. A fractional development right, $(N - W)/A$, is then issued to each landowner for each acre he owns, counted to the nearest acre. It might be issued to him when he pays his annual property tax, to simplify administration, and as a further incentive to pay. He might also receive one right for each existing unit on his land which he demolishes or which is destroyed, although in some situations this could put a premium on the destruction of old but sound low-cost housing.

(Note: It may seem more logical to distribute rights in new growth according to the development potential of land holdings. Under this rule, a town would calculate the maximum number of dwellings allowable on any tract according to its zoning rules, and subtract those already built to give those which could legally be added. The owner would then share in the total pool of rights according to the proportion of his potential new dwellings to the total town potential. Areas fully built up would receive no rights, and areas zoned for low densities would receive few.

We argue for a distribution based solely on acreage for reasons in addition to administrative simplicity. We intend to equalize the costs and benefits of development, as far as they are due to public regulation rather than to characteristics inherent in the land. We hope thereby to improve equity; to take some of the heat, and chance of windfall profit, from zoning changes; to separate rights of development from those of land use as far as possible; to permit public zoning of areas to a zero or a very low density without a taking; and to give some of the value of development to landowners who cannot share in it but who must share in its costs via their taxes. Thus we advocate a simple distribution in proportion to land area owned.)

The holder of such rights now has several options. He may lose the rights or destroy them, either because of carelessness or because he is motivated to retard development in the region, even at some cost to himself. Thus some leakage of usable rights may always be expected. He may hold the rights, and accumulate enough to build on his own land, as permitted by the locational zoning. He may buy additional rights from others, so he can build at a greater density (again, if so permitted at his location). He may hold or buy up rights in order to speculate in them, although speculation will be difficult due to the time limits imposed on the rights, their widespread ownership, and the block of rights withheld by the local government. Finally, a landowner may sell his rights to someone who wishes to use them in another location or to a developer buying for future use on land not yet purchased. Since the rights are interchangeable, and of equal value, it should be possible to organize an orderly local market for them.

The local authority, meanwhile, may sell its withheld rights, W, to developers in particular locations to stimulate development there, or grant (or be compelled to grant) them to developers of low-cost housing as a subsidy. The accumulation and release of such rights might also become a normal secondary function for a regional or state land bank, and so be used to stimulate metropolitan growth in desired directions or to break the suburban exclusionary ring. The land bank, in effect, would have a special power to speculate in rights. The use of rights by the state in this way might logically be tied to state subsidies to localities, for the expansion of public services.

In effect, we propose that the right of development be separated from the right of land ownership, except that ownership is the source of an annual grant of generalized development rights. The development right is now made transferable, marketable, and subject to regulation in time as well as in space. Thus the community has a much more effective and yet flexible way of coordinating public and private investment, and can do so with less injustice to particular landowners. At the same time, part of the rights in land now enter a freer and more rational market, conferring greater flexibility on the developer. The right to develop is a right given to all owners equally, once a feasible total quantity is set, and not a right which can be partially and unequally confiscated by variable zoning rules.

Neither the separation of the development right nor the control of development rate [is a] new idea. Great Britain nationalized all development rights in 1947. But this required a gigantic task of assessing the value of such rights throughout the nation, their purchase, and then the detailed burden of passing on each proposed new development. Development rights have already been transferred at a small scale in the regulation of historic sites in New York City and in Chicago. (See J. J. Costonis, *Space Adrift*, Urbana, University of Illinois Press, 1974.) In 1970, a group at MIT proposed a state-wide market in development rights in Massachusetts, in their publication, "Urban Development Policies." A bill to establish transferrable development rights has been drafted in Maryland.

But the control of development *rate* has been linked to none of these recommendations. Control of the rate of growth has long been a subject of planning discussion, and recently towns such as Ramapo, New York, have instituted controls of this kind, tied to public investment plans and a rather elaborate set of "points" assigned to proposed development schemes. Linking development rights and rate control in an organized system seems to be a new possibility.

Many questions arise, of course. There might be administrative difficulties. But since rights are easily calculated, could be issued when taxes are paid, and could be an actual instrument which is later deposited by a developer when requesting a building permit, the difficulties do not seem to be very large. Other ways of rationing a limited amount of development—such as a lottery, a policy of first come first served, an auction, or a distribution based on development merit (as in Petaluma)—are either more complicated, more unjust, politically more tender, or less subject to public control. Someone would have to organize the local market in rights, however, and this might be a problem in a small town.

The courts might consider the scheme a confiscation of existing rights in land without compensation. But once the control of rate is accepted (and this is the key point which is not discussed here), then the distribution of rights based on ownership is perhaps the most equitable means that can be devised, with a lottery as a second choice. To the accepted concept of public control of density in space, we are adding the control of density in time. It must be subject to the same test of reasonableness, however. It is true that a development right cannot entirely compensate for the loss of any absolute right to build. But it spreads the loss, and softens the blow of restrictive zoning, since the owner is at least left with marketable rights, as well as the right to use his land without building on it. As a result, courts may take a more lenient view of low-density or agricultural zoning in this situation.

The proposal might be considered an unfair redistribution of land values, since owners of inaccessible or unusable land get as many rights as the owners of "ripe" land. But the owner of the unusable land is still unable to market it, and this may be reinforced by the enactment of "non-development" zones. Differential market values still reside in the variable qualities of the land itself, which cannot be moved about. We have already argued for some equalization of development benefits.

The setting of the development rate, of course, would now be a high political act, similar to the setting of the tax rate. But, especially if it is directly linked to budgets for the expansion of public services, it probably should become so. Since the rate is set year by year, mistakes can be corrected fairly rapidly. The fluctuation in the market price of rights will in itself be a useful index.

A local government might consider *selling* the rights, instead of granting them, at a price which would compensate it for the additional public costs of private development, But this is a more radical shift in taxation, and might more easily be considered confiscatory by the courts. Moreover, the markets in rights will then become less responsive. However, a community might be justified in selling some of its withheld rights at a level consistent with the cost of servicing higher densities. Thus all owners are given the right to undertake moderate growth, but more intense growth must be paid for at its social cost.

The spatial "clustering" of new development, which has many advantages, can now only be encouraged where land ownerships are very extensive. The development right proposal would allow this to happen even where ownership was fragmented, since zones of concentration can be mapped which may only build up as rights are drained away from surrounding owners, or, more loosely, high densities might be allowed anywhere in certain general areas, provided that all or a proportion of the development rights had been drawn from land within a close-in radius.

So far, the proposal has been discussed as it would apply to local government. It might be even more useful at the regional level, where some collective authority would set growth rates for the region, or for its sectors, linked to regional development budgets and to regional policies for the location and timing of growth and the opening of social and economic opportunity. Public service costs might be supplemented in the various towns according to the number of rights used there. Moreover, the market in rights would now be large enough to be organized more easily.

The proposal has been keyed to urbanizing areas. Might it also be used in some form in "mature" developed areas, where renewal or intensification of use is contemplated? Could the use of rights not only have a time limit, but the rights themselves in some cases be time-limited? That is, could development rights be leased instead of sold or granted? At first look, these ideas seem to have some useful features. What might be some of the unanticipated consequences?

City Design: What It Is and
How It Might Be Taught (1980)

I think of what I call city design as skill in creating proposals for the form and management of the extended spatial and temporal environment, judging it particularly for its effects on the everyday lives of its inhabitants, and seeking to enhance their daily experience and their development as persons. In a sense, this is a return to that old-fashioned field of physical city (or land use) planning, but it is simultaneously more focused and yet also more amply connected to other concerns, and given a sharper sense of humanistic purpose. It deals primarily with people acting and perceiving in the sensuous, four-dimensional physical environment, and yet it is familiar with all we have learned about institutions, process, and social consequences, during planning's Long March from its original base in land use control.

City design is no longer confined to the public regulation of private actions, or to the design of public works, or to map-like arrangements of legally defined uses—although these continue to be important. It expands to include such topics as programming for activity and character, creating prototypes for elements of the environment as they will be used, making "framework" plans, engaging in environmental education or participatory design, thinking about the management of places, using incentives and building the institutions of ownership and control. Saying that it is concerned with the extended environment does not mean that it is preoccupied only with big things, like superhighways, coastlines, or new towns. As often, it deals with small things which may be seen as a general problem: the use and paving of local streets, the shape of front porches, planting streets trees, making curb cuts, regulating signs. It differs from architecture and landscape design, not in the size of the actions it proposes, but in the way it deals with them: as things connected over extensive spans of space or time, and formed by policies, programs, and guidelines, rather than by blueprints which specify shape and location in detail. Thus city design is distinct from object or project design; but not by any monopoly on bigness, since object designers may also deal with large elements, such as regional parks, big bridges, or extensive housing projects built at one time.

City design is appropriate to those managers, users, and developers of medium to large areas who have a continuing interest and responsibility: institutions of all kinds, community organizations, long-term private developers, regulatory and planning staffs, public works agencies, large industries, local commercial associations, park agencies, and the like. The

Reprinted, with permission, from *Urban Design International* 1, no. 2, pp. 48–53.

purposes and typical strategies of city design are critical for the quality of life. They are stable and recurrent through all the coming and going of such public programs as urban renewal, coastal management, energy conservation, urban forestry, new towns, historic conservation, Third World housing, downtown revitalization, transit schemes, housing rehabilitation and so forth. Any good educational program will keep abreast of these shifting interests, but must represent a more permanent core of knowledge and professional skill.

I have called this field city design in some desperation, since a succinct name is essential. City design is catchy enough, but it unfortunately implies that one deals only with center cities, and not with the entire habitat. It is not very different from the term "urban design," which has been captured by the field of large-scale project design. Moreover, while the word "design" is important to me, it may alarm people who have a misconception of that process. We have used the more awkward term "environmental planning and design" at MIT. That name is too long, and "environment" has also been captured for the narrower meaning of "concern with the natural ecology and with the pollution of water, air, and land." Titles are always being appropriated by particular interests, and perforce we join in that piracy. "City planning" might do, but now that word has very broad and confusing connotations. There are other words to juggle with, such as "conservation," "settlement," "management," or even the older British terms: "town and country planning" and "civic design." City design is the best I can think of just now, but it has its faults.

The field has been an ambiguous one, seeming to lie between city planning and architecture or landscape architecture, something to be practiced by the latter after receiving a finish coat of law, economics, sociology, politics, and planning. The typical "urban design" school in this country is a one- or two-year graduate course for architects, which applies that finish and gives the students some studio experience in dealing with large, complex projects such as new towns, urban renewal, or downtown rehabilitation.

I would not recommend this training, since I think city design should not be restricted to architects (or even landscape architects), and because I think there is a central skill to be taught instead of a finish coat to be laid on. Lastly, I am fearful of the human consequences of "big architecture." Moreover, most urban design departments or programs are in an uneasy, marginal position—deviled by isolation, lacking support or critical mass, worried about accreditation and the fluctuations of student interest, and deprived of a sure institutional basis for implementing their designs.

The city design program at MIT began with interested people in the city planning department, took first in architecture, and led to an informal interdepartmental group which has its own locale and group feeling. There are about 60 students involved from either department, some of whom are candidates for a joint Master's degree, and a few of whom seek a doctoral degree in planning. Three of the faculty are full-time and perhaps four are part-time. No separate degree is given. There is no separate, formal control over budgets, staff appointments, or admissions. Of course there is a vocal lobby. This informality has led to a strong group spirit and easy intercommunication, but an interdepartmental group is always exposed to departmental shifts in interest and emphasis. Moreover, it is not easily visible from outside the school.

Now I would be inclined to propose a program in city design which is firmly centered in one of the professional departments, rather than being a floating bridge. I think it should be centered in city planning, which has the institutional basis for that work and some hard-core knowledge about the planning process, about dealing with institutions, and about the social and economic consequences of physical strategies. Yet in order to focus on city design, the evolutionary drift of most city planning schools must be reversed (or at least reversed in part, to make a pushmi-pullyu). Among other things, faculty must learn how to teach design of this peculiar kind. Nevertheless, I would lead from the present strength in physical city planning, transforming, narrowing, and yet also enlarging the sense of that bollixed field, and only then bridging outwards.

The way to begin is to assemble a critical mass of faculty, at the right place, who have a common passion for the subject. "Critical mass" means two, or better three, good people. Once they have established their center they can grow, and can reach out to the other design fields, as well as to engineering, social sciences or the humanities. Part-time faculty or students from other disciplines can join the group temporarily. But a center comes first, to my mind.

It should be a two-year graduate professional program, I think, although it might also offer introductory undergraduate courses (or just refuse to care about that distinction) and harbor a few doctoral students doing advanced research. Students should be accepted from any background as long as they want to design. While there should be an understood intellectual core (see below), and recommended sets of courses, depending on background and destination, I am very nervous about inflexible requirements. Good discourse is a better guarantee of competence. I also think that a common *place* is extremely important: a single location for faculty offices, studio space, student desks or lockers, secretary, lobby, small seminar, coffee, mail pickup—all with a single entrance. Most good teaching is informal and personal; it happens in the halls and on the stairs. It is equally important that students and faculty undergo some common *experience*, whether it be a first studio, a joint seminar, a common excursion, or some other thing.

While a long list of relevant courses can be written, one should also remember that students (even faculty) have a lifetime to learn. The important features of a school are good colleagues, a common passion, a common experience, access to knowledge, a few central, elementary skills, and just enough fancy technique to carry one well into some first job. In the case of city design, I think of three central, elementary skills which seem to me indispensable:

1. A sharp and sympathetic eye for the interaction between people, places, place events, and the institutions that manage them. One learns to observe, understand, and have strong feelings about that interaction, and one continues to learn throughout one's career. The focus of intervention is place, while the source of value is the person and his experience. Some knowledge of the findings and techniques of environmental psychology and microsociology are most useful, but these scientific fields are nevertheless not truly central. Sensitivity and openness to the subject is central, and constant awareness of it is the basis of design. Prolonged field observation and conversation with people is a very good way to learn it. One acquires . the habit of wandering through a city for the sheer joy of discovering places, hearing voices, seeing people in action. We become ourselves engaged, and sense our own emotions. We learn to empathize with the feelings of others, to see how places must seem to them. In dialogue, we begin to discover collective images of the possible.

2. A thorough grounding in the theory, technique, and values of city design. This means designing the policies, programs, incentives, guidelines, and prototypes that are appropriate to the field. There is a prevalent idea that design is only concerned with site plans, buildings, or smaller objects, that it is non-analytical, socially irresponsible, concerned with pictures, and reserved for the gifted few. Worse, designers are taught to be egocentric and to prize originality.

I think that none of these features is inherent to design, although I admit that they are very often attached to it. Design is a way of thinking—a habit of imaginative, almost child-like, playing with possibilities in complex and ambiguous situations, in order to find a fitting solution. In that general sense, it is a good education for any field. It can be applied to city design specifically, by using images of process, management, and four-dimensional form in active use. City design will stress user participation and will almost always be done in interaction with a multiplicity of clients and other professionals. Pure design cannot to be taught in the abstract, but only in relation to some concrete content. Being competent in one design field is a useful introduction to design in another, but it is perhaps better to learn to design directly in one's own area, from the start. Shifting from architecture to city design requires some unlearning, for example.

City design is not a well-developed skill, and I know no school where it is adequately taught. It will be hard work to develop that teaching. It will require both studio experience and seminars on the theory and practice of interactive, process design. I am not certain how to do it, and yet I am convinced that it is fundamental.

3. Finally, I think that a city designer must be skilled in communication, and have a passion to express and to learn. So should any educated person, of course, but it is especially critical for someone who will spend his or her life exchanging ideas with clients, residents, opponents, and decision makers. I think of four social languages: written words, spoken words (quite a different language, at least in English), mathematics, and graphic images. There are other languages, of course, but these are the important ones for us. One must be fluent in all four, and this means fluent in sending and receiving—that is, in writing *and* reading, speaking *and* listening, computing *and* understanding numbers, drawing *and* seeing. The first three languages are by now thought respectable, and an educated person is assumed to be competent in all of them, even if in fact most people are not. But our culture has a blind spot for the graphic language, which is thought to be specialized, concerned only with art, and confined to the talented. On the contrary, it is just as fundamental as the others, can be learned by anyone, and, like the others, has its own special powers and limitations. Like the others yet again, it is essential to thought, especially to thinking about city design. A city designer must be introduced to any of those languages in which he is illiterate (dumb, innumerate, or iggraphic), and his competence must be developed by constant use.

I think of those three as the fundamental skills for a city designer. They are not taught in City Design 101A (spring term, $7\frac{1}{2}$ units). Concern for developing them must permeate the whole stream of teaching and learning, although particular courses may introduce or focus on them. Of course the city designer must learn (or be learning, or be able to learn) much more: city politics, urban economics, law, sociology, psychology, engineering, ecology, landscape design, architecture, site planning, urban history, project management, planning implementation, community organization, etc., etc. At least she must have been exposed to *some* of them (always choosing courses where the good teachers happen to be), while having heard of the others and knowing how to learn about them when necessary. In addition, she must have some specific skill that will carry her through her first employment. At the end of this note, I have made a list of some appropriate courses that seem to me to be capable of filling a two-year curriculum, but that list must be received with skepticism.

Some of this learning will be in studios, some of it in lectures and seminars, but much of it occurs informally. The normal academic structure, composed of interchangeable, free-standing courses, forces students to split their heads five ways each term, even while it permits co-ordination between teaching programs. It is itself a powerful lesson in disconnection. It might be better if there were long periods and short ones, intensive and extensive courses, springtime and wintertime ways to teach, the freedom to focus and the freedom to explore at random, stimulating visitors now and undisturbed inwardness then, temporary course mergers, times for fantasy and times for hard grappling with stubborn realities. But such flexibility is very hard to come by in a complex university. MIT's "independent activities period," which replaced the lame-duck, post-Christmas tail of the winter term, was one successful move in that direction. At other times, hidden joints in the official structure can secretly be forced open and exploited.

The city design group should have some regular connection to public and private agencies, preferably local ones which are actually engaged in shaping the spatial environment. A continuing relationship means that students can be placed to gain experience, realistic studios can be mounted, research problems for whose solution there is an actual demand can be identified, and working professionals or staff can be brought in to teach or to learn.

At the same time the center should be engaged in research of its own. Not all of that research—perhaps even the lesser fraction of it—need be designed for immediate application. A good school will primarily be engaged in fundamental research. But I think that the proper research for a program in city design is its own subject matter and not psychology, sociology, economics, ecology, engineering, or whatever—all of which have their own bases of operation. City design research will of necessity connect with those fields, but its central concern would be with imaginative possibilities for the form and management of the everyday urban habitat, with evaluating the human consequences of those possibilities, and with strategies for designing and implementing them.

As I have said, the center should welcome the presence of students and faculty in other departments who have connecting interests—not only those engaged in architecture and landscape architecture, but also [those engaged] in graphic design, public works engineering, geography, anthropology, the study of perception and cognition, literature, politics, business administration—wherever the interest appears. Some students may be taking joint degrees. Other departments might develop program centers of similar outlook which are based on their own fields. Bridges are built from secure foundations.

City design, in my view, is a new, more developed and focused version of physical city planning. It has a definite core and an important task to do; it is an art and not a science. There are many real obstacles to achievement in it: the scarcity of institutions responsible for the way whole environments affect people, the emphasis on quantitative criteria rather than on quality, the lack of user participation, the demand for packagers and glamorizers of large-scale projects. Yet good city design *is* being done against odds, and the schools can at least build the knowledge base for it.

What this personal view of the training for city design means for Berkeley is beyond me. Every institution has its own history, resources, and structure, which must be taken into account. In my brief abortive stay, I received a strong impression of wide interest [and] able teachers, and some sense that there is an opportunity for creating a school of city design here which could be one of the best of its kind in the U.S.[1]

I append a list of courses of relevance to city design which could fill a two-year graduate program. These subjects can be packaged in many ways, depending on teaching resources. In my opinion, they should *not* be required, but recommended as subjects likely to be useful. Nor do most of them follow any necessary sequence: they are listed neither in an order to be taken nor in an order of importance. Intelligent students choose courses primarily for their teachers. Everyone has a different background, trajectory, and destination. No student could take all these courses. No school could give them all. No one knows everything she is supposed to know. Beware of lists.

1. Constant practice in graphic communication; drawing, seeing, and basic design (and why not also in reading, writing, speaking, listening, and mathematics?)

2. Laboratories and studios:

    a. the holistic analysis and evaluation of real city places in the field; their sensory quality, behavior, history, economy, politics, sociology, technical structure; all to the end of developing a sharp eye, a delight in city-watching, a habit of seeing wholes, and a stock of environmental models;

    b. site planning—a realistic program, a real site, and possibly some real clients;

    c. community or area design on a participatory basis with a real client; and

    d. city design proper, a real problem again.

(While studio problems should be realistic ones, students should be encouraged to make at least brief flights into exploration and fantasy).

3. Courses in allied fields

    a. land and real estate economics

    b. microsociology of the environment

    c. environmental psychology and behavior

    d. traffic and site engineering

    e. urban landscape design and urban ecology

    f. project organization, initiation, and management

    g. urban history; the physical city in relation to its politics, sociology, and economics.

4. Seminars in city design
    a. case studies of city design processes, models, and outcomes
    b. land use and transportation analysis and planning
    c. the techniques of team and participatory analysis and design
    d. environmental programming and evaluation
    e. the analysis and management of environmental quality
    f. theory and history of city design.

Note

1. This paper was written for an urban design colloquium at the University of California at Berkeley in 1979.

VI City Design: Projects

It has not been an easy task to select from the professional projects of Kevin Lynch, who was an active practitioner throughout his life. He was involved in a wide range of projects, as a consultant or as the principal. He wrote many of these reports, and he contributed sections or chapters to others (as is common when professional planning reports are produced by consulting firms). In collaborative work, Lynch's contributions are often easy to spot because of his distinctive writing. Yet in other instances it is less clear exactly what Lynch wrote, and to make matters worse it is not clear who his co-authors might have been. Some of these reports were written many years ago, and even Lynch's former associates may not accurately recall who did what. But since the restrictions of space did not allow us to include everything, we had to be selective. And in selecting these pieces we chose to include those reports that were clearly written by Lynch, alone or with a colleague, and those studies he talked about in his interviews or other writings as his own work.

There are seven selections in this part of the volume, organized in two groups: projects in the Boston area and projects elsewhere. With the exception of "Performance Zoning: The Small Town of Gay Head Tries It," these pieces are either abridged or excerpted from lengthy documents. In excerpting we have left out the routine descriptive materials and the dry technical details that normally are included in planning reports. What we have included is representative of the more significant aspects of Lynch's contribution, or maintains some continuity with the theoretical views expressed in other articles in the present volume.

For the Government Center, Columbia Point, Boston Tomorrow, Cleveland Circle, and Rio Salado projects, we have provided some additional introductory text to explain the background and the overall content of the main studies from which the texts have been excerpted. The two other pieces—the Gay Head performance zoning (written with Philip Herr) and the San Diego study (done with Donald Appleyard) did not require that, since they are included in their original form, although they are somewhat abridged.

Government Center and the
Waterfront, Boston

In the Government Center plan the old market area and Scollay Square (a seedy entertainment center and the home of the famed Howard Athenaeum, a burlesque theater) were studied as a site for a new government center. The district is the setting for some of Boston's most cherished landmarks, including Faneuil Hall, Quincy Market, the Durgin Park restaurant, the Union Oyster House, and the Hancock House (the treasury of the Continental Army). The major goals of the plan were to provide for new city, county, state, and federal office buildings; to preserve and renovate historic sites and monuments in the area; and to create a new civic square. There was also a desire to improve the functioning and the economy of the district.

Lynch's research for *The Image of the City* had pointed out several structural problems in this area of Boston. People had difficulty imagining the connections between Downtown, the West End, and the Waterfront, probably because the street pattern was so circuitous and there was no intervisibility between the districts. The plans strengthen the visual and functional structure of the districts in several ways. The old tangled web of streets is simplified, providing improved vehicular connections between Downtown, the West End, and North Station. Several streets are realigned; for example, Tremont Street is connected with Cambridge Street in one grand curve, whose sweep is reinforced by the curved office building at the base of Beacon Hill. In clearing out much of Scollay Square, the plan opens up view channels to several of the landmarks. Faneuil Hall and the spire of Old North Church can now be seen from outside the Government Center subway station. At the same time, care is taken to retain and blend the most significant elements of the old city into the new development. The plan does much to preserve and enhance many landmarks, activities, and meaningful objects, such as the huge steaming teakettle that serves as a sign for a coffee shop, the statue of John Quincy Adams, the Italian pushcart market, and the fine-grained seventeenth-century street pattern of the Blackstone Block. All modes of access are addressed, with special consideration for the needs of pedestrians. A system of public paths and spaces linking Beacon Hill with the Waterfront and the North End is proposed.

The Waterfront plan was proposed at a crucial time in the history of the waterfront. Boston's sea-trade economy had declined, leaving behind the derelict shells of many historic wharf buildings. Charles Bulfinch's famed India Wharf buildings, dating from the early nineteenth century, had just been demolished. The Central Artery had recently been built, cutting the Waterfront and the North End off from the rest of the city. Thus, the Boston Chamber of Commerce commissioned a study to examine ways of redeveloping the waterfront. Lynch was a member of the planning team. One major goal of the plan was to make the waterfront more accessible for public recreation and enjoyment through links with the Government Center and the Financial District; another was the creation of a new open space on the waterfront. The plan also advocated the preservation of the old wharf buildings for commercial and residential use and the construction of new housing to create a vital waterfront community.

The Government Center and Waterfront plans are among the more successful urban renewal plans in the United States, and have been largely implemented. The final Government Center plan, by I. M. Pei and Partners, incorporates most of the original plan; however, Lynch strongly objected to the size of the Government Center Plaza as built—he felt is was too large. The following excerpts from the Government Center plan focus on special concerns of Lynch: the spatial structure, the symbolic environment, and pedestrian spaces.

Sources: *Government Center—Boston*, in association with Adams, Howard & Greeley; Anderson, Beckwith & Haible; Sasaki, Walker & Associates; John R. Myer;

and Paul D. Spreiregen (no date); *Report on the Downtown Waterfront–Faneuil Hall Renewal Plan*, by Greater Boston Chamber of Commerce (1962). Excerpts reprinted by permission of Boston Redevelopment Authority. Sketches with dates are by Lynch, courtesy of Institute Archives and Special Collections, MIT Libraries.

Boston itself has a scale and a quality that transcends the sum of its individual historic buildings or sentimental locations. This scale of structure and open space, this intimate mixture of historic symbol and busy commerce, must be maintained and acknowledged in the new plan. Due to the great size and functional demands of the new buildings, this is no easy task.

Movement on Foot

At present, pedestrian circulation is just as confused and just as irritating as is the circulation by car. It is even more dangerous: the area is notorious for its fatalities. Nevertheless, there is heavy foot movement, particularly up and down the Pemberton Square–Court Street–State Street axis, and along the north-south line of movement for commuters between the central business district and North Station.

By its basic street system, the plan clarifies the pedestrian flow as well as the vehicular movements. In addition, the upper end of Washington Street is kept open for those on foot, to allow direct access from the principal shopping street into the Government Center. The new space in front of the federal building would be connected by a footway to the principal square, and also by a path through King's Chapel burial ground and thence by a pedestrian easement to Pemberton Square. The present tidal wave of commuters, who at the peak hours now press through many narrow streets and alleys on their way to or from the trains at North Station, would now be directed along the new Congress Street. To shelter and invite this movement, a handsome pedestrian arcade is proposed along the east side of this street.

The plan also provides a major new pedestrian axis, which would drop downhill from Pemberton Square, through the new city square, through Cornhill, and into the space before Faneuil Hall. Except for two street crossings, this axis would be entirely given over to the man on foot. The new squares themselves would be delightful places through which to stroll, as would the board walk and arcade along Tremont Street at the foot of Beacon Hill, or the narrow ways of the historic area to the east. Although the area as a whole must continue to be a zone of thick-set traffic streets and transit lines, it would provide far more for the pleasure of those who choose to go on foot.

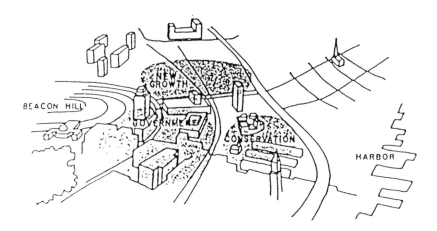

The Governmental Zone

The basic concept of the government zone proper, lying roughly between School, Congress, and Sudbury Streets and Pemberton Square, is that it be the general locus of the major public buildings, but interwoven with private offices, shops, and restaurants. The latter uses would be in somewhat smaller buildings but would be sited in the key commercial spots. These private uses would draw on the trade of the Government Center, replace the taxable values eliminated by its construction, and give the area the life and movement that a purely official zone often lacks.

Most of these uses would face in upon a new civic square, some 250 by 500 feet in dimension. This new square should have a new name consistent with its importance as the central focus of the Government Center area, the principal event on entering or leaving central Boston from the north.

The city hall, as the seat of government, is considered to be the principal symbolic building. It would have the key location on the downhill side of this square: Cambridge Street, Tremont Street, and Court Square being visually focused on it. It would dominate the area, not by its height, but by its position with respect to the open spaces around it and by the quality of its design, just as the Old State House is presently the head of State Street despite the vastly larger size of the surrounding buildings. The architectural design of the city hall will indeed be crucial to the success of the whole, and should be attended to with great care. The exterior envelope here recommended is the result of careful three-dimensional study. It calls for a six-story structure with a central courtyard.

The Conservation Area

The area lying between Hanover Street, the new Congress Street, the back side of properties on State Street, and the Central Artery has been designated as a "conservation area."

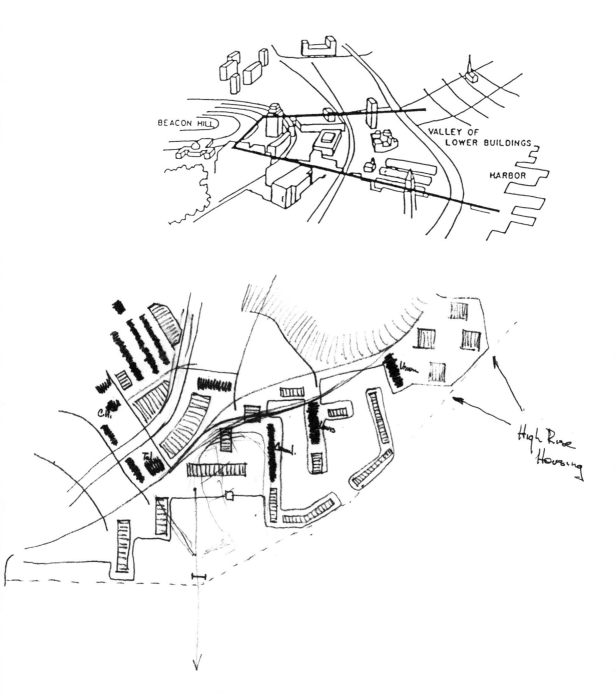

Waterfront study (8/8/61).

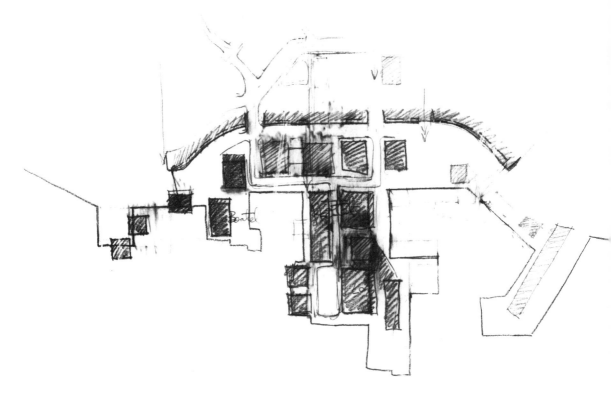

Waterfront study (9/29/62).

What might be developed here is a quarter characteristic of Boston, but unusual in its intensity: where the symbols of the past stand in close contact with a lively present. Here the tourist would come to see the historic sites and the colorful market activity; the Bostonian would come to buy or to dine in intimate surroundings. The shops would thrive on the presence of both. Here could be the principal spot in the city for the retail-wholesale dealer in food, for speciality food and drug stores, for push-carts and fine restaurants. The area could provide unique services for Bostonians and visitors of many classes and interests. Most of these services are already there: it only remains to capitalize upon them.

The Union-Hanover-Blackstone-North block would also in large measure be preserved, with a restoration of the original internal street pattern as a pedestrian system for tourists and shoppers. As has been noted above, this is the last portion of the 17th century street pattern remaining in the city. Hatter's Square would be opened up to Union Street by demolition of the building between Salt Lane and Marsh Lane, a building which is out of character with the block. A new square, which might be named Hancock Square, would be opened in front of the historic Hancock House by clearance of the small triangle of buildings between Union, Hanover, and Marshall Streets.

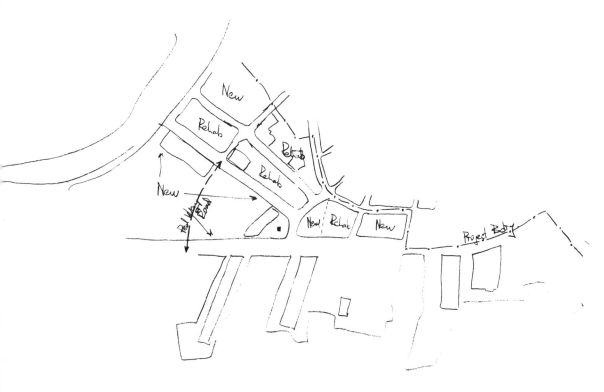

Treatment of edge of North End (7/6/63).

Both of these spaces, plus the present opening behind the Hancock House (the site of the former Hancock Row), would act as pleasant pedestrian enclosures, setting off the historic structures such as the Hancock House, the Old Corner Book Store, and the Union Oyster House, and suitable for such activities as outdoor dining or marketing. Being intimate in size, they would be in scale with the old buildings.

The Union Oyster House, the Hancock House, and the Boston Stone would be preserved. Present activities would be encouraged to continue as at present, or even to expand, as long as the architectural scale of the whole were not destroyed. In fact, the character of the area would only reach full maturity when many more food specialty shops had been encouraged to set up business there. An attempt at restoration which displaced the present retail activities would not only be historically false, and cause economic loss to the city, but would destroy an essential ingredient of the area's life and character.

This policy should include the push-cart activities along Blackstone Street. Although the plan indicates that a portion of their present stand near Haymarket Square must be taken for access roads, it more than compensates for this loss by suggesting a push-cart market which might be covered, between North Street and Clinton Street. The core of the present push-cart activity would be maintained as at present, free from traffic intrusion, with its links to both downtown and North End shoppers undisturbed.

The pedestrian underpass under the Central Artery at Hanover Street would be retained and broadened, so that it would connect with Hanover Street at both ends and would be of sufficient width to be used for food sales. Thus a continuous retail food market might be developed, stretching from Salem Street, under the Artery, along Blackstone, to the new Dock Square.

The System of Public Open Spaces

The fundamental objective of the plan has been to provide for the functional and economic requirements of the Government Center, and to do so in such a way as to enhance the beauty of the city, and to provide pleasant places for Bostonians to walk and to congregate. To meet this desire, provision has been made in the plan for a chain of public open spaces noted in the diagram. This chain of spaces will not only add to the delight of the city, but will be reflected in the increased attractiveness, and hence economic value, of the surrounding parcels.

The chain leads downhill from the crown of Beacon Hill at the State House, via Ashburton Place to the future Pemberton Square and then, via a flight of steps to the principal new square, and finally through a new Cornhill, across Congress Street and its arcade, into Adams Square in front of Faneuil Hall. In the future this footway might be extended through the market area out to the waterfront by means of an underpass at South Market Street. It would extend sideways as well, to link up with the pedestrian areas in the historic block, and with the new square on School Street. All these squares and footways would be furnished with fountains, sculpture, trees, and benches. . . .

This chain of spaces down from Beacon Hill would occur in a great "valley" of lower buildings, opening out like a wedge from the foot of the hill, with Hanover Street as the northern edge and the South Market–Cornhill line as its southern edge. This would enable the city hall and the structures at Pemberton Square to look out to the sea and to be visible from the Central Artery, and would visually connect the North End and the harbor to the center of the city. Moreover, it would retain the present dramatic sense of a "wall" of buildings along State and Court Streets, which marks the beginning of the city's business center. Finally, it would prevent any further intrusions on that part of the skyline where they would destroy the silhouette of the State House dome as it crowns the crest of Beacon Hill. For all these reasons, it was felt important to maintain a wedge-shaped valley of lower buildings here, down through which the chain of small open spaces might run like a river, and to confine the higher structures to locations on or north of Hanover Street. This reinforced the location of the conservation area, and the choice of a lower envelope for the city hall itself.

In all this work it is important to keep in mind the connections to the surrounding areas. All too many renewal projects result in bright new developments, completely divorced from the fabric of the existing city. Therefore every approach into the area or into the city center has been carefully studied for its effect, as well as for the views to be given to drivers on the Artery. The pedestrian entrances have also been considered, such as up Court Square from the King's Chapel burial ground, down Washington into Cornhill, or up from the subway station into the new square itself. Each space was thought of, not by itself alone, but as part of a sequence which would be seen by people in motion. The Government Center has been brought as close up to the old central area as possible, and tightly related to it. The resulting contrast of old and new would be one of the more pleasant features of the scheme.

The approaches and links, the major chain of spaces, the wedge-shaped valley of controlled height, all of these would come to their climax at the new square. Here would be located the principal buildings. Here are recommended the most precise controls over facades, bulk, shape, and disposition on the ground.

Negative controls alone will not do the job, however. There must be positive encouragement and stimulus for good design, and cooperation should be developed between architects designing the various buildings fronting on the square. The details of the square itself will also be crucial: the paving, planting, lighting, fountains or sculpture; the form of the subway station or the shape of the street furniture. Therefore, there must be continuing design advice, which can guide the project in every detail until its final completion.

Community Revitalization Plan for Columbia Point

with Carr/Lynch
Associates, Inc.

This plan has much in common with Carr/Lynch's Franklin Field project, also in Boston. Both dealt with ways of improving ill-designed low-income public housing developments that were in miserable condition. In both cases residents of the projects were involved in the planning process. The Columbia Point residents were represented by an eight-member elected task force, a basic goal of which was to guarantee decent and affordable housing to Columbia Point's current residents. Columbia Point was New England's largest public housing development. According to Lynch, it was "one of the two worst public housing projects in Boston." With 1,504 apartments on a 37.7-acre site on the north shore of the Columbia Point peninsula, it was intended primarily for family housing; however, the units were about half the size specified in current standards, and the density was considered too high for family living. When the plan was prepared, the project was largely vacant, with over 1,000 unoccupied units. The site was a wasteland, lacking services, access to the rest of the city, and any kind of amenity.

The revitalization plan called for at least 450 units of low-income housing within a mixed-income family housing environment. Existing buildings were to be thinned out and redesigned, and all seven-story buildings were to be demolished or lowered to three stories. New buildings were to have from one to three stories. All flat roofs were to be replaced with pitched roofs to erase the institutional feeling. The site plan was to be modified from the fort-like clusters of the original plan, which residents felt represented entrapment, to create the feeling of houses along a tree-lined street. Areas behind buildings were to be treated as large open common greens. New commercial and recreational facilities were to be added, including small beaches, a boat ramp and a marina, and a waterfront pedestrian and bicycle path. This excerpt from the plan discusses the planning principles. It is reprinted by permission of Greater Boston Community Development, Inc.

Planning Principles

To establish an understanding of the unmet housing needs of current resisdents, the Task Force carried out a resident needs survey. Designed and analyzed with the assistance of Ms. Gayle Epp, an experienced analyst of housing user needs, the Task Force surveyed a substantial percentage of current residents. . . . These needs are reflected in this plan and must be addressed in any redevelopment at Columbia Point. Based on this information and the Task Force's subsequent work with its planning and design consultants, Carr/Lynch Associates, Inc., the Task Force considers the following to be basic planning principles for the revitalization of Columbia Point.

A Predominantly Low-Rise Family-Oriented Community

As discussed above, it is of great importance that a substantial family housing environment be provided at Columbia Point. The vast majority of these family units must be in low-rise buildings: two- or three-story townhouses, walk-ups, or garden apartments. They should have a clear front entrance side and on the other side face an open green area which is at least 80 feet wide. All dwellings with three or more bedrooms, and as many other units as possible, should have direct ground access and small semi-private outdoor living spaces. No unit should have its main floor more than two stories above ground. All units should meet MHFA and HUD design standards.

The strong preference of current residents is for clearly identified units which look like "homes." Thus, low-rise buildings should have pitched roofs and old and new buildings alike should make use of entry porches, balconies, and window grouping to identify individual units.

In addition, to create a balanced community and to serve current and future senior citizens as well, there must be homes for both younger and older single people and couples, some of which can be in elevator buildings. New high-rise buildings should be located only at the extreme east or west ends of the community where they will not shadow any low-rise housing, overlook their private spaces, disturb them with their traffic and parking, or exclude them from the shoreline.

No Separate Areas by Income or
Racial Group

The revitalized Columbia Point community must not perpetuate the social stigma and isolation of public housing. There must be no visually distinct buildings or areas for one income or racial group. In the new community, tenant selection and assignment procedures should be designed to implement a policy of full income and racial integration. The success of this key policy will depend not only on design and on tenant selection and assignment, but also on the presence of supportive community-controlled social services, including progressive schools, a security force trained in mediating conflict, and family counseling. Such services must be combined with strong community-oriented management which does not tolerate vandalism or other forms of behavior destructive to the community.

No Distinct Separate Areas of Development

New development at Columbia Point must be planned for functional and visual continuity with the existing buildings. The existing Columbia Point development must be modified to make its site use pattern and massing consistent with that planned for the now vacant land parcels on the peninsula. To do this will require thinning out existing buildings as well as cutting most of the seven-story elevator buildings down to three stories. New townhouses should be distributed among the remaining older buildings, utilizing where possible the existing foundations of buildings to be demolished. The lines where the predominantly older development and the new development join should be treated as spatially interlocking seams, so that visual and functional continuity are established.

No Sharp Visible Differentiation Between
Old and New Buildings

As with the general pattern of development, new and old buildings on the site must be designed for maximum visual continuity. There should be a continuity of materials: in particular, the brick exteriors and the materials used for porches or balconies. Within this continuity, identity may be enhanced by using a variety of compatible colors for trim, doors, porches, and balconies.

A Single, Connected Circulation System

The streets and walkways of the community must be continuous to allow free movement to all parts of the site. The system should be easily understandable in form, well related to the buildings, and have varied views, including views of the Bay. It must be possible to operate a public bus along a continuous route which serves the University of Massachusetts and the entire community and connects to the Columbia MBTA station, major shopping, and regional facilities. In addition to sidewalks along all roads, there should be continuous separate pedestrian ways within the community and along the shore. There should also be a bike way along the shore. All low-rise units should have vehicular access and parking within 100 feet of the front door; and all high-rise buildings, particularly those for elderly residents, are to have direct vehicular access to the front door and parking within 100 feet.

A Continuous and Ample Flow of Open Spaces

The lack of attractive, well maintained, and usable open space is one of the major deficiencies of the present development. Its ground is broken asphalt. The reconstructed community should be opened up by means of a continuous and ample flow of green open space. It must be possible to overlook open spaces from the public streets. The streets themselves should be lined with trees. Interior spaces wihin each block should be accessible from the street and should be of varying width—at least 80 feet—and have green lawns and clumps of trees flowing through the community. Green fingers should connect the open block interiors to the shore, but no continuously wide belt of open land should divide the community from the water. At least 12 acres of this open ground should be reserved for active recreational and park uses, distributed in several parcels convenient to the dwellings. All dwellings with three bedrooms or more should have playlots for pre-school children. There should be no continuous road along the shore and no large parking areas there. The shore itself should be developed with several small protected beaches and fishing piers for community use. If there is to be a large regional marina, it should be located at the extreme eastern end of the point so its traffic does not intrude within the residential community. A buffer should be created between the residential community and the Kennedy Memorial Library and the proposed State Archives building.

Appropriately Located Community Facilities and Services

There should be enclosed spaces in the heart of the community for local services such as daycare, management, and indoor recreation, including a pool, gymnasium, and community hall. Area-wide services, such as a health center, alcoholism unit, teen center, job training unit, and local commerce, as well as maintenance supply areas, should be located along Mt. Vernon Street, with adequate parking. Assuming appropriate funding can be secured, the former pumping station should be converted to shopping, restaurants, community, and recreational uses, for joint service of the community, the University of Massachusetts, marina users, and visitors to the Kennedy Library.

Boston Tomorrow:
Draft Development Policies

with the Boston
Redevelopment
Authority

Kevin Lynch completed the draft of policies and the work program for the next phase of the "Boston Tommorow" project shortly before his death in 1984. The project came about as a result of the pressure for development in Boston and the need to reassess the impact of development on the city and the framework within which it should take place. This document is remarkable for its humanism and for the connection of the policy statements with values and goals. Although the policies are aimed at the central business area of Boston, they emphasize the support of human physical and psychological needs rather than the needs of vehicles and buildings. This is an uncommon, almost unique, perspective in the context of American planning for business areas, where vehicular, engineering, and economic requirements almost always take precedence. These policies are derived from goals which are in turn derived from basic human values; they reflect Lynch's theoretical work in *Good City Form*, where he attempted to develop performance dimensions for urban form. It would have been fascinating to see this wonderful policy statement begin to have an impact on Boston's future and to see what political debates it would stir. The next phase would have been to develop operational standards and guidelines, but unfortunately the project was abandoned, to be replaced with a conventional zoning plan. Perhaps it will become a model for another city! The following is reprinted by permission of the Boston Redevelopment Authority.

Policies for the Public Environment

The first set of policies deals with the direct impacts of development on people in the public environment. Guidelines to implement these policies will be based on notions of performance: How understandable is the central city and what meaning does it convey? How well does the public environment fit common behavior and provide for human comfort? How easily can people reach their destinations?

A Sense of Place and Time

Central Boston should be understandable and delightful for all its people, enlarging their sense of community, history, and nature. To that end, the following policies are proposed.

1. *Maintain and strengthen district and neighborhood character.*
Most districts and neighborhoods in the city have a recognizable and memorable character, determined by their history, cultural identity, landscape and architecture, and by activities located there. In concert, these factors can confer a strong sense of place and meaning. District character makes areas remarkable and coherent so that they serve as a basis for pride, affection, and a sense of continuity.

Guidelines should be prepared which will conserve or create the qualities of district character. They will necessarily deal with building height and bulk, with use mix, [with] relation to the street, and [with] the quality and pattern of open space. They will also be concerned with facade design, landscape and streetscape, surface materials, and views. To accomplish this, those areas will be identified which, through their scale, use, and character, are clearly recognized in people's minds. Guidelines will be based on the essential existing features that confer that particular sense of place. Areas of less distinct character will also be identified, and guidelines would be prepared to clarify or supercede the existing form of such areas, and thus to create a stronger sense of place. In both cases, analyses would be based on field inspection, on consultation with the people who use these areas, and on the knowledge of district character accumulated by the Landmarks Commission and the BRA [Boston Redevelopment Authority] staff.

2. *Maintain the human scale of Boston.*
Maintain and enhance those qualities often referred to as "human scale" which allow people to feel comfortable and not overwhelmed in the city. These qualities derive from the patterns of neighborhoods, blocks, buildings, and facades being broken down into sizes and shapes that feel familiar and to which people can relate.

The sense of human scale is an important aspect of a livable city and is apparent in a broad range of experiences, from the forms and patterns perceived when arriving in the city to the details of architectural refinement perceived when entering a shopfront. In general, there should be no abrupt changes in building height and massing, and the scale of new development should reflect the predominant features of the surrounding area.

As a means of ensuring human scale, guidelines for streetscapes will be prepared regarding continuity of the street wall, the size and rhythm of buildings and spaces, and facade design and landscape elements such as lights, sidewalk furnishings, and paving patterns. Guidelines will be prepared for neighborhoods and for overall district organization with regard to building height and massing, patterns of open spaces, and views.

3. *Establish and maintain connections among parts of Central Boston and between Central Boston and outlying neighborhoods.*
Along with its vivid character, the growth of Boston has produced some confusions and disconnections. It can be difficult to find some location, in imagination as well as in reality. It can be a puzzle to go from the Back Bay to the South End, for example, or to picture where the water goes as it passes from the Charles River into Boston Harbor. In some places, neighborhoods have been cut off from the core by large development projects and highways. A sense of a connected whole is important for building a sense of community, as well as for personal orientation. Linking the elements of Central Boston and strengthening ties between [the] downtown and [the] neighborhoods will require an analysis of the existing connections and a plan and guidelines for mending and extending these connections. Such a plan would employ such elements as new or clarified pedestrian and transit access, focal points, view corridors, and the extension of activity across barriers or "empty" areas. Much of this can be implemented as new development takes place.

4. *Preserve a sense of continuity with the past within a context that allows for change.*
Over time, economic, cultural and technological changes have altered the physical organization of the city. Nonetheless, much of Boston's form is still derived from earlier periods. Today the city is a collage of time, which gives Boston a special character and provides people with a sense of continuity between past and present. This special sense of time merits protection.

Several methods of implementing this policy are in place and additional ones could be created:

Landmarks and historic districts have been designated in Central Boston. The Boston Landmarks Commission has completed an inventory of structures and districts in the Central Business District and has identified those meriting preservation in some degree (approximately 33 percent of the total buildings). Many of these have been designated or put under permanent stewardship through other mechanisms, and the process of designating additional buildings is ongoing. Finishing the inventory and evaluation for incomplete areas of Central Boston is essential. The system acknowledges that changes will occur, and permissible changes are outlined in some designation guidelines. However, there is a need for more specific guidance in advance of, rather than in response to, proposals for new development.

In addition to historic designation, there are other ways of communicating a sense of time. New development could express the changing times by incorporating traces of former structures and uses, including urban design patterns, and architectural and landscape elements. Graphic and written descriptions of previous use would also be welcome. Predictable and imminent future changes, such as the location and design of new structures, could be conveyed with appropriate signs and symbols.

5. *Encourage visible human activity along the streets and street frontages, of a variety, intensity, and duration appropriate to its location.*
The sight of other people and their activity is one of the enduring delights of the city. This policy could be implemented by guidelines such as the following:

a. Require large development projects to include publicly accessible activity on the ground floor and to make that activity visible from the street.
b. Encourage housing downtown, as well as that of other uses which would make streets active over a greater span of the day.
c. Encourage a range of street activity—selling, performing, play, or resting. To ensure room for such activities, developers could be required to provide public open space and improvements for public spaces. Public projects, such as street closings, could add to the inventory and variety of such spaces. New techniques for open space management could be instituted.

This policy is currently implemented by the BRA in its review of development proposals and plans for specific areas, such as Downtown Crossing. It could be more effective if it were based on a survey of street fronts and street activity, [the] timing and seasonal variation [of street activity], and an inventory of those streets where additional activity would be welcome.

6. *Enhance Boston's natural and manmade geographic features, in particular the attractiveness and accessibility of the water's edge.*
The topography and river and harborfront are the basis of Boston's urban form. The overall massing and patterns of development and the park system fit upon this base to create the city's special geography. The edge of the Boston peninsula is its prime natural asset and its most visible geographic feature. From this vantage point, one can see the city in its setting; enjoy sky, sun, and water; and participate in waterside activities.

The BRA mandates public access to the waterfront in its development projects, implementing policies and recommendations [from] its 1980 study of the waterfront. A truly effective policy would require an updated study of the present use and accessibility of the entire water's edge, an analysis of potential access and its difficulties, and an assessment of ways to promote appropriate water-related and water-dependent uses. Public and private actions should make it possible to walk along the water's edge without hindrance and to approach it at frequent intervals from nearby public ways, should ensure that there are frequent views out to the water, and [should] encourage attractive public uses to locate there, along with water-dependent uses which are open to public view.

Public Safety, Health, and Comfort

It is the public purpose that Central Boston be fit for the people who use it, allowing them to conduct their activities safely and in good health and comfort. To that end, the following policies are proposed.

1. *Ensure sunlight in the public ways and spaces, and adequate daylight and views of the sky along the city streets.*
a. Sunlight
Sunlight is key to the use of public ways and spaces. To maintain sunlight in public open spaces, a guideline could stipulate that no new building or addition cast a shadow onto public open spaces during certain seasons, at the times of day when those open spaces are most heavily used. For example, a general rule might prevent the blocking of sunlight in public spaces during the middle hours of the day at the spring and fall equinox[es]. Alternatively, more detailed rules for different hours and seasons might be based on the actual use, size, and situation of particular public spaces.

In either case, the sunlight guidelines will be based on a study of the existing conditions of sun and shadow in public open spaces, on the use of the space, and on how those sunlight conditions affect that use. In addition, the consequences of the guideline on development must be analyzed.

b. Daylight
Ensuring the presence of sunlight along all the narrow, winding streets of Boston, however desirable, would be impractical. Nonetheless, it is important to maintain adequate daylight and views of the sky.

One possible guideline which would protect daylight on the streets without imposing rigid controls on architectural design could be stated as follows: If any part of a new building were to have an angle of elevation, as seen from the opposite sidewalk, which was greater than some standard angle, then that piece of the sky dome which was blocked above the standard angle would have to be replaced by a least an equal area of visible sky below the standard angle by means of a setting back or a lowering of other portions of the building.

The standard angle could vary by district to reflect predominant and desirable building heights and street widths. Determining the appropriate standard angle will require a study of the influence of adjacent building heights on light levels, as well as analyses of the impacts of various angles on building form and the character of the streetscape.

2. *Prevent heavy winds in public areas but ensure that light prevailing winds and sea breezes are not blocked out.*

a. Winds

Boston is one of the windiest cities in the country, and the ill effects of its strong winds are made worse in locations where tall buildings create gale-force gusts at the street level. Moreover, dense concentrations of large buildings can convert narrow streets into wind tunnels. The effect is not only unpleasant but can be dangerous for the elderly and infirm.

Standards exist for regulating the wind impacts of development: A commonly accepted limit for winds in pedestrian areas is that the "equivalent speed" of the wind (an equivalent which allows for variable gusts) should not exceed 35 mph more than 0.1 percent of the time, or about 10 hours in the year. This is a safety rule. Additional limits could be set to ensure comfort in public seating areas. Once guidelines are agreed upon, it is important to determine what projects must comply. Because wind tunnel tests are expensive [and] time-consuming, and must be repeated each time a design is modified, it is desirable to give advance guidance to designers and to set a threshold of height or location which would trigger the need for wind tunnel tests. Formulating the guidelines and implemention methods will require the advice of wind experts.

b. Light prevailing winds and sea breezes

It is important to minimize strong winds on city streets, but it is also important to enhance the flow of light prevailing winds and sea breezes, which have a cooling effect in hot weather and which prevent the accumulation of air pollution.

The effects of development on air flow can to some degree be predicted from the location, massing, and height of buildings. Specific guidelines to maintain air circulation will be based on a study of the influence on air flow of existing air channels and the urban geometry of Boston.

3. *Prohibit undue noise in the public environment.*

Daily transportation, commercial, and industrial activities all generate background noise. Occasional activities, such as air traffic, heavy trucks, and construction work, create intermittent louder noise. Both sorts of noise can be irritating and, depending on their volume and frequency, can damage hearing.

Boston's Air Pollution Control Commission has established a comprehensive set of regulations concerned with the generation of noise by various uses, vehicles, equipment, and construction operations. The rules vary according to the time of day and the location. For the most part, the rules set acceptable noise levels at specified distances from the source of the noise, and in some instances they are stated in terms of what percent of the time noise can exceed those limits. The rules are based on generally accepted national standards backed by substantial research. Compliance with the rules can be objectively measured.

Thus the problem with regulating noise is enforcement, and not the lack of well-formulated rules. A commitment to reducing noise levels will require an administrative budget that will support an adequate staff to monitor noise and enforce the existing regulations.

4. *Reduce air pollution, particularly that generated by construction activity and vehicular traffic.*

Air pollution is a principal health hazard in cities, and its serious effects are well known. Traffic generates approximately 70 percent of the hydrocarbon emissions and 90 percent of the carbon monoxide emissions in metropolitan Boston. For both types of emissions, Boston's air [pollution] exceeds federally acceptable levels.

There are two primary means of controlling pollution by vehicles: reducing the emissions from individual vehicles and reducing the number of vehicular trips or the times that engines are idling. The City has greater control over the latter source of pollution. The policies and guidelines suggested in the Access section of this document and which are aimed at congestion are reinforced by the need for clean air.

In addition, the policies suggested for maintaining open channels for prevailing breezes in the city have the intent of protecting air quality through the dispersal of pollutants. Construction operations are dealt with directly by city regulation, which require that the release of dust and fumes be minimized by well-established procedures of wetting and storing materials.

5. *Ensure that the public environment provides adequate seating, shelter from wind and rain, and toilet facilities.*

Some simple conveniences are needed in public places: it should be possible to sit down when tired, to take temporary shelter from the wind or rain, and to find a clean, safe public toilet. Detailed guidelines could provide criteria for the amount and design of seating that should be provided, based on the anticipated use of an area. Temporary shelters should be available at transit stops and at some reasonable intervals in heavily used areas. The form of the shelters can vary from deep doorways to awnings and arcades. More specific guidance about the provision of shelter would be based on a study of existing shelters to determine the characteristics worth replicating. Clean, supervised toilets should be easy to find downtown.

While criteria for the design and location of public amenities may be relatively simple to define, the provision and maintenance of the amenities is a more controversial issue, particularly the provision of public toilets.

Thresholds could be set to determine what level of amenities would be required of various size projects, and what is best provided by public actions.

6. *Enhance existing open spaces and create new ones.*

Boston's public open spaces, ranging from the Common to Angell Memorial park in Post Office Square, are universally enjoyed as places to rest, to play, or simply to observe in passing. Some areas are bereft of such space, and the existing parks need better maintenance.

Implementing the open space policy will require guidelines for open space acquisition, including opportunities for creating them out of existing public rights-of-way. Guidelines must be founded on a study of the present distribution and use of open space, and how use is affected by design and by accessibility. In particular, the working and resident population of the central area should be consulted. The study would identify areas where public open space is needed most. Design guidelines concerning materials, form, light and sun, wind, vistas, maintenance, and other open space qualities would be prepared.

Implementing the policy will also require new administrative devices for maintaining, enhancing, and creating public open spaces, including ways to coordinate public and private responsibility for those functions. When new development would significantly increase the population of an area, for instance, the developer could be asked to provide funds for public open space. Boston is familiar with innovative management on a project by project basis, as evidenced by the process to redesign Copley Square and by the management techniques for Downtown Crossing. Such processes could be extended to improve parks city-wide.

7. *Ensure that the public ways and open spaces are safe.*

a. The design of ways and spaces and the buildings which border them can help to discourage crime in the streets and to give people a greater sense of security. Adequate lighting, secure footing, no hidden spots, and a sense of "eyes on the street" from storefronts and upper floor windows contribute to safety. Forms and materials can clarify circulation routes and can define the public, semi-public, and private realms, adding to the self-policing of areas. Round-the-clock activity and the programming, maintenance, and direct and indirect surveillance of public ways and spaces also enhance security.

Implementing this policy will require guidelines for the design and administration of public areas for visible activity and for the design of the street wall.

b. Conflict between vehicles and people on foot is another major urban danger. Creating pedestrian zones, such as Downtown Crossing, is one strategy to ensure the safety of pedestrians. Other strategies include restrictions on the number and location of curb cuts, design controls for parking ramps and truck loading areas, and traffic management plans which direct heavy traffic away from residential areas and minor streets. Special pavement treatments and pedestrian signals at crosswalks help to protect pedestrians. The location of building entrances affects pedestrian safety, particularly in areas with heavy traffic. For some of these methods, specific rules can be written and compliance easily measured. For others, general guidelines can be written and the means of meeting them left more flexible. In all cases, the safety and comfort of the pedestrian must be given priority.

Access

The activities and facilities of Central Boston should be accessible to people who visit, live, and work in the city. To that end, the following policies are proposed.

1. *Relate the density of development in any area to the access capacity of that locality.*
Physical access to and within the city is affected by the conditions and capacity of the streets, parking facilities, walkways, [and] public transportation, and by the location and density of activity relative to the different modes of access. The number of people coming and going in some areas downtown has surpassed the capacity of the various circulation systems. Guidelines are needed which relate the density of development in any area to its access capacity, while giving priority to transit access and ensuring that the Central Business District remains the continuously active core area. Large projects should be built in areas convenient to public transit and expressways to avoid circuitous routing of vehicles via local streets. Implementing such a guideline will require analysis of the variables which determine the access capacity of an area, how densities should relate to these capacities, and what the desirable form of Central Boston might be.

2. *Minimize vehicular traffic and congestion.*
While the basic premise of the access policy is to make it easier to get to and move about Central Boston, making vehicular access easier would create a contradiction: The more smoothly automobile traffic flows, the more people will choose to travel by car. Any increase in vehicular traffic will only exacerbate the existing problems of pedestrian safety and air pollution. Hence, access policies are intended to minimize congestion, but by substituting for travel by car rather than promoting it.

Implementing this policy would focus on the following:

a. A proposed amendment to the Zoning Code would require developers of projects over 100,000 square feet and which require a variance, conditional use permit, exception, or zoning map amendment to formulate an access plan. Prior to development, the plan would estimate the traffic impacts of a project and would specify measures for minimizing vehicular person-trips. The plan would set targets for the number of daily commuter trips, which would be monitored in a post-development access plan.

b. Controlling parking is a second means of reducing traffic and congestion. Restricting the number of parking spaces downtown is a strategy employed by the Boston Air Pollution Control Commission. The restriction, imposed in 1975, currently is being reassessed.

Some methods for allocating scarce parking and street space are already in use: non-residential parking in neighborhoods is discouraged; parking is reserved for the handicapped; and curb space is set aside for buses and taxis. Guidelines could set priorities for the allocation of spaces within parking garages so that commuting to work by car, especially with only one person per vehicle, would be discouraged. Employee parking adds significantly to peak-hour congestion and air pollution at times of day when transit service is most frequent. The proposed access plan requirement would include strategies to allocate scarce parking.

In addition, the location and form of parking facilities can help to minimize congestion. When parking structures are designed with efficient internal circulation and fee payment systems, queuing is minimized. As well, careful siting of entrances and egresses cuts down on traffic jams. Peripheral parking convenient to expressways and arterials reduces traffic in the center. The Boston Air Pollution Control Commission (BAPCC) has established criteria for the location and form of parking facilities which serves as the basis of their review of parking proposals.

c. The policies for improving public transit outlined below should also help reduce vehicular traffic.

3. *Improve access by public transit*

Public transit remains a primary mode of travel to and within Boston. Unfortunately, the system (and its riders) suffer from old equipment and scheduling problems. As Central Boston [develops], some aspects of the system could be improved and the use of transit could be increased.

To that end:

a. Major development projects should be located in areas convenient to transit, as noted in the first access policy.

b. Transit improvements, including new stations, ferry terminals, and pedestrian connections, should be integrated into large development projects. A general guideline to that effect is frequently made part of development review. In some instances, more specific advance guidance could be offered, based on a study of the need for new transit stops, stations, and terminals.

c. It may also be possible to restrict certain streets to transit vehicles, or to transit and taxis only.

4. *Make pedestrian access easy, direct, and inviting*

Boston is a city for walking. The compactness of the central area, the design of streets and pedestrian ways, and the difficulties of driving encourage people to travel by foot. Walking could be made more pleasurable. Actions to improve pedestrian access will include the following:

a. Sidewalks should be designed to accommodate the anticipated volume of foot traffic, with minimal obstacles to pedestrian flow, adequate space to wait at crossings and corners, and no barriers for the handicapped, the elderly, or people transporting children or goods. Some general standards exist for sidewalk design, and they could form the basis for guidelines for pedestrian access. However, guidelines should reflect the anticipated volume of foot traffic and the character of specific areas.

b. The pedestrian network should be strengthened. This would require a study of the existing pedestrian network and a plan for establishing critical connections that currently are missing. As part of this effort, additional pedestrian streets could be designed. Guidelines will be developed to improve the design of pedestrian ways and adjacent open spaces and to make the routes more legible.

5. *Facilitate access for bicyclists*

Despite the obstacles presented by Boston's streets, a number of people regularly commute by bicycle. Their ranks could grow. The barriers which currently deter would-be riders include conflicts with vehicles, unsafe pavements, and the lack of cycle parking facilities. Some of the problems can be resolved easily and for relatively little cost; others will require time and substantial investment.

a. Secure parking facilities should be provided at all major buildings. Standards could be set to specify the number of spaces required based on the potential volume of use.

b. Given the narrow streets and limited space available for cars and pedestrians downtown, creating separate lanes for bicyclists is seldom feasible. However, major changes in the road network, such as the proposed Central Artery depression, present opportunities to develop safe bicycle routes. Standards for bike lanes should be developed in consultation with bicyclists and should be incorporated in the design of specific large-scale projects.

Proposed Work Program Outline

The work program will focus on formulating guidelines for three major issues of development:

1. Character of districts and the pedestrian environment;
2. Density;
3. Microclimate conditions.

A sketch of the anticipated scope of work follows; more detailed information on the district character and microclimate study is attached. The three studies will be coordinated so each informs the work of the others. A final effort will review the existing development guidance system [and will] determine what changes [and] mechanisms would be required to implement the new guidelines.

1. *Character of Districts and Pedestrian Environment*
To prepare detailed guidelines for development which will enhance district character and the pedestrian environment, the following work program is proposed.

a. *Scoping*
• Review pertinent existing studies and regulations for Boston and other cities.
• Map districts and select priority areas for analysis with assistance of an advisory group.
• Establish purpose, assumptions, [and] methods of study in detail and conduct initial charette on possible guidelines, also with an advisory group.

b. *Field Reconnaissance*
• Evaluate character of priority districts, locating key assets and problems through observation of how a place is used.
• Interview a small sample of users regarding their experience of districts.
• Consult with police and other managers of public environment regarding street design and use, safety, maintenance.
• Collate and review information with advisors, formulate tentative guidelines, and identify conflicts between districts or with results of microclimate and density studies.

c. *Guidelines*
• Formulate initial guidelines; designate assets to conserve and problems to address.

• Test initial guidelines, assets, and problems in the field and for consistency with density and microclimate studies. Review with advisors, city agencies, and the public.
• Revise guidelines.

2. *Density*

To minimize problems of overbuilding in parts of Central Boston, a study will be undertaken to determine on what basis, where, and how development should be distributed. The work program, yet to be elaborated on, will focus on the following:

a. *Capacity* of circulation networks on the sewerage system.
• Review existing data on access and infrastructure capacity, noting problem areas on which to focus.
• Investigate options for alleviating capacity problems, including plans of relevant agencies, management techniques, new technologies.
• Map areas where the access and infrastructure capacity would support or discourage growth.

b. *Urban form*
• Review relevant design plans and concepts which have directed the density of development.
• Through public discussion and with input from designers and other Boston Tomorrow studies, explore notions of desirable urban form based on character and geography.
• Map consequences for density of development.

c. *Public policies*
• Review plans, policies, and regulations—such as those for enterprise zones, neighborhood revitalization, and historic districts—to determine their impact on density.
• Map areas where existing public policy would encourage or discourage growth.

d. Determination of appropriate distribution of growth.
• Discuss and analyze growth capacity, form, and policy maps and information to develop final map indicating areas for growth and conservation.

3. *Microclimate Conditions*

Technical studies, to be conducted by microclimate consultants, will be initiated to investigate the effects of the form and location of development on sunlight, daylight, pedestrian level winds, and air circulation. The studies will culminate in acceptable standards, such as allowable wind speeds, and in urban design and architectural guidelines.

Performance Zoning: The Small Town of Gay Head Tries It (1973)

with Philip Herr

Gay Head occupies the western tip of the island of Martha's Vineyard, and it is nearly detached from the island. It is an area of six square miles. Its winter population was 118 persons at the last census, and the summer population swells to about 1,000. Gay Head has no industry and no commerce except for some tourist stands at the western cliff. The permanent residents live along the main road on the central ridge not far from town hall, and the summer cottages are spread around the sea margins. The land is terminal moraine; and the soil is a jumble of boulders, clay, and sand.

Gay Head was an Indian reservation until 1872, and today many of its permanent residents are descendants of the original Wampanoags. The average per capita income is one of the lowest in Massachusetts, but the visiting summer residents are relatively affluent.

Martha's Vineyard is only 45 minutes by ferry from Cape Cod on the mainland, half an hour by air from Boston, and an hour by air from New York City. In the crowded Eastern Seaboard, the recreational development pressures on the island have increased tremendously in the past few years. Due to this pressure, the past few years have seen many of the Vineyard towns hastily adopt their first zoning and subdivision regulations. Others have stiffened existing controls. A county planning commission has been established. A county plan was prepared, but it was not adopted. There are many different interests in conflict and there is a lot of controversy, as is usual with these things.

Rural Attitudes

Gay Head is under the same pressure as the other towns on the island. Typical land prices have gone from $1,000 to $10,000 or more per acre in a few years. Many new lots have been recorded. Housing starts, while still moderate, have multiplied. Years ago, most of the land had slipped out of Indian ownership, although some local families still have moderately large holdings. Many of them have deep feelings about the land as their ancestral home, and they dislike its transformation into a summer colony. On the other hand, some of them stand to gain by the speculative jump in land prices. There are political factions within the permanent community, typical grudges between summer and winter people, a common resentment of the more transient visitors using the once-empty beaches, and signs of a rising Indian consciousness. All these conflicting streams unite in a strong affection for the town and an anxiety for its future.

Until 1972, there had been in Gay Head no control of land development in any form, beyond state health regulations and a state electrical code. Enforcement was informal. A local conservation commission had just been instituted, but there was and is no planning board, no subdivision control, no building code or local health regulations. No local permits of any kind were required. Gay Headers valued their independence and saw hidden pitfalls in formal legislation. They were wary of outside interference. There had been an attempt to institute zoning in 1967, but it had died quietly, by consensus, even before reaching a town meeting.

In 1972, however, Gay Head was doubly threatened: by the impending flood of summer houses, and also by the possibility of state and federal intervention through legislation which would control its land use from above. The established summer residents were clamoring for protection. An unsightly clump of "Garrison Colonial" houses had just gone up at a prominent seaside location.

The townspeople reluctantly concluded that a zoning bylaw was necessary. But they wanted it simple and flexible. They mistrusted boundary lines and complicated provisions. They wanted to keep Gay Head quiet and rural, without a business or an industrial district, a place where each person might carry on his trade on his own land. Moreover, they were too few and too busy to man any complex structure of boards and agencies.

Gay Head's attitude towards regulation is not peculiar to it, but widespread in rural towns suddenly threatened by development. This attitude follows from the nature and history of such places.

First, the people who have chosen to move to or remain in rural communities often have done so in part because of their attitude towards government and regulation. A not inconsiderable part of the attraction of rural living is the relative freedom to act without constantly encountering governmental licenses and rules and procedures and prohibitions to which urbanites have become inured. Adoption of any zoning entails for rural people a reluctant surrender of a part of that freedom.

Second, hesitancy over conventional zoning stems from resident knowledge of the town's terrain which, by urban standards, is awesome. Ownership patterns and history, income and use, soil qualities, wildlife habitats, drainage patterns, and vegetation are known with an intimacy which causes distrust of any scheme which, like zoning, lumps together for similar treatment areas known to be different, or which arbitrarily divides, for geometric convenience, areas known to share many attributes.

Third, such towns characteristically have a low level of land use precommitment. They are early in their developmental history. There isn't much existing land development to set the pattern for future land development. Commonly there is little investment in service systems: paved roads, water, or sewerage. This makes the initial division of the town into zones appear even more arbitrary. A new boundary line would be taken as a visible, personal affront by land owners on at least one side of it.

Fourth, the only serious plan-making in such towns usually focuses on implementation, normally zoning. There is little patience for abstractions like long-range future land use plans, a perspective professional planners are now catching up with. In these towns, zoning normally precedes formal plan-making at least by years, often by decades.

Fifth, personalities have enormous importance. "Judging each case on its merits" is the favored system of administration, leading to a preference for laws which can be used selectively, which constitute no barrier to known people doing things to be good but yet are an insurmountable barrier to unknown outsiders doing things presumed to be damaging. Any law, no matter how clear will to a degree be administered in this way.

On the other hand, there are certain relationships or rules about which people can agree. The rural character should be retained, and it is about to disappear. Traffic should not be too heavy at any one location. Extensive or dense development is not wanted. Noise, dust, odor, and pollution should be controlled, regardles of location. In some towns, unmapped location rules can be agreed upon, such as ones stating that businesses may only be located next to other businesses (or, on the other hand, are prohibited from doing so), or that they may not be near clusters of existing dwellings. With heightened environmental awareness, new rules are being added to protect wetlands, steep slopes, or other environmentally sensitive areas. Ingenious definitions of "family" and "dwelling unit" are concocted to discourage communes, [which are] now common in parts of rural Massachusetts and which often seem threatening to rural people.

Highly discretionary zoning bylaws have become common in some parts of rural Massachusetts. The town is mapped as a single zoning district, with use and dimensional regulations uniform throughout the town. Despite the obvious legal and practical problems, the Board of Appeals is then given untrammeled discretion to allow commercial and industrial uses anywhere by exception. While allowing each case to be judged on its merits, this approach could probably be overturned if challenged in the courts.

All of this suggests that development might be guided through rules governing how activities must perform, and perhaps through rules relating activity performance to locational attributes. But, these rules would have to avoid unjust exclusion, administrative caprice, complex measurements, involved procedures, arbitrary boundaries, or lengthy statutory provisions. Such rules would control the town-wide mix of activities, and provide a modicum of environmental control; but they would not fix the spatial pattern of land use, leaving that, as before, to be determined by the inter-play of the market, the qualities of the land, and accident.

The Gay Head Bylaw

Gay Head appointed a Zoning Committee of local citizens in March of 1972, who minutely debated and drafted a bylaw for a special Town Meeting in October. Parallel ideas developed in Vermont and in Franklin County, Massachusetts,[1] were pointed out and used. The simplified bylaw finally proposed passed the meeting almost unanimously. In many of its features, this bylaw is like most conventional zoning regulations. It regulates use, lot size, setbacks, building height, structural density, drainage, land clearance, and the occupation of sensitive conservation areas.

But in two ways it is unusual.

First, the town is practically a single zone. There is a second zone, "Marine Commercial," but this is confined to a small, marginal section of the town, most of which is still owned by the Wampanoag Tribe. This second zone is intended to protect traditional fishing activity. All the rest of the town is designated "Rural Residential."

The traditional uses, such as single-family houses, schools and public buildings, agriculture, fishing, and their accessory uses inclusive of small trades, are allowed anywhere by right. Any other use, including all commercial and industrial ones, are also allowed anywhere by special permit, subject to a set of performance conditions. These conditions are:

1. The use cannot be likely to generate more auto trips both to and from the premises at the busiest hour of a normal operating day than is given by the number 10 multiplied by the number of acres contained in the lot. The estimation of likely auto traffic will be based on current available experience with the type and size of the use in question.

2. Space for off-street parking will be provided which is at least twice the floor area of all structures on the lot, and this parking arrangement will require no backing out onto the public right of way.

3. All outdoor parking, storage, loading, and service areas will be screened from the view of the public roads and from adjacent residences.

4. There will be no odor, dust, fumes, glare, or flashing light which is perceptible without instruments more than 200 feet from the boundaries of the lot in question, except for warning devices, construction or maintenance work, or other special circumstances.

5. The use will not cause continued erosion of the land or increased surface drainage from the lot.

6. No pollution of the water or the air will result which is greater than that caused by a use which is allowed without a special permit.

7. No temporary or mobile structures not otherwise permitted under this bylaw will be used or stored, except if incidental to a fair, a special event, or a construction project, and then only if for no more than 60 days.

8. Where possible, the site design will preserve and enhance existing trees over 12 inch caliper, water courses, hills, and other natural features, as well as vistas, ocean views, and historic locations, and will minimize the intrusion into the character of existing development.

Throughout the town, then, a few listed uses are automatically allowed, while any other is permitted if it meets the listed performance standards. The list includes most of the items likely to be a problem in a town such as Gay Head, given wetlands, health, and air pollution controls adopted at the state level.

Traditional zoning by named category of use was largely abandoned in favor of flexible and uniform controls on performance and density. Rather than developing any concentrated commercial areas, the town might continue with its mix of use at low densities.

Some Comments

Some of the rules deserve comment.

Rule #1 limits the density of traffic generated by any single non-residential lot to the average traffic densities generated by town houses or apartments at 15 to 20 units to the acre. Yet an intensive traffic generator of any size is allowable, so long as enough land is reserved along with it. Baltimore County has been working on a somewhat parallel approach, though vastly more complex.[2] The Franklin County studies provided some data for the estimates of traffic generation, and current Dukes County studies may provide more.

The town would have preferred to include the word "noise" in Rule #4; but it was dropped on advice of town counsel because of a recent adverse ruling in a Massachusetts court.

Rule #8 has, subsequent to adoption, been buttressed by publication and wide endorsement of a study of the visual landscape, *Looking at the Vineyard*, sponsored by the Vineyard Open Land Foundation, which provides a datum and more operational guidelines for the esthetic intent of the rule.[3]

The nature of the development pattern in the town, and the operational simplicity of the rules (save, perhaps, the traffic estimates in #1 and the generalities in #8) made it seem that the number of special permits required would be small, and that the required decisions would be simple ones. In fact, no applications have yet been made under this section.

The second unusual feature of the bylaw is a provision for the special review of large developments, which are defined by thresholds on the total floor area or the number of lots (over 10,000 square feet, or 3 lots). That an off-island developer may one day, without warning, open up an extensive second-home subdivision in the town is one of the town's persistent fears. Yet the town cannot prevent that development if it meets all legal requirements. Therefore, a review process was provided, using a version of the now-familiar environmental impact statement. The review will give the town some early warning, while slowing down the development process. It is designed to open the process to public view, and to allow town officials or town citizens to urge changes, or to bring pressure to bear. Before a large development can be approved, a developer is required to submit detailed site plans, plus an impact statement covering the probable effects of the development on the following points:

1. attendance at public schools;
2. increases in vehicular traffic;
3. changes in the number of legal residents;
4. provision of housing for Town residents and for persons of low and moderate income;
5. increases in municipal service costs;
6. load on public utilities or future demands for them;
7. public safety;
8. changes in tax revenues;
9. changes in surface drainage;
10. increased consumption of ground water;
11. increased refuse disposal;
12. pollution of water or air;
13. land erosion or loss of tree cover;
14. disturbance to other aspects of the natural ecology;
15. blocking of views;
16. harmony with the character of surrounding development.

Cluster development may also be permitted under this same procedure. The impact statement and its review is simply an advisory process: one might even comment that it is "zoning by bluff." The town cannot stop large developments which follow the stated rules, although that would have been the town's intent. The control of the *rate* of development, and its scale, are surely the critical items here, but it is not apparent that present Massachusetts zoning enabling legislation can yet be stretched so far. (The proposed new Dukes County Land Management Act will, however, if passed by the legislature, empower a county-wide commission to put special controls on large projects.)

Experience and Evaluation

There has been little experience in Gay Head to date, by which to evaluate the new bylaw. There was the expected flurry of land subdivision and building starts just prior to its enactment, and some normal permits were granted in 1973. While one routine variance has been acted on, nothing has yet happened to test the new features of the law.

Indeed, the principal test has been that of organizing a permit and appeal process in such a small town so unused to land regulation. Making that process orderly, and containing the conflict between summer and winter people, will occupy the town's attention and, at least for the time, obscure the particular effects of the bylaw itself. The bylaw has made no immediate detectable difference, except that it may be changing the expectations of residents and builders. It is widely known in the region as an innovative bylaw.[4] Most likely, it has already dissuaded some developer somewhere from moving in on the town.

The one-district feature of the bylaw, based on performance standards, may be useful as an approach for other small rural towns, where the pattern of development is still fluid and the nature of development not likely to be complex. A normal zoning map implies that the pattern of future land use is predictable and offers psychological comforts which this approach cannot give. Some state officials have opposed the Franklin County model on the grounds that it represents an abdication from planning and from providing predictability.

But amendments, variances, and administrative lapses make the definitiveness and predictability of conventional zoning maps more apparent than real. The one-district performance rule bylaw has substantial advantages of flexibility (since it responds to changing demand and to local condition), equity (since all locations are treated alike, and not by rules which vary sharply across district boundaries), and clarity (since the bases for regulation are directly stated, not buried in the assumptions which lie behind the land use rules). Since the performance reasoning is openly avowed, it is easier to judge effectiveness and to make improvements.

In more complicated localities, this approach to zoning would probably have to be improvised with some simpler form of districting. Densities and performance rules, for example, might be varied between districts. The rules themselves would have to be carefully considered, to see that they covered the items of concern without being so complex that their administration would be cumbersome or capricious. Clinton, Massachusetts, an industrial town of 13,000 population, developed such a hybrid in 1972, by adopting a two-district performance rule bylaw as its original zoning. A computer simulation has demonstrated that the operation of a conventional five-district bylaw adopted by suburban Blackstone can be approximately replicated by a relatively short set of performance rules, though that would not be the case with all such bylaws.

The impact statement is by now a familiar device at state and national levels, and was here simply brought down to the local level. It will be useful in opening up the development process to citizen review, as has occurred in hearings at higher levels. It will force developers to consider impacts often ignored. But it will also jam the decision process unless it is confined to particularly critical classes of decision.

The sixteen points listed in the Gay Head bylaw describe the town's concerns, and call for information in a form easily read by a local board. They suggest to the developer how to be well received. The list doesn't, of course, tell the developer how to resolve the conflicts: for example, how to provide low- and moderate-income housing, the need for which is widely recognized on the island, and at the same time show a positive fiscal effect and a low impact on schools and traffic. Nor does it make the town's perplexities entirely clear: summer homes, despite their fiscal attractiveness and importance to the economy, are the form of development felt to be out of hand, growing too fast. Yet it is precisely because the required statements are only informative, only the subject of advice, that they can comfortably encompass the town's uncertainties. As experience accumulates, these and other factors may be converted to performance rules, or weighted for use in a cost-benefit calculation.

But until we know more, the problems remain. We don't wish to write zoning which precludes all uses which are fiscally disadvantageous, such as low-income housing, or even all those which are large and therefore large consumers of ground water, road capacity, and schools.

A special permit approach would be strikingly parallel to current land-control legislation in Vermont and elsewhere, where large-scale development is subject to regional or state review, based on non-location-specific performance criteria. A body of experience is now being accumulated at higher government levels on land control without districts, but with required impact studies and with performance rules. Proposed Massachusetts legislation would create a similar system for all of Martha's Vineyard.

Useful as it will undoubtedly be, the new zoning bylaw is not a fundamental solution for a town as threatened as Gay Head. Until the quality, rate, and scale of development can be regulated, preferably at a regional level, and land ownership can be kept out of speculative hands or its speculative profits siphoned off, the peculiar and attractive qualities of this town may yet succumb to the tidal wave of summer houses. Beyond the town's reach, these larger battles will be fought out in Congress and in the legislature of Massachusetts.

References

1. Philip B. Herr and Associates, *Performance Zoning II*. Franklin County, Massachusetts, June 1972.

2. Jacob Kaminsky, *Environmental Characteristics Planning*. Regional Planning Council, Baltimore, 1972.

3. Kevin Lynch and Sasaki, Dawson and Demay Associates, Inc., *Looking At the Vineyard*. Vineyard Open Land Foundation, 1978.

4. David Vickery, "A Computer Program to Aid in the Evaluation of Development Controls." Master's thesis, MIT, 1973.

University Circle Area Planning Project, Cleveland (1957)

Completed in 1957, the master plan for the University Circle area in Cleveland was one of the earliest professional projects of Kevin Lynch. As a key member of the Cambridge-based Adams, Howard and Greeley planning consulting team, he was instrumental in developing the physical planning and design concepts for the future development of a major urban institutional complex situated on a 488-acre site.

Located only four miles from downtown Cleveland, the University Circle area includes Western Reserve University, the Case Institute of Technology, the University Hospitals, the Cleveland Museum of Art, the Musical Arts Association, the Cleveland Museum of Natural History, the Western Reserve Historical Society, the Cleveland Institute of Music, the Cleveland Institute of Art, Benjamin Rose Hospital, the Academy of Medicine, Mount Sinai Hospital, and several important churches. When the study was initiated, the universities were expected to double their size in twenty years, the hospitals and other institutions were expected to have much larger staffs during that time, and in general a much greater demand for cultural activities was expected from a growing leisure-oriented population. All of this presaged demands for additional space and parking from various institutions within the complex. Efficient and safe circulation of cars and people, and appropriate locational linkages between various institutions and facilities, were seen as important. Above all, it was believed that the complex should function as a "total unit" symbolizing a model "cultural center" for urban America.

After working out various space standards and requirements, the plan recommended development of the University Circle area in two distinct but linked areas: an academic-medical complex, and a public-oriented leisure-activity zone consisting of museums, performance centers, parks, and gardens. A small core area with common facilities, strategically located between these two areas, was seen as the main link. In addition, a pedestrian network organized around two principal axes was to provide linkage and unity. The plan also stressed strategies for maintaining visual continuity and harmony over the long-term development of the area.

We have selected two sections from the plan that reflect Kevin Lynch's distinctive contribution to its development. One of these sections is about the theoretical performance criteria for the physical planning and design of the campus. The other has to do with the more specific and tangible design strategies for organizing the physical form of the complex. Few contemporary physical-planning reports could match the strategic design thinking expressed in these passages.

These passages were written only a few years after Lynch's travels in Europe, and shortly before *The Image of the City* was published. Thus, one wonders whether his use of "pathways" and "nodes" to strengthen the visual form of a developing campus was not really an advance notice of his seminal work on city form, and whether his prescriptions for locating buildings along a pedestrian axis in a "sweeping curve" were not influenced by his experiences in Bath and Venice, and whether his design linking two parts of a campus by means of a pedestrian bridge over a major arterial road were not a distant echo of Ponte Vecchio in Florence, which he had studied so intently.

The following is reprinted by permission of University Circle Inc.

If a distinctive, harmonious institutional center is to emerge at University Circle, functional and aesthetic considerations are just as important as the satisfaction of quantitative space needs. An effective environment will not only be of sufficient size that each activity can grow without interference; it will be rationally arranged, and it will also be beautiful, full of sensory experiences ranging from excitement to repose.

The cultural center, conceived as a total unit, can become a powerful symbol for urban America of the future. Leisure time and the growing importance of education will make the cultural center a major activity core for the metropolitan area. As a physical entity in which people "enjoy" the city, it can fulfill a function similar to [that of] the cathedral squares of medieval times or the village greens of 18th century New England. Such an area can provide essential experiences which are impossible to achieve in the helter-skelter, formless development of contemporary cities. University Circle, in becoming this kind of cultural center, will set an example for other cities.

If the long-range plan is to guide development toward this aim, it must be based on certain fundamental principles. These are the tests by which the ultimate quality of the plan may be judged:

1. Each pair of activities which are functionally linked should also be connected in their physical locations. Activities which have substantial student flows between them at class time, for example, should be within easy walking distance. If spontaneous contacts between professionals are vital, then separations between activities should shrink down to even smaller distances. In other cases, the linkages may be served by supply movements, access for visitors, infrequent special servicing, or emergency patient movements. Since there is always competition for the most highly accessible places, the plan will reflect the relative value of these connections. This principle is the touchstone of a good arrangement.

2. As an extension of this principle, it is important, not only to provide for existing linkages, but also to encourage the development of new, desired ones. Thus one of the prime advantages of a good plan will be to bring about meeting and communication between isolated professionals. Each group now tends to move in a close, self-contained world. The physical environment should encourage links between doctor and engineer, physicist and painter, historian and minister. Similarly, a far greater use by the general public should be encouraged, not only of the public museums, but also of other facilities: in postgraduate education, art, health, and technology. Clear access points are needed and increased emphasis on activities for general participation is required. The people of Cleveland must be invited into the area, so they may become aware of the vast new possibilities of knowledge and pleasure that are opening to them.

3. Adequate circulation is a basic functional requirement. Each activity must be adequately serviced by internal roads, and the whole complex must be accessible to the great flood of metropolitan traffic that will eventually be directed to it. Both automobile ways and transit connections must be as effective as possible. On arrival, there must be an efficient distributing system that will sort out people to their final destinations. Within University Circle, a system of pedestrian ways should permit walking from sector to sector with ease and without hazard.

Because of the location of University Circle in relation to the city, and particularly because accessibility for cars must be kept high, through traffic cannot be eliminated from the cultural zone. Disadvantages of noise, fumes, and potential hazards arise from this. These disadvantages may be minimized by routings, or by lowering the level of pavements with proper pedestrian bridges above the roadway.

Large open parking areas, which are likely to destroy any vestige of environment quality, would preferably be located at the fringe, with internal land left for building sites and open space. Fringe parking can also serve as a cushion for future expansion. Internal parking should only be provided in small, intensive, controlled areas, as in parking ramps or underground sites.

4. Each major activity must have space to meet its presently foreseen needs, and in addition have a direction open for the unforeseen future growth that is bound to come. Past experience shows that urban institutions invariably underestimate their ultimate growth requirements. This is a twenty-year plan, but expansion will not cease in 1977. Each major function, therefore, should have at one side a region of vacuum or low pressure, into which it can some day grow without interfering with the operations of any other major function. Parking zones, open athletic fields, or temporarily conserved regions of older housing can all serve this purpose. Flexibility in general is an essential quality, and yet most difficult to achieve in an area as complex as this, built up over a long period of time. Initial open spaces, the preservation of axes of growth, and the erection of general-purpose buildings where possible all help to retain this elusive quality.

If University Circle is to play its role as metropolitan center of culture it must be outstanding visually as well as functionally. It must present itself as the symbol of the values it stands for; it must make a sharp and unforgettable image for both inhabitant and visitor alike. This means that it should be unique, and also harmonious within itself, united in one whole in a way that is evident to the senses.

This does not require such mechanical devices as uniform roof lines or keeping all buildings in some predetermined style. Such rules would fail of their end in a complicated area, and as long as they were adhered to, would only be a source of frustration to future designers. Use can rather be made of devices such as dominant foci, ordered open spaces, or continuous pathways, which bring together the whole in a meaningful way, without attempting to dictate the exact form of future parts, and without suppressing the identity of individual institutions.

6. Finally, and by no means least of all, the future University Circle should be a delight to see and to be in. This is a simple and straightforward requirement, no less important than traffic or sunlight. It is a result of many things: landscaping, the play of spaces, textures and colors of walls and ground surface, mass and scale of buildings, and many others. The general plan can insure some of this; in particular it can promote a positive visual use of the open spaces between buildings, and can set the key for

landscaping or ground textures. Also much depends on the design of future buildings and details. To insure excellent physical form each new project should be conceived in relation to the surrounding structures and open spaces; its architectural quality analyzed from every side, "rear" as well as "front." This will necessarily be a constant concern of the institutions in University Circle, and of any continuing planning staff. The Fine Arts Garden is an outstanding example of what can be done: of the beauty that can be created, and of the everyday joy it gives to those who walk through it. Unfortunately, this Garden now stands alone in the area.

The Physical Form

[The] chief determinant of University Circle's distinctiveness as a cultural center will be its physical form. Design of individual structures and open spaces is the province of architects commissioned for special projects, but an overall form concept, governing the basic pattern of open space and building type, can only be established while considering the area as a whole.

Such a form concept is essential if University Circle is to have a distinctive, unified visual character. At the same time, such a concept cannot be achieved by imposing formal, balanced compositions or detailed building shapes on long-range future development. Future needs cannot be foreseen in detail, and a region such as this is too complex in its function ever to fit in any force-ordained architectural bed. The past history of campus designs is strewn with the wreckage of long-range but rigid site plans.

We face a new kind of problem, therefore: how to gain continuity and harmonious character over a long period of development, without sacrificing that flexibility to meet new demands in the future. We propose that this be done by setting guides for the general shape and character of such characteristics as use, pathways, nodal points, density, and three-dimensional open space.

The two major use clusters would be defined and organized by the character of their activity, the surrounding roads, and the major open spaces. The leisure-time area would enclose the large central open space of Wade Park, which could provide a single setting for the diverse public buildings. This open space should be developed to the pitch of landscape excellence exemplified by the Fine Arts Garden. The academic-medical area, also a region of inter-dependent use, would have just the opposite shape: a solid center of structures and activities, clearly marked off by the loop road, or by such large unbuilt-on areas as the new park in the Stearns Road region, the Fine Arts Garden, and the Western Reserve athletic fields to the west.

The Pathways

A system of pedestrian pathways whose lie and visual character would be set and preserved from the beginning would run through these two large forms, and interconnect them with each other and with surrounding area. This system is shown in the figure. These pathways or "greenways" would have various characters, so that each is distinct from the other. In time the paths would stand in clear contrast to the denser development through which they pass. Among these distinctive paths should occur a whole sequence of exciting visual experiences: small space openings, gardens, sculpture.

One basic element of this pathway system would be the north-south mall, running from the bluff under the Christian Science church, along the present lie of Cornell Road, across Euclid without interruption, and through the Reserve north campus to Wade Park. This formal axis, passing through medical, housing, academic, and cultural areas, would thus connect two important natural features of the site. A second basic part of this system would be the curving line of contrasting character, which would begin at the Rapid station, cross the railroad, pass through Case and alongside the Reserve Science Center and the University Hospitals, cross Euclid on the landscaped plaza at the common core, and sweep through the Reserve north campus in a great arc paralleling the line of the loop road. Through much of its length, it would pass along or under elevated buildings. On the north of Euclid, the greenway would have functional as well as visual or circulation aspects, being intended as the locus of general-purpose classrooms and offices.

It would be vital, if the pathways were to be effective, that not only their line but also their visual character be carefully preserved and regulated. The greenway through the Reserve north campus would be particularly important in this respect, since it encompasses a broad belt of structures rather than a relatively narrow path. As a suggestion for limitations that might be put upon individual designers in this particular zone, we recommend the following:

a) all structures to be long and narrow rectangular masses, not over three stories in height or over 50 feet in width, and with a minimum of 25% of their ground floor left open for passage or view;

b) buildings to be oriented generally perpendicular to the curving axis of the greenway, and to reach more or less across the width of the zone;

c) departure from these limitations, where necessary, to be confined to minor structures not over one story in height.

d) F.A.R. to be kept below 0.5, and no two major buildings to be placed closer than 200 feet apart.

e) buildings in this zone to be designed for classroom, office, or other activity which uses rather flexible, standardized space; and

f) particular attention to be given, in the design of an individual building in this group, to preserving a sense of unity in the group as a whole by the use of harmonizing materials and colors, similar fenestration patterns, harmonious roof lines, and similar bay sizes, and by careful consideration of the pattern of the exterior spaces. Within these limits, the design and style of successive buildings might vary substantially.

Nodes and Spaces

In addition to the pathway system, strong nodes, or cores of heightened activity, should occur at several points in the area. These would be distinctive places, the condensation points to which the areas around them can relate. Such nodes are the suggested core area between East Boulevard and Euclid, with its services for institutional personnel, the small pedestrian "square" in the Fine Arts court in the northwest corner of the Western Reserve campus, or the terrace on the Case campus, overlooking Rockefeller Park. Like the pathways, these nodal areas would also be located and designed from the beginning.

The density provisions of the plan would serve a functional purpose as outlined above, but would also have aesthetic results. Uniform general densities throughout the north campus, for example, can in the end tend to support the basic harmony desired. Both building heights and the distribution and character of minor open spaces are tremendously important if one wishes to weave a common visual texture.

Thus it may be necessary to lay down common suggestive regulations, not only for floor area ratio and building height, but also for the general character of open ground space desired: for example to recommend generous use of courtyards of a certain range of proportions. Such ideas remain to be worked out in the further development of the plan.

At any rate, we must emphasize that small landscaped areas are essential to good visual character. They set off the buildings, are the intimate places where one can take one's ease, and provide good visual contrast to the larger spaces such as a greenway or a Fine Arts Garden. These smaller spaces are particularly important in association with classrooms, laboratories, and hospital facilities.

Planting, Signs, and Details

Still another means can be used to give University Circle its own proper character, distinct from its surroundings and harmonious within itself. This may be done by the design and control of landscaping, exterior details, and the sign and other elements of communication. Thus a common policy as to the types of trees to be used in the area can give a sense of visual

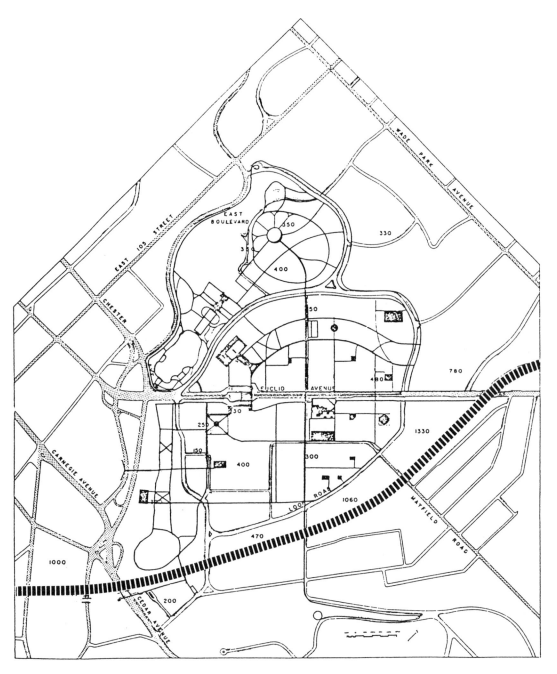

PROPOSED CIRCULATION

PEDESTRIAN WAYS AND SPACES

THROUGH ROADS

LOOP ROAD

U N I V E R S I T Y   C I R C L E

AREA PLANNING PROJECT

CLEVELAND OHIO   AUGUST 1957

ADAMS   HOWARD & GREELEY
AND   ANDERSON   BECKWITH
& HAIBLE   CONSULTANTS

unity. The whole area or parts of it may be designated as having a common texture of planting: dominated by tall columnar forest trees, for example, or dotted with lacy groves of birch, or marked by the mottled bark of the sycamore. A coordinated landscape plan is an important part of the overall design that should be developed.

Similar attention should be given to exterior details: the material and texture of paved surfaces, for example, which may recur throughout the area, and the design of such street furniture as benches, lamp standards, and waste containers.

A critical kind of detail which receives a disproportionate amount of attention and thus speaks loudly of the character of an area to a visitor, are the signs and other elements of visual communication. The size and style of all signs in University Circle should be designed as a single group, [with] a controlled use made of lettering, color, and form to symbolize the location of various functions. This shaping of the forms of communication might also go over into the layout of maps and publicity. All such means, if carefully handled with professional help, are instrumental both in explaining and [in] orienting the area, making clear the rich resources which it has for the potential user and impressing him with the unity and style of the whole.

By controlling use, certain paths and nodal points, density, open space, planting, and signs, we can impose on future development a general harmony, without dictating precise forms for activities which cannot be predicted with equal precision. Within this general framework, new structures of highly varied shape and setting can fit without disruption. It should be repeated again, of course, that while such action will help to create overall unities, total visual character is equally dependent on the individual excellence of particular architectural and landscape design, now and in the future.

The Rio Salado Development Plan (1985)

This project represents the last major professional involvement of Kevin Lynch. His firm was retained to prepare a development plan for the flood plains of the Salt River, which runs through the middle of the Phoenix metropolitan area as a shallow but wide (1–3 miles) wash. Although dry most of the time, this barren and neglected wasteland undergoes periodic flooding, which allows very little productive use of its shores other than for sand and gravel mining.

The Arizona legislature created the Rio Salado Development District and gave an authority the responsibility for changing the essential character of the Salt River so that it could serve a more effective and productive purpose in the development of the Phoenix metropolitan area. Although the financial, political, and technical prospects of constructing flood-control devices and the other improvements needed to change the character of the river corridor were uncertain, the authority invited the consulting team to prepare development proposals for the river corridor.

Although Stephen Carr was the project director, Kevin Lynch was very much involved in the development of design ideas. What is particularly significant about this project is that it was a truly collaborative design effort, involving not only Carr/Lynch Associates but also many other professionals assembled by them. Gary Hack and Misty Canto have described parts of the design process in their article "Collaboration and Context in Urban Design" (*Design Studies* 5, no. 9 [1984]: 178–184, copyright 1984 Butterworth & Co. Ltd.; excerpts in the following pages are reprinted with permission).

This may have been the only instance where a taped record of discussions involving various aspects of the design process in which

Kevin Lynch participated was kept. In the article cited above, Hack and Canto use segments of these conversations as exemplars of how collaborative design processes evolve through the resolution of conflicts and contradictions. The following transcripts of some of the taped conversation, reproduced from their article, show the critical role Kevin Lynch played as a senior designer, and his role in the group dynamics and in influencing conflict resolution.

Lynch was influential in the exploration of ideas about the future possibilities for the river. When a flood control expert (CB) expressed his preference for an uninterrupted channel to handle 100-year floods, the following interchange occurred:

KL: You could have lakes in the channel. Not ground water lakes but you could . . .

CB: The problem is—let me explain this clearly . . . What happens with other lakes in this kind of situation is that a lake is like a shotgun. The water comes in very strongly with intense magnitude, and then dissipates. And once it dissipates all the transported material falls out of the transporting flow and just settles . . .

KL: But excuse me. But if you have a big channel the water's not coming in with heavy force. It is only coming in at several hundred cubic feet per second.

CB: But it's flowing.

KL: But that's similar to what's happening in Indian Bend Wash.

Later, when those charged with exploring the overall image of the Salt River and its connection to the day-to-day experience of the Phoenix residents presented the idea of a great green oasis in the middle of the desert landscape, Lynch resisted the conventionality of that idea:

KL: But I think of having the desert in the city . . .

SW (events planner): And having that oasis . . .

KL: Yeah . . .

SW: And I think one thing I like is that this is the oasis for the whole town. This is our special place. I think it has to be special. I think what we are talking about is this special place.

SC (project director): The only problem with the "oasis" is that most people won't think of it as different, even though there aren't many places where they can be.

KL: Uh hum.

SW: And maybe nodes of high intensity with connectors of re-creation . . . but they are going to have to be able to see the water coming . . .

KL: . . . Tidal waves going down the river (laughter), I mean that is more odd . . . The largest safeguard . . .

SC: . . . The channel running ahead . . .

KL: White water . . . how about white water?

SC: Somebody suggested maybe one of the things we ought to do is find a way of celebrating the floods when they come!

As the discussion progressed, new ideas emerged, Lynch providing pivotal ideas along the way:

CB: The main flow channel, the primary flow channel over there has landscape and trees. It has a very thick flow and it has an upward tilt.

SW: I was going to ask you about what they did in Turtle Creek in Dallas; where they have hung onto the streets, some of the main flow goes into the tunnel . . . Have you seen anything like that?

CB: No, not around this scale?

KL: Yeah, um hum . . .

SW: Not in that configuration?

CB: Most of the water—if we look at the section—in the channel is not ground water. For flooding, the channel is full of rip-rap . . . The lake could be created from the ground water . . .

KL: And the water coming down into the lake can come down in a fall . . . a waterfall! . . .

SC: Which is OK!

The discussion led to a new concept, stripped of earlier conventionalities, of a broad flood channel with armored edges, landscaped with desert plants and embellished with falls and lakes fed by groundwater pumped to the surface:

CB: Even there you could put in small channels and widen them and expect a washout of landscape and the cost would be minimal. You might be talking cost of . . .

KL: Uhmm . . . I say, I am much attracted to the idea of another world down there, a linear world within a great big city and wild desert life which has golf courses in it—unfenced courses because you have got this bank. You can let cattle and horses run free. The image in my mind is of a . . . (the group is laughing) . . . I am riding through there, you know (louder laughing) . . .

SW: He is really down in there!

The discussions ultimately led to two broad alternative schemes for the river: an "intensely developed braided river landscape periodically widening into small lakes with rapids and white water" and a "dry but rather lush desert landscape capable of regenerating itself after major floods." Both of these ideas were subtly introduced by Lynch. Although the project staff agreed on these ideas, there was some uncertainty as to how to "sell" them in the face of a strong predilection for a green park:

> *SC: You know that grand design with big lakes and so on had the virtue of being something that people could really image and say, "Wow"!*
>
> *KL: That is OK. But don't forget, the idea of good image and so on doesn't have to be big lakes.*
>
> *SC: No. I am not saying that . . .*
>
> *KL: That's their grand image now. That is what has a lot of power.*
>
> *TM (senior economist): Yeah. But it's a powerful image and it's environment. But then . . . look at Central Park. Look at any of the major urban parks and the kind of development they typically get next to them.*
>
> *SW: But Central Park is to be contrasted . . . This is never going to be Central Park . . .*
>
> *KL: Yeah. But that is what is in their minds at the moment. They are thinking of parks . . . "*

These excerpts are indicative of Kevin Lynch's vivid imagination, his visions for creating unique and unconventional human experiences that can be memorable and stimulating, his affection for nature in the raw, and his gentle but persuasive abilities to direct creative thinking. The following text is reprinted by courtesy of Carr/Lynch Associates, Cambridge, Massachusetts.

Summary

The Rio Salado Development District runs for 40 miles along the dry riverbed, from which it derives its name, through the heart of metropolitan Phoenix. It passes through several political jurisdictions: the cities of Phoenix, Mesa, and Tempe, Maricopa County, and the Salt-River, Pima-Maricopa, and Gila River Indian Communities.

The District was created as an official planning and development area by the State Legislature to bring to life and productive use what is now, with the exception of productive sand and gravel mining, a dry, empty scar. The District Board of Directors has been charged with developing a Master Plan for the reclamation of this area.

Occasionally, a city has been able to convert a waste land into a fine recreational landscape. One thinks of San Francisco's Golden Gate Park, New York's Central Park, or Scottsdale's Indian Bend Wash. To have that opportunity on such a scale that the conversion will actually reverse the development of the entire city, as well as convert the waste land itself, is an extremely rare event. The Phoenix area has this opportunity on [a] gigantic scale. The conversion of this broad expanse into a park and water landscape can literally turn the metropolis inside out.

This astonishing redirection of the Rio Salado will draw vigorous new development to its edges. It can also show how the careful use and re-use of water in an arid land sustains and enriches life.

The change will not come easily. It will require a long, intricate ballet of coordinated public and private moves: engineering works, landscaping, planning, development, land acquisition, water management, financing, institutional and legislative changes, and sharp shifts in public attitude. But what a magnificent spectacle that ballet can produce!

This Master Plan document is presented as a guiding vision for the development of the Rio Salado. It serves as a policy guide for an extended sequence of actions. It lays out a strategy of action: where and how to begin, what forces to assemble to set the whole in motion, and how to move from phase to phase. The results at each stage of development will be sufficiently attractive to motivate the continuing effort. And yet the plan keeps the future open by explaining which actions to take and which to avoid, in order to prevent the loss of desirable future options.

This work is purposefully general and makes proposals for only that portion of the District which is likely to develop within 25 years. As implementation proceeds, additional, more detailed plans and studies will be required before various elements can be realized.

Highlights

This Master Plan involves a major reclamation of nearly 10,000 acres of land, including transformation of the present riverbed into a continuous regional park, and intensive development of its banks for industry, housing, recreation, tourism, and cultural and education uses. Reclamation depends on the construction of additional upstream flood control, which would reduce the predicted 100-year flood to no more than 55,000 cubic feet per second (cfs). This control will be provided by the Central Arizona Water Control Study (CAWCS) Plan 6, the financing of which is now under study. Cost for this work has not been included since that information is not yet available. However, the cost for this additional flood protection will be substantial, and this expenditure will be necessary if the Rio Salado Plan is to be fully implemented.

This plan provides that the riverbed be transformed into a chain of narrow lakes, connected with drops and brief rapids, all set in a grassy bed

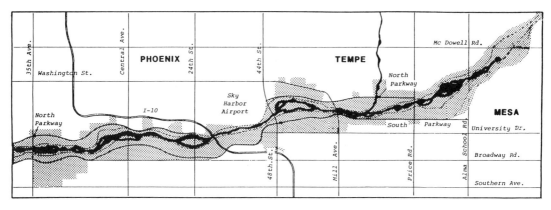

Rio Salado development district.

and enriched with lush low water planting along the waterways. The riverbed will become a continuous regional park, and [will] support many diverse recreational activities, including swimming, fishing, camping, horseback riding, cycling, picnicking, small boat sailing on the larger lakes, golf, and organized sports. It will also feature clusters of planted islands and a canoeway. The banks on either side will be intensely developed, within two flanking parkways. [The accompanying figure] is an overview of these features.

Various special elements of this plan are described in detail below. They include:

a special mix of industry, housing and recreation;

a continuing education and conference center near ASU;

a "water garden" associated with special new museums;

a new Southwest Cultural Center;

a possible national or international Exposition;

a desert arboretum;

future new urban settlement extending to the west;

lakes for boating and swimming;

campgrounds;

"white water" rapids;

equestrian trails;

archaeological and historic sites;

and many other associated features.

Physical Image

This plan assumes that the additional upstream flood control will be in place within ten years, and that subsequent development will have to deal with a flood of no more than 55,000 cfs. The plan shows the eventual conversion of the floodway into a long succession of narrow, interlacing lakes, for the most part one-quarter to one mile long, linked by a continuous boating waterway. Drop structures would occur about every two miles, as shown on the plan, but in two locations, below 7th Avenue and between Mesa and the Mill Avenue Bridge, the slope of the river allows a longer length of quiet water. At each drop, the waterway would pass through rapids, which could be attractive features for those who enjoy white water boating.

Lakes and waterways pass alongside or among clusters of small planted islands, in a grassy bed, and within planted banks which are gentle or steep depending on the width of the waterway. In a new and more dramatic form, these lakes and islands recall the old braided stream. Trees border the lakes, and desert plants create a new landscape in the streambed. The Rio Salado flows again, using a minimum of water and affording multiple new recreational opportunities. Most of 17 miles of riverbed (4,085 acres) is devoted to recreation: swimming, boating, fishing, picnicking, camping, hiking, riding, and field sports. A shallow, grassed low-flow channel protects lakes or sensitive planting where necessary. It can take urban run-off and up to 15,000 cfs of water, the normal five-year flood.

Paralleling the riverbed are two curving parkways—generally within 1,000 to 2,500 feet of the streambed on the south side and rather closer on the north—within which the District or other public agencies will have acquired most of the land, and where the new riverside development gradually unfolds. The southern parkway is continuous, from 35th Avenue to Alma School Road, while the northern road is interrupted by the airport. The southern bank is less affected by noise, has more generous space available, and can more easily be connected to a residential hinterland.

Above Country Club Drive, within the Indian community, the Rio Salado is shaped into a broad sedimentation basin in which flow velocities are sufficiently reduced that the water will drop its load of silt, sand, and gravel, and so will not damage the lakes and plantings located downstream. This basin will be an extended landscape, clothed in native desert plants, in places mined for the retained sand and gravel, but for the most [part] a wildlife refuge, open to camping and horseback riding.

Below the wide drop structure of this retention basin, the streambed can be planted with grass. The first large lake occurs at Alma School Road.

It lies wholly within the Indian Community, and is open to recreational use on a fee basis. Effluent from the expanded Dobson Road sewage plant in Mesa feeds that first lake, after undergoing tertiary treatment. South of this lake and its borders within the city of Mesa is low density residence, a resort hotel, a new Mesa public golf course, and industrial development along the Price/Pima Freeway. North of it, the land is given over to sand and gravel mining and industry, in accord with present Indian plans. The area within the City of Mesa between Country Club Drive and Granite Reef Dam will be the subject of additional planning immediately following the approval of a permanent financing vehicle for the District.

At McClintock Drive, we arrive at the historic, picturesque location where the Buttes and the Indian Bend Wash join the Rio Salado, across from Arizona State University. On the south, ASU will build its new golf course.

At the junction with Indian Bend Wash, the largest lake in the Rio Salado system provides a sheet of water a mile and a half long. It will be used for swimming, fishing, and boating. The Wash itself is complete with a stream and small lakes to its junction with the Rio Salado. This junction would be marked by a monument or observation tower set on an artificial elevation. Large rock formations cross the streambed along the course of the reef of bedrock, just below the surface. By its history and its geology this is a unique location along the river. Development of this site will depend upon the satisfactory completion of a detailed investigation of its hydrological condition.

Just south of Papago Park and the old Indian Bend Canal, recreational facilities and restaurants may locate along the north bank of the Rio Salado. To the east, between Scottsdale Rd. and Indian Bend Wash, on what is now an unincorporated county island, there would be a hotel with conference facilities that could serve activities related to ASU. Such a development might also include recreational features. This facility would allow the University to house visiting scholars and guests and provide room for those attending alumni events, symposiums, special courses, and conferences. Nearby offices could rent meeting rooms for their own special conferences and briefings. North of this complex, additional new townhouse developments are anticipated.

On the east bank of the Indian Bend Wash, a special mix of industry, recreation, and housing would develop. It would have connections to Arizona State University, to the entertainment and resort functions along Hayden Road and further north in Scottsdale, and to the high technology industry developing around the airport.

Development at Mill Avenue in Tempe should take advantage of the elevation of the Tempe Butte. The site should be evaluated for its value to the community for its research, education, and tourist potential. Pilot

Project No. 4 of the Tempe Rio Salado Plan should be evaluated for inclusion here. A downtown commerical revitalization area will include at least one major new hotel at this point. The old Tempe Bridge may be renovated to carry pedestrians to the center to look out over the lakes or to reach the north side.

Below the bridges at Mill Avenue, the river opens into a broad expanse, filled with a dense cluster of islands and interlacing lakes. Here we are under the noisy approach zone of the airport, and so this stretch will be devoted to a park and a golf course within the islands. North of this, between Mill Avenue and the airport in Phoenix, the area along Washington Street will be dominated by a mix of industry, offices, and commercial ventures. This is an area already under development, and subject to high airplane noise.

Once past the Mill Avenue bridges, a continuous band of new development on the south bank begins, between [the] parkway and the river, which will extend to 35th Avenue and beyond. Along Priest Drive, development is devoted to industry, an equestrian center, and a clubhouse for the golf course which lies in the streambed below.

Moving westward along this southern line, the industrial and office uses begin to be mixed with housing, once I-10 is crossed and the airport noise diminishes. Described in more detail in the section on New Development, this is a blend of residence, work place, and recreation. This mix extends to the new Rio Salado Industrial Recreational Park and proposed park golf course at 12th Street, and through it, connects to the special uses at Central Avenue.

At 24th Street, the river broadens to form a large new island, occupied by offices, high density housing, and one or more hotels. This will be a prestige location [and a] principal event along the course of the river. The development is centered on a public pedestrian spine which can be expected to include retail and recreational uses. At both ends of the island are public parks.

At 7th Street and Central Avenue, we approach the existing new industrial development on the north, and the river is confined between steep banks. But it still sports lakes and a waterway on a grassy bottom, all part of the continuous regional park. On the north bank, an effort will be made to strengthen and preserve the existing neighborhood between 12th and 16th Streets.

At Central Avenue, one of key features of the plan occurs on the south bank of the Rio in the form of an island which stretches from 7th Street to 7th Avenue.

Coming from downtown Phoenix, crossing the bridge over the new lake in the riverbed, the magisterial entrance to the island is marked by high jet fountains. Shaded promenades and lookout points along the north edge of the island will provide a view of downtown and uptown

Phoenix. Another, more narrow lake along the southern edge of the island creates a southern approach to this special place. Boats will shuttle between stations, connecting the southern island promenade to parking and attractions on the South Phoenix shore.

All along the central pedestrian spine of the island a series of "water events" are connected by waterways running under lath-roofed arcades. On one end, this pedestrian axis will lead to an open amphitheater for public festivities and concerts. The other tip of the island will be occupied by a discovery museum for children. A special watergarden at the junction with Central Avenue will provide freshness and shade.

Like the "Ile de la Cite" in Paris and the "Isola Tiberina" in Rome, this island will bridge the gap between north and south Phoenix. It will attract a variety of public institutions, special industries, entertainment, shopping, and recreation.

The new regional institutions here should include a Southwest Cultural Center, dedicated to the research, conservation, interpretation, and communication of the southwestern heritage. There could also be a museum and research study on the world-wide role of water: its physics and chemistry, its connection with living things, and its practical use and key importance throughout the world. Here might also be located Discovery Place, a museum for young people and their elders in which they could learn about the sciences and the arts by participation. There could be computer shops, bookstores, and an ethnic market of food crafts.

This central island location will also feature an alternative school—a special technical high school open to students throughout the city, but with a particular focus on students from the Rio Salado District and from areas of high unemployment. Such a school will encourage families to settle in the district, and will stimulate investment here by technical industries interested in a recreational setting and an educational link. These industries would benefit from participation in developing a skilled work force, would be linked to advanced research, and might themselves be designed to explain their functions to the public. Restaurants and other entertainments would keep this true "industrial park" open in the cool of the evening. All this will be directly connected to downtown Phoenix by means of a shuttle bus system. During Phase I, a special exposition will work as a launching platform for an exceptional concentration of public features.

The opening of the exposition would be timed to coincide with the building of the upstream flood control dams.

Beyond 7th Avenue, the river opens up once more to a landscape of small hills along the north edge of the riverbed, containing a desert arboretum displaying the life of the desert and the possibilities of desert flora. It would contain oases, dunes, mesas, and hidden "canyons," and might support a number of restaurants and other entertainment facilities.

Adjacent to this, there is a lake in a park, and an equestrian center. Certain choice sections fronting on the park are given to new housing. A golf course has been built on the old landfill west of 27th Avenue. South of the arboretum, the parkway runs for a stretch along the present Broadway, then swings wide to give space to several major new resorts along the braided stream and its lakes. These resorts, along with new low density housing, replace the auto junk yards now located there. This plan does not fix the disposition of the District beyond 35th Avenue, but recommends that this ground should be preserved for a major future development. One of the strategic aims of the entire plan, implemented by the inital occupation at Central Avenue and followed by the progressive westward extension via the desert arboretum and the parkway, is to open up this empty western territory, now abandoned by the northward and eastward drive of Phoenix. New settlement might extend along this completely unexploited growth axis of the metropolis. It could be carried out according to a careful general plan, and make maximum use of the recycled water released by existing urban settlement. District strategy should be designed to unlock and to control that great opportunity. Preparation of a plan for this area will become a priority immediatey following the realization of a permanent financing vehicle for the District.

Temporary Paradise? A Look at the Special Landscape of the San Diego Region (1974)

with Donald
Appleyard

sketches by
Donald Appleyard
and Roger Kavana

In Brief

This is an illustrated discussion of the landscape of San Diego, made by two newcomers. The city's magnificent site, for which its citizens have such strong affection, is still intact, but may be losing its best qualities. In this report, we analyze these qualities, the history of the regional landscape, its meaning to its people, and how it stands today.

We make many suggestions about saving the valleys and the canyons, restoring the Bay to the people, rebuilding the neighborhoods, and renewing the major centers. We recommend slowing down and changing the form of suburban development while redirecting growth to the present urban areas, and thence along the coast. We suggest ways of doing it that will conserve water, energy, and the land, while making the landscape more humane. We discuss airports, highways, better transit systems, walkways, and cycle trails. We try to show that Tijuana is an integral part of the San Diego landscape, and that the rapid changes going on there must be managed by strong joint action.

The situation of the region is chancy (when are human affairs not so?). But San Diego has a very possible future in which its splendid assets have been conserved, and its amenities shared more equitably among all its people. The city should begin to take thought for the long-term quality of its environment. We suggest a way to do that, and end up with a few questions and a few basic principles.

We hope San Diegans will find this report provocative, will agree and disagree with it, and will make their feelings known. Most of all, we hope that San Diego takes charge of its future.

What Is This About and Who Is It From?

This is about the land and how people have settled on it, and what this means for the quality of their lives. How does this physical place, San Diego, satisfy the needs of its people? What [do] its land, its water, and all its buildings and its streets mean to those who experience them every day? The human quality of the environment is fundamental to any decisions about the city. We will look at the city region as a whole, since this is the arena within which the real forces shaping the environment are acting today.

What follows is a personal statement, based on a reconnaissance of the San Diego region. It is a report to the city, made possible by a generous grant from the Marston family. It is not city policy. It has no detailed proposals in it. It is a general analysis of the quality of San Diego and some ideas for preserving and improving it. . . .

San Diego's Natural Base

Look at the land as it was before any major settlement occurred upon it. This is the basis of the city's quality. We must work with that base, or pay an unremitting price.

This is an arid coast, with a dry mild Mediterranean climate. If you add water, and prepare the soil, this land will bloom. But its natural vegetation is, for the most part, low and dully colored.

At a distance of 20 miles, bold, rocky mountains parallel to the seacoast, a handsome backdrop for the landscape. Through the intervening mesas, small streams in deep valleys carry the intermittent mountain water back to the sea from which it came. Santa Margarita, San Luis Rey, Buena Vista, Agua Hedionda, San Marcos, Escondido, San Dieguito, Penasquitos, San Clemente, San Diego, Sweetwater, Otay, Tijuana—the musical river names speak of an earlier occupation.

The ocean shore is a long arc of sand, which foots bold bluffs, or seals off the dune-sheltered salt lagoons into which the rivers empty. This is still a clean ocean: the undersea fauna are luxuriant, the lagoons and bays full of life.

Two large hills stand forward of this ocean arc: Mount Soledad and Point Loma. By interrupting that sweep of beach, they shelter the two great bays into which the San Diego River once alternately emptied. Thus the ocean shore is "doubled" here in the center of the region, forming the harbor that is the reason for the city's existence. But this "doubling" has also had important consequences for the quality of the region, since it saved at least one shoreline for public enjoyment, and produced a unique setting for the city. San Diego Bay has a very special scale: ample and yet intimately enclosed, changing its quality with every shift of light. The sunset is visible; one sees the relation of land and water; the city center can be seen from a distance, in its maritime setting. These views of the Bay are the symbol of San Diego. . . .

Upland from the shore, above the first bluffs, the flat mesas rise gradually to the mountains. The ground is dry, and the soil, for the most part, thin and poor, covered with a tough, dull brush. What water there is [is] in the valleys, and here one finds the water-loving vegetation. The streams are quite small, but on occasion they will fill their valley with a wild torrent. The mesa tops are intersected almost everywhere by a branching network of deep, dry, V-shaped canyons, leading down to the flatbottomed valleys and so breaking up what otherwise might be a rather monotonous terrain. Behind all this lie the mountains, with their picturesque ridges and green valleys. Behind them is the desert.

At the shore the climate is mild and extremely stable. There is a steady breeze from the sea. Mornings are often cloudy, and afternoons bright. But there is little rain. Not far inland, the sea breeze dies away. The even climate becomes progressively more extreme as one goes inland: hotter in the summer and colder in winter. There is a little more rain, but still the air and land are dry and the sun shines almost without ceasing. The climate is harsh, more desert-like, the air still. This warm, stable air is very susceptible to haze and smog.

If we look at the natural region as a whole, we see that it is a very simple unit—mountains, mesas, and sea—across which the water is cycled. Yet it has great variety within that unity: a variety of coastal form, the juxtaposition of mesa and canyon, the complex mountain shapes. Above all, it has strong contrasts within short distances as one goes inland. The natural gradient, therefore, is *west to east*.

This bold site, its openness, its sun and mild climate, the sea, [and] the landscape contrasting within brief space are (along with its people) the wealth of San Diego. They are what have attracted settlers to the place and still attract them. They must not be destroyed.

A Miniature History

This natural base has been settled in a special way, which also helps to explain the quality of San Diego. The Indians who originally occupied the land hardly disturbed it. Of necessity, they respected the power and spirit of the place, and fitted their lives to it. Those few of their myths that have survived mirror the grandeur of the setting. Overrun and all but extinguished by the Spanish occupation, they have hardly left a trace, although they were among the more advanced of the California Indians. Even their name, the Dieguenos, is an imposition, a name transferred to them from their conqueror's name for their land.

The Spanish colonists and missionaries came up from the south, looking for grazing land and souls to save. They held the land for less than a century, and their occupation was thin and precarious compared with other regions of Mexico, or even with the other California to the north. The land was too dry, and the Indians resisted, although dying of the white man's epidemics. There was some cattle ranching in the watered valleys, and a presidio and [a] mission were established on a strategic spur of the mesa, commanding both bays and the mouth of the San Diego River.

The North Americans came down the coast from above and took the land once more. A land speculator moved the town from its strategic site to a characterless location along the edge of the southern bay and shaped it on a thoughtless gridiron, designed for profit. The San Diego River was blocked from entering the southern bay. The center of the city still suffers from the indecisive relation to sea and land which resulted. . . .

Even the North American town was precarious until the late 19th Century. Repeated declines of population came very close to causing its extinction. A direct and permanent railroad connection to the east was only completed in 1919. San Diego was outpaced by Los Angeles, her rival to the north, and never developed as an important port. Still today, it is much more dependent on exotic activities, that is, on the Navy and on tourism.

With the Indians gone, the Spanish settlement obliterated, and the early U.S. growth slow, the deposit of history on the landscape is quite thin and deceptively recent. There is no visible tradition of form, or style of life. It is hard to realize that this place has been a site of human occupation for millennia. Just the same, there *is* a substantial heritage of fine turn-of-the-century buildings in the center city. These buildings are ignored today or carelessly destroyed.

When the growth of San Diego finally began, the bay shore was the natural location for the railway, the wharves, and the industries. This initial capture of the inner sea front was confirmed by military claims, then by the highways and the airports. The physical and visual barriers created by these uses, their noise, [and] their smoke and smell carried inland by the sea breeze are a detriment of the city. San Diegans are cut off from one of their principal landscape assets.

Luckily, the outer shore remained untouched. Except for military holdings, all of this is in civil public hands today. With a car one can reach a public beach, although one may have to pay a bridge toll or annoy other people living at the shore. San Diego has a tradition, beginning with the first Nolen plan, of reclaiming its oceanfront for public enjoyment. Those who have no car, or are caught behind the military-industrial front along the south bay, are at a disadvantage. Much has been lost, but much has been saved or regained.

As the city grew, houses at first grouped about the center, or were sprinkled in other speculative town sites down south along the bay. Then the streetcar came and pushed inland toward the existing settlement of El Cajon, encouraging the growth of a finger of urbanization eastward from Hillcrest. The arterial shopping streets were created, and the houses pushed into a more difficult climate. But there was very little north of the San Diego River, except for some settlement in Clairemont, and La Jolla.

When the private car became available to most people, growth moved inland at many points. It jumped the river, and spread to the vast north space. As migrants poured in, attracted by new jobs and especially by the setting, they wanted houses of their own, just like the ones back home. There was no tradition to oppose that, and, technically, it could be done.

The results were heavy traffic, smog, noise, expensive extension of schools, roads, and utilities, [and] a necessity for air conditioning. In general, this was a wasteful use of land, energy, water, and public funds. Along with the rapid suburban growth came the first signs of central decay and abandonment.

In most places, the new suburban growth occurred on the tops of the mesas, where the land was extensive, cheap, and flat. The watered valleys at first were left alone, and many still are empty today. This historic reversal of development, from farming the valleys to suburbanizing the mesas, offers San Diego the possibility of a two-level city, as we will see later.

Unfortunately, this historic resource has already been squandered in some places. The most dramatic loss was the conversion of historic Mission Valley in the 1950s into a chaos of highways, parking lots, and scattered commercial buildings. The city should erect an historic monument to that tragic event. It struck a double blow: one directed both at the landscape and at the economy of the center city.

But during these same years of growth and intermittent mismanagement, San Diego also did much to preserve its site, and, more noteworthy still, even to create fine new landscapes. Mount Soledad and Point Loma were kept open for public enjoyment, along with much of the shore. Balboa Park is a breathtaking transformation of a dry, rather featureless mesa. Mission Bay is a huge man-made marine park, yet incomplete. The African landscapes of the zoo are nationally famous. The city has a knack for acting on a big scale.

Across the arbitrary border line, in the same natural region and the same terrain, the small agricultural settlement of Tijuana began to grow in the 1920s and 30s, when Prohibition was enacted in the U.S. and as prostitution, gambling, and boxing were pushed out of the Upper California cities. From this start as the "dark side" of U.S. society, Tijuana has recently grown into a center for family tourism and now has begun to attract a flood of migrants from farther south, who come looking for work or a chance to cross the border.

Today Tijuana is one of the fastest growing cities in the world. Its mushrooming subdivisions and squatter settlements fill the valley and the canyons, and spread out over the slopes and mesas to the south and east. Its form of settlement is in startling contrast to the neat single-family houses of the San Diego region.

Where the Region Stands Today

This is a special landscape, yet much of the development on it is a faithful copy of U.S. models. Freeways, arterial streets, airports, industries, shopping centers, the downtown renewal zone—they all look familiar. The new suburbs are quite the same, if more closely built and barren. At first glance, this is a standard American city, still new and clean, without trees, rather dried-up, dropped onto a big landscape.

But the fine climate and the dramatic site are not yet destroyed. Large open areas remain: underused military and industrial lands, numerous airports, flood plains, steep slopes, discontinuous urbanization, farms, waste lands waiting for development. San Diego is not yet committed, not yet seriously congested.

Within the city, a number of older communities, by slow growth and adaptation, have evolved a memorable character of their own, a character which is modest, comfortable, and humane. The city is a collection of communities, and the qualities of these communities can still be conserved. Indeed, in comparison with most U.S. cities, San Diego is still remarkably clean and quiet. Abandoned buildings or derelict areas are still relatively rare.

Finally, there are great civil enterprises accomplished or in process. Balboa Park is a stunning achievement. Mission Bay is in the making. The University of California is creating a new center of activity. The very growth of the region, while it creates tensions and threatens the land, also has given San Diego a new sense of life and excitement.

If one looks to see where these fine new man-made landscapes are located, one will see that they are almost all north of Mission Valley. Indeed, this has recently been the general pattern of public investment. The natural gradient may be west to east, but the *social* gradient is clearly north to south. This social slope is becoming steeper, and public actions tend to steepen it. South of the border are the extensive slums, and the pattern runs right up to the North County. For prestige, a home buyer will locate as far "upstream" as he can afford. . . .

Some Images of San Diego

What do people think of when they imagine San Diego? How do they view their city? How do they use it? An earlier survey by the Comprehensive Planning Organization showed that people were especially concerned about air pollution, open space, and transportation. Since we were strangers, we wanted to learn more, so we sent out a simple questionnaire, mostly to community leaders, professionals, and high school students in various parts of the city.[1] They drew a map of San Diego, and noted how frequently they used different parts of it. They were asked what symbolized the city for them, what they liked and disliked about it, and what suggestions they had for the city's improvement. Some 200 people generously gave their time to complete this questionnaire. It is not a scientific sample of San Diego opinion. The sample is undoubtedly biased, and the questions were open-ended rather than precise. But it gave us useful insights into how different groups perceive and use their city.

Overwhelmingly, those interviewed said that the first things that came to their mind when thinking of San Diego were the ocean, the beaches, and the climate. Then they spoke of parks, the zoo, the recreational activities, the bays, and the whole natural landscape setting. It is a remarkably consistent picture. Moreover, these are just the things that they most like about their city. San Diegans are fortunate, for their image of the city is generally positive, and full of affection. The physical setting appears as the most important feature. In many other cities, when asked to symbolize a place, or to recount what they like about it, people will mention relations with other people, or making a living, or a historic tradition. Here, it seems to be the land itself that is remembered and enjoyed.

Yet this natural paradise is beginning to suffer the same problems that are experienced in other California cities, problems which undermine the very things for which people have so much affection. When asked what they most disliked, people wrote on the questionnaire about the smog which pollutes the climate, the urban growth which transforms the landscape and crowds the beaches, the traffic congestion and poor transit which impedes access. Most often, these problems were attributed to low quality development, poor planning, and weak government. . . .

San Diego's problems are not so very dissimilar from those of other cities, but, so far, many of them are seen more as signals of worse that might come. Already there is a nostalgia for the place that was. . . .

And so, when they were asked to suggest improvements, these people naturally emphasized the control of growth, the preservation of open space, the improvement of public transit, with a lesser but still quite significant plea for smog control, more parks, the improvement of downtown, and more control over building. It is a strong, coherent plea, indeed.

More diverse problems show up among the different groups when they talk of their own communities. Those in Southeast San Diego are also concerned with the lack of jobs, with "corporate control pushing out small businesses," with poor housing, needed recreational facilities, the lack of shops, problems with the police, children on the street, dogs, freeways cutting through the area, and large apartment buildings. Clairemont people are worried about the "bull-dozing of canyons and hills," "run-down areas," "the military," the schools, decreasing open space, billboards and signs, the lack of the arts, and the lack of rain. . . .

There are places that are used in common. Centre City is still visited regularly by the people of most communities, even as far out as Mira Mesa. Mission Valley is almost as heavily used as is La Jolla. Public recreation is the other focus, especially Mission Bay and Balboa Park. Those splendid public investments are much used and widely appreciated. The downtown centers, the resort of La Jolla, and the great parks, to which so many people gravitate, give San Diego its sense that, unlike Los Angeles, it is still one city.

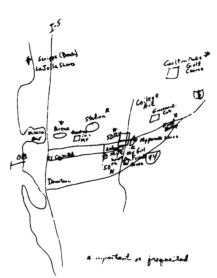

Map of San Diego by a San Diego State University student.

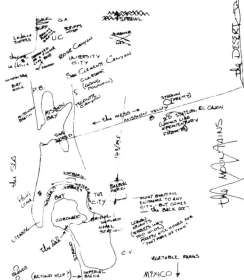

Map of San Diego by a University City resident.

Map of San Diego by a La Jolla High School student.

Map of San Diego by a Logan Heights resident.

Images of San Diego.

We have frequently been asked our impression as to whether San Diego is "really a city." That is a double-edged question: It reveals the wish for a sense of regional community and coherent character; but it also reveals an equal wish for a more ample scale and greater contrasts. The common use of places is one sign of unity, but some people complain of the lack of cultural diversity in San Diego. The frequent visits to Los Angeles and Tijuana suggest that many people use the whole Southern California/Baja California region as their resource and range. The Point Loma group, for instance, frequent Los Angeles and Orange County more often than they do El Cajon.

While this small survey told us that there were some strong common feelings about the quality of San Diego's environment, they also gave us some insights into the diversity of environmental problems faced by each community. A true environmental plan for the city should be based on a far more careful understanding of each community than we have been able to gain through these few interviews.

San Diego will grow and change, but the city is already here and what is here will continue to be a major determinant of quality. A careful look at what should be saved and repaired in the existing city is our first task. Conservation of the natural setting is surely an urgent priority, and the finer parts of the city can also be preserved. But much of San Diego needs repair and restoration. As in any city that has grown fast, mistakes have been made. Public use and public access have been pre-empted. The public environment is all too often simply the left-over space between.

The Valleys and Canyons

The valleys and canyons are San Diego's priceless asset. The flat-floored valleys hold the water and the vegetation, and have been left open until very recently, since new housing has avoided the flood plain and occupied the high mesas. But now it is the turn of the valley: highways, shopping centers, stadia, industries, and parking lots are beginning to appear there despite the flood dangers.

Fingering out from the long valleys, the narrow, brushy canyons, too steep for building, penetrate almost everywhere in the inland city. They are a naturally connected system of open space that is close to almost every locality. Many canyons show signs of use by local children, and a few have walking trails. Most lie unused—inaccessible to their neighborhoods and most likely severed at their base where they connect to the valley. What's more, heavy machinery can now fill them over or terrace them to make flat building sites. But cost, flood danger, erosion, and respect for the land all argue against tampering with this natural drainage system.

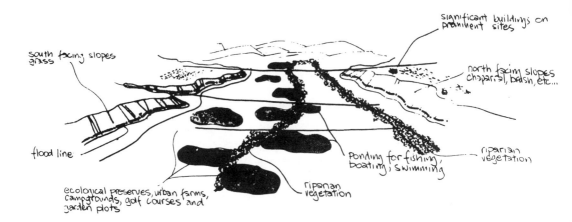

Labels on the drawing:

south facing slopes grass

significant buildings on prominent sites

north facing slopes chaparral, brush, etc...

flood line

ponding for fishing, boating, swimming

riparian vegetation

ecological preserves, urban farms, campgrounds, golf courses, and garden plots

riparian vegetation

The valleys and canyons.

It is of great importance that San Diego now, at the last moment, preserve all the remaining undeveloped valleys and canyons. Keep the building up on the expansive flats above. Protect the valley sides and rims, as well as the floor, so that the rural character of the valley is preserved, even within the city, and erosion and flood damage [are] prevented. Flood plain and hillside zoning will help, particularly in saving the canyons, but the codes must be specifically applied and much more tightly drawn than they are today. Public purchase of valley land will also be necessary, and perhaps the use of transferable development rights, as discussed below. Structures should be kept back from the rims, unless perhaps for some small landmark on some prominent nose where canyon and valley intersect. Valley sides should be left to their natural vegetation, and the flat floor [should] be devoted to open uses which are unharmed by flood. No further channeling of the streams should be permitted.

No more highways, not even transit lines, should be carried along these green fingers, however reasonable that may look at first glance. Not only do highways destroy the natural character, they inevitably bring further development. The uses which most need their access are up above, on the mesas, and this means even more ramps to get up there. Except for short local ways serving valley uses, roads should cross canyons and valleys at right angles—dipping down perhaps, or even using a canyon mouth to ease a descending grade—but staying above the valley floor, leaving the floodway open. San Diego has a unique opportunity to develop as a two-level city—one level a greenway undisturbed by city traffic—an opportunity that other cities must create laboriously by artificial means.

Parts of the valleys should be ecological preserves, others campgrounds and wild lands for children to explore. The watercourses could be ponded with small dams to be stocked with fish or used as swimming holes. The bottoms can be grazed or cultivated, perhaps in subsidized urban farms that provide educational jobs for the youth of the city. Or they might be parceled into garden plots for the people nearby. Parks and sport uses could be located there, wherever the natural character can be maintained. But uses which mean large gatherings and extensive parking lots— even public uses—would not belong.

A complete trail system—for walking, cycling, and horseback riding—should be developed along these natural valleys. Since they penetrate the region at regular intervals and run from mountains to the sea on easy grades, they are ideal for recreational travel, and might even be a component in the movement of commuters. The trails will have their own rights-of-way, safe from cars and free of fumes, unlike those presently designed which flank the highways. Selected canyons could be developed as connectors between mesa communities and the valleys, while others will serve for strolling, exploration, and local connections. Wherever there are major flows, there can be steps, benches, lights, and a clearance of vegetation. The canyon trail leading up to Presidio Park from the Camino del Rio is an excellent example of this treatment. . . .

The Seacoast

In people's minds the ocean shore is the most important asset of the city, as evidenced in our interview and in tourist literature. Beach attendance in the region has recently been increasing with giant strides: for the last decade at a rate which doubles every six years. Most of San Diego's outer shore is in public hands, although some of that is military ownership, and in other cases access is difficult because of bluffs and steep slopes, or indirect routes, or the hostility of local shore communities. San Diego is one of the few cities in Southern California with a fairly wide range of income and housing in its coastal neighborhoods, but the pressures for higher densities and higher rents are increasing. Some objectionably large buildings have already appeared. Mission Beach and Ocean Beach could, like Miami, erect a solid line of high-rise hotels and luxury apartments along the beach, walling it off from the people behind. The local opposition to this is quite justified. . . .

This is the basic question: how much of the shore should be accessible to whom, and by what means? For our part, we believe that **the ocean shore should be the possession of all those who live in the region.** Shore communities should not have exclusive rights, nor should tourist accommodations be able to appropriate special frontages. The diversity of beach character and [the] diversity of access should be maintained. We think there will in the future be less reliance on the car, and more on feet, cycle wheels, and transit lines. Maintain the mix of income and type in the present coastal communities, and give a greater number of people—of all

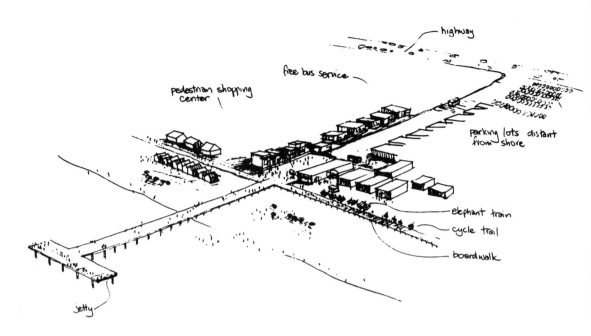

The seacoast — perspective view.

incomes—the chance to live near the sea. Commercial, industrial, and military uses should be on the water only when they make active use of it, and then not for long, continuous reaches. This is a plea for open and equal access. Pursuing that principle, we recommend:

Keep private development back from the water's edge—whenever possible, private land should be at least 100 yards back of the beach or shore and set well behind the brow of the bluff. In many places it should be set farther back. Forward of that line, the land should be given to water-related public recreation, or occasionally leased to moderately priced commercial recreation open to the general public.

Make the beaches accessible without destroying the local communities behind them—major transportation and parking should be kept well back of the beach, with free transit forward and frequent foot access. Elephant trains, bicycles, mini-buses, and boardwalks should predominate along the coast, reaching back to the major routes, while discreet public stairs and escalators run down the bluff faces. Continuous shore roads are not needed, but a connected cycle and foot trail should run along the ocean.

Encourage housing of mixed price and type to locate along the shore—densities may be allowed to increase moderately in this favored zone, but bulk and character must be controlled as noted below. The existing mix of income should be protected, and a mix ensured in any new development. To replace lively, low-rise Mission Beach with high-rise, high-rent towers, for example, would be a serious step backwards. Quotas of moderately priced housing may have to be imposed, for the privilege of developing shorefront property. Residential use and its attendant services and small-scale employment should be the natural dispostion of coastal land, except where there are fragile estuaries to be maintained in their natural condition.

Control the height and bulk of shorefront development—tall buildings and massive beachfront walls block the view and impair access. In general, buildings should be low at the beach, and higher up on the bluffs and mesas in order to give everyone a look. Buildings close to the water should be limited in their dimensions parallel to the shore. Stairs, plantings, and other works on the highly visible face and rim of the bluff should be controlled to maintain the natural aspect. At the same time, and while maintaining their intimate character, residential densities could be increased in many beach communities. Prototype designs for shoreline residence and for combinations of recreational and residential use should be examined.

In the long term, remove all uses from the shore which are not water-related, and are not residence or recreation—much of the shorefront industry, military, and transport is there for historic reasons, and not because they use the water today. The people of San Diego will lay increasing emphasis on access to their Bay, and these uses hedge them out. Some, like the airfields, are noisy and dangerous. In the long run, large-scale industry can be dispersed to inland locations and the military uses consolidated or removed to Camp Pendleton or other locations. . . .

Productive activities actually related to the water—such as shipping or commercial fishing—should be retained, not only for the obvious functional reasons, but also because their presence adds to the liveliness and meaning of the Bay. Even where industrial or military installations have moved away, some of their large structures might be saved to be used for other purposes. Their presence will remind us of the historic use of the waterfront. Vast areas of land by the Bay could thus be opened up for residence and recreation—some 2,500 acres and six miles of beach in North Island alone (which is sufficient for a population of 100,000 to 150,000 people, at moderate densities). Lindbergh Field and the Marine Corps Depot, together with some of the cluttered growth just north of them, would furnish another 2,000 acres in a strategic location through which waterways might run to relink the bays. None of these moves will be easy, and many will take a long time, but returning the Bay to San Diego will maintain the inner city as a prime place to live and ease the pressure for suburban growth.

Existing Communities

The San Diego region contains communities of all sizes, levels of cohesion, incomes, races, ages, and environmental qualities. A study by R. D.

NO   YES

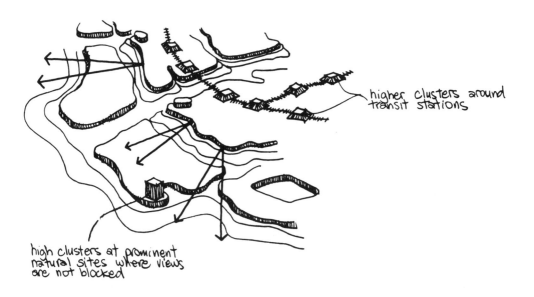

higher clusters around transit stations

high clusters at prominent natural sites where views are not blocked

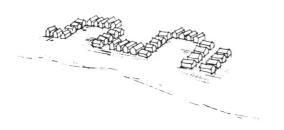

Design guidelines for coastal development.

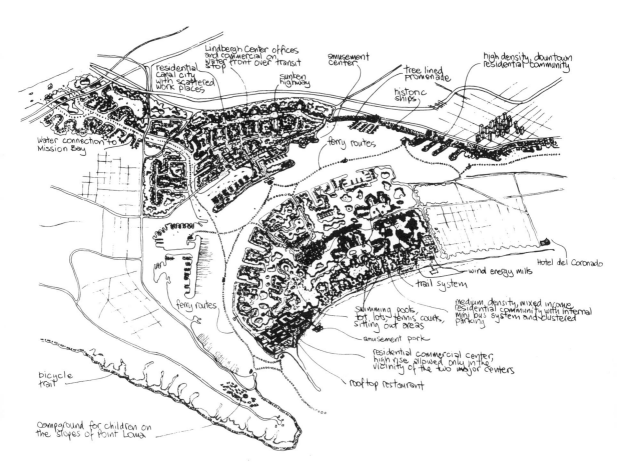

Area development ideas — a coastal district.

Jones[2] identifies 34 communities in the City alone, each with its own profile of problems. Many of them have already been the subjects of plans worked out with community groups, but visits to some of them reveal that many recommendations have not been carried out. However, people are more aware of environmental problems than they were even a few years ago and less willing to accept poor conditions. Respondents to our questionnaire told us of many of these problems and offered many suggestions. Repair and restoration should begin where the people are living today.

Brief visits to Logan Heights and Harbor 101 told a typical story of regional invasion, inadequate public facilities, and poor neighborhood conditions. The environmental problems of these areas have been well articulated. A recent study reports that community concerns were particularly directed towards the threat of more freeways passing through the area, the long-promised educational-cultural facility, the lack of other public facilities, poor medical services, shopping centers, internal circulation and neighborhood conditions, unpaved streets and sidewalks, [and the] lack of landscaping and street lighting. Our own surveys confirmed much of this. The residents of southeast San Diego are as aware and concerned about their environment as any other group in the city. By reason of their lesser mobility, they must spend more time in it. The solutions they propose are sensible and reasonable: they only cost money. The city must give these areas greater priority in making public environmental investments.

When neighborhood improvements are proposed for other areas, the question should always be: are these needy areas getting their share?

Freeways, tuna fish plants, and parking lots for patrol cars end up here, when there is nowhere else to go. They take away housing and community facilities, and give in return a sense of loss and resentment. The proposed freeway link between I-5 and I-805, for example, for which the right-of-way is already cleared, will not benefit southeast San Diego. But if that land were combined with Los Chollas Creek and the present rather ominous expansion areas for the cemetery, it could provide valuable housing and recreation.

We look more closely at North Park as a typical inner city community. North Park began in 1911 as a settlement of small single-family houses built to a gridiron pattern on the flat mesa top. With the extension of the trolley lines eastwards, its main street shopping grew to regional importance, but [it] was bypassed in the 1960s by the Mission Valley freeways. The population is mixed in age, race, and income. Many elderly people live there. Densities have increased by infill and piecemeal replacement: backyards are filled with second houses, and many walkup apartments have been built.

The community is concerned about its aging housing, the dangerous traffic, the heavy parking, the lack of parks, the threat of uncontrolled apartment growth, the aircraft overhead, the poor walking conditions, the deteriorating commercial strips. The arterial streets, in particular, have been neglected in the push to build freeways, but they are the work horses of the transportation system, the main arteries of city life—as well as a chaos of traffic and a disreputable front door. A 1969 plan attempted to improve access to the shopping but was quietly shelved. Still another proposed traffic control and a reduction of allowable densities.

But the area still has an intimate scale, well-grown trees, and quiet back alleys. The streets are wide, and many single-family houses survive. The population is diverse. Balboa Park is nearby, and the neglected canyons. Downtown is not far. What can be done to conserve an area such as this?

Maintain the existing residential character—Make a community survey to identify and then conserve the streets, landmarks, and areas that have a sense of place or history. Develop guidelines to keep new development in character, in regard to such things as height, bulk and setback, use, open space, parking, landscaping, roofs, wall materials, windows, balconies, and detail.

Protect the residential areas from through traffic—Studies show that an increase of traffic on residential streets causes families to move, to withdraw from the street, to reduce their feeling of responsibility for it. Cars are noisy, polluting, and dangerous. There are simple ways of controlling traffic volume and speed. Diagonal diverters can be built at four-way intersections; street entrances can be necked down, traffic islands erected. By making some gridiron streets into cul-de-sacs, while using the alleys for auto access, clustered parking can be provided, as well as open space for neighborhood use. Changes of this kind will increase livability and attract new families. The capacity of the arterials may have to be increased, of course, to take the diverted flow.

Bring more open space into use—Street parks can be created by traffic management, [and] vacant lots or canyons [can be] brought into use. Block groups may be encouraged to make and maintain their own mini-parks for children or to cultivate block gardens for vegetables or flowers. Individual yards are often too small for these amenities.

Improve the conditions for walking and cycling—Closing off streets can provide more pleasant, safer walkways for children going to school and adults on their way to shop. Cycle trails can be built down these closed streets or along the alleys. A network of cycle trails on separate rights-of-way should connect shopping, bus stops, public facilities, the access canyons to the valleys, and, in this case, Balboa Park.

Improve the surroundings of schools, libraries, churches, and community facilities—In San Diego's climate many of the activities of these local institutions could have outdoor learning environments far more rich and interesting than the current asphalt-and-cyclone-fence playgrounds. Libraries and churches could have quiet sitting out spaces for contemplation and reading. Outdoor exhibits and local art could be placed in public open spaces. Pedestrian precincts around these institutions could also protect them from traffic and noise.

Improve the pedestrian environment in the commercial strip—Inner city shopping is designed as a string of sales outlets where automobile riders may stop off to buy. There are no trees, benches, or human amenities of any kind. Yet these streets are the local service centers. Facilities for those who walk, bike, or come by transit are urgently needed. Indeed, shopping can be a pleasant social activity. Wider sidewalks, shade, arcades, pedestrian crossings, and pedestrian signs can begin to create a human atmosphere. Convenience clusters at bus stops can be furnished with benches, rest rooms, shade trees, fountains, newsstands and bulletin boards, and even some local works of art.

Increase the traffic capacity of the arterials—An increase in arterial capacity will become urgent as present freeways fill up, and as residential

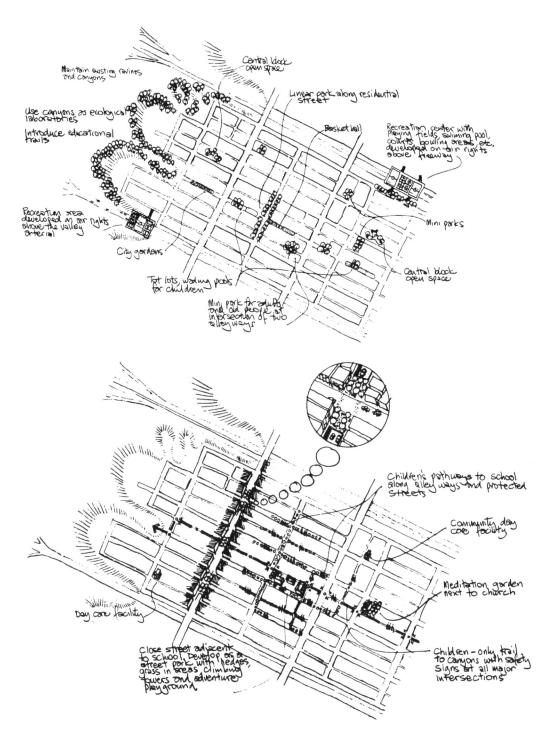

Existing communities — design improvements
(4 sketches).

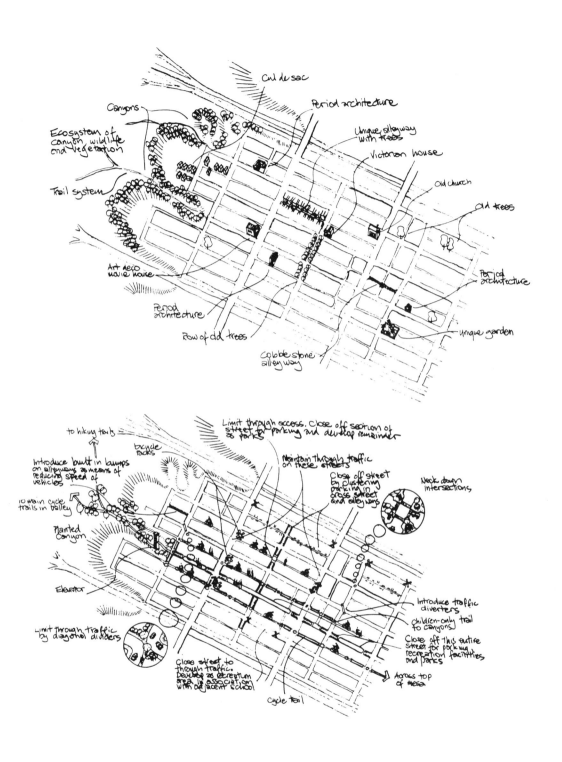

Cul de sac

Period architecture

Canyons

Ecosystem of canyon, wildlife and vegetation

Unique alleyway with trees

Victorian house

Old church

Trail system

Old trees

Art deco movie house

Period architecture

Period architecture

Row of old trees

Unique garden

Cobble stone alleyway

Limit through access. Close off section of street for parking and develop remainder

to hiking trails

bicycle racks

Maintain through traffic on these streets

Introduce built in bumps on alleyways as means of reducing speed of vehicles

Close off street by clustering parking in cross street and alleyways

Neck down intersections

10 main cycle trails in valley

Planted canyon

Elevator

Introduce traffic diverters

Children-only trail to canyons

Limit through traffic by diagonal dividers

Close off this entire street for parking recreation facilities and parks

Close street to through traffic. Develop as recreation area in association with adjacent school

Across top of mesa

cycle trail

areas reject through traffic. Handled in the usual manner, i.e., by increasing the width of the traffic pavement, this can negate any other improvement of the strip, and finally destroy its social and commercial function. If through traffic is diverted around the shopping street, the street is then cut off from its neighborhood. In this case, it is better to maintain and enhance the pedestrian turf on either side. Fortunately, San Diego's arterial rights-of-way are wide. Median strips and side strips, the prohibition of curb parking and curb entrances, better traffic control, shifting traffic pavements off-center to give a wide walkway on one side, the use of pedestrian overpasses, and a lowered street all can help to increase capacity without reducing pedestrian amenity. Capacity in terms of persons transported (which is our aim, rather than the transportation of cars!) can be still further increased if special lanes are devoted to buses or bicycles.

Planting alone could raise the quality of San Diego's arterials far above their present mediocre level. Streets need not be lined with trees on the standard model. Problems of maintenance and the use of water set limits to this. But there could be frequent oases of lush planting, not located for visual reasons alone, but where they also serve to shade pedestrians. It is striking to the observer how few plants San Diego has along its major streets.

Signs can be more lively, more informative, and yet less cluttered— Billboards are out of scale with the strip, and most signs simply confuse and detract. The chaos can be controlled by reducing sign size and movement, and by limiting signs to those building facades to which they refer. Signs about particular people and local establishments can be encouraged to develop an individual style. Mass-produced signs and those for products not related to the place can be clustered at places where they do not submerge the local scene. Other signs which convey information of general interest—time, the weather, the news, local history, local ecology, schedules of buses or events—can be added to the commercial ones. Signing is a necessary art and can create character and sparkle, instead of simply assaulting the eye.

Lights and graphics can enliven the scene—High, cold, uniform lighting benefits the passing traffic and no one else. Warmer, smaller lights grouped in clusters are more useful for those who walk along the sidewalks and gather at the bus stops. Special night lighting can create a new mood, or enliven a community event. Street murals can be painted on the walls of buildings, or on screens around the parking lot.

Coordinated management can bring people out to use the street— The streets of San Diego, except for a few locations such as Horton Plaza, La Jolla, or Mission Beach, are remarkable for their emptiness at almost any hour and all the more remarkable when we consider the mild climate. Where an arterial street is the principal shopping [center] for a community, coordinated management by community groups or merchant associations could arrange for street events and provide the places for social contact so that people can once again take possession of their public space.

In sum, North Park, as one typical example, offers many opportunities for restoration. Conservation treatment in the residential areas can protect threatened residential character and make use of unexploited resources. More thorough-going treatment of the commercial streets would transform those neglected arteries into useful social centers. Indeed, instead of subjecting large areas to public renewal, destroying housing and uprooting residents, we might consider renewal projects which focus on these long commercial strips, so vital to the city, so deteriorated, and so amenable to change without social dislocation.

The Major Centers

The centers of a city are the places that people identify with, sharing reflected glory or shame, depending on their quality. People are proud of cities whose unique centers present a clear image to themselves and to visitors. In other cities, they say there is nothing to see, nowhere in particular to go.

Downtown San Diego presents a clear image from the outside. Its buildings, although moderate in height and not unique, cluster well together. Horton's choice of the original site was not a happy one, and yet the Bay is close enough to provide a setting. Some recent structures which cross above the streets, and the prison tower at the critical corner nearest the Bay, have begun to seal the center away from that principal setting. Establishing a comfortable connection is still possible but will not be easy. Moreover, any further structures like the Royal Inn will disrupt the clustered image of downtown and destroy its outward views. Center City renewal will have to be handled with care.

The new office area downtown has elegant buildings, well-designed landscaping, and elaborate street furniture. Most of the time, it seems empty of people, while Horton Plaza, brash and tawdry, is packed with action. It will be unfortunate if the renewal program banishes this liveliness and substitutes for it an empty space ringed by bank fronts.

Downtown suffers from a dichotomy of use. Its principal economic function is that of an office center, whose workers come and go in brief periods and are most of the day indoors. (But even those who work in the high-rise buildings in other cities find them "cold, impersonal, oppresive.") Investments in the environment, naturally enough, are made to enhance this office function.

Yet downtown is the principal shopping and entertainment center for the lower-income neighborhoods around it. Their residents are more dependent on the facilities that downtown affords and use its public space more intensively. Yet they have least to say about its transformation.

Mission Valley is the second "downtown" of the region, and its future appears gloomy. It presents a fragmented and uninspiring image. High or bulky buildings are scattered about like pieces of an uncompleted jigsaw puzzle. Parking lots, storage yards, and fast roadways fill the spaces between. This central valley, the largest and most dramatic in San Diego south of the Penasquitos Canyon and the superb San Dieguito Valley, is now just an urban trench. The freeway approach promises some excitement, but that promise quickly collapses. Down in the trench one must drive from one store to another; it is impossible to walk. . . .

The scattered fragments should be connected with shaded pedestrian walkways and sitting out spaces, outside and between the complexes, not hidden in their interiors. One of our informants told us that it took her a year to discover that there were any pedestrian walks in Mission Valley; she usually drove in, shopped, and drove out again. A field investigator was convinced it was illegal to walk there. A slow moving transport system such as an elephant train could connect these separate islands.

The north-facing slopes of the valley are still untouched, and could be saved. The center of the valley is still miraculously open; the creek flows unseen. Unbelievable as it may seem, a wooded trail could still be laid out along that creek, following it past the stadium and the shopping centers, through the country club to Mission Bay. Cycle elevators could link the creekway with cycle trails on the mesa above. In the region of the shopping centers, it would be relatively easy to create some large lakes on a grand scale on the site of the main floodway. One lake could be used for quiet boating—no motor boats—[and] another could be ornamental. This area could take on the relaxed and delightful character of the Tivoli Gardens in Copenhagen. The lakes could reflect the numerous lights of the shopping centers and surrounding hillside communities—a mirror of dancing activity.

High and bulky buildings should be confined to their present domain and height envelope, thus concentrating the external image of this center. The character of new buildings should be much more responsive to pedestrians who have to walk by them, with active frontages at street level [and with] human scale in the details, rather than huge faceless facades.

The south-facing slopes, already quarried and eroded, could in the exceptional case be recovered with a cascade of housing and new planting. Sites on the valley rim could be reserved for significant buildings at fine locations like that of the University of San Diego. Even the giant underpinnings of the freeways could be dramatized with light and color. Mission Valley is a landscape disaster, yet few disasters are beyond all repair. It is only that repair demands money, time, and effort.

Growth Where? Of What Kind?

The continuing rapid growth of San Diego is a serious issue, as it is in much of the U.S. Environmental quality is only one element to consider in thinking about growth, but it is a key one. The growth of the region probably cannot be stopped, short of drastic national, even international, action. Although there are indications that the national populations may soon approach zero growth, the relative growth of the southwest is still a strong trend. Regional actions *might* be able to modify the rate of growth to some degree. But the region can certainly redirect the location of growth, and modify its nature. At this point, the considerations of environmental quality become crucial.

As one example, we looked at the rapidly developing suburb of Mira Mesa. What did we see?

First, that rapid growth has outrun public services. There are not enough schools, even though there may be empty classrooms in the inner city. The main roads leading out of the community are congested. Community institutions are lacking. The *rate* of growth is too fast.

Second, the landscape is being carelessly destroyed. The tough natural cover and [the] thin soil are being stripped off, leaving dusty, barren surfaces. Hills and banks are cut off, canyons buried. All the potentialities of the land are lost.

Third, the form of settlement itself, which is borrowed from the humid East, is inappropriate. Streets are too wide; yards are empty; houses and people are unprotected from the sun. The plants struggle with drought and poor soil. The public spaces are barren; the resulting landscape is hot, arid, empty, and monotonous. At the same time, it is wasteful of space and wasteful of water.

Fourth, development is at such a huge scale, and of such a single type, that not even skilled design could prevent a sense of endlessness, of remoteness from the natural setting. This in an area that is in fact still largely open! Small design decisions, such as a choice of roof form or wall color, become overwhelming when repeated so often. More serious, perhaps, the scale and homogeneity of development isolates people from work, from services, and from people who are not like themselves.

Finally, the location of this inland development puts more people in a climate which is hotter in summer and colder in winter, where they must expend more water and more energy to remian comfortable. It is farther from the sea, and [this] increases their dependence on the car, with its attendant road congestion, oil consumption, [and] smog and its reduction of the independence of children and the elderly. These areas are more expensive to serve, while facilities in the inner city lie underused. In the process of relocation, people are uprooted from their familiar communities, and increasingly segregated by class.

Please note that these suburbs are *not* substandard in any legal sense. Their form abides strictly by the public rules for construction, street widths, setbacks, street walls, bulk, and type of use. Their road patterns have been carefully reviewed. In official terms, they are properly done.

In sum, if we judge by Mira Mesa, it seems that the present suburban growth is too rapid, too poorly coordinated with public services, too extensive and homogeneous, too destructive of the land, inappropriate in form, and in the wrong place. Then why does it happen?

The immediate cause is speculative profit, of course. But why do people buy these houses, and so provide the opportunity for profit? Clearly, because in the suburbs they can get a new house at a price they can afford, one which they cannot find in the inner city. They can have the security and satisfaction of owning a home, and that home can have a familiar form which fits with the nuclear family. Along with this they have an initial sense of spaciousness, as they are the first occupants of the big mesas. That sense of space is illusory, however, and declines as development proceeds. The satisfactions of home ownership and of adequate housing at a reasonable price are more lasting. Might it be possible to discover a form of housing which is more appropriate to the site and climate, and which also gave the same satisfactions?

It is also likely that a good number of people who move out to the mesa do so because they prefer the bright sun and dry air to the coastal climate. Such a preference is perfectly reasonable, if they realize how precarious is the clarity of that still, dry, haze-prone air and are willing to discipline themselves to preserve it—and also if they are willing to pay the social costs of more water, energy, and public service.

Moreover, there is a logic in the land that suggests something about development here. The flat mesa tops are easy to reach and to build on. They are not precious in any ecological or landscape sense. The ubiquitous canyons, if left alone, are historic, watered, rural, seemingly remote. They divide the huge mesas into many smaller places.

This analysis suggests some policies to us:

Slow down the inland suburban growth, but do not try to stop it. Extend public services gradually, on a phased basis, and not automatically, on the request of developers. Tie the pace of development strictly to that extension of service so that all public services (schools, utilities, roads, fire protection) are budgeted and provided *before* houses are complete. Find ways of levying the real public costs of extension directly onto the suburban developments that cause them—not only the initial construction costs, but the running costs, and those more intangible losses of traffic, smog, wasted water, and so on. Use timed and transferable development rights to impose a control on the regional rate of development, while maintaining equity for all those land owners who would prefer that their

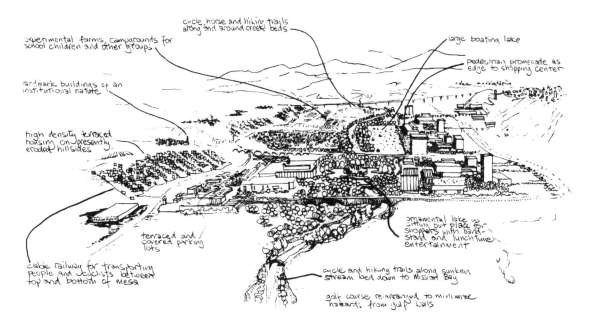

Mission Valley as it still could be.

The following labels appear on the illustration:

experimental farms, campgrounds for school children and other groups

cycle, horse and hiking trails along and around creek beds

large boating lake

pedestrian promenade as edge to shopping center

landmark buildings of an institutional nature

high density terraced housing on presently eroded hillsides

terraced and covered parking lots

cable railway for transporting people and cyclists between top and bottom of mesa

cycle and hiking trails along sunken stream bed down to Mission Bay

ornamental lake as sitting out place for shoppers with band-stand and lunchtime entertainment

golf course re-arranged to minimize hazards from gulf balls

land be the next to develop.[3] In other words, don't rely on zoning and subdivision control to stem the tide. Experience shows that those familiar devices are often impotent where development pressures are strong and there is no established community to make a resistance.

Encourage smaller, less homogeneous development. When development happens in smaller pieces, when there is a greater mixture of house type, and of employment and services with the housing, then a more interesting landscape is produced, as well as a community which is more varied in age and social composition. The journey to work and to shopping can be correspondingly reduced. This means much more flexible and fine-grained zoning and other public rules. It indicates a greater reliance on planned unit development techniques, and on performance standards rather than on use zone boundaries. Permits to develop land should be released in smaller pieces, perhaps in the same compartments which are formed by the canyons. Or a limit might be put on the maximum size of any contiguous development that could be carried out by any entrepreneur in a given period of time. It may even be sensible to *require* some minimum percentage of land use mixture. Fundamentally, this means a change in the way the land development business is organized, which will come harder. Could there be public ways of encouraging small builders and community enterprises?

Use a more appropriate form of settlement, based perhaps on the Mediterranean prototype, which developed in this type of landscape. What is wanted is much more compact site planning, narrow (even shaded) streets, [and] the use of roofs, interior courts, and small intensive gardens in place of lawns and yards. In this dry air, rely on breeze and shade for coolness in place of air conditioning. Use native plants, and concentrate the application of water. Collect the abundant solar energy to power the houses. All this can be done without sacrificing family privacy, home ownership, or reasonable cost. But prototypes must be built to show how it can be done. It may be necessary to impose *minimum* densities, as well as the usual maxima, to encourage compactness and save the land. Minima would have to be accompanied by other rules, of course, to prevent that equally inappropriate form: the high tower set in an arid parking lot.

Respect the land. Keep the valleys and canyons, and their rims, out of development, using public purchase and flood plain and hillside zoning with real teeth. The canyons automatically provide an open space network for recreation, food production, trails, small inland oases, and room for children and adults to wander, in contrast to the urbanized mesas above. Work *with* the ground; use native plants. Where possible, do not disturb the existing plant cover or the skin of the earth. This skin is very tender in an arid country. When disturbance is necessary, confine it to the flat tops.

Save water and energy. Concentrate the use of water, and recycle it to the canyons. Develop solar energy inland (and wind energy on the coast?). Minimize the use of the automobile by dispersing employment and services to local areas, by developing cycle trails, [and] by installing small-scale, demand-activated transit ("dial-a-bus") which can operate at suburban densities. Perhaps it may even in time become necessary to ration, or to sell, a temporary right to park a car in a local area. We have had glimpses of the impending shortage of water and energy, but that shortage is still largely hidden to view. When it appears again, in a sharper form, it may have serious social, economic, and environmental consequences. New suburbs should be designed so that they can adapt quickly to a low-energy, low-water regime.

But the policies we have outlined for regulating suburban growth could be extremely dangerous, if no alternate location for growth were provided. San Diego cannot stop migrants at [its] borders, nor forcibly reduce its birth rate. A check in suburban growth alone will simply raise the price of housing and confine moderate income families to a shrinking, inadequate, inner city stock of houses. If there were acceptable ways of controlling the mix of house prices and rents, preventing discrimination against the less affluent, or directly supplying low-cost housing, then growth could be more severely contolled without loss of equity. As it is, a suburban slow-down must be accompanied by the encouragement of new growth in present urban areas.

Where could that happen? Isn't the building of new apartments just what the existing communities are most desperately resisting? Look at

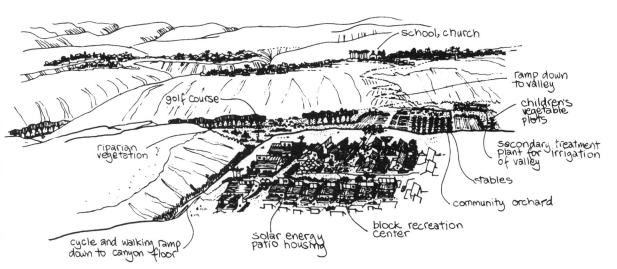

Labels on illustration:
school, church
ramp down to valley
children's vegetable plots
golf course
secondary treatment plant for irrigation of valley
riparian vegetation
stables
community orchard
block recreation center
cycle and walking ramp down to canyon floor
solar energy patio housing

Future development possibilities.

North Park again, to see an example of where "densification"—the gradual addition of dwellings to an existing community—is happening, and to see its problems.

The most visible kind of "densifying" happens where new apartments built on old single-family lots invade a block en masse. They transform the population, and thus overturn the community. They steal each other's light and air, display their tawdry fronts, and appropriate the curbs with their parked cars. They make a new, rather unpleasant, single-use area, which will in time be ripe for its own decline.

But, except for its wide streets, North Park is already quite dense for its type of housing, due to the gradual accumulation of rear houses and converted cottages, all still in good repair. The original density in the area shown, perhaps five dwellings per acre, has already come near to doubling. Indeed, this is an illustration of how a *slow and scattered* process of increase can come without disruption. Speaking purely in visual terms, the narrow alleys with their varied rear houses and garages are often the most interesting part of the North Park scene.

Even North Park can take more housing, but only if it is gradual and dispersed, so that the change does not upset the present mix of people and buildings, and only if most new buildings are low—except at some special location such as a transit station. And only if the community is compensated for the new population load by corresponding new public investments: schools, parks, transit, street improvements, new services.

Given all that, existing houses can be rehabilitated, new units can be added in rear yards or filled in between existing single family units, and occasional apartments can be built. The "densification" we propose is not massed apartments at 40 units to the acre, or high-rise towers at 80, but a mix of individual homes and low, small, rental units at 10 to 15 units per acre. This will require new performance standards to handle such additions, plus means of preventing the conversion of extensive areas of apartments, and new ways of managing and discouraging parking. The automatic alarm of communities to a threatened increase in density could be converted to acceptance, if only they could be sure that the increase would be moderate, controlled, and in keeping with what they have.

Elsewhere in the city and county there are much better opportunities for "densification." There are plentiful waste lands between the developed zones, and frequent vacant lots. There will be opportunities at future transit stops. In the longer term, there are magnificent opportunities to bring people "back to the Bay," to occupy Lindbergh Field, North Island, or the south Bay shore with housing.

Unless there is a concerted policy for densifying the present urban area, suburban growth cannot—and should not—be checked. Based on surveys of the relative ability of city and rural lands to absorb growth (due to water, soils, energy use, climate, visual quality, hazards, transport, amenities, potentials, etc.), compared with the need for housing expansion, public agencies must indicate where densities may increase, and where they may not. Then agencies must key their land assessments and investments to those decisions. Any "densification" should follow certain rules:

It should be by the consent of the local community, a consent gained in return for public investment and services. We are not advocating total neighborhood control, since regional reasons must often prevail, as in building a connected transit system, for example, or in trying to diminish social segregation. But we do advocate a negotiated settlement when regional and local interests clash.

Its rate and character should not destroy existing community character. Particular guidelines will be needed for each community. Guidelines can deal with the control of parking and paved areas, the provision of balconies and planting, the prevention of buildings which overlook or overshadow smaller neighbors, the use of materials, the activities which front the street, and indeed many other things. It all depends on the neighborhood character to be preserved. In general, additional units should be low, scattered, and added gradually. Relaxed spacing and density rules must be accompanied by new performance standards. A scattering in space and time might be ensured by requiring new apartments to purchase development rights from adjacent property owners, a sale which would then preclude higher densities on those adjacent sites. Some clustering could be allowed, however, as at major transit stops.

Public improvements should focus on the present urban areas, and not on the open land north of Mission Valley, as is presently the case. The old arterial commercial streets should be renewed, local streets and alleys reformed, small parks added, schools and libraries rebuilt. Suburban restraint and the revitalization of the existing city must go hand in hand.

How to Get About

. . . In many parts, San Diego's freeway system is magnificent. It was put in place largely prior to development, and is still today not badly congested, except in certain locations and at certain times. Great ribbons of concrete snake through the canyons, pass over valleys and the Bay on splendid, massive supports, [and] intersect in giant curves over sheets of ivy and ice plant. They are the masterpieces of 20th century engineering. The Cabrillo Freeway, as it passes through the lush canyon of Balboa Park and into the beautifully landscaped intersection with I-5, was described by many of our respondents as their favorite piece of freeway. But then it arrives at that jumble of signs and buildings which is the back door of downtown—a true anti-climax.

Other parts of the freeway system are less successful. Although almost all our respondents used the automobile, few of them found their journeys a very enjoyable experience. . . .

At times, it even is difficult to know which freeway one is on. Gravel pits, bare hills, [and] graded cuts not yet recovered scar the natural landscape. Elsewhere than in the confined Cabrillo canyon, with its lavish use of water and its old trees, the effort to create a green setting is abortive. The spaces are too big, too bare of trees, too open; it takes too much water. The adjacent urbanized land, which has its back to the freeway and yet is undergoing a rapid change due to that freeway access, is the effective visual setting, and it is nondescript. In some stretches, as for instance through La Mesa, the freeway is flanked by telephone poles and signs for steak and whiskey. When the glare from the concrete is coupled with this open, dry landscape, the experience can be arid and eye-scorching.

The freeways clearly cannot be replaced or relocated. But they need *repair*.

The city should pay attention to its highway landscape. This means a detailed evaluation, to see which settings should be preserved, and which can be rehabilitated. It means thinking of the highway in terms of the way it approaches important centers, the landmarks and gateways that are visible, the views of the ocean, the bays, valleys, and hills. Easements should be established to protect these better views. Landmark structures might be encouraged at significant locations.

Cluster vegetation, use native plants. It is too expensive and water-consuming to plant the freeways continuously. Intense clumps of vegetation are more effective than slim lines of trees, or narrow bands of ice plant. Native plants or drought-resistant trees may take time to grow, but it may be possible to use irrigated planting until the native species take over. Look at the old trees along the former Pacific Highway north of La Jolla to see how an unwatered planting of trees can in time give strong character to a road.

Use highway detail in non-standard ways. Coloring the pavement and the guardrails in dark green, blues, and browns could do much to relieve the sense of glare and heat. Varied lighting systems, or signs which had local character and conveyed local names and information, would support a sense of place in the city.

Accommodate other uses, other modes of travel. Express bus lanes can be designated, to support a fast transit sytem. Bicycles, even pedestrians, might have a lane across the Coronado Bridge. On very special occasions, a section of freeway, such as in the Cabrillo canyon through Balboa Park, might be closed to cars and used for some public event. A street fair, perhaps, to reassert possession of these car ways and to give the trees a breath of air.

Incorporate the freeway into the community landscape where feasible. Noise, fumes, and visual intrusions can be reduced by buffers and walls, but a consistent sound-proofing would lead to miles of monstrous, continuous walls, much like the walled-off arterials in Mira Mesa, but more gigantic. Buffers must be applied with care, and locally fitted. Communities can also be encouraged to make use of the supporting freeway structures. The murals applied in the Harbor 101 district humanize the enormous pylons of the Coronado Bridge approach. . . .

The remainder of the freeway program should be delayed once 805 is completed, thus precluding construction, at this time, of the outer circumferential freeway. EPA pollution standards may also limit large new auto-oriented activities. In the longer term, charges for the use of the freeway system may be levied on drivers or on the large traffic generators.

The bus is the fundamental unit of a public transportation system, but people will be attracted to buses, and away from cars, only if the frequency, character, and location of service [are] much improved. . . .

Long distance commuting buses might use their own freeway and arterial lanes. Bus stops could have seats, shade, parking, food and drink, rest rooms, newsstands, information, night lighting. Mini-buses could operate in the suburbs on flexible routes. The internal comfort of vehicles could be improved, and made easier for the elderly to move about in. It should be possible to carry bicycles and vehicles for the handicapped. Some buses could be double-deckers, or have open tops for the pleasure of riding in them.

Fixed rail transit, now under serious consideration in San Diego, can offer a fast, comfortable trip and, if above grade, a fine view of the city. It frees the rider to read, think, or daydream in ways which are difficult in an automobile. If the system is safe and usable for children, and if it presents information about the areas it is passing through, it can be a unique resource for public education. The social image of the system must be attractive to a wide range of San Diegans; the quality of materials and detail should bring some glamour to the everyday commute and the recreational journey. . . .

Stations should be located where they can reinforce existing centers and where higher densities are possible. Rather than surrounding stations with vast parking lots, bus, pedestrian, and bicycle access to the stations should have equal consideration. Parking garages could compact the areas devoted to the automobiles.

The detailed location and form of the lines and stations must respect the local fabric. Carelessly done, they can be as destructive as highways. Experience with the BART system in San Francisco shows that a system fits poorly into the landscape, and is unlikely to satisfy a broad range of travelers, if engineering criteria are dominant during design. Environmental surveys of the corridors should locate sensitive areas, areas of change, neighborhood and community territories, valued places, and good crossing points. Where possible, the lines should be elevated for the benefit of the traveler, preferably on light support structures, and along wide commercial streets or other less sensitive edges. This will depend on how noise-free the system can be.

The general location of routes and stations will affect the form of regional growth. Since a transit system induces growth, just as a highway system does, the location of its routes and stations is critical for the future form of the city. Since we recommend that growth be directed to the present urban areas, and especially along the coast and southwards toward the border, **the highest priority rail transit line, from our viewpoint, is that which will run from Mission Bay to Tijuana.** This will serve much of the denser city, Mission Valley, Centre City, the industries, and the water-based recreation. It would make a link to Tijuana and the proposed international airport, relieve some of the border congestion, and bring isolated communities like San Ysidro closer to San Diego. It would encourage "densification" all along the coastal plain and to the south, and in the future to be the spine for residential renewal of the Bay shore.

From that same viewpoint, **the next priority would be the eastern line through North Park to San Diego State University,** to serve that heavily settled area. Extending north from Mission Bay could be held back, in early years, to slow the northerly growth. In any case, congestion on I-5 above La Jolla is not predicted until after 1995.

Cycle trails in the valleys and canyons have already been proposed. **Cycling to work** is also possible—the climate is ideal, and the grades are flat if one can move either up on the mesas or down in the valley. Transit vehicles should be able to carry cycles so that the cyclist can extend his range. A system on the mesas will require more than just setting up a few signs, however. Cycle rights-of-way which are separate from those for automobiles will be needed, along or in parallel with the arterial system. . . .

Dispersing work places into residential districts may make it feasible to walk to work. Pedestrians in San Diego are a rarity today. It takes courage and stamina to walk. . . .

If as much attention were given to sidewalks as to streets, the walker would have a chance. For instance, since cars climb more easily than people do, streets should be raised or lowered to allow level pedestrian crossings, rather than vice versa. Footways need not always hug the road system. The importance of street-front activity, trees, seats, signs, lights, and walk surfaces [has] already been underlined.

Airplanes dominate San Diego. They are constantly overhead. To see them come down over the Laurel Canyon onto Lindbergh Field is a dramatic spectacle, but the noise and the danger of a crash threaten many people. Miramar's noise blankets large areas north of La Jolla. Indeed, airplane noise may affect as many as 100,000 people in the region.

Airports should be separated from residential areas. Since the coast and the Bay are prime locations for residence, and airplanes find no real pleasure in them, the airports should be moved. Lindbergh, as the most dangerous and annoying one, and the one now requiring expansion, should be the first. Of the three alternative sites which have been studied, the Carmel Valley and Miramar would continue to threaten residences, and would at the same time induce a northerly spread.

It may be that some site well inland would be the best of all, but of the three places examined, consolidation with the Tijuana airport at the border is clearly to be preferred. Flights can come in over underdeveloped land to the east, and over the flood plain of the Tijuana River to the west. Some 6,000 persons in San Ysidro will be affected, but that number is small relative to other locations, and none will be directly under the flight patterns. A border airport will be no more than 30 minutes from downtown San Diego, and could have a transit connection. It would encourage the industrial development needed to employ residents of Tijuana and of the South Bay communities. . . .

The Mexican Connection

All the official maps go blank at the border. The U.S. maps are white below the line, while the Mexican maps are white above. Even the special Border Area Plan of 1966 shows nothing across the line! Newspapers on either side give no more than 4% of their space to what is happening on the other side. To see the border from the air is a visual shock. The fence runs ruler-straight and heedless across valleys and mesas: open fields on one side, crowded settlements pressed right against the fence on the other.

But this is a single natural region, and a connected social landscape as well, despite the barrier. San Diego thinks of itself as a border town, but in reality it is part of the functioning metropolitan region of San Diego/ Tijuana. Tijuana, with its estimated 400,000 people, is almost one-quarter of the total regional population today. It is one of the most rapidly growing cities in the world—perhaps 6 or 7% per year, although there is no sure information. At these current estimated rates, Tijuana will have a population of 1.4 million by 1990 and will be as large as San Diego in 40 years.

Over 30 million persons cross the border every year, the largest volume of flow across any international border in the world. U.S. citizens go south for shopping or recreation; Mexican citizens go north to shop or to work. Legal and illegal immigrants move over the line, and many other things as well: piped water, sewage, smoke and dust, money, goods, floodwater. . . .

The relation between these two halves of the landscape, belonging to two separate nations and to two vastly different economies, goes far beyond this report. But we hope that officials and citizens will begin to *see* the division, to understand that it is artificial, and that it is urgent that they attend to it. The destruction of the natural landscape in Tijuana, the pollution, poverty, and social disruption to be found there, as well as the hopes and the vital energy, are the problem and the opportunity of the whole metropolitan region and will be so increasingly. . . .

The key actions that are needed are economic, social, and political ones. Stable, equitable regional institutions must be built up. But actions in the environment might help to lead off, and might alleviate some present problems. For example:

Establish an international airport on the Otay Mesa to provide a major focus for growth. The airport could be located on or near the border, just north of the present Tijuana Field, and surrounded by a joint free-trade zone on both sides, with a new crossing for goods and workers. The industries which would be attracted here by the access and the freedom from customs duties would revitalize this relatively stagnant end of San Diego County, and give jobs to Mexican workers. The airport could be connected by rail transit to the centers of Tijuana and San Diego. . . .

Keep the lower Tijuana River valley open for joint use. The floodplain of the Tijuana should be kept open for agriculture and for recreation, and the estuary protected as a nature preserve. Tijuana is desperately short of open space. For its 400,000 people, there is one tiny central plaza, a narrow beach at a distance, and one golf course for the well-to-do. The floodplain is a precious resource for joint open-air use, to the degree that it will no longer be used for agriculture. For example, the extensive flood dissipator area that will be built on the U.S. end of Mexican flood channel might be made into a unique outdoor sculptural park and playground. Pedestrian trails and bikeways could lead into the open plain from both sides, connecting with the south Bay and the Otay River, Tijuana center and the upper valley, Tijuana residential areas, and the shore trails.

Build bicultural institutions on the mesas above the river valley. The sites at the tip of the mesas overlooking the valley from the south are magnificent locations with sweeping views. They are easily accessible from the Mexican side, and that area is still lightly occupied. These are fine locations for one or more international institutions, such as an Interamerican University which would focus on the two cultural heritages.

Let the new center of Tijuana become the major southern sub-center of the San Diego/Tijuana region. This commercial center, to be built along the new flood channel, can complement San Diego's Centre City, Mission Valley, and the central functions likely in time to develop somewhere north of the University of California. . . .

Joint action to protect the natural setting. Cooperative studies of pollution, of water and air movements, of the ocean, [and] of the general ecology of the international region are sorely needed. So are joint efforts to manage those phenomena: to control air and water pollution, treat sewage, supply water. Water is desperately short in Tijuana: the city can supply only some 60% of the requirements of its people. . . . The water requirements of the whole metropolitan region must be considered as one unified system of supply and demand. Waste on one side of the line and shortage on the other cannot long continue. Creating a water-conserving landscape in San Diego is important—even if for no other reason—in order to meet the urgent needs of the whole region.

What the Region Could Become

Dreams have some use. They give us hope, but they also move us to act. Can one dream about a region as large and as complicated as San Diego/Tijuana? We think so. There are dreams for the future region that one might realistically work for.

San Diego de Baja California

San Diego/Tijuana could be the center of a large international region, a vital meeting point of two living cultures. The metropolis would share its water, its energy, its landscape, its culture, its economy. The border would be converted into a zone of confluence.

The public sea. The entire seafront would be in public ownership, accessible to everyone by all modes of transport. Many San Diegans would live near it, within reach of the sea breeze, within walk of the beach. Productive activities that depended on the water—shipyards, boat docks, ferry slips, fish piers—would still be there, to give the water life and variety. But the sea would be given to the people of the city, of all

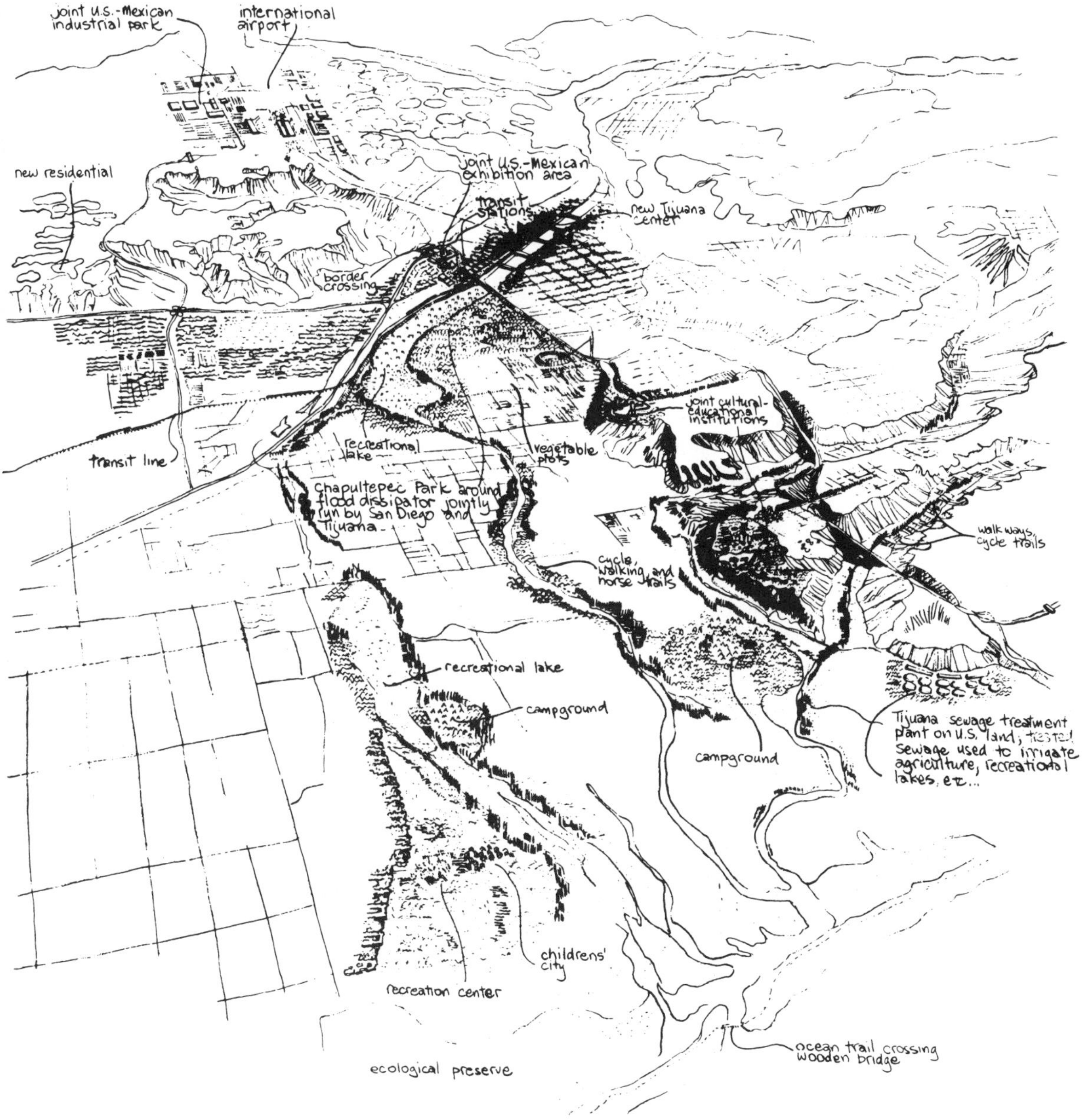
joint U.S.-Mexican industrial park
international airport
new residential
joint U.S.-Mexican exhibition area
transit stations
new Tijuana center
border crossing
transit line
recreational lake
Chapultepec Park around flood dissipator jointly run by San Diego and Tijuana
vegetable plots
joint cultural-educational institutions
walk ways, cycle trails
cycle, walking and horse trails
recreational lake
campground
campground
Tijuana sewage treatment plant on U.S. land; tested sewage used to irrigate agriculture, recreational lakes, etc...
childrens' city
recreation center
ocean trail crossing wooden bridge
ecological preserve

Looking across the Tijuana River Valley at the border region as it might become.

classes, to live near and to enjoy. The Bay is cleared of its airports, vast factories, and gloomy naval installations. It is an urban bay, surrounded by residences, an everyday sight and pleasure.

The coastal band. The great majority of San Diegans live in a compact low-rise urban band along the shore, a band rarely more than two or three miles deep, except where it projects along the present chain of communities out towards El Cajon or has moved up the Tijuana Valley. Thus, most people live within easy reach of the sea and the sea breeze, in a mild climate free of smog. Most of this is urbanized land today, except for the coast north of La Jolla and Clairemont, and this north coast would be held back from development until a late stage. The growth was a "densification" of the older areas, and was especially encouraged south to Tijuana and around the Bay. By regional policy, the north-south social gradient has been flattened out, Tijuana has been integrated into the region, there is a greater mix of people. All incomes and ages have opportunities to live throughout the coastal zone. . . .

Communities of character. The growth of the older areas has been fitted to community character, and based on local advice, so that the distinctiveness of the local communities has been preserved. Fine existing buildings have been saved, and the new ones fit with them in intricate and interesting ways. Public reinvestment and private rehabilitation are continuous and complementary. The worn areas of Tijuana have been rebuilt and reoccupied, by citizens of both nations. The old commercial arteries are now fine shopping streets and community centers. Small workplaces are widely distributed. There are many small parks; the canyons are open and green, the sea not far. Most structures are low. The high towers are clustered at a few strategic places: the major centers and sub-centers around the transit stations, or at some visual keypoint such as a strategic break in the coast, or on some prominent nose at the branching of two major canyons.

The inland kingdom. Inland of the coast the land is much more lightly occupied. No more than 20% of the region's population live here. They occupy low, dense communities of modest size and mixed income, many of them new but which have grown only slowly. They are separated by large tracts of open land, used for farming, recreation, heavy industry, the collection of solar energy, military reservations, or airports. The residential communities are compact, designed for a minimum use of water in a hot, dry climate. Intense planting is concentrated in small courts and gardens, or in the canyons. Elsewhere, the land is undisturbed, the natural plant cover in place. The canyons and valleys thread the region, and lead from mountains to sea. Trails pass along them; food is grown there; water is collected in verdant oases. So the landscape expresses our ultimate dependence on water, and on power from the sun. Traces of the earlier Indian and Spanish occupation have been preserved. One senses the connection to the land and its history, to the mountains behind, the sea before, and the sun and stars above.

Traveling light. People go to work by cycle, bus, and ferry, and some can do it on foot. Since work weeks are flexible, there are no tense commuting peaks, nor any frantic weekend race. People can use the same varied means to shop, or to meet their friends, reach the sea, or explore the countryside. Cycles are easy to rent and can be carried on any public vehicle, as can shopping packages. By foot and cycle, one can range the entire coast, go up any valley or major canyon. Rail transit is for longer trips up and down the urban band. Light aircraft and dirigibles go from center to center. Automobiles are for trips *out* of the city, or for the handicapped, or for special deliveries or emergencies. The arteries and freeways give as much space to buses and bicycles as they do to cars. Traveling has become a pleasure, a way of enjoying the region, and no one is confined.

Why Have Things Gone Wrong?

Many people might agree with us that this would be a desirable future. But it will never happen unless we understand how the the city is actually built, and thus how it might be built differently. Why have so many mistakes been made? Why are so many parts of the city deteriorating? There are a number of reasons:

1. When a city is built rapidly, mistakes are inevitable. Developers, private or public, do not foresee the consequences of what they do.

2. Vast social changes—immigration, the search for subsistence or comfort, new technology, shifting social and economic patterns, new ways of living—are revolutionizing how we use the land. Public agencies cannot cope with these changes. Indeed, they are often unaware of them.

3. There are real conflicts between sections of the community, e.g., employment vs. conservation, city vs. county, rich vs. poor, growth vs. non-growth. Even so, many groups are not spoken for.

4. Private desires and profits are satisfied at the expense of the public environment and the natural environment. Thus the city becomes a collection of private islands, which ignore each other and ignore the general public.

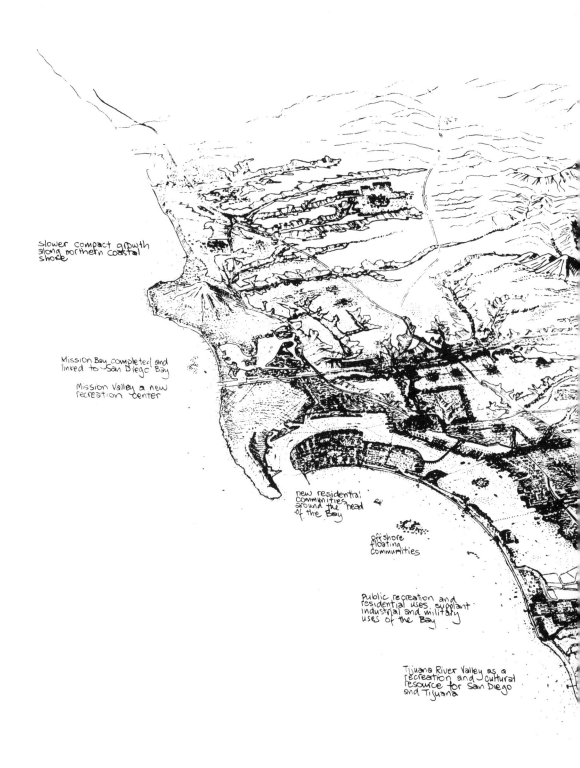

slower compact growth
along northern coastal
shore

Mission Bay completed and
linked to San Diego Bay

Mission Valley a new
recreation center

new residential
communities
around the head
of the Bay

offshore
floating
communities

public recreation and
residential uses supplant
industrial and military
uses of the Bay

Tijuana River Valley as a
recreation and cultural
resource for San Diego
and Tijuana

*A bird's-eye view of the San Diego region as
it might become.*

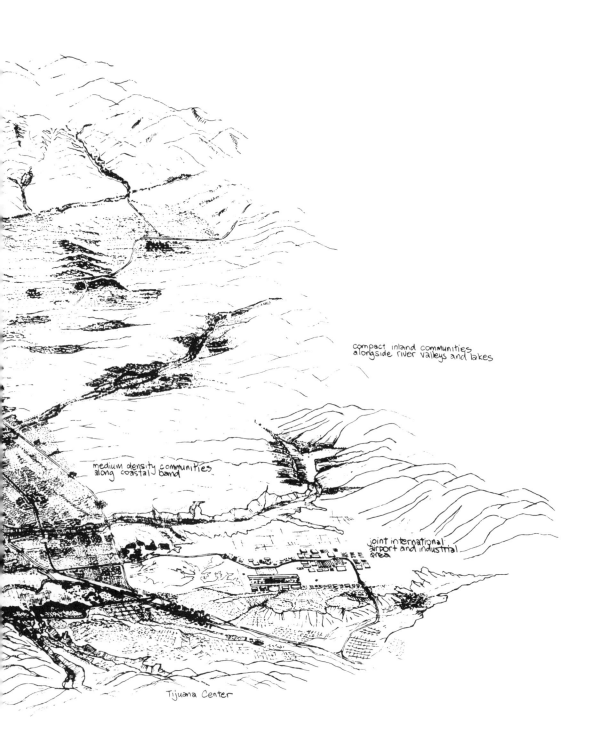

compact inland communities
alongside river valleys and lakes

medium density communities
along coastal band

joint international
airport and industrial
area

Tijuana Center

5. Public development agencies, as well, concentrate on direct costs and their own main interest, ignoring the side effects of their activity on the environment.

6. Planning agencies and citizen interest groups are too weak and disorganized to control these single-purpose agencies and builders; they are reduced to the desperate defense of scattered amenities.

Still, things are changing. The real costs of disjointed, incremental building are coming home. People find they can no longer buy their way out of deteriorating conditions. Even the well-to-do cannot easily escape air pollution, traffic, and aircraft noise. The energy crisis, and the threat of inundation by Los Angeles, have added to the sense of disquiet. The first reaction, understandably, has been defensive and piecemeal: To preserve the Santa Fe railroad station, or to stop the building of high-rise towers along the coast. But *creative* action is required, and more comprehensive issues are at stake.

New agencies and departments have been created to deal with the new problem. Their creation sharpens our attention on selected aspects of the environment but further fragments the decision process. Over 20 agencies now deal with some important aspect of San Diego's environment.[4] Very few of these agencies have trained environmental designers on their staff. Tijuana's planning is equally fragmented, and, to make it worse, much of it is conducted far away in Mexico City.

The two agencies best situated to deal with environmental design issues in San Diego, and to relate them to general planning issues, are the CPO at the regional scale and the Planning Department within the City. The CPO concentrates on large scale issues of regional growth, the distribution of land use, alternative transportation systems, and the saving of regional open space. It advises local governments, makes predictions and gathers information, and exercises control primarily through the review of proposals requiring federal funds.

The Planning Department is more directly responsible for the quality of the city's environment. But it cannot cope with the sudden surge of public interest. It cannot maintain liaison with all the community groups formed to make community plans. Its environmental design staff consists of only three professionals, much of whose time is committed elsewhere.

While large-scale regional questions are beginning to be faced, their relation with the detailed quality of the physical environment must not be ignored. It is no use to save large open spaces if they lie unused or unseen, nor to sketch a regional bikeway system if its detailed-design will preclude its use, nor to propose higher densities unless there is a way in which they can be achieved without community opposition. Many regional schemes have dreary outcomes because they neglect the impact of their general proposals on the everyday environment.

An Environmental Plan for San Diego

We recommend that these concerns be confronted more directly by forming a special Environmental Planning and Design Section in the Planning Department of the city. The Section would have two jobs to do:

1. To produce, within two years, a plan for the environmental quality of San Diego;

2. To begin a continuous environmental planning process, in liaison with other public agencies, encouraging them to set up their own environmental design staff.

Within the first two years, the Section would:

1. Make the first detailed assessment of the quality of San Diego environment and how it is perceived and used by its people.

2. Analyze how the city's environmental quality is created today, and propose strategic changes in that process.

3. Propose images and policies for the future city that will stimulate public discussion and provide a framework for the present scattered efforts to improve the quality of San Diego.

4. Recommend effective public actions for some of the most urgent environmental issues (for example, [the] priority items we list below).

The environmental plan will not simply be a plan for conserving nature, [or] just for beautifying the city (although it will include those). It will deal with six basic values, which might be thought of as the environmental rights of any citizen:

Livability: An environment in which one can act with competence, free from such dangers and discomforts as noise, pollution, accident, heat, glare, and fatigue.

Access: A region in which all groups—including, the young, the old, the poor, the handicapped, and the Spanish-speaking—have equal access to work places, educational and medical facilities, recreation, and open space, and to public environments of equal quality.

Sense of place and time: A landscape which has that definite sense of place and history of which citizens can be proud, and where the different communities take pride in their own territories.

Responsiveness: An environment in the human scale, which allows for personal control and the expression of personal values.

Pleasure and Sensibility: A landscape that is a pleasure to live in, where the senses are heightened by its richness, esthetic quality, and sense of life.

Conservation: A place in which all valuable resources, both natural and urban, are cared for and conserved. . . .

A Few Issues, A Few Principles

In conclusion, we see four questions that seek an answer:

1. Will San Diego and Tijuana continue as border towns, each at the end of its nation's line of development, and each dependent on an exotic and uncertain economy? Or can they realize their role as a bicultural metropolis, the center of a great natural region, safely sustained by the resources of that region?

2. Will San Diego grow as an extension of Los Angeles, and in that city's image, or can it find a new form, adapted to its own site and climate, a form which conserves water, air, and energy, and supports the well-being of its people?

3. Will the region make sure that its amenities are available to all its people, regardless of nationality or income, or will present inequities continue to grow at the regional scale?

4. How can this region organize itself to conserve and enhance the quality of its environment, without losing touch with the local people in whose name that quality is being conserved?

In the course of discussing those questions, we have presented many suggestions and possibilities. Our ideas can be reduced to just a few principles:

1. Begin now to manage the environmental quality of the whole region in a coherent, effective way.

2. Save the shorelines, bays, valleys, and mountains, and restore them to everyone.

3. Retard suburban development, and change its form to one better adapted to the site.

4. Redirect growth to the existing urban neighborhoods. Restore and enhance the special character of each one. Shift public investment to those existing localities and increase the measure of local control.

5. Reduce dependence on the automobile, encourage all forms of nonpolluting lightweight transportation.

6. Reach across the border. Treat San Diego/Tijuana as one unified metropolis.

7. Flatten the north-south social gradient, and exploit the east-west natural one.

8. Conserve water, conserve energy, conserve the land.

Notes

1. Point Loma and La Jolla along the shore, Clairemont and Mira Mesa to the north, Navajo and Patrick Henry High School to the east, and Uptown and South East San Diego in the inner city.

2. R. D. Jones, "Community Organization and Environmental Control," unpublished manuscript, San Diego State University, 1973.

3. Timed and transferable development rights are a new idea, not yet tested in practice, whereby growth might be more strictly controlled in location and timing, without giving windfall profits to some landowners and causing severe losses to others. In brief, a total maximum growth rate would be set for some region, and specific, limited zones [would] be designated in which that growth would be allowed to happen. At the same time, all landowners in the region would be given marketable development rights on some equitable basis. Developers in the favored areas would have to buy up rights from other owners in order to proceed with anything more than low-density building on their land.

4. The City Departments of Planning, Parks and Recreation, Environmental Quality, Community Development, Engineering, Police, Fire, and Sanitation; the Port District, the School District, the Gas & Electric Co., and the Transit Corporation; plus, at a larger geographic scale, the County Planning Department, the Local Agency Formation Commission, the Comprehensive Planning Organization, the Air Pollution District, the Water Quality Control Board, the Coastal Commission, State Parks and Recreation, Caltrans, the U.S. Corps of Engineers, the U.S. Navy, the Border Patrol, and the Environmental Protection Agency.

VII Utopias and Cacotopias

In this last part of the volume we gather a very special group of essays written by Kevin Lynch, mostly in the later years of his career. As the title suggests, these writings are all about the future—the possible, the probable, and even the unthinkable. Some are full of hope and optimism, others are sad and frightening.

Lynch was fond of utopias, and apparently even thought about writing a book on them, although he had gone on record once saying "Utopias are out of fashion." (See "Quality in City Design," in part IV.) But when you read the lines following this statement you realize that he was merely commenting on the architectural and social utopias as being too rigid, too definitive, too deterministic: "They were not useful as guides for action: they were unreal, they were static, they dealt with a very narrow range of objectives."

In "Grounds for Utopia" (in this part of the volume) Lynch talked more about how he felt about these utopias—architectural or social. What he rejected in them were the dogmas that leave very little room for individual initiative or creativity, or are incapable of accommodating future institutions and innovations, or are inert to the flux of life and the spontaneity of human intuition.

Lynch was interested in a different kind of utopia: a "place utopia" that allows freedom and choice for life experiences and experiments with living. In Lynch's utopia, people and places bond naturally. People are deeply involved in making places and caring about them; and the places in turn come alive, provide for ongoing life, become memorable.

In many ways the utopia Lynch dreamed of was the natural extension of the normative theories of good city form and good city design he developed in the essays reprinted in part IV. In fact, the essays in that part and this part can be seen as in a continuum. But Lynch himself did not see all of his speculative writings as necessarily utopian. In fact he used to be disappointed, yet clearly amused, when reviewers considered some of his normative writing utopian. He once fired a letter back to a journal editor saying "...I simply discount the fear of 'utopian' speculation," and then adding within parentheses: "Lord, they should see what we do when *we* think we are operating in the utopian mode!"

Indeed we shudder to think what those critics would have said if they had read, for example, the piece on "fantasies" about waste, written more recently and included here.

Two of the five articles in this section are in the "utopia" category. "The Possible City" was written to speculate about how cities might transform with technological advances and changes, and how cities can be designed to keep up with and take advantage of such changes. "Grounds for Utopia" was written as a more complete scenario for a place utopia, integrating Lynch's earlier normative ideas of various form characteristics. Lynch had argued that utopias are not flights of fantasy, nor are they idle daydreaming. Utopias are results of creative processes. Utopian thinking is in a way an act of designing, it is not an idle act of "reciting wishes."

If utopias are more than a recital of wishes, of hopes for the future, "cacotopias" are sad and fearful scenarios of doom and despair. In Lynch's own words, cacotopias are "imaginary descriptions of horrifying worlds to come" (*Good City Form*). To one who intensely believed in life and living, cacotopias could not have been a favorite subject. Yet Lynch, in the final years of his life, wrote some remarkable essays about cacotopian futures. The tenet of these may seem uncharacteristic of him. One may wonder: Did Kevin Lynch lose his optimism, his unwavering faith in the possibilities for human society? Did he finally give up dreaming about a good society?

We think not. Lynch's cacotopias were educational in purpose: he meant for us to see the worst, so that we would know what to want, and what we should avoid. There is no question, however, that he was deeply troubled by the increasing talk of "limited" nuclear war and "survivable" atomic exchanges immediately after the Reagan administration took office. Two of these essays, "What Will Happen to Us?" and

"Coming Home," were written as part of an effort by a coalition of concerned scientists and professionals to mobilize public opinion against such foolish nuclear defense policy. Thus, in a way, these essays were written to jar our consciousness ("Hell is more impressive than heaven," as Lynch wrote in *Good City Form*), to nudge us from the inertia of apathy, to shake us up a little so that the dreams he had dreamed earlier could still be saved, or at least salvaged. We don't think he abandoned his dream. The scenarios of doom he wrote were in fact intended to preempt such eventualities.

Lynch let his creative talents loose in writing these scenarios. "What Will Happen to Us?" (written with Tunney Lee and Peter Droege) is a manual to help communities plan for coping with the disaster of a "limited nuclear engagement." Grave and sobering, the essay assembles all the relevant objective facts of a nuclear explosion and what (little) a local community can do to survive it. The essay "Coming Home" begins with a critique of the kind of official studies of "post-attack" recovery of urban communities that have been sponsored by government agencies from time to time, and the absolute futility of such studies. And in order to underscore the futility of such efforts Lynch wrote perhaps the most powerful fiction of his life: a narrative in which he himself tries to find his way home to Watertown, a suburb of Boston, after a nuclear attack has leveled the entire metropolitan area. Finally, "Fantasies of Waste" explores the consequences of too much and too little waste. Bizarre yet humorous and entertaining, this essay is part of the prologue of Lynch's posthumously published book *Wasting Away* (edited by Michael Southworth and published by Sierra Club Books). The book ultimately develops into an insightful piece on waste—a subject Lynch had been researching for some thirty years—and presents some creative ideas about how to waste well.

The Possible City (1968)

The issue for the future city is how it affects the growing of human beings. If we knew better, we might add: and the survival and development of other living organisms. But our knowledge and our ethics are still too limited for that. Growth occurs (or fails) within a spatial pattern of activities and spaces, and that pattern plays a role in the growing. There are various world futures which we can imagine: Does any of them include a city suited for growth? Can we make that possible city a probable one?

Social changes cause environmental problems—congestion, discomfort, obsolescence, pollution, abandonment, overload—and in return environment frustrates change. The changes themselves are disturbing. Landmarks are swept away, associations dissolve, we lose our roots in particular places, our values waver. We may be poisoning the world with our technology; and so we fear our power as well as delight in it. The changes occur unevenly: groups are exploited or left behind; in a relative sense they become poorer, their ways of life more archaic and despised. They are excluded from the common opportunities. The bitter contrast of the ghetto will become more visible as advantaged groups gain mobility.

So we hope to make environments which accept change, and also to manage that change so that it occurs in the areas of need, and does not degrade the living community. Environment might be used to decrease deprivation and segregation, rather than to sharpen it. It might create more intricate ecologies. Indeed we might learn, not simply to accept change, but to see its possibilities and delights.

Our fear of change is accompanied by a fear of powerlessness, the loss of meaningful participation and control. The individual makes only marginal alterations in the system in which he lives. Perhaps there were never more than rare periods in history when the individual had any autonomy, but we feel that he should have, and does not now. Fears of impersonal control are evoked by recent advances in biology, in psychology, in information systems. People are aware of the extent to which their lives are already manipulated. Alienation and loss of purpose are talked about; they also exist. The increase of leisure and material production threatens to exaggerate those feelings by detaching men from the work that has been their central purposeful activity.

Environment can counteract this loss. Surroundings can be designed to be open and responsive to the user; they can encourage him to learn and to become involved; they can be a vehicle for autonomy and local decision, an object of creation and purposeful absorption. Technology might increase individual option and control, rather than decrease it. None of this will of itself solve these dilemmas, and yet it can countervail.

Reprinted, with permission, from *Environment and Policy*, ed. W. R. Ewald, Jr. (Indiana University Press).

Our possible city must therefore have certain characteristics: adaptability coupled with a sense of past and future continuity; equalization of opportunity; a diversity of species, habitats, and ways of life. It must be open and responsive, experimental and engaging. These are crucial qualities for the future. However general, they direct attention to particular possibilities. But these possibilities will not come of themselves. Our cities become more rigid, segregated, and unresponsive. Are there chances to move in an opposite direction?

For the future, I assume a steady growth of the world population, and, in the developed countries at least, rising incomes and expectations. I hope for an increase in international cooperation, and a flow of resources to reduce international and intranational inequalities. I do not hope for radical political shifts in this country, although they will occur elsewhere in the world, but for increased public intervention and investment in city development. I expect a continuance of the current restraints on how cities grow: a diversity of users, a dispersion and conflict of decision, institutional and environmental inertia. I hope for some shift in the attitudes of people toward each other: a greater mutual tolerance, concern and delight, a desire to see human potentialities realized. We might even progress from a human-centered ethic to one which values the whole interdependent living community, to an attitude which welcomes diversity, both human and non-human. Quixotic, perhaps, but possible; a development in which the city could play a role.

The Edge of the Metropolis

We can expect the metropolis to be the normal environment of the future: the realized desire of those seeking space, better services, congenial neighbors, and a home of their own. Present estimates are that 80 percent of our population will be living in such regions by the year 2000, and that the largest of these metropolises will coalesce into four giant megalopolitan regions—on the Atlantic seaboard, along the lower Great Lakes (these two may even grow together into a single belt), in Florida, and in California—four regions containing 60 percent of the U.S. population on $7\frac{1}{2}$ percent of its land. The horror of critics is unjustified: This is a superior environment by past standards. It doesn't "eat up" land, nor will it cause the end of civilization. It frees large areas of the country for rural and recreational uses. The apparent threat of extended urbanization can in fact be turned to our great advantage—can be but may not be. The metropolis has serious problems. Social groups are increasingly segregated in space. There is a lack of diversity and a lack of identity. If you have no car, you are stranded. There are no concentrated centers. But none of these difficulties is inherent in the metropolitan form.

If you ask anyone to imagine a city of 50,000 square miles, 600 miles long (as the Californian megalopolis is projected to be), he feels desperate because he imagines a mechanical enlargement of the present city. But one need not feel lost in a region, simply because it is encompassing. Setting limits is only one way of structuring. Such a region could be a very diverse place, it could be clean and open, the quality of its life could be pleasant and challenging. It could be a homeland, a beloved landscape. We cling to the notion of the rural-urban dichotomy—small cities in a rural hinterland, a world with an outside and an inside. That world is fading before our eyes. The sense of being at home depends neither on size nor on traditional form, but on an active relation between men and their landscape, a landscape which they made and which speaks to them. How can we achieve this in such vast areas?

Guiding the development of these great regions will be a staggering task, considering our difficulties in managing the growth of much smaller and less complex areas. Even by 1975, we can expect new construction to double the present rates. The sheer quantity of new environment, which will be most striking at the fringe but also substantial in the city interiors, is an opportunity and a threat. There will be a growing body of used environment, which must be continually adapted and maintained, or painfully rebuilt, while attending to a great diversity in user wants and needs. If anything, this diversity appears to be increasing. No central agency can direct the details of this process.

The most effective opportunities for environmental quality are at the point of development. One such opportunity is at the edge of the metropolis, where public (or mixed public and private) authorities might assemble and plan large chunks of undeveloped land for diverse urban uses, which would then be transferred to private and public development agencies for actual construction. These would not be "new towns" in the old sense. The authorities would work with the normal urbanizing process, much as several large private land developers are doing today, but on a far more comprehensive scale. The private developer works under severe limitations of market and political control, yet his product is the environment of the future.

Here at the growing edge our evolving ideas for clusters of mixed low density housing, for the maintenance of ecological balance, for intense diversified centers or continuous open spaces, for new modes of transport or the control of climate, light, and sound, could most easily be put into practice. Any existing social, or built, or natural identities could be preserved. The authority could create a sense of place by specifying particular environmental characters to be built into various zones. The region would become a mosaic of distinctive and well-fitted districts, a human landscape built from the beginning. No one is building it today. All large developing areas at the metropolitan fringe should pass through the hands of capable public authorities, but not through a single central authority. It should be a public responsibility to see that an adequate supply of land for development is constantly available throughout the metropolitan region, that it is well planned, well serviced, and free of speculative surcharge.

This public power must only be used if it will reduce the growing segregation of our population by race and class. Rather than straining to entice the middle class to return to the central city they have left behind, we should make it possible for others to move out to the suburbs that they would like to reach. This will be a long effort, contending with resistance from the suburbs and fear on the part of the movers. It will require concerted action on jobs, housing, and transport—a massive resettlement. It will mean the construction of substantial quantities of new housing within the reach of lower income groups. Technology promises future reductions in building costs, and we should press to realize those promises. Until they are realized, the construction of housing must be subsidized. We must create development agencies which can take on those resettlement tasks, in the newly organizing areas, but also in scattered locations throughout the inner and outer zones. They will necessarily be engaged in the provision of social services, the improvement of transportation, and the distribution of employment, as well as in building houses. Grants to local authorities to pay for the additional services required must accompany these movements, to make them politically palatable. "Sister" relations between inner and outer districts, with exchanges of services and visitors, might precede permanent population movements. It may be unrealistic (even undesirable) to hope for a fine-grained mix of social groups, but we must destroy the one-color school district and the single-class town. We are already building the future metropolis. If we refuse to intervene decisively, that future is an even suburbia and a frayed interior. It will have its amenities. It will have its costs—not least being a denial of growth to a sizeable number of people. And it will be a splendid opportunity gone by.

The System of Centers

Strenuous efforts are being made to "save the downtown" as a last vestige of concentrated urbanity. Indeed there is something lost, if we should no longer have places of intense activity, of diverse services and opportune encounters. The outward dispersion of high intensity activities to widely scattered sites deprives us of social and visual meeting points, as well as of the opportunity to live close to the action or to enjoy a rich array of supporting facilities. But to maintain a single center as the dominant focus of employment and services is to swim against the flood. As far as it is successful, it will preserve commuter congestion and the ghetto.

We have a better opportunity: to channel high density housing, services such as health, education, shopping, culture, and entertainment, and concentrated and interlinked employment, such as offices and business services, into a galaxy of metropolitan centers, each large enough to provide substantial diversity and to support a local transit system, provided with structures linked at many levels, pedestrian carriers, and climate control. To the extent that these centers had a special character of activity and form, they could stand for differentiated areas of the region, and might encourage social interactions over a broader geographic base, less tied to class and race.

In and near these centers people might live who, by choice or necessity, wished to be close to work and services. The centers might also serve as points of reception for families escaping from the central ghetto. Centers could be built out of older incomplete foci, or encouraged to coalesce in the regions of new growth. Their range of activity and their physical character could be guided in a way which would be impractical over larger areas. Building or rebuilding the important focal points is another crucial development task which might be undertaken by public authority. There are significant advances to be made in the design and maintenance of such intensive locales.

Change and Renovation

Activities that occupy the older areas are constantly changing, and we have burned our fingers in trying to manage that change. Even the oldest areas are rarely completely abandoned, but become specialized for other activities, often more diverse than the original ones. The contrast of activity and setting can be quite evocative. If we do anything here, it should be to facilitate these shifts in use, to assist in the gradual specialization and decrease in density of the central areas. The danger lies in the attempt to cling to the present—to save the downtown, for example, or to congeal our problems by rebuilding at higher densities. We must encourage the central areas to open out, to become the locus for particular uses and institutions, the residence of people with special tastes, or attractive vacation areas in which open space and intense urban activity are closely mingled. Some concentrations of high density housing will persist, particularly at the core, but we can expect to see apartment living widely distributed throughout the metropolitan region. Areas of particular historic interest or environmental character should of course be conserved, but they occupy a small fraction of the land. The central ghettos might be transformed, not only into centers of political power and social reconstruction, but also into settings of prestige, the symbolic centers of cultures newly visible in our society. As a prerequisite for unlocking this process of change, its costs must be openly accounted for and justly allocated. The burden now falls on deprived and powerless people.

One promising avenue for dealing with the existing city is the search for underused space and time, and its readaptation for a desired activity. We can explore the use of streets as play areas, or the possibilities for using roof tops, empty stores, abandoned buildings, waste lots, odd bits of land, or the large areas presently sterilized by such mono-cultures as parking lots, expressways, railroad yards, and airports. We may find room for new modes of transit, additional housing, schools, or special recreation.

Another strategy is to find ingenious ways of adapting or reconditioning the existing environment with a minimum of disturbance to existing users. Rehabilitation techniques have not yet proved very promising, except where the degree of improvement desired is small, or where it has been done piecemeal by the user-owner employing his own labor and capital and making a fit to his own particular desires. New techniques which aided this latter process—packaged amenities which are easy to insert; tools, power, and materials for use by the individual; training and guidance in rebuilding—would all be useful. Technical services and information must be made available directly to the user of environment, particularly to those who presently have no voice in political and developmental decisions.

Perhaps we can organize a rebuilding and maintenance industry, and begin to conserve our still-useful environmental stock in a more systematic and efficient way. Renewal-and-rehabilitation has traditionally focused its attention on the oldest parts of the central city. The problem for the future is the conservation and improvement of what are now the new suburbs. Surely there are ways in which sophisticated technology could be employed in such essential tasks as the cleaning or refacing of outdoor surfaces, the modification of noise and climate, routine housekeeping, the prevention of fire, the removal of waste, the provision of local communal services, or the insertion of small gardens or micro-recreation facilities. It is just this kind of environmental renewal that can provide jobs for many of the lowest skilled or racially excluded workers. Maintenance technology should be designed to make use of such men, and then to train them in more complex skills.

We will always be concerned with the problem of obsolescence. Technology and styles of life will shift in the near future at least as rapidly as they have done in the near past. One reasonable response is to make sure that any new environment is highly adaptable, able to accommodate new functions at low economic or social cost. We know very little about how to do this. We can only make vague guesses: building at low density, providing growth room or surplus capacity; providing a high capability for circulation and communication; separating functions and structures that are likely to change from those likely to be permanent; using temporary or movable structures (only if we are later able to control their disposal, however); establishing a neutral grid to regulate locations and connections; setting up a monitoring system which will call for adaptation at the first signals of change. We have much to do to develop and test these ideas. The urgency and permanence of the problem would make full-scale research worthwhile. For example, we would like to be able to specify levels of adaptability as performance standards for new construction.

Mobility and change add novelty and adventure to living, but exact an emotional price. The sense of continuity with the past, the feeling of "home," of belonging and commitment, has some relation to geographical fixity. Change must be made psychologically tolerable. One may be trained to live in a changing place and with changing social relationships. One may shift his point of reference from a small spatial community to a larger unit (a metropolis, a nation), or to a stable but spatially shifting social unit (the traditional solution of the nomad), or to a stable set of connections with persons who are dispersed and shifting in space, or even to a symbolic home occasionally visited (a function that summer cottages may be taking on for some of our mobile middle class).

In any case, environmental form must take account of these stresses: providing clear orientation for the newcomer, with a proportion of familiar stereotypes; clarifying the image at larger and larger scales, so that the individual may feel that he is only moving about within his permanent "home"; providing symbolic landmarks of continuity with the past; making change legible in itself. Behavior changes rapidly; physical form may be used symbolically to stabilize it and give it continuity, as well as to support it functionally. By expressing what shifts are going on, how they arose out of the recent past and are likely to continue into the near future, the environment can help us to live with change, and even to enjoy it.

It will also be necessary to establish and protect areas of little change, of archaic ways of life, for those who do not choose to follow the common pattern. Tenure of a second home in a stable setting may make change elsewhere more acceptable. In a shifting world, one must know how to forget and how to remember, how to conserve and how to dispose of environment. The problems of change and mobility will be fundamental ones for the future city. They tempt us with new possibilities as well.

Design for Mobility

Mobility, access, and communication are indeed the essential qualities of an urbanized region—its reason for being. Cities can be most simply described as being dense networks of communication, and the movement of persons is the critical process. Thus the system of movement is strategic for the quality of the future environment. We are spending large sums on highway systems, and are encountering increasing resistance from those who are dissatisfied with highway performance. Despite troubles of parking and congestion—he can go from door to door at will, over very large territories and in a short time—the car owner is far more moblie than he ever has been. If the car kills, if it pollutes the air and occupies big space, it also confers a new personal freedom. So we become more and more dependent on a single mode of transport, although many cannot use the car because they are too young, too old, too disabled, or too poor to own one.

One of the most efficient ways of enhancing the adaptability of an environment (and to improve the chances and choices of its citizens) is to increase the accessibility within it, so that activities can easily shift from one location to another, or as easily shift their linkages, for example, so that workers can move from job to job without moving their home, or vice versa. Good accessibility is a psychological as well as a physical fact. Fast transport is not enough; people must also feel free to enter, and the location of activities and the system of access must be perceptually legible. To increase the level of accessibility will be to continue an historic trend which is freeing more and more persons from the tight bonds of place, and increasing their scope for action. The future difficulty will not be how to prevent traffic jams (which should ameliorate as urbanization disperses and flow patterns become omni-directional), but how to prevent relative disadvantages from increasing: children locked into suburbs, low-paid workers tied to scarce jobs, old people shut in golden age corrals. Public policy should increase the access for all groups to a wider and wider area. We should have a free transit system, operating over extensive regions. The evolving new communications services should be brought to everyone, via accessible local terminals.

Rather than dream about a return to "efficient" mass transit, we should build a diversified system of small-unit, flexible transport which caters to all groups: safe vehicles in which children can roam or that are suitable for the infirm, programmed mini-buses that will work in low-density areas, special carriers for high-density centers, recreational vehicles, or those that challenge the user by requiring skilled control. The automobile need not be abolished, but [should be] modified and regulated to prevent pollution, increase safety, or decrease noise, congestion, and the preemption of valuable space. The routes themselves can be diversified: direct lines for people in a hurry, slow leisurely tours for pleasure, challenging routes to test your skill, safe easy ways for children or the elderly: motor ways, bus tracks, bicycle paths, horse trails, moving belts, waterways, footpaths. Innovation in vehicle and channel design should be a public function.

We can expect the mobility of population to increase both in frequency and in range. People will be on the move for better jobs, but also for better climate and environment. Distant vacations, pilgrimages, temporary and seasonal communities will be commonplace. Environmental quality will become more important for the economic survival of a place, and places will be liable to receive sudden shifts in load. The Easter mobs on the beaches of Ft. Lauderdale, or the influx to the Sunset Strip in Los Angeles, are signs of the future. Adaptability and the rapid organization of environment will be crucial. We must be able to shift services, personnel, and equipment, even to employ mobile settlements. These pose new problems of design, which should now be under study. As a simple example, we are presently unable to deal with the design of the trailer park, even though it is by now a common residential environment.

Traveling is traditionally considered an unfortunate necessity, a "waste of time" to be minimized. Yet recreational travel is widespread, and ordinary routes could easily be designed to make traveling a delight, and not just a necessity. The sequence of open spaces, motions, visible activities, lights, planting, textures, [and] views could be managed to the pleasure of the moving observer. Views can pick out the principal elements of a city region, its most interesting activities, its history, geology, and fauna. Highways might move through giant sculptures. Our existing arterials, unpleasant and illegible as they are, are with us for another generation or more. They can be improved with the same techniques. At little additional cost, the metropolis may be endowed with a network of scenic corridors. Air travel is a more resistant problem, since present technology is directed toward anesthetizing the experience. Even here, there may be ways to exploit the act of flight.

Our roads have a single purpose, and are driven heedlessly through the landscape. We could use rights-of-way for many other purposes than circulation: for housing, for example, or for recreation or commerce. Roads can be designed to enhance their flanking areas to make space for local facilities. They could be an integral part of the landscape, rather than a scar. Roads are the observation platforms of a city, the prime means by which people organize large regions, making them psychologically as well as physically accessible. The design and development of the entire movement system, including its vehicles, its associated facilities, and its multi-purpose rights-of-way, is one of the great environmental opportunities: it touches on vital interests; its construction is a customary public function; it is an object of great interest for many citizens; it reflects and makes possible a new way of life; it offers unexpected possibilities of form.

An Open Environment

It is crucial for our purpose that the future environment be an "open" one which the individual can easily penetrate, and in which he can act by his own choice. Development of the individual has been an historic role of the city, but it has never been articulated as a conscious goal of environmental policy. The growth of leisure, the economic demands for high skill, [and] the danger of leaving a section of our population behind in helpless ignorance combine to make this humane ideal an urgent social requirement. An education is gained in many ways, not least via the city itself.

The provision of a new kind of open space would be one strategic and yet tolerable way of building an educative city. Here also there is a tradition of government action, although I am not speaking just of the spaces colored green on official maps, but of the areas which are open to the freely chosen and spontaneous activity of city people. I include vacant lots, sandbanks, and open dumps, as well as parks, woods, and beaches. I do not mean tennis courts or baseball diamonds, which, however desirable, are designed for standardized activities, but the uncommitted complement to the system of committed uses which make up an urban region— the ambiguous places of ill-defined ownership and function. There are many possible kinds: pits, mazes, raceways, heaths, woods, thickets, canyons, beaches, allotments and do-it-yourself cabins, rooftops, hobby yards, caves, marshes, canals, dirt piles, junk yards, aerial runways, undersea gardens, ruined buildings. The zones between contrasting regions are of particular value, because of their ambiguity, flux, and range of choice: shore lines, quiet gardens in city centers, the edge of woods, the meeting of salt and fresh waters. This kind of open space may even be within doors: in barn-like buildings where people can organize various activities at temporary stands.

Space of this kind extends the individual's range of choice, and allows him to pursue his purposes directly, without elaborate prior planning or community constraint. Since social investment is low, he has a chance to demonstrate mastery and to participate actively in a way usually denied him in the protected and expensive, committed environment. Here he can act at his own pace and in his own style. Open space is a place of stimulus release, withdrawal, and privacy, in contrast to the intense and meaning-loaded communications which confront him elsewhere. Modern information techniques threaten to submerge our privacy and individual autonomy. In a preferred environment, one can deny communications, as well as seek them—one can protest, even rebel. The guerillas of the future will need a base of operation.

This kind of open space is a place for the try-out of new roles without too serious a risk. It permits the user to learn in a dialogue of action and response. It corresponds to our desire for an autonomous, creative environment. I am not speaking simply of places for "fun," but of places where people may develop commitments and run risks of their own choosing, where they may invent their work and their play, learn to care about things and people, and exert the effort that care demands.

Open space is also a means whereby other species may be preserved and observed in their appropriate habitat. It is crucial for maintaining water resources, and for moderating climate. Widespread areas of low economic commitment, particularly if they are planned to follow distinct natural divisions, will ensure a diverse set of ecological communities. Open space is of obvious service in preserving future flexibility, and it should be public policy to maintain such a land reserve.

For all these reasons, the acquisition and development of a set of uncommitted spaces throughout the urbanized region is a strategic action. As our metropolitan regions expand, we should reserve an extensive web of them. In the older areas, now lean of public ground, there are a variety of lands that can be turned to this use. Our cities might take on a porous texture, embracing open and rural uses, so that the boundary of city and country is erased, and the urban region becomes a complete human environment. Many of these spaces might be in public hands, but much of it could be private, given suitable easements, agreements, or public incentives. They need not be of great size, but should be ubiquitous, highly accessible. Many of them could be based on land presently discarded and unused. Some of them might be only in temporary open-space use, between clearance and recommitment, being part of a continuously maintained land-reserve inventory. While control of such spaces could be dispersed, there should be central agencies concerned with maintaining the "openness" of the region as a whole, constantly monitoring the quality, quantity, and use of the open lands.

The open space system is a clear subject for action. But in the city we wish to make possible, we can go further. We can think of the entire environment as a means to education, a place where learning and working are indistinguishable and absorbing activities. Such an environment would be highly diverse, offering rich sources of information and experience in the midst of everyday life: working processes and styles of life exposed, human and natural history explained, unusual trips and experimental actions facilitated. It would invite exploration but allow periodic withdrawal. The awareness of things and people, direct perception and communication, would be encouraged. Small groups should be able to build and care for their own surroundings. This would be a manipulable world, inviting action and responding thereto; a domain where people could see the results of what they do; a social world with open niches; an array of teaching machines, through which people might gain and structure skill and information at their own pace and for their own purposes.

Surely this redefinition of working and learning will not be brought about by changes in city form, but form can reflect and support it. These policies may sound innocuous but are in fact dangerous. Change and growth are disturbing; they upset vested interests and are painful (as well as exhilarating) to undergo. If we engage in them, we must be prepared for trouble.

Experimental Communities

Just as we look for an environment conducive to growth and learning by its inhabitants, so we also want one that will itself "learn," that will respond to the varying needs of its users and provide a stream of new possibilities for trial and evaluation. Think of a room which responds to the man who enters it: his preference for temperature, his need for light according to the task, his mood for color. We already have some of these devices: the light switch, the thermostat. At the city scale, the task is technically far more difficult, and complicated by the variety of simultaneous users.

We can conceive of large environments which respond to outside changes to maintain some average preference, as the facets of a geodesic dome become opaque or translucent as the sun moves across them, or as street lamps turn on when darkness falls. It would also be possible to build public spaces that would respond to the cumulative effects of users: opening up, or decreasing the accoustical reflectance, or lowering the temperature, as crowds change in size. Alternatively, we might amplify an effect, as by re-projecting views of a crowd to itself, or re-broadcasting its noise, or by allowing its actions to program changes in light and sound. Where the outdoor environment can be controlled on a fine scale, and users are relatively sparse, there are other openings: outdoor radiant heat or light which can be turned on or off at will (or even "track" a traveler), retractable shelters which open out at need. Over a longer time interval, buildings might grow, contract, or otherwise adapt to the activities they contain. People should be able to take on environmental control as they wish, up to the level of intrusion on their neighbor. Ingenious design and technology could open some new possibilities for us.

The symbolic environment might be similarly organized; signs could expose only the most general information to the casual viewer, and respond with details when queried (a directory, a map with locations that light up on call, [and] a programmed teaching device are examples). The creative use of ambient factors—artificial light, sound, modified climate, even smell—is a large and unexploited realm in city design. For example, much of the city experience is a night-time experience, but no city has yet attempted to design the nightscape. City people are vocal about their climate, but no efforts are made to provide a varied outdoor climate, not even an indoor one which is more than a single monotonous standard. A rich and varied responsiveness is what we mean when we plead for a more "human" environment.

If environment should respond to the user, it should also suggest to him new modes of action and perception. New shared experiences may bring men together over the gulf of traditional divisions. We should be trying out settings which offer the possibility of different styles of life: residential areas based on new ideas of family organization; new systems of space organization; new ways of sensing the surroundings; schools completely dispersed throughout other activities of the community; mobile temporary and shifting environments; very-high-density areas using new techniques for communication and privacy; moderate-density zones in which families have the independent control and access now associated with the single-family house; or "isolated" rural settings in the midst of the urban region. Once built, they must be evaluated for their effects; indeed the means of evaluation must be built into their design. They will improve our skill in constructing environment, while expanding the choices that people have. They could be the "museums of the future."

To take one example, new technology will soon allow us to occupy marginal areas on which increasing wealth and population will soon place mounting pressure. We should prepare for the rational exploitation of these hitherto "waste" areas. This means exploratory design and pilot experiments for settlements in the desert, on (even under) the water, in extensive swamps, [on] high mountains, [in] arctic regions, underground. Use of these areas may be forced upon us, here or elsewhere in the world, but they may also turn out to be highly desirable habitats once the adverse conditions are removed. We shrink at the thought of such places—they would be strange, artificial. But the problem is not one of a natural versus a synthetic world; all human environments are natural, and most of them are synthetic. The problem is how to make these new worlds humane, by taking account of our psychological limits and abilities, and how to give them a rich and stable ecology. Occupation of sea or mountain may increase the diversity and delight of our landscape. Certainly we should like to prevent their casual spoliation. Important new technical systems should never be employed before they have been tested for their human and environmental side effects.

Thus there are cogent reasons why we should begin now to make environmental experiments on a substantial scale. They will be expensive. They will be seen as disturbing to the existing order (indeed they are), even immoral. They may have to be geographically isolated, or located in areas where tolerance is high, or restricted to spatial experiments without obvious social connotations. They will attract peculiar people, making generalizations to the rest of the populace more difficult. Experimentation will have to be undertaken with care. The risk is high, and the period of fruition uncertain. Yet this is a most effective way of keeping our future options open. The combination of risk, requirements, and importance means that this work must be institutionalized by government, foundations, or universities. Experimental communities might become the laboratories of our society, a new sort of university, where people are not experimented upon, but join in conducting experiments in which they learn about themselves and their own possibilities.

New Cities

It may be apparent from this that, while I see metropolitan growth as a magnificent future opportunity for the improvement of our environment, I do not advocate a special form nor a single strategy. On the contrary, I

propose a plurality of actions, and many levels of control. I do not emphasize restriction of size, nor starting with what seems to be a "clean slate."
The critical problem is to manage the metropolis as a vast ongoing system,
monitoring the growth and quality of the environment as a whole and
concentrating public efforts at the key points of development. There are a
number of strategic opportunities, of which the most attractive seem to be
planned development and resettlement at the fringe, creating new open
space and transportation systems, organizing a new set of intensive
centers, building a sophisticated disposal and maintenance technology,
developing the techniques and institutions which will facilitate environmental change and also justly allocate its costs, and conducting environmental experiments. These opportunities are easily lost, but the act of
changing the environment can be a potent weapon for mobilizing hope
and social action.

The deliberately planted, independent new city has been much discussed as a remedy for urban ills. In the United States, however, "new
towns" are simply planned chunks of the existing metropolitan regions,
and are functionally integrated with those regions. They illustrate how
new growth can be better organized physically, but they do not deal with
our more refractory social problems. It seems unlikely that new cities, in
their original sense, will be an important device for development in this
country, unless we are prepared to program them to grow at the rate of,
say, one million people in a decade—unless, that is, we are ready to build
new metropolitan regions. Such a task would require a national effort,
based on a policy to change the national distribution of the population. We
would then be seeking to exploit some potential, human or physical, that
could only be unlocked by this means. At present we are unable to say
whether such a massive effort is indicated, whether we can concentrate the
resources for development at that scale, and whether we know how to do it
well. The need for considered national policy of that kind is evident.

New cities are likely to be more important elsewhere in the world,
where urbanization is just gaining momentum, and where there are glaring regional inequalities. Planting a new city can be a critical weapon in
revolutionizing a backward economy. Were there to be a serious world-
wide attack on poverty (and how can we face the possibility that there
might not be?), then international consortia for new cities would be a
potent device. One or more of the developed nations might join with a host
country, furnishing technical aid and part of the capital but leaving political control in local hands.

New cities could be built for political reasons, as they have been in
the past. Cities cut by national boundaries are thought of as disturbing
anomalies. And yet, if we had more of them, joint action on urban problems might tend to keep international communications open. Urban
regions could deliberately be planted across boundaries, either where

current relations were reasonably amicable or even as internationalized buffer zones between nations in conflict. New cities have been suggested as an alternative to American destruction in Vietnam, to turn war expenditures to productive ends, to offer a haven for refugees, and to give us a less embarrassing means of exit. New urban regions might be a constructive way of settling Arab refugees in the Middle East.

This paper has focused on the problems of the city in this country. I do not imply that we can ignore the convulsive changes occurring elsewhere in the world. Morally, we cannot turn our back on the poverty of the colonial world, nor refuse to support the awakening of its people. Realistically, if we do, we will spend our attention and our resources on destruction and "defense." Urban policy is tied to foreign policy. Our predicted affluence and decline in the need for human labor is either chimerical or fragile, in the face of the desperation inside and outside our borders. Whether due to commitments for international aid, or cost for war, we can expect that our resources for internal urban development will continue to fall short of need. Our aim must be to use those limited resources to encourage human growth, and not to find ways to "use up" goods or leisure time. Urbanization in the developing countries poses problems at a different material level, and yet the basic purposes and dangers seem surprisingly similar. Indeed, in the midst of social revolution, those purposes may there be easier to attain.

In the United States, however, the core problem is the quality of the metropolis as a device for supporting the activities of a complex population and for promoting the growth and autonomy of the individual and the small group. This requires an open, adaptable, diverse, autonomous, responsive environment. The necessary actions range from national policies, through the guidance of metropolitan development and the development of certain kinds of large environmental systems, to experimentation and the creation of new prototypes at the site-planning scale.

Opportunities for Action

I have outlined some opportunities for future city form. Do we have the leverage for them? The strategic impression is imposed at the point of development. We need to build the agencies which can carry out development at the scale now required, while avoiding the centralized control over detail that such large-scale action seems to imply. To concentrate the necessary skill and capital, these agencies will probably have to be mixed public and private authorities, with special powers of acquisition and development, but operating under local and national regulation. They need not be tied to one locality, but should be free to apply themselves throughout the nation, and perhaps elsewhere in the world.

I have indicated the crucial points of intervention: the growing edge, the open space system, the circulation system, the intense centers, the insertion of new activities at under-used places in the existing fabric, the building of experimental communities and of new cities in the under-developed world. Development agencies would probably specialize in particular kinds of problems, and there should be a sufficient number of such agencies to encourage competition.

They would be called in by localities—cities, small neighborhoods within cities, or metropolitan regions—or perhaps by other nations—to carry out specific development tasks. Some authorities might be quite large and comprehensive in their abilities, others small and specialized. All of them, by virtue of their public component, and in return for such powers as condemnation, would have mixed criteria of performance, including the well-being and development of the user as well as the return on capital. They would, moreover, be constrained to work within the policy guidelines of the locality engaging them. In any event, they must be motivated or constrained to build with adaptability, diversity, and openness.

Regulatory and planning agencies, tied to units of government, will still be essential, recommending broad policies, monitoring the environmental system and disseminating information about it, proposing controls, and using economic devices such as user charges and user subsidies, or the allocation of block grants to local units. Thus a city, following its general policy, might call in a development agency to acquire and build a new center, or a part of the open space system, which would afterward be turned over to the control partly of public agencies, partly of special institutions, [and] partly of private owners. The center, or the open space, would then operate within the general controls and incentives of the governmental unit.

Planning agencies, attached to a public base of power at that scale, are particularly needed at the metropolitan level, the functional unit where a new environment is actually being built and where the opportunities therefore lie. Their functions will probably include recommendations for the application of user charges and the allocation of federal grants to minimize inequalities and bring out-of-pocket costs closer to social costs, as well as recommendations for key development actions in the region. Similar agencies will be wanted at the other end of the scale—the local intra-city neighborhood. These local areas, working within the constraints imposed by the larger units, should also be able to call for, and control, development and change within their own territory. Finally, since policies for urbanization at the national scale and for international development assistance are prerequisites for action on new cities and for the intelligent use of federal grants as a lever for environmental improvement, the environmental planning functions are also required at the national level.

We need a means for accomplishing environmental experimentation. Work must be done on new techniques for adaptability, as well as on the innovative design of centers, of open spaces, of circulation systems, and of local site planning. Exploratory design should be underway on possible new habitats, and experimental communities must be designed, built, and tested. Laboratories should be engaged in fundamental research on the interaction of user and environment, developing new criteria, and acting as "lookouts" to discern new opportunities and possible futures.

Some of these activities may be carried out by the development authorities in their own area of specialization, since they would now be large and flexible enough to make in-house research reasonable. But much of the exploratory and basic work is too risky to fit into their calculations. Environmental design laboratories and exploratory planning units must therefore be established by universities, foundations, and governments, with sufficient funds and abilities to test their explorations in actual use.

Environmental research and development will not come cheap. The yearly bill for the new urban development and redevelopment that we should be doing will rise to the order of $250 billion in the next generation. If 1 percent of this were to be devoted to research and development, then $2.5 billion per year would be devoted to basic and developmental research on the city environment.

There are severe administrative problems to be met, particularly in regard to metropolitan planning and government, but also in developing national urbanization policy and in making possible semi-autonomous development at the neighborhood level. We will suffer from shortages of skilled manpower when we seek to staff these agencies. However difficult, this is a secondary problem, which will be met once a decision is made to embark.

When massive new powers or funds are applied to a problem, there is always a danger that they will be diverted to ends far removed from their original ones. Urban renewal is a well-known example. Many of the above proposals could be deflected in ways not now foreseen. Their exploration must therefore include a study of how they could be turned to other purposes. The proposed development agencies, for example, might become centers of irresponsible power, unless they were carefully regulated at the national and local levels, and numerous enough to be affected by competition.

A fundamental difficulty will be the resistance to change that will be encountered: the privileged interests, the fears of racial integration or of other social change, the just apprehensions of the displaced. Since our possible city is based on change, there must be provisions for identifying the social and economic costs of change and for fairly allocating them by charges, subsidies, or replacements. Since we will also encounter less rational fears, we will be constrained to begin at points where there is already some consensus: circulation, open space, new suburban development, insertion of new activity into unused interstices in the existing fabric, attacks on pollution, climate, and noise, experiments with new possibilities for the physical fabric of the city.

I have not tried to program the necessary actions, at various scales, for periodic times throughout the next fifty years. I believe that a long-range program of that kind is both impossible to construct (given our present state of knowledge about environment) and useless if constructed (given our inability to control the programmed actions at the scale and over the time suggested). I think it more useful to scan the future for likely dangers and constraints, and particularly for appealing possibilities, and then to suggest present actions calculated to meet those problems and to keep open those opportunities. The opportunities I have outlined above. The critical present actions are to establish the developmental and experimental agencies which will begin to unfold those opportunities; to imbue them with positive attitudes toward growth and diversity; to give them the backing of finance, power, and skilled men that they need for the task; and to begin to prepare environmental policy at the metropolitan, national, and neighborhood levels.

If I seem to prophesy a bright new technological future, I am misread. My purpose is to encourage human beings to grow into their diverse potentialities, and to find a possible city to do it in. Technology and environment might be exploited to that end. They will subvert it, if left to develop in their present course.

Grounds for Utopia (1975)

Most utopian proposals fail to keep space and society simultaneously in mind. There are architectural fantasies—such as those by Soleri, Le Corbusier, and Fuller—which revel in the intricacies of environmental form. Creative, forward-looking, sometimes brilliant when discussing the physical setting, yet they accept society as it is, and simply give it a new home. And any society would in all likelihood become even more autocratic, were it called on to manage those gigantic, intricate structures. (Indeed, this may be one subconscious intention of those dreams.) Among the rare exceptions to this disregard for the social consequence of architectural fantasy are the three brief caricatures of society and place to be found in the Goodmans' "Communitas."

The classical social utopia, on the other hand, preoccupied with creating a new (or, more often, recreating a superseded) social structure, will only sketch a few disconnected features of the spatial environment. The fragments add color and the semblance of reality, or they demonstrate the conviction that physical forms, like all other subordinate things, follow automatically from social organization. The pattern of social relations is far and away the prime determinant of the quality of life. It is hardly surprising, then, that their spatial proposals are as banal and conventional as are the architects' thoughts of society.

In contrast, we find strong descriptions of place in most anti-utopias, where physical oppression abets social oppression in a very direct and circumstantial way. Hell is always vivid and convincing. Heaven, unfortunately, tends to be vaguely sweet, tenuous, and monochrome.

No one can easily resolve this great estrangement. It is difficult to unfold a coherent vision of a desirable new society in a desirable new world. We will attempt something more modest: to show how some utopian features of space might be generated from thinking of how people relate to their surroundings, rather than out of a self-absorbed technical fantasy, or as a mechanical consequence of social prescription. Values can spring from the relation of people to things, as well as from the relation of people to each other. This does not deny the importance of values socially generated, but simply shifts attention to an aspect traditionally neglected. To ask which of the two is more important is worse than asking for a preference between ice cream and bicycles. It is like asking whether bicycle frames or bicycle wheels are most useful.

While the literary utopias traditionally neglect or misread the influence of the spatial setting, the efforts to build utopias in reality made no such mistake, or were soon forced to correct it. Not only did they find that questions of setting had to be confronted if the society were to have a real

Reprinted from *Responding to Social Change*, ed. Basil Honikman (Stroudsburg, Pennsylvania: Dowden Hutchinson & Ross). Copyright 1975 by Kevin Lynch.

existence. They also discovered that the setting could be used to advance their utopian aims, and that it might even generate aims on its own. Thus they consciously designed the communal setting to heighten community identity, to promote social interaction, to encourage creative participation, to express the balance between the individual and the collective, or the link between production and consumption, or the alternation between discipline and ecstasy. True to their heritage, the social critics of utopia have hardly noticed this conscious use of space for utopian ends, but recent scholarship has made it quite evident.

The spatial setting does not merely set limits to our actions. It is also the source of positive satisfactions: the pleasures of creation and maintenance, sensuous delights, the joy of intimate relations to things outside ourselves. Ask someone how they would like to live, and the reply is usually replete with spatial detail.

The spatial environment is not composed solely of inert and permanent physical objects. It includes plants and animals, events, and the presence of human activity, as well as the timing of all those things—the daily changes, the seasonal changes, the progressions of history. This is spatial environment in the broad sense. Moreover, when we seek to analyze its human implications, we find we must include those human attitudes and institutions which are directly connected to the environment—ways of controlling it, maintaining it, changing it, or giving it meaning—land ownership, nature worship, or accepted ways of behaving in a place. (Critics will now object that we have smuggled society back in again. So we have; we can't help it.) Our subject, then, is the implications for utopian thought of the pattern of the spatial and temporal physical environment, including how it is used and managed, and what it means to its users. Beginning as is customary, with a few generalities, we will try to illustrate these possibilities by sketching out a utopia of place.

Fitness, Openness, Connection

A good setting would be biologically *fit* for human beings, and also for other species (but not all living things— we have some enemies!). This has many environmental consequences, ranging from climates and daily rhythms which are amicable to man, through the control of pollution and the conservation of resources, to changes in our attitudes toward nature and waste. Some implications are obvious, others more obscure, especially as we try to balance the conflicting interests of different persons and groups of persons, and then of different species. But there are many common requirements. A hope of survival, and a reverence for life, underlies them.

Secondly, a good world would be *open*. Resources, places, occasions, persons, and information would be accessible to everyone. This statement, too, has broad consequences—in ownership, in transportation, in the density and diversity of use, in the nature of open space, in customary ways of dealing with mobility and access. It means decentralized decision, flexibility, and relative equality. It implies the removal of barriers and injustices, but also those positive actions that enlarge opportunity and our ability to seize it.

In the temporal dimension, it means adaptability and resilience, a landscape easily changed by incremental effort and tolerant to experiment. The ability to change must itself be conserved, and that requires the avoidance of any dead-end, irreversible transformation. Note that this emphasis on dynamic openness is quite different from the typical "environmental" emphasis on a stable ecology, as well as from the usual assumption of utopias that they will last forever.

Third, the ideal setting would be a connected one that is intimately linked to its inhabitants, meaningful to them, expressive of time, of the place and its function, of the society that occupies it. This implies a congruence of use, control, and feeling between human groups and the territory they occupy. It requires symbolic, legible form. It rests on an attitude of caring and relation—a sense of sacredness in the world, and of our nakedness to it. It has consequences for the form of things, for the social institutions of environmental control, for attitudes, beliefs, and customs. Indeed, it is in these mental states that the achievement of this criterion may be judged. Social and environmental characteristics are linked, and the links are ideas in the mind.

Connection, openness, and fitness are values that spring from how men relate to places, and to non-human life. Ethical influences run from place to man, as well as vice versa; our ideas of what is right may derive from the nature of things around us, as well as from the nature of ourselves. We go directly from these generalities to a more circumstantial environmental prescription, prosaic in places, perhaps, but coming from a vision of how men might relate to non-human things.

An Urban Countryside

Imagine, then, an urban countryside, a continuous, highly varied, and humanized landscape. It is neither urban nor rural in the old sense, since houses, workplaces, and places of assembly are set among trees, farms, and streams. The average density of occupation is moderate or low, within which there is a network of intensive centers of small or moderate size. This countryside is as functionally intricate and interdependent as any contemporary city.

It flows over the old political boundaries, and occupies, or is in the process of settling, many kinds of habitat now avoided: mountain slopes, shallow seas, deserts, marshes, the polar ice. In that sense, the world is more evenly inhabited, and even those places not permanently settled are more frequently used than before. Cities are no longer islands encircled by suburbs, sitting in the midst of a featureless rural space—an empty space to pass through, something to be mined for food, timber, minerals, vacations, or the space to grow in. No longer do most people think of a "home town," but of a "home region," regions which contain a complete range of function, but which vary tremendously in their landscape characters, since each habitat is developed in its own mode, and each cultural tradition has its distinct expression.

This expansion of settlement has not come easily, since a fit between men and a strange place requires a modification of both. Settlements at the poles, and on the high seas, faced serious difficulties of boredom, illness, and social strain, until people learned how to respond to the pleasures and problems of those places, and found a way to endow them with human meaning. Efforts to occupy the deep sea permanently, as well as the moon and the planets, have so far failed. We have not yet been able to domesticate these alien places. But there are labyrinthine underground environments, complete with gardens, internal weather, intriguing lights, intimate and awesome spaces. People born to them are homesick on the surface.

While almost all types of terrain (and some waters) are somewhere successfully occupied, and while settlement is continuous in the sense of being interconnected, most of the world's surface is lightly occupied by man. Large areas, in all types of ground, are given to extensive and shifting agriculture, forests, pasturage, open space, wilderness, and waste. These open lands and seas are also continuously interconnected, and so are closely woven everywhere with the occupied surface. The air is clear, waters run clean, and the host of living things, great and small, still flourish on a fertile earth. Even outlaws and deviants can move freely throughout the world.

This did not come about in some titanic cataclysm that wiped away the stains of human occupation. The older, declining urban areas and inner suburbs were gradually rebuilt as community ownership took hold—opened out with gardens and recreations, their specialization diminished, their infrastructure converted to new uses, private preserves opened to the public, their buildings weeded, transplanted and rebuilt. Centers have been built in the outer suburbs and rural lands. Old village centers, formerly drowned in the tidal wave of metropolis, have emerged again. Buildings have been clustered, and productive activities brought in. The old intensive urban cores have for the most part been retained, but radically rebuilt and reused. They are considered to be natural landscapes of as special and difficult a type as a tropical rainforest or an alpine ridge, and special settlements and ways of living have been fitted to their peculiar characteristics. Some have been converted to wilderness, and a few preserved as historic monuments. They are pruned and shaped to bring out their special character, just as any landscape might be. Some specialized, obsolete buildings—skyscrapers, tenements, luxury apartments, huge mills—have proved difficult to adapt, and have been abandoned, or wrecked in some dramatic spectacle. But most old buildings, still structurally sound, turn out to have interesting new uses. Each place has visibly *evolved* from what it was before, and these multiple directions of growth, overlaid on the diversity of land and of society, [have] resulted in a rich variety of habitat. The history of human settlement is vividly inscribed.

The Ownership of Land

The land (or rather, the spatial volume, now that there are settlements underground and undersea, and more recently in the air) is owned, naturally enough, by those who use it. But ownership simply means the right of present control and enjoyment, and the responsibility of present maintenance. The myth of eternal and absolute individual possession has evaporated, since the life of an owner is ephemeral, in contrast to the abidingness of place, and many other creatures have their own overlapping territories. In concept, all the habitable places of the earth are held in permanent trust by various public or semi-public regional bodies. The land has been regionalized, rather than nationalized. Typically, the intensive central areas and major transport routes—i.e., the more heavily "humanized" grounds—are held by local governments, while the remainder is in the hands of special land trusts.

These regional trusts, self-perpetuating but subject to public supervision, are almost like religious bodies. Their aim is to conserve basic environmental resources, protect the variety of species, and keep the environment open for future use. They are not simply preservation societies. They look on themselves as long-term managers, concerned neither with "development" nor with "preservation," but with keeping the settlement system fluid and open. They are trustees for the non-represented—other species and future human generations—whose motives are obscure and whose chances must be preserved. They do rather little planning, control, or improvement, except to assure this. They have the power, and the narrow-mindedness, of concentrated purpose. They will parcel their lands out among stable resident groups where they can. They feel themselves as belonging to the land, as much as the land belongs to them.

These trusts grant leases of present ownership of space to individuals, corporations, and other private and public agencies, and to resident social groups, such as families, group families, groups of families, communes, and the like. There are limits to the volume that may be leased to any one. The leases vary in length, but those made to resident groups are the longest. The latter are renewable, and generally run for the lifetime of members, so that a vigorous group, which regularly replenishes its membership, may hold a settlement space indefinitely. Old resident communities of this kind are commonly encountered. They are organized, not only around kinship or ethnic ties, but also around joint activities of production and consumption, or around commune life styles, and these latter bonds are often related to the nature of the place. Social ties and place ties are closely associated, and tend toward stability. Non-resident land may be in public hands (roadways, schools), or be allotted to semi-public agencies, individuals, cooperatives, or private corporations. Resident groups often maintain their own services and productive facilities, however.

Thus while some space is temporarily controlled by a variety of functional agencies, individuals, or corporations, more of it is in the hands of resident groups, and these holdings are more long-lived. The great majority of people belong to resident groups, although they may work or study elsewhere, be part of some other institution or corporation, and have many other social ties. Yet all holdings change, in response to changes in function, society, and ecology. No assignments are permanent, except for some few sacred or symbolic locations, the publicly held central areas, some permanent wilderness, and the broad rights-of-way of the major transportation routes. As land holdings and uses shift, the pattern of local government and public service also shifts, while the trust territories endure.

The user-lessees plan their own turf, while regional governments plan for the routes and the central areas, the necessary infrastructure and services, and control local users where necessary to prevent external harm. National, even international, bodies may override regional decisions on crucial issues of resource allocation, transport, or social exclusion, particularly where a region has some quasi-monopoly of site, materials, energy source, or amenity. But the management of space is primarily a regional affair, rising out of the interplay between three principal kinds of actors: the land trusts, the regional governments, and the resident communities.

Any person or small group may, in their own region, obtain a lease on a modest but adequate residential space, since the control of most land is recyling regularly, and interregional policies control the basic ratios of men to space. Everyone may have a private indoor space, and a private outdoor one. Children have this right as well as adults. But no one may multiply his residential domains, or continue to hold them when no longer used, or after joining a resident group, or on leaving a region. Migration to other regions is always possible, although supra-regional bodies may use controls or inducements to stablize regional rates of growth or decline.

Residential space may be a piece of land; a space underground, underwater, or in the air; an unused dwelling; or even a volume within a structural framework.

No rent is exacted for the relatively few permanent assignments of land (main rights-of-way, symbolic locations, isolated wilderness). Rents are zero for the modest residential spaces allotted to individuals and small groups, including that space devoted to any minimum subsistence activities such as the production of food and clothing for internal consumption, or the education of their members. Such leases are not transferable; they return to the trust or government on death or abandonment of the space. The costs of maintaining essential services to such space, and of administering the land allocation and planning, are borne generally, via regional taxation or lease revenues. Residential space and service are considered to be public utilities.

Space for larger, or non-resident, activities, including space which is particularly desirable or in short supply, and space leased to individuals and agencies in the center and along the main routes, is leased for some definite term to the highest bidder, and the proceeds used for trust or government purposes. These leases are transferable, are limited in size as well as to term, and are subject to restrictions to maintain future usefulness. Such lease allocations are not allowed to pre-empt the supply of minimum residential space. Public and semi-public agencies and institutions compete in this same lease market. This loss of the hidden subsidies associated with the indefinite possession of unpriced land has been especially difficult for large public agencies such as the military, but all institutions have found their costs inflated thereby, and must come closer to justifying them.

No one controls the living space of anyone else, unless by the latter's choice, or because he is legally incompetent or his residence is temporary. Specially desirable locations are not permanently pre-empted. Everyone may have his own place if he wishes, or may join a resident group. Permanent ownership is regional, and the basic strategy of land management is set at that level, albeit by two different entities. Landscape creation and maintenance, as well as the provision of local service, is decentralized and shifting. Within the framework of centers and main routes, the region is a mosaic of small, diverse territories, where inhabitant, user, manager, and temporary owner all tend to coincide.

This system of land allocation did not appear overnight, of course, and certainly not without resistance. Land began to be regionalized quite early, at first by scattered trusts set up by foundations or local governments. Although at first they took charge primarily of open lands to be conserved, major public funds were later put into areas ripe for development (such as at the edge of the metropolitan regions), in order to squeeze out speculation and promote orderly planning. Later still, local resident communities began to take their sites by seizure or purchase, and then conveyed them to trusts to insure their title. The trusts themselves had also begun to acquire vacant and abandoned lands (many of them urban) as a matter of policy, as well as to regionalize development rights.

Next, they moved to take larger holdings. Here, of course, they encountered the stiffest resistance, and the conflicts that arose were only resolved by forceful political intervention, softened by cash and by grants of life tenure, or of a terminal period in which rents could be received by former owners. Resistance also flared from small holders, who were fearful of eviction, or emotionally attached to their possessions. Here again, the transfer was sometimes forcible, but more often it relied on persuasion, purchase, and grants of life tenure. Thus the control of land changed radically, but its use changed more slowly. Even in terms of ownership, the trusts expanded their holdings only gradually. Border disputes and overlaps arose between the trusts themselves, which required patient negotiations. There are numerous enclaves and border areas not yet in trust, but it is by now clear that most lands—again excepting some permanent reservations or special cases—will eventually fall into their hands. This piecemeal, local growth has meant that trust administration and control has many local variants, from region to region, even if the basic principles of land management are very general.

The Character and Mix of Settlement

Each small territory may have its own style of living, its own types of buildings and landscape, even its own pattern of utilities and transport. These localized patterns are controlled by the land trusts and the regional governments to insure safety and health (both of men and of the land), and to prevent interference with neighbors. Otherwise, there is little regulation of internal form. Thus the occupation is "patchy" in many ways: small open spaces, farmlands, and forests are everywhere. There are strips and pieces of "waste" land, under no group's direct control, and so open to spontaneous (or deviant) use. They are a reservoir of species (including pests, of course), a balancing divide, a living museum and yet also a place where new ways of life can easily be started up. Clearly, they must be so located and insulated that the relatively uncontrolled activity within them does not disturb the even tenor of life within the residential areas. They carry out a function once performed by the abandoned farms of declining rural areas, and by the decaying "gray areas" of the inner cities.

Thus some small, untended wasteland is always somewhere close at hand, while "wilderness" (in the true sense of an area untouched by human intervention) is at least within one's mind and one's extended reach, although the access to it may be difficult. The wilderness may be an island, a mountain, a great swamp, a trackless scrub, a deep sea canyon.

Other lands are devoted to isolated rural retreats, or to enclaves where people may live, if they choose, in retarded or exotic modes.

In the inhabited areas, there is a fine-grain mix of activity. Production, consumption, residence, education, and creation go on in each other's presence. No one need travel far to engage in any of these activities, although he may range widely if he wishes. The spatial and temporal integration of activity supports its functional integration. Teaching and learning occur in the factories, fields, and offices. It is not confined to school buildings, nor to childhood, nor consigned to one agency. Any productive task has its educational and recreational aspects. Children see the world at work, and working parents watch their children learn, or they work and learn together.

This new, muddled landscape contrasts sharply to the extensive mono-cultures of the past: the big fields of agro-industry, the great pine forests grown to be cut over, the mining regions, the empty lands, the extensive suburbs, the specialized summer resorts, the splendid hospitals and university campuses, the great office districts, the gigantic industrial estates, airfields, ports, and switching yards—all those places whose inhabitants were so often isolated, specialized, or temporary: migratory workers, tourists, lumberjacks, farm laborers, housewives, students, passengers, patients, secretaries. Large-scale specialization of the land is now avoided, or, where inescapable, it is mitigated by encouraging some other temporary use, or by providing some other home base for its temporary users. There are workshops in the fields, and quiet ones among the houses. Next to them are the swimming holes, picnic places, and cottages for people on tour and on vacation. Crops are often set out in mixed plantings, garden style. The borders between different things are the most interesting parts of the landscape. This mixing of use occurred rather naturally once the nature of ownership began to change and large single-purpose agencies lost control. It reduced the efficiency of production until the measure of efficiency was recalculated.

The lack of functional segregation is matched by a relative lack of social segregation. Small local territories are distinct in their landscape and way of life, but they are set together. No larger region is closed to any group of people. Everyone is aware of the diversity around him. Safe on his home ground, he can maintain the norms and behavior he values. Yet he is at least in visual contact with other ways of life. And since many communities cohere around characteristics which are not permanently assigned to the person—such as a set of beliefs and interests, or a way of conducting life—it is possible for people (at some cost, of course) to shift from one group to another. Moreover, large numbers of partially like-minded people—Finnish descendants, camera enthusiasts, homosexuals, radical theologians—will at times congregate temporarily to revel in their special kind. All these ways of distributing social groups in space could have been seen in the earlier cities, but they were marginal compared to the great ethnic and class distinctions. Indeed, spatial segregation by economic class was becoming sharper and coarser. It broke down only after revolutionary changes, both in the economy and in popular values.

While the general density of land occupation is now rather low, due particularly to all this mixing of use and waste, the diversity of building type includes towers, factories and meeting halls of moderate size, and intricate compact group dwellings. Smaller buildings may occur in tight clusters, and there are the intensive public centers devoted to offices, high-density residence, specialized production, communication, distribution, and sophisticated consumption and entertainment. Footloose cosmopolites choose to live there, or perhaps along the main routes, and so do many adolescents and young adults, as well as a few older persons. (Not "retired" persons, however, since it is difficult to disengage from activity now, unless one is seriously ill. Sick and disturbed people are only rarely and reluctantly shut off from others. Lives are not segregated into eras of education, production, and rest, any more than space is.)

These centers of stimulus and decision are active throughout the twenty-four hours. Most of them are an outgrowth of the earlier central places, although new centers have been established in sparsely occupied regions, so that they are as accessible to everyone as are the wastelands and the quiet places. Indeed, there will often be a quiet, isolated area in immediate contrast with a center. In such centers, and along the main routes, space is leased on a temporary basis from the public owner, which is also the local government and provides the common services. Resplendent, active, and alive—changing constantly in their internal structure—these centers occupy an historic site in an unchanging way. Many kinds of people walk their streets. Some people feel alienated there, and rather enjoy it.

Regions are multi-centered; there is no single dominant, and everyone is within reach of several of these active points. But the centers are partially specialized in function, and each has its own character which arises out of its long history as an inhabited place. They are the symbolic points around which the continuous, loosely patterned, and shifting urban countryside is mentally organized, the foci of regional identity and pride. Natural features are intensified to strengthen that symbolism, or may even be manufactured where no remarkable form exists.

Communications

We have seen that parts of the region are secluded and difficult of access, while the developed lands, and particularly the centers, are highly accessible. The landscape is an alternation of rest and movement, of privacy and sociability. A major grid of public transport, within a broad right-of-way, covers the entire region. It is distorted to accommodate to natural features, to avoid the wild lands on the one hand and to serve the centers on the other. Yet it is regular and continuous. This grid is permanently located, as are the centers, [the] wilderness, and certain symbolic sites. Within the grid run the major conduits which carry people, goods, messages, wastes, and energy.

A great variety of transport modes are in use. Noise and pollution have been bred out of them, or their use has been strictly confined. The space they occupy and the energy they use is in proportion to the work they do. There are trains, moving walks and seats, escalators, buses, minibuses, trucks, group taxis, boats, horses, low-powered carts and wheelchairs, dirigibles, gliders, and light noiseless aircraft. More often than not, people walk, cycle, skate, or ski, using their own energy to get about. This utopian world has failed to invent any major new modes of transport, except for fun. It has improved the old modes, makes better use of them, and is dependent on none.

There may be regional networks, separate from the main grid, which are devoted to slow, safe movement, or to the pure pleasure of motion, or which are composed of historic pathways. Many of these special roads are maintained by volunteer "way societies," while the main grid is normally controlled by some regional government. Beyond that, a capillary network of roads and paths, held in many temporary hands, perfuses the region, and this network expands and contracts as uses change. In the centers, the transport network erupts into three dimensions. In the air, it is channeled and does not pass over certain zones. Underground, there are fantastic passage systems, while underwater one moves with less restriction. But all roads are designed to make travel interesting; all are an integral part of the landscape. They make no scars.

All people are free to move. There are vehicles for the very young, the very old, and the handicapped; there are easy ways of carrying parcels or conveying small children. Except in the wilderness, the private retreats, and the local territories, the barriers are down. No high curbs block a wheelchair, no drop-offs endanger the blind, there are no streets that a child cannot cross safely. Indeed, children are encouraged to roam—watching, listening, testing, wondering, learning. The right of public access, if without damage to the landscape or direct intrusion on privacy, is well established. Seacoasts, lakes, and streams are open. Anyone can travel abroad. Accordingly, most people have spent a few years of their life in world-wandering. Travel still takes time, however, and personal energy. Daily [and] weekly purposeful travel has lessened, since people are closer to their work, and recreation is less a running away than a renewal of self in the familiar locale. Yet people also have a greater experience of distant travel and are more likely to walk or to journey for pleasure, to roam freely at irregular times.

Outside the retreats and the wilderness, simple communications devices are easy to find and free to use: telephones, videophones, radios, TV cameras and screens, computer outlets, postal boxes, notice boards. Message sending is decentralized, and two-way channels are favored. Broadcasts originate at local levels; there are wall newspapers, small printing presses, street theater. The determined use of the landscape for diffuse communication has broken the hold of the mass media. It is easy and safe to locate and converse with a like-minded person, in a public place, by a conference call, through notices and the mails.

The basic infrastructure of transportation and communication is a free public utility, supported by public funds. Not only are the streets free to walk on, but transit, telephone and radio, the mail, [and] even the simpler kinds of vehicles, like wheelchairs, bicycles, and roller skates, are free to be used where found. Of course, the same is true for drinking water, baths and toilets, basic food and medicine, small amounts of heat and power, utility clothing, and minimal shelter (or the components of which to make it). These are the commune ground of existence, and the common charge. While the simplest kind, they are for the taking in public places. Their production, distribution, and maintenance are a public enterprise.

The Consumption of Material Goods

In many domains, we find these same two tiers of consumption: the one limited, cheap, standard, simple, and necessary, provided free as a common good, and the other more costly or varied, acquired by individual effort. One can live with very little labor, but few have the stamina to do so.

Most buildings, whether simple or elaborate, use a minimum of imported material and energy. Structural technique is advanced, but it has advanced to the use of abundant local material—sand, earth, clay, rock, brush, grass—to the harnessing of local forces, and to the devising of building systems which are easy to erect and to modify. Most buildings now are simple, light, and low. They are extensively warmed and cooled by sunlight, geothermal heat, evaporation, and the movement of natural currents of air, rather than by imported energy expended in sealed structures. Building skins respond to the fluctuations of weather: opening and closing, paling and darkening. Spaces, inside and out, are arranged to produce a variety of microclimates. Pollution is reduced to levels easily absorbed by the natural processes of transformation.

True enough, many massive, uncomfortable structures remain from an earlier time. Cities cannot be transformed overnight; their inertia is very large. Much ingenuity has been expended in making these older buildings habitable—thinning them out, breaking through their walls and roofs, reducing their density of use, rehabilitating them internally. Some still require wasteful amounts of energy. In some localities, people who live in surviving apartments, or must work in old factories or skyscrapers, may receive some bonus of income or prestige. Occasionally, as we have seen, the older city areas have become a wilderness, or are mined for their materials.

Recycled material is more frequently employed than raw material. Wastes are converted, or their breakdown accelerated. Structures are designed to be reused, or to be wrecked and reconstituted easily. Thus the testing and evaluation of a design or material includes a consideration of how it can be reshaped or destroyed. The whole process of waste, elimination, and conversion is seen as being interesting and useful, as worthy of celebration as production. Sewering, wrecking, cleaning, and repainting are trades as glamorous as cooking and building.

The low average density, the high degree of accessibility, [and] the patchiness of development all mean that the environment is easily changed to fit new uses and new users. Adaptations can be made with small applications of power and effort. This quality of adaptability is also prized in the design of equipment, [which is] made to be repaired and modified by simple means. Looking at a new machine, the first question is "how can I fix it when it breaks down?" The second question may be "can I run it by hand?"

Despite an occasional individual extravaganza, the material standard of life is not elaborate, except in a symbolic sense. World levels of consumption are below resource replacement rates, or allow ample time for resource substitution. Since regions turn increasingly toward using their local resources, there has been some deflation of the international carriage of goods and energy, and this has been most marked for those things that are scarce and irreplaceable at the point of origin, or which required the exploitation of human labor. Oil and gas, for example, are now traded in very small amounts, a shift which brought on very disturbing changes in the use of power (and in the balance of power) all over the world.

While the world's people now have enough food and shelter, and the material basis of a decent life, citizens of the regions once called "advanced" have had to give up many customs and luxuries. In a quantitative sense, there has been a marked leveling down of consumption, although not an homogenization of its form. So there have been surprising changes in diet, clothing, transport, and equipment, and an even more profound change in attitudes toward material acquisition.

Since fundamental physical requirements are assured to everyone, owning a great quantity of material goods is no longer a sign of prestige, although some older people, secretly defiant, still feel it to be so. To the amusement of the young, they hoard objects, and are disappointed when their descendants seem indifferent to an inheritance. They still make wills, but the wills are read as expressions of feeling, as "last words" rather than as legal documents. This shift in attitudes towards the possession of material goods has proved to be one of the more difficult obstacles to communication between the generations.

People have by no means turned to a life of ascetic spirituality, however. On the contrary, they find great pleasure in the physical world, in creating and consuming fine things in an elegant way. It is the exclusive control of goods, and their sheer quantity, which has lost its savor. Greater attention is now paid to the material environment, even as the quantitative level of consumption has receded.

The Use of Living Things

People are aware of the ecological process around them, and feel part of that process. While not afraid to disturb it—as indeed they cannot avoid doing—they are accustomed to watch the ripples that spread out from their own gestures. They are actors and fascinated spectators, active and passive. They use a trail and watch how trailside plants respond to the passage of men; abandon a building and note the succession of flora and fauna which reoccupy it. Studies of this kind occupy the free time of many people, particularly in the older urban areas. Some conduct experiments, or try to communicate with other species. But the ethical issues involved in these experiments are a matter of some controversy.

The responsibility of a group for its territory includes the well functioning of other living things there, just as much as care for its continued human usefulness. Residents may be brought to account by a trust for the demise of a marsh, for example, as well as a government for injury to a neighbor. They can be required to maintain or replenish the soil, or the water table, or a stand of trees, since men and land belong to each other. Particularly in the early days, some residents might so misuse their land as to be dispossessed on that account. But the non-resident lands have proved the more resistant problem. Maintenance can more easily be brought to a formal standard, but it is not easy to foster an attitude of caring within a non-resident organization. On the other hand, a volunteer group will sometimes ask to take on the care of some piece of public land.

Plants and animals are controlled to serve human purposes, but not heedlessly. People keep few pets, and those that remain coexist with humans on a much more independent footing. Animals which work cooperatively with man are still common, of course: horses, milk cows, seeing eye dogs, rescue dolphins, rats trained to find breaks in pipes and wires. The consumption of meat has fallen, although strict vegetarians are still only a large minority. Some advanced sects distinguish between the "lower" and the "higher" plants, which may and may not be eaten.

Since there are small strips of waste between the developed lands, many species survive which are intolerant of man. Temporarily threatened species may be held in reservations, or introduced elsewhere when the consequences can be foreseen. This is not done to prevent species changes, but simply to conserve diversity and to prevent catastrophic change. In brief, men are no longer an uncontrolled disease of nature, but have come to accept some responsibility as a dominant and aware species. What those responsibilities may be remains a puzzle. That they might even include a furthering of evolution is a thought just beginning to trouble people.

Moving and Changing

Even as attention is paid to the recycling of material, so it is also given to the periodic cycling of human settlement. The rate of regional growth and decline may be tinkered with, but no one tries to get a death grip on some "optimum" size or character. Change is expected; places evolve, although explosive or irreversible change may be derailed. There are strategies for decline, as well as for growth. Processes of settlement, resettlement, and unsettlement are all attended to. The recent celebrated devolution of Manhattan into a set of small communities dependent on fishing, specialized recreation, and the mining of used building materials has aroused world-wide admiration. Even though the stifling urban investment of the island has been melted away, it still retains that magic sense of power and excitement which draws many to visit it, or to live there for a brief time.

How people can be free to move, to shift their living group and their locale, and yet maintain their sense of continuity, is a much debated issue. Temporary gatherings are normal, and world travel [is] encouraged. But world sophistication is founded on secure local attachment, just as social ease depends on a robust sense of personal identity. High mobility, and frequent temporary residence, are tempered by strong local ties, by permanent symbolic locations and retreats. Some groups, of course, are mobile by nature, and their stable territory is a route or sea along which they regularly pass, and the succession of places at which they regularly pause.

The great majority of people will pass their lives in one group and place, broken by periods of travel. Yet many have had the experience of a permanent transfer, or some of their close kin or neighbors have done so. A transferral is always a well-remembered event, carefully prepared. A move will be preceded by lengthy reconnaisance and trial. Social groups often move together. There are accepted rituals for "closing" an old location and "opening" a new one. Given such preparation, the moves may be quite distant ones. Not only is the size of the world population being regulated, but its pattern is constantly being adjusted to make better use of world resources.

Environmental change has also been institutionalized in special experimental centers. Volunteers give a trial run to some hypothesis about a coordinated modification of place and society—a type of group family in a specially designed structure, for example, or a free-running temporal rhythm of activity in an underground habitat. The experiment is monitored, and may be abandoned or modified, by these same volunteers. If it proves workable, the experiment becomes a demonstration. Others can repeat the experience for themselves—for pleasure, for confirmation, or to help them choose a way of life. Numerous locality groups have had their origins in some successful place and group experiment, although in their own evolution they may have moved quite far away from the original pattern. In this way, paths to the future—good and bad—are being run out and their consequences openly examined.

The Congruence of Place and Sense

All but the youngest can remodel their own setting to some degree, and are to that degree responsible for it: the young child for his corner of a room or garden, the adult for a complex landscape. Particular kinds of people are charged with particular environmental functions. Older adolescents may be the fire fighters, while the blind regulate noise pollution. Children manage small animals, or gather trash. Tasks are found for the retarded, the ill, and the handicapped, so that all people find meaning in the common care for place. This participation brings people to understand themselves, and binds them together. The environment is the occasion for cooperative effort; it is consciously designed to reinforce cooperation—sometimes even to require it. Since most social groups have defined spatial territories, the mental images of place and of community are congruent with each other. Centers and landmarks are symbols of common values. They are deliberately shaped to receive those meanings.

The elements of the landscape are also shaped to be memorable in their own right. Roads, for example, no longer have a single standard form, a standard cross-section, an approved set of details monotonously imposed. Each path has its own character. It fits into the cultural and natural landscape in its own way, and reveals a sequence of expressive views. Buildings have strong personalities. Places have distinctive sounds and smells at special times.

Landscape design—place creation—is a much admired social art. Small teams are eager to take the responsibility for shaping and managing some piece of the "public" region, since this is one route to renown. New efforts at landscape are widely criticized. Old settings are reworked, or, if considered to be classics, are preserved and made the subject of critical appreciation. Some early landscapes are especially revered, because of their historic role in generating the first excitements and transformations which ultimately helped to fuel the utopian change.

Graceful land management, the way a place is used, maintained, and modified through the seasons and the peaks and valleys of activity, is as much appreciated as fine design. In fact, design and management are not distinguished. Both intend to clarify and deepen the common image of a region, to give its features a vivid presence to which meanings may attach. People learn to be aware of their surroundings, through all their senses. They perceive places actively: digging into them, moving over them, making them echo. Other arts—theater, poetry, sculpture, music—sharpen this awareness, make the landscape resonant. Tales and poems develop the meaning of a place; paintings and photography cause it to be seen in some new way. Guidebooks of a hundred specialized kinds are written and read with interest. These are also considered as place-creating arts.

Light, motion, sound, and smell are manipulated to increase the "sensibility" of places, that is, to make them more engaging to the senses. Dim white sculpture may inhabit a dark pine grove, wind-driven mobiles play with a water surface. A particular tree is hung with its own distinctive chimes, gives off an augmented odor, has a special way of being lit at night. Even a special bird, one associated with that tree in some memorable poem, may be attracted there. Local climate is dramatized, or made more distinctive by local weather control. Special celebrations are reserved to special places.

Where it will not interfere with privacy, the landscape is made more transparent, or clues to its hidden functions are left on view. Economic processes are normally exposed. The connection between production and consumption is as immediate as possible: corn roasts are held in corn fields, people put up their own houses, fashions are modeled alongside the looms, bicycles are chosen off the assembly line, with the advice of the assembly teams. But it remains difficult to present more remote and abstract activities in some tangible way. How does one communicate the work of a public accountant? Or of a trader in futures?

Public activity is visible, and the nature of resident groups is displayed. The inner workings of significant functional elements—a water main, perhaps, or a clock—is there to be seen if one is interested. There are guidebooks to the sewer system, for example, with instructions on how to read the time of day by observing the flow. The nature of local ecology can be read on the spot. Signs, obscure marks, the traces of the activity itself, recording and listening devices, symbols and diagrams, remote sensors, television, magnifying glasses, slow-motion films, periscopes, peepholes—all are used to make organic and mechanical processes perceptible: not immediately apparent, of course, or presented in some canned condensation. Learning is a process of discovery. But the clues are available, the threads are there to follow if one desires to do so. The environment is a great book, a drama—a rich display of information about place, function, human society, the stars, the concert of living things. It is an education, and not simply an illustration of the knowledge in a book, or the subject of an occasional field trip as a relief from school.

Everyone is trained to read a place, just as they are trained to read a book. Reading a place means coming to understand what is happening there, what has [happened] or might happen, what it means, how one should behave there, and how it is connected to other places. This environmental tale is not a single, fixed text. Coming to understand its complexity is continuous and cumulative. Contending factions read their surroundings differently, and press their own readings on others. Thus, two contrasting interpretations of the social function of a place may be presented simultaneously to the bewildered observer.

The setting is neither a unified nor a static record. Historic traces are preserved, and modified as concepts of the past are revised. Records and artifacts which explain the cultural traditions are considered to be important landscape resources, like timber, soil, or coal. Most often, they can be conserved within the living, changing setting without any interference to its current function. Current history is marked out as it occurs. Present trends and future possibilities are displayed. (These can be mutually contradictory, of course.) Time of day and season [are] dramatized, and so are the important social events and pervasive rhythms of human activity. Thus the environment is a celebration of place and time and process.

There are "slow" places and fast ones; ones whose day begins at dawn and others which are most alive at night. Even the periodic measures are diverse: one location may have 90-minute "hours," or its weeks [may] contain thirteen days. In some locations, periods may not be sharply measured, but be elastic, to fit the work at hand, or a common mood. There remains a "standard time" of reference, which can be used to maintain social coordination, just as there is a main road system that links diverse territories. Yet people are encouraged to match their lives to their own rhythms and preferences for timing.

And so the world is closely fitted to human feeling. There are sacred places, mysterious and tragic ones, landscapes of aggression and of love: a place for each feeling and perception. Through the customs and rituals associated with those places, people can experience and express their most profound emotions. One setting can be a symbol of paradise, of the highest human values, while another expresses our deep fears and anxieties. Special features of the land are deliberately exploited to produce these emotive places—caves, sea-coves and promontories, mountain tops, deep lakes and forests, gorges, waterfalls, arid mesas, jumbled badlands—as well as small locales deep within the built environment—secluded courts, pinnacles, underground rooms, tiny pools.

A world network of holy places is beginning to emerge, which together are weaving an image of the earth as a richly diverse and sacred unit. They celebrate the basic elements and processes of earth, their connections, their context in space. They can be found in volcanoes, under-seas, or in the high air; they are cold, hot, wet, or dry. They expose earth time, and the time of the universe. Some look at the stars, and there are sacred satellites which regard the earth. People make pilgrimages from one holy place to another, at various stages in their life. They may visit briefly, to experience that special meaning, or stay longer to contribute to the evolution of the place. Some remain to devote themselves to the locale, becoming, in a sense, priests of wind, fire, earth, or water. The places speak to each other by vibrations through the earth or sea, by lights and air waves, by exchanging material substances, by messages carried by birds and fish.

Environmental rituals, customary ways of acting in these special places, are as much a part of the design as the place itself. In some, or at certain times, actions are rigidly controlled; speech, gesture, posture, clothing are minutely prescribed. Others are devoted to exuberant spon-taneity and disorder. Sacred actions are proper to the sacred cave, the ritual of tea to the tea house. They are actions that every member of a community can hope to perform. Outdoor events celebrate the spring or the solstice, floods, or the breakup of winter ice, the return of swallows and tourists, the shared mourning of a people at some place of common tragedy. The planet is a festival, a high drama, a remembrance.

The mental attitudes of men and women have grown to include this awareness, this care. People feel exposed to their surroundings. They enjoy nakedness. Many seek out places which challenge them, even at risk of life. Tall buildings are scaled like mountains. The polar ice is a test of survival. Nature is not tamed to hand.

People use places to develop their own potentialities—the plasticity of the environment, its richness in available information, its strong emo-tive and social character, its openness and its challenges, are all adapted to this end. People learn by doing, and by thinking about what they are doing. They are discovering new human abilities, new ways of perceiving, moving, feeling, new games and resources.

Some even consider themselves, like very limited gods, to be re-sponsible for the development of other forms of life. Watching the changes in the animals and plants around them, they protect and encourage those changes that seem beneficial [and] which appear to increase the viability and capability of the species itself, rather than just its economic usefulness to man. Although most do no more than to observe and select, or to train individual organisms, others may even seek to stimulate evolutionary changes, thinking of themselves as conscious agents of evolution. Luckily, the license to practice is still quite restricted, both by custom and for lack of knowledge. But the development of oneself, of one's own social circle, and of the living place is thought to be high art and high science, the fun-damental ethical action.

Place Without Society

Since our utopian recital has been focused on the spatial environment, it leaves many features unexplained. Clearly, there would be important social and economic prerequisites and consequences. Levels of production and consumption would be quite different than they are today. Most of the productive system would probably be communally owned, albeit in some mixed local/regional/international way. Population levels and migrations would be managed. Political power must have been radically reorganized. Some form of world government or federation is implied, as well as governmental territories which fit more closely to the natural or functional organization of the land, and are thus more nearly regional and local than national. The renewal of the earth, and of the human settlement upon it, would have been the greatest human enterprise since the Neolithic. It would have been a world task, which not simply required, but also called forth, a world-wide unity and joint endeavor.

The proposals imply—or at least allow for—new forms of the family. Social groups would have many diverse bases for their coherence. They would be place-oriented, and yet jointly mobile. New social means for dealing with mobility and change would be required, ways of dealing with strangers and neighbors, ways of managing social transformations. New institutions focusing on the environment would develop. Age and sex roles would shift. The temporal organization of society would be different. And so on.

The utopian notes are inadequate, because they deal with the relationship of man to place, and only tangentially with those of man to man. They are no worse in this than other utopian discourses, which commit the opposite error. Like other utopias (but here is a critical flaw indeed), they do not say how the millenium is to be reached, nor if it really all fits together. Useful strategy requires a deep analysis of the present situation as it is now maturing, the construction of an integrated future pattern rather than a fragmented one, and a surer knowledge of the dynamics of social and environmental change.

We pretend to none of these. This has been a recital of wishes. Reciting wishes, mind you, is not an idle act, despite what the critics of utopia might have you believe. First, of course, because it is a pleasure to dream. Second, because wishes are part of the mechanism of action. Thinking of them is one way of learning how to act better in the present. Wishing is a way of finding out, a way of communicating.

It is interesting to see that these environmental proposals do not have an absolutely tight and necessary relation to social proposals. Physical environment and society are not simply mirrors to each other. The former, in particular, is slow to bring forth its reflections. It carries the images of many previous historical states, and willfully emanates images of its own. So one could conceive of a number of societies which might support our environmental ideas. But not an extremely large number. Our criteria—fit, openness, and connection—have some definite social counterparts.

Where We Are

There is small resemblance between these proposals and the organization of environment in societies which have been radically restructured in recent times, such as the USSR, Cuba, or China, although Havana's "Cordon" is a landscape symbol of the integration of work and recreation, and the Chinese agro-industrial commune may prefigure the mixed-use urban countryside, organized into local territories. The spatial settings of the socialist world seem to be, from a distance at least, much like those of the capitalist one, and their environmental attitudes not so very diverse. The small communes, which cling to the crevices of the western world, exhibit some more advanced features, but the gap is still wide. The indifference of utopian thought to the qualities of place is reflected on the plane of reality.

Yet these themes are not new; they are not revelations. They come from many historic and contemporary sources: from the commune, indeed, but also from the farm, the garden, the "urban village," the tribal territory, the summer house, the wilderness camp, the weedy vacant lot and the remembered landscape of childhood, the sacred precinct, the historic city, the meadow, seashore, wood, and stream, the lively plaza, and even (here we blush a little) the despised North American suburb. The ideas come from novelists, painters, poets, and the critics of environment. I hear them from students, and see them in guidebooks and reminiscences and anthropological notes.

The picture has little resemblance to the contemporary metropolis, yet those great settlements cannot simply be wiped away (unless we are to go with them). Total rebuilding is impossible—politically, economically, and psychologically. Moreover, not all current processes and conditions are perverse. The spreading metropolis itself, for example, sets the stage for a more dispersed style of life. The technical infrastructure for the urbanized countryside is already being laid down. While it is beyond us to lay out a strategy of transformation, at least we want to be sure it is possible, that we are not in some dead end. Moreover, there are many preliminary, holding, or exploratory actions that would continue to keep the future open.

Moves to protect the environment, and to preserve and extend the fabric of open space, are holding actions of that kind. Better control of development at the fringes by the public acquisition of development rights in the urbanizing areas could be an important early step. So are measures which will make it possible for all classes of people to live in these new areas. Fringe development could be directly coupled with the renewal of central areas, and controlled by a coalition of center and edge inhabitants. Cooperative ownership and management would allow people to control the places they live in.

New devices for land tenure can be tried out which keep areas in permanent trust while granting long leases for autonomous use and development by resident groups. New settlements can incorporate innovative land patterns, support treatment of the urban landscape as a collective work of art, or show how it can be used as an integral part of the process of education. National and international efforts can be applied to reverse the pattern of decline in lagging areas, making them attractive enough to hold their people and to encourage resettlement.

Much better use can be made of all the underused spaces and times which are so pervasive in our cities: the vacant lots, empty yards, rooftops, empty buildings, excessive streets, the land under the viaducts, the barren parking lots, the many specialized areas. New transport modes can give access to the isolated—the young, the old, the handicapped, the poor—instead of reinforcing their disabilities. Environmental information can be amplified, and people [can] be trained to read it.

Nor is it too early to consider the unthinkable: the rehabilitation of the vast intermediate areas and suburbs of our cities. Could groups of people begin to infiltrate that enormous landscape, begin to build a network of small counter-environments in which consumption and management were shared activities? Which would demonstrate new ways of living together, and of caring for the landscape? More formal experiments in the connections between a modified life style and a modified setting might be conducted under institutional sponsorship. At another scale, we can already begin to design and manage imageable regional landscapes. And soon.

These separate items do not make up a grand strategy of transformation, which must deal with man and his setting together, based on an understanding of how change in one promotes change in the other. Remaking the environment is a compelling idea just because it embraces so many issues: inward feelings and outward form, the integration of science, art, and ethics, the relation of the individual to his local community and also to the unity of mankind, the interaction and development of human and non-human life. The renewal of the world landscape, if coupled with the renewal of society, would indeed be an exhilarating enterprise.

What Will Happen to Us? (1983)

with Tunney Lee and Peter Droege

This is a guidebook on how to instruct your community on the effects of a nuclear war. It is directed toward those professional planners, community organizers, or civic leaders who have the motive and the analytical or organizing skill to initiate and guide a community effort of self-education.

This manual stems from the conviction that the possibility of nuclear conflict is an overwhelming threat to mankind, and indeed to all of life on earth. Yet American military doctrine has shifted from deterrence by means of "mutually assured destruction" to the concept of a "limited" nuclear war, and "survivable" atomic exchanges. This policy shift only increases the likelihood of a preventive surprise attack in times of heightened international tension. There are scores of imaginable provocations, ranging from confrontation in the Middle East to accidental launchings or the detonation of a terrorist weapon, any one of which could lead to an international nuclear conflict. These are the dangers that prompt this manual.

The nuclear threat will not be turned aside by proclamation, nor by a bit of diplomacy, but only by the determined, organized, and continuous political actions of people from this and other countries. To be most effective in expressing opposition to nuclear attack, people should have a thorough understanding of the probable consequences of nuclear war as well as the current mode of protection from such an attack.

Thus, the manual's main objective is to direct citizens themselves to examine the effects of a nuclear war. Nothing is so convincing as what one learns for oneself through applying general ideas to one's own life and circumstances. Communities will be convinced when they see that their own survival is at stake. Self-education is an extended process which takes time and effort. But once aroused and aware, communities can speak with a powerful voice.

The exercises outlined in this manual cannot be done quickly, nor should they be done in isolation by a handful of experts. They should involve individuals at all levels of the community. These are precisely the people who must be brought in if a coherent and informed political opposition to the present drift toward catastrophe can be built.

This manual does not assume an all-out exchange of nuclear weapons, since that would amount to describing the instant annihilation of nearly 400 million Americans, Russians, and Europeans. Rather, it describes the effects of a "limited" bombardment of military and industrial targets alone. Our assumption here is that an initial wave of missiles might seek to destroy the economic base of the United States, along with its strategic nuclear force. In that case, the potential targets would be the

Reprinted, with permission, from *Space and Society*, no. 22, pp. 87–97.

● HIGH-RISK AREAS

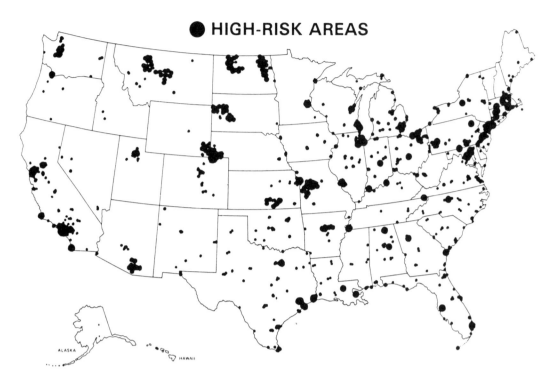

*The 380 "high risk" areas of the U.S., in which
about two-thirds of the population live.*

"high risk" areas containing high technology research and manufacturing
industries, transportation and communication centers, and the major science libraries and institutions, missile silos, launching pads, Air Force
fields, Strategic Air Command posts, and submarine bases. These areas
make up about 2 or 3 percent of the land area of the country and include
about two-thirds of its population.

What a nuclear detonation does

Before commencing your community study, you should have an understanding of what a nuclear explosion will do to the surrounding region and
population. Actual experience and nuclear testing have provided a base
for predicting these results; you must apply them to your own locality.

A nuclear detonation destroys in at least five ways:

Blast. The explosion causes sudden changes in air pressure and
ensuing high winds. The excess pressure crushes rigid objects such as
buildings, while people, trees, and other light or flexible things are destroyed by the wind. People will be killed as buildings collapse over
them, as they are blown into things, or as things are blown into them.

Thermal radiation and fire. Approximately one-third of the energy of the explosion is given off in an intense burst of heat and light. The light is strong enough to produce temporary blindness to those observing it from as far away as 13 miles on a clear day.

Skin burns from the flash are more serious, ranging from first degree burns (causing bad sunburns) at 7 miles to third degree burns (those destroying skin tissue) at 5 miles depending upon the amount of shielding one has from the explosion. While a single nuclear attack can produce up to 10,000 burn cases that would be fatal without medical care, this country's medical facilities can treat no more than 1–2,000 such cases at any one time.

The burst of heat will also ignite any exposed combustible material, which, in the absence of any organized firefighting response, will spread from building to building; blast damage to stoves, water heaters, furnaces, etc. will ignite further fires. When the flammable material is sufficiently close together, individual fires may unite into a mass fire or firestorm. Available oxygen is consumed, and living creatures are asphyxiated.

Direct nuclear radiation. The explosion emits an intense, brief burst of ionizing radiation. Depending on the amount of radiation one is exposed to, short-term effects include nausea, severe radiation sickness, marked susceptibility to other diseases and infection, and death. In the long term, even a low exposure to radiation will induce an incidence of fatal cancers in 0.5 to 2.5 percent of a large population, and there will be serious genetic damage inflicted on others. The only persons who will not receive this radiation will be those who are protected on all sides by massive barriers of earth, concrete, or the like, which can absorb the flux of neutrons and gamma rays. Ordinary walls will reduce this but will not eliminate it.

The combination of nuclear radiation, thermal radiation, and mechanical injuries will kill still more persons who might have survived only one cause by itself.

Radioactive fallout. The effects of radiation received from particles made radioactive by the explosion are the same as from direct radiation, but this type of radiation is more persistent and affects a wider territory. Fine radioactive dust particles not falling back into the eye of the explosion comprise the upper portions of the mushroom cloud; they are carried in whatever direction and at whatever speed the wind may be blowing and [will] eventually fall back to earth in an elliptical pattern. Local rains will carry down concentrations of the radioactive particles and create "hot spots" of higher radiation. The outer edges of the ellipse might become safe (by peacetime standards) in 2 to 3 years, and the inner areas in 10 years.

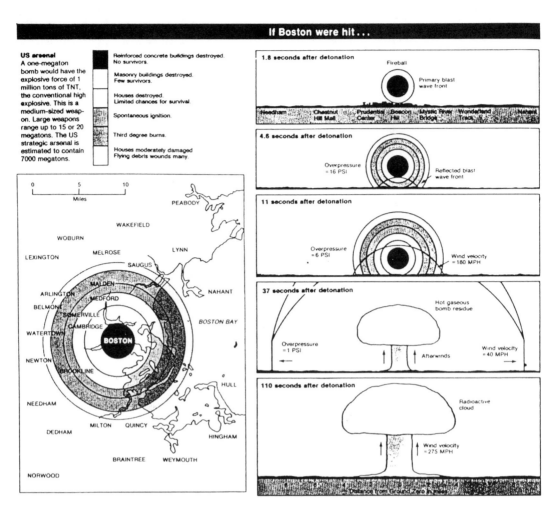

US arsenal
A one-megaton bomb would have the explosive force of 1 million tons of TNT, the conventional high explosive. This is a medium-sized weapon. Large weapons range up to 15 or 20 megatons. The US strategic arsenal is estimated to contain 7000 megatons.

Reinforced concrete buildings destroyed. No survivors.

Masonry buildings destroyed. Few survivors.

Houses destroyed. Limited chances for survival.

Spontaneous ignition.

Third degree burns.

Houses moderately damaged. Flying debris wounds many.

Plotting the zone of destruction: "If Boston were hit."

Electromagnetic pulse (EMP). This is an electromagnetic wave carrying thousands of volts in a single pulse, like the signal from lightning, but rising far more rapidly in its voltage. EMP is not a direct threat to human beings, but it will short out or shut down electrical or electronic systems, computers, radio and TV stations, and perhaps telephone lines.

If a nuclear weapon goes off overhead, what would happen to your community?

If you live in a metropolitan area of over 50,000 people, or are near an important military or economic installation, then you are in one of the "high risk" areas. In case of war, you are likely to have a bomb detonated over your head. This section shows how to analyze the effects on your community in the case of such an event taking place.

1. *Locate likely target point* (ground zero): e.g. major military base or center of population in your urbanized area.

2. *Plot on a map the resulting zones of destruction*, extending about 10 miles from the target point. Note the buildings and scenes within each zone, as well as places of importance to the community such as schools, hospitals, churches, and government buildings. The locations of other centers of crucial activity should also be mapped out, such as telephone centrals, television stations, pumping stations. Note the location also of any officially designed shelter, but disregard those in the first three zones. People in them will be asphyxiated or roasted to death. In this way, it will be possible to estimate the number of people who will be immediately killed or injured, the number of structures destroyed or damaged, roads blocked, and utilities and services disrupted.

3. *Estimate the physical and social consequences of such destruction*. Canvass those specialists in your community who have an intimate knowledge of local services: doctors, police, the mayor and councilmen, engineers, utility men, firemen, transit drivers, civil defense, and military. Assume that there will be no outside help, since in such a preventive strike all the other major targets will also have been hit. Ask each specialist to tell you what they would be able to do and in what time period, given the destruction of people and facilities that you have estimated.

What would happen to those who survived? Consider that families might be divided; children could be in schools, the elderly at home, the sick in hospitals, etc. How would people still alive escape the devastation? How could they get out if streets were blocked? How far could they walk and where would they walk to? Where would they get food and water? What epidemics might occur and how could they be dealt with? Answers to these questions will be impressionistic, but it is vital to raise them.

Evacuation prior to an attack

Since the protection of a population subject to a direct nuclear attack is clearly so hopeless, civil defense plans are being prepared, and in your community may be well advanced, to evacuate the population before an attack, given several days notice. It seems doubtful that such notice would be given, and the elaboration of such evacuation plans is more a dare in the cold war nuclear bluff than a realistic plan for defense. Yet you should be thoroughly familiar with those plans, in order to analyze them and to include them in your report.

If there *were* a timely warning, who would go, and who would stay to operate essential services and keep key industries going? Of those who would stay, where would they stay, and how could they be protected? How would they be persuaded to stay? Would families be divided? Of those who would go, by what means would they be moved, along what routes, and to what points? Would there be sufficient gasoline and vehicles? Would public transportation be operating? How does the capacity of the escape routes compare with this probable load of traffic? Could the moves in fact be controlled according to plan? How would vehicular breakdowns be dealt with, or panic, or those who don't know where to go, or those physically handicapped who are unable to move?

The evacuation of a large urban area is quite different from the usual evening traffic jam. It involves moving all the population at once, rather than some fraction of the workers. Something like one-half of the people of the US would have to move, from the most threatened locations. Many will be lost, or be moving with difficulty, and everyone must pass outward through the whole region, along a few arteries, rather than in many balancing directions, as in the normal return from work. Knowing the escape routes designated in the evacuation plan for your area, and the number of people by district, you can calculate the probable dimensions of the traffic, and its relation to the capacity of the route. Once arrived at the designated reception point, what reception may one expect? You should inquire of the communities designated to receive your refugees about their plans for reception.

Since it must occur well *before* an attack, if it is to have any value at all, evacuation would be a serious and probably irreversible step in the escalation to the ultimate conflict. It would advise a potential opponent that he must attack now if he is to strike first and be most effective. A general evacuation (which is quite different, for example, from the partial evacuation of women and children from London in World War II, which itself had such serious social repercussions later) is not only difficult to accomplish, it would have a stunning effect on the economy and on the social fabric. Production would close down and unemployment would soar. All but emergency transportation would come to a halt. Central management would be completely disrupted, including banking services. Food supplies would quickly run short. The distribution of goods would break down, unless it were completely reorganized, and local social services would be totally inadequate. The receiving communities would be overwhelmed, and underlying racial and class conflicts would very likely emerge. The dispersion of citizens, and their loss of the normal means of communication, would make any democratic political response or protest impossible, until mass desperation had developed. It is estimated that it would require one or two years for the economy to recover from even a one or two week general evacuation. A more protracted exodus would be far more disruptive. And yet, when would it be safe to return, and could fearful people be persuaded to do so? What would occur if a second evacuation were called? Civil defense plans consider only the first move. In Great Britain, when only $1\frac{1}{2}$ million women and children , not essential to production, were evacuated in the "phony war" in 1933, serious social tensions developed

If a missile hit Boston . . .
Chart (right) shows local fallout pattern that could result from a MIRVed missile with 10 warheads hitting the Boston area on a day with a northwest breeze. If fireballs touch ground, huge amounts of dust and debris are drawn up into mushroom clouds. Within a few hours, as the clouds drift downwind, much of the radioactive material settles back to earth, creating "plumes" of local fallout. Weather, the nature of the weapon and height of the burst affect fallout patterns; exposed persons would get lethal doses for many miles downwind.

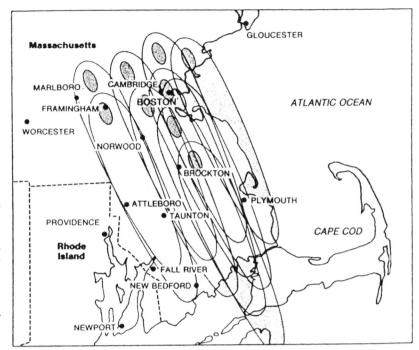

"If a missile hit Boston" . . . the fallout pattern on a day with a northwest breeze.

which affected over one-quarter of the entire population. Such a general move was never repeated, even at the height of aerial attack. Many of the systemwide effects of a general evacuation would resemble those long-term post-attack effects discussed below.

Having mapped your town, estimated the destruction and the loss of life, [and] considered the likelihood of immediate recovery and support, the consequences of mass evacuation, and the possibility of post-attack escape, you have a reasonable picture of the immediate effects of a nuclear explosion, or the preparation for such an explosion, on your community. If you find that a complete analysis of all these effects is beyond your capability, it will still be useful to carry out certain parts of this study: a mapping of the town by the rings of destruction, for example, or a series of discussions with local service people, or an analysis of existing civil defense plans. But it is better to think through the total effect.

What will happen if you are not in a high risk area?

You do not live within 10 miles of an urbanized area or a major target. All locations in the United States may receive radioactive fallout, and most communities will receive crowds of refugees fleeing from the stricken areas.

Radioactive dust and debris from the nuclear blast is sucked up into the mushroom cloud and carried great distances. Gradually these particles settle, far from their origin, and [they] continue to emit dangerous invisible radiation in threatening amounts for periods of from two to eight weeks.

Since you cannot escape the fallout, your only recourse is to occupy a shelter whose walls are thick enough to absorb the gamma radiation. This must be a prepared underground shelter, or one that is improvised in the basement of a building or, with greater difficulty, on its ground floor.

A basement shelter requires several feet of earth piled against any exposed exterior wall. Also, one foot of earth must be heaped over the entire first floor, supported by the reinforcement of the floor joists. A strong table covered or surrounded by boxes of earth or other massive objects, should be placed in the most protected portion of the basement. The basement must have some means of ventilation which includes a special filtration device to keep out radioactive particles. The shelter must also contain a several weeks' supply of food and water, plus some way to dispose of waste.

Begin your community survey by finding out the following:

1. Are there any officially designed fallout shelters in the town? How many people will they protect, and how will these people be chosen? Are these shelters adequately equipped and supplied? How will residents reach these shelters? What will they bring with them?

2. Consider the possibility of improvised basement shelters. How many people in your community live in buildings with full basements? How many will be able to move the quantities of earth needed to convert these basements into shelters? Will these shelters have supplies of food and ways to deal with waste disposal? How many residents live too far from possible shelters or would be incapable of reaching them?

3. Would basic services such as water and electric power supply, medical service, and telephones continue to operate? Whose presence would be required above ground to maintain these services?

4. Consider the flow of refugees likely to enter your town. Consult your civil defense headquarters to find out whether your community may already be officially designated as a host community in case of attack. In addition to a planned influx, there will be large numbers of disoriented people fleeing other large population centers. Judging from the size of nearby centers and likely escape routes, you will be able to make an estimate, however rough, of how many might drift through to your community.

5. Inquire what official plans have been made to receive these refugees, to register them, to lodge them, and to move them to shelters once the attack occurs. How will your town deal with the hostilities that will erupt since many of the refugees and many of your own people will possess guns?

REAGAN GUIDEBOOK FOR CIVIL DEFENSE

"The Reagan Guidebook for Civil Defense":
Cartoon by Dwane Powell, 1982.

6. Beyond this first shelter stage, there will be many more considerations. When should the survivors emerge? Who will reestablish public services? Who will dispose of bad food and water [and] decaying corpses? Can your community maintain a self-sufficient economy till the shattered national one has been reestablished?

Afterwards

Predictions about a nuclear attack stop after the bombs have gone off, as if there were nothing more to say. By using some recent studies of the probable long-term effect of a nuclear attack, you can sketch out how this might affect your communities. A good reference for this is Arthur Katz's book, *Life After Nuclear War*, based on his estimates of the effects of a "modest" attack (using some 3 to 400 megaton and 100 kiloton weapons) unleashed on some 71 largest metropolitan areas and some key industrial and military targets. One can expect the following:

- The economy will have been shattered.
- Food supplies will be seriously affected.

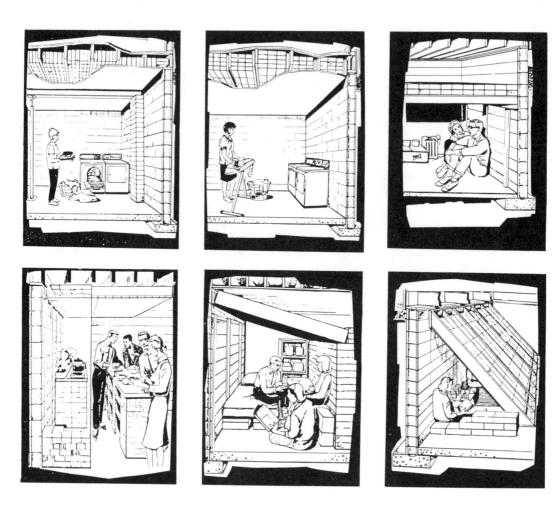

Images of the quality of life in various fallout shelters designed by the U.S. Office of Civil Defense in 1966.

- Most hospitals will have been destroyed in the urban attacks, particularly the more specialized ones.

- Housing will be in very short supply, due to massive destruction and the vast shiftings of population.

- One should be prepared to expect severe psychological disturbances. That the danger of radiation will be invisible will make it all the more terrifying. There will be apathy, disorientation, antisocial behavior, and feelings of guilt, isolation, and helplessness. Morale will plummet; there will be competition for food and other necessities.

- Leadership will lose its legitimacy and democratic procedures will be threatened.

Impressionistic as these predictions may be, they are well grounded in our experience of smaller disasters. Using them, and your knowledge of your own area, you can translate them into likely outcomes for your community.

For example, what will happen to your local banking services? Will credit be obtainable? How long will food inventories last? Will there be electric power? What will be the housing supply? Outside help can be assumed in none of these situations.

Organizing and communicating your study

This manual is meant to help you make vivid a possibility to your own community which may otherwise seem a distant nightmare, and then to come to its own conclusions. For reasons of accuracy and community support, as well as for the power of self-education, don't try to make this analysis alone, or within an exclusive group. Before your begin, bring together an advisory committee of local citizens and professionals who will review your plans for the study, discuss its results as they accumulate, comment on the final draft and your plans for distribution, and stand behind the accuracy of the work when it is made public.

Take photographs of the important buildings, bridges, roads, and utilities, and also of typical houses and other buildings which would be in the various zones of destruction. They can be compared to [photographs of] the remains of similar buildings, in similar zones. These photographs of your own locality, matched with the [comparable] photos and drawings, could be the illustrations of your report, supplemented by the statements of local people, which you have gathered. If you wish, your report can follow the same outline which has been followed by the substance of this manual. It may conclude with a recommendation for action, or you may let it stand as a statement.

Given the devoted energies of a few organizers, and the occasional labor of dozens of volunteers, it might take four to six months to produce and distribute a report of this kind. Your principal costs, again assuming volunteers, will be for printing and distribution. Some reports will be mailed out, but most will be hand-delivered. Your local government might be willing to pay part of the cost. Once the report is out, you will probably want to hold an open community meeting to discuss it, and to talk about what action should be taken.

It is not our purpose to tell you what you should do. Your results and recommendations for action must be your own, coming out of your own locality and your own analysis. We simply hope to help you bring home the reality of nuclear war to your neighbors, and let their good sense guide them from there.

Coming Home: The Urban Environment After Nuclear War (1984)

A few official studies have considered the world after a nuclear holocaust, when the survivors, shaken but resolute, come back to rebuild America. The thinking about this time at the end of the rainbow is peculiarly thin. Resettlement seems to be a technical problem, something compounded of heavy machines, roads, idle factories, power lines, debris, and such abstract factors as labor, money, food stocks, and managerial skill. But under such awesome conditions, what will resettlement mean to human beings? Who thinks about the links that develop between people and place and how grotesque those links might then become?

One lengthy, careful study[1] considers the likelihood of recovery of the economic system, given nuclear attacks of different dimensions. In the "best" case (one in which less than half of the nation's population might die), the survivors "would have no difficulty in supporting themselves" and in rebuilding the national economic system. This excludes, of course, any such "esoteric" effects as changes in the ecosystem after the burning over of more than 50 percent of the nation's surface and the widespread contamination of its soil and water.

These predictions explicitly put aside any "psychological or organizational effects." The study is a discussion of the *technical* limits of production, not of reality. People are considered to be factors like any other. Space is a nuisance, an "inappropriate distribution" of productive factors, a matter of transport costs.[2] The supreme problem, then, is to rebuild the nationwide market economy while preventing any lapse into barter, self-sufficiency, or the loss of work incentives.

A second report looks more directly at the problem of urban resettlement but does so through an even narrower aperture.[3] Given the probable physical damage in any urban area after a nuclear attack (damage that is described in exquisite detail), what would be the technical problems of clearing off the debris? Within 2.5 miles of ground zero, it would simply not be tried. Up to 9 miles out, in the heavily built up zone, the debris might be 20 feet deep and full of steel beams and reinforced concrete, making it difficult to handle. But the main roads could be cleared and the other debris left until later. Any early rescue operation would not be feasible, of course, in all that rubble. However, the heavy machinery necessary to open the main roads and level the strategic locations could probably be recovered and set to work. Farther out, things would be easier.

The reader is left with two concrete images. The first one consists of two large bulldozers, working blade to blade, opening a 20-foot swathe

From *The Counterfeit Ark: Crisis Relocation for Nuclear War*, ed. J. Leaning and L. Keyes. Copyright 1984 by Physicians for Social Responsibility. Reprinted by permission of Ballinger Publishing Company.

through the ruined city, pushing the layers of debris into two great ridges at the sides of the road. In the second image, we see a huge power shovel methodically eating away at those piles, loading them into waiting trucks, and thereby opening up a 20-foot channel without creating great windrows at each edge. In one day, the shovel could clear 40 feet; the bulldozers could clear 20 miles. The images are haunting: there is no one there but the big machines and heaps of smashed buildings.

In the final section of a third report, there is a brief consideration of the problem of rehousing the homeless after attack.[4] Once more, the study draws back from an unsettling reality. The question is reduced to a global, quantitative one: Would enough houses be left, somewhere in a metropolitan region, for the people that remain? The authors assume a "relatively light attack," consider only the larger U.S. metropolitan regions, and further assume that (as if due to the thoughtfulness of the attacker) no nearby regions would be hit if that would preempt houses needed for some larger region. Under those assumptions, they calculate that the survivors in the average U.S. metropolis could be settled in any remaining houses that had received radiation of 2,000 rems per hour or less, by moving these people 60 miles or less (transported how?), and by crowding them into those houses at up to four times the original occupancy rate. But people who move, two weeks after an attack, from shelters into houses that received, one hour after attack, fallout doses of 2,000 rems per hour, will themselves be irradiated by 100 rems per week, assuming protection factors of two and continual occupancy. This is sufficient to cause long-term effects, nausea, and lowered resistence to disease, but probably not sufficient, the authors postulate, to bring on the severe radiation sickness that requires immediate medical treatment. As the authors note, there will be some additional difficulties of allocation, of moving the survivors, and of deciding when to move, how far to move, and what level of contamination to expose people to.

We have two actual experiences of nuclear devastation: Hiroshima and Nagasaki. The record of those assaults focuses on the terrifying physical and medical consequences,[5] but it also has some information to our purpose: a brief account of the days immediately following the explosion and some material on its extended social and psychological effects.

The first days are only sketchily described, since no comprehensive records remain from that chaotic time. But the photographs and personal memories are stark and vivid. One sees the desert of burnt rubble, the blackened corpses and the wounded on the ground, the dazed and mutilated survivors wandering aimlessly over the terrain. Military teams came in early (telephone service for the army was restored on the first day), but they could do little beyond simple first aid and the burning and burying of the dead. Contrary to orders, people from outside streamed into the ruins, looking for kin and friends, even as others stumbled out. The early entrants into the wreckage themselves fell prey to radiation sickness. A "black rain" fell shortly after the explosion, chilling the weakened people and carrying the radioactive dust back to the earth. Those days made a deep impression on all who survived them, as hundreds of diaries and drawings bear witness.

Almost every family in those two cities lost at least one member. Children remember the successive deaths of their parents and siblings. A blank, indifferent state of mind was followed by deep depression and a sense of guilt for surviving when so many had perished. Orphaned children suffered discrimination, drifted from odd jobs into delinquency, felt conspicuous for their deformities. The "orphaned elderly," bereft of kin, lived in makeshift shacks for years. Adult survivors lost their wealth and social connections and in time became laborers and petty employees, regardless of previous skill and position.

The charred trees sprouted from their roots, and new associations of herbs sprang up in the ruins, but it was a year before people began to return to the edges of the burned out area, and three years before houses were rebuilt. Even by this time, only 50 percent of the original population had resettled in Hiroshima. It was the Korean War that brought the city back to its former size.

The surrender of Japan, shortly after the attack, made it more difficult for the victims, since there then was no possibility of revenge. Their suffering had been converted into a senseless sacrifice. Subsequent suppression of information by the authorities made it difficult for survivors to understand what had happened to them or to find support for their confusions. Only as the antinuclear movement developed could they begin to work out their anger and fear and find common cause with others. They are still a marked group in the Japanese society. Many of them have moved away to other cities, perhaps to lose themselves in more anonymous surroundings.

The official reports, and others like them, have given no thought to the human experience, even as it will rebound directly on their management concerns. In particular, there is no conception of the role of *place*, of the intimate linkages that develop between people and their location.

The issue is neither abstruse nor trivial. To be an active human being, one must know where one is—be able to identify one's present location and know how to get to a neighboring place. Each place has its meanings, some superficial and some profound, that connect it to our everyday lives. This ordinary knowledge will strike back at us whenever we are lost. We are mobile, meaning-creating animals. If we cannot recognize places, know what they mean and how to move through them, we are helpless and disturbed.

It can be a pleasure to wander through a new city looking for surprises, but only if one is certain that a secure order of meaning and location underlies the novel form—that one can refer to a map, or ask one's way, or at least will in time come out on some recognizable feature, whence the way home is clear. To be lost in the woods is not fearful for a trained woodsman; he knows the signs of the woodland and the strategies for coming out. But to be truly lost, unable to recognize anything or any direction, brings us to panic and often to physical nausea.

Being truly lost is for most people an unusual experience, and normally only a temporary one, soon safely buried, if remembered with fear. We have too many resources to fall back upon, social as well as physical, should any one link be severed. In times of great stress, however, the physical environment provides an image of stability to which we will cling, in our grief and inner disorientation. It is our anchor until the inner storm subsides. This is well known in the experience of deep mourning and in neurotic or psychotic disturbance. But if the physical setting is disrupted at the very time that the inner storm is raging, the combined effect can be devastating. In calmer times the environment serves as a religious symbol, or the symbol of a joint culture, or the visible cement of some complex institution. What may seem to be no more than a pleasant landscape may have an important functional role.

In childhood we form deep attachments to the location in which we grew up, and [we] carry the image of this place with us for the remainder of our lives. Features of the childhood place have been shown to influence many later decisions—where to live or how to arrange the home, for example. Many people have suffered the shock of finding their childhood home obliterated by some recent development. Even for those long past childhood—effective adults well supplied with social and locational links—the shock is peculiarly disturbing. *Home* is a powerful idea, a fact of which real estate agents are well aware.

In old age, as active social links fall away, we are notoriously dependent on the stability of our physical surroundings. An abrupt move can literally kill a person unless it is carefully prepared for and softened by the carriage of personal property and the maintenance of social ties.

Great waves of immigrants have poured into this country. Even when they came voluntarily, they felt the pain of separation. Immigrants dream about home while they struggle to find a place for themselves in the confusion of a new world. Where they can, they settle in landscapes like those they left or reshape places to resemble the lost ones. They never forget "the old country," however miserable their existence there may have been. For the remainder of their lives, most of them never feel that the new country is truly home. And yet these were willing migrants, in the main, coming *to* a place that had meaning and opportunity—a country that they were proud to be part of. They could return if they wished, or at least they thought they could. For many Africans, of course, none of this was true, and the pain and fear of the kidnapping has carried down through the generations.

While we are accustomed to the presence of migrating people (and "looking for roots" is one of our commonplace expressions), we are not familiar with any situation in which *everyone* is uprooted—none willingly, all under stress and without hope of return. Nomadic tribes move en masse, but they keep their social ties intact. It is true enough that a tidal wave of displaced refugees is now sweeping the world, but many of them have maintained their essential social connections or have been able to reestablish them in the camps, where they are supported by outside services. Yet disorientation persists, and effective production is poor.

Major disasters give us some further insight into the role of place. A great fire, earthquake, or inundation will cause much damage and suffering, but society can be reknit if the people and their connections survive: if they still have kin and institutions, if they can return to a familiar landscape. When everyone returns to a customary, recognizable place, they begin from a solid base. Thus the typical rush to return by an evacuated population and its stubborn insistence on rebuilding a place "just as it was." London after the Great Fire and Warsaw after its razing by the Nazis are well-known examples of this phenomenon.

But where the home place has been poisoned—when it is too dangerous to resettle or has been obliterated or made unrecognizable— then the trauma can be deep and lasting. In the Buffalo Creek disaster in West Virginia, a ruptured dam loosed a tidal wave of sludge down a narrow mountain valley. Residents yearning to return were held back by the fear of being trapped in another rush of debris. Those who did go back were always aware of the close valley walls and the single exit far downstream. Many remained afraid to go outside. Their familiar valley had become a place of menace; they were caught between attachment and abandonment.

Making a new place in the wilderness—the recurrent American image that may seem appropriate to the reoccupation of our cities after a holocaust—is a serious business. It involves far more than a functional modification of the landscape. The wild place must be made psychologically safe and familiar: cleared of danger, bounded, named, oriented, given a center, planted, and furnished with familiar things. This is a protracted, demanding task requiring the taming of the land and the reorientation of how the newcomers see and feel about the land. Many rituals of blessing and of town founding are used for just that purpose. It is only the second or third generation that begins to feel entirely safe and at home.

Settlement is more disturbing if the ground is studded with the evidence of a previous occupation. The ground must then be conquered and purified. There are frequent historical episodes of razing earlier symbols and of occupying old sites with dominant new symbols. Until the land is psychologically secured, people are uneasy. Interest in the previous remains comes later. To wipe out an enemy, one does not stop with murder; one razes their place as well. Geocide is auxiliary to genocide.

So the role of space in human affairs is far more than the economist's "location space" or "spatial friction," far more than the Cartesian space of the engineer within which machines work on materials. The sense of place is a human experience and will be a crucial ingredient in any resettlement after a nuclear holocaust. To foresee the nature of that experience, we must draw on all these previous experiences: of disaster and immigration, childhood and old age, neurosis and mourning, genocide, refugee camps and place making in the wilderness. Yet coming home after a widespread nuclear war will be unique—not only for its terrifying magnitude but also for the heightened interaction of so many negative features.

It will be a return to a poisoned home, and people will be caught between fear and desire to return. The home place will have been shattered, [the] survivors will know it to be tainted with radiation by the malice of the enemy, and the enemy might return. The environment will be shapeless, largely unrecognizable, bereft of orientation, and yet vast. Most social ties will have been broken by death and the confusion of evacuation and relocation. Ethnic groups will look on each other with suspicious hostility, and government will have lost its legitimacy. There will be no support from outside, since there will *be* no outside. Technically, the survivors are returning, yet psychologically return is impossible. Home is gone; there is no going back to it. Nor is one going to some organized place. The destination is all gray, shapeless, home and not home—a strange, dangerous, uneasy, confusing place.

Survivors will have to cope with this as best they can, but it will be another burden to add to all the medical, social, economic, and technical burdens they must carry. Even in a callous sense, one cannot manipulate these "labor factors" without thought for the interaction of laborer, place, and society. Such an analysis is unreal, not just inhumane. Experiences of this intensity are unpredictable, but one can at least make an attempt to imagine oneself there:

★ ★ ★ ★ ★ ★

We had walked in from Northfield. Much of the countryside had been burned away, but I knew the general direction to the city, and we found the main road. Others were moving with us, since orders to return had been announced. Everyone seemed too tired to be dangerous. A few were coming the other way. We asked them why and got confused answers.

We had already decided to return, when we came out of our burrow. Northfield was hostile to the refugees, and the locals had gotten control of the food supply. They said that there was food and work in the city, it was time to get out. I was glad to go, but my older son was sure that it was still too dangerous in the city and said that he would join us later. We appointed a rendezvous, but the place we named proved to be unrecognizable. I never knew what became of him, after the city people had gone.

Closer in, the smashed buildings had been cleared off the road. By then, a file of people were walking between the piles of debris. Here and there, there were temporary signs pointing to different headquarters. It was like a silent battlefield.

I wasn't sure where I was: probably some northern suburb. It had been my intention to put up a shelter on our own land, but now I knew that I would not find it easily. Everything was covered with shapeless, broken, burnt debris. The few cleared roads were marked with strange numbers. At times, these tracks followed old streets, at others they ran over broken foundations. One cracked pavement looked like another, and, since the sky was overcast, I had no sense of direction. I tried to remember the shape of the ground, but without the buildings and streets I could not connect the litter with my memories of shops and houses and different districts. I had never seen this ground before. An old street sign on a wooden pole said Broadway, which was a street I knew. But how could it be on this side of town? It occurred to me that it might be a joke.

Eventually, we came to a cleared space by the side of the road, where some boards and canvas had been set up to keep off the wind and the rain. We settled there for the time. There was a water tank, and we scavenged in the ruins for some lumber and plastic to patch our roof and make a partition around ourselves.

A mile down the road they were clearing away a shattered building. If you were there early you got bread, cheese, and coffee for helping to lift and load the beams and wall fragments. We worked slowly enough, not very sure what we were doing. The work seemed pointless.

Day and night we could hear the crash of the big machines working nearby, chewing away at the trash, making a clearing or a new road. It wasn't obvious to me which roads led out of the city and which ran in, or if any of them went to any particular place. The world had lost its shape, but luckily the sun still gave me directions. I had a map of the old city, and I worked evenings with it to puzzle out where we might be.

Perhaps it had been a mistake to come. Northfield was hostile, but it was real and recognizable. We had food here and were out of our hole, but we were nowhere, drifting with other people we hardly spoke to. There were little signs posted here and there, asking about someone who had disappeared. I never found a familiar name. The loose piles of wreckage could shift suddenly when we were out on them. If our shoes wore out, it would be difficult to walk over the sharp-edged trash, so we tied on pieces of wood or rubber to make them last.

We knew that the ground was radioactive, but not how much. What effect was it having on us? We watched for nausea and looked for dark patches on our skin. Once a soldier went by, holding a dosimeter, but he would not tell us what it read. Official communications had been reestablished, but we lived in two worlds as far as information was concerned. Officials used telephones, radios, printed reports, computers. We lived on rumors, handwritten notices, graffiti, and public proclamations. We went hungry for news. Maps and papers were luxuries. I remember that a man came by with a camera, taking pictures of us and our camp. He must have been from some newspaper, though I had never seen one. They smashed his camera, not wanting any pictures taken, and I was just as glad.

Our world was our clearing and the road that passed it by, just as if we lived in the wilderness. From time to time, we moved to some new clearing, closer to work or food, or because they told us to move on. I can't remember all those places, not that they were better or worse. Some people moved out to the far edge of the city, where there were houses still standing. Others came back, because the houses were crowded with strangers, and there was no work nearby. Just south of us, a small group—perhaps they were old neighbors who had found each other—decided to settle on a piece of land. They cleared a lane around it, and then a central street. They marked each corner with stones, and put up a large stone at the entrance. They found a priest and made a procession around their bounds, saying a prayer at every mark. They cut the date on the entrance stone, and so declared the land their own.

I was determined to find our own land. I had a strategy: find the river, which must still be recognizable, and go up it until I reached the place where our street ran down the saddle between two hills. Once that close, I was sure that I could find the clues. So I worked up and down the network of cleared roads, counting turns and distances so that I could make my way back. And I came on the river, full of debris, wandering out of its banks, but still flowing. It was difficult to move along it. There were small hills, or perhaps piles of wreckage, but in the end I came to a familiar slope. When I searched over the rubbish, I found a familiar street corner, exposed by the blast, and then a slate from our neighbor's roof. With that, I located our lot, and I was home.

We moved some bulky things off the top of the litter and packed loose rubbish into the holes. Perched up above the old ground, we put up our poles and roof. It was an uneasy foundation since I did not know what was beneath us. When the city was first evacuated, I had reached my sons at work, but I never found my wife and small daughter. Perhaps they had succeeded in joining each other, perhaps not. Perhaps they were buried in the trash on which we camped.

I could not be sure just how our street ran, but we marked it out as well as we could. Then we laid out our lot, since I didn't want to encroach on my neighbor's land. None of our neighbors had returned, however, and it annoyed me that others camping nearby thought that this was some other street. We argued over the clues and landmarks. But I dug a hole down to the old ground at one point. I felt that I must touch it somewhere. I found the burnt stump of our apple tree, and it released a flood of memories.

Now I felt in place again, and I could look for permanent work. Up till then, I had worked at whatever casual job turned up. Now I looked more systematically, and yet I could never find work where I could use my former experience. Sometimes I heard of such jobs, but they were far away, or their location uncertain. I did not have the energy to chase after them, and so I descended to the unskilled labor that I could find. We stole our food when we could. Organized gangs worked on a larger scale, ambushing convoys or raiding supply dumps to supply the black market.

We had to walk some distance now, over and through the trash, to reach water, food, and even fuel, since the firestorm had burned over this area. To find our way through the waste, we made new landmarks out of odd fragments and gave them names and shapes and histories. Gradually, the cleared roads were being extended to connect the workplaces, camps, and depots. The city was slowly taking on a form: clumps of sheds, clearings in the rubble. When we gave directions, we used turnings and small details, which might shift from day to day. All the historic places were gone. Even the natural features were dismembered. Sometimes I thought of the old view down the river valley but could not connect it to the blocked and flooded land, and the memory of what it once was like was beginning to escape me. I saw desolation.

The city center was Ground Zero, an absolute emptiness, still dangerous to enter, but seemed to draw us as if it were a black hole in space. Cold, wet, and mud were our commonplaces, and so we dreamed about smooth clean floors. Waste water ran down the streets, since the sewers were blocked. People relieved themselves on the debris, or at times in the gutter, like dogs. There were epidemics, and illnesses. People were still dying, one by one, leaving their children or their old ones to go on alone. Unidentified bodies occasionally appeared, and space for proper burial was hard to find. Our cemeteries were buried; we were cut off even from our dead.

"Before the bomb" was long ago, a time that had hardly left a trace. We could not describe it even to ourselves. Any structure saved by some quirk of the explosion, any tree still living, took on an immense importance. We lived in a timeless, endless wasteland and slept on the buried past. Where were the old names? Weren't there hidden dangers down below? We had to develop a science of places: signs of power or safety that could be read in the remains. Some people said that the streets were safe enough, if you kept off the debris. Others said that everything was radioactive. We all knew some special signs of danger: where rust had flaked off the steel and exposed the bare metal, then you kept your distance. A peculiar weed with spiked, downy leaves was known to thrive in hot spots. We refused to work where such signs appeared. We felt the presence of the enemy, whose power and malice had made all this. Would he come again? Should we stay or go? There were frightening and enticing rumors about other cities.

Surveyors began to lay their invisible lines along the roads. Some squatters paid them bonuses, to confirm their land. When they came to us they found (was it true?) that we were not where we had thought, not even in the same district. For me, it was as if the ground were jerked away. Hills were valleys, and valleys hills; we were in a different city. I felt a confusion of the senses, and that night I was ill again.

As soon as I was up, we moved down to a more convenient, nameless clearing. Then my son said that he was sick of this aimless life, and that he would just walk out to see what was outside. I never saw him again, nor any other member of my family.

So then, it was clear that I would live alone, in empty places. The future went with a flash, and the past was gone. When there was a call for labor to clear destroyed cities overseas, I left without looking back. I could dig out the rubble of a strange city, with all my heart.

★ ★ ★ ★ ★ ★

All the above is imaginary, or, to give it a more dignified name, it is a "scenario"—one that emphasizes only a single factor. But imagination may be all we have to use in thinking about stress at such levels, in such a synergism of negative influences. The survivors who return to rebuild production will not only be ill and exhausted; not only lacking in information, shelter, power, and food; not only be separated from their kin, or have seen them die or left them to die. They will have been twice uprooted, subject to further random moves, returning and yet unable to return, since home will be unrecognizable. There will be hostility in the "host" area, and unknown dangers in the burned out city. The city itself will be a chaotic landscape of rubbish—disorienting and without discernible parts. It will be a junkyard and will communicate all that deep aversion in our culture for waste and excrement. It will utterly fail to convey any of that sense of exterior stability so important for people under stress. There will be no outside support moving in to deal with the disaster and no undamaged environment outside. *All* the land will be devastated; everyone will be uprooted.

The survivors will come back to a pulverized, poisoned place and be subject to conflicting emotions of attachment and flight. Clearance will be difficult; for long periods there will be no firm floor underfoot. Beneath the rubble there will be dead bodies, some of them abandoned kin and friends. The psychologically necessary operations of purifying and reclaiming the ground will come slowly. All sacred and meaningful landmarks will have disappeared, and the fear of hidden danger will be reinforced by the fear of renewed attack. These pathologies of place are only additions to all the social and biological stress survivors will encounter. Our fantasy hardly alludes to those other stresses and, thus, it underplays the effect. Anger and alienation may be the best that can be hoped for. For those that remain alive that will be the "healthy" reaction. Only after people have been reduced to that level of despair can they act their part as that neutral, mobile, "labor factor," on which the economic calculation of recovery depends.

Even if we should forget how people will feel, the destruction of place raises serious difficulties for management, on top of all the expected problems of epidemics and food, shelter, and transportation shortages; puzzles of restarting production; finding energy and material resources; directing resettlement; dilemmas of distribution; problems of control. The survivors will be frantic or numbed. They will settle where they should not and shift on rumor. They will have irrational perceptions of places, get lost, and consume time in aimless travel. Authority will be in doubt, official information discounted, rumors abundant. Social disorder, violence, theft, and the wastage of resources may be expected. There may be a tendency to underoccupy the built up city and to squat in the outer fringes, where there is cleared space and some surviving buildings. Transportation and the linkage of labor and production will then be a greater burden. Fuel will be scarce, and usable buildings will be picked apart and burned. Many other disturbances of the recovery process may be imagined. Recovery may not be possible.

The distant results of these dislocations are unfathomable. Would survivors stay for long in the burned areas? How would their underlying attitudes toward the land and toward each other shift? Would the nation become, in the minds of its people, that "dark and bloody ground" that the Cherokee prophesized for us? What would be the repercussions on common neuroses, on childhood, on the family, on our sense of past and future, and on a thousand other things? I cannot answer these questions precisely. But to analyze the reoccupation of cities as if it were an economic redistribution, or a clearing of debris from the streets, or even an heroic resettlement of the wilderness, is surely a stupendous error.

Notes

1. S. G. Winter, Jr., *Economic Viability after Thermonuclear War: The Limits of Feasible Production* (Santa Monica, Calif.: Rand Corporation, September 1963).

2. Most economists look on space as an exotic cost that disturbs their balancing equations. In that tradition, Winter believes that space would have no economic consequences at all, if only transport were free and instantaneous (p. 142). This observation turns its back on human experience. We depend on the "friction of space" just as we depend on the friction between our shoes and the ground. Imagine a world in which anyone could instantly, and without cost, be anywhere they wished to be! A nightmare.

3. P. D. LaRiviere and Hong Lee, *Postattack Recovery of Damaged Urban Areas* (Menlo Park, Calif.: Stanford Research Institute (SRI), November 1966) [prepared for the Office of Civil Defense].

4. Richard L. Goen et al., *Potential Vulnerabilities Affecting National Survival* (Menlo Park, Calif.: SRI, September 1970) [prepared for the Office of Civil Defense].

5. Committee for the Compilation of Materials, *Hiroshima and Nagasaki: The Physical, Medical, and Social Effects of the Atomic Bombings* (New York: Basic Books, 1981).

Fantasies of Waste

Wasting is a necessary part of living, yet if the processes are not well managed, life itself is threatened. Even when waste is prevented, the results can be deadly, but in a different way. What would a world be like where waste was out of control? Two fantasies explore the consequences of too much and too little waste, both of them nightmares.

A Waste Cacotopia

The inhabited buildings slowly extrude their continuous ribbons of compressed garbage and trash. The ribbons fall onto the cargo belts which move steadily toward the high ridges at the city boundary. In these populous continents, each city presses against the next, and so the waste ridges form a network, through which tunnel the intercity roads. Each city posts frontier guards, to prevent a neighbor from tipping its trash over the crest.

The waste ribbons are unloaded high up, and are shaped to settle compactly, at a high angle of repose. As the base of the waste-belt expands, it presses the settlement into a narrower territory. Few extensive uses remain, since food and water are shipped in from a distance, with consequent leakage and spoiling. Yet the ground is encumbered with abandoned buildings and weedy lots of uncertain ownership, so that it is difficult for a city to contract efficiently into a denser formation. Men wearing respirators and mounting big machines are at work daily in this no man's land, demolishing buildings, slashing weeds, and spraying dangerous insects and vermin. Truant children play in these jungles, too, and deplorable accidents are common.

At greater expense, a city may have its trash carried to some distant uninhabited sink. The Grand Canyon is partly full, a permanent conduit having been reserved for the Colorado underneath. The Mindinao Deep is shallow now, and Holland is well above sea level. However, as wastes have been piled over the Arctic snowfields, the surface darkening, along with the greenhouse effect of the polluted atmosphere, has caused melting of the ice and a rising sea level.

The inhabited settlements jut out over the seas, or are built over the larger rivers, which have been straightened and lined with a glassy coat in smooth cross section, to carry the flow more rapidly to the ocean. Thus, the settlements can evacuate directly into the liquid medium below. Filters remove the coarser ejecta, however, so that stream or tidal flow will not become too viscous. Imported water is added to the channel, to keep the whole in motion. Since buildings are sealed, the resulting odors are not so noticeable. The ocean itself, too corrosive for the hulls of ordinary ships,

From Kevin Lynch's *Wasting Away*, ed. Michael Southworth. Reprinted by the permission of Sierra Club Books.

and so littered with floating debris as to make navigation hazardous, is traversed by long submarine tunnels.

Ordinary fumes are vented to high altitudes; toxic dusts and gases are sealed in thin bags and ejected into space. These bags are strong enough to confine their contents until well away from earth, and are highly reflective, so that passing craft can easily avoid them. Aerial sweepers keep the approach lanes open through the air around the major landing sites. These sites are also favored locations for vacation hotels, since the sun or moon can frequently be glimpsed through the aerial openings.

To replace the material so rapidly consumed, the earth, the moon, two planets, and several asteroids are mined for minerals, oxygen, water, and hydrocarbons. As the earth is hollowed out underneath and the wastes pile up on its surface, there is concern that its rock beds may collapse downwards, vulcanism in reverse. To prevent this, wastes are injected into the empty mining galleries. Later, however, they are drilled out again, as the productive appetite swells for new minerals or for lower grades of previously mined material.

This massive transport and transformation of matter requires a corresponding expenditure of energy. Once expended, it is vented as pervasive noise, or as waste heat. Since the earth's radiation into space cannot match the flow, this venting energy has resulted in a persistent warming of the climate. Recently, radiators have been transported to the troposphere, to step up this outward flow.

Fossil hydrocarbons are almost depleted, and the forests are stunted or cut over. Nuclear and solar power are now the prime sources of energy. The former is constrained to the rate at which its by-products can safely be spewed forth into space, since far too much of the earth's surface is already contaminated by radioactivity. Solar power, on the other hand, is inhibited by the increasing opacity of the atmosphere. For the most part, solar energy is now collected by orbiting panels flying above the smog. In order to increase this source of energy, and since the earth is now more securely shielded from solar radiation, new destabilizing compounds are being shot into the atomic furnace of the sun to speed up the rate of nuclear fusion, accelerating the sun's stellar evolution. This shortening of the active life of the sun is not considered likely to affect the life span of the human species.

More than half of the more recent living species are now extinct, due to complete disruption of their habitats. Some few, most dear or useful to man, have been brought inside, or live in protected areas, or have been fitted with respirators and other prosthetic devices. The parasites of man have done rather well, and cluster in and near his defended settlements. Other surviving creatures, especially those of the more primitive orders, have evolved rapidly under the stress, taking advantage of the rich flow of toxins, wastes, and heat. These new organisms, which bloom and subside, periodically invade the human territories.

Human beings themselves must be more active and aggressive. Women bear ten to twenty children, so that the strongest may be selected and the weak put away. Life is short and full of incident. Riots and demonstrations are frequent; cities contend against each other, their armies trampling back and forth.

Celebrations, displays, and the trading of possessions sustain the passage of goods, so necessary to the system of production. Splendid feasts are prolonged by vomiting. The casual destruction of valuables before the envious eye of many spectators is the best evidence of wealth and power.

The houses of the rich are spotless, kept clean by sophisticated machines in the hands of the low class sweepers. Surroundings grow somewhat dirtier as one descends the income scale. Multiplying the rate of consumption by the degree of cleanliness gives the measure of social rank. A sophisticate eats rapidly, washes often, and dons fresh clothes after every meal.

Waste and death are not mentioned in polite society. Unwanted infants are exposed at night in remote places. Adults die in special hospitals, to which they have been sent, nameless, to be purified. Children are taught to excrete unnoticed, in the secret places hanging over the sewer streams. They learn not to speak of rivers. Among themselves, they may snigger over the fat tubes of waste squeezed out beneath the buildings, or the teasing way in which the smoking chimneys poke up into the air. The shame of wasting keeps the social ranks in place.

A Wasteless Cacotopia

Escape that nightmare to dream of a society freed of waste. No more garbage, no more sewage; clean air, an unencumbered earth. Everything fully used, no rotting food, no loss in storage. Plants and animals will be bred to reduce their useless parts: stringless beans, boneless chickens, skinless beets. They will be shipped in cubes, but not far. Food is produced where it is consumed, and is just ready at the moment of consumption. Leftovers are unknown. There is no deep mining. Things are made of wood and bone and animal hair. Energy comes from food, or directly from the sun. Fire has been given back to Prometheus, and the air is clear.

Weeds and useless animals will not be found, even in the most remote areas: no crabgrass, bindweed, cat briar, water hyacinth, goldenrod, hedge rose, ant, or shrew. Nor are there any parasites. Mice, rats, cockroaches, raccoons, sparrows, gulls, mosquitoes, fleas, weevils, germs have all vanished. Dogs and cats are not kept, and strays not tolerated. Useful plants grow in evenly spaced rows, many of them in extensive glasshouses. No plant shades another. Deciduous plants are no longer favored, for fear of autumn leaves. Mirrors distribute solar radiation to the north sides of hills and buildings.

There are no empty buildings or vacant lots, no useless side yards or barren rooftops, no long corridors, crawl spaces, or odd nooks. Buildings have regular shapes, without misfit additions. They last for generations, so that everyone lives in an ancestral home. It is built to a standard plan, of the material taken from its foundations. When it wears out, it does so completely, crumbling into deposits of useful material. Indoors and out, all space is competely used. Rooms are small and low, a close fit to body dimensions. Settlements are compact and ordered, intricately miniaturized, just as Soleri[1] predicted. They are dark, cold, and silent, warmed by the sun and by body heat, which is retained by bundling and by thick clothing. Buildings are completely insulated, and vent no gas. There is no city heat island, no smog. When on infrequent occasion a change is necessary, it is planned to happen rapidly in some clearly bounded area. As a space is abandoned, it is immediately taken up.

Time is as efficiently used as space: factories run continuously, streets are just full, beds always slept in, meals prepared and eaten in continuous shifts. Gardens grow all the year, since mirrors in outer space have equalized the flux of solar radiation. Fur storage is a lost trade. It is generally bright but cool. Violent storms never occur. Rains are light drizzles, falling entirely on the agricultural areas, leaving dry the mountainsides. The wasteful hydrologic cycle has been minimized by taking up the flowing water for continuous closed cycling within the buildings and great glasshouses. So rivers are dry at their mouths, and the sea has fallen. The ocean surface is now less than that of the land. Sea travel is by sail, but this is slow, due to diminished winds. Land travel, of course, is restricted to walking, cycling, or animal traction. But, since travelers are scarce and few goods are carried far, little time is thereby wasted.

Cautious genetic manipulation has allowed body size to be standardized, with enormous savings in all clothing and equipment. This size is smaller than before, bringing it closer to an efficient balance between heat loss and the intake needed for body maintenance. Smaller size has created additional savings in settlement space and the size of gear. Children reach this normal size rather rapidly, making leaps from one standard intermediate size to another, thus reducing the range of required children's sizes. The awkward period of immaturity, which is a wasteful time for all organisms, is accomplished expeditiously. People are passive and calm, a personality trait reinforced by selected depressants.

Symbiotic bacteria help the body to recycle much excrement internally, so that human waste is slight, and the intake of food is reduced. Cooking is accomplished by solar heat, and much food is eaten raw. Children are taught to eat lightly and to retain their body wastes until they can be discharged at approved recycling stations, at times that allow a continuous, efficient run. Feasts are of course immoral, vomiting quite shameful even when involuntary.

There are no sewer flows and extremely little trash. There is no dirt on the streets, no dust in the houses, no spills, no breakage, no smoke or smog. Street cleaning is no longer necessary, and all the streams run pure (although their flow is diminished, as we have said, to reduce the waste of water). An occasional recycling station is the only reminder of the old waste ridges.

Even sweat is reduced, since the air is cool and equable. Tears are not proper. The body is sweetly tuned, the vermiform appendix removed at birth. Even if some energy is expended in action, since body mass is not large heat loss through the skin is low, and unnecessary movement is avoided. No leaps or pirouttes. Walking, an inefficient mode of motion, is now most often replaced by unicycles. People do not move far, of course, since transportation is wasteful. Symbols substitute for journeys, and most people work where they live.

Soap is a lost commodity, bathing and laundry forgotten indulgences. Brooms, mops, and vacuum cleaners are museum pieces. Informative sounds, smells, or light waves are beamed directly to their receivers, instead of spreading wastefully through the air. Those signals that are void of information are suppressed at the source. Machines are noiseless: the sounds of traffic, leaves, and water cannot be detected. This is a silent world, disturbed only by soft, precise, symbolic communications. Friction has been reduced to the minimum needed to keep us erect and keep things in their place. The edges of the continents have been smoothed to reduce the tidal losses. All moving parts slip silently over each other. People do not rub their hands for warmth; fires are prohibited; artificial lights are cold.

There are no waste words or motions: everything is meant to be attended to. Decorations, music, and other superfluous displays are forbidden. No celebrations break the normal round. No one is subjected to repetition, noise, or misinformation. The Congressional Record is abolished, along with advertising, gossip, and scholarly papers. There is no inattention, no idleness, no mental drifting. Everyone is either sound asleep or fully awake. Insomnia is the ideal, but it has not been widely achieved. The hours for sleep are short and are set at birth. They are spread evenly throughout the 24-hour day, among equal groups of the population. Since schedules are completely regular, social contacts between these time groups are rare, except where there are overlaps. Mistakes are never made. Although that has eliminated one mode of learning, the accumulated information store is accurate and accessible.

Clearly, the supreme waste is the loss of a wise and experienced person. Efforts have been directed toward immortality. Other researchers look for a way of transferring memory and personality to a successor. One outcome of this research is that the active life span has been lengthened to several hundred years. Another outcome is that many of the cognitive and emotional patterns of one person can successfully be recorded, and even internalized by a new person. Thus one generation is much like another. Since the life span is long, any accidental death, although rare, is a catastrophe. The approach of natural death is predictable, which affords time for a complete debriefing and a careful settlement of affairs. It is a rather hushed and fearful event.

The birth of a new individual must, in turn, be carefully controlled, in order to replace the dead at one-to-one. This demands detailed prediction and planning. No time is spent in courting or other sexual preliminaries. Sperm and ova are not to be wasted. While intercourse for pleasure is surely not prohibited, it is clearly unnecessary, and must be registered, so that proper precautions can be taken. Many women never bear a child, although the male to female ratio is kept low, few males being required. The proper development of embryo and child is unfailing. Early death, or birth defects, are unknown. The child is carefully shielded to prevent them.

Since accidents are rare, they merit headlines. In general, the news might seem a little dull to us. Papers have no riots, disorders, wars, disasters, or struggles of any kind to offer to their readers. All issues are decided expeditiously, without heat or rancor. There is no economic or social competition, no battles over status or the division of resources, no bankruptcies, no business cycles, no unemployment. The great insurance companies are gone with the advertisers, their office towers converted to dovecotes and chicken factories. The old military reservations are farms, or ordered forests where old drill sergeants keep the trees in line. The suppression of military waste alone has raised world living standards as much as the abandonment of all other forms of conspicuous consumption. Even the police are few in number, because controls are internalized in this well-managed world. Each person is very careful not to do less or more than is wanted. No one suffers any psychological depression, confusion, neurosis, or psychosis.

Since nothing is forgotten, it is difficult to manage the growing store of information, and scholarly emphasis now lies on the efficient restructuring and elimination of knowledge, rather than on its acquisition. Due to the perfection of memory and the longevity of individuals, learning must be restrained. Time is not wasted, but still it is not overvalued. People content themselves with a slow pace of existence and languid communications. Only perverts want something new. Digusting images are passed along the underground circuit: titillating descriptions of feasts, dirty hands, warm fires, slaughter, and wild laughter.

This is a predictable world, in which surprise is rare. Elaborate games of chance have been developed in compensation, although of course no material outcomes are staked upon them. While not officially encouraged, they have become quite complex, in order to cope with the powerful predictive abilities of the age. A vicious hunger for novelty and uncertainty, a reminder of our old foolishness, can be slaked in an array of wildly inventive arts. Sadly enough, many people still indulge in them, deep in caverns, at times when they are programmed for sleep.

One fantasy has bred another, and neither seems attractive.

Note

1. Paolo Soleri, visionary 20th-century architect and author of *Arcology: The City in the Image of Man* (MIT Press, 1969).

Index

Carcassonne, *44*

Carr, Stephen, 6–7, 21, 233, 251

Carr/Lynch Associates, Inc., 21, 674

Castello Sant'Angelo, 132

Cathedral squares, 702–703

Celebrations, 505, 596, 805

Centers, 62–63, 64, 69, 78–80, 82, 84–85, 91–93, 95, 129–131, 214–215, 297, 303–305, 422–423, 500, 529–530, 643–644, 719, 741–742, 775, 798, 804

Centers and districts, *290*

Central Park, New York, 413, 414, 714

Chain of spaces, 672–673

Change, 407, 518, 775, 777, 790

Changes of grade, *611*

Channels of movement, 57, 63–64, 69, 84–85, 528–529, 584

Character, 93, 217, 279, 306–307, 338, 690

Charleston, 406

Chicago, 10, 19, 38, 40, 42

Children, 99, 142, 154–184, 241, 825

Children's neighborhood maps, *176, 181–182*

China, 536, 550, 809

  agro-industrial commune, 808

  cities, 231

  courtyard house, 231

Choice, 59–62, 65, 296, 368, 370, 379, 398–401, 432, 453, 457, 518

Circulation, 48, 79, 361, 475, 521, 563–578, 642, 676–677, 703–704, 785

Citizen image, 240, 287, 340

City appearance, 465–497

City Beautiful movement, 487, 553

City design, 7, 254, 430–458, 465–534

City design education, 652–659

City

  floor, 118–121, 123, 129, 146, 156–157, 185, 189, 195, 362

  form, 35–46, *44*, 65, 352, 370, 420–458, 465–497, 499

  furniture, 505–506

  image. *See* image

  landscape, 247, 296, 519

  man, 537–538, 544

  noise, 516, 684

  orientation, 248

  parks, 407, 409, 541

planning, 535–562, 653–654

  size, 35–36, 39, 137, 142, 551

  villages, 41

  walls, 137, 406

Cityscape, 195, 569

Ciudad Guayana, 240, 463, 634–640

Ciudad Lineal, 42

Civic design, 531, 653

Civil defense plans, 815

Cleveland, 701–709

Climate, 640, 722. *See also* Microclimate

Cluster zoning, 334

Coastal form, 723

Cognition, 233

Cognitive

  anthropology, 253

  development, 468, 518

  geography, 253

  image, 584

  psychology, 240

Collage of time, 681

Colonia San Augustin, 175, 180, 184

Colonia Universidad, 174, 178

Color and texture, 146, 157–158

Columbia, Maryland, 463, 641–645

Comfort, 60–61, 65, 68, 295, 683

Commercial strips, 462, 541, 579–616, *580, 586–587, 589, 593–594, 601, 606–614. See also* Arterial streets; Strips

Communes, 533, 809

Communication, 403, 420, 472, 477, 514–515, 597, 656, 703, 777, 782, 798

Communication substitutes, 391–392

Communitas, 533, 789

Community, 726, 748, 812

  character, 748, 756

  facilities and services, 677

  identity, 790

  revitalization, 674

  spatial form, 534

  visual survey, 260, 263–286

Competence, 420, 517

Comprehensive

  plan, 287, 309

  zoning, 646

Compressed garbage, 832

Congruence, 457, 804

Connection, 790–791, 809

Maillart, Robert, 570
Maki, Fumihiko, 490
Management of places, 417, 597, *601*, 652–653, 740, 804
Managing the Sense of a Region, 6, 34, 255
Manhattan, 38–40, 46, 74, *160*, 163
Mapping, 233, 235, 242, 249, 283
Mardi Gras, 415, 505
Marston family, 8
Martha's Vineyard, 8, 11, 261, 316–337, 342–343, 692, 699
 road experience, *268–269*
Mastery, 402–403
Meaning, 240, 253, 287, 296, 457, 471, 519–520, 804
Medieval city, 40, 119, 139
Melbourne, 174, 177, 180, 183
Memory, 155, 187
Mental health, 396, 453
Mental images, 234, 248–249, 279, 293
Mesas, 722, 725, 729–730
Metropolitan
 form, 33, 47–86, 483, 541, 549, 772
 growth, 211, 550, 783
 image, 62, 67
 pattern, 47–64, 70–82
 region, 67, 69, 211, 396, 422, 557, 753, 775, 786, 795, 814
Mexico, 174, 752
Mexico City, *179*, 537, 540, 760
Microclimate, 310, 514, 640, 690
Minimum standards, 438, 444, 451, 456, 746
Minneapolis, 339, 343
Mira Mesa, 743–744
Mission Bay, 725, 742, 751
Mission Beach, 731–732, 740
Mission Valley, 727, 742, *745*, 748
MIT, 19, 20, 653, 657
Mitchell, James, 11
Mix of social groups, 639, 731–732
Models for metropolitan form, 76–82
Mohenjo-Daro, 46
Mono-cultures, 776, 796
Monumental places, 465, 541
Moore, G.T., 253
Moors, 322–323
Mosaics, 73, 773, 795
Moscow, 54, 538, 550

Moses, Robert, 160
Movement, 94, 95, 135, 149, 667
Mumford, Lewis, 19
Myer, John, 5, 666

Nagasaki, 823
Nanjing, 226–232
Naples, 38
National economic planning, 551, 624
National urbanization policy, 624, 786
Natural landscapes, 33, 148, 205, 217, 274, 308, 338, 549, 682, 722–723, 729–733, 746, 761, 792
Negev Desert, 547
Neighborhood unit, 3, 36, 454, 643
Neighborhoods, 59, 157, 171, 241, 244, 596, 643, 680, 721, 735–736, 748
Neolithic village, 536
Network of scenic corridors, 779
New cities, 783–785
New England, 42, 590
New Orleans, 415, 505
New towns, 463, 547, 641–645, 773, 784
New York, 36, 39, 42, 169, 414, 416, 714
Nicollet Mall, 600
Night lighting, 274, 782
Nodes, 69, 71–72, 211, *613*, 707
Noise, 118–121, 129, 310, 516, 563–564, 597, 600, 603, 610, 684, 694, 696, 752
Normative theory, 351–352
North Carolina, 19, 36
North Island, 733, 748
North Park, 736, 741, 747, 751
Nuclear attack, 811–821, 823–833

Oak Bluffs, 321
Objectives, 433–436, 439–441, 445–446
Ocean Beach, 731
Odor, 695
Olmsted, Frederick Law, 2, 260, 414, 532
Open
 environment, 413–417, 546, 779–781, 790
 plains, 327–329
 space, 77–82, 85, 92–93, 231, 303, 308, 338, 353–354, 386–387, 396–417, 424, *609*, 645, 683, 686, 703–704, 726, 737, 780–781, 785–786. *See also* Parks
Open Land Foundation, 333